W9-ADZ-750

EDUARD FARBER, Ph.D., University of Leipzig, is Adjunct Professor of Chemistry at the American University, Washington, D.C. Dr. Farber has served as Vice President and Director of Scientific Research of the Polyxor Chemical Company and Chief Chemist of the Timber Engineering Company. He has been a consultant to the Smithsonian Institution and an Associate Editor of *Isis,* one of the world's foremost scientific periodicals. An internationally recognized chemistry historian, Dr. Farber was presented with the 1964 Dexter Award by the American Chemical Society for his services in the advancement of the history of chemistry.

The Evolution of Chemistry

A History of its Ideas, Methods, and Materials

EDUARD FARBER, Ph.D.

Second Edition

THE RONALD PRESS COMPANY • NEW YORK

Copyright © 1969 by
THE RONALD PRESS COMPANY

Copyright © 1952 by
THE RONALD PRESS COMPANY

All Rights Reserved

No part of this book may be reproduced in any form without permission in writing from the publisher.

MP

QD
11
.F34
1969

Library of Congress Catalog Card Number: 69-14669

PRINTED IN THE UNITED STATES OF AMERICA

Preface

This book is a survey of the historical development of chemistry, from its origins to the present time. The aim of the Second Edition, like that of its predecessor, is to provide a deeper and fuller understanding of the ideas and methods of the science by integrating the evolution of chemistry into the context of history in general. A review of man's first recorded interest in the chemical transformation of materials that lay at hand is followed by a description of the ways by which chemical beliefs developed into ideas, how ideas developed into theories, and how practices evolved into experimental methods of research. The searching and experimentation of the past are so described that they may well provide both stimulation and special examples for solving present-day problems.

Experimental activities in the laboratory together with the broad advance of technology on all fronts have permitted the chemical industry to make tremendous strides. Thus industrial developments as well as the theoretical and experimental elements of the evolutionary process are given close attention.

Investigators through the ages have contributed to our present-day knowledge of the nature of substances, affinity, and chemical reactions. Throughout the volume, so far as possible, the story has been told by letting old records relate what actually took place. This has been done by making a careful and objective selection of pertinent material for early books and periodicals that are not readily accessible, and from the professional papers, lectures, and letters of great chemists. In this way, the chronicle constructs a solid basis for interpreting the manifold connections between imagination and necessity, between theory and experiment. Yet the history of chemistry itself is not a static subject. New discoveries and fresh insights continue to add to the rich lode of material available to the historian. Thus the Second Edition contains the results of the latest investigations and writings in the field. Sources of material cited in the text are keyed by number in parentheses to a list of references at the end of each chapter.

The reader of these pages will soon discern that the development of chemistry has from earliest times gone hand in hand with progress in other sciences and philosophies, especially medicine, mineralogy,

57000

botany, zoology, physics, and engineering. For this reason it is hoped that this volume will be found useful not only by students of chemistry and by professional workers in the field but also by all who have an abiding interest in the advancement of human knowledge.

EDUARD FARBER

Washington, D.C.
January, 1969

Contents

PERIOD III

Expansion of Synthesis and Analysis:
From the Latter Part of the Nineteenth Century to the Present

The Evolution of Chemistry

A History of its

Ideas, Methods, and Materials

Not from the beginning have the gods
shown all to mortals,
But only with time do they searchingly
find improvement.

—Xenophanes, Fragment 18

1

The History of Science and Chemistry

The Four Kinds and Dimensions of the History of Science

The scientific approach to reality consists of separating our experiences into simple parts so as to see them more clearly and of connecting these parts so as to knowingly reconstruct what impressed us. This seems to be a complicated kind of approach. We use two steps, analysis and synthesis, and we have to create intricate relationships between them because separately they are contradictory and sterile. Is it not better to use the direct method of understanding reality as one whole? The inspirational feeling that refuses both analysis and synthesis is strong, but it is mute. The German poet Friedrich Schiller expressed our inability to communicate our deepest feelings with these words: "When the soul speaks, alas, it is no longer the soul that speaks!" Science is the effort to find the language of the soul.

It is an effort that has needed time for its development. The process is still going on. Its accelerated pace does not seem to bring us closer to perfection. There is a meaningful irony in the fact that the more exact the methods of science we develop, the more inaccessible does living reality appear to become. In art we have attained perfection at various times. Works of painting, sculpture, and music created centuries ago have remained unsurpassed. They are ageless parts of our culture. Science is always moving away from its past. New discoveries, while adding to the treasure of our knowledge, at the same time reveal wider fields of our ignorance. As a consequence, what seemed to form the end of an inquiry means only the possibility of a new beginning.

Thus time plays a dominant and continuous role in science, and history should therefore be an important part of the equipment we use in continuing to build science. A. N. Whitehead (1861–1947), the mathematical physicist and philosopher, once said: "What our students should learn is how to face the future with the aid of the past." The history of science can furnish this aid when it is presented as the story of human development. When teaching present-day science, we often leave out the human element. We have to bring this human element back into focus when we talk of history in a realistic manner.

I use the term "realistic" with some hesitation because it is generally very much misused. Here its meaning can be clarified by comparison with three other methods of presenting the history of science. These can be called the analytical, the critical, and the absolutistic kinds.

The analytical kind of history collects and assembles the evidence that is available in facts and documents. It performs an important part of the whole task, but it becomes insufficient when this part is taken for the whole. When this is done, history appears as a number of statements that are no longer true or of curiosities that may at best furnish material for quiz programs or after-dinner speeches. All this is irrelevant for our scientific pursuits today. Such analytical history cannot fulfill the task of giving aid in facing the future.

The critical kind of history has more appeal because it is more emotional. Critical history uses the present state of science as the solid platform from which to cast an impatient glance at the past. Why did it take so long to arrive at our insight, why has science not developed more freely, more rapidly, and along less circuitous routes? The Greeks of classical times are blamed for not having made use of the experimental method; the alchemists are condemned for retarding progress; contemporaries of great men are reproached for not recognizing values that later became apparent. Criticism of the past has value in stirring up interest and discussion, and although we cannot change the past, we can shape a better future by learning to avoid what we recognize as error.

Absolutistic history claims that past events could not have happened differently under any circumstances. The premise from which this kind of history starts is the one that the German philosopher Hegel (1770–1831) characterized when he said that everything that exists is reasonable; it exists or it did exist through inescapable necessity. Every event occurred as the manifestation of reason. Since from the standpoint of the absolute there is no reasoning about reason, critical history becomes impossible and analytical history is deprived of its innocence by injecting a generally preconceived idea.

Realistic history is the attempt to see past events as the result of human reactions, as human efforts to observe and understand, to produce and use materials and forces. Historical reality includes the motives and feelings that were involved in creating science. In order to be historically realistic, we should reverse the usual manner of speaking of "older times" when we mean earlier times. Then science was younger, not older. We are here trying to follow it as it grows to its present age.

In selecting a realistic approach to the history of chemistry, I do not wish to indicate that the other three approaches should be categorically denounced and dramatically rejected. Much analytical work, some criticism, and even a little absolutism are needed in the attempt to recount this history realistically.

Such an attempt will always remain unfinished. Of the overwhelming amount of material, only a fraction can be selected, and of the mystery of life, only that abstraction can be given which is accessible to science. The history of science has the privilege and the duty to indicate that it is not the entire soul that speaks; only for a part of it have we found a language in science. What is true for science also applies to the description of its history. I concur with the words of George Sarton (1884–1956): "To write without passion or prejudice does not mean to write without feeling. The author has not been afraid to express his feelings, indeed he has sometimes considered it his duty to express them; but his feelings are always unmistakably separated from the facts." (1)*

In describing how science changed in the course of time, we also have to consider the men who caused the change and the surroundings in which they worked. Thus we have four directions, or dimensions, in which the history of science moves. These four dimensions are man, time, place, and object. The emphasis can be on any one of them, throughout or during a part of the story.

1. *Man.* In addition to recording scientific truths in their relation to time, the history of any science includes the men of science, the society in which they lived, and the influence exerted by the one upon the other. It is regrettable that in this dimension, history is particularly incomplete for the more distant past, just at the time when personal conviction was the source of evidence to a much larger extent than it is today. The increasing objectivization of science seems to render the effect of personality less important. The ideal scientist apparently became the passive mirror of observations, and for this he was alternately ridiculed and praised.

New developments in physics have made us see the scientist in

* The (1) indicates a reference at the end of the chapter.

a different role. Niels Bohr (1885–1962) recognized an influence by the observer on the observed; Wolfgang Pauli (1900–1958) declared that, to a certain degree, it is arbitrary where we trace the dividing line between subject and object. (2) In selecting a place for this dividing line, the historian can report more or less extensively in the human dimension. If he reduces it too much, he may get involved with the mystical concept of a *Zeitgeist,* which is something like a compelling inhuman force; if he expands it too far, he will be in danger of making science appear as a collection of emotions and imaginings. Obviously, we need additional dimensions for the history of science.

2. *Time.* In a story of this kind, a chronological date means a symbol for a state of knowledge, for a confluence of efforts made until then. Besides, all the unknown circumstances that gave rise to the advance of science are involved. The efforts to discover more of the hidden causes make the task of writing history as endless as science itself. To determine accurately the date of an event is as necessary as it is to measure a quantity of matter with utmost care, although in both cases, at the time of the determination, we do not know of the connections that may later make it important. Thus the actual meaning of the time factor in a development is not completely expressed by the calendar date. In our experimental work or in more general respects, we rarely live fully at the date the calendar indicates. This can be exemplified by the case of the inventor who believes that he is the first in the field, but may find from Patent Office records that his invention had been made public long before. In writing about history, we often assume, as does the Patent Office, that the expert is fully conversant with the state of his "art." In some parts of our work or ideas we may live in advance of our time.

The deviations in both directions are particularly frequent for the distant past when the interchange of information among scientists was scanty and slow. Although the volume of new results to be exchanged was smaller and fewer persons were participating in the pursuit of science, the special results had greater influence on general concepts of science. Who has not envied the men who lived at the time when the invention of a new form of laboratory glassware or a new kind of analytical solution gave everlasting fame? Or were there times when it was particularly easy to make far-reaching inventions?

The German historian Karl Lamprecht was convinced (1910) that a definite connection between time and event exists. When the time was ripe for the growth of atomic theories in chemistry, an atomic theory of society was simultaneously developed, and attention began to be focused on the individual, the atom of society. The paleontologist Edgar Dacqué tried to prove (1915) that time, not place, was a determining influence in organic developments. Certain forms of plants and animals became dominant all over the earth at the same geological period. It was fashionable to be an ammonite in a particular part of the Paleozoic Cambrian period.

Attempts have been made to interpret historical development by comparing it to the growth of an organism. Generally speaking, the comparison is either too superficial or too deep. It fails because it assumes that the activity of human consciousness and will is the same, in order and form, as the natural events occurring without human interference. Such speculations about the time dimension will here be avoided.

3. *Place.* In our times, a biochemist from Budapest can continue his work in Stanford, California. The soil of Illinois has no visible influence on the development of the university's betatron. Berthollet was born in Talloire, a beautiful French mountain town. Did this fact help in shaping his concept of affinity? It would be absurd to ask whether he could just as well have come into this world in Lyons or Paris. There is only one reality, this birthplace, whether or not we can find a meaning in it. Very rarely and sketchily can we sometimes connect such local origins with an influence they might have exerted on scientific work. In most cases the places of study and work are important because of the men who came to live there or because of some industry or natural resource. This dimension is closely connected with nationality. The genius of a nation is more easily felt than described in scientific language. Political events influenced the course of science very greatly, and local developments in science found application of wide political and social consequences. This dimension will be somewhat neglected in this book.

4. *Object.* The change of knowledge with time might be presented by two fundamentally different methods. One consists in separately following the development of each special object; the other describes all that occurred at one specific date and then starts again at the next following date. The first involves an artificial separation between objects, and therefore requires frequent reference to influences from neighboring fields. General theories cannot be shown in the context from which they grew. The method leads to a bundle of monographs. The second method would be arbitrary in selecting

the time periods for which the crosscuts through the state of science were to be made. The story would have to repeat itself partly for each of the succeeding periods. The result would be a collection of yearbooks.

Monographs and yearbooks can be very valuable, but they do not fulfill the function of a survey of the history of science since they present it in only one dimension. A two-dimensional history would be better but still not sufficient. It would omit values and efforts and give only the shadows of real developments, like two-dimensional graphs for, say, the yearly production of a commodity or the rate of growth of inventions. In order to give more than shadows we have to include, or at least to indicate, all of history's four dimensions—man, time, place, and object—although this makes the task of writing the history of a science particularly difficult.

Is it worth the effort to approach such a task? Hermann Kopp, the German historian of chemistry, compared the value of history to that ascribed to elixir, the fabulous life-prolonging agent. History is a kind of elixir with the effect reversed in time: "In a certain sense, we are able to prolong our life backwards by acquiring the experiences of those who were before us and by learning to know their conceptions as if we were their contemporaries."

The good that this can do depends upon the personality of the student. Will he be burdened or will he be aided by the treasures of history? A knowledge of zoology can be of great value to an architect; mineralogy can be of help to a linguist. Any field of science could stimulate any other field if it were possible to re-create that understanding of unity which we have exchanged for specialization. The history of science can recapture the foundations of that unity. It can be productive in many ways. To see how we attained our present state of knowledge may yield the power of liberating forces for continued progress and of contributing to the rehumanization of our work and life.

The Three Periods in the History of Chemistry

Chemistry is a young science as compared with medicine, astronomy, or mathematics. Man's occupation with separating and changing materials in practice and theory emerged slowly from connections with religions, philosophies, and arts and so became a science. This process was completed in the latter part of the eighteenth century. At that time chemical methods and explanations were so related to one another as to create a new fund of knowledge. The immediate cause of this great event was the success in determining the composition of the most common, and therefore most important, materials of our earth: air and water. A century of exuberant growth of the new science followed. Soon after chemistry had been established as a distinctly separate system of science, it had to be divided into special systems which increased in number. This development of chemistry has a significant analogy in the fate of the atom, which was no sooner scientifically established than it began to be divided into smaller units. Specialization and industrialization proceeded with particular vigor towards the end of the nineteenth century. Three periods thus appear in the history of chemistry: the periods of emergence, of systematization, and of expansion.

The First Period. The first period comprises the emergence of chemistry as a science out of the experiences of the workers and artisans and out of the thoughts of the philosophers. Artisans with the tradition of a special craft, and philosophers with an intutive understanding of the universe, combined their knowledge and reasoning. These men felt, as men obviously always did, that they possessed complete explanations for their experiences. When we look back to these early times at what was to emerge as chemistry, we may expect to find that people felt the absence of "real" understanding. Actually, there was no such absence. The place of scientific explanations was firmly occupied by strong convictions of a different kind. The feeling of an intimate bond with communal groups which each human being had was transferred to the things and experiences in the world of objects. The individual substances were regarded as being completely governed by their connections with the universe. Intuitions that related to cosmic forces and events were the source of knowledge of the substances. The observed realities appeared to be deeply imbedded in universal dependencies.

The Second Period. The second period shows the widening of chemical facts and the construction of systems. Actual experiences are idealized so that they acquire a general meaning. Single facts become models for others not yet observed. Great as is the change from the first to the second period, nevertheless we recognize how similar they are in their tendency toward universal unity. When each single substance represents and exemplifies a group, the observation of a few reactions is sufficient to derive general laws. These laws are idealizations. In the general conviction of the men of this period, they have greater dignity and are more reliable than practical measurements which suffer from shortcomings of our equipment.

What we measure in our experiments may constitute only an approximation to the content of the laws.

THE THIRD PERIOD. The third period is marked by the expansion of chemical work by specialization and industrialization. With the improvement of our measuring devices, we notice important deviations from the previously established laws. Individual characteristics of the substances have to be taken seriously. In a reversal of the former attitude, our laws come to be considered as only approximations to the realities.

These three periods represent stages of a development that leads from a unity of universal participation to a separation into groups and finally to emphasis upon individual singularity. Dividing the development of chemistry into such periods is artificial, but it is not arbitrary. Compromises are involved, and the rich diversities are left to the telling of the real story. The question might be asked whether it would not be more realistic to divide the history of chemistry into periods according to great men. We could find a period of Paracelsus in the sixteenth century, of Boyle in the seventeenth, of Lavoisier in the eighteenth and would thus deal with the reality of personalities instead of abstractions of concepts. It is obvious that such divisions would use the persons as symbols that would include influences from predecessors and contemporaries. The results of their work, however, which are more appropriate than their personalities, serve as a basis for organizing the whole story. Speculation and interpretation are involved when employing either method of division.

The objective changes from one period to the next are not abrupt and uniform; the borders between them are not straight lines in the time dimension. The discoverer feels that revolutions in science are sudden events; when the historian shows that they are rooted in the past, he does not aim to disparage personal achievements; he wants to describe their greatness in true perspective. (3)

REFERENCES

1. From the introductory chapter of George Sarton's *Introduction to the History of Science* (Baltimore: The Williams & Wilkins Co., 1947), Vol. 3, p. 10. A publication of the Carnegie Institution of Washington.

2. Bohr, *Atomtheorie und Naturbeschreibung* (Berlin, 1931). W. Pauli, "Die philosophische Bedeutung der Idee der Komplementarität," *Experientia,* **6,** (80) (1950); *Collected Scientific Papers by Wolfgang Pauli,* (New York: Interscience Publishers, Inc., 1964), Vol. 2, p. 1157.

3. E. Farber, "Historiography of Chemistry," *J. Chem. Ed.,* **42,** (3) (1965), pp. 120–6.

Period I

The Emergence of Chemistry:

From Oldest Records to the Eighteenth Century

2

Survey of Period I

Documents having to do with purposeful operations in the use and modification of natural materials can be dated back to before 3000 B.C. Chemistry as a distinct, self-supporting scientific system appears in the eighteenth century A.D. The five thousand years between these dates, so rich in fundamental changes of religious, political, cultural, and economic matters, are comparatively poor in scientific developments, particularly chemical. Many speculations could be based on this amazing fact. When we deplore the use of science for destruction during wars, when we advocate more attention to human pursuits than to scientific, we should bear in mind that there have been long periods in the history of mankind when science was a very minor influence. I do not mean to disparage the plea for a rehumanization of our institutions. On the contrary, this whole book has as its main purpose the strengthening of such a plea by trying to understand a part of the great human experiment which history represents. There were times when religious convictions prevailed, when the human aspect of our experiences was the only source of explanation, when universal community of activity excluded specialization. These attitudes, which are now frequently proclaimed as ideals for further developing or for supplanting science, historically preceded science. They proved unsatisfactory. The development of chemistry is an example that shows how that happened. This development took place in the first period of the history of chemistry. It is characterized by the following three main directions:

1. Substances, originally thought to have been derived from gods and planets, acquire independence of such influences. The properties or "virtues" of metals and minerals are revealed by handling and observing them. References to gods and constellations gradually become unnecessary and meaningless. This process, *the emergence*

from deification, was completed with the final abandonment of alchemistic ideas—a relatively recent event, in the eighteenth century.

2. Analogies with human feelings are gradually replaced by objective forces in explaining material changes. This process, *the emergence from anthropomorphization,* starts with the Greek philosophers of the sixth century B.C. Its end was prepared by new speculation about motion and particles of matter, which began in the thirteenth century A.D., and by the mathematical abstractions which were mainly introduced by Newton and Descartes in the seventeenth century.

3. Elements, originally introduced as the philosophical counterparts for the continuous flow of change, lose their character as universal principles and become distinct substances. This process, *the emergence from universality,* lingered behind the other two processes. It was stimulated by Robert Boyle's skepticism concerning the classical elements (1661), but its main advance took place during the eighteenth century.

These three main processes went through several stages during which the original ideas changed in content and significance. Spiritual and human connections with the world of materials were not easily given up. They retreated to make room for allegories and symbolism until, mainly after the seventeenth century, the impact of new experiences became sufficiently recognized. A preceding, wildly digressing play of alchemistical speculation could not retard this recognition for very long, but it demonstrated how painful it was to sever the old ties.

Parallel to the developments concerning the qualities of substances ran a change of thought about the structure of matter. The smallest particles of matter, the atoms of Leucippus and Democritus, represented limits of the logical process of dividing matter, just as the classical elements expressed the logical opposite of permanence to continual change. These were not only or even primarily scientific theories in the present-day sense; they had broad religious and political implications. The theories of atoms were understood to refer to the structure of human society. The philosophical atomists discovered the importance of the smallest particles of matter, but the suspicion soon arose that what they actually meant was the importance of the human individual as the smallest unit of society. This suspicion accompanied the development of atomistic theory up to the end of this period. Perhaps there is a particular significance in the fact that this end of our first period can be placed about the time when the American and the French revolutions began to take shape.

3

The Fourth Millennium B.C. to the Third Century A.D.

Techniques and Ideas

Who started chemistry? When, where, and how did it begin? Following our scheme of the four dimensions, the question takes this simple form, but we would not expect that it has a simple answer. Usually, origins are not easy to discover. First, we would have to state what the word "chemistry" means. For a time, it appeared that the problem had been definitely and finally solved.

The first record in which we find *chemia* mentioned as a secret art occurs in the writings of Zosimos, a Gnostic Christian from Panopolis in Upper Egypt, who taught and wrote in Alexandria about A.D. 300. He claimed that the name of this art was derived from that of a legendary man, Chemes, to whom fallen angels had revealed great secrets.

Such legends have a way of hiding the truth and sometimes indicating it. *Kême,* meaning the land of the black earth, was the hieroglyphic name for Egypt. Chemistry was the art of treating the pregnant mysteries of blackness so as to develop out of it the shining brightness of gold and silver. Zosimos summarized a long development of techniques and thought. They belonged together and were more intimately interwoven than are industrial and theoretical chemistry today.

In his commentary on Zosimos, Olympiodorus (fifth century A.D.) coined the name *chymeia* ("hidden art"), and he emphasized that this was the art of melting and casting metals. Julius Ruska concluded that its root was *chyma* ("metal cast"). (1) The word became widely used; its original meaning, however, was found much too narrow. In the new meaning, which we resolutely extend back in time, chemistry was the art of combined selection, separation, and substantial modification of materials. Since heat was the most important means for carrying out such operations, Prometheus, who brought fire from heaven to earth, would have to be considered the First Chemist.

In this sense, we have to date the beginnings of chemistry at the time of the earliest civilizations, at the places where they arose. Baking, brewing, and brick making are among the oldest arts. Among the oldest inventions are those of the furnace, of the mortar and pestle for grinding, and the use of clay for making pots. A large pot with a double rim on top was excavated in Mesopotamia and dated 3600 B.C.; it was probably used for the sublimation of mineral or plant materials. Clay tablets of about 2000 B.C. contain recipes for extracting plant materials in heated water. Hides were steeped in salt, mechanically worked, and treated with alum, grape juice, gall nuts, myrrh, oak, or sumac, and the leather so produced was made supple by oil and grease. Hide scraps furnished the material for glues. Edible oil was pressed from sesame in Mesopotamia, from olives in other places. Recipes for dyeing specify the use of vitriol, copper salts, juices from myrobalans or pomegranates. Other tablets tell of perfumes, medicines, and cleaning agents. (2)

At the time of our records, these things were already traditions. They were passed on through generations in a form that perhaps left an unnamed artisan free to add his own innovations. We can get a perspective of time when we learn from a cuneiform tablet of about 1700 B.C.: "In days of yore, a farmer passed these instructions to his son." (3)

When we search for general thoughts connected with these practical operations, we find wide-ranging analogies with religious concepts of gods and stars. For one of these analogies we have to go to Egypt. This land of the black earth was devoted to the cult of the dead. The god Osiris is revived from death after he has been ritually wrapped in bandages. To the Egyptian's mind, this indicated a valid analogy to the fact that minerals are bandaged and entombed in black lye to revive them into metals. Salt was used in the important art of embalming. Salt, therefore, "conserves the body and is second in rank next to the soul," according to Philo of Alexandria (30 B.C. to A.D. 50). Matter is endowed with power by which it affects life. It has this power from the connection with universal forces which are personalized and sublimed into gods.

In one of the deep mysteries which shock and convince by combining the greatest contradictions, the blackness of death and the tomb is pregnant with life, like the dark menstrual blood. All colors have vital importance. The direct sensual effects lead in the operations for obtaining colors. Purple is monopolized by the emperors. Red, blue, and green stones for jewelry, pigments for cosmetics—all have a direct emotional value before their use becomes merely traditional. Thus we do not find a tiny model of our chemistry in ancient times, but a world in which forces are alive instead of being abstracted into laws of nature. The work carried out by technicians (called *technítes*) and their manual helpers (the *ergátes*) is influenced by these forces. Since they are also personalities, these forces are not entirely predictable, but they can be invoked, appeased, and flattered. The reproducibility of more than the most common events and operations is not at all certain. When gods can change from the form of an animal to that of a plant, the identity of stone or metal is also variable. The variability of substances leads to two different kinds of result. In one case the properties of a material change, as when wine turns sour. In the other case, uniform appearance is offered to our senses by materials that are not really the same. The first is easily observed; the second presents a technical problem. For gold it can be solved, because, besides its color, its behavior in the fire is important for its use.

Furnaces for melting gold were used at the time of the Old Empire of Egypt, between 2895 B.C. and 2540 B.C. The Babylonian Tell -'el-Amarna tablets of the fourteenth century B.C. contain a report about the purity test for gold in the fire. The king of Babylon informs the king of Egypt that of twenty *mines* (about 500 grams each) of gold sent to him, only five came out of the furnace as "real" gold. The Papyrus Harris (of the thirteenth century B.C.) mentions "two-thirds gold, fine gold, and white gold," of which the latter, containing silver, was called *electron* by the Greeks.

The refining of gold and silver was so widely known and so highly regarded in the sixth century B.C. that many of the Biblical prophets used it in metaphors. Ezekiel (22:22) exclaims: "As silver is melted in the midst of the furnace, so shall ye be melted in the midst thereof; . . ." Malachi's vision (3:3) sees the Lord "as a refiner and purifier of silver: and he shall purify the sons of Levi, and purge them as gold and silver. . . ." (4)

When Solomon planned to build a temple, he called for men who knew metals and colors. "Send me now therefore a man cunning to work in gold, and in silver, and in brass, and in iron, and in purple, and crimson, and blue. . . ." (II Chronicles 2:7).

Lapis lazuli was a highly valued blue stone. Inscriptions of 2500

Fig. 1. Wooden chest of cosmetics containing salves and makeup belonging to Tutu, the wife of the scribe Ani. On the floor below are red sandals made of antelope leather. About 1400 B.C. (London, British Museum.)

B.C. already mention a genuine blue stone, obviously to distinguish it from an imitation. Even the imitated stone must have been very precious because glass in small pieces and as beads was a gift fit for kings in the fifteenth century B.C.

Alkanna, the dyestuff from the plant *Lawsonia inermis*, is reported in the thirteenth century B.C. Whether the name was restricted to material of this origin, however, appears doubtful. Sandyx, at first the name of a bright red plant pigment, also designated other red colors including the minerals cinnabar, iron oxide, etc. Indigo, the name of the most important of the old dyestuffs, was originally an Egyptian word; it was later erroneously connected with India.

To the techniques of working with stones and dyes we have to add those of preparing hides by tanning, of baking, brewing, and making wine and cheese, of forming, drying, and firing pottery, bricks, and tiles. The traditions on which these industries are based go further back than recorded history.

Connection with religious origins survived into late medieval times, when saints were claimed as the patrons of these trades. Since the time of Hesiod, an Ionian poet of the seventh century B.C., it has been thought that the development of civilization could be divided into four consecutive periods or "ages," those of stone, copper, bronze, and iron. The change from the first to the second was supposed to have occurred about 2500 B.C.; the beginning of the Iron Age was placed at about 1100 B.C. Actually, however, the historical variations are too great to permit such a general statement. Bronze figures from the fourth millennium B.C. have been discovered. The oldest specimens, from Mesopotamia, contain only one-third percent of tin, while later ones contain considerably more. Lead appears as a component of bronze in the third millenium B.C. King Gudea of Lagos constructed a temple basin in which stone and lead were used. Large lead plates have been discovered in Assyrian tombs of the thirteenth century B.C. Among the offerings that the Egyptian king Ramses III (twelfth century) made to the gods were 9000 pounds of lead. Antimony metal was known at the time of the Sumerians and in oldest China. The Semitic Chetites produced iron in the fifteenth century B.C., at the time when the Egyptian king Thutmosis conquered the Retenu in Lebanon and brought iron weapons home in triumph. In India, ironworking was so well known that commentaries on the religious Vedas (1000 B.C.–500 B.C.) use as a simile ". . . just as a lump of iron, overcome by the fire and hammered by the workmen, takes on manyfold shapes." The famous Kutub Column of Delhi was made from seventeen (long) tons of

Fig. 2. Servant brewing beer. Painted limestone statue from Sakkara, Egypt, VI Dynasty, about 2500 B.C. (Florence, Museo Archeologico.)

wrought iron, with such an elaborate technique that a lengthy development must have preceded its erection in the fourth century A.D.

In the *Iliad* (eighth century B.C.) Homer describes the adornment of weapons with tin. The Greek word for this metal, *kassíteros,* comes from the Babylonian *kastira,* which itself goes back to the Akkadian *Ik-kasduru.* The islands near Britain, whence the Phoenicians imported the metal, were therefore called the Cassiterides.

Mercury was found in an Egyptian tomb of the sixteenth or fifteenth century B.C. The land of its origin was perhaps Spain. Cinnabar was highly valued because of its red-gold color. The stone of Tarshish, mentioned in the Biblical "Canticle of Canticles," is a crystallized cinnabar. Aristotle (384 B.C.–322 B.C.) mentions mercury, the "molten silver," and its use in a magic wooden statue of Aphrodite.

Knowledge and use of the metals, like those of the minerals, remained quite stagnant during these millennia. A Babylonian clay tablet of the seventeenth century B.C., which lists the ingredients for a pottery glaze and which has been called a "glass text," differs very little from the "glass text" of the seventh century B.C. The thousand years between these two texts brought no change but only confirmation of the prescriptions, an essential part of which consisted of placating the spirits. The younger text contains a description of two types of ovens for which the fuel wood should be cut in the hot month of Ab so as to give high heat. (5)

A development in the art of alloying metals consisted in an increase in the falsification of gold. A Chinese imperial edict of 144 B.C. proclaims punishment by execution for the private coining of money and for making counterfeit gold (6). Among the laws that the Roman consul and dictator Sulla promulgated in 81 B.C. was one against false gold (*Lex Cornelia de falsis*).

These measures indicate that the misuse of chemical arts for making false gold was considerable and aroused great attention. It is much more important, however, that chemical arts made it possible to create objects of lasting beauty. Artisans joined with artists to produce beautiful weapons, tools, containers, and ornaments from metals, stones, and clays. Some of the painted vases of the seventh to the fourth century from the country around Athens even bear the names of the artists. For these vases, we also know a date, about 530–500 B.C., when the painting was changed from black on a red ground to red on a black ground. The technique required the use of special, iron-rich earths, and a control of the firing to produce flames that were oxidizing or reducing at the proper time. A Scyth-

Fig. 3. Chinese bronze from the Shang dynasty, a ceremonial vessel of the type *p'an*. Decoration cast partly in relief but mainly in intaglio. Single character inscription. Green patination with some cuprite in the artifact. (Courtesy of the Smithsonian Institution. Freer Gallery of Art, Washington, D.C.)

Fig. 4. Attic amphora, or vase, with black figures, from about 550 B.C. (Courtesy of the Dumbarton Oaks Collection, Washington, D.C.)

ian prince in Asia Minor was so impressed with the beauty of one of these vases that, as payment, he filled with grains the Attic ship that had brought it. (7)

Constant Elements and Changing Substances

Authorship for the chemical activities of the most ancient times can be described only vaguely within national units. The great personalities of those days, named in later reports, are fictitious or legendary, like the god Hermes, the great Chemes, the priests Ostanes and Johannes, and the alchemist Moses. It is different for ancient Greece. Homer still belongs to the dim period of the past, but beginning with the sixth century B.C. personalities begin to become clearly recognizable. Here is a list of some of these, with as much as can be ascertained about the dates of their lives.*

PROMINENT MEN OF ANCIENT TIMES

Name	Place	Date (B.C.)
Solon	Athens	600
Thales	Miletus	600
Anaximander	Miletus	611–545
Anaximenes	Miletus	585–525
Pythagoras	Samos	570–490
Heraclitus	Ephesus	540–?
Leucippus	Miletus	*ca.* 500–?
Anaxagoras	Clazomenae	500–428
Protagoras	Abdera	485–411
Zeno	Elea	490–430
Empedocles	Akragas (now Agrigento)	483–430
Parmenides	Elea	*ca.* 500–?
Herodotus	Halicarnassus	484–424?
Socrates	Athens	470–399
Hippocrates	Kos	460–377
Democritus	Abdera	450–420
Plato	Athens	427–347
Aristotle	Athens	384–322
Epicurus	Athens	342–271

When we turn from the Egyptians and Babylonians to the Greeks, a great change in the problems and in the methods for their solution

* Refer to this table for information about the authors mentioned in this chapter. Xenophanes, whose Fragment 18 is quoted as the motto of this book, is not listed because so little is known about his life dates.

is recognizable. Old concepts of the stars being gods remain alive; the sun, the moon, and the five planets are animated beings in Plato's *Timaeus.* The new emphasis, however, is on the nature of man and his ability to know the forces and objects on the earth and not only those in the heavens.

Plato felt the fundamental difference between the Hellenic love of science as against the love of utility which characterized the Egyptian approach. This difference has since been confirmed by many historians. Abel Rey stresses the positive part of it when he says that Egypt had established "a positive and human science, all technique without theory, without philosophy . . ." (8) Theory and philosophy were the contributions arising out of the new period. "The Egyptians could not conceive of nature as a universal whole, as the Ionians could and did." (9) Human existence takes part in this unity of the universe. Human society can be understood as an organism. Both man and society are in a healthy state when the basic elements are in a harmonious admixture. From this basis, Solon proceeded in promulgating his laws.

The new emphasis on man as a natural part of the universe can also be seen in the founding of the medical schools at Kos and Cnidus in the Greek Archipelago. The founders called themselves the Sons of Asclepius (around 600 B.C.). From Thales to Democritus, the ardent endeavor is to penetrate to the foundations, to define words, to establish meanings. The basis for the definitions is found in our human existence, in our relationship to cosmic powers, in the response of our senses to the events of this world. Together, these attempts try to find the human equation. Consciousness of the equipment that we, as observers, bring to our task preceded the experimental way to knowledge. These Greek philosophers first ask themselves about the world in order to lay the foundation on which they could then, by means of experimentation, ask questions about objects.

The search for definition is guided by poetic visions and carried out with strong convictions. The philosophers of those times were imbued with the feeling that they had found the absolute truth. They pronounced it in the form of laws, not as tentative working hypotheses or as useful fiction. For Thales, water was "the inexhaustable substance from which everything is born and into which everything passes!" (10) Anaximander proclaims that air is the universal matter which, in his words, "includes everything in itself and guides everything." Air is thus not to be taken in the sense of a primitive substance, but as an active "element" in the role that was formerly ascribed to the gods. Air is a principle, immortal and indestructible.

Objects arise out of air and pass away into air, according to the strict necessity of penitence and atonement.

What is constant behind change is not a substance, like water, but an invisible *apeiron,* the law of birth and death in time, the objective order of the world.

Anaximenes combines the visions of a definite substance and of infinite change by the universal processes of thickening and thinning, or contraction and expansion. Matter and life are connected, not absolutely separated, by differences in degrees of this scale of change, and the unity thus formed allows us to compare the great cosmos of the world with the small cosmos of the individual.

Pythagoras agrees with these thoughts and strengthens their application through the concept of numbers. The world is quantity and measure, and our knowledge of the world is based on the definiteness of numbers. Anaximenes saw the link between matter and life; Pythagoras proclaims that number mediates between the thinking mind and the perceived things. *Apeiron,* according to Anaximander, is the essence of matter; what makes it knowable to us is number, through which the world becomes a system of forms and movements.

There is a continuation of thoughts from Thales to Pythagoras, but there is complete opposition between those of Heraclitus and Parmenides. For Heraclitus, the order of the world is an eternal fire, now alight, now extinguished, gradually changing into water and earth and periodically turning the whole world into a state of fire. Between these conflagrations the world temporarily consists of fire, water, and earth. We could easily rationalize that these three elements mean the three states of matter—gaseous, liquid, and solid. Such a meaning is only a small part of what Heraclitus tried to express. The fire, which for a time assumes the form of water and earth, is not just a physically real state of matter, its reality is that of a god. Empedocles calls fire "the shining Zeus," and he identifies air with "the life-bringing Hera" (a Greek goddess). For Parmenides, the basic truth is that we can think only of being, of that which exists. We can neither think nor say anything about nonbeing. Being is immovable, indivisible, and unchanging. We have to seek this pure being in our world of appearances, in which being is intermingled with nonbeing.

Empedocles was a philosopher and a medical doctor. His theory of the four elements influenced chemistry as much as medicine, where belief in the basic four humours: blood, phlegm, yellow bile, and black bile, predominated for many centuries. Plato used medicine as an example for true rhetoric. He quotes, in the *Gorgias,* the teachings of Hippocrates, "careful analysis of nature, enumeration of its types, and definition of the appropriate treatment for each." In the first stage of the creation of the world, the primordial matter was formed into four elements—fire, air, water, earth. The smallest particles of earth, as the heaviest of the elements, consist of cubes, those of fire are tetrahedrons with their sharp angles and cutting edges. Ether is the fifth, the celestial element. Demons, who are transitions between man and god, mostly consist of ether and air.

According to Empedocles, there once existed a primordial state in which all the elements were mixed in an all-embracing sphere held together by love. Hatred gained entrance into it and separated the elements into individual beings. Anaxagoras replaced the emotional forces, love and hatred, by spirit (*nus*) which arranges the uniformly scattered parts according to their natures. Not four elements, but infinite numbers of primary substances, exist. Anaxagoras called them *spermata.* Aristotle later gave them the name *homoiomerei,* which can be translated as "equal particles." We can divide a bone, a piece of gold, into even-smaller particles, but we never reach a smallest particle nor can matter cease to exist by being subdivided.

With their respective single elements, Thales, Anaximander, and Heraclitus express recognition that existence is real; whether the element is called water, air, or fire is of secondary importance. The change of substances in this reality is the problem that Heraclitus and Parmenides solve in such opposite fashions. Love and hatred are the forces that cause the change, according to Empedocles. In Plato's *Timaeus,* the elements are means by which the creator translates eternal ideas into realities. Plato here agrees with Pythagoras on the importance of numbers and mathematical forms, and he follows Leucippus and Democritus in his thoughts about the ultimate, indivisible, smallest particles of matter. It is Aristotle, at one time a disciple of Plato, who gives tangible reality to the elements. It is the reality of our sensations, of cold and warmth, of wetness and dryness. The cause of these sensations is ascribed to the object and called "quality." Each element has two of the qualities.

To the scheme devised by Aristotle, the Stoic philosophers added another distinction: fire and air are light, water and earth are heavy. Thus, in addition to two qualities residing in one element, there were two pairs of elements that shared one quality each.

In the teachings of Hippocrates, dryness and wetness, cold and warmth were the elements of the human body and its food. The four are used by Aristotle either with the same meaning, as elements,

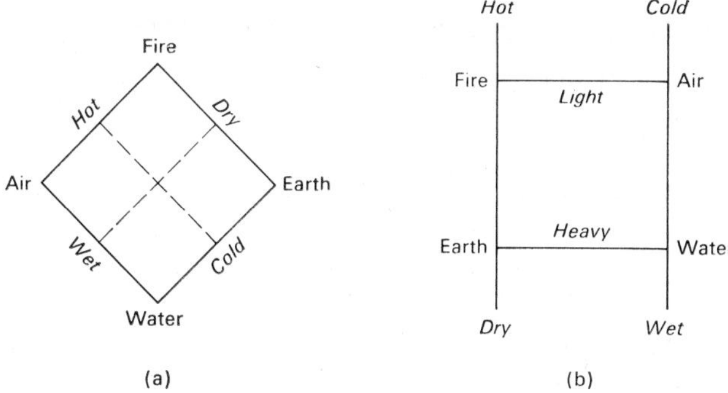

Fig. 5. The four elements according to (a) Aristotle, with their four qualities, and (b) the Stoic philosophers, whose elements had six qualities.

or in a different role, as qualities that constitute the elements. In separating out these four from the great number of qualities, Aristotle differs fundamentally from Anaxagoras, who included all qualities. Black and white, or sweetness and bitterness, for example, are rejected by Aristotle because they are too subjective.

The proportion—Fire : Air = Air : Water = Water : Earth—which Plato postulated, is here completed into a cycle. The idea of the four elements recurs in medicine as the theory of the four essential liquids or humours. The four qualities, therefore, also had medical importance. Two books of the time before Aristotle, *On Regimen in Health* and *On Diet,* prescribe food of much warmth and dryness to counteract the effects of winter, which is cold and wet; the opposite composition of food is advised for summer. For massage, oil, which heats the body, should be used in winter; in summer the oil should be mixed with cooling water. The number four recurs as that of the principle of all being: form, matter, moving cause, and design (or purpose). Matter is a potential existence, made real by form which is called *entelechéia* or *energéia* . Movement or change, called *kinesis,* is the transition from the potential to the real.

Epicurus' metaphysics is based on Democritus' atomism. In contrast to Anaxagoras, he argued that there must be limits to the possibility of dividing bodies, otherwise we could dissolve them into nonexistence. The indivisible particles, or atoms, are too small to be seen singly, but their number is infinitely great. Their only properties are extension, shape, and weight. From eternity these particles move in empty space between them. Through the chances of aggregation they create all the diversity of existing things. Aristotle exemplified this by saying that the same letters can be combined to write either comedy or tragedy.

"The inventors of the atomistic theory either must have discovered at the outset the key to events in nature, or they have hit upon a concept which is dictated to the human mind by its very nature." (11) The same might be said about the "inventors" of the other great theories brought up between the sixth and the fourth century B.C., the theories that change is continuous, that in all change there is a core which remains permanent, that matter is composed of elements. The first led to laws of continuity, of causality, of conservation for matter, and later for energy. After a long digression during the period of alchemy, the last developed into a modified theory of elements.

Greek philosophy contained more theories than these that have just been set forth. The contradictory views of Heraclitus and Parmenides, of Empedocles and Anaxagoras, indicate that they, together, express general, human possibilities of thinking about god, man, and nature, asserted by strong personalities and proved by intuitions. They establish a decisive advance from the reign of mythos to the predominance of reason, from fear and fantasy to thoughts and perceptions, the way to the human side of the method of science. It proved to be a difficult way. From the beginning, the proponents of the theory of atoms had to fight against the suspicion that they were low and subversive characters. And it was not the fault of Aristotle that "schoolmen," centuries later, converted his philosophical thoughts into unreasonable dogmas.

The successors of Aristotle at the Lyceum were Theophrastus of Eresos (372–288 B.C.) and Strabo of Lampsacus, who was head of the Lyceum from 287 to 269. Diogenes Laertius, who wrote ten volumes of *Lives of Eminent Philosophers* (third century A.D.), ascribes 227 treatises to Theophrastus, among them books on fire, on stones, on the senses, on the history of plants. He points out that fire is quite different from the other three elements: we can generate fire, and it requires a substratum. He is also interested in such technical things as the preparation of "white lead," the much-used pigment consisting of lead acetate. Strabo called atoms "the dream of Democritus, who could not prove them but only desired them."

A different form of the theory of elements came from China. It is ascribed to Dzou Yen, who lived in Shantung from 323 B.C. till 298 B.C. Influences from Mesopotamia may have helped to shape it, particularly to include emphasis upon colors, while the place attributed to the elements appears to be characteristic of Chinese thinking.

The five elements, with their corresponding colors, metals, and places, are as follows (12):

EARTH = YELLOW = GOLD = CENTER
WOOD = AZURE = LEAD = EAST
FIRE = RED = COPPER = SOUTH
METAL = WHITE = SILVER = WEST
WATER = BLACK = IRON = NORTH

These concepts were combined with the old principle of the contraries, *yin* and *yang*, which are variously identified with female and male or moon and sun.

> The doctrine of the two contraries in its general form, as philosophy and science, as religion and nature theory and world concept, seems to have prevailed in Egypt from the earliest times. It appeared in China in the third or fourth century B.C., full-grown and already associated with numerous occult connotations, in a state of maturity which indicates that it was probably an importation into that country. (13)

The experience of cold and warm as opposites is commonplace. To connect it with other opposite or contrary sensations, to conclude that all existence is made up of contraries, was a great revelation. A universal structure of the world, a common link between all the contraries was discovered, and chemical change could be explained by saying that the balance of the two opposite qualities in matter had undergone a change.

Elements and principles were created by great intuitions. Their meaning seemed clear and precise within a system of thinking. Their place in material reality was quite another thing. The correlation of elements with metals was variable. A favorite assumption was that mercury is water plus earth, and that sulfur is made of fire plus air. Both aspects of such formulas were vague enough to be exciting.

In China particularly, gold was assumed to have great "virtues" as a means for prolonging life. Is it necessary to have real gold, or does any substance with the color of gold have the same effect? On the other hand, since substances change, since the elements combine in varying proportions, would it not be possible to convert lead, copper, or mercury into gold? Experience with fermentation appeared to offer a great analogy. A small amount of zyme (yeast) transforms large quantities of flour. In writings ascribed to Democritus but originating in the first or second century of our era, and for a long time afterward, the thought is expressed that actions similar to those of the small quantities of yeast can be produced. There is a powerful powder which, when thrown upon the prepared metals, will convert them into gold. Its name is *xerion* in Greek, *al-iksir* in Arabic. From this latter word the term "elixir" was derived. The more that materials and methods became known, the more those men who were trying to explore the secrets of nature seemed to lose their grip on reality. The artisans were safe; they followed traditions in dyeing and glassmaking and the other trades. Explorers found an apparently chaotic world in which ritualistic exhortations and a strong will to achieve great work remained as guides. Hidden forces, changing elements, magic converting-powders became parts in the great tragedy of alchemy. From small beginnings it grew during many centuries until it came to dominate the scene to such an extent that the Roman emperor Diocletian (A.D. 284–305) denounced chemistry as the abominable are of falsifying gold and silver.

We recognize here a great division in the evolution of chemistry. Technical experience and religious endeavors during an untold number of millennia provided the source for fundamental thoughts about man and the universe, mind and matter, constancy and change. These thoughts were proclaimed as the final truth, but they were even greater as the starting positions for the continuing search. The philosophers had to satisfy the thirst for knowledge; the artisans were confronted with the thirst for gold, and they made the thoughts about elements and qualities useful for the purpose of converting lower metals into gold. This "practical" application later led to its own kind of theories, with deep roots in religious concepts, and yet under the fascination with the one metal: gold.

REFERENCES

1. J. Ruska, "Neue Beiträge zur Geschichte der Chemie. 1. Die Namen der Goldmacherkunst," *Quellen zur Geschichte der Naturwissenschaften und der Medizin,* **8** (3, 4) (1942), pp. 1–31.

2. G. Sarton, *A History of Science* (Cambridge: 1952), p. 150.

3. M. Levey, *Chemistry and Chemical Technology in Ancient Mesopotamia* (Princeton, N.J.: D. Van Nostrand Co., Inc., 1959).

4. Robert Eisler, "Metallurgical anthropology in Hesiod and Plato and the date of a 'Phoenician Lie'," *Isis.,* **40** (1949), p. 108.

5. R. Campbell Thompson, *A Dictionary of Assyrian Chemistry and Geology* (London: The Clarendon Press, 1936).

6. Homer H. Dubs, *Isis,* **38** (1947), p. 62.

7. J. V. Noble, *The Techniques of Painted Attic Pottery* (London: 1966).

8. Abel Rey, *La science orientale avant les Grecs* (Paris: La Renaissance du Livre, 1930), p. 331.

9. Werner Jaeger (translated by Gilbert Highet), *Paideia, the Ideals of Greek Culture* (New York: The Oxford University Press, 1944), Vol. 3, p. 5.

10. For these and subsequent quotations, see: Hermann Diels, *Die Fragmente der Vorsokratiker, griechisch und deutsch* (6th ed., by Walther Kranz; 3 vols, Berlin: 1951–52). Giorgio de Santillana, *The Origins of Scientific Thought from Anaximander to Proclus* (Chicago/London: 1961). S. Sambursky, *The Physical World of Late Antiquity,* (New York: 1962).

11. A. Cournot, *Traité de l'Enchaînement des Idées Fondamentales dans la Science et dans l'Histoire* (Paris: 1861), p. 245.

12. Homer H. Dubs, *Isis* **38** (1947), pp. 62–86.

13. Tenney L. Davis, *Isis* **28** (1938), p. 73. Joseph Needham (with the research assistance of Wang Ling), *Science and Civilization in China,* Vol. 2: *History of Scientific Thought* (New York: 1956).

4

The Third to the Sixteenth Centuries

It may appear strange that all-embracing theories were sought before the attempt was made to explore the actual behavior of substances. Should not direct, patient observation have instigated the beginning of chemistry? Was it not the wrong approach to reality to start from gods and mysteries, logical principles, and the philosophical organization of ideas? The answers to such questions are given by the history of the science. What we call simple facts were not so real to our predecessors as were mysteries and ideas. The latter gave meaning to single observations; they formed the system that we always need for relating isolated facts. Even our most empirical work is imbedded in systematic correlations through which experiments become possible. Before correlations and understanding could be objective, they obviously had to be humanly subjective, but we could never do without these additions to the "simple facts."

To some extent, and apart from the influences of the old astrology, Ptolemy (Claudius Ptolomaeus) attempted to develop and carry out a scientific method in astronomy. He failed where he had no system to support him. "Ptolemy illustrates well the fact that a mere mechanical application of the various steps in scientific method is no guarantee of infallible conclusions. The weakness of Ptolemy's work lies, paradoxically enough, not in the fact that he was not empirical, but that he was too empirical in a naïve sense." (1)

A great philosophical system, particularly that of Aristotle, functioned as the basis from which creative experimental work could start and in which it could find coherent meaning. The work of a slightly younger contemporary of Ptolemy, the physician Galen, is proof of that. Galen was born at Pergamum about A.D. 130. With an interruption during the plague of 166, he lived in Rome from 162 and died there (or in Pergamum) in 201. His writings, almost four hundred in number, coordinate his experiments with the teaching of a philosophy that was closely connected with religion. His physiology employs the old theory of the four humours. As in ancient times, health was a result of the right mixture, qualitatively and quantitatively, of bodily components. Respiration brings the "pneuma," the principle of life, into the body. There it is differentiated into the three kinds of pneuma, those of liver, heart, and brain. Galen distinguishes between grades of the action of medicaments. Both fire and pepper are characterized by the quality heat, but the former is actually hot, the latter only potentially. He considers the stone of the magic king and god, Nechepsus, a powerful remedy even without its being engraved with pictures of stars and magic signs which was formerly thought necessary. The greatness of Galen is not characterized by originality but by the erection of a comprehensive system which coordinates older theories. The amount of medical experience was so great that the work of the encyclopedist was urgently needed, and he found help in his heroic task by using the traditional method of forming groups with three of four members.

When we consider the development of chemistry from the standpoint of arithmetic, it becomes obvious that the beginning is a simple division into two parts. Preformed in many old concepts, like the *yin* and *yang* of the Chinese, the male and the female take on the significance of matter and form, of substance and energy. We have only recently overcome this particular stage in recognizing the relationship that unites these two. Establishing four elements was an advance of such importance that it remained dominant into the eighteenth century. Another attempt at bringing theory and observation closer together consisted in representing the form principle as a seed, which was intimated by Anaxagoras and later expressed as the *logoi spermatikoi* of Aristotle. The conversion of copper into bronze by the addition of tin became an example of the action of these sperms of the logos or of form. They were simply identified with the metal tin. Copper consisted of primitive matter with a certain number of qualities added. The introduction of a further quality, tin now being considered as having only one quality, changes the number of qualities of the primitive matter and thereby converts it into bronze. (2)

The figures three, four, and seven frequently recur in efforts to conquer reality by dividing it. The fabulous Hermes has the surname *Trismegistos* because, according to Zosimos, he reconstructed the world from the three units—cold, warm, and liquid. For Pliny (Caius Plinius Secundus, author of *Naturalis historia,* who died at Stabiae

Fig. 6. Cane sugar manufacture, A.D. 1100. (From *Li Ch'ioa-p'ing*, "The Chemical Arts of Old China," *J. Chem. Educ.*, 1948, p. 157.)

in A.D. 79), magic has three parts: religion, medicine, astronomy. In writings ascribed to Hermes and dating from the third century A.D., one of the books is devoted to the seven plants on earth that correspond to the seven planets. A. Manlius Severinus Boethius (480–524, consul under the Ostrogothic king, Theodoric) (3) defined knowledge as having four stages: sense, imagination, reason, understanding (*De Consolatione Philosophiae,* written shortly before he was put to death). Spinoza, more than eleven hundred years later, described this fourth stage of knowledge, understanding, as our feeling and enjoying the thing itself, its essence. In treatises composed by the Brethren of Purity, a kind of philosophical association founded in Basra (Iran) in 983, the seven hundred kinds of minerals are divided into seven classes.

Against or above these divisions by traditional numbers, the idea of a fundamental unity persisted. One of its proponents was Olympiodorus, of whom it is reported that he acted as a special envoy to the Roman emperor Honorius in A.D. 412. The great symbol for the unity in matter and processes was the serpent that bends its body into a circle and bites into its own tail. This symbol, with its background of myths about serpents and dragons named Ouroboros, signifies many things in their basic and encircled unity. For Olympiodorus, the symbol means the common prime matter that transforms and regenerates itself, and he identifies it variously with lead or with sulfur, this "principle of all things."

Theories and abstractions were related to experimental work by the use of equipment, of which descriptions are ascribed to Dioscurides (about A.D. 75) and the slightly younger Maria the Jewess. A very important part of the technique consists is producing the correct degree of heat. The chemist is a philosopher of and by fire, a *philosophus per ignem* in the commentaries to Zosimos. Robertus Vallensis, who reported about the foundations of chemistry in a book which may represent the first attempt at writing a history of chemistry (1561), identifies the name of this "art" with the Greek word for fusion: ". . . that art of fusion is part of the natural philosophy of mineral things and is a more secret art, called by the ancients 'Secret Philosophy' or 'Sacred Art,' which examines the causes and natures of minerals which liquify in fire; and from those in particular, it shows how to prepare a certain powder, fusible even in the gentlest flame, like melting wax: it may be called either stone, or salt, oil, sulphur, elixir, medicine, or potable gold. It has a marvelous power over the animal, vegetable, and mineral kingdoms. . . ." (4)

For very gentle heating, materials are placed in horse manure. The water bath is used in other operations. Ovens are built to special requirements, and heat from burning wood is increased by blowing air into it, through pipes by the mouth or by means of a bellows. The vessels are made of clay or, strongly recommended by Zosimos, of glass. By connecting the neck with a vent tube of clay, glass, or copper, and leading this to a receiver, an apparatus for distilling is constructed. The arrangement of the three parts and the method of cooling the vaporized materials were varied in many ways.

Materials are digested in solutions of salt or of ashes. They are cooked, as in the preparation of soap (Greek *saponion*). They are "sweetened" by being washed out with filtered water.

One of the basic materials used in the operations is lead. It shows its nature of being a primitive or primordial matter by being black and easily fused. A great favorite is pyrite, the Etesian Stone, which Zosimos describes as "the most glorious stone, beloved of god . . . composed of everything." A complicated line of analogies and allusions connects the name of this stone with that of the Etesian Winds, the annual desert winds which brought fertility to the black soil, so that this stone is at the same time a symbol of extreme blackness. Mercury is "water" because it is liquid and thus one of the fundamental elements. The other fundamental element is sulfur, with which mercury forms cinnabar. Sometimes mercury is also identified with sulfur. Arsenic "whitens" metals and is a male principle, since its name is so similar to *arren*, the Greek word for "male." "Asbestos of the ancients" is lime, but it is different from "white asbestos," which is artificially burnt lime.

Color Schemes in the Conversion of Metals

All these materials are variable. Mercury can have several degrees of liquidity, sulfur can be light or dark, arsenic can be made to rise as a sublimate. Greater still are the variations produced when these materials act upon one another. Fascinated by the red color obtained from lime and sulfur, the yellow produced by *stimmi* (antimony sulfide) on metal alloys, the operators sought understanding, that fourth stage of knowledge which goes beyond reason to the essence of things. This essence was found revealed in a change of color or in a transition from liquid to solid. The great process of making gold was divided into four steps, according to colors:

1. *Melanosis,* the production of the black metal, as from a mixture of lead and copper treated with sulfur.
2. *Leukosis,* the whitening, as by the action of arsenic.
3. *Xanthosis,* from "silver" to the yellow of gold, as with a lime-sulfur concoction.
4. *Iosis,* turning gold to violet to obtain a super-gold, one which is so powerful that it converts other materials by a yeastlike action.

This classical Egyptian process was later changed into the sequence black—white—red, and the Ios became Elixir at the time of the Islamic alchemists of the ninth century. (5)

The material converted into vapor during distillation was considered to be the spirit, a part of the universal pneuma; the dead body remained behind. When we today describe the distillation of a substance in terms of its vapor pressure, we thereby place this substance in a system of other substances. Without such systematic context, the words "vapor pressure" would only duplicate and be identical with what we strive to explain. In these alchemistical times, a reference to coordinating groups of facts was not possible; they were not known. The reference was to human feelings and ideas because these were known.

Alexandria was a focal point for the combination of Egyptian practice and Greek thought. From there this alchemy spread to the Roman province of Syria. Greek writings were translated into Syraic from the fourth to at least the eighth century A.D. After the death of Mohammed in 632, the Arabs conquered Persia and spread Islam to the East and the West. Hebrew, Greek, and Syriac were replaced by Arabic as the language of the scientific world until Latin began to dominate the scene in the twelfth century. Baghdad in the East and Cordova (Spain) in the West were great centers of learning in the ninth and tenth centuries.

Perhaps during this time the oracular pronouncements of the *Tabula Smaragdina,* the "green tablet," may have been composed. The "tablet" carries the explanatory subtitle *De operatione Solis,* which means "working with or for the production of gold"; it contains ten short paragraphs like the following, which is the fourth: "You will separate the earth from the fire, the subtle from the compact, with great skill. It ascends from Earth to Heaven, then descends again to Earth and receives the force of those above and those below." (6)

It is impossible for us to understand why such pronouncements acquired great fame in the thirteenth century and later unless we try to participate in the deep emotion from which they originated. This is not simply a description of a process of sublimation in the physicochemical sense of a laboratory procedure. We speak of sublimation when we heat a thin layer of a dry material and thereby obtain a vapor which solidifies or crystallizes on a cold surface. Sulfur can thus be separated from a mixture as a sublimate. The original connection with the meaning of "sublime" is not yet forgotten in the "green tablet" or Emerald Table.

Here, allusions to religious feelings and philosophical ideas serve as the bridge between the technical work and its theoretical interpretation. The authors who wanted to describe the chemical methods and materials had to develop a language that was appropriate for the special job while being adept in conveying meaningful connections with the past. The ambiguities in traditional names, like that of Hermes, the god of merchants, thieves, and writers, helped; they became specific by being pinned down during subsequent use. A rich source for the developing language was the usual designation of an obvious and impressive quality. Thus, *anthrax* was the name for indigo, and the lustrous, shiny surface of indigo in blocks led to the extended use of the word for other things of similar surface appearance, e.g., for the coal named anthracite and later for that terrible disease that is characterized by glossy carbuncles. The name "crystal" for a transparent solid was thus also applied to water and air of high transparency. The effort to develop a language for talking about chemistry is shown in the copious literature of the period we are considering here; it is a continuing effort that accompanies the evolution of science.

Only a few of the many authors will be mentioned here, and

from their writings about the universe of thoughts and experiences only the specifically chemical parts will be selected.

The center of interest was the operation with metals and the production of colors. At least, one would judge so from the titles and contents of several anonymous collections of recipes from the time of Charlemagne (742?–814). One of them describes compositions for coloring mosaics (*Compositiones ad tingendum musiva . . .*), another promises to give a key to the prescriptions for making gold (*Mappae clavicula de efficiendo auro*). They give recipes for "gilding" metals by alloying with gold, for making cinnabar by heating mercury with sulfur, and for using resins and petroleum as incendiaries; and the *Mappae* warns not to forget appropriate prayers, particularly when trying to multiply gold.

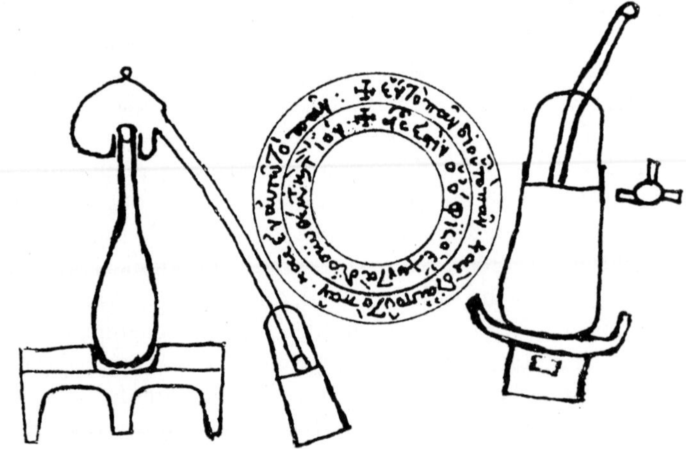

Fig. 7. Alembic with long condensing tube to receiver, concentric circles with inscriptions, and a vase for "Fixation" standing on furnace. A fifteenth century copy of Zosimos. (From M. Berthelot, *La Chimie des Anciens et du Moyen Age*, p. 136.)

These compilations are based on still-unknown sources, which were also used by authors of Persian, Iranian, Turkish, and Arabic descent, all writing in Arabic.

Jabir ibn Hayyan, also known by his Latinized name Geber, was born in Kufa, a town 90 miles south of Baghdad; he died in 815. Among the many books ascribed to him is one on alums and stones. According to him, blood or the excrement of men of choleric temperament are the best materials from which to prepare elixir, but substances obtained from animals or plants can also serve. This precious material must combine 17 forces, distributed over the four natures, composed in weight and measure like animals from the four elements:

1. Spirit, which is hot and moist, represented by mercury;
2. Soul, which is hot and dry, the principle of color, situated in heart, liver, blood, and gall;
3. Body, which is cold and dry, like bones and metals, and holds the light spirits down by its heaviness;
4. Humidity, which as water is the solvent for al-iksir's parts.

Al-Razi (865–925) (latinized name: Rhazes) gave clear and precise descriptions of the ingredients and utensils he used in his experiments. Hair, blood, and bones were converted by digestion and distillation. Hartshorn salt was considered the artificial equivalent of natural salmiac. It appeared so important to al-Razi that he added it as a fourth alchemistical spirit to the older three, namely, mercury, sulfur, and arsenic. (7)

The kind of preparations he describes is similar to those in the writings of Jabir and al-Kindi (800–870). Usually, they state that an operation has to be repeated a certain number of times, such as 7 or 13, to give the desired product. This seems strange for many cases, but it becomes technically appropriate in the following recipe for making "sharp waters": Put 4 "ratl" (1431 grams) of sweet water into a pure vessel, throw in 1 ratl of finely ground, sifted kali, let settle, and add one handful of "nura," i.e., lime. After one day and one night, separate the water from the substance that settled to the bottom, throw in another ratl of kali and a handful of nura, and repeat this procedure three times according to Jabir, seven according to al-Razi. Weigh the water, add as much as one third of this weight of good, crystallized sal ammoniac, and keep it in a lightly stoppered bottle. After the salt has dissolved, the water is very sharp. The repetitions here serve to increase the concentration in the desired product.

A "sharp vinegar" is made from the water separated over curdled milk, mixed with lemon juice, distilled, and mixed with sal ammoniac distilled together with copper green.

Most of these descriptions are quite precise in the weights and measures of the operations, but they are vague or exuberant as to the uses for the products, except when metals and gold are involved. In general, the aim is to replace expensive materials, such as used in perfumes, by cheap substitutes. These "practical" aspects are interwoven with lofty ideas about cosmology, as in the Turba Philosophorum, written about A.D. 900. (8)

Ibn Sina, also known as Avicenna (980–1037) (9), wrote over a hundred books, among which the *Canon* remained authoritative in medicine for centuries. While he discussed the contribution of our thinking to our seeing, Alhazen (965–1038) dealt with the physical, physiological, and psychological problems of optics.

The compilators of this time wrote in Arabic but were not all of Arabian nationality. (10) They transmitted the heritage of Plato and Aristotle and influenced chemistry indirectly. For example, Algazel (Ghazālī), who lived in Baghdad from 1059 till 1111, discussed the theory of fire. Combustion follows exposure to fire and is a change caused by it, but fire does not enter as an element into the material that is burnt.

Alchemy in China developed from old indigenous concepts and was influenced by the countries to the West. The old Taoist *Canon* contains volumes on alchemy, as do the Tao Tê Ching and Pao P'u Tzu, which antedate the T'ang dynasty (A.D. 618–906). Frequent in Chinese alchemy is the division into nine parts, (11) with three subgroups, which also occurs in the treatises of the Islamic Brethren of Purity in the tenth century.

Fundamentally, the recipes are similar to those of the Western schools. For many centuries, even into the eighteenth, they are repeated and embellished with increasingly complicated allegories. Where we find apparent attempts at a new departure, as in the writings of Roger Bacon, the English Franciscan and alchemist (1214–1292), they should be read in the context of their meaning. "The earlier ideas are often given significance only by later events which they may or may not have influenced. They may have had no significance in their own time, or one different from that which they later acquired. Thus the experimental method and the acquisition of power over nature advised by Roger Bacon make him a forerunner of the scientific revolution of the sixteenth and seventeenth centuries. Yet his ideas were of their time, and for him the unity of science was theological." (12).

In a book on universal science which was perhaps written by one of Bacon's disciples, the last three of the nineteen treatises refer to the four elements and qualities, meteorology (including the saltiness of the sea), and lastly, minerals (precious stones, seven metals, sulfur, and mercury). The main part deals with truth and science, matter, form, and virtue, the rational, sensitive, and vegetative souls, and nature in its universal and particular aspects.

Theology dominated the interest of men in the Middle Ages.

Philosophy, a receptacle for all kinds of knowledge, gradually freeing itself from complete dependence upon Aristotle, arrived at conclusions that differed from the teachings of the Church. Experience was no longer completely guided and justified by tradition. Something else had to take the place of the strong support that the framework of tradition had provided. The change did not result from experimental demonstration alone, nor was it caused by pure reasoning alone. Advances in knowledge of the universe, of mathematics and physics, are the complex products of observation and presupposition. If I may continue the analogy to mechanics suggested by the words "support" and "framework," the greatest change consisted in the influence that results of individual observations were permitted to exert upon the universal framework itself. The authors of the twelfth century did not use such an analogy; they expressed the same relationships in their concern with the individual and the universal. These words are meant to designate a very general reality, not any specific one. One Nature, although it is divided up into substances, is common to all Matter. Our intellect finds the universal in the particular existences, and it is the character of science to see the universal in the particular. In stating this as the function and attitude of science, Averroes (the Arabic name is ibn Ruschd, 1126–1198, Cordova) relies on the authority of Aristotle. Averroes was persecuted and confined for teaching that religion contains the philosophical truth under the veil of images, and that what we have to admit theologically may differ from what philosophy reveals.

Similar thoughts were expressed even more forcefully by Moses Maimonides (born 1135 in Cordova, died 1204 in Cairo). After fleeing from Spain in order to keep his Jewish faith, he antagonized the orthodox school by declaring that knowledge may have precedence over the letter of the Bible. This influential theological philosopher was also great as a medical doctor. In his book, *The Venoms and Their Antidotes,* he distinguished between two kinds of poisons. Those of vipers produce high temperature, those of scorpions and snakes low temperature. The remedy is the animal bezoar, a stone found in the bezoar goat. It helps in both cases, but it has to be taken in vinegar, which is "cold," in the first case, and in wine, which is "hot," in the second.

Ramon Lull (1235–1315), who lived in Majorca, saw in logic the Great Art (*Ars Magna*) which enables its disciples to obtain encyclopedic knowledge almost automatically. He applied it mainly to the conversion of the infidels. Between his apostolic missions to

North Africa he wrote on philosophy, religion, and science. He was later considered a great alchemist, although he declared in his genuine writings that the changes produced by alchemy are only superficial.

The thesis of the *Ars Magna* was an exuberant expression of strengthened confidence in reason. Long and sometimes violent discussions in the philosophical schools of France, England, Germany, and Italy sought to define the value of experience. What is the source of general theories? Experience or philosophy? How can we understand matter with its individualized properties in a universe that is eternal in substance but changing in qualities? A deep conflict began to be felt between the acceptance of universal truths in faith and the access to science through reason. Thomas Aquinas (1227–1274) crystallized this conflict into the sentence: "It is not possible that there be of the same thing faith and science." The distinction between the potential and the actual leads Aquinas to a precise formulation of the principle of causality. Each effect has a cause; that which is warm in actuality is cold potentially. Wood itself is cold; after it changes, it becomes fire.

These philosophical investigations carry the old Greek ideas forward toward experimentation. William of Conches, who was born in France in 1080 and died in 1145, combined Democritus' atom theory with the theory that the elements are simple and minimal particles existing in four kinds, as understood by the distinction of reason. Robert Greathead (1175–1253), called Grosseteste, the bishop of Lincoln, explained the causes of everything by means of mathematics, according to his pupil Roger Bacon. Light, the finest and nearly incorporeal substance, is the source of force and action. Through the extension and disaggregation of light, the thirteen spheres develop, namely, the nine celestial and the four terrestrial—fire, air, water, and earth. Nicolaus of Autrecourt, who was a member of the Sorbonne in Paris from 1320 to 1327, and who later, upon orders from Pope Benedict XII, recanted and burned his own books in 1347, rejected many teachings of Aristotle. He maintained that the objects of our senses and the contents of our experience are the only sources from which knowledge of substances flows.

Nicolaus, like William of Conches and other members of the University of Paris, discussed the problems inherent in the movement of atoms and declared that atoms are held together like a magnet and iron. (13) This physical analogy now replaces the classical one of love and hatred.

New foundations on which to build an understanding of chemical change were thus laid. The question of the transmutation of metals was left undecided. Thomas Aquinas posed the hypothetical question, if true gold were made by alchemy, why should it be illegal to sell it as genuine? Nothing forbids art to use natural causes for the production of natural effects! The alchemists declared that they were using "natural causes," but were they producing genuine gold? Albertus Magnus (1193–1280), who became Bishop of Regensburg in 1260, did not answer with a definite "No!". Manuscripts from the fourteenth and fifteenth centuries ascribed to him a definite "Yes!" as answer to this question.

The art of dealing with substances is described there (14) as the imitation of nature. Nature does its work in the viscera of the earth; art tries to duplicate it in alembics and crucibles. The ingredients in nature and in art are the same, sulfur and mercury. They have to be washed and purified by decoction in caustic waters. Sublimation carefully removes the watery and oily parts which would be harmful in the final operations. Lead may be prepared for the red tincture by calcination with sulfur and sublimation with sal ammoniac. Silver is closer to gold than any other metal and is mutated to gold more easily than any other. The method of analysis in these writings consists of a comparison of colors and an observation of behavior when the substance is heated. Silver has much of the substance of sulfur with little of its virtue, and little of the substance of mercury with much of its virtue. If silver had more of the virtue of sulfur, it would be yellow, but it is white and thereby shows the virtue of mercury; but again, the high degree of heat required to melt silver proves that only little of the substance of mercury is present. Tin melts and corrodes easily because it is not well mixed out of its components. Lead is very heavy and cold, and has a powerful action on the kidneys. Twelve parts of lead heated with one part of mercury, when boiled in milk of almonds and juices of yellow flowers, acquires the color of gold. (15)

Technical methods for producing changes in substances are now considerably increased. Some of the authors of the fifteenth century concentrate their attention on the precipitations, filtrations, calcinations, distillations, and sublimations, perhaps realizing rather than admitting that the results have no generalizable meaning. Others, however, expand the old claims and cover a lack of practical achievement with words that distort old allegories and lose connection with either thought or experiment. The German mystics Khunrath and Jacob Boehme (end of sixteenth century and beginning of seventeenth) follow Peter Bonus of Ferrara (about 1330) in identifying the philosopher's stone with Christ. Books on alchemy are published which in word and picture show neither art nor science—fantastic tales which may be of interest to the psychoanalyst (16) but which contribute to chemistry only by demonstrating that this way leads nowhere. Intuition does not produce a knowledge of nature sufficient to carry out the avowed purpose of "imitating" it in the alchemistical art.

The alchemistical dream of the exalted position of gold, and of elixir as the concentrated essence of gold, lingered on into the eighteenth century. In no sense can radioactive disintegration and nuclear fission be called fulfillments of this dream. So far as our work has such a relationship to old thoughts, it is to the theory of light, in which Robert Grosseteste crystallized the teachings of myths and philosophies.

The progress of chemistry during these thirteen centuries is small. The extension of knowledge was not the aim of the men of this period. In contrast to much political change, to uncertainty of existence, and the migration of nations, constancy and security of knowledge seem to have prevailed as the ideal. Science is revealed, not developed, and Aristotle, together with the other old sages, had possessed and proclaimed it. All that can possibly be achieved through experimentation is to confirm the teachings of reason. What E. O. von Lippmann writes concerning the *Summa Theologiae* of Thomas Aquinas is true of many other famous books of this time. "The impartial reader who sees this book for the first time will be extremely disappointed: the author does not seek the truth, he possesses it already, i.e., true for him is immediately that which the church and its representatives have stipulated. . . . The philosophical sham-investigation self-evidently furnishes always and unfailingly that result on which the author was fixed from the beginning." (17) Yet, to his contemporaries, Thomas appeared to be a great renovator whom "God illuminated with the rays of a new light." We might say with Lynn Thorndike: "Perhaps it would be well to read it and think of what the future historian may say of the mentality and scholasticism of the present era, and with what sympathy or antipathy he would be justified in regarding us." (18)

Thus the general concepts of matter remain stationary. Techniques, however, are expanded and diversified. Sometime in the eleventh century, and perhaps in Italy, it was found that old, strong wine, when distilled with the addition of salt, gives a "water" which can be ignited to burn with a flame. Ramon Lull is credited with the method of strengthening this "water" by adding to it the ash obtained from cream of tartar. Vitriols, on heating with chips of brick or with salts, yield a vitriolic spirit which dissolves metals. When sal petrosum, the niter of ancient times, is used in such an operation, a liquid is obtained on cooling the vapors. This dissolves silver, and with the addition of salt it even dissolves gold. This mineral spirit is therefore called *aqua regia.* These acids are described in the books ascribed to Geber, who was already a legendary figure when al-Nadīm wrote his compilation *Fihrist ul-ʾulūm* (completed in 987). Numbers of books were published under Geber's name during three centuries. They form a library of alchemistic experiments and speculations. The basic Arabic texts comprise several books in which the author promises to write perfectly clearly and without any allegories. If he really made an effort to do that, then the difference between his writings and the dark and allegorical language of his predecessors is not very noticeable to us. This is, at least in part, our own fault. Perhaps the unknown author of the *Summa Perfectionis Magisterii* and the other four books ascribed to Geber does not mean it as an allegory when he explains chemical transformations by the action of spirits on dead bodies. A little gold, added to the correctly prepared mixture of such metals as lead, copper, and iron, acts like a seed to produce more gold, and elixir is like yeast in its ability to convert many times its own weight into other materials. At that time these were not mere analogies but discoveries of real explanations. Methods of purification by washing, distilling, and particularly the techniques of sublimation are described in detail, but in order to be successful they have to be accompanied by the right words and formulas. The world of substances is strongly linked to the world of spirits.

Very inflammable oils were known and used in rituals and warfare. (19) The Roman historian Livy (about 186 B.C.) mentions torches that ignite upon immersion in water. They contained a mixture of naphtha with finely powdered burnt lime, the so-called "Greek fire." Used as a weapon, it saved Constantinople twice, from the Arabs in 678 and from the Russians in 941. Explosive mixtures in paper cartridges were shot from tubes in Chinese wars of the eleventh century. The use of an explosive powder obtained by mixing saltpeter, sulfur, and charcoal is established for 1232 when the Mongolians were defeated by the Chinese by means of this frightful weapon. (20) By way of Byzantium, the news spread to Europe. In writings ascribed to Marcus Graecus (eighth century) but perhaps dating from 1250, the composition is given as six parts saltpeter, two parts charcoal, and one part sulfur. (21) Roger Bacon talks of this powder in a letter written in 1265. The German monk

Berthold of Freiburg, who was devoted to the Black Art and was therefore called Berthold Schwartz, did not invent the black powder itself but arranged for its use in guns. The thirteenth century thus brought about the development of using chemical forces with great consequences for methods of warfare.

For centuries, these new forces appeared dangerous and sinister; prayer must accompany their use. Charles Quint, who was Emperor from 1519 to 1558, issued "regulations for the artillery school at Burgos," which included the order to invoke the aid of Santa Barbara at each loading of a gun and each detonation of a mine. (22)

REFERENCES

1. Louis G. Kattsoff, *Isis,* **38** (1947), p. 22.

2. E. O. von Lippmann, *Entstehung und Ausbreitung der Alchemie* (Berlin: Julius Springer, 1919), p. 319.

3. Agnes Arber, "Spinoza and Boethius," *Isis* **34** (1943), p. 399.

4. T. S. Patterson, J. D. London, Adeline M. Cook, *Annals of Science,* **6** (1948), pp. 1–23.

5. Arthur John Hopkins, *Isis,* **29** (1938), pp. 254–326.

6. Julius Ruska, *Tabula Smaragdina* (Heidelberg: C. F. Winther, 1926); and E. J. Holmyard, *Nature,* **2,** (1923), p. 525.

7. Al-Razi, *Opera,* Paul Kraus, Ed. (Cairo: 1939).

8. M. Plessner, "The Place of the Turba Philosophorum in the Development of Alchemy," *Isis,* **45** (1954), pp. 331–38.

9. Aiden M. Sayili, "Was Ibn Sina an Iranian or a Turk?" *Isis,* **31** (1939), pp. 8–24; and Paul Kraus, *Mém. présentés à l'Inst. d'Egypte,* T. 44 and 45 (Cairo: 1942–43).

10. G. Sarton, *Introduction to the History of Science* (Baltimore: The Williams & Wilkins Co., 1927), Vol. 1, p. 524.

11. Roy C. Spooner and C. H. Wang, *Isis,* **38** (1948), pp. 235–42.

12. A. C. Crombie, *Ann. of Science,* **6** (1948), p. 55.

13. Julius R. Weinberg, *Nicolaus of Autrecourt. A Study in 14th Century Thought.* (Princeton, N.J.: Princeton University Press, 1948). See review in *Isis,* **40,** pp. 265–69.

14. Pearl Kibre, *Isis,* **35** (1945), pp. 303–16, discusses and transcribes a Latin text from the Sloane Collection at the British Museum (Sloane 3457).

15. W. J. Wilson, *Osiris,* **2** (1936), pp. 220–405, describes a manuscript from the library of Lehigh University, in which Arnaldus de Bruxella (fifteenth century, Naples) copies from Albertus Magnus, Geber, Lullus, Arnaldus de Villanova, and Ortulanus, Italian sonnets about *lapide philosophorum* and other pieces.

16. C. J. Jung, *Psychologie und Alchemie* (Zürich: Rascher Verlag, 1944).

17. E. O. von Lippmann, *Entstehung und Ausbreitung der Alchemie* (Berlin: Julius Springer, 1919), p. 493, footnote 3.

18. Lynn Thorndike, *A History of Magic and Experimental Science* [New York: Columbia University Press, Vols. 1, 2 (1923); Vols. 3, 4 (1934); Vols. 5, 6 (1941)]; Vol. 6, p. 615.

19. E. O. von Lippmann, *Abhandlungen und Vorträge* (Leipzig: Veit & Co., 1906), pp. 125–89.

20. Li Ch'ia-p'ing, *The Chemical Arts of Old China* (Easton, Pa.: *J. Chem. Ed.*, 1948), pp. 113 ff.

21. Tenney L. Davis, *The Chemistry of Powder and Explosives* (New York: John Wiley & Sons, 1941), p. 39. L. Carrington Goodrich and Fêng Chia-Shêng, *Isis,* **36** (1946), p. 114. J. R. Partington, *A History of Greek Fire and Gunpowder* (Cambridge, England: W. Heffer & Sons, Ltd., 1960).

22. E. O. von Lippmann, *Abhandlungen und Vorträge zur Geschichte der Naturwissenschaften* (Leipzig: 1906), p. 174, cites this from Pfleiderer, *Die Attribute der Heiligen* (Ulm: 1898), p. 169.

5

The Beginning of the Sixteenth Century to the Third Quarter of the Eighteenth

The progress of science in the Middle Ages was slow as seen from the modern point of view, but this vewpoint is not the proper one for a realistic history of science. This period brought about a thorough investigation of the mental equipment that we can apply in developing science. The scholastic philosophy is an effort to secure the foundations of science. It is an effort on a large scale in the realm of ideas and reasoning. (1) Plato's thoughts about the relationship between ideas and matter are crystallized into a doctrine known as "absolute realism" because it ascribes primary reality to universal concepts. On the authority of Aristotle, this doctrine was modified into a moderate realism. This realism is the conviction that ideas have real existence in individual things but not before or without them.

According to absolute realism, our knowledge of individual things is only based on belief and conjecture. Nominalism rejects this position and proves that we know only individual things, and that general concepts are the result of combining individual experiences according to similarities and by means of subjective notions. The framework of chemistry was erected on this foundation. The supports were formed by Plato's ideas of the relationship between form and matter, Aristotle's concept of the elements, and Democritus' atomism.

Atomism was widely discussed in the fourteenth century, and it began to become important for chemistry from the seventeenth century onward. The special observations gained by means of experiments were fitted into the philosophical framework. It gave them

Nī sollicher massen magstu ouch eyn
i offen machē dz du mit holtz dar ī b:ē
nest also dz d offen lāgt ist/vñ von d
höche des rosts biß zů dem blech soll sin ey/
ner ellen hoch/vnd für die blech so werd ge
nummen basel tach/vñ dz mūtloch des of/
fens sy vff einer siten in d wyte ein halb ellē
vñ in d höhe.iii.viertel eyner ellen der offen
hab ouch zwei groß reuchlöcker.sollichē offē
magstu machē mit wie vil helmē du wilt
oder begeren du bist nach dinem gefallen.
vnd die figur hie zeigen ist.

Fig. 8. Distillation apparatus. (From Hieronimus Brunschwig, *Kunst zu Distillieren*, First Edition, Strassburg, 1500.)

The oven is described as "one ellen" (that is, two feet) high between the grating and the top cover; the front opening is one foot wide and one and one half feet high; "provide two large vent holes, and put on as many helmets as you desire."

Brunschwig, born *ca.* 1430 in Strassburg, was a municipal doctor there. His book on the art of distilling was reprinted in several editions for more than a century.

the support without which they would have fallen apart into meaningless accidents. At all times, the goal was completeness in a system of knowledge. This completeness could not be derived from experiments alone; they needed the addition of magnificent connections with the greatness of the universe. From the ancient reference to gods, the emphasis now turns to man and to that nature in which he participates. Because of this participation man can understand nature. He has to be taught. In the process of learning, a prominent subject of Greek philosophy, not man himself but nature is the teacher.

The authors of books on chemical developments were in general not inventors but systematizers; their work was not simply reporting but placing the new inventions into the light of great ideas. When John of Rupescissa (Jean de Roquetaillade, fourteenth century) writes about distilled alcohol, he praises it as an incomparable quinta essencia, "related to the four qualities as heaven is related to the four elements." (2)

A pronouncement like this was helpful and illuminating when accepted as an inspired intuition; when that was lost and the intuition turned into the dead letter of a school doctrine, it became a useless burden. Instead of guides and signposts, the ideas of great men of the past acted as barriers to new insights. Those who felt impeded by the burden and wanted to overcome the barrier advocated a return to the sources. For Thomas Aquinas, that had meant a return to the real Aristotle from the teachings of his interpreters. For men of the fourteenth and fifteenth centuries, it meant a revolt against Aristotle himself and the return to nature. In the sixteenth century, the revolt found a powerful expression through Paracelsus. He discovered the sources of wisdom not at the schools and not in the books but by travel through many lands, by following the Dutch armies and caring for wounded soldiers, by listening to miners and farmers. He taught and wrote in German, not in the language of the classics. "Follow me! You follow me, not I you! Follow me, Avicenna, Galen, Rhasis, Montagnana . . . you Greeks, you Arabs, you Israelites. . . ." (3)

The Imitation of Nature by the Chemical Art

Theophrastus Paracelsus, or Theophrastus Bombastus von Hohenheim, was born in Switzerland in November, 1493, the son of a doctor who later moved to Villach in Carinthia. Paracelsus broadened his medical school education by working in mines. In Italy he was deeply impressed by the Neoplatonic teachings of Marsilio Ficino (1453–1499). Rejecting the crude methods of the practicing doctors of that time, Paracelsus achieved cures which appeared marvelous to his friends, suspect to the much greater number of his enemies. Thus he saved the life of a prominent citizen of Basel, the printer and publisher Johannes Froben, the friend of Erasmus of Rotterdam, the great humanist (1466?–1536). The University of Basel thereupon invited him to become a municipal physician there. In June, 1527, he began his courses with a violent declaration against those who, instead of studying nature, relied on old books and long-established authorities. The highest source of knowledge is experience: *Summa doctrix experientia!*

Like Galen, whose system he wanted to overthrow, Paracelsus had the unfortunate habit of antagonizing those who would have liked to be his friends. Too intent upon his own ideas, he was not able to consider a belief in authority and the display of pompous formality as human traits worthy of as much study as natural phenomena. Instead, he denounced his professional colleagues as wicked, harmful, and ignorant. He aroused so much enmity that he was forced to leave Basel after little more than a year. "I must be and remain a wanderer through the lands!"

At this time syphilis was ravaging Germany. A book about this scourge was one of the few of his writings that the censors permitted to be published during his lifetime (1529). Juices and extracts from plants, mercury, antimony, and their salts, are the remedies that he selected according to their secret nature and administered at a propitious time. While he taught the physicians to use chemistry, he told the chemists that the purpose of alchemy is not to make gold but to prepare medicines. The alchemist must know about the processes of nature and how to continue them in imitation of nature. He has to make the hidden virtues of things appear. His model should be the natural alchemist, summer, which brings out the leaves and fruits that were hidden in the dark roots.

After erratic travels, always teaching, healing, and writing, Paracelsus returned to Salzburg. He died there September 24, 1541. His writings (Basel: 1589–1591), edited by Johann Huser, are collections of aphorisms, autobiographical sketches, and theological tracts. He felt himself to be a reformer who frees man from the fetters of the past and leads him to harmony with nature. Experiences can teach him because they communicate with each other in the one great unity. With this background, intuitive feeling for the sick is a more successful guide for the physician than is traditional medicine. His indebtedness to the past is, however, greater than he realized. He continued an old idea when he proclaimed that man is a small world, a microcosm which is an image of the larger cosmos and dependent on it.

This was also what Nicolaus Cusanus (1401, Cues, Germany –1464, Todi, Italy), the great cardinal, bishops of Brixen, had taught, and what Marsilio Ficino had continued. Since the relationship of the large and small world was reversible, Ficino spoke of the hair, teeth, and bones as parts of the anatomy of the earth. Paracelsus derived from this wide analogy his access to the correct magic, to the real nature of plants and metals and their medicinal use.

Ancient Greek medicine proposed to compensate for excesses of heat and cold by their opposites. Paracelsus added a compensation for age. Use young herbs for an old illness, but for a new one, apply old herbs and medicines! (4) The thought that nature indicates the essence and virtue of things through forms and signs has its roots in old Egypt. It acquired new vigor in Paracelsus' theory of the signatures. (5) In a special application, this theory interprets the form of leaves and flowers as signs of their medical "virtues" because of the unit of form and force. In its kindness, nature speaks to man, at least to the natural philosopher, and reveals its secrets to him in forms and colors. Open appearance and hidden character are one. This triumphal discovery was accompanied by such deep emotion that it did not call for much experimentation to verify it. For a long time after Paracelsus this discovery of signatures was repeated, just as Paracelsus himself had repeated his predecessors in the theory of signatures. Chelidoneum, being yellow, must be good against jaundice; kidney-shaped leaves should be remedies for kidney troubles. A great law of nature was here revealed. And when science later found that such humanization of natural forms was entirely arbitrary, there still remained some mystical shadow of the old conviction.

The beginning of an advance over the old mysticism of colors appears in the following discussion from Paracelsus' *Liber de Imaginibus:*

> . . . And even if you knew the four principal colors which belong and are ascribed to the four elements—as Blue to the Earth, Green to the Water, Yellow to the Air, Red to the Fire—nevertheless there are many other accidental colors and mixed colors of which one may scarcely recognize the real color. . . . Black is the root and the origin of the other colors. Like an herb which, after winter, cannot yet be seen in spring, and its roots stand in the earth still hidden, black, lean, and unshaped. As soon as the warmth of summer grips it, it is thereby driven to grow, and it changes through the heat of the sun and acquires all four principal colors, one after the other. This you now understand more clearly, thus: First the herb grows out of the root, then out of the herb the flower, lastly out of the flower the seed; this now is the tincture, or the *Quintam Esse,* of the herb.

All things, and man too, derive their substantiality from three substances.

> Now to experience things, begin with wood. This is a body, now let it burn, then what burns is the Sulphur, that which smokes is the Mercurius, that which becomes ash is Sal. . . . Now you have man, that his body is nothing but a Sulphur, a Mercurius, a Sal. In these three things rests his health, his sickness, and all that concerns him. And as there are only three, therefore there are three causes of all sicknesses, and not the four Humores, Qualitates, or so on. . . . Where there is no salt, at that same place putrifies that which is not salted. And like dead flesh which has been salted, it is protected from putrescence. Thus you should know that the salt which God has naturally implanted in us guards our body from putrescence."

These three "things," from which, like everything else, the seven metals are composed, are variously "elements" or "principles" for Paracelsus. As elements, they are represented by sulfur, mercury, and salt; as principles, they are the counterparts of spirit, soul (anima), and corpus. A counterpart also exists in nature for the "alchemist." He is the Archeus, a living spirit of many shapes, who causes fruit to ripen and who presides over the processes of digestion and respiration. In Archeus, the forces and patterns of life take on a human form, or more than that, the form of an intermediary between God and his created things. Archeus is the workmaster who directs the functioning of an organism.

Living agents are present in all active things, spirits of life can be found everywhere. Since this life can influence other lives, medical virtues can be found everywhere, provided that the time and the dosage are correctly chosen. The words of Friar Laurence in Shakespeare's *Romeo and Juliet* (Act II, scene 3) express the thoughts of Paracelsus (6):

> O, mickle is the powerful grace that lies
> In plants, herbs, stones, and their true qualities; . . .
> Within the infant rind of this small flower
> Poison hath residence, and medicine power;
> For this, being smelt, with that part cheers each part;
> Being tasted, slays all senses with the heart.

Speculation about the unity of nature, which identifies spirit, soul, and body with the principles of matter, has a practical application. It makes it possible to predict the medicinal action of metals or herbs. While Paracelsus exclaims against practice without correct philosophy, he does not mean to praise philosophy without practical use. We do not attain it by dissecting, but by unifying. Anatomists, who rely on the results of dissecting the human body, are misled in medicine because they destroy the essential forces which correspond to cosmic unity, human feeling, and natural form.

Paracelsus had enthusiastic followers and violent opponents, but he could not be ignored. Andreas Libavius (1550, Halle/Saale–1616, Coburg), a teacher and inspector of schools who wrote the first systematic textbook of chemistry, (7) tries to defend himself against the influence of Paracelsus. After all, chemistry was not invented by Paracelsus! (*Chymia non est inventum Paracelsi!*) Yet he bases his system on the three principles, sulfur, mercury, and salt, as Paracelsus did. The living operators of chemical change, the Archei, however, find successors which are no longer formed in the image of a workmaster. Libavius takes a step in the direction of objective and more abstract agents. He calls them *magisteria.* Alchemy becomes the art of extracting pure magisteria and essences from mixed bodies. There are several kinds of magisteria, those of substantiality and those of qualities—color, weight, odor, and sound, like the sound that a bar of tin produces on bending.

In describing the operations involved in chemical work, Libavius could draw on a considerable number of books on metallurgical techniques. The two most outstanding were those by Vannoccio Biringuccio (1480–1539, Rome) and Georg Agricola (1494–1555, Chemnitz). (8)

The French "ouvrier de terre," Bernard Palissy (about 1499–1589), wrote his work on enamels and the crystallization of salts out of their solutions. The solidification of certain liquids, the *succi concreti,* had puzzled previous observers. Palissy showed that this is not a transmutation of the water but the separation of substances that were present in the solutions. The name of Libavius himself was later connected with that of a *spiritus fumans* which he had not claimed as his discovery, a sublimated spiritus which contained the product of heating tin with mercury sublimate.

Greater still was the influence of Paracelsus' thoughts and practices on books published around the turn of the century under the name of "Basilius Valentinus." The identity of the author is a riddle. It can perhaps be stated negatively that the editor, Johann Thölde, who composed a "thorough and definite description of all salt minerals" in 1603, was not the author. In the *Triumphal Chariot of Antimony* (1604), Basilius Valentinus exalted the virtues of the metal and its salts for medical purposes. Antimony had been an important medicament for Paracelsus. A special experiment, which Basilius Valentinus learned from Paracelsus, was that great cold is able to freeze out the water (phlegm) from a wine distillate and leave a strong "spirit" in liquid form.

A last attempt to combine the passionate presupposition of unity in nature with special experiments in the Paracelsian spirit was made by Robert Fludd (1574–1637) who studied in Oxford and practiced medicine in London. Again the aim was not to make gold but to study nature, and through it to search for God and His truth. "God clearly appears as the chief chemist with nature as His laboratory. . . . Therefore true practical theology is nothing but mystical chemistry . . ." (9) The primary element is water, as told by the Biblical story of the creation. The key to the explanation of the world is the principle of expansion and contraction.

Robert Fludd thus reaffirms the viewpoints of Thales and Anaximenes. The result is not new discovery, nor is this the aim. The study of nature only confirms the knowledge with which we begin it. The question arises whether that is all we can expect from experimentation. Does not preconceived explanation hide the results in their specific value instead of revealing their universal importance? Sir Francis Bacon (1561–1626, London) proclaimed in his anti-Aristotelian *Novum Organum:* "Neither the naked hand nor the understanding left to itself can effect much. It is by instruments and help that the work is done, which are as much wanted for the understanding as for the hand." A new departure is necessary, a new concentrated effort at experimentation. In his *New Atlantis* he describes the activities of a Utopian learned society, living in "Solomon's House." "We have high towers, the highest about half a mile in height . . . with baths and gardens, with workshops and furnaces of great diversities . . . ," and a staff organized as Merchants of Light—who bring new books and patterns from foreign sources, Depredators—who collect the information from these sources, Mystery Men—for new mechanical invention, Pioneers—who try new experiments, Compilers, Benefactors, Lamps, Inoculators, and Interpreters of nature.

The struggle against the authority of the ancient thinkers was ineffective as long as it had only the alternative of either proclaiming the negation that we do not possess such complete knowledge or trying to substitute the newer author's philosophy for the old one. Thus it was of great importance that Galileo Galilei (1564–1641, Pisa and Padua, Italy) demonstrated the new ideal of science in producing new specific and definite results and not only a general method of

D.O.M.A

ALCHYMIA

ANDREÆ LIBAVII, RECOGNITA, EMENDATA, ET aucta, tum dogmatibus & experimentis nonnullis;

TVM COMMENTARIO Medico Physico Chymico:

QVI EXORNATVS EST VAriis Instrumentorum Chymicorum picturis; partim aliunde translatis, partim planè nouis:

In gratiam eorum,

QVI ARCANORVM NATVRALIVM cupidi, ea absq; inuolucris elementarium & ænigmaticarum sordium, intueri gaudent.

PRÆMISSA DEFENSIONE ARTIS: opposita censuræ Parisianæ:

Cum Gratia & Priuilegio Cæsareo speciali ad decennium.

FRANCOFVRTI,

Excudebat Joannes Saurius, impensis Petri Kopffii.

Anno cIↃ. IↃ. VI.

Fig. 9. Title page of the *Alchemia* of Andreas Libavius, 1606 edition.

approach. In all previous chemical work, the qualities of substances were interpreted as indicating some kind of personality in the substances. Galileo argued that odor, color, taste, and sound are human sensations, not qualities inherent in matter (*Il Saggiatore* = "The Weigher of Gold," 1623).

Galileo wrote his *Dialogues* in Italian, not in Latin; René Descartes (1596, La Haye, France –1650, Stockholm, Sweden) often used his native French. Both wanted to reach "those who avail themselves only of their natural reason in its purity" rather than those who "believe only in the writings of the ancients." They followed the examples set by Paracelsus, who wrote in German, though he felt he had to add many new words of his own creation, and set by Simon Stevin (1548–1620), who described his mills, sleuces, and fortification constructions in Dutch.

Descartes seeks the certainty that we reach after subjecting everything to doubt. He finds this certainty in our reason, not in the world of experiences. "The first principle of the philosophy I sought is: I think, therefore I am. Our certainty rests on our thoughts, not our substance." Descartes explained it by saying, "This thinking 'I' is an immaterial substance, one that has nothing corporeal." The thought of Anaximander on the universal that he called "apeiron" is recognizable in the new application to the human existence. In the atomic theory of Descartes there are Pythagorean thoughts concerning the importance of number, here used in contrast with the idea of qualitative differences between the atoms. The qualities are my sensations; they are not present in the things I experience or observe. He showed this in striking examples like the following:

> Although in approaching a fire I feel heat, and approaching a little too closely I resent the pain, there is nevertheless no possible reason that could persuade me that there was something in the fire resembling that heat or that pain; rather I have reason to believe only that in fire there is something, whatever it may be, that excites in me those feelings of heat or of pain. (10)

Like Galileo, Descartes advocated the use of mathematics in science, particularly for the understanding of motion. This was necessary since the Creator has endowed the particles of matter with motion. It is in motion that these particles, which are not substantial atoms, acquire reality. The laws of motion are the laws of nature, and we can understand them mathematically. The most general of these laws is the conservation of the magnitude of motion, which Descartes defines as the product of volume and velocity. By arbitrary acts of thinking, we separate the reality of continuous extension into bodies, but they remain connected with universal matter. Thus when such a body moves from place to place, it does not leave a vacuum behind; other matter moves in.

Between Established Authority and Experimental Evidence

The prominent role ascribed to motion in this great philosophical system is, at least in part, created by the deep impression produced by the development of explosives and the use of projectiles in warfare. Descartes, although not a strong man, took part in several of the earlier battles of the Thirty Years' War.

Descartes' "I think, therefore I am" could be interpreted as not only the function but the right of the individual to think, and to think freely, even if the result came in conflict with the authority of the classical philosophers. This authority had been established on the premise that they had discovered and formulated the truth for all times. Liberation from this authority was sought in the sixteenth and seventeenth centuries not as a rejection but rather as the reconstruction of these truths, together with the recognition that while they were valid as foundations, they were not complete with regard to the new experiences. In other words, these truths were necessary but not sufficient. The new experiences themselves were, however, not sufficient to give the new complete picture of reality that was the aim. To reach this aim, free assertions were needed, and their justification seemed to rest on a modified Cartesian sentence: I think them, therefore they are.

In this way, Pierre Gassendi (1592, near Digne en Provence –1655, Paris) extended the atomistic theory of Epicurus. Gassendi (11) was a professor of philosophy at the age of nineteen, later a high dignitary of the Church, and, from 1646 on, a professor of mathematics. Although he rejected Descartes' system, he regarded matter as constant, simple, and without qualities. Atoms, however, are real particles, not mere numbers. They have extension, form, and weight, and they move in empty space.

Gottfried Wilhelm Leibniz (1646, Leipzig –1716, Hannover) (12) created his work not in seclusion like Descartes, but in the midst of the stream of life. He took an active part in theological and political controversies; he was in correspondence with great princes and famous scientists. This active life in the company of powerful personalities is reflected in his philosophy of nature. Substance is a being capable of action. We must think of substance by means of the concept of force (*vis*), in imitation of the notion we have of souls. Ultimate units of matter are monads, each of which expresses the entire universe according to an inherent point of view. Mathematical points are the ways in which the monads express the universe. The continuity of mathematics is universal; the law of continuity is the general law of nature. All the properties of matter are the result of motion. In the continuous scale of existences, substances are "momentary spirits," as if arrested in the flux of time, while real spirits have a history. Spirits connect past and future. The arrested tendency for the motion of matter is a dead force (*vis mortua*) which is converted into living force (*vis viva*) in actual motion.

The philosophical concept of a law of continuity, first expressed in a letter to Pierre Bayle in 1687, was a generalization of mathematical efforts which were to some extent influenced by Newton and which culminated in a method of infinitesimal calculus.

Leibniz tended to unite the philosophies of Aristotle and Democritus. He also reconciled the differences between Heraclitus and Parmenides, and what Nicolaus Autrecourt had called "impetus" was here separated into dead and living force, *vis mortua* and *vis viva*.

The discussion of motion, of continuity in its relationship to permanence, leads to thoughts about growth and development. For Leibniz, development is not an endless continuation of change but a past and closed history of present things. In the construction of the alchemists, change found its definite end when the transmutation reached the stage of gold.

The highest title accorded a chemist was that of a "philosopher by fire," the creative man who uses the most godlike element as his tool and guide. The title was bestowed upon Robert Fludd, who did not experiment, and upon Jan Baptista van Helmont, who proclaimed water as the primary element. The original connotation of the words was already changing into mere symbolism, like that of the retort which remained the symbol of chemistry long after its use had receded into the background. Van Helmont, the Belgian physician (1577–1644, Brussels) was not a *philosophus per ignem* (by fire), he was a biological philosopher. (13) Fire is a violent and destructive agent for processes of life; they depend upon water and air. The Paracelsian elements, sulfur, mercury, and salt, are only qualities, although van Helmont also calls them particles which, through their arrangement in space, cause the differences between the substances. The first elements from which everything is created are, originally, water and air. Archeus, the governor, the force of life, shapes them into organisms.

"All growth from the earth" is directly produced by the Archeus from water. That was what Nicolaus Cusanus had thought, and Paracelsus had proclaimed that water is the matrix of all creatures. Van Helmont tried to prove it experimentally. (14) He planted a young willow tree in a weighed amount of earth. For five years only water was added to the earth, and it was carefully shielded from falling leaves. After this period the weight of the tree was found considerably increased, but that of the earth was unchanged. Did this not demonstrate that the tree was only water which had been transformed by the life process? And does not the creation of fish in water show that they also are nothing but water in substance?

These organic changes, it was thought, begin with seeds, which contain the life principle. The beginning from seeds, the *initium seminale per quod,* is exemplified by fermentation. The action of a ferment in making dough and wine, in which alchemists saw an explanation for the action of elixir, is used by Van Helmont as an analogy to organic transformation.

Such processes are very different from those that occur by dissolving substances in water. Salt is still present, as such, in its solution, from which it can easily be recovered. Even aqua fortis (nitric acid), in dissolving metals, does not change them "in their essence." "Because even though silver, when dissolved in aqua fortis, seems to be gone completely since it looks like water, it still remains in its former essence." (15)

Water can be converted into the solid material of a tree or into impalpable vapor, but it can assume still another form, for which van Helmont created the name "gas." Whether he formed it in resemblance to the Chaos of which Paracelsus spoke occasionally, or whether he derived it from the word "ghost," (16) he intended it to indicate a particular state of matter. He sees it in the mist that can be observed over water in cold air. He discovers it in fermentation, in decomposing organic materials, in the products that result from burning charcoal. The gas from fermentation is dangerous; it kills animals. The gas from decomposing organic matter is flammable; he calls it *gas flammeum.* Gas is a spiritus in its subtleness, without mystical connotations. A great field for further investigation was thus opened up.

The old four elements of Aristotle, or the three of Paracelsus, which van Helmont had found unsatisfactory in his medical work, were rejected by the physician Franz de le Boë [Franciscus Sylvius]

(1614, Hanau –1672, Leiden). Instead, he chose as the two chemical principles a "secret" acute acid and an alkali. The contrary *qualities* of the old medical theory were thus replaced by contrary *chemicals.* Health is bound up with the right equilibrium between the two; when one becomes prevalent, sickness is the result, just as it was in the old theories.

Holland, a haven of peace during the ravages of the Thirty Years' War, attracted philosophers and practical chemists. Rudolph Glauber (1604, Karlstadt –1670, Amsterdam) (17) founded a large manufacturing laboratory in Amsterdam. It was magnificent, of prodigal grandeur and particular construction, according to the report of a French visitor in 1660. The title of Glauber's main work, (18) *New Ovens for the Philosophers,* indicates that he was truly a philosopher by fire. He obtained *oleum acidum vitrioli* by heating vitriol. When he added this "acid oil" to saltpeter and exposed the mixture to fire, he produced a different kind of spirit, the spirit of saltpeter (*spiritus nitri*). This again was different from the spirit distilled from common salt and alum, the *spiritus salis.* These spiritus were wonderful medicines; they cooled the members of the body from the inside! When metals were dissolved in oleum acidum vitrioli, they could be converted into the vitriols. What the fire had separated could thus be regenerated through reactions in solution at lower temperatures, and a cycle of chemical reactions could be closed.

Glauber's practical work in the manufacturing laboratory emanated from universal thoughts which it in turn strongly confirmed. The reason for combination and separation is a difference in the strength of attractions. Fire is the universal purifying agent; God himself is a fire: Did He not appear in the shape of a fire to the Saints? The sun is a fire. Everything is contained in and governed by sun and salt: *In sole et sale omnia.* This sounds like metaphysics, but it leads to practical consequences. A plant needs the sun and a fiery salt in order to grow. A salt, made fiery in the laboratory, is better than manure, in which the nutritive agent is *ein urinosisch Salz,* and it can be advantageously replaced by such urine-related salt. Glauber prepared a *sal mirabile* that would multiply the seed corn from a hundred to a thousand fold.

While the methods for distilling, digesting, and extracting were expanded and improved, the theory for selecting herbs for medicinal purposes was still the same as a hundred years earlier. Guided by the signatures, Glauber developed great ingenuity in recognizing the auspicious signs. Against pellagra he gave hellebore, against calculus, the extract from *Semen fraxini,* against diseases of the uterus he recommended henbane (*Hyoscyamus niger*).

From such strong and poisonous plants as henbane and other members of the nightshade family (*Strychnos nux vomica*), or from "worms" and beetles, Glauber prepared a panacea, namely, a medicament which "can be profitably used in all sickness." (18) The universal solvent for such purposes was *nitrum,* i.e., saltpeter.

In the search for a universal solvent, Glauber continued an old alchemistical objective. Paracelsus and Van Helmont believed they found it in a mystical alkahest which was variously identified with an essence of salt or a philosophical fire. Glauber gave a more precise definition for alkahest by identifying it with nitrum, or rather with the strong solution obtained when nitrum becomes liquid through moisture attracted from the air.

The violent reaction of saltpeter with coal dust was used in gunpowder. Glauber experimented with the salt that is left after this reaction is over. This salt becomes liquid in moist air and forms a *liquor fixus.* When the spiritus of niter (nitric acid) is added to this fixed liquor, both lose their strength and form saltpeter. The substance from which the spiritus and the fixed salt had originally been made was thus restored.

This cycle of operations was repeated by Robert Boyle (1627, Munster, southern Ireland –1691, Oxford). The calx, the residue from the distillation of saltpeter, is mixed with the distilled spirit, and saltpeter is regenerated. The news of these results was communicated to the philosopher Baruch Spinoza by his and Boyle's mutual friend Heinrich Oldenburg (1663). To them, chemical changes had a direct bearing on the philosophical concepts concerning matter. Spinoza tried to prove experimentally that the calx was only saltpeter freed from some finer particles. The controversy, brief as it was, expresses one of the deep changes that shaped the new chemistry. The question that the old "philosophers of fire" had asked was directed toward the essence of things. Paracelsus, with all his revolutionary attitude, was still intent upon finding, or feeling, the hidden absolute characters in all that exists. Agricola sought the reason why metals melt, and he found it in the water the metals contain as an element. Spinoza attempted to find the nature of saltpeter. The answer can only be given by connecting the special substance with its universal background, by seeing the one substance in relation to all matter. Robert Boyle was concerned with a different question: What does a substance do when brought together with other specific substances? "The volatile liquor and fix'd salt into which it [the saltpeter] is reduc'd by the fire, are endowed with properties exceeding different both from each other and from those of the undissipated Concrete. . . ." Saltpeter is a solid substance, a "Concrete," but it can be decomposed or dissipated into two products. One of them is acid; it turns the blue extract obtained from violet petals red, and it evolves a kind of "air" by its action on iron. The other is "alkalizate." The two principles of Franz de le Boë are thus obtained in a specific example.

In his experiments on respiration, Robert Boyle showed that a bird can live only for a limited time in a closed vessel.

> Paracelsus indeed tells us That as the Stomack concocts Meat, and makes part of it useful to the Body, rejecting the other part, so the Lungs consume part of the Air, and proscribe the rest. So that according to our Hermetick Philosopher . . . we may suppose that there is in the Air a little vital Quintessence . . . which serves to the refreshment and restauration of our vital Spirits. . . . But though this Opinion is not . . . absur'd . . . it should not be barely asserted, but explicated and prov'd. . . ." (19)

The man who wrote so cautiously was not adverse to philosophy; he wanted to demonstrate the usefulness of "chymical experiments to contemplative philosophers." This was the result of a classical education, part of which he received in Switzerland and Italy. He was in Florence at the time when Galileo Galilei died there, January 8, 1642. After returning to England he devoted himself to theology and chemistry with equal ardor. In 1660 he declined an offer to enter exclusively into the service of the Church. (20)

His studies and experiments showed him that many substances can be characterized and identified by chemical reactions, except for the elements, the three of the spagyrikei (following Paracelsus), or the four of Aristotle, or the five of the Peripatetics. Are these elements chemical realities? This is the foremost question in his *Sceptical Chemist* (21) where Boyle discusses it under five points of view.

1. Is fire the "universal analyzer" of all substances? The old saying that fire combines that which is equal of nature and separates that which is unequal, although ascribed to Aristotle, is not true. Fire does not separate the mixture of silver and gold, which are unequal, and it combines the unequal substances alkali and sand in making glass.

2. Are the products obtained under the action of fire really elements or principles? Fire causes a violent motion of the particles

of matter. Its results depend on the intimacy of the mixture. Van Helmont had concluded from his experiment with the willow tree that all plant growth consists of the element water. Boyle repeats the experiment and carries the conclusion much further. The plant yields all the elements on heating, namely fire in its combustion, air in the form of smoke, water in the distillate, and earth as the residue. Thus the element water appears to have been transformed into the other elements! But this is inconsistent with the concept of an element.

3. Is the number of the elements really three, four, or five? Who has separated gold or glass into those elements? It is true that salts can be made from metals, even from silver and gold, but the metals can easily be recovered from these salts. They are therefore not "elemental salts," they are "mixed bodies." And which of the products of distilling wood are to be called elements? The acid distillate, mixed with powdered coral (calcium carbonate) and gently heated, gives a new distillate which is entirely changed, which does not taste acidic or turn the color of violet extract. If the substance of the distillate were an element, it would be impossible to change it.

4. Are there really elementary salt, elementary sulfur, and elementary mercury? All descriptions of these are indefinite and variable. Some call sulfur what others designate as mercury, and anything soluble in water passes as salt. The chemists know, however, that distillates differ in specific gravity; some are liquid, others congeal into solid masses. Salts differ in medical action or in usefulness for making glass.

5. Are there elements or principles at all? With all the uncertainties about number, character, and method of separation, do we need elements and principles for explaining certain prominent qualities of the substances? It is assumed that heaviness depends upon the earth-element; actually it is a result of the compactness of the particles. Color is explained by the mercury content, but sometimes salt and sulfur are also made responsible for it, and Boyle himself has shown that color may be produced by certain arrangements of the surface particles without any color-giving element.

Chemical elements "are certain primitive and simple, or perfectly unmingled bodies, which not being made of any other bodies, or of one another, are the ingredients of which all . . . bodies are immediately compounded, and into which they are ultimately resolved." This was what those who talked clearly understood by elements; whether there were such elements, or whether the world "as it now is" showed only the three principles, matter, motion, and rest, or simply matter and form, that remained to be decided.

This definition of what an element is does not represent Boyle's original contribution. A few years before, Joachim Jungius (1587, Lübeck –1657, Hamburg) had cited Aristotle as the authority for the statement that "principles should not be composed of one another, nor of others, and everything should consist of them." (22) Jungius attempted to find the realities that correspond to the thoughts expressed in classical Greek philosophy, and he ended with the general warning to go about it with "conscientious, unrelenting diligence, penetrating into details through observation." More than this general prescription was necessary, and as Boyle demonstrated, was possible at this time. The advance in chemical certainty was, however, connected with a resignation in philosophical universality. The new method that led to this change was chemical analysis which characterized a chemical substance by its reactions with other chemicals. The new thought, which overcame traditional concepts, considered qualities as a human convention which was more arbitrary than we may think. (23) Still Boyle felt that "there may be a real Transmutation of one metal into another, even among the most perfect and noblest metals."

Goethe said about Boyle that "his attitude was much too gentle, his expressions vacillating, his demands too broad, his purpose too involved." These words may well indicate a reaction that was strong and prevalent without being just. Boyle was modest and courageous enough to remain a sceptical chemist, that is to say, one who does not give bold and final answers. The legendary figure of Faustus, to whom Goethe was so strongly attracted, is an example of an entirely different attitude. The absolute was his goal, without which he could not bear to live. If he could not penetrate to the core of nature with the help of God, he appealed to the devil.

On the other hand, Goethe's characterization of Boyle may help to explain the fact that the latter's influence on the immediate course of chemistry was quite limited. Men of the seventeenth century continued to construct absolute and complete explanations. Nicholas Lémery developed a mechanistic theory of chemical behavior (1645, Rouen –1715) which made use of the "corpuscular philosophy" without Boyle's caution. Johann Joachim Becher (1635, Speyer –1682, London) based his speculations on the old "principles," which Boyle had rejected because they vacillated between being definite elementary substances and hidden causes of qualitites. These men were not convinced by a criticism that rejected universal concepts because they failed to correspond with the results of experiments, and the principles of matter and form were too general as Boyle offered them to the chemists.

In his *Cours de Chimie,* which appeared in 1675, Lémery explained taste and the chemical activity of acids by ascribing a sharp, pointed form to their particles. Finely ground little knives attack our senses and produce a sharp taste, just as they attack metals and corrode them. When spirit of salt precipitates silver from solutions of its salts, it does so because the coarser particles of the acid break off the fine hooks by which the silver is held in solution. Fire owes its nature to its especially fine particles. They can even penetrate the walls of vessels in which metals are heated, and attach themselves to the metals. When fire attaches itself to limestone, this mild material becomes caustic. It is the fire we feel on the tongue when we taste burnt lime (or quicklime).

According to Becher, the qualities of substances are produced by the primordial principles they contain. These are not exactly the old three independent principles. He reduces them to the state of modification of one primitive earth. The three modifications are the mercurial, the vitrifiable, and the combustible. Wood burns because it contains combustible earth. Since fats are very combustible, the principle that causes combustibility is also called "fatty earth." Acids owe their most prominent character to a principle of acidity, and to make it clear that this is a substance, it is called the generator of acidity (*acidum primogenium*).

Translated into simpler language, this means that substances are acids when and because they contain something that makes them acid. Such a translation, however, is not quite true because it leaves out the main features, the unification that causes the theory to become more than a mere repetition of the problem. Unification is the strength of this theory as philosophy, but it is its weakness as chemistry. In chemistry the principles had to be demonstrated as substances. Vinegar, the oldest of the known acids, became identified with the *acidum primogenium,* and fat, the best known combustible substance, became identified with combustible earth. In this term, the name of the ancient Aristotelian element was reduced to a mere allegory; a fat can not really be called an "earth." That the old word was retained only indicates that the task was still the old one, to explain the "origin" or "cause" of qualities. Now, however, more than the old qualities were important, not only those called cold and humid, hot and dry, and not only solidity and fluidity, represented by salt and mercury. The way to achieve the new task was the old familiar identification of the quality with the substance that showed it for everybody to see. On the other side of the identity was the paradox that a substance such as acetic acid should also be a principal and an element. The identity satisfied for the moment, the paradox led on to continued search. The paradox had the additional advantage that it left room for the ingenuity of the individual. For Georg Ernst Stahl, the universal acid was sulfuric acid.

Acidity was interesting but much less important than combustibility and its manifest result: fire. Strabo (page 28) had already pointed out that, as an element, fire had an exceptional position. The property of combustibility, such as that of sulfur, needed something else to produce the actual event of combustion. Paracelsus said that air is the life of fire. In his "De morbis metallicis," about the ailments of metals (1535?), he stated that in respiration a part of air is consumed and another part is released as a kind of excrement. The part that is consumed has the nature of niter, i.e., saltpeter, because this is known to be necessary in gunpowder. (24)

Some analogies were seen between respiration, combustion, and the conversion of a metal into a calx. In this process, according to several observers, the metal increases in weight. The French apothecary Brun, of Bergerac, one day heated two pounds, six ounces of the best tin in an open kettle and after a few hours recovered two pounds, thirteen ounces of a purely white calx. A similar experiment with lead, however, resulted in a loss of weight. He asked Jean Rey, a physician and experimenter (d. 1645) to find an explanation. Rey discovered it quickly enough. (25) The power of fire refines the air and separates it into light particles which evaporate like the spiritus of wine, and a heavy part which is comparable to the heavy residue from wine distillation. Thus densified by heat, air then attaches itself to the calx and makes it heavy, like water added to sand. The limit of the increase in weight is the capacity of the calx to take up densified air. The loss that Brun found with lead was explained as being caused by its impurities. The Italian mathematician and philosopher, Hieronymus Cardanus (1501–1576), had developed a different explanation in his book *De Subtilitate* (1554). Among the subtle things he discussed in this book were air and fire. When the metal lead is heated, it dies, it loses the celestial fire that made it alive and light. Therefore lead becomes heavier when it is heated. Biringuccio had held the same view and both had pointed to the analogy between this increase and the increase in weight of animals after death. Rey believed and explained this fact for animals, but he refused to ascribe life to a metal.

Experiments on flames and respiration were carried out at meetings of the newly formed (1662) Royal Society of London. Much skill and ingenuity went into devising and building the apparatus for these investigations. Robert Hooke (1635–1703), who assisted Boyle in his work on the compression and rarification of air, devised new methods for collecting gases. Bladders were pressed flat and then inflated by the air developed in fermentation or in the reaction of oyster shells with acids. Another arrangement was to place a vial with the reacting mixture under a large glass filled with water and inverted with the opening under water (Stephen Hales, 1727).

Saltpeter quickly "dissolves," that is, burns, sulfurous bodies. When air acts in this way, Hooke assumes it does so "by a substance inherent, and mixed with the air, that is like, if not the very same, with that which is fixt in Salt-peter." (26)

Robert Boyle continued his experiments on the behavior of air which in 1662 had led to a confirmation of his hypothesis that pressure and volume are in reverse proportion. In 1673 he described "Some experiments to make fire and flame ponderable." For example, tin, on calcination, increases in weight due to "absorption of the material of fire which had passed through the glass." John Mayow (1643–1679) assumed that niter is present in the air (1668), which he later (1674) changed into "nitroaerial particles." These particles strike, rub, and comminute the saline particles of burning sulfur so that they are "at last sharpened like small swords and are moreover so attenuated as to be changed from rigid and solid into flexible and fluid particles," thus producing the acrid and acid spirit of sulfur.

These events are not the result of an abstract mechanism; they are governed by the "hostility" between the partners: "The nitroaerial spirit and sulphur are engaged in perpetual hostilities with each other, and indeed from their mutual struggle when they meet and from their diverse state when they succumb by turns, all changes of things seem to arise." (27)

This is one of the dramatic periods in the development of chemistry. A connection between combustion and respiration is revealed. Boyle finds the volume of air reduced by both. He supposes the presence in air of "a little vital Quintessence" which Hooke recognizes as similar to or identical with a substance that is "fixt" in saltpeter. Mayow, and this is his real contribution, states that the air remaining after having served for respiration is still "elastic" with the same "spring" that Boyle had measured. Later historians succumbed to the temptation to interpret these attempts as the solution, which was not found for another hundred years.

The old philosophical idea of elements as the expression of unity in nature had remained the basis of chemical thought for two thousand years. During the course of this time, however, one great defect in these ideas appeared. They identified as elements one, or a small group, of those substances known from everyday experience. With the growth of experience, this identification proved unsatisfactory if not impossible. To be valid, a concept of universal elements would have to be much bolder, it would have to rise above the tangible and commonplace. A philosophical sulfur or a universal salt as elements were contradictory in themselves. Could sulfur, with its now better known specific combination of qualities, at the same time represent only one of these qualities everywhere? Could salt remain a universal element when so many particular salts were distinguished? The tension between individuality and universality, which formerly contributed to the value of such ideas, now became so great that it tore them apart. Boyle saw the difficulty and found no other way of overcoming it except to renounce the chemical concept of element. He knew that to explain chemical experience by matter and form alone and directly was at best an ideal program. He did not make the attempt to carry it out for chemistry, nor did Descartes or Leibniz do this for philosophy.

A universal element which was not identical with any one of the known substances arose from speculations about the universal chemical reaction of combustion. Six years after Boyle's death, the German physician Georg Ernst Stahl refined Becher's combustible earth into "phlogiston" as the element involved in combustion. (28) This new theory was soon widely accepted.

REFERENCES

1. Guy Beaujouan, *L'Interdépendance entre la Science Scolastique et les Techniques Utilitaires* (Paris: 1957).

2. R. P. Multhauf, *Isis,* **45** (1954), p. 364.

3. Paracelsus, in his preface to the book *Paragranum* (1531). See also Jolande Jacobi's *Paracelsus: Selected Writings* (New York: Pantheon Books, Inc., 1951), and Walter Pagel, *Paracelsus, an Introduction to Philosophical Medicine in the Era of the Renaissance* (Basel/New York: S. Karger, 1958).

4. Johann Huser, *De Natura Rerum,* Vol. 6, p. 344. A complete German edition of *Paracelsus Sämtliche Werke* was edited by Karl Sudhoff and R. Oldenbourg (Munich and Berlin: 1922–1933). *Four Treatises of Theophrastus von Hohenheim* edited by Henry E. Sigerist in *Publications of the Institute of the History of Medicine,* 2d Series, Vol. 1 (Baltimore: Johns Hopkins University Press, 1949). *Volumen Medicinae Paramyrum* appeared

separately as a supplement to the *Bulletin of the History of Medicine,* No. 11 (Baltimore: Johns Hopkins University Press, 1949).

5 Johann Huser, *Astronomia Magna oder Philosophia Sagax der grossen und kleinen Welt,* Vol. 10.

6. Shakespeare's source probably was the translation of Pliny's *Natural History,* by Philemon Holland, 1601; see H. N. Wethered, *The Mind of the Ancient World, a Consideration of Pliny's Natural History* (New York/London: Longmans Green & Co., 1937).

7. The first volume of the *Alchemia* was published in Frankfurt in 1597. It was followed by additions, commentaries, and an appendix, which completed the work in 1615.

8. Biringuccio's *De la Pirotechnia* (Venice: 1540) was translated and amplified by Agricola in his *De Re Metallica* (Basel: 1556). Both books have been translated into English, *The Pirotechnia of V. Biringuccio* by Cyril S. Smith and Martha T. Gnudi (New York: American Institute of Mining and Metallurgical Engineering, 1942). Agricola's book was translated and edited by Herbert C. Hoover and Lou H. Hoover (London: *Mining Magazine,* 1912). This later appeared in book form (New York: Dover Publications, 1950).

9. Walter Pagel, *Bull. Inst. Hist. Medicine,* **3** (1935), p. 268.

10. René Descartes, *Discours de la Méthode pour bien Conduire sa Raison et Chercher la Vérité dans les Sciences,* Méditation Sixième, 1637 ("Discourse on the method of well using one's reason and seeking the tiuth in sciences").

11. B. Rochot, A. Koyre, G. Mongredien, and A. Adam, *Pierre Gassendi, sa Vie et son Oeuvre* (Paris: 1955).

12. H. Peters, "Leibniz als Chemiker," *Archiv f. Geschichte d. Naturwissenschaften u. d. Technik,* **7** (1916), pp. 85–108, 220–35, 278–97.

13. Franz Strunz, *J. B. van Helmont* (Vienna and Leipzig: 1907). W. Pagel, *Jo. Bapt. van Helmont, Einführung in die philosphische Medizin des Barock* (Berlin: 1930).

14. Herbert M. Howe, "The Roots of van Helmont's Tree," *Isis,* **56** (1965), pp. 408–19; Howe traces the idea of such an experiment back to about A.D. 400.

15. J. B. van Helmont, *Ortus medicinae, id est initia physicae inaudita* (edited by his son), (Amsterdam: 1648). Translated from the German edition by Christian Knorr von Rosenroth (Sultzbach: 1683), p. 820.

16. Max Speter, *Chem. Ztg.,* **34** (1910), p. 193.

17. Kurt F. Gugel, *Johann Rudolph Glauber 1604–1670* (Würzburg, 1955). Erich Pietsch, "Johann Rudolph Glauber," *Deutsches Museum* **24** (1) (1956).

18. J. R. Glauber, *Furni Novi Philosophici* (Amsterdam, 1648–1650); *Opera Omnia* (Frankfurt am Mayn: 1658), *Pharmacopoeae Spagyricae,* 2d part.

19. Robert Boyle, *New Experiments, Physico-mechanical, Touching the Spring of Air and Its Effects* (Oxford: 1660), p. 363.

20. Marie Boas (Hall), *Robert Boyle and Seventeenth Century Chemistry* (London: Cambridge University Press, 1958).

21. *The Sceptical Chemist* was first published in 1661 (Oxford), with many later editions in Latin. See J. F. Fulton, *A Bibliography of The Honourable Robert Boyle* (Oxford: University Press, 1932).

22. Joachim Jungius, *Disputationum de principiis corporum naturalium,* prima (March 30) et altera (April 2) (Hamburg: 1642).

23. Robert Boyle, *The Origin of Forms and Qualities According to the Corpuscular Philosophy* (Oxford: 1666).

24. Allen J. Debus, "The Paracelsian Aerial Niter," *Isis,* **55** (1964), pp. 43–61.

25. Jean Rey, *Essais sur la recherche de la cause par laquelle l'estain et le plomb augmentent de poids, quand on les calcine* (Bazas: 1630). (Investigation of the cause from which tin and lead increase in weight when calcined.) Pierre Lemay, "Jean Rey, précurseur de Torricelli, Pascal, et Lavoisier," *Bull. Soc. Française de l'Historie de la Médecine,* **32** (3) (1938), pp. 148–63.

26. Robert Hooke, *Micrographia* (London: 1665), p. 103.

27. John Mayow, *Tractatus Quinque Medico-Physici* (Oxford: 1674). Translated in *Alembic Club Reprints* No. 17 (Edinburgh: 1907), pp. 25, 49. J. R. Partington, "The Life and Work of John Mayow," *Isis,* **47** (1956), pp. 217–30, 405–17.

28. G. E. Stahl, *Zymotechnia fundamentalis sive fermentationis theoria generalis* (Halle: 1697), and *Specimen Beccherianum* (Leipzig: Joh. Ludov Gleditsch, 1703).

6

Phlogiston and Dephlogisticated Air

Boyle was deeply dissatisfied with his own theories and those of others. "But though I agree with them, in thinking that the air is in many places impregnated with corpuscles of a nitrous nature, yet I confess that I have not hitherto been convinced of all that is wont to be delivered about the plenty and qualities of nitre in the air: for I have not found that those that build so much upon this volatile nitre have made out by any competent experiment that there is such a volatile nitre abounding in the air."(1) Others were less troubled by skepticism. For Mayow, and similarly for Lémery, elementary atoms acted by means of specific forms of which everyday tools gave satisfactory models.

For Becher, the cause for the combustion of a substance was its content of a principle of combustibility. This principle had to be an "earth" (*terra*), like the other principles, and a *terra pinguis*. Becher endowed it with the property which he tried to explain. Georg Ernst Stahl (1660–1734, Berlin) enlarged the theory of this universal substance of combustibility. He called it *phlogiston,* a word that van Helmont had used somewhat vaguely. While Becher said that a substance actually burns because it is potentially combustible, Stahl carried the theory through for a cycle of operations.

When sulfur burns it becomes a volatile acid; when salts of this acid are heated with coal dust, sulfur is regenerated. The phlogiston theory explains this cycle:

Sulfur − Phlogiston = Volatile acid
Volatile acid + Phlogiston = Sulfur

It follows that phlogiston is about the same as coal. A combustible substance contains phlogiston, loses it on combustion, and has it restored from the product of combustion when the lost phlogiston is returned to this substance. Thus metallic lead loses its phlogiston on calcining, and coal (or oil) restores the metal from the calx. Lead is, therefore, a composite of lead-calx with the phlogiston, of which coal is a representative. Air dissolves the phlogiston liberated when a candle burns. That the candle goes out after burning for a while in an enclosed air chamber is explained by the limited capacity of the air to hold or dissolve phlogiston. That the air around us is not gradually becoming saturated with phlogiston is due to its absorption by plants when they grow; van Helmont must be criticized for having disregarded this effect in his experiment with the willow tree.

The quantity of phlogiston in a metal or in other heat-sensitive substances need not be great. It acts in the manner of a quality substance and is thus directly connected with the ideas of olden times which Paracelsus and van Helmont had in part transmitted. Although rejecting the opiates and metal salts which Paracelsus used for medication, Stahl was deeply influenced by him. Paracelsus' Archeus and spiritus recur in Stahl's system as the anima which distinguishes living from dead bodies and which is active in mental as well as in vegetative processes.

Phlogiston can variously be coal, heat, or light; it is not identified with one particular substance. This concept is, perhaps, influenced by the new philosophy of Leibniz, who declared that *vis est substantia* (force is substance). Isaac Newton (1642–1727) was opposed to such explanations with occult qualities. "To tell us that every species of Things is endowed with an occult specifick Quality by which it acts and produces manifest Effects, is to tell us nothing: But to derive two or three general Principles of Motion from Phenomena, and afterwards to tell us, how the Properties and Actions of all corporeal Things follow from those manifest Principles, would be a great step in Philosophy, though the Causes of those Principles were not yet discover'd. . . ." (2) To derive qualities from principles of motion, to express observations in the language of mathematics, was easier in astronomy and physics than in chemistry. Newton himself uses phlogistic language when he discusses "the refractive Power of the Body in respect of its density." He calculates a value of 5000 to 8000 for many "bodies," but 10,000 to 14,000 for oily materials. "Spirit of wine has a refractive Power in a middle degree between those of Water and oily Substances, and accordingly seems to be composed of both, united by Fermentation; the Water, by means of some Saline Spirits with which it is impregnated, dissolving the Oil, and volatalizing it by the Action . . . And as Light congregated by a Burning-glass acts most upon sulphureous Bodies, to turn them into Fire and Flame; so since all Action is mutual, Sulphurs ought to act most upon Light." (3)

In line with these thoughts, Newton concluded from the high refractive index of diamond that it must be combustible. His general rule, "all Action is mutual," has deep roots, going down to the philosophy of Empedocles (page 25).

The philosopher John Locke (1632–1704) once wrote to his cousin, Lord King: "Mr. Newton is really a very valuable man, not only for his wonderful skill in mathematics, but in divinity too and his great knowledge in the Scriptures, wherein I know few for his equals." (4)

Voltaire (François Marie Arouet) (1694–1778), the French poet and philosopher who did much to explain Newton's "philosophy," described the differences of prevailing viewpoints in a letter of 1728: "When a Frenchman arrives in London, he finds a very great difference in philosophy as well as in most other things. In Paris he left the world entirely full of matter; here he finds completely empty spaces. In Paris they see the universe beset with ethereal whirls, while there the invisible forces of gravitation act in the same space. In Paris they paint a picture of the earth oblong like an egg, and in London it is flattened like a melon."

Chemistry was taught "according to the principles of Newton and of Stahl," (5) with one exception. The words "attraction" and "affinity" were banned in France, so that Étienne-François Geoffroy (Geoffroy senior, as he was called, 1672–1731, Paris) called a compilation of substances in the order of the strength of their compounds a *"Table of Relations."* (6) This table, which is here reproduced and explained, does not derive principles of motion from chemical reactions, but it abstains from referring to "occult qualities" and in so far fulfills at least the negative part of Newton's requirements. In his theory of the metals, however, Geoffroy uses a combustible principle which combines with the specific metal-earth to constitute the metal itself. It is this principle, universally distributed in nature, that causes the characteristic properties of metals.

The *Table of Relations* gave a comparative gradation for the "love and strive" between the substances. For a more precise tabulation, new tools and techniques were needed. Foremost among the new tools was the thermometer. This development is connected with Boyle's work on the elasticity of air. (7) Guillaume Amontons (1663–1705) used the pressure of air as a measure of its state of heat and constructed an air thermometer (1699). Gabriel Daniel

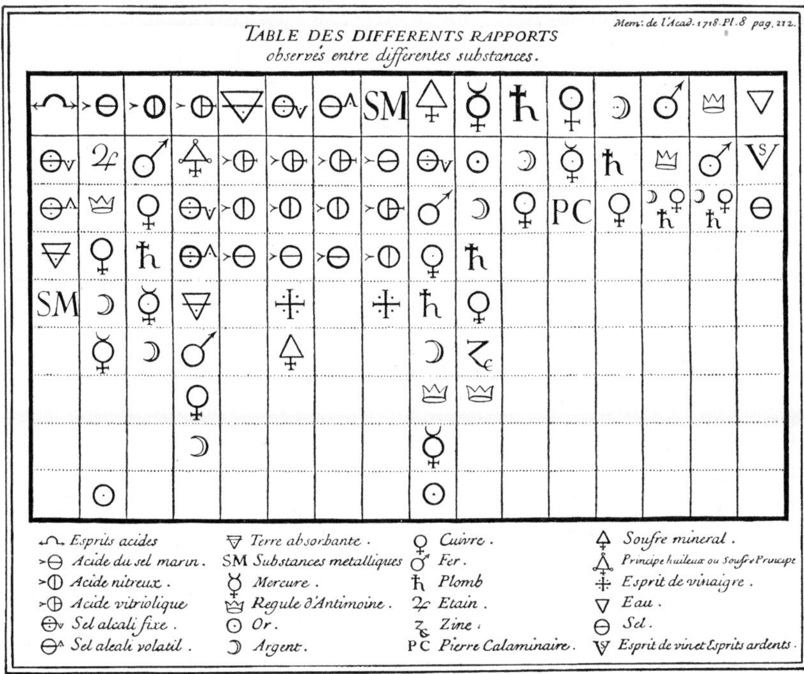

Fig. 10. *Geoffroy's Table* of the different relations observed between different substances, 1718.

The first horizontal line lists the substances used in chemistry; under each of these, substances are arranged vertically in the order of decreasing reactivity. For example, in the first vertical row, spirits of acids have the strongest relationship to soda, less to ammonia, absorbent earth, and metallic substances. Gold is the noblest metal with the lowest inclination to react with the acid of sea salt (Row 2) or sulfur (Row 9), except for its readiness to combine with mercury (Row 10) to form amalgams. In the combination with acids, the fixed alkali drives out the volatile alkali (Row 1), in combination with alkali or metallic substances, vitriolic acid displaces nitric, and nitric displaces marine acid (Rows 6, 7, 8). The "principe huileux ou soufre Principe" is the principle contained in oily or charry substances, similar to phlogiston.

Fahrenheit (1686–1736) introduced mercury (1714) instead of the previously used alcohol in a liquid-based thermometer. For the fixed points to determine a scale, Christian Huygens (1629–1695) had proposed melting ice and boiling water (1665). René Antoine Ferchault, Sieur de Réaumur (1683–1757), accepted these fixed points (1730). While Fahrenheit called zero the indication in the coldest mixture which he could produce by adding sal ammonia to melting ice, Anders Celsius (1670–1756) defined boiling water as zero and melting ice as 100 degrees, which Linnaeus (Karl von Linné) three years later (1745) reversed. To be historically correct, the degrees of our centigrade scale should therefore be called "degrees Linné," not "degrees Celsius."

When two equal quantities of water of different temperatures are mixed, the resulting temperature is the arithmetic middle. When, however, equal volumes of water and mercury are brought together, the resulting temperature is closer to that of the water than to that of the mercury. These experiments had been carried out by Fahrenheit for Hermann Boerhaave, the famous professor of chemistry and botany at the University of Leiden (1668–1738): (8) Joseph Black (1728–1799, Edinburgh) concluded that the quantity of heat should be distinguished from its force or intensity. In experiments like those of Fahrenheit, the quantity of heat which the water gained was the same as that which the mercury lost. The temperature change then indicates that one volume of mercury contains a smaller quantity of heat than an equal volume of water. In other words, mercury has a lower capacity for heat than water has. When ice melts it takes up a considerable quantity of heat without changing its temperature. Water is thus a quasi-chemical compound of ice with an amount of heat which becomes latent. Black points out the disastrous consequences that the melting of ice and snow would have without the delaying action caused by the absorption of latent heat. The conversion of water into steam requires a still greater quantity of latent heat. Black presented these results in his lectures of 1762. James Watt developed an important practical application of the findings of his teacher and friend in his condenser for steam engines which he patented in 1769.

The use of this simple tool, the thermometer, thus had great consequences. Another new tool was the pneumatic trough, an improvement over earlier methods for collecting gas, which the clergyman Stephen Hales (1677–1761, London) developed. Its usefulness was later extended by replacing the water in the trough and in the collecting flask by mercury. With this apparatus, Hales showed that alkaline salts give off a large quantity of "air" when added to pure acids. This air was also formed when limestone was calcined. The resulting quicklime lost its caustic taste when exposed to this air, became "mild," and in this state effervesced with acids.

The renewed interest in these reactions had a rather strange origin. A secret medicine which had marvelous effects in gallstone afflictions was revealed as consisting mainly of burned egg shells and seeds of herbs. Hales, who was a member of the royal commission

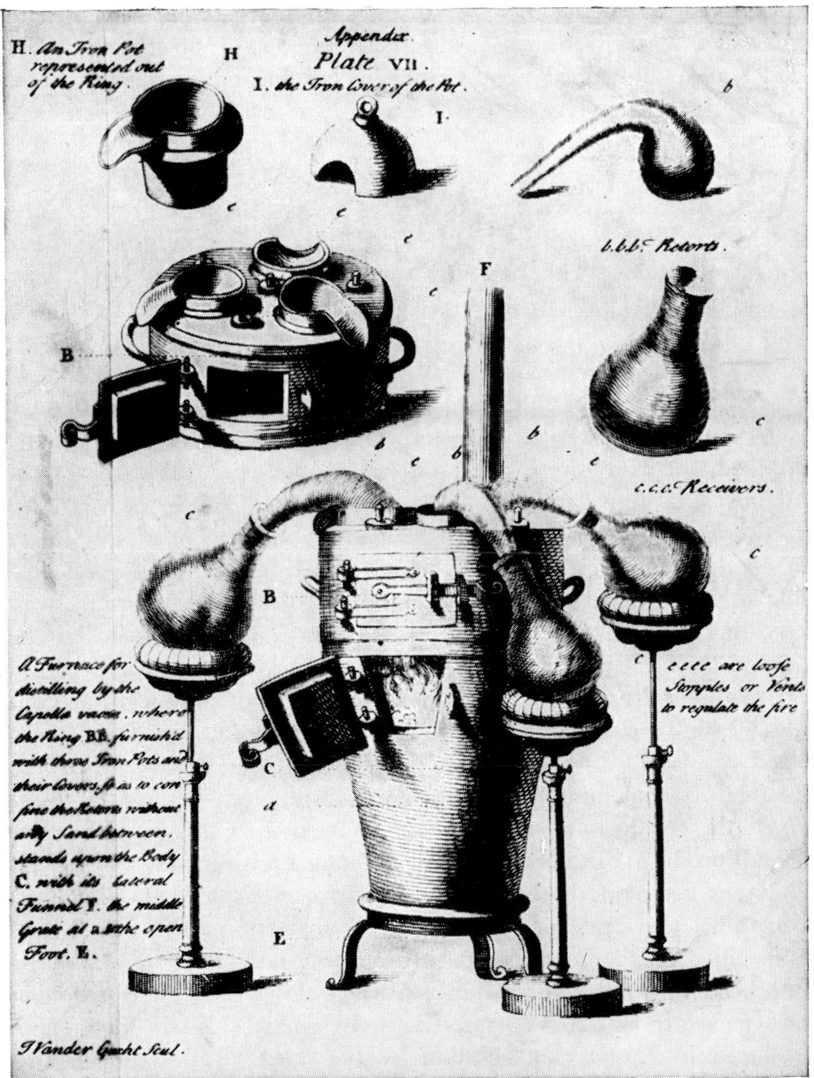

Fig. 11. Boerhaave's furnace with retorts and receivers. (A reproduction of Plate VII from *A New Method of Chemistry,* translated from the original Latin of *Dr. Boerhaave's Elementa Chemiae* by Peter Shaw, 2d ed., London, 1741, Vol. 2.)

Compared with Brunschwig's arrangement, the oven now has a brick lining, a fire door, stoppers on the vents to regulate the fire, pots, and covers to hold the retorts in place without the use of sand.

to examine this medicine (1739), was thereby led to experiment with limewater. At this time Friedrich Hoffmann (1660–1742, Berlin, then Halle), the colleague of Stahl, showed that magnesia is different from lime because the salts that they form with sulfuric acid can be separated according to their different solubilities. This again was of great interest to the medical profession. Magnesia was a famous laxative, already known to Hippocrates in the fifth century B.C. The water of a spring discovered in 1616 at Epsom (England) had similar beneficial action. The botanist Nehemias Grew crystallized a salt, called *sal anglicum,* from this water (*De salis cathartici in aquis Ebshamensibus* . . . , 1695). This bitter-tasting salt was also found (1707) in the saline liquor, called "bittern," which was left after crystallizing common salt from seawater and in the mother liquor from the purification of saltpeter. Precipitates from such liquors, obtained, for example, by "alkaline salts," namely, soda or pearl ash (mainly potassium carbonate), were designated as "magnesia." This word originally meant any half-solid material, a *magma* or, in Arabic, an *amalgam*. What is the magnesia from Epsom salt, and is it possible to make a stronger limewater for dissolving gallstones? These were the questions that Joseph Black, a student of medicine at the University of Edinburgh (1751–1754), was asked to investigate.

Alkaline salts added to a solution of Epsom salt produce a precipitate which reacts with sulfuric acid to regenerate the Epsom salt. Fixed air is liberated in this regeneration. The same air can be obtained by calcining the precipitated white magnesia (*magnesia alba*), thereby forming *magnesia usta* (burnt magnesia). This preheated product dissolves in acids without forming gas. Magnesia alba thus corresponds to limestone, and magnesia usta to quicklime. Limestone, the crude or "mild" lime, is an acid "earth" which loses its "acidity" in the fixed air that is driven out on calcining. Calcined lime becomes mild again when it attracts this air. Crude magnesia loses fixed air when it becomes burnt magnesia. In the precipitate produced in Epsom salt solution by the fixed alkali, "the air was forced from the alkali by the acid and lodged itself in the magnesia." The fixed alkali contained the kind of "air" which passed over to the magnesia in the precipitate and which could be liberated from this precipitate through heat. The burnt magnesia had to be considered as analogous to the burnt lime. The "remarkable acrimony" of quicklime was not acquired from any added matter received from the fire "but seemed to be an essential property of a pure earth." (9)

It was this latter point from which the apothecary Johann Friedrich Meyer (1764, Osnabrück) started his opposite views. Calcining consisted in combining the crude lime with a particular matter from the fire for which he invented the name *Acidum pingue.* The presence of this acidum pingue in quicklime manifested itself in its "acrimony" and solubility. In the reaction with mild (or fixed) alkali, this acid is transferred from the lime to the alkali, which thereby becomes caustic.

JOSEPH BLACK:

$$\underset{\text{(in solution)}}{\text{Epsom salt + Fixed alkali}} \longrightarrow \underset{\text{(precipitate)}}{\text{Magnesia}} + \underset{\text{(dissolved)}}{\text{Salt of alkali}}$$

$$\text{Crude lime} \xrightarrow{\text{heated}} \text{Quicklime} + \underset{\text{(gas)}}{\text{Fixed air}}$$

$$\text{Magnesia alba} \xrightarrow{\text{heated}} \text{Magnesia usta} + \underset{\text{(gas)}}{\text{Fixed air}}$$

J. F. MEYER:

Crude lime + Acidum pingue ⟶ Quicklime

Quicklime + Fixed alkali ⟶ Crude lime + (Alkali + Acidum pingue)

The heat substance, in whatever new form, seemed so much more real to Meyer than the fixed air on which Black had based his explanation! To Black, fixed air was a definite chemical substance. He measured the quantities involved in the reactions. He weighed a piece of chalk, dissolved it in just the sufficient amount of dilute acid, and found that "the loss in weight by the effervescence" was very nearly equal to the loss the same quantity of chalk showed when it was heated in a crucible. Whether by dilute acid or by strong heat, the relative amount of fixed air removed from chalk is the same, and its measure is very nearly 40 percent by weight. Black proposed to add a new column to Geoffroy's *Table of Affinities,* with fixed air at the head, followed by the alkalies in the order of their affinity to it. This order should be calcareous earth, fixed alkali, magnesia, and volatile alkali (ammonia).

The new technical methods made it possible to measure and characterize *other gases* which had been observed in earlier times. Henry Cavendish (1731–1810, London) found that fixed air has a specific gravity of 1.57, inflammable air 0.09, compared with air as unity (1766). He also prepared a pure "mephitic air" by passing common air over glowing coal and removing the fixed air through absorption in lime.

Several investigators reported such a "mephitic" or spoiled component in the air. In 1772, Daniel Rutherford (1749–1819), a student of Black, let mice remove the respirable part, removed the fixed air by alkali, and found a large residue that was incapable of absorbing the phlogiston. Torbern Bergman made similar statements. For its inability to sustain the life of an animal (zoon), the gas was named azote. The name persists in the French literature. In his *Elements de Chimie* of 1790, Jean Antoine Claude Chaptal (1756–1832, Paris) recommended the name nitrogen, derived from nitric acid.

Joseph Priestley (1733, Fieldhead, England –1804, Northumberland, Pennsylvania) measured the contraction of air after it reacted with the nitrous gas which Hales had already produced and tested in his eudiometer, i.e., an apparatus for measuring the quality of air.

Karl Wilhelm Scheele (1742, Stralsund –1786, Köping, Sweden) heated "calcined red mercury" and thereby obtained a particular kind of air "in which fire burned beautifully." This proved to be the same air as that developed on heating the salt formed from magnesia and nitric acid. He called it "fire-air" because it is that part of the common air that sustains combustion. When sulfur burns, it becomes an acid and loses its phlogiston. The old theory went on to declare that this phlogiston is "dissolved" in the air. His new findings caused Scheele to modify the theory. Phlogiston combined with the fire-air; heat and light are the products of this combination. When metals are calcined, they absorb fire-air, which explains the increase in weight. Either the phlogiston in the metal attracts this air or phlogiston is abandoned to the air. In the first case heat is synthesized; in the second case it is decomposed. The reverse reaction occurs, for example, on heating the calx of mercury under a burning glass in the sun, when heat releases its fire-air and yields its other component, phlogiston, to the calx. With the abbreviation "phl" for phlogiston, the reaction is:

KARL WILHELM SCHEELE:

$$\text{Calx of mercury} + \underbrace{(\text{phl} + \text{fire-air})}_{=\text{ heat}} = \underbrace{(\text{calx of mercury} + \text{phl})}_{=\text{ mercury}} + \text{fire-air}$$

Scheele heated a solution of the "acid of salt" together with "brownstone" (manganese dioxide) in a retort. An effervescence followed, and the gas, that was not fixed air, proved "most oppressive to the lungs; by smell it resembled warm aqua regia." In bottles connected with the retort, the air turns yellow; green vitriol of iron is turned red, vegetable leaves and flowers are bleached, all metals are attacked. The yellow gas is "acid of salt" deprived of its phlogiston by the brownstone.

The main part of these experiments was carried out in 1771–1772, the manuscript was ready in 1775, but publication was delayed for two more years. (10) Antoine Laurent Lavoisier (1743–1794, Paris) raised strong objections: "In the work of Scheele, nothing less is claimed than to change all our accepted ideas in chemistry and physics; to deprive fire and light of the quality of elements which has been attributed to them by ancient and modern philosophers; to decompose and recompose the fire in our laboratories, and thus to extend considerably the domain of physics and chemistry." Lavoisier further pointed out that this theory was first conceived by Meyer in his acidum pingue, and that the priority for the discovery of the fire-air belonged to himself, having called it "vital air." (11)

The first part of this criticism is more valid than the priority claim. In a note of April 6, 1773, Lavoisier still confused fixed air with this new kind of air: "Lime, in my view, is a calcareous earth deprived of air; the metallic calces, on the contrary, are metals saturated with air. Yet both produce a like effect on the alkalis; they make them caustic." (12) Early in 1774 Pierre Bayen (1725–1797, Paris) described the quantities of "elastic fluid" which he had obtained on heating the red precipitated mercury, and Joseph Priestley, on August 1 of the same year, showed that this air reacts with nitrous gas and causes flames to burn very brightly. On April 26, 1775, Lavoisier confirmed by exact measurements what Bayen had already demonstrated qualitatively, namely, that the gas obtained from heating this red mercury precipitate alone is different from that which it develops when heated together with coal. The first is a new kind of air, the other is identical with fixed air.

PIERRE BAYEN:

$$\text{Red mercury precipitate} \xrightarrow{\text{heat}} \text{Mercury} + \text{New air}$$

$$\text{Red mercury precipitate} + \text{Coal} \xrightarrow{\text{heat}} \text{Mercury} + \text{Fixed air}$$

Now Lavoisier was ready to explain "the nature of the principle which combines with the metals in calcination and which increases their weight." Two years later he gave new names to the "eminently respirable air": acidifying principle or oxygine principle.

Thus Lavoisier was not the first to discover the gas to which he gave these names. Priority may be assigned to Boyle or Hooke or Hales, who produced the gas long before Scheele or Priestley, Bayen, or Lavoisier did. However, Scheele was the first to recognize it as the air of fire, and he obtained it from several different chemi-

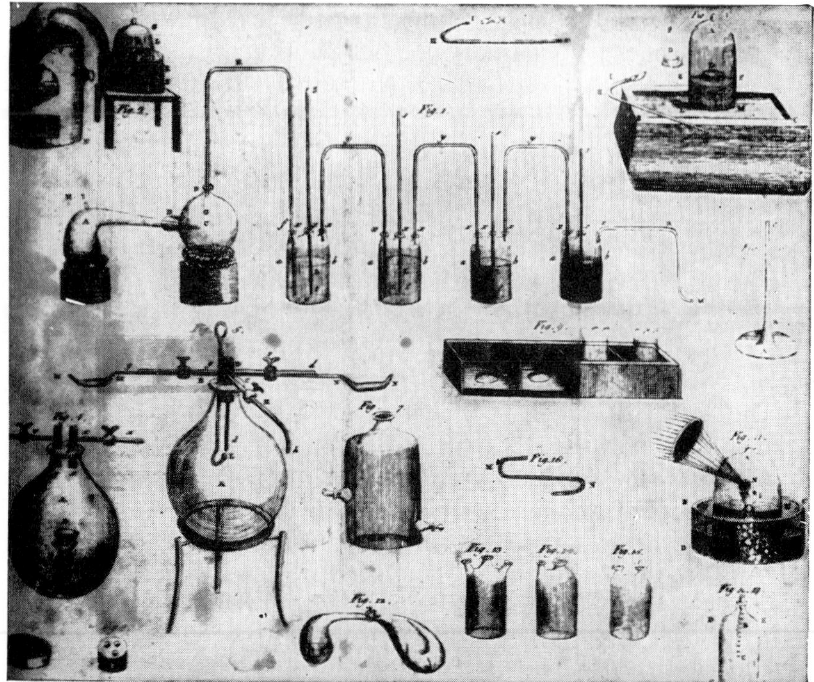

Fig. 12. Laboratory equipment used by Lavoisier. (A reproduction of Plate IV from *Elements of Chemistry* by A. Lavoisier, translated by Robert Kerr, 3d ed., Edinburgh, 1796.)

Fig. 1 (upper center) shows an arrangement "for the most complicated distillations." The tubular glass retort at the left has its beak fitted into its recipient, which is connected to a train of four bottles containing limewater and the like for absorbing the gases. These bottles have capillary tubes in the middle neck, upon the suggestion of J. H. Hassenfratz, to equalize air pressure in the system.

The outlet from the last bottle may be connected with a jar in a pneumato-chemical apparatus, such as shown in the right half of Fig. 2 (upper left).

Fig. 3 (upper right) shows a bell jar placed over mercury. Just to the left of the bell jar may be a piece of Kunckel's phosphorus, or charcoal to which a bit of tinder has been added so that it can be ignited by contact with a red-hot iron. The glass tube is used to regulate passage of air into and from the bell jar, one end being covered by a piece of paper to prevent the entrance of mercury.

Fig. 11 (far right, near bottom) is designated as representing Priestley's method for burning a metal in porcelain. The porcelain cup is under a jar, which is standing in a basin of water. The focus of a burning glass is being brought to bear on the metal in the cup.

cals. Priestley learned not before March, 1775, that the reaction with nitrous gas proved the new air to be better than common air. The first to organize all these observations, those of others together with his own, into a comprehensive system was Lavoisier; he is the discoverer not of the substance but of its place and importance in chemistry. All the other investigators, with the exception of one, adhered to the phlogiston theory. Bayen declared in April, 1774, that calces are formed from metals when they combine with an elastic fluid of the air, about which no accurate knowledge was available.

The function of Copernicus in astronomy was performed in chemistry by Lavoisier; he reversed the prevalent system in its theory of combustion and the relationship of metals to their calces or "earths." Where the theory of Stahl in any of its modifications, including that elaborated by Scheele, assumed a loss of phlogiston or its gain, the new system demonstrated a gain of oxygen or its loss. The reversion was, however, not a revolution, it was not radical enough to abolish the universality at which the old concept aimed. Lavoisier transferred universal functions from phlogiston to the new element, and to the old function as producer of color he added the new one of producer of acidity.

What Lavoisier retained of the old concept of universal elements was formulated in his theory that oxygen gas is a compound of the oxygine principle with heat. (13) The "principle" itself never occurs free. When the red precipitate of mercury is heated, the reaction is:

Red precipitate of mercury + Heat = Mercury + (Oxygine + Heat)

Thus, oxygen is literally and figuratively a compound of the old with the new chemistry.

The new insights into the composition and effect of air resulted from efforts in many countries by men who differed greatly in character and mode of living. Cavendish, the rich, solitary nobleman, sought the information through exact measurements of physical properties. He was convinced that nature was governed by number, measure, and weight. In his way he continued the vision of Pythagoras and the work of Galileo and Newton, not the way of Paracelsus or Stahl. He discovered new relationships but no new substances. In an experiment to determine whether the dephlogisticated part of air was really uniform, he found a residue, only $1/120$ of the air, that was neither phlogisticated nor dephlogisticated air. He had enough confidence in his measurements to consider this residue as real and different; it was rediscovered and identified a hundred years later. (14)

Scheele started under very modest financial conditions as an apothecary's assistant, yet he soon found the time and the means to indulge in chemical research. His method for preparing pure tartaric acid from cream of tartar (wine lees) was published by his friend Anders Jahan Retzius (1742–1821) in 1770. Friendships with Torbern Bergman (1735–1784) and Johan Gottlieb Gahn (1745–1818) may have been responsible for several fine offers he received but did not accept. From 1775 to his death in 1786 he remained in Köping as superintendent of the pharmacy. In a sample of Bergman's *lapis ponderosus*, i.e., heavy stone, in Swedish: *tung sten,* he discovered a new earth; it dissolves in alkali, and on treating with zinc, tin, or iron, the solution turns blue, similar to the solution of the terra molybdena that he obtained from molybdenite (MoS) with nitric acid. For plumbago, which had often been taken as being identical with molybdenite, Scheele proved that it is graphite and consists of "aerial acid" combined with phlogiston. In the water that had been used for boiling oil with litharge to make a lead soap, he discovered a "sweet principle" of the oil; the name glycerol for this "principle" was later derived from the Greek word for sweet.

With Cavendish, from whom he is otherwise so different, he shared the belief in phlogiston, although Scheele was disturbed by doubts. In 1780 (March 13) he wrote to his friend Peter Jacob Hjelm (1746–1813, Stockholm): "If pure air has taken up phlogiston in respiration, why has the air not disappeared or, which is the same thing, been converted into heat? If the air has, however, lost phlogiston, why does it not attract phlogiston afterward? How strongly should not fire burn in it [the spoilt, exhaled air], since we know, e.g., of the nitric acid that it attracts phlogiston the better, the more of it [the nitric acid] loses." (15)

Priestley's wide interests in languages and theology did not prevent him from studying physics and chemistry. The University of Edinburgh gave him the degree of doctor juris for a thesis on the history of electricity (1767)! His work on gases began with investigations of their electrical conductivity. The French Revolution influenced his life considerably. He had to flee from Birmingham because of his sympathies with the movement. First he went to London (1791), and three years later he sought and found freedom in the United States.

Lavoisier combined the gifts of experimenter with those of administrator and financier. In the same month in which he was nominated to the Académie in 1768 he joined the "Ferme," the committee that collected taxes for the government and was later accused of amassing huge profits. Always interested in public affairs, he assisted Turgot, the minister of war, in his efforts to increase the production of saltpeter. One day of his busy week was devoted to experiments for which he spent large sums of money. During the French Revolution he fought bravely for the security of scientists and the Académie, of which he had become a director in 1785. He was arrested under the decree of November 24, 1793, against the "Fermiers," and executed on May 8, 1794. The efforts of his friends were in vain; it is doubtful whether the accusations of his enemies were decisive. His biographer, M. Berthelot, is bitter about the silence of men like Monge and Guyton de Morveau, and particularly about Fourcroy's actions against Lavoisier. (16).

REFERENCES

1. Robert Boyle, *The General History of Air,* published in 1692, after his death. See Birch, *Robert Boyle's Works* (1744), Vol. 5, p. 117.

2. Sir Isaac Newton, *Optiks,* (London: 1704).

3. Sir Isaac Newton, *Opticks,* in the reprint from the fourth edition (London: 1730) (London: G. Bell & Sons, Ltd., 1931), p. 275.

4. The Royal Society, *Newton Tercentenary Celebration,* 15–19 July, 1946 (London: Cambridge University Press, 1949).

5. Jean Sénac, *Nouveau cours de chimie suivant les principes de Newton et de Stahl* (Paris: 1723).

6. Presented August 27, 1718, at the meeting of the Académie Royale des Sciences and published in the *Mémoires* for that year, which appeared only in 1741.

7. This was connected with the revived interest in Hero of Alexandria's *Pneumatica* (1st century A.D.). See Marie Boas, *Isis,* **40** (1949), p. 38.

8. Hermann Boerhaave, *Elementa Chemiae* (Leiden: Isaac Leverinus, 1732), Vol. 1, p. 268. English edition, *A New Method of Chemistry . . . Translated by P. Shaw and E. Chambers* (London: Osborn & Longman, 1727).

9. Joseph Black, "Experiments upon Magnesia Alba and Other Alkaline Substances," in *Essays and Observations . . . Read Before the Society in Edinburgh* (1755), Vol. 7, Art. 8. Henry Guerlac, "Joseph Black and Fixed Air, *Isis,* **48** (1957), pp. 124–51, 433–56.

10. K. W. Scheele, *Chemische Abhandlung von der Luft und dem Feuer* (Upsala and Leipzig: 1777), p. 95. English edition by J. R. Foster, *Chemical Observations and Experiments on Air and Fire* (London: 1780).

11. A. L. Lavoisier, *Mem. Ac.* Paris: 1781), p. 396; *Oeuvres de Lavoisier,* M. Dumas, Ed., (Paris: 1862–1868), Vol. 2, p. 391.

12. Douglas McKie, *A. Lavoisier* (Philadelphia: J. B. Lippincott Co., 1935). Henry Guerlac, *Lavoisier—The Crucial Year, the Background and Origin of his First Experiment on Combustion in 1772* (Ithaca: Cornell University Press, 1961). Denis I. Duveen and H. S. Klickstein, *A Bibliography*

of the Works of Antoine Laurent Lavoisier, 1743–1794 (London: Wm. Dawson & Sons, 1954); *Supplement* (by Denis I. Duveen, ibid., 1965).

13. E. Farber, "Wärmestoff und Sauerstoff," *Studien zur Geschichte der Chemie, Festgabe fur E. O. von Lippmann* (Berlin: Julius Springer Verlag 1927), pp. 122–31.

14. A. J. Berry, *Henry Cavendish, His Life and Scientific Work* (Hutchinson of London, 1960).

15. A. E. Nordenskiöld, *Carl Wilhelm Scheele* (Stockholm: Norsted & Sons, 1892), p. 393. (Translation and parenthesis by E. F.) Otto Zekert, *Carl Wilhelm Scheele, Apotheker—Chemiker—Entdecker* (Stuttgart: Wissenschaftliche Verlagsgesellschaft, 1963).

16. For the relationships between Priestley and Lavoisier, see S. J. French, *J. Chem. Ed.,* **27**(1950), pp. 83–89. W. A. Smeaton, *Fourcroy: Chemist and Revolutionary 1755–1809* (London, 1962). With great risk to himself, Fourcroy tried to save Lavoisier: G. Kersaint, *Rev. Gén. des Sciences pures et appliquées,* **65** (1958), pp. 27–31. F. W. Gibbs, *Joseph Priestley, Adventurer in Science and Champion of Truth* (Edinburgh: Th. Nelson & Sons, 1965).

7

Mines, Pharmacies, and Manufacturing Plants

The production and use of materials by chemical means comprised metals, salts, alkalis, acids, extracts, and distillates from plants and animals. The development of these materials, particularly from the sixteenth to the eighteenth century, occurred in reciprocal connection with the thoughts, theories, and investigations that have been outlined.

The most universally used source of energy was the heat of burning wood and coal. The operations of separating metals from their ores, of "thickening" (concentrating) solutions of alkali and saltpeter, of distilling leaves and bones were all carried out by heat and fire. The prominence of this tool corresponds to the primary role assigned to it among the elements.

The purpose of these operations was to obtain substances having certain qualities. The direct human appeal of color and odor, the direct application for human needs and achievements, formed the basis for the inquiry into the nature of qualities. The question was: Why do substances act upon our senses and feelings? The answer had a general form: They act through the presence of an agent. This answer seemed only to restate the question, yet it did more than that. Independent characteristics of the agent were sought, its occurrence in different materials was investigated, and as soon as it began to be measured it became depersonalized. The recognition that connecting qualities with mathematics would lead to more satisfactory answers grew in spite of many difficulties and after many attempts, of which Newton's was the most prominent. Goethe found consolation in the thought that sciences will finally return to "life," although they appear to withdraw from it at first. The way is long, perhaps endless. It has not become shorter in our time when we hear the

Fig. 13B. (Above). From the back of the altar of the Annaberg Miners Guild, St. Ann Church, Annaberg, Saxony, 1521.

Left-side panel: Smelting operations in a shaft furnace and an open hearth by two men in white coats and caps.

Right-side panel: The mint. The man at the right brings the metal plates to the coiner at the left.

← **Fig. 13A.** Mining operations. Painting from the back of the altar of the Annaberg "Bergknappschaft," 1521. (From Ernst Oswald Schmidt, *Die St. Annenkirche zu Annaberg*, Leipzig, 1908, Plate XIII).

Upper panel: In the right foreground, two men are winding up a bucket filled with ore from one of the closely spaced shafts. The ore is broken by hammer (middle) and carted by wheelbarrow to the shed. The patron saint (top of upper panel) watches the operations.

Lower panel: The ore is washed and screened.

urgent appeal to the scientist to come down from his ivory tower—the tower that Sir Francis Bacon so poetically described.

In the development of the practical arts, we find the same trends as in the growing science. The old metallurgist thought that ores and metals grow in the earth as plants do on its surface. In a book on mines—the Bergbüchlein of 1500—Ulrich Rülein von Calw summarizes old opinions when he declares that under the influence of sun and stars, mercury and sulfur grow together, as if forming the seeds for ores and metals. The differences between them consist in the fineness and permanence of the components, besides those in the governing star. The typical old pharmacist was permeated by the spirit of alchemy and suffered from its excesses. These practitioners relied upon traditions of the "art" just as the theorists depended upon the ideas of early philosophers.

The relationship of the practical to political events was in many cases very complex. Raw materials and manufactured products, gunpowder and arms, had less influence on wars and trade agreements than politics had. Geographical location and personal enterprise, not advance in manufacturing, gave a predominant role in the chemical trade to the Italy of the eleventh to the fifteenth centuries. The Thirty Years' War disrupted German production for at least a century

The discovery of America brought new materials to the European markets. The Spanish physician, Nicolo Monardes (1546), founded a museum for products collected in the Americas. During the years from 1545 to 1560, four times as much silver was imported from Peru, Mexico, and Bolivia than was produced in all of Europe. Peru at this time began to compete with Spain for predominance in the production of mercury. Gold from America increased in importance as the productivity of Austria and Hungary declined towards the end of the sixteenth century.

Trade between distant countries assumed such surprising dimensions that the French historian and political philosopher Jean Bodin (1530–1596) declared, "Through universal commerce the world was turned, as it were, into a single state." (1)

A heavy stone called *platina* (little silver) used to be mined in Peru. The first report about it came from Don Antonio de Ulloa, a member of the French commission for geographic measurements that visited Peru in 1738. Only small quantities of this material were obtainable. The Spanish government ordered the mines closed and exports stopped so as to prevent the adulteration of gold by adding platina to it! The assumption that it consisted of gold and iron was disproved by the reaction of its solutions in aqua regia and by the fact that its whiteness increased with purity. If purification had consisted in the removal of iron, platina should have turned yellow. It could safely be called "the eighth metal." (2)

It would have been the ninth if the discovery of the new metal, *nickel,* by Axel Frederic Cronstedt in 1751 had been better substantiated at that time. It was confirmed twenty-five years later by Johannes Afzelius Arvidson. Nickel had been suspected of being a modification of iron because of its magnetism, which had been thought to be an exclusive property of iron. Arvidson used the methods common in metal purification, heating with alkali to produce a calx and slag, reduction with fine coal dust, evaporation to remove arsenic and sulfur, and again calcining with the addition of saltpeter. Since these melts always seemed to result in an impure metal, he dissolved it in acids and noted the change of color with varying states of phlogistication, and the green precipitates with alkali. Is nickel a particular modification of iron? He attempted to synthesize nickel from iron and copper to prove its composition.

Similar difficulties existed in the chemistry of *cobalt.* Originally cobalts (or kobolds) were dangerous spirits in mines and were harmful to the miners. This was later rationalized to mean minerals that contain arsenic, and was then confined to those minerals that give a blue color when melted with glass. An additional characteristic was the ability of its salts to form a sympathetic ink which is colorless unless heated. Georg Brandt, the Swedish chemist, obtained a white, metallic cobalt "king" after roasting the mineral, washing it, and heating it with potash at high temperature. Both nickel and cobalt were considered to be only half-metals until about 1780 when Torbern Bergman showed their specific reactions in solutions.

A third "dubious metal" was that obtained from *manganese.* Its Latin name was *magnesia nigra,* black magnesia, to distinguish it from the white magnesia of talcum. It was known in antiquity that the addition of a small quantity of the black manganese to molten glass made it colorless. Too much of it, however, produced a violet color in glass. By heating magnesia nigra, Scheele obtained his fire-air. Its pronounced attraction for phlogiston was considered the cause of its action on sulfur, which produces vitriolic acid. The volatile product of heating marine acid with this magnesia, a greenish-yellow gas, was consequently called "dephlogisticated marine acid" by its discoverer, Scheele. The little-known Viennese chemist Ignatius Gottfried Kaim melted the ore down to a regulus which proved to be different from iron. (3) Another method utilized the insolubility of iron calx in strong acetic acid, which distinguishes it from the soluble manganese calx.

At that time England and Sweden were among the greatest metal-producing countries. England was particularly prominent for its *lead* and *tin*. The annual output of tin in England was about 6800 tons in the sixteenth century. Towards the end of the eighteenth century the imports from India increased while domestic production declined considerably. Tin was the favorite metal for cups and dinner plates, and some quantities were used for tinning sheet iron and nails, a technique described by Agricola (1556) from older sources. The annual English production of *copper* was about 1000 tons at the beginning of the eighteenth century, 8000 tons at its end, which was about ten times the tonnage from the German mining district of Mansfeld at the corresponding periods. Fahlun, in Sweden, produced 3500 tons of copper in 1650. The production of *iron* began to develop from small hand-operated manufactories in the forests to large industrial-size plants after the close of the fifteenth century. New kinds of ovens, water power to drive the hammers and blowers, and new processes using coal and coke instead of charcoal raised production from a few thousand tons at the end of the sixteenth century to about 400,000 tons at the end of the eighteenth. At that time England made about 125,000 tons of pig iron, Russia 85,000, France nearly 70,000, and Sweden about 60,000 tons.

The conversion of iron into *steel* was known to the authors of the books ascribed to Geber in the fourteenth century. More detailed information is contained in the literature of the early sixteenth century. (4) The main chemical agent is the *oleum philosophorum* obtained by heat-decomposition of fatty oils with bricks and therefore also called "oil of bricks" (*oleum laterni*). The operation was "cementation," since a "cement" designated any kind of powder or dough capable of producing certain changes of the materials with which it is heated. Réaumur investigated mixtures of coal dust and salts for this purpose. The tempering of steel by rapid cooling was an old art.

These experiences, which showed how easily the properties of iron can be modified, were in part responsible for doubts concerning the nature of the newly discovered metals. They were based upon the old idea that there exist substances of which a very small proportion exerts a powerful influence on the material in which it is present. This idea is recognizable in the "small vital quintessence" that Boyle suspected in the air, and it is the same idea that made Torbern Bergman hesitate when he wrote, ". . . there are many and mighty reasons which induce us to think that nickel, cobalt, and manganese are perhaps to be considered in no other light than modifications of iron." However, "these metals possess distinct properties, and always preserve their own peculiar nature." (5)

The suspicion that a modified iron forms the metallic basis in *tungsten* was finally dispelled by the Spanish brothers Juan Josef and Fausto de Elhuyar, who had spent six months with Bergman in Upsala in 1782. The acid that Scheele obtained by melting tungsten with alkali and decomposing with nitric acid is the same as that from the mineral wolfram, and it is reduced under strong heat with coal to form a metal. (6)

In Pliny's time, *molybdena* was the name for dark and heavy minerals or even of lead itself. The Latin equivalent, *plumbago,* later on designated mainly one kind of molybdena which occurs in a more flaky or granular form. This material was used as black crayon. Our present word "lead pencil" preserves the old usage. Scheele found in this plumbago a very large quantity of combustible which he converted into fixed air. The other more metallic-appearing mineral, to which the name "molybdena" was now restricted, gave a white residual calx after heating with nitric acid. Solutions of this acid of molybdena turn a deep blue upon the addition of tin and iron. Heated with oil or with coal and copper, the calx yields a characteristic metal. What had formerly appeared as one group, united by outward resemblances and designated by one name, was thus separated into individual substances distinguished by chemical reactions.

Metals and their salts had a prominent place among medicines. Arnoldus Bachuone de Villanova (1235?–1312) used mercury in the form of a salve, an *unguentum hydrargyrae,* prepared by triturating mercury with saliva. Paracelsus digested mercury with oil of vitriol and distilled it with spiritus vini. To this preparation, with which he achieved great success in combating syphilis, he gave the name "turbith" because of its tradition. The physician of ancient India, and later the Arabs, called the root of the plant ipomea (turpethum) turpith, and used it to treat worms.

Antimony was highly praised by Paracelsus. Since about the twelfth century, this metal had been prepared from the mineral that the ancient Egyptians knew as *stimmi.* It is so dangerous as a medicine that the faculty of medicine of the University of Paris prohibited its use (1566). The eminent doctor, Turquet de Mayerne (1573, Mayerne, near Geneva –1655, London), wrote an *Apologia* of antimony in 1603 and was condemned for it. In Germany, however, the virtues of the metal were exalted in the *Triumphal Chariot of Antimony* of 1604. Adrian von Mynsicht (1603–1638, Mecklenburg) introduced a new form of it, tartar emetic, which Glauber somewhat later (1630) explained how to prepare more easily from vitrified antimony and tartar. It is characteristic of these times that such a violent name is given to the innocent precipitate formed by fermenting liquors. The French playwright Molière helped the cause of antimony so effectively that it was admitted for use in 1666. Forty years later, Lémery described five hundred preparations of antimony in his *Traité de l'antimoine* (1707).

A great variety of *iron salts* found particular favor when the color resembled that of gold. A solution of iron treated with marine acid and sal ammonia went under the pretentious names *sedativum Archei* or "Tincture of Mars."

Several books on mining, assaying, and refining appeared in the sixteenth century, the most successful one by Lazarus Ercker (ca. 1530–1594). It first came out in Prague, 1574; a hundred years later the Royal Society of London sponsored an English edition, and new German and English editions continued to be in demand until 1738. The title changed from "Description of the foremost mineral ores and species of mines" to "Aula Subterranea" or "Fleta Minor." Ercker freely communicated his own experiences with tools and processes for assaying gold, silver, copper, lead, bismuth, antimony, and mercury. He gives many practical details for the distillation of saltpeter with vitriol to prepare "parting acid." For the production of saltpeter by leaching of the proper "earth," evaporating the liquor, and crystallizing, Ercker recommends his own invention; it consists in reusing the raw liquor on fresh earth and then following up with weak liquor, finally with water. This manner of producing an enriched liquor before boiling it down should also be used for "all roasted ores." The main advantage was the saving in costly fuel. (7)

Metals and medicines are the two dominant topics in the technical chemistry of the sixteenth century. Later on, acids and alkalies play a growing role, and chemistry begins to influence the fields of foods, textiles, and dyeing. This historical sequence will be the order in which the most important of these developments are to be considered here.

The expanding use of *alcohol* in medicines is described by J. C. Wiegleb. "At the beginning of the fourteenth century, the foundation was laid for the prolifically growing number of essences. This was done by Lullus who, induced by the great concept of the *spiritus vini,* called it quintessence or also *mercurius vegetabilis* and used it in several of his quintessences. (See his *Liber de secretis naturae sive de Quinta Essentia.*) At the beginning of the sixteenth century, Philipp Ulsted expanded the number of these preparations still more and gave numerous prescriptions for gold tinctures (*Coelum philosophorum, sive de secretis naturae Liber, Argentorati,* 1528). Finally,

Fig. 14. Soda extraction: Leaching soda from plant ashes. The eight wooden tubs *A,* charged with the ashes, are filled with water from *B.* The solution runs through *C* into the sumps *D.* From the small tub *E* the solution flows into kettle *G* in oven *F,* which is heated by the wood *L* on grid *K.* The door in the background is also marked *L.* (From Lazarus Ercker, *Beschreibung allerfürnemsten mineralischen Ertz und bergkwercks Arten,* p. 129, Franckfurt am Main, durch Johan Feyerabendt, 1598.)

Libavius, at the end of the sixteenth century, carried this matter still further and published more detailed instructions for this kind of medicines (*Alchemia,* Vol. 2, tract 2), whereupon, at the beginning of the seventeenth century, the pharmacies were gradually drowned in the tremendous number of essences." (8)

In addition to the tinctures containing metal salts or extracts from plants, powerful remedies were obtained by distilling alcohol with mineral acids. Valerius Cordus (1515–1544, Rome) gained experience in the making of these preparations which is said to have started in Ramon Lull's work. The ether thus made from alcohol became an official part of the pharmacology. Many formulations containing ether brought fame to their authors, e.g., Hoffmann's Drops, the mixture of alcohol with ether, introduced by Friedrich Hoffmann (1660–1742) in Halle.

The pharamcists of the fifteenth century were called *aromatarii* because they made and sold *aromatic extracts* and *oils* from many herbs and kinds of wood. Every new discovery of plants or chemicals was soon employed for healing or fortifying the human body. André Thevet brought the first tobacco plants from Mexico to France in 1556 as the herb *petum*. It was later named not after this first messenger but after Jean Nicot, the man who planted it in his garden and described its medicinal effects in 1559. Further publications on extracts and distillates from tobacco soon followed. (9)

Two new kinds of *phosphorescent substances* were discovered in 1674. One was obtained by Balduin by calcining the nitric acid salt of lime, the other by the alchemist Brand, in Hamburg, by distilling concentrated urine. Johann Kunckel (1630–1702) soon discovered the secret of producing this *Phosphor Mirabilis* (1678). Urine must be left to putrefy and then mixed with sand in order to avoid the excessive foaming which otherwise makes it impossible to separate the phosphor on distillation. This miraculous substance should also be wonderful as a medicine! After its extremely high price had been somewhat reduced, its solution in alcohol or mixture with rose oil appear as pharmaceuticals in the early eighteenth century. Andreas Sigismund Marggraf (1709–1782, Berlin) tested several additions to the urine and found that they are unnecessary. The phosphor is also obtained from the seeds of plants, for example, from wheat. This demonstrates that the phosphor in the urine comes from that in food. (10)

In spite of the great number of available medicaments—Ibn Baitar (1197–1248) had already mentioned about two thousand of them—there were doctors who thought that one medicine could cure all diseases. Pierandrea Mattioli (1501–1577, Trient) derisively called such doctors *pseudomedici*. Hermann Boerhaave quotes the great van Helmont who, in a book, *De Vita Longa*, asserts that "cedarwood, reduced into an *ens* by the alcahest, is that *primum naturae*, one or two drops whereof absterges the matter of all disease . . . so that with the use hereof it were impossible for him to die. . . ." (11) On his travels to the Bermudas, George Berkeley (1685–1753) had learned that the natives used tar water in many diseases. As bishop of Cloyne, Ireland (after 1735), concerned about the epidemics following the severe winter of 1739–1740, he tried tar water successfully and explained the philosophical reasons for it in a "chain of philosophical considerations." (12)

In cases of heart failure, "an old woman in Shropshire" produced spectacular effects with her secret mixture of herbs. The physician William Withering (1741–1799, Birmingham) found that among the twenty ingredients, the leaves of the common foxglove (*Digitalis purpurea*) were most important. He himself combined the treatment by foxglove with pills made from mercury, soap, and decoctions of dandelion, followed by crystals of tartar and ginger. (13)

Increased cooperation between theoretical investigators and technical manufacturers characterized the development from the sixteenth century onward. The old methods of manufacturing soap, glass, textiles, flour, sugar, and paper were expanded and improved. Demands for a greater quantity and a better quality of the products grew. Physicians, pharmacists, and chemists found it highly interesting as well as remunerative to investigate materials and methods of manufacture. Thus they prepared the way for providing the larger supplies of raw materials and the better products that were required.

For the manufacture of glass and soap, more alkali was needed. *Soda* was obtained from natural deposits in Egypt and by burning plants that grow near the sea. Large quantities of plant ashes were produced on the Spanish coast (Alicante) as well as in France and Ireland. Bernard Palissy (1499–1589, Paris) concluded that crops generally remove salts from the soil, which will therefore lose its fertility unless salts are returned to it in the fertilizer. To throw salt on fields may be effective as punishment for heinous crimes in some countries, but in general salt is needed in the soil. In 1747 Louis Henry Duhamel du Monceau (1700–1781) found that potash replaces soda when plants rich in soda while growing on the seashore are moved farther inland. Duhamel devised a method for converting Glauber's salt (sodium sulfate) into soda by heating with coal, treating with acetic acid, and then calcining it. So great was the shortage of soda that in 1775 the French Academy promised 12,000 livres to the inventor of a commercially feasible method of producing soda from common salt.

A few years before (1770), Scheele had obtained soda from salt ($NaCl$) by heating it with litharge (PbO) in solution and then exposing it to the air. The process gave a yellow lead compound (the oxychloride) as a heavy by-product, and this was not good enough as a pigment to carry the financial burden. In other efforts described at that time, the common salt was first converted into Glauber's salt, i.e., the *sal mirabile* that Glauber had discovered (1658) in spring water near Vienna and that was later "artificially" made from salt and sulfuric acid. Shannon received British patent 1223 of 1779 for a process of heating Glauber's salt with charcoal and lime. James Keir (1735–1820) passed a solution of sodium sulfate slowly through a sludge of lime and, "by calling in the aid of a chemical agent, . . . Time" made soda. In this case, however, time meant not simply waiting, but providing a large installation; otherwise the production would be very small.

Of the many other attempts at making soda, only that initiated by Nicolas Leblanc (1742?–1806) acquired technical importance. It was an improved Shannon process. Technical, financial, and political difficulties frustrated Leblanc. His name remained linked with the process after the many contentions were resolved in his favor by Dumas in 1856. (14)

Saltpeter was imported from India. Increased domestic production from decomposed earth and animal wastes developed in the seventeenth and eighteenth centuries. When John Winthrop planned to make gunpowder in Boston (1642), he induced the General Court of Massachusetts to pass an order decreeing that "every plantation in the Colony shall erect a house in length about 20 or 30 foote, and 20 foote wide . . . to make saltpeter from urine of men, beastes, goates, hennes, hogs, and horses' dung." (15)

The soot from burning camel's dung was the source of sal ammoniac in Egypt. Duhamel showed that it could be obtained from the aqueous part of the distillate of wool rags or bones (1735).

The production of *nitric acid* remained small, although two special applications in technical manufacturing were found. English hat makers discovered that the solution of mercury in nitric acid made a good felting agent for hair. This was kept as a great secret, but it found its way to France in 1730. The other application involved the method of cochineal dyeing. The versatile Dutch inventor Cornelius Drebbel (1572–1633). (16) once prepared an extract of cochineal for the purpose of filling a thermometer. By accident, some aqua regia dropped into the solution, dissolving tin from a window frame during its fall into the solution. This changed the purple color into a bright scarlet. From this fortunate accident a method was developed which consisted in adding the solution of tin in aqua regia to the dyestuff bath. Later, Peter Joseph Macquer (1718–1784) treated silk first in the salt solution and pointed out that the metal should be dissolved by introducing it slowly into the acid without allowing the temperature to rise too high (1768).

Sulfuric acid (oil of vitriol) was needed in great quantities after its use in wool dyeing and in bleaching cotton and linen had been discovered between 1740 and 1750. The old method of distilling

Fig. 15. Preparing clay. (From Duhamel du Monceau *L'art du potier de terre,* 1773, Plate IV.)

Clay, from the pile (upper right) is washed, mixed with salt and a little lime, and then worked either by hand (upper left) or with an iron bar (upper center). A glaze or "varnish" is prepared (lower right), screened (lower center), and ground to a fluid condition (lower left).

it from vitriol was carried out in banks of small stills. A new method followed all those earlier investigations about the burning of sulfur. A mixture of saltpeter and sulfur was heated in glass jars containing water. The process was repeated with new charges until the water had absorbed a considerable quantity of the acid formed. This acid production brought the price down to about two shillings per pound, while formerly that much had been paid for an ounce. Around 1736 Esaias Ward started it in Richmond, near London, and John Roebuck (1718–1794) extended the size of plants manufacturing this "English" acid by using lead chambers (1746).

Charles Bernard Desormes (1777, Dyon –1862) and his son-in-law Clément Desormes (d. 1841, Paris) proved that nitric acid is only "a tool" for the reaction of burning sulfur with air. The "nitric gas" takes oxygen from the air, offers it in a convenient form to the sulfur dioxide, and then returns to its original state. (17) This first theory of the sulfuric acid process was published in 1806, "and it cannot be said that we have advanced beyond it in any essential points" until 1879. (18)

When Scheele in 1774 found that *marine acid* could be dephlogisticated on heating with manganese, he also observed that the new product destroyed the colors of plants. This was soon (1785) developed into a method for bleaching textiles, and Charles Tennant absorbed the gas in lime (1798, St. Rollox, near Glasgow). Jean Antoine Claude de Chaptal, professor of chemistry and a great industrialist, applied this bleach to paper. This constituted the first chemical progress of the *paper* industry. A great improvement in equipment had been made in the seventeenth century when the old method of pounding rags had been replaced by rotating mills, particularly the "hollander," developed in Holland and driven by windmills.

The production of *sugar* from cane shifted from Egypt to the new American colonies in the early sixteenth century. Refineries in Italy were partly replaced by those in France, Holland, England, and Germany. In 1788 France imported nearly 50,000 tons from Santo Domingo and re-exported a little over one third of it to Hamburg refineries. Marggraf extracted sugar from beets (1747). The method was expensive, however, and yields were low. Another domestic source of sugar was discovered by Fabrizio Bartoletti (1581–1630, Bologna). He obtained a *manna,* or *nitrum seri lactis,* by crystallization from whey (1619). In his description of this sugar from milk, Guillaume François Rouelle (1703–1770, Paris) mentions a milk-salt from Switzerland which was on sale in France.

Wheat flour can be separated into *starch* and *gluten.* The method, according to Jacopo Bartolommeo Beccari (1745), consists in kneading the flour, contained in a coarse filter cloth, with water and renewing it until it runs off free of starch. The residue is gluten, which resembles animal glue. Both give a characteristic odor, oil, and sal ammoniac on distillation. Starch has this in common with sugar that it is converted into saccharic acid by nitric acid (Scheele, Bergman). Both starch and gluten are necessary in order to obtain a good dough and to bake bread.

The search for greater food supplies caused Antoine Augustin Paramentier to investigate the uses of potatoes (1787), from which he made bread. Potatoes as a raw material for the manufacture of alcohol had been proposed by Becher in 1682 and are said to have been used in the Palatinate from 1750 on.

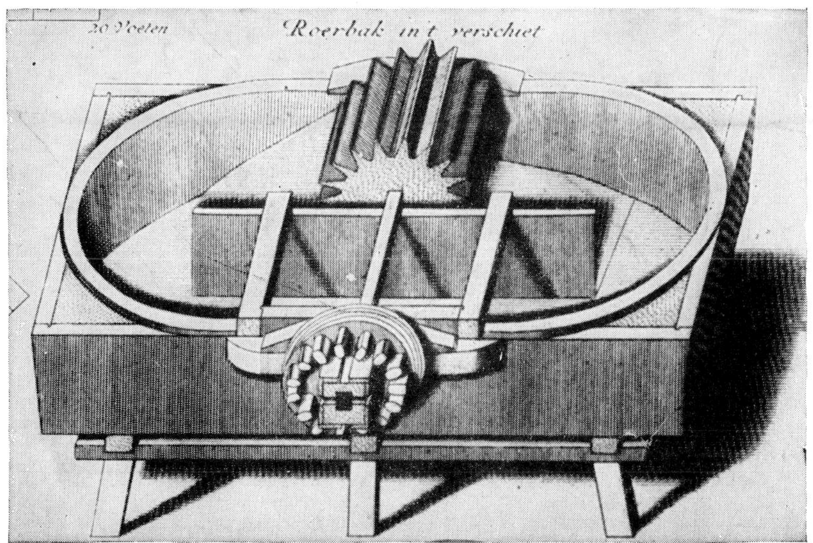

Fig. 16. Papermaker's hollander, or stirring trough, 1734. (Courtesy Hercules Powder Company, Wilmington, Del., and Mr. H. Voorn, Amsterdam, Holland.)

The cooking or coking of *coal,* in analogy to the distillation of wood, is mentioned in a British patent in 1589. Abraham Darby produced coke for blast furnaces in 1713. When, due to the war, wood tar from America was cut off in 1775, England used coal tar instead.

Terebinth was the collective name for the resinous fluids obtained by tapping certain trees. The Cyprian product came from the terebinth tree proper (*Pistacia terebinthus*), the Venetian from a larch, others from fir and pine. Dry distillation gave a cruder product than distillation in the presence of water, which separated the raw material into an ethereal spiritus and a residual balsam. The spiritus, turpentine, was used as an external and internal medicine,

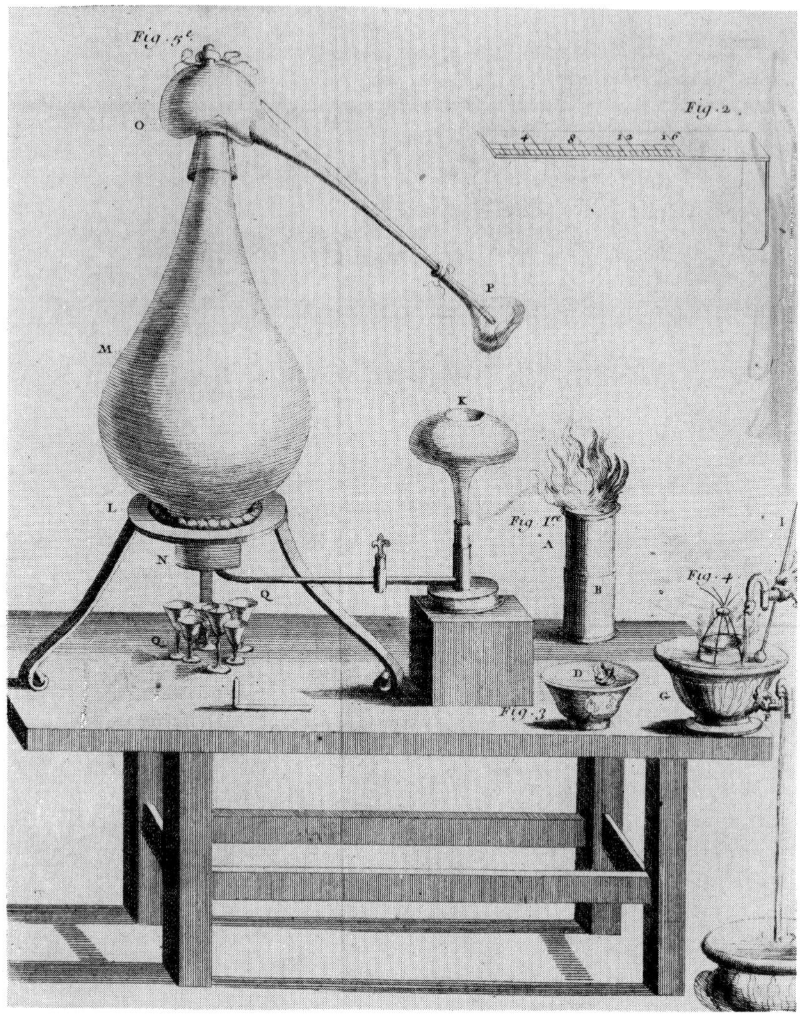

Fig. 17. Chemical analysis. Illustration attached to the article by Geoffroy le Cadet (Geoffroy, Junior): Method for knowing and precisely determining the quality of the alcoholic liquors (*liqueurs spiritueuses*) that carry the names *eau de vie* or *esprit de vie.* (In *Histoire de l'Académie Royale des Sciences,* 1718, *Mémoires de Mathématique et de Physique, Paris,* 1719, pp. 37–50.)

The five drawings are explained as follows: In *Fig. 1, A* is a cylindrical vessel in its support *B*; alcohol is burnt to test its strength. *Fig. 2* shows gauge for measuring the depth of the alcohol put into *A*. In *Fig. 3, D* is a very thin gondola, made of silver or copper, that floats as a vehicle for paint and a softener for leather. Although insoluble in water, it could be emulsified in it by the addition of egg yolk or oily fruit kernels. The balsam, called *colophony,* had many applications, in pills and plasters and as a solder in tinning sheet metal.

The soot deposited in the incomplete combustion of resins or pitch and twigs formed a low-cost black *pigment.* Old techniques for producing white pigments from lead and acetic acid, and green colors from copper kept in fermentation residues, added variety to the natural minerals used as pigments. Nothing could take the place of lead white for oil paints, although it caused a dreaded colic to its users. The blue pigment, called Prussian or Paris blue, was discovered by accident. Its basis was the phlogisticated alkali obtained by heating potash with blood, leather, or other animal waste materials. The blue pigment was precipitated from solutions of this alkali with green iron-vitriol. Alum was also added. Many investigators tried to solve the riddle of this phlogisticated alkali. Scheele distilled a volatile acid from it after adding vitriolic acid, and Bergman considered it as being a specific *acidum coeruli tingens,* a blue-producing acid.

Dissolved *dyestuffs* were made from a variety of plant materials, many of them being subjected to fermentation before extracting the dye. Importations from India, and particularly from the Americas, assumed such proportions that the domestic cultivation of dye plants was threatened. On several occasions government regulations attempted to protect the local growers. A discovery like that of scarlet dyeing with cochineal and tin salt as the mordant—instead of the usual alum—had considerable economic consequences. Indigo, which was produced in South Carolina, gradually replaced European cultures of woad. Decrees forbidding the use of the devil's dye, which destroyed fabrics because sulfuric acid was too freely used in its preparation, had no permanent effect.

Tests for the fastness of dyes by boiling sample pieces in water and with soap were developed. The precipitation of the dyestuffs

---

on fresh water to measure how much "phlegm," or moisture, is in the alcohol. *Fig. 4: I* is the thermometer that tells how the temperature of the water in *G* changes when alcohol is burnt in the inner container while outlet *F* is open and fresh water enters from *H* at the rate necessary to keep *G* full. *Fig. 5* shows the lamp *K* containing the alcohol and the support *L* for the flask *M,* which connects at the top with head *O* and receiver *P,* and which is open at the bottom. The condensate forming on the walls of *M,* when the alcohol is slowly burnt underneath, can be collected in the vases *Q.* (Compare the "Zosimos" alembic in Fig. 7 of this book.)

from solution by adding alum caused some chemists to wonder whether such precipitations would not also remove the medically useful parts of plant extracts. (19) The same substances that contain the dyeing particles also contain those substances that exert the healing actions!

Tools for testing chemicals gradually came into use. Examples are the hydrometer, described by the mysterious Frater Basilius Valentinus in 1612; the blowpipe, for which Torbern Bergman cites the year 1738 and (Anton) von Swab as a beginning; and tests by distillation. (20)

Robert P. Multhauf remarked: ". . . it can be said of the seventeenth century medical chemist, as it can of Paracelsus, that he constantly emphasized the *preparation* of drugs as the key to therapy." (21) The number of old materials now more clearly distinguished, and of new materials discovered by direct search, increased considerably during these two centuries. Unintentional discoveries were made quite frequently. Although not understood, they could be applied in new techniques because of a wider technical and scientific background. We may sometimes shudder to learn what kind of substances were used as medicines. Many of the technical developments appear to us like raw materials to be refined by deeper investigation. Expanding experience in mines, pharmacies, and manufacturing plants began to burst out of the confines of the old theories. Modification of elements, or innate qualities, became inadequate to explain the growing insight into differences of qualities and specificity of actions.

References

1. Jean Bodin, *Methodus ad facilem historiam cognitionem* (Paris: 1566). See E. Kahler, *Man the Measure* (New York: Pantheon Books, Inc., 1943), p. 468.

2. L'abbé Jean Morin, *L'Or blanc ou l'huitième Métal* (Paris: 1758). Paul Bergsoe, *The Metallurgy and Technology of Gold and Platinum Among the Pre-Columbian Indians.* Injeniorvidenskabelige Skrifter No. A 44 (Copenhagen: 1937).

3. I. G. Kaim, *De metallis dubiis* (Vienna: 1770).

4. Ernst Darmstaedter, *Berg-, Probir-, und Kunstbüchlein* (Munich: 1926). English edition by A. G. Sisco and C. S. Smith (New York: American Institute of Mining and Metallurgical Engineers, 1949).

5. Torbern Bergman, *Physical and Chemical Essays,* translated by Edmund Cullen (London: 1784, pp. 261, 264.

6. E. Moles, *El momento científico español 1775–1825* (Madrid: C. Bermejo, 1934).

7. P. R. Beierlein, *Lazarus Ercker* (Berlin: Akademie-Verlag, 1955). A. G. Sisco and C. S. Smith, *Lazarus Ercker's Treatise on Ores and Asseying,* translation from the German edition of 1580 (Chicago: University of Chicago Press, 1951).

8. In Torbern Bergman's *Geschichte der Chemie* (1792), p. 158 ff.

9. W. H. Bowen, *Isis,* **28** (1938), pp. 349–63.

10. A. S. Marggraf, *Histoire de l'Académie royale de Berlin* (1746), Tom 6, p. 84.

11. H. Boerhaave, *A New Method of Chemistry . . .* (London: 1727), p. 35.

12. George Berkeley, *Siris* (London: 1744).

13. William Withering, *An Account of the Foxglove* (Birmingham: 1785). This booklet has been published (in translation) by the firm of C. F. Boehringer und Söhne, Mannheim, 1929, with a survey of the further history of digitalis alkaloids. See also F. A. Flückiger and D. Hanbury, *Pharmacographia, a History of the Principal Drugs of Vegetable Origin Met With in Great Britain and British India* (London: Macmillan & Co., 1879). T. W. Peck and K. D. Wilkinson, *William Withering of Birmingham* (Bristol Baltimore, 1950).

14. C. C. Gillispie, "The discovery of the Leblanc process," *Isis,* **48** (1957), pp. 152–70.

15. See William Haynes, *Chemical Pioneers* (Princeton: D. Van Nostrand Co., Inc., 1939), p. 22.

16. G. Tiery, *Cornelius Drebbel* (Amsterdam: H. J. Paris, 1932), p. 76.

17. C. B. Désormes and Clément, "Théorie de la fabrication de l'acide sulfurique," *Ann. Chim.,* **59** (1806), pp. 329–39.

18. Georg Lunge, *Handbuch der Soda-Industrie* (Braunschweig: Vieweg & Sohn, 1879). Vol. 1, p. 415.

19. J. P. Macquer, *Chymisches Wörterbuch* (2d ed.; from the French 2d ed., translated and with notes and additions by D. Johann Gottfried Leonhardi [Leipzig: Weidmann, 1788]), Vol. 2, p. 420. Many French, Swiss, English, Danish, German, and Italian editions of the Dictionary are listed by Roy G. Neville, "Macquer and the first chemical dictionary, 1766, a bicentennial tribute," *J. Chem. Ed.* **43** (9) (1966), pp. 486–90.

20. The blowpipe quickly became so important that its history formed an interesting subject as early as 1790; see Chr. Weigel, "Versuch einer Geschichte des Blasrohrs und seiner Anwendungen," Crell's Beyträge **4** (1790), pp. 262, 393; **5** (1794), pp. 198 ff.

21. Robert P. Multhauf, *The Origins of Chemistry* (London: Oldbourne, 1966), p. 222.

Period II

The Development of Chemical Systems:

From the Late Eighteenth Century to the Late Nineteenth

8

Survey of Period II

A new period in the evolution of chemistry begins in the last quarter of the eighteenth century. It is characterized by the introduction of a new system, which proved stable while flexible enough for growth and modifications.

These characteristics do not fit the earlier great innovations, like those contained in the work of Paracelsus, Robert Boyle, or Joseph Black. Paracelsus, who proudly declared: "Yatrochimista sum" (I am a medical chemist), stormed against the authority of the ancients and advocated reliance on nature as a guide in our own experimenting. Boyle showed that the philosophical, universal elements are not confirmed by experiment; he proposed, instead, the combination of a still more universal concept of matter with the infinite variety of structure. Black followed Boyle in the method of carrying out cycles of chemical operations, and he solved old problems by adding quantitative measurements. Each one of these advances was important; only their new combination really initiated a new period in chemistry.

It began at a time of other great changes in politics and science. The American colonies declared their independence on July 4, 1776. The French Revolution started with Bastille Day, July 14, 1789. Did these events by accident almost coincide and have nothing at all to do with the chemical revolution? The same question, with hope for a more specific answer, can be raised with regard to attempts at constructing systems in botany and zoology. Carl Linnaeus, later named von Linné (1707–1778), published his *Systema Naturae* in 1735, and he followed it by the *Classes Plantarum* in 1738. Many others sought the basis for systems in comparative anatomy and physiology.

The search for system also found expression in the great organization of extensive encyclopedias. Denis Diderot (1713–1784) and Jean d'Alembert (1717–1783) with a large group of collaborators, published their multivolume work from 1751 to 1772, with later additions. Its subtitle was "Explanatory Dictionary of the Sciences, Arts, and Manufactures." (1) A Swiss encyclopedia in 58 volumes came out in Yverdon, 1770–1780.

All these developments were the work of strong personalities, yet they did not remain in isolation. The connections sometimes took the form of heated discussions and violent oppositions. The aim of the highly personal efforts, however, was the objective truth, and science became independent of individual scientists and their conditional opinions. Through personal efforts, objective truth is changed in time. During this period, the change extended to all the main concepts. The philosophical element and the speculative atom became chemical realities, but at the end they were quite different from what they had been at the beginning. The search for unity in a system was successful, but individual characteristics grew in importance. The role of time in chemical reactions was discovered and elaborated, (2) and this again coincided with an outstanding development in biology, the theory of evolution.

Still more generally, the period can be characterized by a change in the concept of objectivity itself. This change occurred slowly in science and became clear only after the end of this period, while in its beginning a new philosophical view of objectivity provided the basis for a revolutionary system.

Immanuel Kant (1724–1804, Königsberg) developed the thought that in metaphysics "the sure path of science has not hitherto been found" because it had been assumed "that our cognition must conform to objects." He suggested a different approach. "Let us then make the experiment whether we may not be more successful in metaphysics if we assume that objects must conform to our cognition." He compared this proposed experiment with the reversion that Copernicus performed in order to explain "celestial movements." In the same sense, Lavoisier's proposal to change the phlogiston theory into the oxygen system can be called a Copernican reversion.

With the enthusiasm of a reformer, with the intuitive confidence of having arrived at the final solution, and backed by his exposition of a new system, Kant expected that "what many centuries have failed to accomplish" might be attained "before the close of the present one"—or within less than two decades. (3) Similar confidence can be found in the chemistry of the new period and not there alone. The foundations of knowledge have been laid, the great problems of philosophy and science have been solved. It only remains to fill in the details, and this can be done by routine work. The feeling of achievement and certainty characterizes many scientific theories of the nineteenth century, perhaps reflecting the effects of greater and more regular food supplies which chemistry helped to provide.

Toward the end of this period, Ernst Mach (1838–1916) spoke of "the adaptation of our thinking to observed facts," an idea in which Kant's metaphysics was combined with Darwin's theory to obtain a new "critique of reason."

Previously, scientific theories sought their justification by conforming to the past; age gave stronger support than did experimental evidence. Now, with greater confidence in the power of reason and observation in laboratory and manufacturing plant, the creed of progress replaced reliance upon the past.

The former reliance of theories on old, established ideas had its parallel in the conviction of the unity of substances in a cosmic universe. This all-embracing unity now has to be abandoned. In its place appear the limited unities of scientific systems. On the one hand it is an analogue to the Declaration of Independence when a scientific system is constituted; on the other hand, however, it contains the admission that instead of understanding the world as a whole we can only investigate its parts. This development is accompanied by occasional protests against resignation, deploring the loss of universality and the accumulation of separate details. The loss is not complete, although the separations grow more distinct and numerous. The old unity still shines through and constructively illuminates useful analogies between separate systems. Thus the separation is clearly defined, but it is not absolute.

The change in the concept of chemical elements manifests this dual aspect. The old elements were found by pointing out qualities that different substances have in common. The purpose was to recognize primordial water and essential earths in their disguises and modifications. New elements are obtained by extending the distinctions. Direct visual inspection is enhanced by instruments; similarities in single qualities become less important than measured differences in quantities. Modifications or vacillating changes of properties find no place here unless they are explained by the presence of definite substances. The purpose of chemistry from now on is to distinguish and to separate as many elements as our finest tools are able to establish as strictly separate units. From the beginning, these efforts have been accompanied by a search for the rule by which we may combine the elements to form a unit of analogies which show the properties of the elements as a function of their place in a system relative to one another.

The old ideal was universal substance. The new ideal is chemically pure substance. This represents a product of the experimental art of separating and of the logical method of idealization. It is not a mirror image which we passively accept from nature, but the human manner of apprehending its laws. Kant's Copernican reversion in metaphysics was here again performed in special theories. The old theories had introduced idealized substances as elements. They had to be rejected, while idealization of substances and reaction paths remained valuable creative efforts, as deeply appreciated in their new forms as the older ones had been at their time. The new idealization pertains especially to the states of gas and of solution; it is present, though less recognizable, in the invention of types and models for molecular structures.

New means and methods for approaching the ideal of pure substances are developed. Chemical change is produced, arrested, prevented by creating selected conditions of temperature, pressure, electricity, and light, by excluding the influences of the natural environment of air and water. The atom theory is first used, to a considerable extent, only as a convenient means for representing the composition of multitudinous new compounds. For this purpose the theory has to be enlarged, the concept of molecule has to be added. A pictorial language in which imaginary valences hold atoms together to form those next smallest particles of matter, the molecules, is surprisingly successful in accounting for fine distinctions. The atom as a mere particle of matter has to be endowed with energy, and the spatial arrangement of atoms in the molecule adds form as a new factor. The result is the old triad of van Helmont—matter, form, and force—with a new, specific meaning.

While chemists need a more complex particle than the atom, physicists look for a subdivision of the atom into still smaller units. Heat, light, electricity and magnetism, which the chemists had claimed as elementary if weightless substances, are given separate status in a system of energies. Ancient times had been divided into periods according to the prevalence of substances—stone, bronze, copper, and iron; the new period gradually becomes the Age of Energy.

With much help from analogies to the chemistry of mineral substances, organic chemistry is building its own system and gradually finds that it does not need to rely on an unknowable force of life; after becoming the chemistry of carbon compounds, it prepares the way for a return to the chemistry of organisms.

The bonds between chemical industry and scientific chemistry increase in number and strength. The rise of a synthetic dyestuff industry brings the greatest economic advantages to the country where the scientific education of chemists is the most highly developed. Agricultural productivity gains with the spread of chemically produced plant nutrients.

More and more men devote themselves exclusively to the new science. The main occupation of chemists is no longer that of pharmacist, philosopher, or medical doctor. The personal anecdote disappears gradually from the reports about chemical work. Authors objectify their presentation to formal accounts published in one of the growing number of special scientific periodicals. The spread of communications over many places creates the need for "central" journals in which abstracts of all pertinent publications are collected. (4)

References

1. A selection of pictures from the 11 volumes of plates has been edited by C. C. Gillispie: *A Diderot pictorial Encyclopedia of Trades and Industry,* 2 vols. (New York: Dover Publications, Inc., 1959).

2. E. Farber, "Early studies concerning time in chemical reactions," *Chymia* 7 (1961), pp. 135–48.

3. Immanuel Kant, *Kritik der reinen Vernunft* (Königsberg: 1781). The citation is from the closing paragraph. From the translation by J. M. D. Meiklejohn, *Critique of Pure Reason* (London: G. Bell & Sons, Ltd., 1930), p. 517.

4. *Pharmaceutisches Central-Blatt,* founded in 1829, became *Chemisch-Pharmaceutisches Central-Blatt* in 1851 and *Chemisches Central-Blatt, Repertorium für reine, pharmaceutische, physiologische, und technische Chemie* in 1870; all were published in Leipzig: Verlag Leopold Voss.

9

Principles and Elements

After a critical survey of what was known and thought about elements, Robert Boyle had come to the conclusion that the world "as it now is" consisted not of elements but of principles. He was perhaps influenced by Descartes' philosophy when he set forth three such principles—matter, motion, and rest. And then he may have recalled the system of Aristotle, because he continued that, instead, the two principles, matter and form, might be sufficient. The attempt to replace the elements by such principles was a result of serious difficulties which could not at that time be solved in terms of elements. The proposed principles were so far removed from chemical practice that the open space invited the construction of connecting links. Such links were the particular forms that Gassendi and Lémery ascribed to their chemicals. The program was to reduce all qualities to mere mechanisms, but not even Newton could consistently adhere to a program involving the exclusion of "hidden qualities." The promise that the program contained for the future was deeply felt, but immediately satisfying ideas were needed. Form and motion were as yet too abstract to explain quality and matter. Better than open form, which could not really be demonstrated, was hidden quality, which could at least be felt and which could be supported by an analogy to the hidden soul. Paracelsus had found direct and indirect expressions for this analogy in the form of the Archeus and the essence. The power that substances exert in medical action, his primary interest, was brought into them by a nearly immaterial essence which can be compared to the slender wire that brings electricity into a large house. That this creates a new problem and that this analogy is in need of explanation later became apparent when the measurements of quantities proved possible and decisive.

M. W. Lomonosov (1711–1765), the Russian physicist and chemist whose work was rediscovered by B. N. Menschutkin in 1904, explained in his *Thoughts Concerning the Causes of Heat and Cold,* written in 1744: "We conclude . . . that it is entirely superfluous to ascribe the heat of bodies to a subtle substance especially invented for this purpose; instead, heat consists in an internal circular movement of the combined matter of the warm body." (1) He expressed his conviction that he had "abolished the heat substance." Most chemists at this time were violently opposed to such ideas.

Physicists might be satisfied with the explanation of heat as a state of motion; it did not solve the chemist's problem of qualities. Chemists were concerned with this question: What causes combustion? The first answer was, the quality of combustibility. As soon as an agent imparting combustibility was introduced, this was not the question itself in a slightly different form. This agent, phlogiston, resembled an essence characterized by the quality it imparts to the substances; the quantity was not important. It was a principle, that of combustibility, and it could be regarded as an element by those who saw elements as identical with principles.

The technique of experimenting with gases developed by Hales, Cavendish, and others led to two decisive discoveries: that air is necessary for combustion, and that the quantity of air is a limiting factor. This could not for long be explained by the limited solubility of phlogiston in air. The qualitative differentiation between fixed air, fire-air, and inflammable air, together with the quantitative relationships in combustion, led to a new interpretation of the nature of water and to a new system of elements.

Formation and Decomposition of Water

Van Helmont had demonstrated the primacy of water as an element by an experiment that only confirmed Boyle in his skepticism. Another experiment apparently showed a conversion of water into earth on heating and evaporating water. Scheele reported in 1770 that this was accompanied by an increase in weight when the quantities of water and earth were added. Somewhat later he found that the earth was qualitatively similar to the glass of the vessel in which the heating occurred. Lavoisier weighed the glass vessel before and after heating water in it for 101 days. The vessel lost 17.4 grains, the deposited earth weighed only 4.9 grains, the water, however, contained dissolved materials. Its evaporation left a residue of 15.5 grains. This, added to the weight of the deposited earth, was too much for an exact balance. In spite of the difference between the 20.4 grains of earth found in the glass and the 17.4 grains lost from it, the problem appeared to be solved. Qualitative and quantitative methods demonstrated that water is not transmuted into another element–earth. The direct observation had been misleading as long as it had been focused on only one of the objects involved in the experiment; the influence of the container had been unduly neglected.

In 1778 Macquer described water as an unalterable and indestructible substance. "Efforts of the art" are unable to decompose water; therefore it is an element. At that time the appearance of water after detonating a mixture of common air and inflammable air had occasionally been observed, but it had not been considered very important. In April 1781, Priestley and Warltire assumed that this water only represented the moisture that the gases originally contained. James Watt mentioned "the idea of water consisting of pure air and phlogiston" in a letter to Priestley of December 14, 1783. (2) This "idea" was not considered by Cavendish to contain the facts of the decisive answer to the water problem.

> As Mr. Watt, in a paper lately read before this Society supposes water to consist of dephlogisticated air and phlogiston deprived of part of their latent heat, whereas I take no notice of this latter circumstance, it may be proper to mention in a few words the reason of the apparent difference between us. If there be any such thing as elementary heat, it must be allowed that what Mr. Watt says is true; but by the same rule we ought to say that the diluted mineral acids consist of the concentrated acids united to water, and deprived of their latent heats. . . . (3)

Inflammable air had meant phlogiston to Cavendish since 1766; now he thought this air to be a compound with water. The reason was that it takes red heat to unite common air with inflammable air, whereas common air absorbs "the phlogiston of nitrous air, liver of sulfur, and many other substances, without that assistance."

The name "inflammable air" was applied to the gas obtained on heating coal as well as to the gas developed in the reaction between acids and metals. Lavoisier had been led into considerable difficulty by the different reactions of inflammable air obtained from these two sources. Carbonic acid was produced in the combustion of the gas from coal and was therefore also expected to be formed when inflammable air was burnt. Analysis disproved this expectation and showed that the same name had erroneously been given to two different kinds of gas. On June 24, 1783, Lavoisier and Laplace demonstrated before a group of distinguished scientists that the inflammable air from zinc and sulfuric acid, burning in oxygen, gives only pure water. At about the same time, and independently, Gaspard Monge stated the same result and added figures for the quantities of the gases consumed in forming water. After later corrections, these figures were that 15 grains of the inflammable air combine with 85 grains of oxygen and yield 100 grains of water. This quantity of water must have been newly formed; it could not have been contained in the 100 grains of the two gases, otherwise these gases would have had to be nothing but water! This conclusion was drawn by Lavoisier, but it was not shared by Monge, the originator of such measurements. Monge believed that other distinguishing components were present in the gases, and that their escape in the form of heat and light left the water behind. (4) Cavendish was greatly concerned with his observation that a small amount of nitric acid is produced in the water from this combustion, and therefore he could not agree with Lavoisier's interpretation.

This interpretation was sensible only within a supporting system that made it possible to assign the right place to the details of experimental results. The proportions of the gases were not at all found to be the same in various experiments. Lavoisier's figures changed considerably as he continued his measurements. They had the merit of indicating the need for greater accuracy, but construction of the system did not have to wait until ultimate accuracy was attained. This construction theoretically completed existing results and in doing so brought out their practical imperfection. To unite past experience and to invite its perfection is the double function of a system.

If it were true that inflammable air and oxygen unite to form water, the reverse should also be true; water should form those two gases upon decomposition. The test of this prediction had not only theoretical importance. In 1782 the brothers Montgolfier had to use the old method of lightening the air in the balloon by heating it with an open fire just as B. L. de Gusmão in Lisbon did in 1709. Could a convenient method be found for producing enough of the very light inflammable air to fill the balloon? Lavoisier and Meusnier constructed an apparatus for decomposing water in a hot iron tube. The oxygen combined with the iron to form the solid iron oxide and the other component of water could be collected as a gas. By replacing the iron by a copper tube, no decomposition occurred, and this disproved Priestley's contention that he could transform water into air through heat alone (1783–1784).

The Basic Chemistry of Organisms

The expression "flame of life" is as old as poetic imagery; it acquired a more specific meaning in the seventeenth century. When

Descartes wrote of "fire that burns constantly in the heart," he did not intend it as a poetic figure of speech; he added expressly that this was the same fire as we know it from inanimate things. Thomas Willis (1621–1675, London) explained the heat of the blood as a combustion through particles occurring in the air. John Mayow observed that when a flame and a small animal are confined together under a bell jar, "the animal does not long survive the funereal torch." The extinction of flame and life occurs through the exhaustion of the aerial nitre, not because of fumes given off by the flame. Joseph Priestley, however, was convinced "that the fitness of air for respiration depends upon its capacity to receive the *phlogiston* exhaled from the lungs." From calcined mercury or the red precipitate of mercury, the first prepared by dry heating, the other by precipitation from solution and also from red lead, he produced a new kind of air "that is five or six times better than common air for the purpose of respiration, inflammation, and, I believe, other uses of common atmospherical air," and he therefore called it *dephlogisticated* air. (5)

That was published in 1775. Two years later, Lavoisier extended these thoughts and added his new interpretation:

> . . . to put it into a simple form that everyone can easily grasp, we can say first, in general, that respiration is nothing but a slow combustion of carbon and hydrogen which, in sum, is similar to the combustion in a lamp or a burning candle, and further, that under this aspect breathing animals are really combustible bodies that burn and are consumed. (6)

Lavoisier said quite clearly that this statement was a highly simplified "sum" of what really happened. Our "common" air becomes "unfit" for flame or life when this air is depleted of its oxygen, not through its saturation with phlogiston.

The red color of arterial blood is due to the absorption of oxygen in analogy to the color produced when mercury or lead absorbs oxygen. Respiration is the source of animal heat, a consequence of internal combustion to which air furnishes the oxygen and blood furnishes the combustible substances. These results were communicated to the Académie on June 18, 1783, by Lavoisier and Pierre Simon de Laplace (1747–1827) who collaborated for many years in calorimetric measurements and theories.

According to Priestley, green plants remove phlogiston from air and thus make it pure. For a green "matter" growing in a stagnant water, he observed that dephlogisticated air was given off. Jan Ingen Housz, a Dutch physician (1730–1799), was greatly interested in this new source of "pure air." The gas was found to develop in sunlight, mostly from the underside of leaves. Jean Senebier (1742–1809) showed in 1782 that saturating water with carbonic acid increases the development of oxygen. Nicolas Théodore de Saussure (1767–1845) concluded that at least part of the carbon dioxide remains in the plant to be assimilated, while oxygen is "exhaled." From these and his own experiments, Lavoisier arrived at the general concept of a great process in all nature. Its basis is a decomposition of water into oxygen, which is given off, and an inflammable constituent, which combines to form the combustible part of all plants. In the green plant, carbon dioxide is also split, and the light required for the process combines with the oxygen to form the free gas. Lavoisier's thought can be presented by the formulation (which is not meant to indicate quantitative relationships!):

$$\underset{\text{(fixed air)}}{(\mathrm{C, O})} + \underset{\text{(water)}}{(\mathrm{H, O})} + \text{light} \xrightarrow{\text{green plant}} \underset{\text{(plant body)}}{(\mathrm{C, H, O})} + \underset{\text{(oxygen gas)}}{[(\mathrm{O}) + \text{light}]}$$

Lavoisier studied a special example in the fermentation of sugar by yeast, in which alcohol and carbonic acid are formed. The combustion of 16 parts of alcohol yielded 18 parts of water, and carbonic acid. Therefore the water could not have been present, as such, in the alcohol. In the process of fermentation, sugar undergoes a redistribution of its elements, the inflammable part being concentrated in the alcohol, the oxygen in the carbonic acid.

The experimental basis for the theory was the quantitative analysis of organic substances by combustion. It was a difficult method. Lavoisier worked on it for many years. The results varied so considerably that they alone could not have led to a generalization. The experimental variations were only temporarily imperfect indications of the general system, and its main support was the universal law of the conservation of matter. The intuition that led to this general law was more trustworthy than the known imperfection of the apparatus.

Light, Heat, and Oxygen

In Lavoisier's system, oxygen is a principle; it never occurs in a free state. As a gas it is combined with light or *caloric*, the heat element. When the gas is decomposed, as by reaction with iron, the metal combines with the oxygen principle, and heat is liberated. The combination with this principle produces acidity in the product.

Lavoisier therefore divided the systematic exposition of his views (8) into two main parts, the decomposition of oxygen gas and the combination of acids with bases under the formation of neutral salts. The third part describes instruments and operations.

He begins Chapter 1 of his *Traité Élémentaire de Chimie* (1789) with a reference to "the English philosophers, who have given us the first precise ideas upon this subject, the capacity of bodies for containing the matter of heat." A gas, he wrote, consists of the matter of heat combined with a basis. Almost any basis can combine with heat and thereby become a gas. If the earth were suddenly transported to a hotter place in the solar system, water and other vaporizable substances would become gases. Conversely, in a colder place, the present gases would be transformed into new hitherto unknown liquids. (9)

Thus oxygen is not a component of heat, as Scheele had speculated, but heat is a component of the gas oxygen, and just this reversion shows the manner in which the new theory depended on the thoughts prevailing at the time of its origin.

The Chemical Language

In 1782, when Guyton de Morveau (1737–1816) undertook to write a dictionary of chemistry, he found that many of the existing chemical expressions had become meaningless and that new words should be created to conform with the progress of the study. Morveau was a lawyer in Dijon. He brought to the new task his experience in carrying out a systematic and orderly reform in law, (10) but he needed the help of chemists. He combined forces with Lavoisier, Fourcroy, and Berthollet.

Antoine François de Fourcroy (1755–1809, Paris) was the author of a very successful textbook of natural science and chemistry (1781). Claude-Louis Berthollet (1748–1822, Paris) had started his career as a physician. He introduced chlorine, Scheele's dephlogisticated marine acid, as a bleaching agent for textiles and found that the reaction of chlorine with ammonia liberated mephitic air.

These four men published their report about the new nomenclature in 1786. (11) Conferences with many other scientists had preceded. The philosophy of Abbé de Condillac and Marquis de Condorcet (1743–1794, Paris) had provided guiding principles.

The name of elements was reserved to a first group of simple substances, consisting of light, heat, and the three gases—oxygen, the producer of acids; hydrogen, the producer of water; and azote, that part of common air, formerly called "mephitic air," in which life cannot exist. Of the other names proposed for this latter substance, only nitrogen survived.

Other simple substances were characterized by the fact that up to this time it had not been possible to decompose them. This was expected to be only a temporary stage. The second group of simple bodies, comprising those which are nonmetallic, oxidizable, and acid-forming, thus listed sulfur, phosphorus, and carbon, and besides, as "unknown," the bases of muriatic acid, fluoric acid, and boric acid.

The seventeen known metals were combined into a third group. The decision to recognize all these metals as simple was a characteristic of the new system as was the creation of the first group. After oxygen and hydrogen had been established as elements, this question still remained open: In the reaction of metals with acids, from which of the reagents did hydrogen originate? The problem was similar to that involved in the oxidation of metals, and the uncertain identification of phlogiston with hydrogen was still at the core of the problem. A few years before, Scheele had been convinced that flammable air was part of the substance of the metals. It cannot be true that this air is contributed by components of the acids because the two alkalies also produce flammable air in reaction with the metals! (12) What Scheele considered to be a decomposition of metals was now explained as a decomposition of water.

The fourth group of simple substances contained the earths—lime, magnesia, baryta, alumina, and silica. The fifth group was considered to be preliminary. All the alkalies were thought to be similar to ammonia, for which Berthollet had just at that time confirmed that it contains azote (nitrogen).

The principles for naming compounds were, first, the division of all chemicals into "combustible" or oxidizable substances and oxygen, and second, the division of all salts into two components, base and acid. Lavoisier explained:

> In short, we have advanced so far that from the name alone may be instantly found (1) what the combustible substance is which enters into any combination; (2) whether that combustible substance be combined with the acidifying principle, and in what proportion; (3) what is the state (of oxidation) of the acid; (4) with what basis is it united; (5) whether the saturation be exact, or whether the acid or the basis be in excess.
>
> It may readily be supposed that it was not possible to attain all these different objects without departing in some instances from established custom, and adopting terms which at first sight may

> appear uncouth and barbarous. But we considered that the ear is soon habituated to new words, especially when they are connected with a general and rational system. The names, besides, which were formerly employed, such as powder of algaroth, salt of alembroth, pompholix, phogadenic water, turbith mineral, colcothar, and many others, were neither less barbarous nor less uncommon. . . . The names of oil of tartar per deliquium, oil of vitriol, butter of arsenic and of antimony, flowers of zinc, etc. were still more improper because they suggested false ideas. . . . (13)

Principle and System

In his successful textbook Fourcroy (14) refers to the view previously held, that there exists a principle of oiliness. This principle was assumed to be combined with different substances that modified it and thus formed the several kinds of oil obtainable from plants. The qualities ascribed to the principle were the idealized qualities of oil, very fluid and volatile, odorless, and insoluble in water. This principle was not an element but a composition of water with acid to which phlogiston had associated itself. Repeated distillation of actual oils yielded the true and philosophical oil, the oil principle.

Such a principle is a real substance, to which the distinctive feature is added that it has the dual function of being productive and representative. A principle produces its special quality in every substance of which it becomes a part. When this part becomes very small, the principle acts like a ferment and is thus conceptually related to the philosophers' stone with its power over a vastly greater quantity of matter. The principle also represents quality, the one designated by its name. Thus, the "primitive" salt stands for all salts, it is the type of everything that can be called salt. As ferment and as type, a principle is unique and universal. In the new chemistry, the word principle remained while its meaning changed.

The chemistry of organic acids offers an example of the transition from principle through phlogiston to the new theory. Acetic acid had been the prototype of all organic acids. S. F. Hermbstädt (1760–1833, Berlin) declared in 1782 that Scheele's tartaric acid was not greatly different from acetic acid. Gradual oxidation by means of nitric acid showed transitions between the organic acids which caused F. A. Carl Gren (1760–1798, Halle) to explain the difference between the acids as one of phlogiston content. (15) Lavoisier was not surprised that vegetable acids can be converted, the one into the other; it is only a matter of changing the proportions of carbon and hydrogen or of oxygen. (16)

Fourcroy continued in the passage cited above that the search for principles is now abandoned by the chemist. "He discovers the intimate nature of substances by submitting them to analysis. He determines the order of their simplicity or composition; he causes sudden variations of the properties which formed their sensible or apparent characters. He studies the attractions which the constituent parts of the substances obey; and, while occupied with molecules so fine and so disconnected that they cease to be visible, he withdraws completely from the naturalist who only observes the regular or organic aggregations of bodies, with their form and structure." Chemistry is no longer an accessory to natural history but it is about to become its compass. (17)

Affinity and Quantity

The new system of elements was founded upon measurement of the volume and weight of substances which undergo chemical change. Solution of the water problem became a model for the importance of quantitative relations. When water was found in experiments, there were two possibilities: it could be either an accidental impurity or it could be the result of chemical change. In the second case, the finding was decisive for the interpretation of the experiments. A little water could come from anywhere; accidental moisture could be expected in all gases and vessels. However, when a quantity of water appeared that was equal to the combined quantities of hydrogen and oxygen consumed in the reaction, it had to be interpreted as newly formed by a complete combination of these gases. The first element in the New System, heat, involved a problem. It is exceptional among the elements because it has no weight. Its degrees can be determined, its quantity can be defined by thermometers and calorimeters, but not by scales. Chemical reactions may absorb or develop heat. The phlogiston theory explained heat phenomena but it conflicted with the measurement of the quantities of the substances involved. The New System coordinated the quantities satisfactorily but it needed amplification to coordinate heat and chemical change.

The attempt was made to accomplish this by considering the heat capacities before and after a reaction. This attempt was based on the assumption that the reagents contained heat as one of their constituent parts. When the reaction product had a lower heat capacity, some of the initially present heat had to be discarded; in the opposite case, it had to be gained from an outside source. Lavoisier proved by calorimetric measurement of the specific heats that this assumption was wrong.

Another approach to the problem started from the old concept of affinity and did not return to the problem of heat in chemical reactions before about 1840. On the way, two new pillars of the chemical system were erected—the law of mass action and the connection between chemistry and electricity.

Affinity is "perhaps a property which is as essential in matter as extension and impenetrability, and about which nothing more can be said than that it belongs to it essentially." (18) This statement by Macquer is not to be taken literally so far as the last part is concerned. Chemists tried to say a good deal about affinity. It is an attraction of the kind for which Newton had developed the general mechanical laws, a kind of gravitation, but it is modified by the form of the primitive particle. In this basic concept, the German chemist of Leipzig, Carl Friedrich Wenzel (1740–1793), (19) and a French count, G. L. Leclerc de Buffon (1707–1788), at almost the same time (around 1775) meant to express chemical specificity. Both apparently felt that the correlation of geometrical form with chemical specificity was sufficiently familiar to require no proof. Buffon visualized as a program for future work the discovery of special forms and thus the fulfillment of the promise contained in the hypothesis. Wenzel sought a measure of affinity in the velocities with which different substances are dissolved by the same solvent. He measured the rates at which metals were dissolved by mineral acids. Even in this limited field too many exceptions upset the rule that affinity should be in inverse proportion to the time required for dissolution.

Heat modifies, sometimes reverses, the result of chemical attraction. At low temperatures ammonia decomposes salts, displaces their bases, and combines with acids; upon heating, however, these bases easily separate the ammonia from the acids and thus reverse the decomposition. Antoine Baumé (1728–1804), who won lasting fame through the construction of the hydrometer (1768), proposed that a distinction be made between affinities in solutions at atmospheric temperature and affinities in reactions carried out under the influence of heat. Torbern Bergman found this distinction very helpful although not exhaustive enough to include the thousands of possible combinations that he tried to bring into systematic order.

If affinity could not be understood, at least it could be described in its several forms. Macquer compiled a list of such forms in which the following six were the most outstanding:

1. Affinity of aggregation, which holds particles of equal nature together and which could also be called the force of cohesion.
2. Affinity of composition, Bergman's *attractio solutionis* and *fusionis,* which acts, for example, in combining iron with sulfuric acid into vitriol. Macquer here points to the change of properties, vitriol being neither iron nor sulfuric acid but composed of them.
3. Complicated affinity, in which three substances are involved.
4. Affinity of intermedium, exemplified by a solution of sodium sulfide in water where the alkali acts as an intermedium to bring sulfur into the water, whereas by itself sulfur is not soluble in water.
5. Reciprocal affinity, also called disposed affinity, by which a substance is brought into disposition to react, as when silver is first dissolved in nitric acid to prepare it for reaction with muriatic acid.
6. Double affinity, which causes two substances together to react with a compound when neither of the two substances could do it alone. A special example for this case is offered by Prussian or Berlin blue (page 103). Its coloring substance can be extracted by caustic soda which is thus saturated with this still mysterious substance. The new compound formed is not decomposed by acid alone. When acid is first combined with iron and the solution of the iron salt then mixed with the compound, its alkali combines with the acid of the iron salt and the coloring substance precipitates with the iron.

The experiments which this classification attempted to summarize were first of all reactions between acids and bases which neutralize each other and form salts. The method for determining the end point of neutralization was the old one, described by Boyle, of observing the color change of extracts of litmus or violet petals. The next in importance were reactions between salts, again easily observed when they resulted in precipitation and crystallization. It seemed ridiculous to Buffon (1775) to divide the great concept of affinity into a number of "little affinities" which introduced descriptive words, without meaning for theory, without support in a general system.

Geoffroy's table of "rapports" or relationships (p. 75) stimulated many chemists to improve and amplify lists of acids and bases arranged in the order of the supposed magnitudes of affinity. Torbern Bergman, and similarly Richard Kirwan (1735–1812, Dublin), sought the measure of affinity in the relative quantities of solvent and dissolved material. It was supposed that the greater the affinity of one base—lime or magnesia or alumina—to different acids, the more of these acids it took to saturate or neutralize the base.

Guyton de Morveau (1786) ascribed numbers to the bases and acids in such a table, hoping to find that reactions occur whenever a compound of higher number could be formed. The variety of known reactions was greater than any of these predictions could describe.

Lavoisier's objection to such tabulations was that they at best represented results at a certain degree of heat; new tables would be required for each temperature. Besides, these investigators neglected the influence of the attraction of water. Together with Laplace, he defined the problem as one of equilibrium between heat and affinity. Heat tends to remove the molecules from one another; reciprocal affinity has the opposite tendency, to unite them. The affinities between an acid and water, for example, can be measured by the ultimate temperatures at which a concentrated acid dissolves ice or at which a dilute acid loses water which separates from the solution as ice.

One of the fundamental six rules that Morveau formulated states: "Affinity takes place only between the smallest integrating particles of the substances." This, like the other rules, was pronounced as an a priori conviction, and insofar as it is, it is a continuation of the old ways of the "philosophers by fire." New, however, was the modifying and moderating emphasis that the proposed theory is only preliminary, the self-criticism that known facts are insufficient to support it, the reliance upon future experiments from which proof of the theory may be expected. Dogmatic assertions were turned into questions addressed to nature with confidence in an affirmative reply.

When two neutral salts react and decompose each other, the products are again neutral. This "common experience" led Jeremias Benjamin Richter in 1792 to "the immediate conclusion which could be none other than that there must be definite proportions of quantities between the components of the neutral salts." Richter (1762–1807), who had started out as an engineer, had shown his mathematical inclination in a doctoral thesis on the use of mathematics in chemistry (1789, Königsberg). The idea that urged him to pursue chemical work was that the method of engineering and geodetic measurements should be applied to chemistry. "Since the mathematical part of chemistry mostly has to do with indestructible materials or elements, and teaches us how to determine the proportions of magnitudes between them, I have not been able to find a shorter or more appropriate name for this scientific discipline than the word stoichiometry, from the Greek στοιχεῖον, which means something which cannot be further separated, and μετρεῖν, which means finding proportions of magnitude." (20) Acetate of lime and tartrate of potash (potassium oxide in later language) are neutral salts. When they are brought together in solution, tartrate of lime precipitates, potassium acetate is formed, and the neutrality is maintained. This means, concluded Richter, that the components in these compounds stand in a definite relation of quantities. In the above example, the quantity of tartaric acid that neutralizes potassium oxide must be in a definite relation to the quantity of acetic acid that neutralizes lime, and the same is simultaneously true for the exchanged bases, lime and potash. When the proportionate quantities of the elements in the starting material are known, they are thereby also known for the newly formed products. A table Richter published in 1793 lists the quantities of bases that are neutralized by one thousand parts of the three principal mineral acids. This table conceals rather than states the law which was so difficult to formulate. At least, Richter's complicated language could not make it clear to many of his contemporaries.

RICHTER'S NEUTRALIZATION TABLE (1793)

	Neutralize Parts of		
1000 Parts of	Sulfuric Acid	Muriatic Acid	Nitric Acid
Potash	1606	2239	1143
Soda	1218	1699	867
Volatile alkali	638	889	435
Baryta	2224	3099	1581
Lime	796	1107	565
Magnesia	616	858	438
Alumina	526	734	374

The figures in each of these columns seemed to Richter to follow algebraic rules. So interested was he in the relationshps between these figures that he occasionally changed his experimental results so as to fit them into the speculative rules. The fundamental discovery was hidden in the mystery of numbers in which he imbedded it.

By eliminating speculation about the numbers, E. G. Fischer found that Richter's results could be concentrated into one table which he first published with a German translation of Berthollet's study of affinity.

One year later, Richter enlarged the table of equivalent weights to include thirty bases and eighteen acids, some of them only recently

FISCHER'S TABLE OF EQUIVALENT WEIGHTS (1802)

Bases				Acids			
Alumina	525	Soda	859	Fluoric	422	Formic	988
Magnesia	615	Strontian	1329	Carbonic	577	Sulphuric	1000
Ammonia	672	Potash	1605	Fatty	706	Succinic	1209
Lime	793	Baryta	2222	Muriatic	712	Nitric	1405
				Oxalic	755	Acetic	1480
				Phosphoric	979	Citric	1583
						Tartaric	1694

discovered compounds of new elements. (21) Each of these bases, in the quantity given by the figures at the right, combines with the quantity of the acids given in the same table. Nothing of theories and speculations survived, yet nobody can say, against the historical reality, that the practical result could have been obtained without them. Richter felt that the mystery of chemical relationship could be penetrated by mathematics. Like Cavendish, Richter had the conviction that nature's secrets are revealed in measure, number, and weight. Therefore the arithmetic and geometric progressions were more important, in his opinion, than the equivalent weights by themselves. Cavendish had occasionally mentioned the equivalent weights of alkalies and acids in neutralization, (22) another proof of a basic similarity in the concepts of these two men who were otherwise far apart in their philosophical attitudes.

Continuity and Discontinuity

Berthollet started out from a different but equally preconceived idea. Affinities are physical forces; therefore, other physical forces can compete with affinities and modify their result. Mass, cohesion, and elasticity are decisive for chemical action. Quantity can replace whatever affinity lacks in "inner force."

Claude-Louis Berthollet developed this thesis after more than twenty years of chemical investigation. After acquiring the degree of medical doctor in Turin at the age of twenty-two, he came to Paris. Boerhaave's pupil, Tronchin, recommended him to the Duke of Orleans, who enabled Berthollet to set up a chemical laboratory. He was one of the first to recognize and adopt Lavoisier's oxygen system. As successor of Macquer (d. 1784) in the governmental position of delegate for the directory of the dyeing industry, he introduced bleaching by chlorine. From the reactions of chlorine with ammonia and with prussic acid (obtained by Scheele from coal, potash, and sal ammoniac), he concluded that ammonia is a compound of nitrogen and hydrogen and that prussic acid contains carbon in addition to nitrogen and hydrogen. Technical and scientific investigations were equally interesting to him.

A particularly stimulating event in his life was his participation in the Egyptian campaign (1798). Like Alexander the Great (356 B.C.–332 B.C.) on his Asian campaign, Napoleon took a group of scientists with him. These scientists formed an Egyptian Institute, and it was before this group that Berthollet first presented his ideas about affinity (1799). (23) A few years later he published them in a more extended form as *Essai de Statique Chimique* (1803). Here he included the improved presentation of Richter's neutralization equivalents which E. G. Fischer had attached to his translation of Berthollet's earlier work. A third part of Berthollet's studies on the laws of affinity appeared in 1806.

The phenomenon of neutralization shows a capacity of acid and alkali to saturate each other. Capacities of saturation are also observed in the relationship of water to a soluble salt. Berthollet considered both kinds of phenomena together, since with the concept of affinity as a physical force, neutralization is not fundamentally different from any other kind of saturation. Affinity is not a qualitatively elective force; it is variable and it depends upon acting masses and circumstances. This leads to the conclusion that chemical combination progresses continuously unless other forces interfere.

> When an obstacle prevents the continuous progression of the combination and requires an accumulation of force, then the compound suddenly, at the instant when the accumulated force is overcome, adopts the whole quantity and all the qualities which it would have acquired had the progression been continuous, comparable to water's taking up all the heat on boiling, which corresponds to the vapor state. In compounds which precipitate because they are insoluble, this obstacle consists in the force of cohesion, but they do not always assume the proportions which would have the greatest insolubility. They can have an excess of one or the other element, in conformity with the quantities which can exert this influence, so that only a small number of insoluble compounds exist in which the proportions could be constant. (24)

Similarly, the force of elasticity counteracts affinity in liquid substances when one of the products assumes the gaseous state. Heat changes the effect of affinities, because it influences cohesion and elasticity. When potassium chloride and sodium nitrate are brought together in solution, potassium nitrate crystallizes out in the cold, sodium chloride under the influence of heat. An exchange of the components of these salts thus takes place because of the change in solubilities with temperature.

Current methods of measuring affinities are criticized by Berthollet. Whenever these methods cause the separation of one of the participants in a reaction, they change the proportions of the remaining substances. The new equilibrium is no longer the same as that which was to be investigated.

In the same year in which Berthollet in Paris announced his theory of the continuously sliding scale of proportions in chemical compounds, Proust in Madrid published observations to prove that the quantities of components in chemical substances are always constant in their proportions.

Joseph Louis Proust (1754–1826, Angers, France) followed his father's profession of apothecary and lectured in Paris at the Musée (later the Lycée) du Palais Royal. Upon invitation by the king of Spain, he built a magnificent laboratory in Madrid. Observations of the commercial process for distilling mercury from cinnabar, and particularly the comparison of natural with synthetic copper carbonate, inspired this generalization: "Copper carbonate made by nature has the same properties and the same proportions between metal and carbonic acid as that produced in the laboratory. This must, therefore, always be so and not only for this compound but for all substances. These always invariable proportions, these constant properties which characterize the combinations of art or those of nature, in one word, this *pondus naturae* which Stahl has so clearly seen, all this, I say, is no more subject to the will of the chemist than the elective law which governs all combinations." (25)

In addition to Stahl, Proust could have quoted Stephen Hales who, in the introduction to his *Vegetable Staticks* of 1727, referred to the authority of Scripture, Wisdom of Solomon 11:20, which reads: "Thou hast ordained all things by measure and number and weight."

Where Berthollet claimed continuity of change, Proust felt that the combining weights stop at definite and discontinuously different levels. The relative quantities in a solution may vary continuously, but chemical combination is fundamentally different. "The solution of ammonia in water can, as I see it, not be the same thing as that of hydrogen in nitrogen, which gives ammonia." (26) On the calcination of lead, the quantities of oxygen absorbed only seem to progress continuously. Chemical analysis, treatment with nitric acid, separates the product into two oxides, each of which always has the same proportions of metal to oxygen. There is a gap between these proportions in the lower oxide and those of the higher oxide. The relative quantity of oxygen in the latter is a simple multiple of that in the lower oxide. Berthollet objected that the method of separation changed the original product so that Proust, not nature, produced constant proportions. Proust answered that since the original product responded to the method of separation, the products of separation must have been present before as a mixture and not as one chemical substance.

"Chemists have frequently considered it a general property of compounds that they form in constant proportions. This is a hypothesis which has no other foundation than the distinction between [chemical] combination and dissolution." In these words Berthollet characterized the basic difference between himself and Proust. To distinguish chemical combination from physical mixture in solution did not justify the "hypothesis" for Berthollet because he started from the premise that chemical forces are not different from physical forces. For Proust this premise was an unjustified hypothesis because he felt the discontinuity distinctly taking effect in chemical combination. The actual figures that he found for the proportional weights of components often showed variations. The underlying law was, however, clearly indicated.

The discussion between Berthollet and Proust continued for about eight years. Its results were (1) a clearer definition of chemical combination; (2) the establishment of a law of constant and multiple proportions; and (3) the recognition of a law of mass action. The first two are the culmination of Proust's arguments and experiments, the third was Berthollet's contribution.

Proust's argument for a discontinuity in chemical combination was greatly strengthened by Dalton's development of the atomic theory. Berthollet's conception of continuity and his explanation of chemical change by physical "forces" led to new theories at various times during the nineteenth century. They were not limited to chemistry. For example, Matthias Jacob Schleiden (1804–1881) intended to make botany a part of "biophysics" and to relate "all physical theories to purely mathematical grounds of explanation." (27) The opposite general laws explicated by Proust and Berthollet thus can be seen as evolutions from the thoughts of Democritus and Pythagoras.

REFERENCES

1. Excerpts from Lomonosov's work have been published by B. N. Menschutkin and M. Speter in Ostwald's *Klassiker der Naturwissenschaften,* No. 178 (Leipzig: 1910).

2. S. Edelstein, in *Chymia* (Philadelphia: University of Pennsylvania Press, 1948), Vol. 1, p. 123.

3. H. Cavendish, *Phil. Trans.* for 1784, p. 140. See also, George Wilson, *The Life of the Honorable Henry Cavendish* (London: 1851).

4. G. Monge, "Sur le résultat de l'inflammation du gas inflammable et de l'air déphlogistiqué dans des vaisseaux clos" (On the result of exploding inflammable air with dephlogisticated air in closed vessels), *Mém. Ac. Paris,* 1783, pp. 78–88.

5. Joseph Priestley, "An account of further discoveries in air," *Phil. Trans.,* **65** (1775), pp. 384–94, esp. 387, 389; three letters dated March 15, April 1, and May 25, 1775.

6. A. Lavoisier, "Expériences sur la respiration des animaux," *Mém. Ac. Paris,* 1777, pp. 185–94.

7. A. Lavoisier, "Réflexions sur la décomposition de l'eau par les substances végétales et animales," *Mém. Ac. Paris,* 1786 (1788), pp. 590–605.

8. A. Lavoisier: *Traité Élémentaire de Chimie* (Paris: 1789). An English edition prepared by Robert Kerr was published in Edinburgh.

9. A. Lavoisier, *Mém. Ac. Paris* for 1780, printed in 1784. *See Œuvres de Lavoisier* (Paris: 1862), Vol. 2, p. 261.

10. George Bouchard, *Guyton-Morveau, chimiste et conventionnel* (Paris: 1938).

11. *Méthode de Nomenclature Chimique de Morveau, Lavoisier,* etc. (Paris: 1787); *Dictionnaire de Chimie* in *Encyclopédie Méthodique* (Paris: 1786).

12. C. W. Scheele, in a letter to T. Bergman, April 4, 1780. See A. E. Nordenskiöld, *Carl Wilhelm Scheele* (Stockholm: 1892), p. 315.

13. A. Lavoisier, *Elements of Chemistry in a New Systematic Order,* translated by Robert Kerr (Edinburgh: 1796), Preface, pp. xxviii and xxx.

14. A. F. Fourcroy, *Elements de l'Histoire Naturelle et de Chimie,* 5th ed. (Paris: 1797), Vol. 4, p. 116.

15. F. A. Carl Gren, *Syst. Handbuch der ges. Chemie* (Berlin: 1789), Vol. 2, 1, p. 154.

16. A. Lavoisier, *Traité de Chimie* (Paris: 1789).

17. A. F. Fourcroy, *Système des Connaissances Chimiques* (Paris: Baudouin, in the year IX, 1801), Vol. 1, p. xliii.

18. P. J. Macquer's *Chymisches Wörterbuch,* 2d ed., Vol. 6, p. 716.

19. C. Fr. Wenzel, *Lehre von der chemischen Verwandtschaft* (Dresden: 1777).

20. J. B. Richter, *Anfangsgründe der Stöchyometrie oder Messkunst chymischer Elemente* (*Outlines of Stoichiometry or the Art of Measuring Chemical Elements*) (Breslau: 1792).

21. See Schweigger's *J. für Chem. und Phys.,* **15** (1815), p. 497.

22. *Phil. Trans.* for 1767, p. 102; for 1788, p. 178.

23. C. L. Berthollet, *Mém. Inst. Nat.,* Vol. 3, and *Ann. Chim.,* **36, 37, 38.**

24. C. L. Berthollet, *Essai de Statique Chimique* (Paris: 1803), Vol. 1, p. 373.

25. J. L. Proust, *Ann. Chim.,* **32** (1799), p. 30.

26. J. L. Proust, *J. Chim. Phys.,* **63** (1806), p. 369.

27. M. J. Schleiden, *Grundzüge der wissenschaftlichen Botanik* (Leipzig: 1842).

10

Galvanism and Voltaism

One of the many important events that helped to form the new chemistry as a science in the late eighteenth century was the connection between electricity and chemical affinity. It started when Priestley and Cavendish used electric sparks from the electrostatic machine to initiate reactions between gases, and it received its greatest impulse from an accident connected with the use of this machine.

The first machine for obtaining static electricity, in which a globe of glass was rotated with friction against the hand, had been built by C. A. Hausen in 1743. This was a considerable improvement over Otto von Guericke's apparatus in which the globe was of sulfur. The Swiss physicist Martin von Planta in 1755 replaced the globe by a glass plate and the hand by pieces of leather. The Leyden jar, invented in 1745 by E. J. von Kleist in Cammin, Prussia, was a small water bottle held in the hand, while an electric charge was applied to a nail stuck into the bottle. It was improved and became widely known through the experiment of Petrus van Musschenbroek in Leyden, Holland.

Benjamin Franklin (1705–1790) adhered to the theory that there is only one electric fluid (1752), whereas those who started from experiments with magnetism mostly preferred to assume two electric fluids. In 1730, Charles François de Cisternay Dufay (1698–1739, Paris) called them the "vitreous" and the "resinous" fluids, corresponding to the well-known opposite charges produced by rubbing glass or resin. (1)

In a letter of May 25, 1747, Franklin explained "some new Terms:" positively and negatively "electrised" bodies. "And we daily in our Experiments electrise Bodies *plus* or *minus* as we think proper. These Terms we may use till your Philosophers give us better. To electrise plus or minus, no more needs to be known than this; that the parts of the Tube or Sphere, that are rub'd, do, in the Instant of the Friction, attract the Electrical Fire, and therefore take it from the Thing rubbing: the same Parts immediately, as the Friction upon them ceases, are disposed to give the Fire they have received, to any Body that has less." (2)

An excess of "electric fire" is here marked plus, and anything less than that is called minus. Henry Cavendish added the idea that what he called "electric fluid" surrounds the bodies as an atmosphere, and this expression itself seemed to make it plausible that this atmosphere can be at various states of compression. ". . . When the electric fluid within any body is more compressed than in its natural state, I call that body positively electrified; when it is less compressed, I call the body negatively electrified." (3) Usually, positive and negative are opposites; Franklin and Cavendish change this into a mere difference.

By means of the torsion balance, a light horizontal metal bar held at its middle by a long fine wire, Charles Augustin Coulomb (1736–1806, Paris) defined a quantity of electricity that attracts or repulses another quantity in proportion to these quantities and inversely proportional to the square of their distance (1785).

Electricity thus appeared to follow the law that Newton had found for gravitational attraction. Chemical actions of electric sparks were explained as due to the light accompanying the discharge. In 1786 an incident occurred that itself acted like a spark and initiated an increasingly widening series of investigations. Luigi Galvani (1737–1798), professor of surgical and anatomical operations in Bologna from 1763, had dissected and prepared a frog. It lay on a table on which an electrical machine was being operated by one of his assistants. Suddenly someone observed that the frog began to twitch when the assistant touched it with a scalpel held in his hand. Although this had been observed before, it was a surprise to Galvani. Immediately he began to investigate what had happened. The accident became as fruitful as the earlier one when acid dripped over a tin frame into a dyestuff solution (page 98) or as the use of contaminated potash (page 103).

Metals are "conductors of electricity," a term that Des Aguliers had introduced in 1740. When a nonconducting material, e.g. glass, was used instead of the metallic scalpel, the frog's leg did not twitch when sparks were drawn from the machine. An apparently nebulous idea, that the open air contains electricity while that in the room does not, caused Galvani to suspend the prepared frog from a hook on his garden fence. He observed that the twitching occurred only when the hook, which was in contact with the lumbar nerve, was of a metal different from the iron of the fence, and when the muscle touched the iron. The best result was obtained when one of the metals was silver, the other iron. This seemed to Galvani to present a perfect analogy to a Leyden jar, with the nerve-muscle system as the source of electricity.

Soon after Galvani published his work (1791), Alessandro Volta (1745–1827), professor of physics in Pavia, rejected its basic results. The animal is only an indicator, an electroscope, not the generator of electricity. Replacing the frog leg by a metallic electroscope in which two pieces of thin gold foil are spread apart when electrically charged, Volta demonstrated that the contact of different metals is sufficient to produce electricity. In 1775, repeating some earlier attempts, Volta constructed an electrophorus, essentially a plate cast from resin, in which electricity is produced when struck with a fox tail. This static electricity induced a charge in a metal plate on which the resin rested. Galvani's new experiences and Volta's explanations led from the old electrophorus to the construction of the electrical pile by which Volta thought to imitate nature's means for creating electricity. Volta wrote in a letter to Sir Joseph Banks, March 20, 1800: (4) "This apparatus . . . which resembles in form more the natural electrical organ of the electric eel . . . than the Leyden jar and the known electrical batteries, I should like to call it Artificial Electrical Organ."

François Arago described this "organ" in his 1831 eulogy of Volta as follows: "In the beginning of the year 1800 . . . the illustrious professor conceived the idea of forming a long column by piling up, in succession, a disc of copper, a disc of zinc, and a disc of wet cloth, with scrupulous attention not to change this order. What could be expected beforehand from such a combination? Well I do not hesitate to say, this apparently inert mass, this bizarre assembly, this pile of so many couples of unequal metals separated by a little liquid is, in the singularity of effect, the most marvelous instrument which men have yet invented, the telescope and the steam engine not excepted." (5)

Another arrangement for producing electricity according to Volta was to immerse a zinc and a silver plate in a cup filled with salty water. Several such cups are combined, the silver of one cup being connected by wire to the zinc of the next. Then when the two end plates are touched, the electric current can be felt. "This circulation of electric fluid without end (this perpetual movement) may seem paradoxical, it may not be explainable, but it is, nonetheless, true and real, one grasps it, so to say, by hand." (6)

Volta was surprised to obtain such a tangible action out of a simple arrangement of two metals and moisture, and the world shared his surprise. What happened in that electric pile seemed to contradict the idea that forces cannot be created without some other change occurring at the same time, the concept of a conservation of force which Lavoisier had again emphasized just a few years before. Voltaic piles were built in many places, the size of metal plates and the number of metal pairs were varied, different alkalies, acids, and salts were dissolved in the water between the metals. The concept of electrical positive and negative charge was generalized. Polarity became a favorite topic of speculation. The original idea of the two contraries (page 29) was thus returned to philosophy after the experimenting scientists had instilled new meaning into it. The hand with which Volta used to feel the electrical action was soon replaced by chemicals.

William Nicholson (1753–1815) and Anthony Carlisle (1768–1840), both in London, observed that the electricity from a pile decomposed solutions of salts and acids in water. Hydrogen gas developed at the wire connected with the zinc pole, and oxygen formed at the wire leading to the copper or silver of the pile. At the Royal Artillery Academy, Woolich, William Cruikshank (1745–1800) explained this as the action of galvanic currents, and he ascribed to them the property of combining with oxygen or hydrogen, carrying these substances to the wires, and unloading them there. (7)

The zinc pole was called negative, the other, e.g., silver, positive. Jöns Jakob Berzelius (1779–1848, Stockholm) and Wilhelm Hisinger reported in 1803 that combustible gas or salt bases accumulate at the negative pole, oxygen and acids at the positive pole. Four years after this, Humphry Davy (1778, Penzance –1829, Geneva) decomposed potash, not in the dilute solutions commonly used in such experiments but in the presence of only a small amount of moisture, just sufficient to help in melting the potash. A large pile, consisting of 250 pairs of metal plates, each 6×4 inches in size, was connected to the platinum dish on which the potash rested, and to a second platinum dish held on the surface of the material. Soon a "vivid action" occurred. Globules of metallic appearance, like mercury, appeared, "some of which burnt with explosion and bright flame." He concluded that these mercury-like globules represented the metal base of potash, potassium. In similar experiments he obtained from soda its metal base, sodium.

Davy's chemical education had started when he was an apprentice of Dr. Borlese, in his native Penzance in Cornwall, and later with

Dr. Beddoes in Bristol (1797–1800). From early youth he liked to talk and experiment before gatherings. He owed his position at the Royal Institution, founded in 1800 by Count Rumford, (8) to the success of an introductory lecture. It may be justifiable to assume that his study of Lavoisier's work on the so-called conversion of water into earth stimulated Davy to investigate whether the acids and bases observed upon the electrical treatment of water were not due to its impurities. In 1800 he found that small amounts of salt are contained in ordinary water. They are the source from which electricity separates the acids and bases. The water, which he prepared by distillation, avoiding contact with glass and air, was not changed by the passage of galvanic current. Thus pure water was made for the first time.

Davy liked the dramatic presentation of chemical experiments. His inclination toward poetry carried him away when he described the effect of nitrous oxide, the "laughing gas." He created in a state of exaltation. His Bakerian lecture of November 19, 1807, in which he demonstrated the new metals that explode on contact with water, was a spectacular success. Shortly afterward his health broke down. He recovered only slowly, probably never completely. After he was knighted (1812) he played the role of the nobleman with a too conscious effort, which has been interpreted as a weakness of character, whereas it obviously was the strength of his sense of drama and poetry.

Many problems were submitted to a scientist of such renown. He found the solution for a safe lamp which could be used in mines without causing an explosion of the dangerous gases. He failed, however, when he tried to improve ventilation in the House of Lords. In 1826 he resigned from the presidency of the Royal Society because of another health breakdown and sought recovery in vain while traveling in Italy and Switzerland.

A powerful pile was required for the decomposition of the alkalies in order to produce their metallic bases. The question arose whether the dimension of the metal plates or the number of the metal pairs determined the magnitude of action. Ten piles, each of the same size, developed ten times as much hydrogen and oxygen from water solutions as did one pile alone. Berzelius concluded that the quantities of decomposition products were proportional to the quantities of electricity, and that the greater these quantities are, the larger the contact surface between metal and conducting liquid in the pile.

The size of the metal plates, therefore, corresponded to the quantity of electricity obtainable from a pile. The number of metal pairs determined the intensity. Davy needed the 250 pairs, and at least

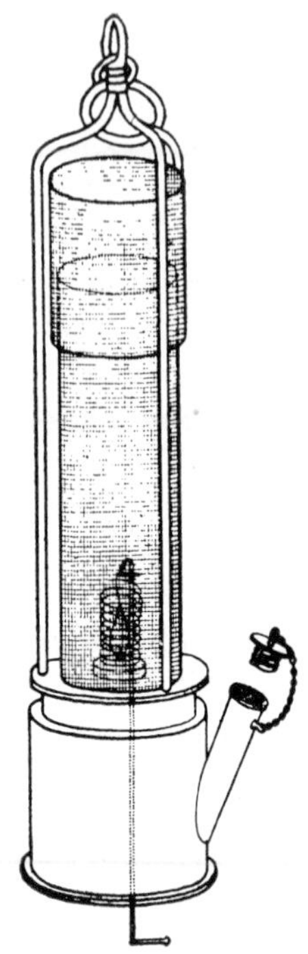

Fig. 18. Davy's safety lamp with a platinum wire (spirally wound) which continues to glow after the flame of the lamp is extinguished, due to lack of fresh air. (From *Gilbert's Annalen*, **56,** 1817, p. 437.)

150, to overcome the great affinity that holds potassium and oxygen together in potash. Berzelius was able to carry out the decomposition with a much shorter pile containing only twenty metal pairs when in 1808 he used mercury at the negative pole. The affinity between mercury and potassium was so great that it reduced the intensity required for the decomposition of potash. The metallic base, or as Berzelius cautiously called it, "the radical of potash," is then obtained, not in the pure state but as a compound with mercury, an amalgam.

This shows, according to Berzelius, the general reason for the electrochemical effect. It counteracts the forces of chemical combination which are themselves of an electrical nature. Each atom has both positive and negative electricity, not in equal quantities but with the prevalence of one or the other. Therefore, elements are either positive or negative, according to the kind of electricity that prevails. The opposite electricities cause chemical combination. Attraction is accompanied by heat and light, as in the discharge of electricity by sparks or through wires. The analogy does not reach very far, however. Heat and light are all that remain after an electric discharge; in a chemical compound the elements continue to be held by a force greater than any mechanical force that could be applied in an attempt to separate them. After the electrical difference has disappeared, destroyed by the attraction, its binding effect remains.

Hegel caustically remarked that in this theory all the chemical qualities "are put aside and sunk in the abstraction of electricity. How can anybody reproach philosophy for abstracting from specificity and creating empty generalities when it is permitted to forget all the qualities of substantiality because of positive and negative electricity!" (9)

Berzelius used the assumption of opposite electricities in the atoms "for systematic purposes. Since it fitted these purposes exceedingly well, this physically nonsensical theory remained dominant for many years and finally collapsed, not because of its physical, but for its systematic weakness." (10) Essential parts of the theory were based on concepts that John Dalton had developed in his atomic theory.

In the explanation that William Cruikshank gave for the electrically produced development of oxygen and hydrogen, electricity was a chemical substance. Berzelius, and to some extent also Davy, reversed this explanation and said that chemical substances are electric. A decisive contribution to this reversal was made by Paul Louis Simon (1767–1815, Berlin) when he showed that the weight of hydrogen and oxygen produced was equal to the weight of the water lost in the decomposition, so that there was no room for an "electric fluid" entering with any weight or substance into this reaction. Another confirmation of the reversed theory was discovered by Davy. When acid, placed in a silver spoon, was neutralized by a stick of caustic soda held in metal pincers while the metals were each connected by wires to the poles of a galvanometer, it indicated an electric charge. The formation of a salt generates electricity. The reversal of the process was thus complete, comprising both the chemical change and the force that accompanies it. On the strength of such findings, affinity was completely identified with electricity, the more easily so because an essential identity of electricity with heat and light was dimly felt to exist.

References

1. William Gilbert (1540–1603, Colchester) described this in his *Physiologia Nova, sive Tractatus de Magnete* (1600). A translation, *On the Magnet,* was published by Silvanus Thompson in 1900 and has been newly edited by Derek J. Price (New York: Basic Books, 1958).

2. Leonard W. Labaree, Ed., *The Papers of Benjamin Franklin* (New Haven: Yale University Press, 1961), Vol. III, pp. 131 ff. See also I. B.

Fig. 19. Dr. Hare's Electrical Machine. (From Robert Hare: "Description of an Electrical Machine," *American Journal of Science and Arts,* **32,** 1837, pp. 272–73.) Robert Hare (1781–1858), professor at the University of Pennsylvania, adhered to the contact theory; Faraday

(Continued on opposite page →)

Cohen *Benjamin Franklin's Experiments* (Cambridge, Mass.: 1941); *Franklin and Newton* (Philadelphia: 1956).

3. H. Cavendish, "An attempt to explain some of the principal phenomena of electricity by means of an elastic fluid," *Phil. Trans.* **61** (1771), pp. 584–677.

4. Alessandro Volta, "On the electricity excited by the mere contact of conducting substances of different kinds," *Phil. Trans.*, 1800, pp. 403–31; facsimile reprint, with introduction by George Sarton, in *Isis*, **31** (1930), pp. 124–57. Valerio Broglia, "Alessandro Volta und die Chemie," Chem.-Ztg. **90** (18) (1966), 628–640.

5. *Œuvres Complètes de François Arago* (Paris-Leipzig: 1854, Vol. 1, p. 219.

6. A. Volta. See reference 4.

7. Cruikshank, *Nicholson's Journal*, **4** (1800), p. 187.

8. Egon Larsen, *An American in Europe. The Life of Benjamin Thompson, Count Rumford* (New York: The Philosophical Society, 1954).

9. G. W. F. Hegel, *Encyclopaedie der philosophischen Wissenschaften* (3d ed., 1830; Hg. Georg Lasson, *Philosophische Bibliothek*, Vol. 33, 2d ed.; Leipzig: Felix Meiner, 1920), p. 295.

10. Wilhelm Ostwald, *Lehrbuch der allgemeinen Chemie* (2d ed; Leipzig: Wilhelm Engelmann, 1903), Vol. 2, Part 1, p. 525.

---

tried to convince him that it was wrong. The following is from the article that this drawing accompanied.

Art. V.—*Description of an Electrical Machine, with a plate four feet in diameter, so constructed as to be above the Operator: also of a Battery Discharger employed therewith: and some Observations on the Causes of the Diversity in the Length of the Sparks erroneously distinguished by the terms Positive and Negative;* by R. Hare, M. D., &c. &c. &c.

The opposite engraving represents a machine with a plate four feet in diameter, which I have recently constructed so as to be permanently affixed to the canopy over the table of my lecture room.

This situation I have found convenient even beyond my expectations, as the machine is always at hand, yet never in the way. In lecturing, with the aid of a machine on the same level with the lecturer, one of two inconveniences is inevitable. Either the machine will occasionally be between him and a portion of the audience, or he must be between a portion of the audience and the machine. Situated like that which I am about to describe, a machine can neither hid the lecturer, nor be hidden by him. With all its power at his command, while kept in motion by an assistant, he has no part of it to reach or to handle besides the knob and sliding rod of the conductor, which are in the most convenient situation.

The object of this machine being to obtain a copious supply of electricity for experiments, in which such a supply is requisite, it was not deemed necessary to insulate the cushions and the axis, as in the electrical plate machine which I employ for experiments requiring insulation.†

† See this Journal for 1828, vol. vii, p. 108; or *London Phil. Mag.* for 1823, vol. xxiii, p. 8.

11

Atoms and Molecules

It was generally understood that all the effects of affinity resulted from the behavior of the particles of matter. To Boyle, Lémery, and Newton, it appeared necessary and convenient that ultimate particles exist, not because there was any possibility of directly visualizing them but, in fact, because of the impossibility of doing just that. Atoms were postulated, not demonstrated. Geometric shapes and physical motions could thus be ascribed to them with the confidence that the men of the eighteenth century had to a much greater extent in their thinking than in their experimenting.

The mechanists rejected "hidden Qualities" and explained chemical change by attractions and repulsions. For these, the old model had been the love and striving, which Empedocles used as the foundation and analogy. The new model did not explicitly refer to human emotions; instead it emerged from the recent experience with vitreous and resinous electricity, and with the magnet. In the theory of Jean-Théophile des Aguliers (1683, Rochelle –1744, London), who was the ardent disciple of Newton, particles of air repel one another because they are charged with positive electricity. Sulfurous, that is, combustible, particles also repel one another, but they do it because of a negative charge. The attraction between air and combustible particles combines them into electrically neutral *moleculae.* (1) The assumption of the electrically opposite nature of charges supported the concept of atoms by connecting them with an impressive new property.

This thought was carried to its philosophical extreme by Roger Josephus Boscovich (2) (1711–1787) who taught in Italy and in France. He combined Newton's theory of forces that act at a distance with Leibniz's thoughts of monads as simplest elements. The transfer of motion from one body to another in collision is so difficult to represent for material atoms that a new hypothesis was required, one that abolished the dualism of matter and force altogether. Atoms then become mere geometric points, centers of force, and nothing else. They produce attraction at a measurably large distance, in accordance with the laws of gravitation. At a very small, immeasurable distance, the force is repulsive and becomes infinitely large as the distance diminishes to infinitely small. These properties of the force, which are again reversed at a very great distances, actually constitute what is commonly called space, and all qualities of matter can be derived from it. This "unique, simple, continuous law for the forces that exist in nature" follows "by direct inference" from the three principles: continuity, simplicity, and similarity (or analogy). The change of force from attractive to repulsive as a periodic function of the distance was the most surprising feature in this bold construction, in which the atom had no real place.

Kant called the atom "a mere idea." It was more than that to the Abbé René Juste Haüy (1743–1822), since he felt that he had opened a physical approach to the realm of the atom. Crystals of Iceland spar can be split in such manner that the smaller fragments retain the same rhombohedrical arrangements of planes and angles that characterize the natural specimen. This, it was reasoned, must be due to a regular arrangement not only of the spar but also of every smallest particle. A crystal consists of a nucleus and enveloping matter of molecules which have the same form as the nucleus, superimposed upon it according to definite rules. (3) Although Torbern Bergman had already noted the "natural joints" or planes of easy rupture in some crystals, Haüy was at first derisively called the crystalloclast—"crystal splitter." He continued, nevertheless, in his efforts, and arrived at the foundations of a law of definite geometric proportions characterizing the situation of the planes of a crystal.

Haüy's crystallographic theory was the basis from which C. S. Weiss (1780–1856, Berlin) constructed "the natural subdivisions of the crystal systems" (1815). Atoms were not necessary for this enterprise; Weiss rejected atomism in favor of dynamism. It had become a fashion, in a sometimes outspoken rivalry between French and German scientists, to consider atomistic theory as the field of the French, and the "deeper" dynamistic theory as essentially German. In England, at that time, William Higgins (4) (1766–1825) and, a few years later, John Dalton (1766–1844, Manchester) explored the meaning of atomism for chemistry.

Higgins based his opinions upon the work on specific gravities and the attractive powers of various salt solutions, and particularly on the composition of nitrous air, of Richard Kirwan (1733–1812,

Dublin), who received the Copley medal from the Royal Society in 1782. Adhering to Kirwan's phlogistical viewpoint, Higgins theorized: "Nitrous air, according to Kirwan, contains 2 of dephlogisticated to 1 of phlogisticated air. . . . I am of opinion that every primary particle of phlogisticated air is united to two of dephlogisticated air, and that these molecules are surrounded with a common atmosphere of fire." Then, further following the trend of using numbers to designate the relative magnitudes of affinities, he "supposes" that not more than five particles of dephlogisticated air (oxygen) can combine with one of phlogisticated air (nitrogen), towards which the former will gravitate "as their common center of gravity. This is the most perfect state of colourless nitrous acid."

John Dalton sought an explanation for Priestley's and his own finding that the composition of the atmosphere is the same at different heights. Oxygen and nitrogen differ in specific gravity; why does this not cause a separation of the two? In the autumn of 1801 "I hit upon an idea" that "the particles of one gas are not elastic or repulsive to the particles of another gas, but only to the particles of their own kind." These particles consist "of the supposed impenetrable nucleus, together with . . . its surrounding repulsive atmosphere of heat." Since it is not known that the specific gravities of substances vary, "we may conclude that the ultimate particles of all homogenous bodies are perfectly alike in weight, figure, etc." (5)

Thus, Dalton's atom is not identical with a "center of force" as it was for Boscovich, and it is not the carrier of electrical charges, as it was for Des Aguilier, but it follows Lavoisier's conception that elements are combined with heat when they exist as gases. For this heat, which is the surviving residue of the phlogiston theory, Dalton visualized a specific place: a sphere surrounding the atomic substance. A sphere is also the place in which several atoms of a substance B arrange themselves around the atom of substance A with which they combine; that is the tacit assumption in the following statement of Dalton:

> When an element A has an affinity for another B, I see no mechanical reason why it should not take as many atoms of B as are presented to it, and can possibly come into contact with it (which may probably be 12 in general), except so far as the repulsion of the atoms of B among themselves are more than a match for the attraction of an atom of A. Now this repulsion begins with 2 atoms of B to 1 of A, in which case the 2 atoms of B are diametrically opposed; it increases with 3 atoms of B to 1 of A, in which case the atoms are only 120° asunder; with 4 atoms

of B it is still greater as the distance is then only 90; and so on in proportion to the number of atoms. It is evident then from these positions, that, as far as powers of attraction and repulsion are concerned (and we know of no other in chemistry), binary compounds must first be formed in the ordinary course if things, then ternary, and so on, till the repulsion of the atoms of B (or A, whichever happens to be on the surface of the other), refuse to admit any more.

The proportions of weights in a compound are the proportions of the weights of the atoms. Lavoisier found 85 percent of oxygen and 15 percent of hydrogen in water; therefore an atom of oxygen is 5.66 times the weight of atom of hydrogen. In ammonia, 80 percent of nitrogen is combined with 20 percent of hydrogen (1788); therefore a nitrogen atom weighs four times as much as a hydrogen atom. The assumption that one atom of each element is present in the compound is made by Dalton without any further explanation.

Where there are two different compounds between the same elements, the atoms are assumed to combine in a 1:1 relationship in one of them, and in a 1:2 proportion in the other. How this applies to the compounds of sulfur with hydrogen and with oxygen is shown in the following quotation from Dalton's *New System of Chemical Philosophy,* Part II (Manchester/London, 1810), pp. 450 ff.

There are two compounds of hydrogen with sulphur; the one, a well-known elastic fluid denominated 'sulphuretted hydrogen,' the other a viscid, oily compound called 'supersulphuretted hydrogen.' The former consists of 1 atom of each element, the latter probably of 1 atom of hydrogen united to 2 of sulphur.

1. Sulphuretted hydrogen

The best way I have found to obtain sulphuretted hydrogen in a pure state is to heat a piece of iron to a white or welding heat in a smith's forge, then suddenly drawing it from the fire, apply a roll of sulphur; . . .

Sulphuretted hydrogen is unfit for respiration and for supporting combustion. . . . Water absorbs just its bulk of this gas; when, therefore, it is mixed with hydrogen, this last will be left after washing in water, or what is still better, in lime water. Sulphuretted hydrogen burns with a blue flame. When mixed with oxygen, in the ratio of 100 measures to 50 of oxygen (which is the least effective quantity), it explodes by an electric spark; water is produced, sulphur deposited, and the gasses disappear. If 150 or more measures of oxygen are used, then after the explosion over mercury, about 87 measures of sulphurous acid are found in the tube, and 150 of oxygen disappear, or enter into combination with both the elements of the gas. . . .

From these facts, the constitution of sulphuretted hydrogen is clearly pointed out. It is 1 atom of sulphur and 1 of hydrogen, united in the same volume as 1 of pure hydrogen. When burned, 2 atoms of oxygen unite to 1 of sulphur to form sulphurous acid, and 1 of oxygen to 1 of hydrogen to form water. The weights of elements confirm this constitution. One atom of sulphur has been found to weigh 13, to which adding 1 for hydrogen, we obtain the weight of an atom of sulphuretted hydrogen = 14; this number likewise expresses the number of times that sulphuretted hydrogen should exceed hydrogen in specific gravity. But common air exceeds hydrogen 12 times; therefore, 12:14::specific gravity of common air; specific gravity of sulphuretted hydrogen = 1.16, agreeably to the preceding determination. Hence this gas is wholly composed of sulphur and hydrogen, as above.

* * *

2. Supersulphuretted hydrogen

. . . When liquid alkali is poured upon supersulphuretted hydrogen, heat is produced, hydrosulphuret is formed, and sulphur precipitated. . . .

OXYGEN WITH SULPHUR

1. Sulphurous oxide

. . . When sulphuretted hydrogen gas and sulphurous acid gas are mixed over mercury, in the proportion of 6 measures of the former to 5 of the latter, both gases lose their elasticity, and a solid deposit is made on the sides of the tube. The common explanation given of this fact is, that the hydrogen of the one gas unites to the oxygen of the other to form water, and the sulphur of both gases is precipitated. This explanation is not correct; water is indeed formed, as is stated; but the deposition consists of a mixture of two solid bodies, the one sulphur, the other sulphurous oxide; they may be distinguished. . . . It will appear in the sequel that 5 measures of sulphuric acid contain twice as much oxygen as the hydrogen in 6 measures of sulphuretted hydrogen require. . . .

As far, then, as appears, sulphurous oxide is a compound of one atom of sulphur and one of oxygen; it is capable of combining with muriatic, and perhaps other acids; when suspended in water, it gives it a milky appearance and a bitter taste, and the mixture being heated, the oxide is changed into sulphur and sulphuric acid.

An atom of sulphur being estimated, from other considerations hereafter to be mentioned, to weigh 13, and one of oxygen weighing 7, it will follow that oxide of sulphur is constituted of 65 percent sulphur and 35 percent oxygen.

Carbon forms two oxides: the first, carbon oxide, contains one atom each of carbon and oxygen; the second, carbon dioxide, has two atoms of oxygen for one of carbon. Since Lavoisier, after several modifications, finally arrived at 72 percent of oxygen and 28 percent of carbon in the dioxide, and since the atomic weight of oxygen was derived from the composition of water to be 5.66, the atomic weight of carbon was 4.4, calculated from the proportion

$$72:28 = (2 \times 5.66):x$$

In 1803 Dalton combined these values in a table of atomic weights which he subsequently corrected and enlarged. He used several kinds of graphical representations of atoms. A small circle, surrounding the initial of the element as the heat atmosphere surrounds the atomic nucleus, designates the atom.

Ⓩ = zinc ©= copper

Later on he reduced the letters to points and straight lines.

⊙ = hydrogen ⦶ = nitrogen ⊕ = sulfur

Oxygen is designated by an empty circle, carbon by a black circle. Thus carbon oxide and dioxide are visualized as

●○ ○●○

Two gaseous compounds of carbon with hydrogen had been investigated at that time, marsh gas and olefiant gas. Volta described the sky-blue flame with which marsh gas burns. This distinguishes it from hydrogen and indicates that its presence is the cause of all flames. Whether paper or wood or alcohol are the burning substances, they are first converted into marsh gas and only then do they give a flame (1778).

In 1794, the "Dutch chemists," Johann Rudolph Deiman (1743–1808), Adrien Paets van Troostwijk (1752–1837), Anthoni Lauwerenburgh (1758–1820), Nicholas Bondt (1765–1796), and Peter Nieuwland (1764–1794) obtained olefiant gas when they heated alcohol with a large quantity of sulphuric acid. (6) Its name was chosen to characterize its property of forming an oil when it combines with

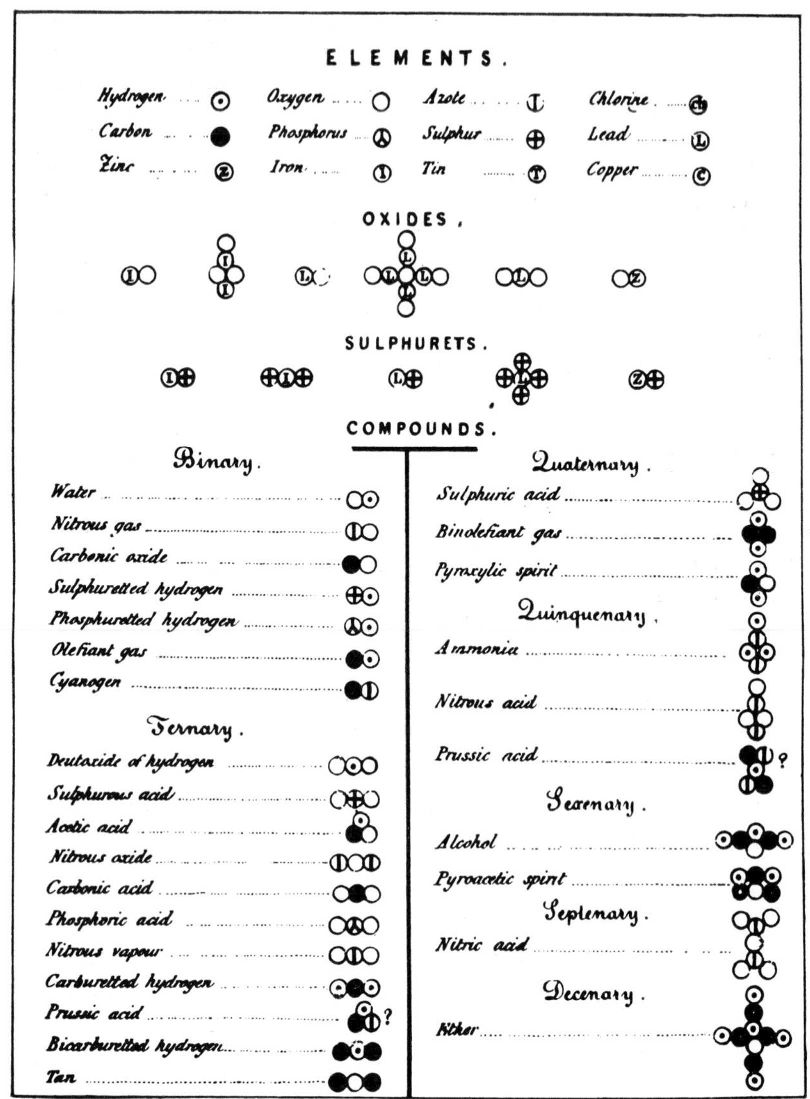

Fig. 20. "Atomic symbols by John Dalton, D.C.L., F.R.S., etc. etc., explanatory of a lecture given by him to the members of the Manchester Mechanics' Institution, October 19th, 1835." From William E. Henry, *Memoirs of the Life and Scientific Researches of John Dalton* (London: Cavendish Society, 1854).

chlorine. The proportions of carbon to hydrogen are 75 : 25 in marsh gas, 85.7 : 14.3 in olefiant gas. Dalton saw that this means 6 : 2 in the first, and, closely enough, 6 : 1 in the second, so that the atomic composition was to be expressed by these symbols: marsh gas ⊙ ● ⊙, olefiant gas ● ⊙. The discrepancy between the atomic weight 6 found here and the 4.4 previously calculated for carbon was not considered critical; Dalton knew that these experimental results were open to great improvement.

Dalton originally intended the theory only for materials "in the state of a pure elastic fluid." In 1810 he extended the atomic theory to solid substances like metals because they react with gases and should, therefore, offer the same kind of ultimate particle.

Dalton's work was not too kindly received by Davy. On March 24, 1811, Davy wrote to Berzelius, who had asked his opinion about it, as follows (7):

> It is not a little curious that the first views of the Atomic Chemistry, which has been so much expanded by Dalton and generally in my opinion after ideas more ingenious than correct, are to be found in a work published in 1789 by William Higgins, *A Comparative View of the Two Theories of Chemistry.*

It is true that Higgins indicated a law of multiple proportions and a heat atmosphere surrounding the atom. These are essential aspects which recurred in Dalton's theory, but they were here amplified by more definite examples and a wider range of applications than Higgins found. Besides that, Dalton's sign language brought the philosophical thought into the form of a chemical theory. If this seemed "more ingenious than correct" to Davy, it was greatly stimulating to his friend and mentor in scientific methods, William Hyde Wollaston (1766–1828). He gave the "directest proof" of the law of multiple proportions by simple experiments with potassium salts. Potassium forms two kinds of salts with sulfuric acid, a supersulfate (bisulfate) and a neutral sulfate. The former is obtained by heating potassium carbonate with an excess of sulfuric acid until the free acid is evaporated. When 20 grams of carbonate were used in this operation, it required just 20 more grams of the carbonate to convert the bisulfate into the neutral salt. By a somewhat different method, the proof for the oxalates was just as simple. Take two equal quantities of the superoxalate and burn the oxalic acid in one of them. The ash obtained is just sufficient to convert the other portion into the neutral oxalate. The supersalts thus contain one part of the alkali for one of the acid, the neutral salts two parts of the alkali for one of the acid. In the quadroxalate, the proportion is four acid to one alkali.

All this could be expressed in Proust's theory without using atomic concepts. For Wollaston, arithmetic relations were insufficient; he needed further explanation for a complete chemical theory. With the new theory it became possible to construct models for the chemical compounds. When the proportion of atoms in a compound is 4:1, the four can be placed in the corners of a regular tetrahedron. (8)

Besides leading to such appealing structural models, the theory also provided a basis for the critical evaluation of experimental results. When Berzelius became acquainted with Dalton's theory, he found that it confirmed the analyses of salts that he had been carrying on since 1807. He saw in Dalton's theory "one of the greatest advances" of chemistry, although he reproached its author for leaving too little for the experiment to decide and for having had "too little distrust in his own way of applying the hypotheses to the system" (1818). Differences between predictions of the theory and the results of experimental measurements arose in the further progress of Berzelius' work. This stimulated him to repeat and to modify the procedures. "Enlightened by the knowledge of my own errors, and with the aid of better methods, I finally found a great accord between the results of the analyses and the calculations of the theory." (9)

It was quite difficult to determine atomic weights. Dalton gave for sulfur figures that varied from 17 and 14.4 in 1803 to 22 and 12 in 1806. Obviously, without the guidance of a theory, experiments alone would not have led to the conclusion that particles of constant weight exist. Therefore it came as a great and almost unbelievable surprise when Gay-Lussac found that the chemical combinations of gases always occur in simple volumetric proportions. Joseph Louis Gay-Lussac (1778–1850, Paris) himself was prepared for such uniform behavior of gases. He had discovered (1802) that all gases have the same coefficient of thermal expansion so that when two substances in gas form had the same volume at one temperature, the volumes remained equal to each other at all temperatures. When he reinvestigated the water reaction, for which Cavendish and Priestley already had indicated simple volumetric proportions, he stated that, by volume, 2 hydrogen combine with 1 oxygen to form 2 water vapor. That he did this work in collaboration with Alexander von Humboldt (1805) was because of an unusual reason. The great German explorer, recently returned to Paris from his travels in South America (1799–1804), had published measurements of the oxygen content in air which Gay-Lussac criticized very sharply. Instead of resenting this, Humboldt sought friendship with the younger man and better chemist.

Simple volumetric proportions were also found for the formation of carbon dioxide, nitrogen oxides, and ammonia:

$$\left.\begin{array}{lll} \text{2 carbon oxide} & + \text{ 1 oxygen} & = \text{2 carbon dioxide} \\ \text{3 hydrogen} & + \text{ 1 nitrogen} & = \text{2 ammonia} \end{array}\right\} \text{ by volume}$$

The neutralization of ammonia by carbon dioxide, or by hydrochloric acid, again showed such simple volumetric relations. Gay-Lussac concluded that similar simple relations would be found if the components of all salts were obtainable in gas form. (10)

Dalton immediately raised two objections to Gay-Lussac's experiments and generalizations. (11) The first objection was directed against the accuracy of the volumetric measurements. Dalton, who had found no difficulty in accepting widely varying figures for the atomic weights of carbon or of sulfur, now insisted that not 2 but 1.97 volumes of hydrogen combined with 1 volume of oxygen, and that this deviation was sufficient to invalidate the law. The second objection was more fundamental. Gay-Lussac's law would necessarily lead to the conclusion that equal volumes of gases contained equal numbers of atoms. Dalton had tried and rejected this assumption. When one atom of nitrogen combines with one atom of oxygen, one atom of oxide is formed, or in Dalton's notation:

⦶ + ○ = ⦶○

Since two atoms thus become one atom, two volumes should become one volume after the reaction if the basic assumption were correct. Actually, the volume does not change in this reaction. This means that Gay-Lussac's law had to be rejected on the basis of the theory which assumed that the atoms in nitrogen and oxygen as elements were simple, while the atoms of nitrogen oxide were complex, just as the graphic models showed. Was this theory more reliable than the measurements? Or was it possible to modify the theoretical concept so that it would be consistent with the experimental results?

Amadeo Avogadro (1776–1856, Turin) assumed that in all gases, whether they are elements or compounds, the ultimate particles are complex. In his language, the particles always consist of a certain number of integral molecules united by attraction. The process of chemical combination, which in Dalton's theory was a simple addition of atoms, involves a step in which the molecules actually present are divided into integral molecules. The particles in nitrogen and oxygen gas consist of two integral molecules. The twins are split when the chemical combination brings one integral molecule each of nitrogen and oxygen together to form the new particle of the nitrous gas. If Avogadro had used Dalton's symbols, he might have written:

⦶⦶		○○		⦶○ + ⦶○
Nitrogen	+	Oxygen	=	Nitrous gas

With an oxygen particle which consists of two integral molecules, as shown by this reaction, the formation of water must be explained as follows: Four integral molecules of hydrogen combine with two of oxygen into two molecules of water. Each particle of water then contains one integral molecule of oxygen with two of hydrogen, and if the atomic weight of hydrogen is defined as 1, that of oxygen must be 15 (according to the best value at that time). It was Dalton's error to assume, from the proportions of the weights of oxygen and hydrogen in water, that the atom of oxygen was 7.5. Unfortunately, after pointing out this error, Avogadro committed it himself at the end of his exposition. (12)

In his work on the molecular volumes of liquids and solids, 1826–1852, Avogadro made assumptions that actually contradicted his hypothesis of 1811. (13)

Gay-Lussac's law, the "French doctrine" as it was called, which the Englishman Dalton said he could not "admit," was thus reconciled with an enlarged atom theory by the Italian Avogadro. He did not make it sufficiently clear, however, that atoms must be distinguished from molecules, which are "particles" consisting of several atoms. This may explain why his theory found little acceptance.

The uniform behavior of all gases, the simplicity of the relationships between volume, temperature, and pressure, indicated to the physicist André Marie Ampère (1775–1836, Paris) that equal volumes of gases contain equal numbers of molecules. The spaces between them are infinitely large compared with the size of the molecules themselves. The chemically active particle is not the smallest unit; it is composed of several, physical molecules, at least of four. Chlorine, for example, must consist of at least eight physical molecules in one chemical particle.

This distinction between physical and chemical ultimate units (14) was not revolutionary. It had a model in the clusters of matter that Robert Boyle had vaguely described. Ampère speculated about the arrangements of these molecules in geometrical forms. Wollaston published similar thoughts shortly before Ampère. Neither impressed the chemists of their time. General theories needed experimental evidence, even if the evidence was quite limited, at least in the beginning. Nor was the idea that atoms consist of smaller units entirely abhorrent. The thought expressed in 1815 and 1816 by the English doctor, William Prout, that all elements are ultimately composed of hydrogen units, did not cause any great astonishment. At that time atoms and molecules still belonged more to philosophy than to physics and chemistry.

Avogadro again presented his views in 1818; Ampère explained his theory once more in 1835. (15) A few years before, Marc Antoine Augustin Gaudin (1804–1880) had tried to clarify the distinction between atom and molecule: "For us, an *atom* shall be a small, spherical, homogeneous body or an essentially indivisible, material point, whereas a *molecule* shall be a separate (isolated) group of atoms in any number and of any nature." (16) With one of his simple diagrams he explained how three H-H and one N-N molecule can form two molecules of ammonia consisting of the four atoms NH_3.

Jean–Baptiste André Dumas (1800–1884) measured the density of gases of mercury, phosphorus, and other substances that require high temperatures for vaporization, and at first (1827) thought that his results could be explained by Avogadro's and Ampère's theories. Later on, in 1837, he declared that he would like to ban the word atom from chemistry because it indicates something that is beyond the reach of chemical experience.

REFERENCES

1. J.-Th. Des Aguliers, *Cours de Physique Expérimentale* (1725–27).

2. J. Boscovish, *Philosophia naturalis theoria, redacta ad unicam legem virium de natura existentium* (Vienna: 1759; Venice: 1763). Lancelot Law Whyte, Ed. *Roger Joseph Boscovich, S.J., F.R.S., 1711–1787. Studies of his life and work on the 250th anniversary of his birth* (London: Allen and Unwin, 1961).

3. R. J. Haüy, *Essai d'une théorie, sur la structure des crystaux* (Paris: 1784); *Traité de minéralogie* (Paris: 1801).

4. W. Higgins, *A Comparative View of the Phlogistic and Antiphlogistic Theories* (London: 1789).

5. John Dalton, *New System of Chemical Philosophy* (Manchester-London: 1808–27. Cf. Henry E. Roscoe and A. Harden, *A New View of the Origin of Dalton's Atomic Theory* (London: Macmillan & Co., 1896). F. Greenaway, "The biographical approach to John Dalton," *Memoirs Manchester lit. phil. Soc.* **100** (2), (1958/9); 98 pages. Arnold W. Thackray, "The origin of Dalton's chemical atomic theory: Daltonian doubts resolved," *Isis,* **57** (1966), pp. 35–55.

6. *Crell's Ann.,* **2** (1795), pp. 195, 310, 430.

7. *Jac. Berzelius Bref,* H. G. Soderbaum, Ed. (Upsala: 1912–16), Vol. 2, pp. 23, 79 ff.

8. W. H. Wollaston, *Phil. Trans.* for 1808, pp. 96–102. Donald McDonald, "William Hyde Wollaston; the production of malleable platinum," *Platinum Metals Review,* **1** (3) (1966), pp. 101–6.

9. J. J. Berzelius, *Lehrbuch der Chemie* (Dresden: Arnoldi, 1827), Vol. 3, Part 1, p. 27.

10. J. L. Gay-Lussac, *Mém. de la Soc. d'Arcueil,* **2** (1809), p. 207.

11. J. Dalton, *New System of Chemical Philosophy* (London: A. Bickerstaff, 1810), Part 2, Appendix, p. 555.

12. A. Avogadro, "Essai d'une manière de déterminer les masses relatives des molécules élémentaires des corps et les proportions selon lesquelles elles entrent dans ses combinations," *J. de Physique,* **83** (1811), pp. 58–76.

13. Linus Pauling, at the meeting of the Academia Nationale dei XL in Rome, commemorating the centennary of Avogadro's death; *Science,* **124** (1956), pp. 710–3.

14. A. M. Ampère, *Ann. Chim.,* **90** (1814), p. 43.

15. A. M. Ampère, *Ann. Chim. Phys.,* **58** (1835), p. 432.

16. M. A. A. Gaudin, "Nouvelle manière d'envisager les corps gazeux, avec application à la détermination du poids relative des atomes," *Ann. chim.,* 52 (1833), p. 133. About Gaudin see M. Delépine, *Bull. Soc. Chim.* (5), **2** (1935), pp. 1–15.

12

Elements and Compounds

Chemical Proof of Elements

The atomic theory, of venerable age as a philosophical concept, proved to be a failure in its application to the new chemistry. It seemed that Dalton had reached out too far. In chemistry we may search for proportions between the combining weights of the elements, but the systematic coordination which the theory postulated in principle could not be achieved by experiment. Davy took this attitude in 1812. In 1813 Wollaston preferred the "practical expediency" of separate analyses to the difficulties of an all-embracing theory. In the same way, Gay-Lussac felt that our experiments gave us only "rapports" and not a universal system of quantitative relations (1814–1816).

However, the new discoveries, made as the result of direct search or by unforeseen accident, exerted great pressure toward systematic unification. The methods of analysis built bridges, and the calculation of proportions connected many different substances. Skill and patience in carrying out chemical analyses were not enough to arrive at an integrating system; "a certain idea which forcefully occupies all thinking" had to be added. Berzelius analyzed substance after substance over and over again. Difficulties were great. Sometimes he was near despair when the results did not make sense, or when the only platinum crucible—actually the only one in Sweden—proved too heavy for his analytical balance. Without "a certain idea" this work could not be done.

Jöns Jakob Berzelius (1) (1779, Wäversunda –1848, Stockholm) was the first full-time chemist. For many of the great men mentioned before, chemistry was an occupation carried on only occasionally, side by side with other professions which often took up much more time and were more lucrative. In the words of one of his many prominent students, Heinrich Rose, chemistry became an exact science through Berzelius. Occasionally, he had to defend his work against the accusation that it consisted of "one-sided and stupid empiricism."

Berzelius was "a child of the Gustavian epoch (in Sweden), and he had obtained his education under the domination of the French fashion. His thinking is preferentially directed toward sober facts; clarity and logical order are the qualities for which he strives most of all in his writing which, besides, does not lack a certain dry humor." (2) Berzelius had started out with the study of medicine and chemistry. In one of his first investigations he tried to use the new electrochemical discoveries for medical purposes. When he began to teach at the War Academy in Stockholm, he felt the need for a good textbook on chemistry. In trying to compose such a text he became impressed by the lack of accurate data. These had to be produced by experimental work. The textbook began to be published in 1808; the last volume of the last (fifth) edition, prepared by his friend Friedrich Wöhler, came out in 1848. From 1821 on, Berzelius also published an annual survey of the advances of physics and chemistry. These *Berichte* gave critical reports, not just abstracts.

Berzelius' own experiments thus became parts in the system of a coherent science. In his opinion, Davy produced only "splendid fragments" because "he was not forced from the beginning to work his way into all parts of science as a whole." (3) Fragments of research, however splendid, were insufficient without a system. The longer Berzelius worked, the more he felt that the system should be the guide and the judge of all new experiences. This attitude brought him into conflict with the advance of his science in the later years of his life. The systems of science are not rigid, predetermined structures; we build them out of experimental results and their interpretation. Berzelius knew this very thoroughly; he reiterated it in the foreword to the last German edition of his *Lehrbuch* (1842): ". . . the history of science shows that an ingrained belief in theoretical concepts frequently did not yield to the most tangible proof of their incorrectness." The difficulty consisted in recognizing when the proof was really "tangible." An important example is the discussion about the nature of newly discovered elements.

Alkali Metals and Chlorine

When Berzelius, together with M. M. Pontin (1780–1858), attempted to repeat Davy's electrolytic preparation of the alkali metals, sodium and potassium, he did not have a sufficiently powerful voltaic column. With mercury as the negative pole, Berzelius' weak source of electricity yielded the alkali metals dissolved in mercury as amalgams. The experiment was also successful with lime and baryta, and it furnished the characteristic amalgams of calcium and barium.

The question to be answered by experiment was whether or not these were really elements. Sodium and potassium react violently with water, hydrogen is released, and the caustic alkalis are formed. Where did the hydrogen originate? Gay-Lussac and Thenard believed it was a component of the metals which were, therefore, not elements. On the other side, Davy and Berzelius held that the hydrogen came out of the water, and that the metals formed the caustic compounds by combining with the oxygen of the water. The discussion was complicated by an apparent analogy with the reactions of ammonia. Its salts, electrolyzed with mercury as the negative pole, gave an amalgam of the ammonia base called *ammonium*. If this indicated a perfect analogy, it was a conflicting one.

Ammonium	= Caustic ammonia	+ Hydrogen	Gay-Lussac
Potassium	= Caustic potash	+ Hydrogen	and Thenard
Ammonium	= Caustic ammonia	− Oxygen	Davy
Potassium	= Caustic potash	− Oxygen	and Berzelius

Which of these two analogies offered the "tangible proof"? Further experiments were needed for a decision. Davy pointed out that potassium or sodium combine with ammonium under release of hydrogen. If this hydrogen came from the potassium, caustic potash would have to be formed, and it was against all expectations that potash should be able to combine with the alkaline ammonium. However, the problem was not yet solved. In the analogy that Davy and Berzelius used, ammonia gas was an oxide like caustic potash or soda. The analysis of this gas showed only hydrogen and nitrogen. Where was the oxygen? The belief in the analogy was so strong that Berzelius suspected nitrogen to be the oxygen compound of a still unknown basis which he thought was the real element azote.

The solution became apparent when the role of water was recognized. Its influence had been neglected, just as in previous instances had the influence of another ever-present substance, air, or the action of the glass of the container in which water was apparently transformed into "earth." Ampère showed (1816) that ammonia gas becomes alkali only after combining with water, and d'Arcet demonstrated the presence of the elements of water in the other caustic alkalies.

Similar difficulties arose from the explanation of the nature of chlorine. It was obtained by the oxidation of muriatic acid. Since in Lavoisier's system oxygen is the universal cause of acidity, muriatic acid should contain oxygen. It was thus to be considered as an oxide of an element, murium. The greenish gas obtained by its oxidation should therefore be a higher oxide of murium. Davy found in 1807 that hydrogen is formed when muriatic acid gas reacts with potassium. He explained it as resulting from the action of this metal on the water which he assumed to be present in the gas as one of its constituent parts.

A solution of chlorine in water develops oxygen when exposed to sunlight and forms muriatic acid. With disregard for the water, the quantity of oxygen contained in chlorine could thus be measured. The decomposition of chlorine could not be produced by passing it over red-hot coal, as Gay-Lussac and Thenard stated. They did not consider this a definite proof of the absence of oxygen in chlorine, for if the affinity of carbon for oxygen was smaller than the affinity of murium for oxygen, a decomposition was not to be expected, according to Berzelius' opinion (1815). Conversely, when the oxidized muriatic acid (chlorine) gave oxygen by reaction with metal oxides, the reason might be that the affinity of muriatic acid for the metallic base was stronger than for its own oxygen.

Muriatic acid, being a member of the systematic group of acids, had to share with them the main characteristic of containing oxygen. This survival of the old notion that a quality of a substance is caused by a component part of this substance, was threatened by finding other acids which did not contain oxygen. Hydrogen sulfide was found to be free of oxygen by Berthollet; hydrocyanic acid does not contain oxygen according to Gay–Lussac (1815). Hydrofluoric and hydroiodic acid were added to the list, against the attempt of Berzelius to deny the elementary character of fluorine and iodine. Muriatic acid was no longer alone in being free of oxygen, and systematic unity no longer required one to write

$$\begin{aligned}\text{Muriatic acid} &= \text{Murium} + \text{Oxygen}\\ \text{Chlorine} &= \text{Muriatic acid} + \text{Oxygen}\end{aligned}$$

Instead, the new discoveries were expressed by the formula

$$\text{Muriatic acid} = \text{Hydrochloric acid} = \text{Chlorine} + \text{Hydrogen}$$

The theory of acids had thus repeated the reversion that Lavoisier had performed in the theory of metals and their "chalks." The central role that Lavoisier had assigned to oxygen was now recognized as exaggerated, and it was in part replaced by that other constituent of water, hydrogen. The expansion to a uniform "hydrogen theory" seemed so alluring that Humphry Davy, about 1807, saw the merits of the old phlogiston theory. (4)

Combining Proportions and Atomic Weights

In the *Traité Élémentaire de Chimie,* Lavoisier listed 33 items in his table of elements. Not counting the first two, light and heat, only 23 in this table were known elements; three were "unknown" radicals of muriatic, fluoric, and boric acid, and five were "simple salt-forming earths," namely, lime, magnesia, baryta, alumina, and silica.

In the first part of his *New System of Chemical Philosophy* (1808), Dalton described 20 elements with their supposed atomic weights. For two of them he added a correction to include Davy's newly discovered sodium and potassium. Two years later, Dalton's list comprised 36 elements for which he gave atomic weights. The number rose to 47 in the account which Berzelius published in 1814.

At this time Berzelius also introduced an improved method of using symbols for the elements. A few years before, Dalton had followed earlier attempts at developing such symbols, and he represented an element by a small circle—a consequence of his belief in the spherical shape of the atoms—inscribed with various geometrical forms such as broken lines and stars as figures for different elements. Berzelius, and Thomas Thomson at about the same time, proposed to use the initial letter or letters of the word designating the elements, with the additional meaning of the atomic weights. Compounds were thus written by combining these initials. Where necessary, figures as subscripts were later added to indicate the number of atoms of each element in the compound.

The following part of Berzelius' table gives the symbols and the atomic weights. Oxygen as "the center of chemical things" was assigned the atomic weight 100.0.

There were two kinds of uncertainty in these values. The first resulted from experimental errors. Berzelius constantly corrected these. The table of 1818–1819 had 6.218 instead of 6.64 for hydrogen; 2486.0 instead of 2688.2 for silver, and many other changes of similar range. Visiting Pierre Louis Dulong (1785–1838) in Paris in 1819, Berzelius complained that his analysis of the oxides of lead and copper gave less water than expected from the known composition of water. Dulong thereupon repeated a careful combustion of hydro-

FROM BERZELIUS' TABLE OF ATOMIC WEIGHTS (1813)

Element	Symbol	Atomic Weight, Relative to O = 100	
Oxygen	O	100.0	
Hydrogen	H	6.64	
Carbon	C	75.1	
Sulphur	S	201.0	
Nitrogen	A + O	179.5	(Azote combined with Oxygen)
Chlorine	M + 3O	439.6	(Murium combined with Oxygen)
Molybdenum	Mo	601.6	
Chromium	Cr	708.0	
Platinum	Pt	1206.7	
Silver	Ag	2688.2	(Argentum)
Mercury	Hg	2531.6	(Hydrargyrum)
Copper	Cu	806.5	(Cuprum)
Lead	Pb	2597.4	(Plumbum)
Tin	Sn	1470.6	(Stannum)
Iron	Fe	693.6	(Ferrum)
Calcium	Ca	510.2	
Sodium	Na	579.3	(Natrium)
Potassium	K	978.0	(Kalium)

gen over CuO (copper oxide) and found 11.1 percent of hydrogen in the water instead of the 13.27 percent previously relied upon.

The second uncertainty which was in some respects still greater consisted in translating the proportions found in gram weights to proportions of atom numbers. Silicon oxide was considered to have the composition Si + 2O in 1813, Si + 3O in 1818. Two rules guided Berzelius in determining the atomic compositions. Rule One was similar to Dalton's assumption of highest simplicity. When A and B combine, assume first that one atom A combines with one atom B. For elements which form several oxides, try 1A + 1B; 1A + 2B, reluctantly, also 2A + 3B and 1A + 3B. Rule Two specified that the number of oxygen atoms in an acid is a simple multiple of the oxygen atoms in the base with which it forms salts. This still left uncertainties in the choice of relative atomic weights. For water or ammonia, the atomic proportions could be settled as the proportions of the volumes of the elements, according to Gay-Lussac's rule. For metal oxides, however, no direct volumetric proportions were available as guides.

Two further rules were discovered in 1819 which brought new systematic connections, one physical and one mineralogical, to amplify the merely chemical analogies.

Dalton's atoms were surrounded by halos of heat substance. It was assumed that the atoms of all gases were combined with the same quantity of heat. This concept was expanded gradually to all elements in all states. If this were true, the quantity of heat taken up per degree and unit of weight, that is to say, the specific heat, of all elements should be the same. The experimental proof was carried out by A. T. Petit (1791–1820) and P. L. Dulong (1785–1838) in Paris. They found that the specific heats of the elements per gram differ widely, but that the products of the specific heats and atomic weights are nearly constant. The table that Petit and Dulong published uses figures for the atomic weights that are not identical with those of Berzelius. The difference is particularly great for some elements for which the new rule requires the chemist to select a weight equal to about one half of Berzelius' weights, as for iron, lead, tin, or even one fourth, as for silver.

SPECIFIC AND ATOMIC HEAT ACCORDING TO PETIT AND DULONG*

Element	Specific Heat for Water = 1	Weight of Atom for Oxygen = 1	Product of Specific Heat by Atom Weight
Bismuth	0.0288	13.30	0.3830
Lead	0.0293	12.95	0.3794
Gold	0.0298	12.43	0.3704
Platinum	0.0314	11.15	0.3740
Tin	0.0514	7.35	0.3779
Silver	0.0557	6.75	0.3759
Zinc	0.0927	4.03	0.3736
Tellurium	0.0912	4.03	0.3675
Copper	0.0949	3.957	0.3755
Nickel	0.1035	3.69	0.3819
Iron	0.1108	3.391	0.3731
Cobalt	0.1498	2.46	0.3685
Sulfur	0.1880	2.011	0.3780

Ann. Chim.* (2), **10 (1819), p. 395.

Most chemists were reluctant to accept this physical method of deciding between possible multiples of atomic weights. The law that the atoms of all elements have the same heat capacity appeared to be too empirical; the proportions that would be required in some compounds were in conflict with some of the purely chemical analogies. A direct relation between chemical composition and the form in which substances crystallize was easier to visualize than the rule of heat capacities because simple mathematical and mechanical reasons could, apparently at least, be given.

Thus, René Juste Haüy (1743–1822) proved "mathematically," and therefore with greatest reliability, that substances of different "nature" never assumed the same crystal form. The regular, or cubic, crystallographical system was excepted as being too unspecific. However, the general rule had to be modified immediately. Components of chemical substances can be replaced without change of form. The replacement of wood by silicates in petrified wood afforded an impressive model. When the calcium of calcium carbonate is replaced by iron or zinc, the resulting carbonates retain their original form. The retention of form in processes of base exchange is as natural as when wood is replaced by silicates.

From the difference in crystal form between barytes (also called heavy spar) and celestine, Haüy predicted that they would be found to be chemically different. (5) The "earth" in barytes had been characterized by Scheele in 1774. Quite similar to celestine was a mineral found in Strontian, a small town in Argyllshire, Scotland. Adair Crawford (1748–1795) converted the "earth" of this mineral into the chloride and found that it was not the same as the chloride from barytes (1790). In the year in which Haüy published his prediction, Thomas Charles Hope (1766–1844), the successor of Joseph Black in Glasgow, demonstrated the red flame given by Crawford's new chloride when it is brought into the spirit lamp. Hope saw this as convincing proof of the presence of a new metal; he named it *strontian* (later renamed *strontium*) after the Scottish town Strontities or Strontian. Humphry Davy separated the metal by his electrolytic method.

This story vindicated Haüy's generalization: "The exterior form and the chemical composition are each other's image." (6)

This statement was, however, limited by the fact that substances of "great force of crystallization" impress their form on other substances. Experiments showed that a little iron vitriol (sulfate) impresses its crystal form on zinc vitriol. Not the passive replacement but the active force of crystallization would thus offer an explanation where Haüy's rule did not hold. This was particularly important when one substance crystallizes in two different forms, as does calcium carbonate, which is found as calcite and as aragonite. A trace of strontium was sought as the cause for this difference.

On the other hand, phosphates and arsenates have the same crystal form. Eilhard Mitscherlich (1794–1863, Berlin) enlarged this observation to a new rule: "An equal number of atoms, combined in the same manner, produces equal crystal forms, and the form of the crystals is determined not by the nature of the atoms but by their arrangement and manner of combination." This was in direct contradiction to Haüy's hypothesis that, except for the mineralogical class of regular forms, crystal form is strictly correlated with chemical nature. Mitscherlich added: "And I shall not reproach myself should it come out at some later time that my thought was more general than experience would then confirm. . . ."

These "remarks" of 1821 were acclaimed by Berzelius as the most important discovery since the theory of chemical proportions had been proposed. In less than twenty years Haüy's theory had thus been completely reversed from the exclusive influence of chemical "nature" to the equally absolute dominance of number and relative position of atoms. However, the new position had to be corrected; the nature of the atoms could not be completely neglected. Mitscherlich coined the expression "isomorphous elements" for those that "belong to the same group" crystallographically in their compounds with equal numbers of other atoms. At the end of the publication in which he introduced this term, he changed it: "not the elements should be called 'isomorphous,' but their compounds." (7)

On the strength of these new experiences Berzelius (1826) reduced many of his former atomic weights by one half. Doubts still remained. Jean Baptiste André Dumas tried to eliminate them by measuring the density of vapors that sulfur, phosphorus, or mercury form at an elevated temperature. The application of Avogadro's law would have made it possible to use the values for the density of these vapors for determining atomic weights. The difficulty was that the high temperatures used for converting these elements to gases might not permit a direct comparison with the results found for "permanent" gases.

The newly established rules confirmed the hope that a uniform relationship between the atomic weights would be obtainable. A complete proof of the atom theory would consist in finding the absolute values of these weights. Such a goal, however, appeared entirely out of reach even to the defender of the atom theory, Thomas Thomson: "All the knowledge that we are likely ever to acquire of the atomic weight of bodies is merely the ratio of these weights." (8)

Methods of Discovering New Elements

Discussions and controversies concerning atomic weights continued into the second half of the nineteenth century. Again it appeared as though the general theory was too broad and too far removed from the experimentally accessible reality. This negative result was compensated for, however, by positive achievements obtained while attempting to arrive at an experimental verification of the theory.

Improved methods of purification, controlled conditions for reactions, preparation of substances for weighing by drying them completely were necessary in order to obtain the same results in repeated analyses. Constant proportions were found only when such precautions were taken. Only by clear and complete separation could the underlying rule be verified. With the greater precision of manual operations, better distinctions between substances became possible, thus leading up to the discovery of new substances and elements. For example, the tests for the behavior of a salt added to melting borax, or the solubilities and colors of precipitates produced from a solution of a compound, indicated the presence of a substance with certainty. When a precipitate looked like that of an aluminum salt but did not have its solubility in an excess of sodium hydroxide, it thus indicated that it did not contain aluminum. When a precipitate that should have been colorless was yellow instead, when an acidic solution of a hydroxide prepared from a new mineral precipitated upon exact neutralization, the presence of new elements could be suspected. Further proof could be obtained by decomposing an oxide with metallic sodium or potassium and comparing this reaction with the behavior of known elements. Such reactions were reliable, provided that the chemist was skillful enough to exclude interfering traces of impurities, e.g., iron, or to select the best proportionate amounts of reagents.

When Franz Joseph Müller von Reichenstein (1740–1825, Vienna) investigated a bluish-white gold ore called *aurum problematicum,* he prepared a fusible metal. He asked Torbern Bergman to find out whether it really was antimony, and the answer was no. Sixteen years later, Martin Heinrich Klaproth in Berlin (1743–1817) dissolved the ore in aqua regia, precipitated the solution with an excess of potash to remove gold and iron, and neutralized the alkaline filtrate exactly with hydrochloric acid. The white precipitate contained a new element. After drying the precipitate and distilling with oil, he prepared a metallic substance. He called it *tellurium.* Zircon, a mineral found in Ceylon, also showed in his experiments (1793) a new element which previous analyses had not discovered—*zirconium.* The white "earth" he obtained from rutil contained another new element, which he named *titanium.* The mineral cerit showed by the specific colors of the oxides prepared from it that again a new element was present. Berzelius, who investigated cerit at about the same time, called the element *cerium.*

In 1797 Klaproth, whom Berzelius regarded as "the greatest analytical chemist in Europe," found a new element in a lead ore from Siberia. In the same year Nicolas-Louis Vauquelin (1763–1829,

Paris) described the many colors of the salts obtained from this ore: red with mercury, yellow with lead, green with stannous chloride. Haüy suggested the name *chromium* for the new element to indicate the many colors of its compounds.

On one occasion, however, even Klaproth was mistaken. He thought, for instance, that he had found alumina in a Peruvian emerald, but Vauquelin discovered (1798) that the precipitate believed to be alumina did not dissolve in an excess of caustic soda. Ammonium carbonate, however, dissolved the precipitate from the emerald, but not alumina. Haüy predicted from crystal form and physical properties that emerald and beryl are chemically analogous. The new earth, first called *glucina* because of its sweet taste, was named *beryllia* by Klaproth. The reaction between its chloride and potassium yielded the new element *beryllium* (1828).

In 1789, when Klaproth analyzed pitchblende, he thought he had reduced the yellow oxide prepared from the mineral to a metal. The name *uranium,* which he gave to this supposed element, was that of the newly discovered planet. The error persisted for more than fifty years. In 1841 Eugène-Melchior Péligot (1811–1890) found that 100 parts of uranium chloride gave 110 parts of the supposed metal. He reduced it with potassium and obtained the real element. The paradox was thus explained, Klaproth had mistaken the oxide for the element.

While most of these discoveries were made by analyzing newly found minerals and ores, the story of *selenium* begins with an industrial operation. Berzelius and Gottlieb Gahn (1745–1828) investigated the method used in Gripsholm for manufacturing sulfuric acid. They found a sediment in this acid which was partly red, partly light brown, and which resembled tellurium. After collecting the sediment, which had accumulated in several months of burning sulfur from Fahlun in the Gripsholm plant, Berzelius digested it with aqua regia and separated the undissolved sulfur by filtration. He added hydrogen sulfide gas to the solution, which then retained zinc and iron, while the new substance was in the precipitate. This he dissolved again in aqua regia and removed the excess of acid by evaporation. From the water solution of the residue, tin and mercury were precipitated by caustic potash. The new substance was now in solution. The solution was then evaporated to dryness, quickly ground to a powder, mixed with ammonium chloride, and heated in a distilling flask. The decomposed residue left in the flask was extracted with water which dissolved all salts except for a metallic residue. After purification by distillation, the metal showed by its unusual behavior that it was a new element. Since it was similar to *tellurium,* the element named from the earth (*tellus*), Berzelius gave his new element a name derived from that of the moon goddess Selene, *selenium.* The new element looked metallic but it had a low conductivity for heat, which was different from the other metals. When it was heated in a large flask containing air, selenium formed a volatile oxide which had the odor of radishes. Nitric acid oxidized selenium to a higher oxide, selenic acid. Selenium also combined with hydrogen; the compound had a peculiar poisoning effect. Berzelius wrote:

> . . . In my first attempt to find the odor of this gas, one gas bubble, perhaps not greater than a pea, came into one of my nostrils. Thereupon I had so completely lost the sense of smell that I could hold the strongest ammonia under my nose without the slightest sensation. The sense of smell returned after five or six hours, but with a strong and wearisome head cold which lasted two weeks. (9)

Andreas Manuel del Rio (1764–1849, Mexico) found (1801) in a lead ore a substance which turned red on heating. He called it *erythronium,* although he was not quite certain that it was not chromium. Friedrich Wöhler described the extraordinary reactions of the substance and wrote to his friend Berzelius: "What kind of a substance can it be which, on admixture, causes that potassium chromate is colorless and dissolves in water without color? But immediately becomes yellow with acids." (10) Nils Gabriel Sefström (1787–1845, Stockholm) separated one-tenth of a gram of this substance out of eighteen and a half pounds of a Swedish iron ore and characterized the new element, *vanadium,* by chemical reactions in Berzelius' laboratory (1830). (11)

In 1803, Smithson Tennant (1761–1815, Cambridge) found indications that two new metals accompanied platinum in its ores. One of them became the first element named for the odor of its compounds, *osmium,* from the Greek for scent or odor. The other one received the name *iridium* because its chlorides have impressively varying colors. In independent work, Vauquelin and Fourcroy confirmed that osmium and iridium are elements.

In 1817, Johann Afzelius, also called Arfvedson (1753–1837, Upsala), analyzed a rare Swedish mineral, petalite. By decomposition with sulfuric acid, he obtained a soluble sulfate that could have been the sodium salt, except that the calculated analysis was too high; therefore, the base in this sulfate must have a lower atomic weight than sodium. This was the first sign that a new alkali was present, and since the solubilities of its salts showed characteristic values, Berzelius recognized the discovery and proposed the name lithia for the alkali and lithion (later lithium) for its metallic element that was isolated a few years later.

Leopold Gmelin (1788–1853, Heidelberg) listed 48 elements in the first edition of his *"Handbuch,"* 1817, and 55 elements in the fourth edition, 1843. These numbers are not quite correct, they include two or three spurious discoveries that had only a short life.

REFERENCES

1. H. G. Söderbaum, *Berzelius' Werden und Wachsen* (Leipzig: 1899). *Bibliographie de J. J. Berzelius,* edited by Arne Holmberg for the Royal Academy of Science of Sweden (1933–36).

2. H. G. Söderbaum in the *Lippmann Festschrift* (Berlin: Julius Springer, 1927), p. 177.

3. *Briefwechsel zwischen J. Berzelius und F. Wöhler,* O. Wallach, Ed. (Leipzig: Wilhelm Engelmann, 1901), Vol. 1, p. 244 (letter of May 3, 1831).

4. Robert Siegfried, "The phlogistonic conjectures of Humphry Davy," *Chymia,* **9** (1964), pp. 117–24.

5. R. J. Haüy, *Ann. Chim.,* **12** (1792), p. 3.

6. R. J. Haüy, *Traité de Minéralogie* (Paris: 1801), Vol. 1, p. xxxi.

7. E. Mitscherlich ("On the relation between the chemical composition and the crystal form of salts of arsenic and phosphoric acids,"), Kongliga Svenska Vetenskaps-Academiens Handligar 1822, pp. 4–79; reprinted in *Gesammelte Schriften von Eilhard Mitscherlich, Lebensbild, Briefwechsel, und Abhandlungen* (Berlin: 1896); partially, in H. M. Leicester and H. S. Klickstein, *Source Book in Chemistry, 1400–1900* (New York: 1952), pp. 306–8.

8. Thomas Thomson, *An Attempt to Establish the First Principles of Chemistry by Experiment* (London: Baldwin, Craddock & Joy, 1825), Vol. 1, p. 16.

9. J. J. Berzelius, *Lehrbuch der Chemie* (Dresden: 1826), Vol. 2, Part 1, p. 19.

10. Letter of January 18, 1829. See *Briefwechsel zwischen J. Berzelius und F. Wöhler,* O. Wallach, Ed. (Leipzig: 1901), Vol. 1, p. 244.

11. For details see Mary Elvira Weeks and H. M. Leicester, "Discovery of the Elements" (Easton, Pa.: *Journal of Chemical Education,* 7th ed.). A. M. White and H. B. Friedman, "On the Discovery of Palladium," *J. Chem. Ed.,* **9** (1932), p. 236.

13

Foundations of Organic Chemistry

Chemical Substances from Organisms

Birth and death, growth and decay characterize organisms; mineral substances are stable and permanent. Living organisms need food and respiration in order to maintain themselves; after death they decompose. A peculiar force must be the active cause for the difference in behavior of living and dead organisms. Life is due to a "force of life," as G. F. Stahl explained. The analogy to his explanation, that combustibility is caused by a principle called phlogiston, can readily be seen. In details there is a difference between the force of life, which is purely a force, and phlogiston, which is on the borderline between force and substance.

Phlogiston made a hesitant exit from the scientific scene in Lavoisier's system. The concept of a force of life persisted much longer. For Berzelius it was the cause of a particular state of matter. According to him, its action explained why oxalic acid, although it is a lower degree of carbon oxidation than carbonic acid, is yet stronger than carbonic acid, against the rules that obtain in the inorganic realm. The force of life is superimposed upon the usual chemical forces; it particularly modifies the electrochemical conditions in organisms, and it produces organic forms, which are very different from those of minerals and crystals.

In the egg of an animal, as in the seed of a plant, there is a dormant force which becomes active during germination and growth. This is the force of life. In such words Justus Liebig (1) (1803, Darmstadt–1873, Munich) continued the old idea and connected it with new concepts. The chemical forces of cohesion and affinity in food substances, the relative position of elementary particles in these substances, are overcome by the force of life which causes them to fall apart and to recombine in a new order of arrangement. Liebig asserted that life loses nothing of its mystery through contemplations such as these. On the other hand, the concept of a force of life becomes less mysterious through comparison with chemical and mechanical forces. Here Liebig follows the thoughts of his friend Friedrich Mohr, which are direct anticipations of the law of the conservation of energy (page 245).

However, the need to find a place for the force of life within the system of energy proved to be fatal for this concept. No quantitative relationships to other energies were to be found, but the need for a scientific expression to describe the mystery of life still continued to be felt. By introducing psychic energy (Wilhelm Ostwald) or by reviving Aristotle's entelechy (Hans Driesch), modern counterparts for the force of life were created at the beginning of this century. The double meaning of force of life, either to reduce life to mere physics or to broaden a physical concept by the mystery of life, was thus dissolved into two extremes. Initially, however, this concept was fascinating because it could fluctuate between extremes.

A similar double meaning was originally combined in the expression "organic chemistry." It was conceived as the chemistry of organisms, and its system was that of the parts of organic beings—bones, nerves, muscles, gall bladder, etc. At the same time, those substances, such as sugars or oils, which could easily be separated from plants or animals, were separately described as chemical substances of a complex molecular structure. Fourcroy (1801) foresaw the time when chemistry would be able to build its own system without depending on the anatomy of organisms. The double meaning also explains the uncertainty concerning analogies between inorganic and organic chemistry. Berzelius, for example, at one time favored such analogies and at other times rejected them. The strict separation of plants and animals lost its chemical justification when M. E. Chevreul, in his work on fats (1811–1823), found the same principles and composition in both realms, or when Doebereiner, in 1822, discovered that formic acid can be obtained not only from the ant (Latin name *formica*) but also by decomposing tartaric acid from grape juice or grape seeds.

From the chemical point of view, all the organic substances have in common the fact that they include in their composition carbon, hydrogen, and frequently also oxygen and nitrogen. Could this not form the basis for a chemical definition for organic substances? Leopold Gmelin (1788–1853) a professor in Heidelberg, tentatively suggested this as a possibility in 1848, and F. A. Kekulé (1829–1896, Bonn) (page 191) stated it definitely in his *Lehrbuch* (1859): "We define organic chemistry as the chemistry of the compounds of carbon. We see here no contrast between organic and inorganic compounds."

Such general considerations did not always occupy first place in organic chemical work. The development of experimental methods and manual skills was at times much more important than relation to basic theories. Attention could be concentrated on a newly discovered substance as if it were an end product in itself. The personal satisfaction with separate new facts could be so great that it excluded all questions of systematic connections. Such situations did not last long. The use or the continued study of the new discovery would invariably point to the practical importance of the background from which it arose and to the new questions that it opened up. Two examples from the beginning of this period will demonstrate these relationships.

Wilhelm August Lampadius (1772–1842, Freiberg, Saxony) was a practical chemist. In his lectures on starch, or on sugar, beer, and wine he discussed the subject of chemistry in everyday life. In 1796 he tried to increase the yield of sulfur from pyrites. When he noticed that the direct heating of the mineral produced a certain quantity of sulfurous gas, he concluded that the addition of coal should bind the generator of acid, oxygen, and thus improve the yield of sulfur. The result was, instead, a liquid of penetrating odor which refracted light with such beautiful effects that he decided to carry this liquid with him in the glass knob of his walking stick. He was satisfied to have found an "alcohol sulfuris," alcohol of sulfur, but others inquired into the conditions for its formation. By combustion they determined its composition to be one equivalent of carbon with two of sulfur. In spite of its nauseating odor, its high solvent power was used for extracting oils from seeds, for recovering grease from wiping rags, and for vulcanizing rubber.

Michel Eugène Chevreul (1786, Angers –1889, Paris) published a book on the chemistry of fats in 1823. (2) This marked the end of a long development and the beginning of a new search. It was an old art to make soap by boiling fat with potash. Pharmacists extended this art by using lead oxide or zinc oxide to obtain plasters for medical applications. Scheele had the curiosity to investigate the water separated in these operations. He found that it contained a sweet-tasting "principle" which remained as a syrup when the water was evaporated. This observation did not change the usual manner of considering soap as consisting of the entire fat substance, combined with potash or other metal bases.

In 1811, when Chevreul was working in Vauquelin's laboratory, he was asked to analyze a sample of soap made from pig's fat. The observation that crystals could be obtained from solutions of this soap led to a plan for systematic investigation. Mineral acids decomposed the soap into salt and organic acid. This organic acid could be purified by crystallizing it out of its solution. A criterion for purity was established. If the melting point did not change after repeated recrystallizations, the substance was constant and pure. The method was extended to the fats obtained from many other animals. Scheele's "sweet principle" was found in the lyes of most fats, while exceptions were found in spermaceti and in bile. The place of Scheele's principle, which Chevreul called "glycerine" to describe its sweetness, was there taken by high-melting crystallizing substances. Chevreul's "ethal," from spermaceti, was later recognized as cetyl-alcohol. His designation "cholesterol" for the solid material from bile was a contraction of the Greek words for "bile" (*chole*) and "solid" (*stereos*); it remained in use even after its presence in many other organs and body fluids was discovered. The acids obtained from the various fats showed great differences in melting points. The highest melting, most solid acid received the name "stearic." The acid prevailing in butter fat was "butyric acid," that from the fat of the goat (Latin *capra*) was "capronic acid," with a lower melting companion, "caprinic acid."

Chevreul summarized the results of over ten years of this work as follows: The process of making soap, saponification, is a chemical fixation of water. In this process glycerine is formed by combining elements of the fat with elements from water. A fat is, therefore, comparable to a salt consisting of an anhydrous glycerine and an anhydrous fatty acid. In saponification, an inorganic salt-forming base replaced glycerine.

Many other substances received names derived from the Greek word for sweet. Glycinium (or glucinium) remained the name for the element from the mineral beryl until after 1921, when it was officially changed to beryllium. Glycocoll is the "sugar from gelatine" which Henri Braconnot obtained by treating with sulfuric acid. Glycogen is the sugar-generating substance investigated in 1857 by Claude Bernard (1813–1878, Paris).

Glycerine and fatty acids are the *principes immédiats*, the direct principles, which constitute the fats. The old philosophical principle of oiliness or fattiness as a substance is thus replaced by a principle of composition or chemical structure.

It was of great practical value to the soapmaker to know what he was doing, and it showed him how he could improve the selection of raw materials, the conditions of boiling, and the separation of the soap. The art of making candles was also stimulated to important progress. Henri Braconnot (1781–1855, Paris) received a patent in 1818 on his process for separating the oily part of tallow by pressing, and hardening it further by adding 20 percent of wax. Gay-Lussac and Chevreul patented the use of stearic acid for non-dripping candles. This became a commercial success after Adolphe de Milly had shown in 1831 that the cost of making stearic acid could be greatly reduced by using lime as the saponifying agent,

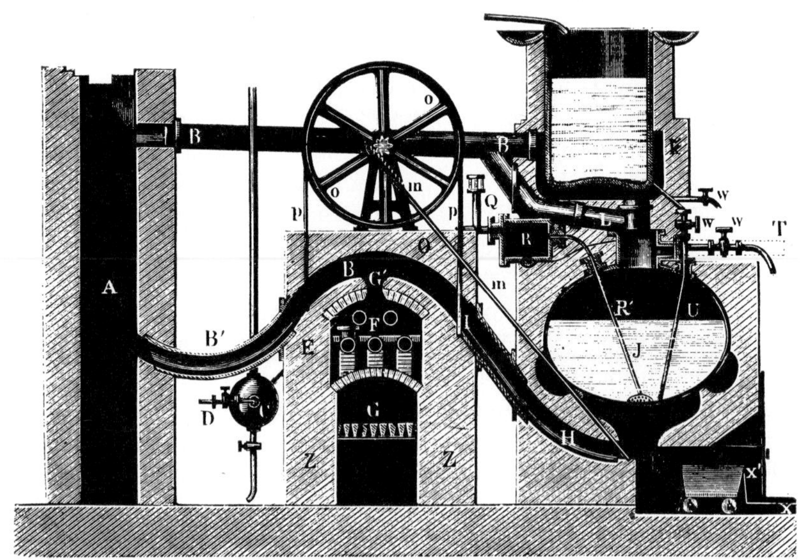

Fig. 21. Vertical section through apparatus for distilling fat with superheated steam, used at Neuilly, France. (From P. Bolley, *Handbuch der chemischen Technologie,* Vol. 1, Part 2, Friedrich Vieweg & Sohn, Braunschweig, 1862, p. 86.)

Steam enters at *D* (lower left) and passes through separator *C* for condensed water and tube *E* to *F*, arranged in the heating zone of oven *Z*. The steam continues through a tube to chamber *R* (which has a fitting *Q* connected with a valve) and thence through tube *R′* and the distributing head in kettle *J*.

This kettle contains the fat, which enters from *k*, preheated through tube *U*. The vapors leave the kettle through *T* to the condenser. The heating of the fat in *J* to 250°–300°C is regulated by moving rod *m*, which moves rods *p* and *p* through wheel *o*, sending the hot combustion gases through *H* or out through *B* to the stack *A*. Distillates of melting points of 40°–55°C are obtained. They are used for making candles.

and that an impregnation with ammonium borate improved the burning of the wick without the need for snubbing.

Chevreul later turned to physical-technical work on colors and philosophical studies on the history of chemistry. At the age of 102, he presented his last communication, on nitrogen in vegetal economy, to the Académie des Sciences.

Chevreul's book of 1823 had on its title page the words of Nicole Malebranche (1638–1715, Paris): *On doit tendre avec effort à l'infaillibilité sans y prétendre* (One must strive vigorously toward infallibility without claiming it). He was greatly interested in the principles of scientific research and devoted much study to it, particularly in his later years. He knew that a name for a new substance that pointed to its natural occurrence was not satisfactory from the chemical point of view. Its relations to other chemical substances, its place in the chemical system had to be found. He saw three steps in defining a chemical "species." The first is the determination of the elements; the second, their relative quantities; the third, and most difficult, the arrangement of the atoms in the molecule. The name glycerine refers to a physiological property, not to a place in the system of chemistry. When M. Berthelot in 1853 showed that one molecular weight of glycerine can combine with three equivalents of acetic acid, he concluded that it is a three-atomic or three-basic alcohol. This result had its foundation in work on spirit of wine and spirit of wood, in findings about phosphoric acid, in studies of the action of chlorine on the oil of bitter almonds, and many other widespread connections. Now it became possible to prove Chevreul's theory for the splitting of fat in saponification by reversing the process and synthesizing fats from glycerine and acids, and it was found that many more "fats" could be made artificially than had been found in nature.

Cholesterol melts at 137°C and can be heated to 350°C before it rises in vapor form and sublimes. With all these distinguishing properties, it has something in common with low-boiling, intoxicating alcohol. Through a small part of its molecule, cholesterol belongs to the family of the alcohols. It took more than one hundred years to find the family to which it belonged with the predominant part of its molecule.

Methods of Analysis

Analysis for the elementary composition of inorganic substances very frequently involved the reduction of an oxide into the element. For organic substances, analysis was based mainly on oxidation.

Lavoisier placed the weighted samples of the few organic substances that he analyzed under a glass jar inverted over mercury, filled it with oxygen, and started combustion by heating the substance in the sunlight, which he concentrated upon the substance by means of a burning glass. From the quantities of carbon dioxide and water formed in the reaction, he calculated the proportions of carbon and hydrogen in the substance. The method was improved by Gay-Lussac and Thenard. They mixed the substance with potassium chlorate and shaped the mixture into small pills; these were introduced into a combustion tube which was connected with a measuring cylinder. The gases collected in this cylinder had to be analyzed for the presence of carbon monoxide, which, if present, would indicate an incomplete combustion, because an incomplete combustion of the substance tested would lead to faulty calculations. Upon Gay-Lussac's suggestion, replacement of the chlorate by copper oxide as the oxygen source made analysis considerably safer. It enabled Chevreul to carry out a large number of elementary analyses in his work on fats. Liebig added (1831) a convenient glass apparatus for absorbing the carbon dioxide in a solution of potassium hydroxide.

For nitrogen-containing organic substances, Dumas developed a method (1833) in which copper oxide was used for combustion, and the gases thus produced passed over metallic copper for the reduction of any nitrogen oxides that might have been formed. Nitrogen could then be measured over a solution of potassium hydroxide. Another approach was the reduction of organic nitrogen to ammonia. Johann Kjeldahl (1849–1900, Copenhagen) found that heating with concentrated sulfuric acid and a catalyst converts the nitrogen of most organic substances into ammonium sulfate (1883). His method became the most widely used.

For the calculation of the elementary composition it was most important to know the relative atomic weight of carbon. This could be obtained indirectly by comparing the specific gravity of carbon dioxide with that of oxygen. According to Dulong, the proportion of these specific gravities was 138.218:100, i.e., 38.218 grams of carbon are combined with 100 grams of oxygen. The relative atomic weight would thus be 38.218, provided that the gas was composed of carbon and oxygen in the proportions of 1:1, as Gay-Lussac and Dumas thought. Berzelius preferred to consider it as being composed of one carbon and two oxygen, because this made it possible to assign the formula CO to the lower oxidation product of carbon, our carbon monoxide, and there were also analogies with the proportions of gas volumes in other compounds.

The relative atomic weight of carbon, or that weight of it which is combined with 200 oxygen in carbon dioxide, would thus be 76.436. However, when Mitscherlich analyzed naphthalene (1836), he obtained 94.34 percent of carbon and 6.26 percent of hydrogen, which added up to more than 100 percent. He simply distributed the excess over 100 percent without seeing more in it than an experimental error. Dumas was more disturbed about this excess, which he repeatedly found in calculating the percentage of C and H in naphthalene from the weights of CO_2 and H_2O obtained in its combustion. Dumas questioned the accuracy of 76.44 as the atomic weight of carbon used in this calculation. Jean Servais Stas (1813–1891, Brussels) was at that time in Paris to work under Dumas' guidance on a substance he had crystallized from extracts of the root bark of apple trees which he called *phloridzin* in allusion to the Greek words for *bark* and *root*. Together they determined the atomic weight of carbon by using diamond and graphite and found exactly 75 (for O = 100, i.e., 12 for O = 16). They pointed out (1840) that previous analyses appeared to be excellent, while actually carbon was lost through incomplete combustion, and the use of the faulty higher atomic weight figure just compensated the error. The new value for carbon confirmed their conviction that William Prout was correct in his hypothesis that all atomic weights should be integer multiples of that of hydrogen. This conviction was later shaken by new analytical work.

Liebig described the advance achieved by 1838 with the following comparison: "For the analysis of seven organic acids Berzelius needed 18 months, and Chevreul was occupied with the analysis of the solid substances he had discovered during 13 years. Using our present methods, Berzelius would have needed four weeks at the most, and Chevreul perhaps two years instead of 13." (3)

With elements that are normally in the form of gases it was relatively easy to measure the relationships in which the elements combine to form compounds. Substances that are liquids or solids at room temperature had to be heated to determine their density in gas form. The importance of doing this followed from the extension of Gay-Lussac's law: Equal volumes contain equal numbers of molecules and are in the relationship of their molecular weights. Dumas continued Gay-Lussac's work on vapor densities at high temperatures, and Hofmann added a more convenient method for easily volatilized substances. He weighed the substance, such as aniline, in a tiny stoppered flask and let it ascend through the mercury in a barometric tube that was heated if necessary. (4)

When Berthollet introduced chlorine as a textile-bleaching

agent, the need soon arose to determine how much chlorine was useful without attacking the fabric. Titrimetric methods of analysis thus began to be expanded towards the end of the eighteenth century. (5)

Chemical Reactions of Organic Substances

A considerable number of substances obtained from animals and plants were in common use at the end of the eighteenth century. Mechanical separation gave fats and oils, starch and gluten. Extraction by water, followed by purification and crystallization, produced sugar from sugar cane. Extraction and distillation concentrated the medically useful components of herbs. Fermentation converted starchy and sugary materials into alcohol. Reaction of alcohol with sulfuric acid led to ether. Oxidation of sugar with nitric acid converted it into oxalic acid. Other organic acids were obtained by the extraction of plants. Dyestuffs were made from leaves, wood, roots, insects, etc.

These substances were known as to origin and use. This was not enough. Commercial and technological requirements called for methods of determining identity and purity and for ways to improve manufacturing procedures. Such requirements could not be met by lucky guess and accidental discovery alone, important as these were. General rules and basic theories were necessary. Whether preconceived by intuition or derived from the interpretation of experiments, their main function was to point out analogies and connections, to move back and forth between the known and the hidden causes for chemical actions. Ultimately, theory had to lead to a basis that needs no further explanation and upon which, therefore, all explanations could be based. Such a basis was provided by the theory of elements and atoms. Since only a few of the elements occur in organic substances, the task of finding the atomic composition of their molecules was particularly in the foreground. This task was only partially solved by elementary analyses. They gave the proportions of the weights of the elements, but not the proportions of their atoms. Assumptions based on analogies had to be added in order to connect the separate analytical results with the theoretical basis.

Even with this addition, however, the explanations were found to be incomplete. This became dramatically evident in 1824, when Gay-Lussac and Liebig in Paris published their analysis of the silver salt of fulminating acid. They soon discovered that only the year before, Wöhler, in Berzelius's laboratory in Stockholm, had found the same composition for his silver salt of cyanic acid. The proportions of silver, carbon, nitrogen, and oxygen in these salts were exactly the same, yet their properties were entirely different. In the following year Faraday reported a similar relationship between the olefiant gas of the four Dutch chemists and a substance which he called "carburet of hydrogen" (*butylene*). He had found this substance in the liquid formed in containers in which gases from distilled fatty oils had been compressed. The reaction of naphthalene with sulfuric acid gave, again according to Faraday, two sulfur-containing acids of different solubilities but with exactly the same composition. When Wöhler treated silver cyanate with ammonium chloride, or lead cyanate with ammonia, he obtained urea (1828). This was remarkable because it was the first time that urea had been made artificially, "without kidneys or any animal at all," as Wöhler wrote. It was at least equally surprising that despite their different chemical reactions, urea and ammonium cyanate were composed of the same elements in the same number of atoms. So far as elementary proportions were concerned, the two substances were identical in chemical composition.

A similar case was observed in 1826 after Gay-Lussac visited a manufacturer of tartaric acid in the Alsatian town of Thann. Solutions of tartaric acid were made there by decomposing the wine lees and concentrating the solution until crystallization of the acid occurred. During the heating of the solution, a precipitate separated out which was thought to be oxalic acid. Elementary analysis showed, however, that its composition was the same as that of tartaric acid, although the solubility of the acid itself was lower and that of its acidic potassium salt higher than known for real tartaric acid. Gay-Lussac called the new product "racemic acid" to indicate its origin from the grape (Latin *racemus*).

When Berzelius repeated the analysis of tartaric and racemic acids and confirmed the previous results, he realized their general meaning. "We shall, therefore, have to study an entirely new field of chemistry, heteromorphous compounds of substances which have the same elements in the same atomic numbers, but which are differently connected with each other." (6) In order to have a handy designation for such substances, he called them "isomeric."

This idea, that the different "mode" in which the atoms are combined with one another could produce different substances having the same number of atoms, was not new. However, what the expression "mode" could mean remained indefinite. At that time

(1830), Berzelius did not discuss it further. The new rule which was implied here, and which Dumas formulated a little later (1832), was that not only the proportions of the elements were constant but also that the arrangement was a definite one in each substance. The thought that carbon, which is found in allotropic modifications in nature as diamond and as graphite, might also occur as different allotropic carbon atoms was published by Berzelius in 1834 but not pursued further.

Analogy to inorganic compounds helped in the task of finding out more about the arrangement of atoms in organic substances. Inorganic compounds were dualistic, or binaric, in chemical structure. Salts were composed of a base and an acid, and these in turn were built from an element and oxygen, or in the case of some acids, of an element and hydrogen. When Gay-Lussac (1815) determined the composition of alcohol by combustion, and compared the result with the laws he had found for chemical combinations of certain gases, he concluded that

1 volume olefiant gas (ethylene) + 1 volume water vapor
= 1 volume alcohol

If this result had had to stand alone, it might have appeared doubtful, but it was confirmed by the explanation for ether, which corresponded to the formula

2 volumes of olefiant gas + 1 volume of water vapor = ether

or

$$2C_2H_4 + H_2O = (C_2H_5)_2O$$

The volatile "salt ether," prepared by heating alcohol with salt (sodium chloride) and sulfuric acid, was found to be C_2H_5Cl. This could be dissolved according to Gay-Lussac's theory into C_2H_4 + HCl. Dumas and Polydore Boullay (1806–1835) saw here a complete analogy between ethylene (which they called *etherin*) and ammonia:

Etherin	C_2H_4	Ammonia	NH_3
Salt ether	$C_2H_4 + HCl$	Salt ammonia	$NH_3 + HCl$
Ether	$2C_2H_4 + H_2O$	Ammonium oxide	$2NH_3 + H_2O$
Alcohol	$2C_2H_4 + 2H_2O$		
Acetic ether	$2C_2H_4 + C_2H_3O + H_2O$	Ammonium acetate	$2NH_3 + C_2H_3O + H_2O$
Oxalic ether	$2C_2H_4 + C_2O_3 + H_2O$	Ammonium oxalate	$2NH_3 + C_2O_3 + H_2O$

They included the ethers (later called "esters") of alcohol with acetic acid and with oxalic acid. Etherin thus appeared as a "powerful alkali." (7)

A group of atoms that held together through all these chemical changes, as if it were an "organic element," was called a "radical." However, the separate existence of the water in the molecule of alcohol was not proved. Liebig pointed out that calcium oxide should react with the water supposedly present in alcohol to liberate the radical. This was not a strong argument if the radical could be considered as being itself a "powerful alkali" which might hold the water more strongly than lime.

Experience with these etherin derivatives suggested that "all" other organic substances likewise had a radical structure. Liebig proved it for a series of compounds which he prepared from the oil of bitter almonds (Latin *amygdalae amarae*). These almonds contain a substance, *amygdalin*, which after digestion with water and distillation produces an oil of agreeable odor and considerable chemical activity. Pierre Jean Robiquet (1780–1840, Paris) treated it with caustic potash and thereby converted it into a crystalline mass. The elementary analysis (1832) of this product, called *benzoine*, was the same as that of the original oil, according to Liebig and Wöhler. In the pure oil itself, when treated with chlorine, oxygen, or ammonia, a substantial part of the molecule remained intact. Liebig and Wöhler designated this constant part by the name "benzoyl" and expressed the composition of this radical as 14C + 10H + 2O (or C_7H_5O, using the atomic weights of carbon = 12, H = 1.0, and O = 16). The oil was the hydride of benzoyl, and only the hydrogen part of the molecule changed in all these transformations.

To consider an oxide like benzoyl as a radical contradicted all analogies with inorganic substances. The theory of dualism between most elements and oxygen required the separation of the "organic element" C_7H_5 from O. The division of the atoms in the molecule of alcohol and ether should be changed in accordance with the new model. The radical should be C_2H_5, alcohol being its oxide and ether being $2C_2H_5 + O$. Dumas' analogy with the ammonia group could still remain valid, with the modification that there the radical is not NH_3 but NH_4, the more so since it is NH_4 that behaves like an element in forming amalgams (Berzelius, 1834).

Though in Liebig's opinion benzoic acid was the oxide of benzoyl hydride, Mitscherlich showed that the molecule could be divided in a different way. Benzoic acid can be obtained from the resins of some East Indian trees (*Styrax*, *Xanthorrea*). When it is heated with much lime, an oil distills which Mitscherlich showed to have the same elementary composition as Faraday's bicarburet of hydrogen (1825) from compressed illuminating gas. Mitscherlich called it *benzene.* One volume of it consists of three (actually six) equal volumes of C and H, and in benzoic acid one volume of CO_2 is added to this molecule. The C_7H_5 radical of Liebig was here replaced by a radical of only six C, and the seventh C was removed into the variable part of the molecule because it was split off by the heating with lime.

Such experimental results demonstrated that the rigidity of the radical concept had to be modified. Berzelius pointed to an example from inorganic chemistry. Manganese forms an oxyd-oxydul which can be separated either into $MnO + Mn_2O_3$ or into $2MnO + MnO_2$, depending on whether the nitric acid used for the separation is dilute or concentrated. It is similarly true that ether can be $C_4H_{10} + O$, or $C_4H_8 + H_2O$. "Now if we take Mitscherlich's and the usual theories of the composition of benzoic acid instead of the example just used, it is clear that in benzoic acid there is neither benzene, nor benzyle, nor a combustible composite radical separate from the rest of the compound; instead, the fractions into which the substance falls apart depend entirely upon the circumstances under which it is decomposed. One must know into which parts it can be decomposed, but it is not correct to say that it is put together from these parts." (8) Liebig expressed the hope that the idea of unchangeable radicals would be abandoned in organic chemistry (1835). Dumas was quite willing to give to "each group its special theory," but he disagreed with Berzelius on the dualistic theory and with Liebig on the role of hydrated hydrocarbons; both men seemed to him as antiquated in their views as those who persisted in assuming that ammonia contained oxygen or potassium hydrogen.

Liebig visited Dumas in Paris in 1837 to discuss the differences of their opinions and to arrive at their scientific solution. These two men had much in common. They were of nearly the same age—Liebig was born on May 12, 1803, at Darmstadt, Dumas on July 16, 1800, at Alais, France. Both had begun their chemical careers in pharmacies; the same human genius, Alexander von Humboldt, had furthered their advance in life; and both underwent systematic university training for chemists. Like Berzelius, Gay-Lussac, and Davy, they had published important works before the age of thirty, although Liebig's career had been more explosive. For him the visit to Paris was a return to the city that had been a political refuge for him in 1822. He started in Vauquelin's laboratory, but it was Gay-Lussac's guidance that helped him to correct his early mistakes. Upon his return to his native land, Liebig was made a professor in Giessen in 1824. The success of the 21-year-old teacher was almost immediate. Perhaps this was not entirely to his personal advantage. He soon developed a strong conviction that his opinions coincided with absolute scientific truth. By thus identifying himself with objective science, he attacked those who differed from him on specific problems as personal foes of science. His violence even shocked his friends, who tried in vain to reason with him. He in turn complained bitterly that his outspoken hatred of "lies and fraud in science" had been interpreted as personal arrogance and vanity. He was similarly violent in attacking the indolence of the governments in Prussia and Austria with regard to chemical education. In his ardor he often committed grave mistakes, but a cautious assertion of the limits of scientific insight never has a general appeal, never stirs the indolent into action. His strength of personal conviction and his courage were necessary to influence the authorities. One of his most dramatic successes was the interest he aroused in England. The Prince Consort founded a College of Chemistry, and Liebig's former student, A. W. Hofmann, was invited to direct it (1845).

Liebig had a strong belief in the law of the conservation of matter, with a premonition of the other law of conservation, that of energy, which began to be recognized in the 1840's. This was the basis on which he built his theory of agriculture and of the importance of mineral plant nutrients. The old theory maintained that organic humus is the important sustainer of plant life. Liebig emphasized that we remove minerals with the plant crops and that these minerals must be restored to the soil. Because the new theory was right, the old theory had to be absolutely wrong. Actually, Humphry Davy had applied chemistry to agriculture, and years before Liebig, Karl Sprengel (1787–1857) and Johann Philipp Bronner (1792–1864) had shown that substances found in plant ashes were to be added to the soil to make for fertility. Furthermore, he overlooked, and later on never realized, the importance of nitrogen for plants and animals. With all these errors and omissions, it was Liebig more than anyone else who initiated the rise of a new industry of fertilizer manufacture. He laid the foundation for the chemical part of the great task of increasing crop yields needed for the growing populations.

After declining a call to the University of Vienna for political reasons ("they have no constitution" in Austria), he went to Munich in 1852. The conditions under which this great organizer of chemical education accepted the call was that he should be free from teaching. The university was too small for the scope in which he wanted to propagate chemistry. He gave general lectures for members of the highest society. With his *Chemische Briefe* (1858) he reached a vast audience. As usual in such cases, there was a definite correlation between the range of the general conclusions and the extent of attention he found for them. He was capable of strong statements which simplified all problems, as when he discovered, through long preparation for an important public address, "that the progress of mankind was due exclusively to the progress of natural sciences, not to morals, religion, or philosophy." (9) Liebig died on April 18, 1873. Adolf Baeyer succeeded him in 1875 and was surprised to find the laboratory in very poor condition.

Dumas and Liebig were equally interested in the application of chemistry to plants and animals. Dumas' lectures on the chemistry of organisms appeared at about the same time (1843) as Liebig's books on agriculture (1840) and the chemistry of animals (1842). Dumas applied his chemical knowledge to tasks of a political nature as Minister for Commerce and Agriculture and as president of the city council of Paris. He died on April 11, 1884.

The relationship between Liebig and Friedrich Wöhler (1800–1882) developed from a scientific dispute into a deep and lifelong friendship. At the chemical start of it was cyan, the gas of which Liebig wrote: "Of all discoveries, the discovery of cyan and its chemical nature by Gay-Lussac has had the richest consequences for organic chemistry." (10) The analytical figures for cyanic acid had been disputed in 1824. Amygdalin, which they investigated together, 1831–1832, contains a compound of hydrocyanic acid. In 1836, Wöhler gently distilled cyanuric acid into a receiver kept at −12°C and obtained an oil of very pungent odor; a drop of it caused painful blisters on the skin while the oil changed into white crystals. (11) Since cyanuric acid is a distillation product of uric acid, the new experiments pointed to a possible way of solving the chemical riddle presented by uric acid. In their joint investigation Liebig and Wöhler discovered so many new substances that they needed a scheme to represent their relationships. They postulated a nonexistent uridylic acid as an analogue of oxalic acid:

$$\text{Uridylic acid} = C_2O_2 + CN \qquad \text{Oxalic acid} = C_2O_2 + O \quad (12)$$

Wöhler first prepared metallic aluminum by treating the chloride with potassium amalgam in 1827 and obtained several grams of aluminum in 1845. As professor in Göttingen (1836), he was also active on technical problems; he guided the production of nickel and proposed that this metal should be used in coins. He prepared a compound of carbon and calcium which reacted strongly with water to give hydrated lime and the gas acetylene, discovered by Edmond Davy (1785–1857) in 1836. (13) The behavior of a similar compound of silicon with calcium led him to the conclusion that there might be a system of compounds derived from silicon similar to the system of carbon compounds (14).

Physical Properties and Chemical Constitution

The agreement that Dumas and Liebig reached in 1837 concerning the theory of radicals did not last. It was completely shattered by the new theory that Dumas developed for explaining extended experiments on the reactions between organic substances and chlorine. This was a continuation of earlier work. Faraday had been investigating such reactions ever since 1821. Liebig himself had found that benzoyl hydride forms benzoyl chloride with chlorine. The further studies of the chlorination reactions developed a fundamental difference in general concepts. This difference may be characterized as one between mechanism and chemism. Dumas and Laurent were inclined toward mechanism, Berzelius and Liebig preferred chemism.

The reaction of chlorine with alcohol gave a new substance which Liebig named "chloral" to indicate its origin from *chlor*ine and *al*cohol. A gentle treatment of chloral with caustic potash yielded chloroform, and when this reacted further with alkali it was converted into formic acid.

Chlorine can be readily introduced into the molecules of benzene, naphthalene, and even acetic acid. In all these reactions, chlorine takes the place of hydrogen, one atom of chlorine substitutes for one atom of hydrogen. For Dumas this was a simple statement of fact; his former student, Auguste Laurent (1807–1853), saw in it the effort of the molecular structure to maintain itself. Thus Dumas interpreted these experiences as revealing a law of substitution, while Laurent concluded that organic substances maintain a relatively stable nucleus. In any case, the role of hydrogen in an organic molecule could be taken over by chlorine and no great change occurred.

In his first publication on the reaction between naphthalene and chlorine (1833), Laurent had pointed out that part of the chlorine is converted into hydrochloric acid. (15) Two years later, he gave a general rule formulated by Dumas and added one of his own:

> 1. Every time that chlorine, bromine or oxygen, or nitric acid exert a dehydrogenating action on a hydrocarbon, the hydrogen that is removed is replaced by an equivalent of chlorine, bromine, or oxygen.
>
> 2. At the same time, hydrochloric, hydrobromic acid, water, or nitrous acid are formed, and they are either evolved or they remain combined with the new radical formed. (16)

Many difficulties would have been avoided if the second law had not been completely ignored. The attention was fixed on the substitution in the organic substance.

To Berzelius and Liebig this was close to nonsense. Hydrogen and chlorine are opposites in chemical nature, therefore the first could not be simply exchanged for the second. Dumas' theory would mean the destruction of the entire chemical system. Dumas argued that this structure was based on a dualistic concept which separated elements into polar opposites. The new experiments, however, showed that this was wrong. "Berzelius ascribes to the nature of the elements the role which I give to their arrangement; this is the main point in our respective opinions. The influence of the *nature* of the molecules has been defined so well by Lavoisier, the influence of their *weight* has been characterized by the immortal work of Berzelius. It can be said that the discoveries of Mitscherlich [isomorphism] relate to the influence of *form*, and the future will show whether the present researches of the French chemists are destined to give us the key to the role which is played by their arrangement." (17)

The future, which would bring an insight into the arrangement of the atoms, that is, their relative position to each other in the molecule, seemed too remote to Charles Gerhardt (1816–1856). According to him, we have to be satisfied with the empirical formulae that we can establish by experiments (1843). This retreat from theory to empiricism recalls an earlier resignation with regard to atomic weights (page 153). In both cases the way to a unifying theory was found somewhat later. For the following few years, however, the achievements of organic chemists consisted in establishing types and groups of atoms, not their arrangement in the molecule.

One of these groups united a number of substances which share with alcohol the property of containing oxygen and reacting with acids so as to form water and esters. Wood spirit, one of the substances obtained in the dry distillation of wood and formerly, even by Liebig, considered identical with *the* alcohol from fermentation, was shown by Dumas and Eugène Melchior Péligot in 1834 to correspond to the formula CH_4O. It was derived from methyl, while common alcohol is related to ethyl. They also found an alcohol of higher carbon content in fusel oil and called it "amyl alcohol."

Organic acids were arranged by Dumas in a similar and even more extended series. A common link was thus formed between Chevreul's solid margarinic acid, $C_{17}H_{34}O_2$, and the highly volatile formic acid, CH_2O_2. From these formulas the existence of fifteen similar acids between $C_{17}H_{34}O_2$ and CH_2O_2 could be foreseen. Seven of them were known in 1843.

Gerhardt generalized this experience into the rule that for all organic acids such serialization could be found. Compounds of equal nature, like alcohols or acids, were homologous when they differed by one or more CH_2 groups. Substances of different nature, such as ethane, alcohol, and acetic acid, derived from the same place in a homologous series, were "heterologous."

Chemistry had formerly distinguished substances by the properties directly observed by the senses; now it penetrated to the unity underlying the physical differences of odor, specific gravity, melting and boiling point, etc. Dumas suggested a program of studying all the physical properties, including optical refraction, in order to find the rules connecting the chemistry and the physics of the molecules. A correspondence between the establishment of homologous series and the amounts in which physical properties vary was to be found. Hermann Kopp (1817–1892, Heidelberg) determined the boiling points of homologous compounds (1842) and reported that the increase by one CH_2 group raised the boiling point "always" by 19°C. Continued investigation showed (1855), however, that this was an oversimplification; there are homologous series in which the intervals are smaller or greater.

The theory of chemical homology had its counterpart in biology. Richard Owen (1804–1892, London) established the term "homologue" for "the same organ in different animals under every variety of form and function." (18) Chemistry and biology had similar developments in other theories, for example, the theory of types, which Georges Cuvier (1769–1832, Paris) proposed for animals (19) at about the time when it was conceived for organic compounds.

Types of Organic Substances

Groups of substances are united by some particular chemical behavior, although they may differ as to other properties. When

Liebig investigated an oxidation product of alcohol for which Doebereiner had observed a characteristic yellow coloration with caustic alkali, he named it *al*cohol *dehyd*rogenatus, "aldehyde" for short. It soon developed that this was only one member of a group of aldehydes. The oil of bitter almonds belongs to it and is, therefore, benzaldehyde. Acetone, a product separated by careful redistillation of wood spirits or by distillation of calcium acetate, was considered an aldehyde in which one hydrogen was substituted by a methyl group. When it was found that similar substances can be made by distilling the calcium or lead salts of other organic acids, Leopold Gmelin suggested the name *ketone* "for acetones in general" (1848).

A group of vegetable alkalies began to be constituted in 1817. It was a great surprise at that time that plant substances should not be neutral or acidic but alkaline. The young pharmacist Friedrich Wilhelm Sertürner (1783–1841), who found an alkaline crystallizing substance in extracts of opium in 1805, was not yet certain that the alkalinity was not due to the caustic reagents used in the preparation of this substance. He later proved it beyond doubt to be a property of what he called "morphium." Gay-Lussac recognized the value of this discovery and induced his associates to search for more of these highly poisonous alkaline plant products or alkaloids. They found that many of the medically used plants contained alkaloids, and in a few years more than a dozen such new substances were isolated. They were found to be strong medicines, and their alkalinity was directly traceable to a content of nitrogen.

Different kinds of alkaline organic substances were discovered in coal tar by Friedlieb Ferdinand Runge (1795–1867, Berlin). He digested the tar with water solutions of acids; when the solution was afterwards neutralized, an oil separated out. By distillation, this oil was divided into three parts: kyanol, pyrrol, and leukol. Another part of the tar was dissolved by caustic soda solutions. By adding mineral acids to the oil separated from these solutions, an acidic carbon-oil which received the name "carb-olic acid" (1834) resulted. This name has persisted in common usage; its scientific counterpart, however, had a more complex history. Laurent saw it as "a hydrate of benzene, or a spirit of tar, analogous with the spirit of wood and the spirit of wine." He preferred the name "phene" for benzene in order to indicate by a derivation of the Greek word for "giving light" that benzene was present in illuminating gas. Runge's carbolic acid thus became "phenic acid." Gerhardt changed this to "phenol" because he wanted to designate an analogy to anisol. Phenol is obtained by heating salicylic acid with lime, anisol by an analogous operation with anisic acid.

In 1826 an alkaline oil which combines with sulfuric acid and forms beautiful crystals was found by Otto Unverdorben (1806–1873, Potsdam) in the distillate from indigo. He called it "kristallin." Heating indigo with caustic potash, Carl Julius Fritzsche in 1840 obtained a liquid to which he gave the name "anilin," because indigo was called *anil* in Spain. Anilin is identical with kristallin and kyanol, and it is the same substance that Nicolaus Zinin (1812–1889, Kasan, Russia) prepared by converting benzene into nitrobenzene and reducing it. This identification was obtained by August Wilhelm Hofmann (1818, Giessen –1892, Berlin) in Liebig's Laboratory in 1843. (20)

Phenol, $C_6H_5O{\cdot}H_2O$ = carbolic acid, had found a companion in phenamide, $C_6H_5{\cdot}NH_2$ = aniline. The corresponding amides of methyl and ethyl are gases which Adolphe Wurtz (1817, Strassburg –1884, Paris) prepared from methyl and ethyl esters of cyanic acid. The alkaline function of these substances was so prominent that they were considered to be like ammonia, in which hydrogen was substituted by organic radicals. Their typical function is that of ammonia, $\left.\begin{matrix}H\\H\\H\end{matrix}\right\}N$. Gradual replacement of its three hydrogen atoms leads to $\left.\begin{matrix}H\\H\\X\end{matrix}\right\}N$, amides; (primary amines) $\left.\begin{matrix}H\\X\\Y\end{matrix}\right\}N$, imide and bases (secondary amines) $\left.\begin{matrix}X\\Y\\Z\end{matrix}\right\}N$, nitrile bases (tertiary amines)

Triethyl amine reacts with ethyl iodide and forms a fourth member of this group by addition to an iodide, in which tetraethyl amine behaves "like an organic metal." (21) When the corresponding free base is heated, ethylene is split off (besides water):

$$\left.\begin{matrix}C_4H_5\\C_4H_5\\C_4H_5\\C_4H_5\end{matrix}\right\}NO,HO = \left.\begin{matrix}C_4H_5\\C_4H_5\\C_4H_5\end{matrix}\right\}N + C_4H_4 + 2HO$$

(with C = 6 and O = 8). "It is clear," said Hofmann, "ethyl amine, diethyl amine, and triethyl amine are composite ammonias, whereas the tetraethylated base represents a composite ammonium compound." (22)

The names first proposed by Hofmann—amide, imide, nitrile—were later redefined and differently applied. The change started from the work of Hugo Schiff (1834–1915) on "basic substances from aldehydes and ammonia." (23)

Atomicity, Combining Number, or Valency

Since 1810, when Berzelius obtained an ammonium amalgam by electrolysis (page 139), ammonium had been considered as the analogue of an alkali metal. The relationship had even been reversed; ammonium, NH_4, became the model that required the presence of hydrogen in the alkali metals. The relationship to ammonia, NH_3, which became a metal through the addition of hydrogen, recurs in the cited words by Hofmann. The partial decomposition showed that the fourth ethyl radical was directly bound to the nitrogen, like the other three; otherwise, not ethylene but ethyl alcohol would have been formed. Besides this result in favor of the radical theory, the reaction also confirmed that the nitrogen in the ammonium compounds binds five radicals or atoms; the nitrogen in ammonia, only three.

In this respect, nitrogen was like several other elements. Robert Bunsen had established that similarity during his work on organic arsenic compounds (1839–41). Edward Frankland (1825 Churchtown, England–1899 Golaa, Norway) brought additional elements into this comparison.

In Leipzig, at the suggestion of his teacher, Hermann Kolbe (1818–1884), Frankland investigated the problem of whether radicals can exist by themselves without being connected with any other element or radical. Can methyl be obtained free of the chlorine in methyl chloride, or ethyl from the cyan in ethyl cyanide? Can the halogen be transferred to a metal? Frankland tried potassium, but since it gave a very strong reaction, he turned to zinc. He obtained very reactive products; they caught fire in contact with air, but they were not the free radicals; they were the metal compounds zinc methyl and zinc ethyl. Similar work was soon extended in several laboratories to organic compounds with tin, antimony, mercury, and magnesium.

In a survey, "read June 17, 1852," Frankland brought the new experiences together with "the formulae of inorganic compounds."

> . . . The compounds of nitrogen, phosphorus, antimony and arsenic especially exhibit the tendency of these elements to form compounds containing 3 or 5 equivs. of other elements, and it is in these proportions that their affinities are best satisfied . . . it is sufficiently evident . . . that such a tendency or law prevails, and that, no matter

what the characters of the uniting atoms may be, the combining power of the attracting element, if I may be allowed the term, is always satisfied by the same number of these atoms. (24)

With the assistance of Baldwin Francis Duppa (1828–1873), Frankland converted ethyl borate ("boracic ether") into boron triethyl ("boric ethide") by reaction with zinc ethyl:

$$\underbrace{2B\begin{cases}C_4H_5O_2\\C_4H_5O_2\\C_4H_5O_2\end{cases}}_{\text{Boracic ether}} + \underbrace{3Zn_2\begin{cases}C_4H_5\\C_4H_5\end{cases}}_{\text{Zincethyl}} = \underbrace{2B\begin{cases}C_4H_5\\C_4H_5\\C_4H_5\end{cases}}_{\text{Boric ethide}} + \underbrace{6\left.\begin{matrix}C_4H_5\\Zn\end{matrix}\right\}O_2}_{\text{Ethylate of zinc}}$$

In 1862, Frankland wrote:

Another but less probable view of the change presents itself in the supposition that the three atoms of ethyl in boric ethide were already present in the boracic ether, the action of the zincethyl being simply to remove the whole of the oxygen from the boracic ether. Kekulé [*Lehrbuch der organischen Chemie*, p. 489] has in fact adopted this latter view of the reaction.

So long as the organic radical of the zinc compound and that of the boracic ether are identical, it is impossible to prove whether the three individual atoms of ethyl in boric ethide were originally present in the boracic ether, or have been derived from the zinc-ethyl. Indicating by an asterisk the atoms of ethyl which finally become part of the boric ethide, it is impossible to prove conclusively whether the reaction takes place according to the first or second of the following equations:—

1. $$2B\begin{cases}C_4H_5O_2\\C_4H_5O_2\\C_4H_5O_2\end{cases} + 3Zn_2\begin{cases}C_4H_5{}^*\\C_4H_5{}^*\end{cases} = 2B\begin{cases}C_4H_5{}^*\\C_4H_5{}^*\\C_4H_5{}^*\end{cases} + 6\left.\begin{matrix}C_4H_5\\Zn\end{matrix}\right\}O_2$$

2. $$2B\begin{cases}C_4H_5{}^*O_2\\C_4H_5{}^*O_2\\C_4H_5{}^*O_2\end{cases} + 3Zn_2\begin{cases}C_4H_5\\C_4H_5\end{cases} = 2B\begin{cases}C_4H_5{}^*\\C_4H_5{}^*\\C_4H_5{}^*\end{cases} + 6\left.\begin{matrix}C_4H_5\\Zn\end{matrix}\right\}O_2$$

Although we cannot thus label, as it were, the atoms taking part in the reaction, we can unerringly trace the movements of the alcohol radicals, if we secure their identification by varying their composition in the two compounds used in the process. The study of the action of zincmethyl upon boracic ether would obviously decide between these views. If boric ethide were produced from these materials, Kekulé's hypothesis would be established; but if, on the other hand, boric methide were the result of the reaction, then the correctness of the view originally taken by Mr. Duppa and myself would be proved to be correct. (25)

The experiment was difficult, but by means of the ammonia compound boric methide was isolated.

In the meantime, another series of studies had been concerned with the relationship between alcohol and ether.

Alexander Williamson (1824–1904), who had studied under Liebig and had later (1849) become professor of analytical chemistry in London, tried to introduce "carburetted hydrogen" for hydrogen into alcohol. The result should be a new alcohol. He replaced hydrogen in alcohol first by potassium and brought the potassium alcoholate into reaction with the iodide of ethyl. Instead of the expected alcohol, he obtained ether. "Thus" said Williamson, "alcohol is $\left.\begin{matrix} C_2H_5 \\ H \end{matrix}\right\rangle O$, and the potassium compound is $\left.\begin{matrix} C_2H_5 \\ K \end{matrix}\right\rangle O$; and by acting upon this by iodide of ethyl, we have

$$\begin{matrix} C_2H_5 \\ K \end{matrix} O + C_2H_5I = IK + \begin{matrix} C_2H_5 \\ C_2H_5 \end{matrix} O$$

Alcohol is therefore water in which half the hydrogen is replaced by carburetted hydrogen, and ether is water in which both atoms of hydrogen are replaced by carburetted hydrogen. Thus

$$\begin{matrix} H \\ H \end{matrix} O; \quad \begin{matrix} C_2H_5 \\ H \end{matrix} O; \quad \begin{matrix} C_2H_5 \\ C_2H_5 \end{matrix} O\text{''} \qquad (26)$$

Williamson confirmed this interpretation by reacting ethyl compounds with methyl compounds and producing an ethyl-methyl-ether $\begin{matrix} C_2H_5 \\ CH_3 \end{matrix} O$. The comparison with water seemed to him generally useful for finding the "rational constitution" of organic substances. He wrote:

> I believe that throughout inorganic chemistry, and for the best known organic compounds, one single type will be found sufficient; it is that of water, represented as containing 2 atoms of hydrogen to 1 of oxygen, thus $\begin{matrix} H \\ H \end{matrix} O$. In many cases a multiple of this formula must be used, and we shall presently see how we thereby get an explanation of the difference between monobasic and bibasic acids, &c.
>
> I will here give a few examples of the application of this universal type to the formulae of common substances. The experiments of M. Chancel, agreeing in result with my own, have clearly proved that the numerous family designated as hydrated oxides are not formed by the juxtaposition of an atom of water with an atom of metallic oxide, e.g. $K_2O + H_2O$, but that the equivalent of the mole-

cule is half of that quantity, namely $\begin{matrix}H\\K\end{matrix}O$; they are not compounds of water, but products of substitution in water.

Sulphurous acid is another radical capable of replacing hydrogen; and the sulphates are thus reduced to our type, being bibasic for the same reason as the carbonates. We have thus for sulphuric acid, $\begin{matrix}SO_2\\H_2\end{matrix}O_2$; acid sulphate of potash, $\begin{matrix}SO_2\\HK\end{matrix}O_2$; neutral sulphate, $\begin{matrix}SO_2\\K_2\end{matrix}O_2$, &c. (27)

Water had been the universal, primordial substance for Thales, the matrix of all organisms according to Paracelsus, and the universal element in van Helmont's demonstration. As the "universal type," water is a pattern of combination. The chemical differences between substances that follow the pattern can be as great as those between potassium hydroxide and sulfuric acid.

Adolphe Wurtz was delighted to put the dibasic radical SO_2 "= sulfuryl side by side with the diatomic radical (C_2H_4)" = ethylene; his newly discovered diatomic alcohol glycol thus became another example of the double water type: $\left.\begin{matrix}C_2H_4\\H_2\end{matrix}\right\}O_2$.

In 1866, ten years after he had first produced glycol, Wurtz combined it with trimethylamine and obtained synthetic neurine. Oscar Liebreich (1839–1908 Berlin) had separated neurine from the products he obtained by treating an alcoholic extract of brain substance with barium hydroxide. (28) Wurtz showed that the chemical reactions of his synthetic product were the same as those of the natural neurine, and by the proper method of splitting he reversed the synthetic procedure. (29)

Such far-reaching developments were based on a combination of the theories of radicals and of types. The combination became still more fruitful when the series of types, H—H, $\begin{matrix}H\\H\end{matrix}\!\!>\!O$, $\begin{matrix}H\diagdown\\H—N\\H\diagup\end{matrix}$, was enlarged by $\begin{matrix}H\\H\\H\\H\end{matrix}\!\!>\!C$; one carbon atom is equivalent to four atoms of hydrogen.

This was, in part, the result of work by August Kekulé von Stradonitz (1829, Darmstadt–1896, Bonn). He had started as a student of architecture; then Liebig won him over to chemistry. "Originally a pupil of Liebig's, I became a student of Dumas, Gerhardt, and Williamson; I do not belong to any one school." He described his chemical education in these words at the celebration of the twenty-fifth anniversary of his publication of the benzene theory. (30)

Carbon is tetratomic, it is saturated by four hydrogen or two oxygen atoms. If one of the four units of affinity is saturated by one of another carbon, six of the 2×4 affinity units of the two atoms remain available. In a chain of n carbon atoms, those within the chain have only two units left, and the two carbons at the ends each have one more, so that the number of hydrogen atoms (or chemical affinity units) in a chain of n carbon atoms is $n(4 - 2) + 2$, or $2n + 2$.(31) Benzene, naphthalene, and certain other substances have a greater number of affinity units saturated between the carbon atoms so that less hydrogen is found in them.

Kekulé added the idea that a carbon atom can saturate some of its affinities by those of other carbon atoms. The idea that carbon can combine with carbon also occurred to Archibald Scott Couper (1831–1892); he published it when he was studying at the laboratory of Wurtz in Paris, almost at the same time as Kekulé. (32) Both used graphic formulas, but in different ways.

Couper insisted that oxygen always occurred as a double atom, combined with itself and with another element:

$$\begin{array}{ccccc} CH_3 & \quad CH_3 & \quad CH_3 & & CH_3 \\ | & \quad | & \quad | & & | \\ CH_2 & \quad CO_2 & \quad CH_2 & & CH_2 \\ | & \quad | & \quad \diagdown & & \diagup \\ O-OH & \quad O-OH & & O-O & \\ \text{Alcohol} & \quad \text{Acetic acid} & & \text{Ether} & \end{array}$$

These arrangements of figures were designed to show the location of atoms in the molecules of these substances. There was nothing in them to indicate those qualities that excited the earlier investigators. The facts that a chemical picture had to explain were proportions of weights, reactions with sulfuric acid or chlorine, conversions into the old olefiant gas, into ether and esters. The figures were obtained from connections with a system of experience, and they had meaning only within this system. The quantities expressed by the symbols C, H, O were relative weights, calculated by the use of assumptions that were still not fully justified. Thus Couper represented C as twelve times and O as eight times the weight of H, while others considered C = 6 or O = 16 in relation to H = 1. They placed two carbon atoms where Couper had one, and one O for Couper's two O atoms.

Kekulé attempted to bring unity into this confusion. A congress which he, together with Wurtz and Carl Weltzien (1813–1870), organized in Karlsruhe was attended by 140 chemists of all countries. (33) An agreement was reached, not at this conference but later, when the participants went home and studied a pamphlet that Stanislao Cannizzaro (1826, Palermo –1910, Rome) distributed at the end of the conference. In this pamphlet Cannizzaro described the plan for a system of chemistry that he used in his lectures in Genoa. It was based on Avogadro's theory so far as the permanent gases and the halogens were involved. Two atoms constitute one molecule in these elements. For the metals, the rule of Petit and Dulong was used to determine the atomic weight. In many cases this rule was valid only when the previously accepted atomic weight was doubled. Zinc, for example, had been considered as having "only one point of chemical attraction," and therefore the weight 32.5, while the value of its specific heat required doubling this figure. Calcium was changed from 20 to 40, lead from 103.5 to 207, potassium and silver remained at 39 and 108, respectively. In vapor form, zinc, mercury, and other metals have one-atomic molecules. Sulfur changes its atomic composition in a relation to temperature, which found its interpretation much later. Cannizzaro linked mercury salts by analogy with ethylene and propylene derivatives; he added that no other chemist had noted this analogy. Actually, this was only a specific application of the analogy between inorganic and organic chemistry that Berzelius had seen as generally valid, that Thomas Graham had used in explaining the phosphoric acids (1831) and Wurtz the amides (1849); obviously, it had to be rediscovered again and again.

The atomicity, or valence, of an atom was also a function of the atomic weight ascribed to it. For C = 12, carbon was tetravalent. The existence of carbon monoxide, however, indicated that C can also act as a bivalent atom. In those organic compounds, such as ethylene, where the quantity of carbon is higher than in ethane relative to hydrogen, Couper assumed that one of its two C atoms was tetravalent, the other bivalent, as shown by the figure $\begin{matrix} C—C \\ H_3\ \ H \end{matrix}$. Lothar Meyer preferred to leave one valence of each of the carbon atoms unsaturated and to write:

$$\underset{C}{\underbrace{.\ H\ \ H}}\ \ \underset{H\ \ H}{\overbrace{C}}$$

The difficulty seemed to be still greater for a hydrocarbon, which Edmund Davy (1785–1857), the cousin of Humphry Davy, had discovered in 1836. He distilled cream of tartar with coal to obtain

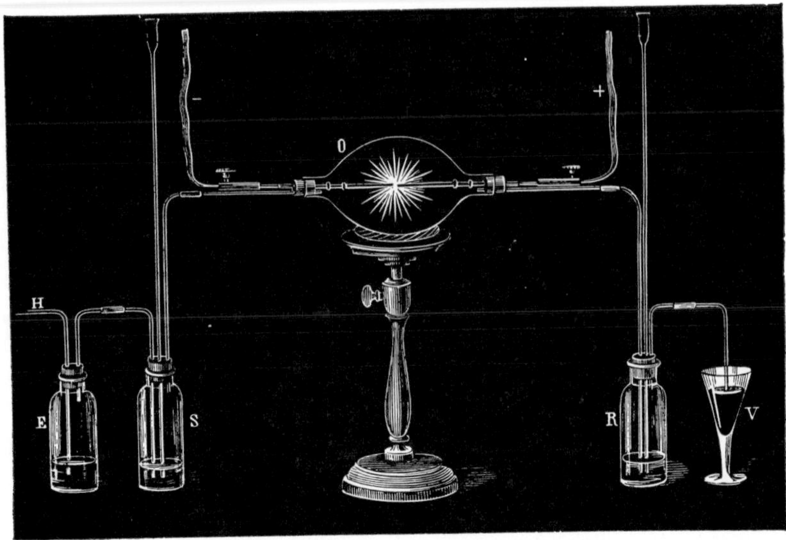

Fig. 22. M. Berthelot's acetylene synthesis. (From M. Berthelot, *Annales de Chimie et Physique* (3), **67,** 1862, pp. 64 ff.)

Hydrogen, purified and dried in bottles E and S, enters bulb O in which an electric arc is burning between electrodes of pure carbon. Current is supplied by fifty Bunsen cells (not shown). Acetylene formed is entrained by the stream of hydrogen. The presence of acetylene is demonstrated by the precipitation of an ammoniacal solution of cuprous chloride in V.

potassium. The residual mass gave off a gas when treated with water. This gas, which ignited when mixed with chlorine, had the elementary composition CH; its molecular formula was C_2H_2. Marcelin Berthelot obtained it synthetically (1862) in the electric arc passing between carbon electrodes in an atmosphere of hydrogen. F. Wöhler observed this gas, called "acetylene," when he decomposed an alloy of zinc, calcium, and coal with water (1862). Berthelot saw in it "an incomplete carburet of the second order," while ethylene was incomplete of the first order, and ethane was complete.

The expressions "incomplete" and "unsaturated" may be considered equivalent; they explain equally well the property of these hydrocarbons to add chlorine or bromine instead of having hydrogen atoms substituted by the halogens, as in saturated compounds. Kekulé felt that "atomicity is a fundamental property of the atom, a property which should be constant and invariable, just as is the weight of the atom." (34)

The obvious contradiction to this stern rule was carbon monoxide. The formula C=O conformed with all its reactions. For example, it adds chlorine to form $COCl_2$, and the light needed for this reaction to proceed obviously acted to dissociate the Cl_2 molecule. With sodium ethyl, CO reacts according to the formula:

$$CO + 2NaC_2H_5 = Na_2 + CO(C_2H_5)_2$$

J. Alfred Wanklyn (1834–1906, a professor in the London Institutions), who discovered this reaction, added that the oil "$CO(C_2H_5)_2$ appears to be identical with propione." (35)

In his *Lehrbuch der organischen Chemie* (Vol. 1, 1861), Kekulé wrote of ammonium chloride and phosphorus pentachloride as "molecular compounds" in which N and P remained three-atomic: NH_3HCl, PCl_3Cl_2. Couper had accepted the change of N, P, and other elements from three to five atomic.

In 1866, Emil Erlenmeyer (1825–1909), then in Heidelberg, 1868–85 in Munich, proposed the term *Werthigkeit*, or value, for atomicity. Elements or radicals would thus be 1-, 2-, 3-, or 4-*werthig*, or valent, which led to expressions like tetravalent in analogy to the long-familiar equivalent. The assumption of a constantly tetravalent carbon atom caused great problems in describing compounds in which carbon atoms were not "saturated."

An organic acid which occurs in apples and is hence called "malic acid" (from Latin *malus*, apple), forms two isomeric acids when water is split off. These acids, "fumaric" and "maleic," both give the same acid by the addition of hydrogen; this is "succinic acid"; it was originally obtained from *succin*, or amber. Since this has the formula

$$\begin{array}{l} H_2C\text{—}COOH \\ \quad | \\ H_2C\text{—}COOH \end{array}$$

the isomerism of fumaric and maleic acid might result from a difference in the place from which two hydrogen atoms are missing as compared with the saturated acid:

$$\begin{array}{l} =C\text{—}COOH \\ \quad\;\, | \\ H_2C\text{—}COOH \end{array} \quad \text{or} \quad \begin{array}{l} HC\text{—}COOH \\ \quad \| \\ HC\text{—}COOH \end{array}$$

These formulae did not account for the chemical differences between the two unsaturated acids, particularly not for the fact that only one of them easily gave off one molecule of water to form maleic anhydride. Such an isomerism, which was outside the available theory, indicated that the theory was not complete.

However, the theory could not be enlarged to fit one special exception so long as it remained isolated. New connections appeared soon and unexpectedly.

Geometric Models for Chemical Formulas in Three Dimensions

The Couper-Kekulé theory extended Dalton's atomism by adding definite valences to the definite weights of the atoms. The consequences of the new theory led to new problems. This could mean that either the theory was inadequate and wrong or that it was incomplete and insufficiently developed. In the present case, the solution consisted in a surprisingly simple construction of the geometric model to express in mathematical language what the words were too weak or too inaccurate to describe. The mere suggestion of geometric models was neither new nor sufficient. Ampère had written about geometric forms of atoms, and he had done so by following a tradition that goes back to Plato. Wollaston had published similar concepts in 1808 (page 152). Gaudin, who had studied under Ampère, specifically suggested a regular tetrahedron with the carbon atom in the center (1865). (36) Kekulé proposed to improve a spherical model of Alexander Crum Brown (1838–1922) by using a tetrahedron (1867). These recurring ideas about a geometric model for the carbon atom meant little in chemistry until they were needed to explain new experiences with isomeric substances.

Two groups of isomeric acids had been isolated; they were the tartaric acids from plants and the lactic acids from animals. Both tartaric and lactic acids have optically active and inactive forms. Tartaric acid and its medically used sodium-ammonium salt (named after Pierre Seignette, 1660–1719, an apothecary in Rochelle, France) were obtained by Louis Pasteur (1822–1895, near Paris) in crystals which showed a characteristic difference. These crystals had the same arrangement of angles and complicated planes, except that one of the forms was the mirror image of the other. The spatial relationships between the two kinds of asymmetric crystals, into which the acid or the salt could be separated, could be compared to the relationship of the right hand to the left. Identifying the asymmetry of the crystals with that of the molecules, Pasteur concluded: "Is it not evident, therefore, that the property of certain molecules to turn the plane of polarization is directly caused by, or at least closely related to, the asymmetry of the molecules?" (37)

Optically active alkaloids, directly extracted from plants, form salts of greatly different solubility with the dextrorotatory or levorotatory forms of tartaric acids. Mixtures of the two active acids can thus be separated by way of their optically opposite salts.

In 1857, Pasteur demonstrated that fermentation of sugars to alcohol or acids (acetic, butyric) does not take place when microorganisms are excluded. For the living organisms, especially yeast or penicillium, "fermentation is life without air." In "life with air," sugar is burned to carbon dioxide and water. Penicillium does not necessarily have to use sugar, it can ferment tartaric acid; but when it does, "it makes a choice. It prefers the dextro compound to the levo compound."(38) This preference for one of the asymmetric forms is only an example of the general law that living nature produces asymmetric substances; the law is a manifestation of the general asymmetry of the universe. (39)

Pasteur's theory that nature produces optically active materials, while the chemist in the laboratory makes inactive ones, is proved true in the case of lactic acid. The acid from meat extract is optically active; it turns the plane of polarized light passing through it. The lactic acid made by synthesis from aldehyde in the laboratory is inactive. Johannes Wislicenus (1835–1902, Leipzig) took the next step toward an explanation of optical asymmetry. He concluded from an intensive investigation of lactic acids that "the difference could be caused only in a different spatial position of the atoms which are connected in the same sequence." (40)

In 1873 Jules Le Bel (1847–1930) and Jacobus Henricus van't Hoff (1852, Rotterdam –1911, Berlin) studied in the laboratory of A. Wurtz in Paris. Without knowing of each other's interest in the problem of optical activity, they both developed similar theories for its explanation. Le Bel started from Pasteur; van't Hoff, who had studied in the laboratory of Kekulé in Bonn for a few months—without seeing much of the famous man, followed in his footsteps. Nevertheless the basis of the two theories was the same. While we are writing chemical formulae on a plane of paper, we must not forget that a molecule has three dimensions. When a carbon atom is linked to four different atoms or groups of atoms (designated as u, v, x, z), the three-dimensional structure becomes asymmetric. Two forms of the same compound $C(u, v, x, z)$ are thus obtained. One is the mirror image of the other. This causes the difference in the behavior toward polarized light. The test for this theory is the reversion: a carbon compound is optically active only when it contains a carbon atom connected with four different radicals. Le Bel extended the theory to nitrogen, which should form active compounds when it is linked to five different atom groups.

Le Bel's publication appeared in November, 1874; two months

earlier, van't Hoff had published, as a booklet of eleven pages, his "proposal to extend the presently used structural formulae of chemistry into space, connected with a remark concerning the relationship between optical rotation and chemical constitution of organic compounds." All previous difficulties disappear by assuming that the four affinities of the carbon atom are directed toward the corners of a tetrahedron, while the carbon atom forms the center of the tetrahedron.

The models show that isomers can also be foretold when two car-

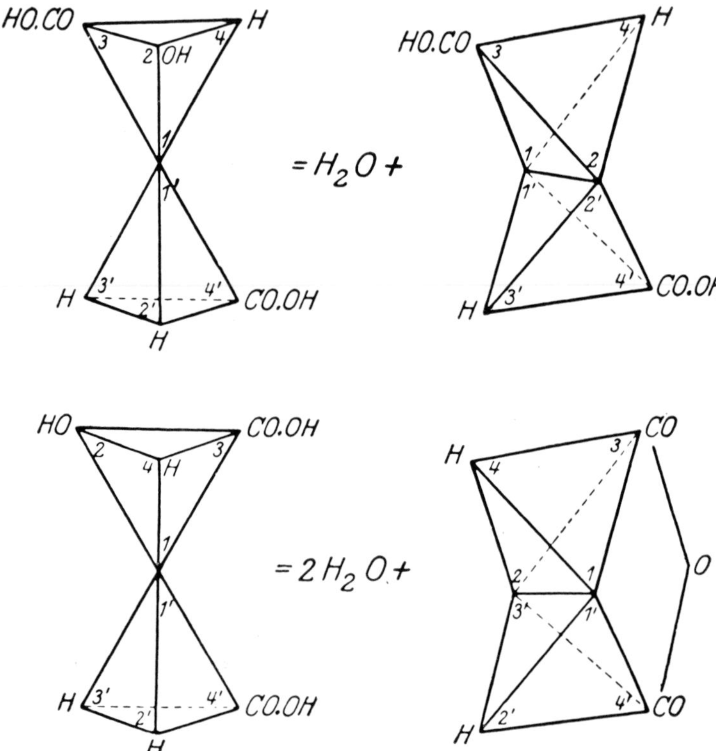

Fig. 23. Steric models for fumaric and maleic acid.

According to van't Hoff's theory, each tetrahedron represents a carbon atom that can rotate freely. At the upper left is malic acid,

$$\begin{array}{ccccccc} & & \text{OH} & & \text{COOH} & & \\ & & | & & | & & \\ \text{H} & — & \text{C} & — & \text{C} & — & \text{H} \\ & & | & & | & & \\ & & \text{HOOC} & & \text{H} & & \end{array}$$

which forms fumaric acid after losing one H_2O. Below, malic acid loses two molecules of water and forms maleic acid anhydride.

carbon atoms are combined by two valences. The relationship between fumaric and maleic acid is thus explained as a spatial or steric isomerism, and it becomes evident that only one of these isomers will readily form an anhydride.

Wislicenus heartily welcomed this theory of the young student who had not even begun to work on his doctoral thesis when his booklet was published. Hermann Kolbe violently criticized this relapse into a speculative nature philosophy which, he said, is close to spiritism. However, the success of van't Hoff's theory soon became overwhelming. Stereochemistry began to form a new branch of the science, the chemistry of the arrangement of atoms to molecules in the three dimensions of space.

REFERENCES

1. J. Liebig, *Die organische Chemie in ihrer Anwendung auf Physiologie und Pathologie* (Braunschweig: Friedrich Vieweg & Sohn, 1842), Part I, p. 208.

2. M. E. Chevreul, *Recherches chimiques sur les corps gras d'origine animale* (Paris: F. G. Levrault, 1823).

3. J. Liebig, *Liebig's Ann.,* **26** (1838), p. 193.

4. A. W. Hofmann, "Über Bestimmung von Dampfdichten in Barometerleere (determination of vapor densities in the barometric vacuum)," *Chem. Ber.,* **1** (1868), pp. 198–201.

5. E. Rancke Madsen, *The development of titrimetric analysis till 1806* (Copenhagen: G.E.C. Gad, 1958).

6. J. J. Berzelius, *Mag. f. Pharmacie,* **31** (1830), p. 260.

7. J. B. Dumas and P. Boullay, fils, "Sur les éthers composés," *Ann. Chim.* (2), **37** (1828), pp. 15–52.

8. J. J. Berzelius, letter to Wöhler of October 6, 1834. See *Briefwechsel,* O. Wallach, Ed. (1901), Vol. 1, p. 590.

9. From Liebig's letter to Schönbein, August 1, 1866. See G. W. A. Kahlbaum and E. Thon, *Liebig and Schönbein, Briefwechsel* (Leipzig: Johann Ambrosius Barth, 1900), p. 221.

10. J. Liebig, *Handbuch der organischen Chemie mit Rücksicht auf Pharmacie* (Heidelberg: C. F. Winter, 1843), p. 18.

11. F. Wöhler, letter from Berlin, March 21, 1830, to Liebig.

12. F. Wöhler and J. Liebig, *Liebig's Ann.,* **26** (1838), pp. 241–340.

13. F. Wöhler, "Bildung des Acetylens durch Kohlenstoff-Calcium," *Liebig's Ann.,* **124** (1862), p. 220.

14. F. Wöhler, letter from Göttingen, June 25, 1863, to Liebig.

15. A. Laurent,"Sur les chlorures de naphthaline," *Ann. Chim.,* **52** (1833), 275–85.

16. A. Laurent, "Action de l'acide nitrique sur la paranaphthaline," *Ann. Chim.,* **60** (1835), pp. 220–3.

17. J. B. Dumas, "Über das Gesetz der Substitutionen und die Theorie der Typen," *Liebig's Ann.,* **33** (1840), pp. 269–300.

18. Richard Owen, *On the Archetype and Homologies of the Vertebrate Skeleton* (London: van Voorst, 1848).

19. Georges Cuvier, *Le Règne Animal distribué d'après son Organisation, pour servir de base à l'histoire naturelle des animaux et d'introduction à anatomie comparée* (Paris: Deterville, 1817). E. Farber, "Theories of types in the history of science," *J. Wash. Ac. Sci.,* **54** (1964), pp. 349–56.

20. A. W. Hofmann, "Chemische Untersuchung der organischen Basen im Steinkohlen-Teeröl," *Liebig's Ann.,* **47** (1843), pp. 37–87, esp. p. 47.

21. A. W. Hofmann, *Liebig's Ann.,* **74** (1850), p. 117.

22. A. W. Hofmann, "Beiträge zur Kenntnis der flüchtigen organischen Basen," *Liebig's Ann.,* **78** (1851), pp. 253–86, esp. 268.

23. Hugo Schiff, "Eine neue Reihe organischer Basen," *Liebig's Ann.,* **131** (1864), pp. 118 f.

24. Edward Frankland, *Phil. Trans.,* **113** (1852), p. 417.

25. Edward Frankland, "On a new series of organic compounds containing boron," *Phil Trans.,* **152** (1862), pp. 175–76.

26. A. Williamson, *Phil. Mag.,* **37** (1850), p. 350.

27. A. Williamson, "On the constitution of salts," *J. Chem. Soc. London,* **4** (1862), pp. 352–3.

28. O. Liebreich, *Liebig's Ann.,* **134** (1864), p. 29.

29. A. Wurtz, *Compt. Rend.,* **66** (1868), pp. 772–6.

30. Celebration in honor of August Kekulé, *Chem. Ber.* **23** (1890), pp. 1265–1312.

31. A. Kekulé, "Über die Constitution und die Metamorphosen der chemischen Verbindungen und über die chemische Natur des Kohlenstoffs," *Liebig's Ann.,* **106** (1858), pp. 129–59.

32. A. S. Couper, "Sur une nouvelle théorie chimique," *Ann. Chim.* (3), **53** (1858), pp. 469–89.

33. A. J. Ihde, *J. Chem. Ed.,* **38** (1961), p. 83.

34. A. Kekulé, "Sur l'atomicité des élémens," *Compt. Rend.,* **58** (1864), pp. 510–14.

35. J. A. Wanklyn, "On the action of carbonic oxide on sodium-ethyle," *Phil. Mag.* (4), **31** (1866), pp. 505–10.

36. M. A. A. Gaudin, *Réforme de la chimie minérale et organique et de la morphogénie moléculaire et de la crystallogénie au moyen de la mécanique des atomes ou synthèse mathématique* (Paris: Germer Balliere, 1865).

37. Louis Pasteur, "Mémoire sur la relation qui peut exister entre la forme crystalline et la composition chimique, et sur la cause de la polarisation rotatoire," *Compt. Rend.,* **26** (1848), pp. 535–8.

38. Louis Pasteur, "Note relative au Penicillium glaucum et à la dissymétrie moléculaire des produits organiques naturels," *Compt. Rend.,* **51** (1860), pp. 298–99.

39. Louis Pasteur, *ibid.,* **78** (1874), pp. 1515–18.

40. Johannes Wislicenus, "Über die optisch-active Milchsäure der Fleischflüssigkeit, die Paramilchsäure," *Liebig's Ann.,* **167** (1873), pp. 302–56.

14

Natural and Artificial Organic Substances

Industrial Materials and Processes

The heating of wood with limited or excluded access of air has long been practiced for producing charcoal. In the last years of the eighteenth century this process of charring became a source of combustible gas, and a few years later, it became a source also of tars and oils. This development into a process of wood distillation had been long in preparation. Rudolf Glauber had recommended it, and Robert Boyle had written about wood spirits and acids. Van Helmont had treated gases as real, characteristic substances, and Stephen Hales had advanced the art of their handling. In 1785 Jean Pierre Minkelers (1748–1824, Louvain, Belgium), in 1792 William Murdock (1754–1839, Birmingham), and from 1799 on Philippe Lebon (1767–1849, Paris) demonstrated that distillation gas could be used for filling balloons, for heating, and particularly for lighting. Large gas-producing plants were erected in the following years. (1)

The heating of coal was also first carried out for the sake of the residue, called coke. In the old distillations, the volatile material had been the only valued product. The recovery of the coal distillates as tars, oils, and gases developed only after coke had been found to be superior to charcoal in the blast furnace for reducing iron ore to iron.

In starting such innovations, the enterprising technicians needed the help of financiers more than that of chemists.

The industrial distillation of wood, wood rosin, and coal furnished products that interested the chemists, and gradually they were called upon to help solve some problems of operations. Thus, for example, Faraday investigated the new gases and their conversions into solids obstructing the free flow. The chemical study of industrial distillates then led to the development of new industrial applications.

The production of materials for tanning and dyeing involved the old method of extracting natural materials with cold or hot water. For the production of sugar, this method was combined with crystallization. Chemists helped develop methods of purifying the raw juice extracted from sugarcane. The economic sanctions during the Napoleonic war with England gave new vigor to the search for domestic sources of sugar. Beets, raisins, and honey were the new raw materials. Gottlieb Sigismund Kirchhoff (1764–1833) in St. Petersburg (Leningrad) in 1811 treated starch with sulfuric acid to make the kind of sugar that Proust in Paris in 1806 produced from raisins.

The development of stills for coal distillation had a counterpart in the introduction by Edward Charles Howard (1774, Sheffield–1816, London) in 1812 of the vacuum pan for concentrating sugar solutions. Under reduced pressure, water is evaporated at relatively low temperature. Purer syrups and higher yields were thus achieved.

On the other hand, Richard Albert Tilghman (1824–1879, Philadelphia) in 1847 purposely used what he called "the decomposing power of water at high temperatures" for making fatty acids from fats, and later, together with his brother Benjamin Chew Tilghman (1821–1901), he used the same process to separate the cellulose out of wood.

In 1822, Anselme Payen (1795–1871, Paris) introduced bone char for removing impurities, especially those of dark color, from sugar juice. This became a model later, when the problem of purifying petroleum distillates arose.

A method for increasing the yield of crystallized sugar was developed by Augustin Pierre Dubrunfaut (1797–1881, Bercy). He purified the mother liquor (molasses) by an osmosis against water through parchment paper, after which additional sugar could be crystallized from the molasses. The name osmosis (from Greek *osmos,* impulse) and the discovery of the process were due to René Joaquim Dutrochet (1776–1847, Paris), who had started on it in 1826 from ideas on diffusion that went back to work by Priestley and Dalton on the diffusion of gases. Thomas Graham (1805–1869) pursued the study of diffusion without and with membranes from 1830. Diffusion and osmosis had been the topic of scientific experimentation and speculation long before 1855, when Dubrunfaut applied them industrially.

Aromatic Substances

The old term "aromatic" was used for a number of plant substances. They had been grouped together because they usually had a pronounced scent. Later on, the word "aromatic" acquired a new chemical meaning when it was found that many of these aromatic substances have only a small proportion of hydrogen compared to their carbon content. Turpentine, for example, the oil separated by distillation of the gum exuded by pine trees, gave upon redistillation a turpentine oil which had the composition $C_{10}H_{16}$. Kekulé's rule that n carbon atoms combine with $2n + 2$ hydrogen atoms to "complete" compounds would have led one to expect 22H combined with 10C. From the crude spirit of *Pinus maritimus* wood, an oil with the composition C_8H_{10} was obtained. Auguste Cahours (1813–1891, Paris) called it "xylene" because it was derived from wood (Greek *xylos*).

Several aromatic substances gave "cymene" (or cymol), with the formula $C_{10}H_{14}$, which was dissolved into $C_6H_4\begin{cases}CH_3\\C_3H_7\end{cases}$. One of its sources was camphor, and its conversion into cymene was a dehydration:

$$\underset{\text{Camphor}}{C_{10}H_{16}O} - \underset{\text{Water}}{H_2O} = \underset{\text{Cymene}}{C_{10}H_{14}}$$

When the tar that settles out from the distillate of brown coal was redistilled, several oils were obtained, and crystallizing substances such as naphthalene could be separated out of the "naphtha" oils.

Not much was known about all these substances; their identity was uncertain, their names were arbitrary, and their uses were imaginary. Liebig considered efforts in this whole field as misdirected. "Science has, especially within the last few years, been enriched with so many bodies of this kind, the products of destructive distillation, that it is much to be wished the labours of chemists were directed to more really useful objects. . . . These substances are not met with in organized nature; they perform no part which fixes our attention." Instead, the laws of animal and vegetable chemistry that present a new world of important discoveries should be the center of interest. "The most remarkable, most interesting, and most important researches in chemistry have little to do with figures." (2)

However, the stream of "products of destructive distillation" continued to flow, and figures were necessary for orientation. By comparing the figures for elementary composition, density of substances in gaseous and liquid state, refraction of light, optical activity in polarized light, behavior on heating, and reactions with simpler substances, the identity of these artificial products and their relations within a system became gradually more definite. The figure of the atomicity of carbon and the concept of carbon-to-carbon linkages led Kekulé to an explanation of the basic structure of aromatic substances.

The explanation came to him in a dreamlike trance after long preoccupation with the problem. He perceived rows of atoms in snake-like motion, and suddenly one of the snakes gripped its own tail. He awoke as if hit by lightning: here was the model for the constitution of these molecules, a closed ring instead of the open chain of carbon atoms.

The vision occurred in 1862. He took three years to convert it into a scientific theory. The final stimulation to do this came from a synthesis of "toluene," the substitution of bromine by methyl in brominated benzene, which Rudolf Fittig (1835–1910, Strassburg) and Bernhard Tollens (1841–1911, Göttingen) published in 1864. A nucleus of six carbon atoms is present in all aromatic substances. The six atoms are linked to one another alternately by one and by two valences. Each carbon atom thus uses three of its valences for its two neighbor carbon atoms and one to bind hydrogen.

The hexagon with a regular sequence of single and double bonds between the carbon atoms resulted from a vision; now it was to be tested as to how well it was able to represent all the facts that were known and all the conclusions that could be derived from it. There was, for example, the problem of isomeric benzene derivatives. Fittig showed that xylene, which has two methyl groups on the benzene nucleus, could be separated into three isomers (1867). This was readily related to the difference in the position of the methyl groups. With the carbon atoms numbered consecutively from 1 to 6, a xylene with the methyls in 1,2 position should be different from one that has methyl groups attached to the carbons, 1,3 or 1,4. Wilhelm

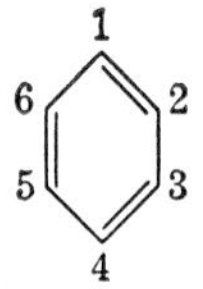

Körner (1839–1925, Milan, Italy) proposed the designations *ortho, meta,* and *para* for such isomers. It became a simple mathematical exercise to figure out the possible isomers for higher degrees of substitution. The experimental verification was considerably more difficult, but it succeeded to a very large extent.

However, the question was soon raised whether position 1,2 should not be different from 1,6; but since such isomers were not found, modified pictures for the benzene ring were proposed. Kekulé said about these formulas:

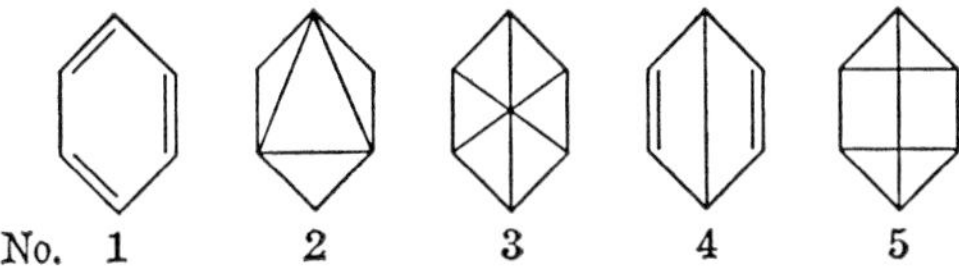

Proposed diagrams for benzene

I had given preference to hypothesis No. 1; Claus had discussed No. 3 and No. 5, but decided in favor of No. 3; No. 5 was again proposed by Ladenburg; Wichelhaus suggested No. 4, as Städeler had done before him. I must confess that to me, too, No. 3 seemed rather evident for quite some time, and that later on I also discovered some beauty in No. 5, however from a different point of view than Ladenburg. In any case I have to say that, up to now, hypothesis No. 1 still seems to me the most probable one. It explains just as easily as any of the others, and, as it appears to me, even more elegantly and symmetrically, the formation of benzene from acetylene and the synthesis of mesithylene from acetone. It shows at least as clearly, if not better than the others, the connection between benzene, naphthalene, and anthracene, and it especially seems to me that it gives a more satisfactory explanation for the formation of the addition products of benzene than the others do. On the other hand, the reasons that were brought forth against the hypothesis seem to me not yet too strong. I think that Ladenburg puts too much emphasis on the possible or probable difference between 1,2 and 1,6. (3)

Synthetic Dyestuffs

Except for the pigments of the Prussian Blue series, picric acid was probably the first "synthetic" dyestuff. Chevreul listed among its names that of "amer de Welter," the bitter principle Welter had made by treating silk with nitric acid. (4)

Chevreul pointed out that several resins, or salicine, and particularly coal-tar, were better than indigo as raw materials for picric acid. Laurent showed the advantage of using crude phenol instead.

"For some time now, picric acid has been used in the dyeing of silk; it gives a beautiful yellow color resistant to washing, provided the fabric has before been mordanted with alum and cream of tartar. Wool also can be dyed by picric acid; cotton, however, mordanted or not, does not take up any color from it." (5)

The second of the laboratory-made dyestuffs was murexide, the ammonium salt of purpuric acid. This was a discovery of William Prout.

The raw material for obtaining murexide was guano. Extraction with potash solution and precipitation with acid furnished about 2¼ kg of pure uric acid from 100 kg of guano. The final yield in murexide is not known; it was obtained with the expenditure of much costly nitric acid. The economy of dyeing with murexide obviously rested on a very high appreciation of the color thus produced.

The raw material for another synthetic dyestuff came from products found by distilling coal tar or alkaloids, which had the common feature of being salt-forming bases.

When Friedlieb Runge separated basic materials from coal tar, he called the first kyanol, because it gave a blue color with chlorinated lime, and the second leukol, because it remained white with this reagent. He also discovered a brown acid and a red acid in the residues from the distillation of coal tar and named them *Brunolsäure* and *Rosolsäure*.

Runge's kyanol was identical with the aniline that Carl Julius Fritzsche obtained as a distillate from indigo and recognized as the same as Unverdorben's Kristallin. Upon oxidation with chloric acid, the almost colorless aniline turned into an indigo-blue material again. (6)

> The interesting behavior of chloric acid, under certain circumstances also of nitric acid, towards aniline induced me to study also the action of oxygen compounds of chlorine on aniline, and this has in fact given noteworthy results. When a solution of an aniline salt, mixed with an equal volume of alcohol, is brought together with a solution of potassium chlorate to which hydrochloric acid has been added, then, after some time and the slower the more certainly, a beautiful flocculent indigo-blue precipitate appears. On filtration and washing with alcohol, the blue color of the precipitate turns green as the free acid is removed, and after drying, the substance has shrunk considerably and is dark-green; it contains about 16 percent chlorine and its composition seems to be expressible by $C_{24}H_{20}N_4Cl_2O$, indicating that from 2 at. aniline, 8 at. hydrogen had combined with 4 at. of the oxygen of chloric acid to form water, while the rest of the atoms had joined to form the new body.

A special raw material was the bark of certain cinchona trees, in Spanish called *quinquina*. Of the two most important alkaloids extracted from this kind of bark, one is "cinchonine," the other "quinine." Both were discovered by two professors of pharmacy in Paris,

Pierre Joseph Pelletier (1788–1842) and Joseph Caventou (1795–1878) in 1820–1821. The two alkaloids could be separated quite easily, since cinchonine itself is less soluble than quinine, while the reverse is true for their sulfates. In the natural state these alkaloids are combined with an acid which was called "quinic acid" before much was known about its chemical nature. It can be decomposed by heat; Alexander Woskresensky (1809–1880, Petrograd) observed the golden yellow crystals that are formed on cooling the vapors from this decomposition. He called the new substance "chinoyl" (1838). Since the ending *–yl* would indicate a radical, Wöhler changed the name to "quinone" (1844). Its composition is indicated by the formula $C_6H_4O_2$. It adds hydrogen in two steps under treatment with sulfurous acid and forms first a green then a colorless hydroquinone, $C_6H_6O_2$.

C. Greville Williams (1829–1910, Glasgow) oxidized derivatives of "volatile bases produced by destructive distillation of cinchomine." (7) He obtained brilliant green and crimson colors, but he did not test their qualities as dyestuffs.

At the College of Chemistry in London, A. W. Hofmann also studied quinine, for which Liebig had proposed the formula $C_{20}H_{24}O_2N_2$. William Henry Perkin (1839–1907) was one of Hofmann's assistants and was particularly occupied with the derivative of aniline, allyl toluidine. Comparing its formula $C_{10}H_{13}N$ with that of quinine, Perkin thought a simple oxidation should lead from one to the other:

$$\underset{\text{Allyltoluidine}}{2C_7H_4(CH_3)NH(C_3H_5)} + 3O = \underset{\text{Quinine}}{C_{20}H_{24}O_2N_2} + H_2O$$

The oxidation with potassium dichromate resulted in an uninviting brown mass. Perkin thereupon tried the same reaction with aniline itself, and from the product he extracted a purple dyestuff. A patent was easily obtained, and the manufacture of the new aniline purple, which he later called "mauveine," was quickly started by Perkin. (8)

The publication of the patent and the appearance of mauveine on the market caused a precipitate rush for similar products. Aniline, usually in an impure grade which contained its next higher homologue, toluidine, was oxidized with different agents, stannic chloride, arsenic acid, permanganate, and others. A preliminary methylation of aniline, according to Berthelot's method of heating aniline hydrochloride with methanol, and subsequent oxidation, gave Charles Lauth (1836, Strassburg –1913, Paris) a violet dyestuff (in 1861). Treatment of some of the purple and violet dyestuffs with aniline, reduction by the "universal fixer," sodium hyposulfite, produced blue and green substances. A black aniline dye was obtained by John Lightfoot in 1863 with copper compounds as catalytic agents. This catalyst was later on (1875) replaced by vanadium pentoxide, of which only about one hundred thousandth of the quantity of the aniline was required for the conversion into aniline black.

The plant of Auguste Poirrier, in Saint Denis, had been manufacturing natural plant extracts as dyestuffs since 1824. In 1861 Perkin's mauveine was put into production. The dyestuff itself, on a pure basis, would have sold for 4,000 francs a kilogram. The commercial product contained about 8 percent to 10 percent of it. The first difficulty of technical production was to obtain the aniline in sufficient quantity. Extraction with acid from coal tar did not yield enough of it. Manufacturers of coal gas had to be persuaded to separate out the benzene from their product.

Benzene was converted into nitrobenzene by a manufacturer in Paris who sold his product to perfumeries from 1856 on under the name of "essence of mirbane." Antoine J. Béchamp (1816–1904) converted nitrobenzene into aniline by treating it with acetic acid and iron filings. This process had to be carefully regulated, otherwise benzene would be formed. The reaction time was soon reduced from eight days to twelve hours with economies in acid and the return of aniline-containing water, so that the price per kilogram could be reduced from 150 francs in 1858 to 2.5 francs in 1868.

An aniline red that sold for 1,200 francs per kilogram in 1859 came down to 50 francs in 1868. It was manufactured by Renard Frères, in Lyon, and was called *fuchsin* because it resembled the color of the fuchsia flower. (9) A typical yield was 0.25 kg of fuchsin from 0.85 kg of aniline, which was made from 1.4 kg of nitrobenzene for which 1 kg of benzene from 1000 kg of coal had to be used.

While businessmen, chemists, and engineers competed in these rapid developments, and lawyers were kept busy with patent suits, A. W. Hofmann tried to determine the arrangement of the atoms in the molecules of these new dyestuffs. From purified fuchsin he isolated a base, "rosaniline," and suggested a threefold ammonia type for the constitution (1864):

$$\left.\begin{array}{c} C_6H_4'' \\ C_7H_6'' \\ H_2 \end{array}\right\} N_3 \cdot H_2O \qquad \left.\begin{array}{c} C_6H_4'' \\ (C_7H_6)_2'' \\ (C_6H_5)_3 \end{array}\right\} N_3 \cdot H_2O \qquad \left.\begin{array}{c} C_6H_4'' \\ (C_7H_6)_2'' \\ (C_2H_5)_3 \end{array}\right\} N_3 \cdot H_2O$$

Aniline red — Aniline blue — Aniline violet

This suggestion was abandoned two years later because of the result found in the reaction of these substances with nitrous acid.

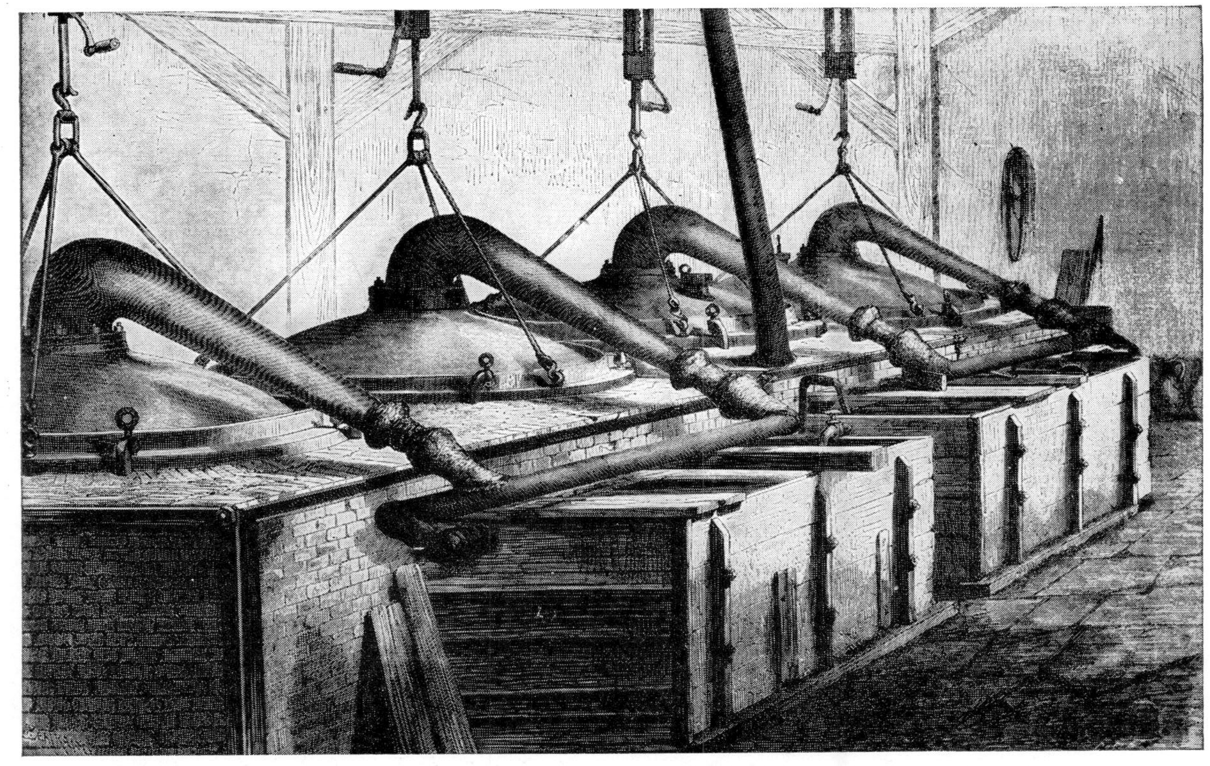

Fig. 24. Stills for a dyestuff intermediate: methylaniline. (From Turgan, *Les Grandes Usines*, Michel Lévy Frères, Paris, 1870, Vol. 9, pp. 312–13.)

Peter Griess (1829–1888) had begun to study the reactions of aromatic amines with nitrous acid in 1858 in Hofmann's London laboratory. When this reaction was carried out with great caution, the product contained two nitrogen atoms for the one in the amino group. Using the old name, azote, for nitrogen, Griess called these new substances diazo compounds. They are very sensitive, some of them even explosive, and they readily combine with phenols and amines. Heinrich Caro (1834–1910, Berlin) was in England at that time and became familiar with the diazotation method. He found (1866) that rosaniline can be diazotized. From this he concluded that it cannot have the constitution proposed by Hofmann.

All these dyestuffs can be converted into colorless hydroderivatives, a so-called "leuko-form," by reduction. Leuko-rosaniline gives a diazotation product from which Emil and Otto Fischer in 1878 prepared the hydrocarbon triphenylmethane. This hydrocarbon had been discovered by Kekulé and Paul Franchimont. Charles Friedel (1832–1899, Paris) and James Mason Crafts (1839–1917, Boston) found a convenient method of combining chloroform with benzene to triphenylmethane under the catalytic action of aluminum chloride. This origin clearly explained the constitution of the new product. The three atoms of chlorine in chloroform are directly replaced by three phenyl groups with release of hydrochloric acid (1877). Aniline dyestuffs were thus shown to be derivatives of triphenylmethane. Benzotrichloride, for instance, can be considered as a phenyl-substituted chloroform. It reacts with dimethylaniline and forms a green dyestuff, malachite green, a discovery of Oscar Doebner (1850–1907). Its leukoform is a derivative of triphenylmethane.

The oxidation of the leuko-forms to the dyestuffs had a simpler analogy in the oxidation of colorless hydroquinone to the golden yellow quinone. The peculiar shift in double bonds which occurs in this transformation must be held responsible for the color. With youthful exaggeration, Carl Graebe and Carl Liebermann (1842–1914, Berlin) made "a more intimate mutual binding of oxygen or nitrogen atoms" responsible for "the physical property of color" (1868).

Graebe and Liebermann had a particularly valuable example for their theory in alizarine. This important natural dyestuff from the madder root, of which about 70,000 tons, worth 50 to 60 million francs, were produced in 1868, had been the object of considerable chemical work. The French chemist François Zacharie Roussin (1827–1894, Paris) tried to obtain alizarine. He tried to synthesize it when he treated naphthalene with nitric acid and added hydrogen to the dinitronaphthalene by reacting it with tin and sulfuric acid. The resulting yellow dyestuff, "naphthazarine," was interesting but it was not alizarine.

Edward Frankland had found interesting organic compounds when he used zinc instead of the more violently reacting alkali metals. Adolf Baeyer had mixed zinc, as a fine powder, with complex organic substances, and on heating he obtained the bare carbon-hydrogen skeleton of these substances, which was a great help in elucidating their constitution. He had used this method in his work on indigo, and he asked his assistant, Graebe, to find out what alizarine would yield when heated with zinc. The product obtained in this reaction was "anthracene," a substance known from previous research by Laurent (1832) and others on the high-boiling components of coal tar. This basic information, combined with the analogy between Laurent's anthraquinone and benzoquinone, enabled Graebe and Liebermann to carry out the synthesis of alizarine from anthracene in 1868 and 1869. They rushed the results of this work to the patent office in London and were just one day ahead of Perkin in filing their patent application. Naphthalene, from which Roussin and others had tried to produce alizarine, later really became the basic raw material in a roundabout way which involved its oxidation to phthalic acid and its condensation with benzene.

The third group of synthetic dyestuffs, after aniline and anthracene dyes, was based on the diazo-compounds that Griess had investigated and from which Roussin developed a host of yellows, reds, and browns. The French plant of Poirrier manufactured them, but at that time (1875) the German Badische Anilin- und Soda-Fabrik (founded 1865) under Caro's direction was also very strong on the market.

The results of the competitive efforts of producing synthetic dyestuffs were displayed at the great exposition of 1878 in Paris. Charles Lauth summed it up in the report to his Minister of Commerce: "The exposition of 1878 has shown that in certain points which formerly had been considered invulnerable, our national industries are seriously beaten by foreign competition. As to the chemical arts, we consider the danger as very grave; it is so much more formidable since the ill is not superficial, it stems from a deep and radical cause . . . the lack of chemists." (10)

Two years later Adolf von Baeyer (1835–1917, Munich) reported the first synthesis of indigo, the king of all plant dyestuffs, and in 1883 he had "established experimentally the place of each atom in the molecule of this dyestuff." (11) This was seventeen years after

Baeyer had begun to work on the chemistry of indigo, years during which new findings were connected and coordinated with investigations of apparently quite different substances, for example, uric acid from the excrement of snakes and birds. When Baeyer, "began his work on indigo, there were no manufacturing plants for organic dyestuffs in Germany; chemistry belonged to the professors." (12)

Baeyer was a student of Kekulé but was entirely different from him. "Kekulé had no interest in the substances themselves, but only in the question whether they conformed with his ideas or not. If such was the case, it was fine; if not, they were rejected. . . . I found that it should be my task to get closer to nature and to regard the things themselves." He was a follower of the old tradition, which combined interest in organic substances with interest in their biological origin. From work on uric acid he thus came to the chemistry of assimilation and fermentation. He found chemical analogues in condensations of phenols with aldehydes or with phthalic anhydride. Experiments carried out in test tubes—Baeyer never used more complicated kinds of laboratory apparatus—gave beautiful dyestuffs from such condensations, "fluoresceine" and "eosine," which had immediate commercial success when their production was taken over by industry.

At the same time he was open-minded to the advantages of using simple mechanical and geometrical explanations. The carbon atom was presented by van't Hoff's theory as the center of a tetrahedron with four valences directed to its corners. The angles between the four valences can thus be calculated. If they are deflected, as in double or triple bonds or in rings of more or less than five carbon atoms, a definite strain should be imposed which becomes experimentally observable in lowered stability of the compounds. This theory of the strain in carbon compounds proved surprisingly successful for many years and can still be used as a first approximation to a general theory.

Baeyer was particularly sensitive to odors. In his report about "the history of indigo synthesis" he mentions that "the peculiar odor of indigo" had impressed him when he was thirteen years old, and that he would never forget "the devotion with which I inhaled the fragrance of orthonitrophenol." In his study on the importance of condensations for the life of plants (1870), he writes that his work "was sustained at every step by the various scents of peppermint, camphor, orange, and oil of turpentine." (13)

From 1875 on Baeyer taught in Munich, and unlike Liebig he continued to teach for forty years more until he was eighty years old. Many of his former students attained prominent positions in science and industry.

Carbohydrates and Proteins

The New System of chemistry marked the great advance of establishing elements, in agreement with the definition that Robert Boyle had confirmed and with resolution of his doubt whether these well-defined limits of chemical separations really existed. With regard to the "composite bodies," such limits of chemical operations still had to be worked out. There, the problem was to find the chemical units in the complexity of the natural substances. For mineral substances, this had been discussed between Berthollet and Proust. For the substances from organisms, the problem persisted all through the nineteenth century. The units that the anatomists prepared were not necessarily chemical units. Chemists continued to search for the "immediate principles" of organisms and their parts. Elementary analysis gave the ultimate parts and thus went too far. Analysis of nuclei and radicals was the next step in finding the intermediate units. Units formed on the basis of general operations, e.g., extractions, were not specific enough. The term "extractives" included too many substances of great chemical differences.

Specific chemical operations, such as oxidation by nitric acid or splitting by sulfuric acid, could not be considered "unit operations;" their products depended too much on the nature of the starting material, unless they were used too strongly, and then they failed to give the specific information that was sought. With the cautious use of these methods, complex organic substances were resolved into still-complex compounds, "elements" at a high level, not too far from the starting material, so that this material could be reconstructed. That was the approach to the uric acid problem by Wöhler and Liebig.

By a cautious treatment with sulfuric acid, Henri Braconnot decomposed cellulose into glucose (1818) and obtained the "sugar of gelatine" from muscle fiber or wool (1820).

The fermentative cleavage of sugar into carbon dioxide and alcohol, however, involved more than Dalton thought when he had the bright idea to reconstruct the sugar from these products (14):

Alcohol

Carbon Dioxide

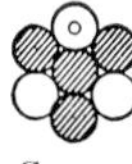
Sugar

Fig. 25. Sugar making. (From William Thomas Brande, *Course of Ten Lectures on Organic Chemistry, arranged by John Scoffern,* London, 1854, p. 194.) The following is from the article that this illustration accompanied.

"This increase of temperature is accomplished by means of the external steam-jacket; and whilst the temperature is getting up, men continually agitate the mass by mean of a paddle of peculiar construction.

"The next operation consists in what is technically called *filling out.* By means of vessels something like coal-scuttles in shape, the contents of the heater are removed, and poured into moulds of copper, iron, or earthenware, the hole in the apex of each mould being plugged by stoppers of brown paper. The next operation varies according to the size of the moulds.

"If the object of manufacture be to prepare that class of sugar-cones to which the term *loaves* is technically applied, that is to say, cones, the weight of which does not exceed fourteen pounds—the sugar-magma, as soon as it has consolidated on the face or *base* of the mould, is broken, and stirred by means of a flat wooden spatula, technically known as a "*hauling knife.*" Cones of sugar exceeding fourteen pounds in weight, are not considered loaves in commerce, but are known under the name of *lumps, Prussian lumps, titlers,* &c., according to their weight. It is not usual for these to be subjected to the operation of hauling.

"As soon as the contents of the moulds have well crystallized (for the accomplishment of which the time materially varies, according to the size of the mould), the paper stoppers are removed, a brad-awl is thrust a few inches up

In this scheme, alcohol is presented as CH_3, a rather incomprehensible formula; Dalton changed it on several occasions.

Albumins and caseins from plants or animals belong together, although they vary much in their properties when prepared from different organisms or by changes of treatment. In Utrecht, Gerardus Johannes Mulder (1802–1882) thought there should be one common material in plants and animals, characterized by forming compounds with sulfur and phosphorus and thereby varying in appearance and properties. "This material has been called "protein," since it produces many unequal bodies and can thus be regarded as a primary compound." (15) Mulder himself coined that name in 1839; he derived it from the Greek word meaning: "I take the first place." It was vague enough to serve for other chemical meanings.

A common name for the related substances—cellulose, starch, and sugar—was derived from their elementary analysis. Carl Schmidt (1822–1894, Dorpat) pointed out that the carbon in them is combined with hydrogen in the same proportion to oxygen as in water; he proposed the name *Kohlehydrate*, or carbohydrates, for the entire group of sugars in which the H_2O relationship exists. There were sugars for which this was not the case and to which Schmidt did not extend the name carbohydrate. (16)

Cane sugar is optically active; its solutions turn the plane of polarized light to the right. Dubrunfaut found that in the first stage of fermentation by yeast the sign of rotation is "inverted." He obtained the same change in rotation by treating the cane sugar solutions with dilute acids. From work extending over the years 1830 to 1856, he concluded that in the reaction one molecule of cane sugar adds one molecule of water and falls apart into glucose and the strongly levorotatory "liquid sugar."

When Alexander Butlerow (1828–1886, Kasan) subjected a new substance, which was later found to be formaldehyde, to a digestion with limewater, he obtained (1861) "the first example of the synthetic production of a substance which behaves like a sugar." (17) Baeyer explained this reaction (1870) as starting from a hydrate of formaldehyde, $CH_2(OH)_2$, and consisting of a combination of six such mole-

---

into the substance of the crystallized contents, and the moulds, thus unstopped and pierced, are placed to stand each over and upon an earthern pot, in order that the non-crystallized liquid matter may drain away. Some manufacturers do not employ pots, but racks—the aggregate, syrup of many hundred, or, it may be, thousand cones, being collected by gutters, all ending in one general reservoir. In either case, the object is similar."

cules with removal of six molecules of water. The sugar thus had the formula $COH(C[OH]H)_4 \cdot CH_2OH$. This speculation used the results of an investigation of *mannit,* an alcohol obtained from manna. As a sequence of his work on the tribasic alcohol glycerine, Berthelot recognized mannit as a hexabasic alcohol (1860); its reduction to the hydrocarbon hexane, by means of hydroiodic acid, proved the arrangement of the carbon atoms in a straight chain. This proof, in turn, was possible only because of the comparison of this hexane with other hydrocarbons.

A. Wurtz applied his findings of aldehyde condensation, in which only two aldehyde molecules were involved, to the problem of the constitution of glucose. Oxidations to sugar acids and reduction to mannit were further helps in solving the problem.

E. C. Jungfleisch, in Berthelot's laboratory, purified Dubrunfaut's "liquid sugar" so that it crystallized. By way of the compound with hydrocyanic acid, Heinrich Kiliani (1855–1940, Freiburg) obtained an acid, and from its structure he arrived (1886) at the interpretation of this sugar as fructose, a 2-ketose. (18)

What Mulder had named protein, that "primary compound," was the intuition of a program; it became a chemical unit after many separate experimental results were recognized as related to each other.

In 1805, Vauquelin and Robiquet discovered a crystalline substance from the hot-water extract of fresh asparagus tips. They called it asparagine, but the same substance was also obtained from extracts of licorice or potatoes. Liebig in 1833 heated it with alkalies, which split off ammonia and gave salts of aspartic acid still containing nitrogen. In connection with his studies on organic acids, Kolbe in 1862 established its relationship to succinic acid. Asparagine emerged as the amide of an aminosuccinic acid:

$$\begin{array}{c} \qquad CH_2CONH_2 \\ \quad | \\ H_2N\cdot CHCOOH \end{array}$$

From stones in the bladder, William Clyde Wollaston prepared a crystalline substance, which he named cystic oxide "to distinguish it from other calculi" (1810). Berzelius changed the name to cystine (1832). M. C. J. Thaulow discovered its sulfur content in 1838. Eugen Baumann (1846–1896, Freiburg) treated it with tin and hydrochloric acid, which reduced it to cystein:

$$\begin{array}{c} NH_2 \\ \cdot \\ H_3C\cdot C\cdot COOH \\ \cdot \\ SH \end{array}$$

The product from casein that Proust had called "cheese oxide" (1819) turned out to be identical with Braconnot's leucine, so named because of its white color.

In his investigation of bile substances, Leopold Gmelin prepared "taurin" from ox gall (from Latin *taurus,* ox). Adolf Strecker (1822–1871, Würzburg), who had been an assistant to Liebig, wrote in 1868: "Taurin, for example, is definitely a sulfo acid without, however, showing the slightest acidic reaction; therefore I assume that the acid at one end is connected with the base of the other end, and that the acidic reaction is thus cancelled":

$$\left.\begin{array}{l} \text{Ȼ}H_2\text{—}NH_2 \\ \text{Ȼ}H_2\text{—}S\Theta_3H \end{array}\right\}$$

Taurin

(Strecker still uses the symbols Ȼ and Θ for the "double" atoms, a style introduced by Berzelius.)

Jakob Volhard (1834–1910, Darmstadt) synthesized "kreatin," a substance previously crystallized from meat extract (Greek *kreas,* flesh), starting from chlorinated acetic acid and methylamine. "Guanidine," a product of oxidation of the main substance in guano, was, according to Emil Erlenmeyer (1825–1909, Aschaffenburg), simply urea in which oxygen was replaced by an ammonia radical.

$$\begin{array}{l} NH_2 \\ | \\ C{=}O \\ | \\ NH_2 \end{array} \qquad\qquad \begin{array}{l} NH_2 \\ | \\ C{=}NH \\ | \\ NH_2 \end{array}$$

Urea Guanidine

Much more complex is the substance that Nicolas Théodore Gobley (1811–1876, Paris) separated out of the yolk of eggs, lecithine (Greek *lekitos,* egg), in 1845. It contains glycerol, phosphoric acid, fatty acids, and choline. Wurtz had shown by synthesis that choline is an alcohol. (Gobley, too, clung to Berzelius' manner of indicating "double atoms.")

$$\begin{array}{l} \text{Ȼ}H_2.\Theta H \\ | \\ \text{Ȼ}H_2.N(\text{Ȼ}H_3)_3.\Theta H. \end{array}$$

According to Strecker, this alcohol forms an ester with one of the acid groups of phosphoric acid attached to glycerol, while two of the alcoholic groups of glycerol are esterified by fatty acids (19):

$$\begin{array}{l} \text{Ȼ}H_2\text{-}\Theta\text{-}P\Theta\left\{\begin{array}{l}\Theta\text{-}\text{Ȼ}_3H_5\left\{\begin{array}{l}\Theta.\text{Ȼ}_{16}H_{31}\Theta \\ \Theta.\text{Ȼ}_{18}H_{33}\Theta\end{array}\right. \\ \Theta H\end{array}\right. \\ | \\ \text{Ȼ}H_2\text{-}N(\text{Ȼ}H_3)_3.\Theta H \end{array}$$

Uric acid and xanthine were the main chemical substances of urinary calculi (stones) in the excrement of snakes and birds. Oxidation of uric acid with nitric acid gave a series of products—alloxantin, alloxan, and urea—and by further oxidation, parabanic and barbituric acid. "The metamorphosis of names in this department of chemistry is at least as perplexing as the metamorphosis of the substances themselves." (20)

These simpler products of chemical conversion could at least be completely identified. Barbituric acid, for example, was urea combined with malonic acid to malonyl-urea. Ludwig Medicus (1847–1915, Würzburg) constructed the molecule of uric acid (1875):

```
            OC—NH
             |   |
       ╱NH—C   CO
    OC       ‖   |
       ╲NH—C—NH
```

The physiological chemist who intended to investigate the role of organic substances in life was confronted with a basic problem. Mulder stated it in these words:

> One particular difficulty in physiological investigations is that to the extent that we leave the field of direct observation and replace it by experiments we run the risk of not finding the truth. And yet, how shall we obtain some kind of scientific knowledge of living nature unless we isolate the effects, unless we separate the influences, unless we strive to study each specialty out of a complex whole? (21)

He exemplifies this situation by describing research on the function of saliva. This alkaline solution of a small quantity of salt, mucous substance, and fat contains a substance that converts starch and dextrines into sugar. Berzelius called this substance "ptyaline" (1832); others considered it to be a diastase, like the starch-converting enzyme that alcohol precipitates from malt extract. A biologically rather unusual salt is also present in saliva, Potassium sulfocyanide (also called "rhodanite" because of the red color which it gives when iron salts are added). Mulder continues:

> If we want to learn about the influence of saliva on digestion, we have to let separated saliva act on foods and follow the changes they undergo; we even have to investigate ptyaline and potassium sulfocyanide and other components of saliva separately, then two and two together, and thus ascending to the whole saliva, concern-

ing their actions. In this way science will come into our knowledge. But saliva does not occur in this form and therefore does not act in this way; such a science, which alone may be called science, would thus teach something quite different from the nature of the influence of the original saliva as it occurs in the mouth.

Still the chemical method consisted in separating influences and ascribing them to substances. For example, diastase was precipitated together with phosphoric acid, expressly added to the extract from malt, by forming calcium phosphate. From the precipitate it was separated by digestion with dilute phosphoric acid. "Emulsine," the amygdalin-splitting agent, was obtained from almonds after pressing out the oil by digestion with water and again pressing the mass. The press-liquor separated into a cream and a water layer. Alcohol precipitated the active principle from the water, together with salts, mainly calcium phosphates. Gastric juice contains "pepsine" (from Greek *pepto,* digesting). It is present there in acidic solution which dissolves albuminous substances (peptides), according to the 1836 report of Theodor Schwann, the German professor of physiology who worked in Louvain (Löwen), and later, Liège (Lüttich). A few years later pepsine preparations were introduced for medical use to help in digestive disorders. "Papaine," from the latex of *carica papaya,* had a still stronger and more universal digestive action on meat, gluten, and other albuminous materials.

Chemical influences on enzyme actions were investigated; borax and heavy-metal salts were found to inhibit them. The temperature ranges were usually around 37°C, although diastase was active even up to 70°C.

A. Wurtz noted that albuminoids absorb papaine or pepsine, and he concluded that temporary combinations between enzyme and substrate preceded and facilitated the decomposing action.

While chemists investigated the carefully separated substances and their actions under laboratory conditions, physiologists like François Magendie (1785–1855, Paris) and Claude Bernard (1813–1878, Paris) used living animals as their test objects. Bernard showed that diabetes can be induced artificially either by the mechanical lesion of a nerve center or by the injection of the alkaloid "curarin," the active substance in curare, which South American natives use to poison their arrow tips.

In 1884, A. W. Hofmann called the main alkaloid in hemlock "coniin" (Latin, *conium maculatum*) because of its natural source, and α-propyl-piperidine, because of its chemical constitution. Albert Ladenburg (1842–1911, Breslau) synthesized coniin, starting from a substance isolated from coal tar, α-picolin, and acetaldehyde. The synthetic product was optically inactive, but it could be separated into two optical antipodes by one of Pasteur's methods. The dextrorotatory component was identical with the natural product in all properties, including the physiological effect. (22)

REFERENCES

1. F. C. Accum, A practical treatise on gas-light (London, 1815).

2. J. Liebig, "Bemerkungen zu vorstehender Abhandlung" (by J. B. Dumas and J. S. Stas, "Über das wahre Atomgewicht des Kohlenstoffs," pp. 141–95), *Liebig's Ann.,* **38** (1841), pp. 195–213, esp. p. 203.

3. A. Kekulé, "Über die Konstitution des Benzols," *Chem. Ber.,* **2** (1869), pp. 362–5.

4. M. E. Chevreul, *Ann. Chim.,* **72** (1809), 113–42; Welter, *ibid.,* **29,** p. 301. J. M. Hausmann is credited with the 1778 discovery.

5. A. Laurent, "Sur le phényle et ses dérivés," *Ann. Chim.* (3), **3** (1841), pp. 195–228.

6. Ch. Gerhardt, *Traité de Chimie* (Paris, 1853–56), Vol. 3, p. 41; he cites Girardin, *Journ. de Pharm.* (3), **21**, p. 30, and the dyer Guinon of Lyons.

7. C. G. Williams, "On the volatile bases produced by the destructive distillation of cinchonine," *Trans. Roy. Soc. Edinburgh,* **21,** (1857), pp. 309–26.

8. W. H. Perkin, British Patent 1984 of August 26, 1856. Sir Robert Robinson, "The life and work of Sir William Henry Perkin," in *Proceedings of the Perkin Centennial,* Howard J. White, Ed. (New York: 1956), p. 41–50.

9. Renard Frères, French Patent 22,706 of April 4, 1859. (The botanist *von Fuchs* died in Tübingen, 1565.)

10. Quoted and translated from A. Balland and I. Luizet, *Le Chimiste Z. Roussin* (Paris: T.-B. Baillière, 1908), p. 43, footnote.

11. Quoted from Richard Willstätter, *Aus meinem Leben* (Berlin: Verlag Chemie, 1949), p. 124.

12. R. Willstätter, in Bugge's *Buch der Grossen Chemiker* (Berlin: Verlag Chemie, 1930), Vol. 2, p. 323.

13. A. Baeyer, "Über die Wasserentziehung und ihre Bedeutung für das Pflanzenleben und die Gärung," *Chem. Ber.,* **3** (1870), p. 63; *Gesammelte Werke,* Vol. 1, p. 501; *ibid.,* pp. xl ff. (Braunschweig: 1905).

14. J. Dalton, *A New System of Chemical Philosophy* (London: 1808–1827), p. 220.

15. G. J. Mulder, *Versuch einer allgemeinen physiologischen Chemie* (Braunschweig: 1844), pp. 300 ff.

16. Carl Schmidt, "Über Pflanzenschleime und Bassorin," *Liebig's Ann.,* **51** (1844), pp. 29–62, esp. p. 30.

17. A. Butlerow, "Formation synthétique d'une substance sucrée," *Compt. Rend.,* **53** (1861), pp. 145–7.

18. H. Kiliani, "My Life and Work," *J. Chem. Ed.,* **9** (1932), p. 1408.

19. A. Strecker, "Über das Lecithin," *Liebig's Ann.*, **148** (1868), pp. 77–90.

20. F. Frederic Daniell, *An Introduction to the Study of Chemical Philosophy* (London: John W. Parker, 1843), p. 665.

21. G. J. Mulder, *Versuch einer allgemeinen physiologischen Chemie,* 2d half (Braunschweig: Friedrich Vieweg & Sohn, 1844–1851), pp. 951 ff.

22. Cf. E. Farber, "Bio-active substances in the nineteenth century," *Chymia,* **3**(Philadelphia: University of Pennsylvania Press, 1950), pp. 63–76. J. M. D. Olmsted, *Claude Bernard, Physiologist* (New York: Harper & Brothers, 1938). Reino Virtanen, *Claude Bernard and his place in the history of ideas* (Lincoln: University of Nebraska Press, 1960).

15

The Periodic System

The search for the relationship among the great number of elements started almost as soon as the new system of chemistry was established. At first it was merely an attempt to find numerical relations. J. B. Richter in 1792 calculated that the neutralization equivalents of the six "earths" could be expressed by the formula $525 + 89n$, in which n is, consecutively, 0, 1, 3, 6, 9, and 19. Doebereiner, who started his search for a relationship in 1817, in 1829 more explicitly described an "attempt to arrange the elements according to their analogy." He found four "triads":

Ca, Sr, Ba; Li, Na, K; Cl, Br, J; S, Se, Te

In each of these triads, the properties of the elements are similar and the atomic weight of the middle element is higher than that of the first member of the group by as much as it is lower than that of the last. At least such a rule seemed to exist; in some cases a more precise revision of the atomic weights might, he hoped, confirm it.

The search for such rules was greatly stimulated by William Prout's hypothesis in 1815 that all atoms were built of primordial atoms, which he tried to identify with the hydrogen atom. Berzelius ridiculed "the fever of the multiples," but it received strong support from the new developments in organic chemistry. Organic radicals had been compared with elements as a kind of justification for that hypothetical concept. Now the process was reversed. Max Pettenkofer (1818–1901), in Munich, 1850, compared metals with organic radicals in order to find "the regular distances of the so-called simple radicals." J.-B. Dumas applied the theory of organic types (page 184) to elements. He saw the "type of fluorine" in the other halogens and the "type of azote" in phosphorus, arsenic, and antimony. Such groups of elements form a progression, like homologous organic compounds. When *a* is equal to initial number or type, *d* to the difference in atomic weights, and *n* to the consecutive number of an element, the progression is $a + nd$, and *nd* defines the place of the member.

These attempts suffered from the unsettled state between atomic and equivalent weights. As long as Cl was given by the atomic weight 35.5, while oxygen was considered as having the atomic weight 8, or magnesium 12 and chromium 26, no reasonable rules for progressions could be formed. The agreement reached through Cannizzaro's return to Avogadro's and Dulong's theory cleared the way for further efforts. Dumas and Stas, who worked on precise methods for determining atomic weights, arrived at a confirmation of Doebereiner's hypothesis of the constant increments in triads (1860).

In his *Handbuch der Chemie,* Leopold Gmelin (1843) proposed an arrangement of the elements in which the triads of Doebereiner are recognizable:

The elementary bodies may be arranged in groups according to their physical and chemical relations; and these groups may be again arranged according to their more general resemblances. The following is an imperfect attempt of this kind. The only way of making a satisfactory arrangement would be to dispose the elements, not on a plane surface, but within an envelope of three dimensions.

	O								N							H		
F	Cl	Br	I												L	Na		K
	S	Se	Te												Mg	Ca	Sr	Ba
		P	As	Sb							G	Er	Y	Tr	Ce	Di	La	
			C	B	Si								Zr	Th	Al			
		Ti	Ta	Nb	Pe	W						Sn	Cd	Zn				
					Mo	V	Cr		U	Mn	Co	Ni	Fe					
							Bi	Pb	Ag	Hg	Cu							
						Os	Ru	Ir	R	Pt	Pd	Au						(1)

In Gmelins arrangement, L stands for lithium and G for glucinium (beryllium). Between niobium and wolfram (tungsten), Pe means Pelopium, which soon disappeared from the list of recognized elements.

The idea to "dispose the elements . . . within an envelope of three dimensions" occurred to others independently.

Béguyer de Chancourtois in 1862 devised an arrangement of all elements along a "telluric helix," a spiral cut at an angle of 45 degrees on a cylinder mantle. John A. R. Newlands (1838–1898), a practical sugar chemist, (2) in 1865 published a table in which 62 elements were listed in order of atomic weights. They were divided into eight vertical columns and seven horizontal families. The number eight seemed to him of deep importance; the relation of the number of analogous elements is that of one or more octaves in music. The first element in the row is similar to the eighth. The relationship to musical octaves, which might have been full of hidden meaning to men of earlier centuries, as it obviously was to Newlands, seemed to discredit his efforts in the eyes of his contemporaries, who were not ready either to accept de Chancourtois' assertion that "the properties of the substances are the properties of the numbers" (1863).

Just at this time (1864) a small book by Julius Lothar Meyer (1830–1895, Tübingen) on *The Modern Theories of Chemistry,* with a table of 28 elements, was published in Breslau. The elements were arranged in six horizontal rows in the order of the atomic weights, and in six vertical columns according to their valency.

At that time it was not possible to include all the known elements because the atomic weights for some of them were doubtful or erroneous. Thallium was only tentatively included at a place in the column where the alkali metals were listed. It was a continuation of Doebereiner's attempt to discover the significance of the differences between the atomic weights in the vertical columns.

In 1868 Dmitri Ivanovich Mendeleev (1834, Tobolsk –1907 Petrograd) undertook to write a handbook of chemistry, and he needed a system of the simple bodies for its organization. In this

LOTHAR MEYER'S TABLE (1864)

4-Valent	3-Valent	2-Valent	1-Valent	1-Valent	2-Valent
–	–	–	–	$Li_{7.01}$	$(Be)_{(9.3)}$
Diff. =				15.98	(14.6)
$C_{11.97}$	$N_{14.01}$	$O_{15.96}$	$Fl_{19.1}$	$Na_{22.99}$	$Mg_{23.94}$
Diff. = 16	16.95	16.02	16.3	16.05	15.96
Si_{28}	$P_{30.96}$	$S_{31.98}$	$Cl_{35.37}$	$K_{39.04}$	$Ca_{39.90}$
Diff. = $\frac{1}{2} \cdot 90$	43.9	46	44.38	46.2	47.3
–	$As_{74.9}$	Se_{78}	$Br_{79.75}$	$Rb_{85.2}$	$Sr_{87.2}$
Diff. = 45	47	50	46.78	47.5	49.6
$Sn_{117.8}$	Sb_{122}	Te_{128}	$J_{126.53}$	$Cs_{132.7}$	$Ba_{136.8}$
Diff. = 88.6	85.5				
$Pb_{206.4}$	$Bi_{207.5}$	–	–	$Tl_{204?}$	–

predicament, which recalls that of Berzelius about 60 years before, Mendeleev decided to base his system on an absolutely objective principle, the atomic weights. At night, in his sleep, he saw the periodicity with which similar elements recur. In March, 1869, he presented his first periodic table to the Russian Chemical Society. It contained question marks and empty spaces for undiscovered elements. "The boldness of thought" which he ascribed to himself proved successful. "The elements, arranged according to the order of their atomic weights, represent a clearly recognizable periodicity of the properties. . . . The magnitude of the atomic weight determines the character of the elements . . . We must expect the discovery of many unknown simple substances, e.g., analogues of aluminum and silicium with the atomic weight 65–75. . . . Some analogies of the elements are discovered by their atomic weights . . ." This is the *Natural System of the Elements* (1870). He used it to predict the properties of unknown elements, and his predictions were confirmed when scandium (1879), gallium (1875), and germanium (1886) were actually discovered. This method of predicting properties from the place in the system was of great help in later work on rare gases and radioactively produced elements. Physical properties, like specific heat, light refraction, melting point, ductility, and metallic character, and conductivity for heat and electricity were found by Meyer and Mendeleev to be functions of the atomic weights. "The numerical value of the atomic weights is the variable by which the material nature and the related properties are determined." (3) Mendeleev discarded all "deeper" speculation about the reasons for periodicity; Meyer felt that Prout's hypothesis might hold the key for an explanation. He

Tabelle II.

Reihen	Gruppe I. — R^2O	Gruppe II. — RO	Gruppe III. — R^2O^3	Gruppe IV. RH^4 RO^2	Gruppe V. RH^3 R^2O^5	Gruppe VI. RH^2 RO^3	Gruppe VII. RH R^2O^7	Gruppe VIII. — RO^4
1	H=1							
2	Li=7	Be=9,4	B=11	C=12	N=14	O=16	F=19	
3	Na=23	Mg=24	Al=27,3	Si=28	P=31	S=32	Cl=35,5	
4	K=39	Ca=40	—=44	Ti=48	V=51	Cr=52	Mn=55	Fe=56, Co=59, Ni=59, Cu=63.
5	(Cu=63)	Zn=65	—=68	—=72	As=75	Se=78	Br=80	
6	Rb=85	Sr=87	?Yt=88	Zr=90	Nb=94	Mo=96	—=100	Ru=104, Rh=104, Pd=106, Ag=108.
7	(Ag=108)	Cd=112	In=113	Sn=118	Sb=122	Te=125	J=127	
8	Cs=133	Ba=137	?Di=138	?Ce=140	—	—	—	— — — —
9	(—)	—	—	—	—	—	—	
10	—	—	?Er=178	?La=180	Ta=182	W=184	—	Os=195, Ir=197, Pt=198, Au=199.
11	(Au=199)	Hg=200	Tl=204	Pb=207	Bi=208	—	—	
12	—	—	—	Th=231	—	U=240	—	— — — —

Fig. 26. Mendeleev's table of 1872.

found some of Mendeleev's arrangements of the elements unwarranted and disturbing, and he warned against "unnecessary hypotheses." Mendeleev quickly accepted the criticism of his first table, and so corrected the positions of several elements in his large table of 1870.

Above all the differences in the details and in the distinction between fact and hypothesis, it was now established that "the properties of the elements are closely related to the atomic weight; they are functions, and periodic functions at that, of the magnitude of the atomic weight." (4)

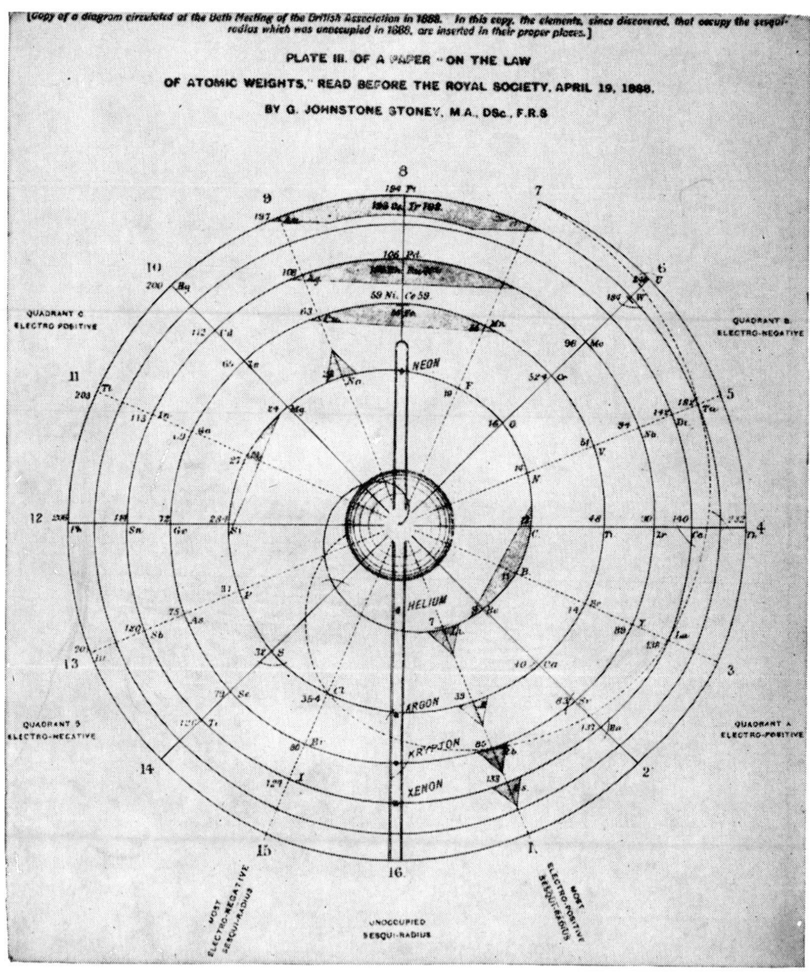

Fig. 27. G. Johnstone Stoney's spiral arrangement of the elements, 1888.

Mendeleev was satisfied with the beauty of a relationship which embraced the actually known elements and formed the systematic rule to which any possible element was subject. If Prout's hypothesis could be verified, which would mean that all elements are built of hydrogen atoms, it would indicate a homology between the elements but not a periodicity. The determination of atomic weights to which Stas devoted his efforts seemed to leave the hypothesis at least debatable for a long time. Finally, however, Stas came to the conclusion that exceptions to the rule were too frequent and too unquestionable to keep it up any longer, and he had to give up his conviction which he had set out to prove.

The spectra of some elements at high temperatures were interpreted as indicating a decomposition into other elements, but this was refuted. (5) Victor von Richter (1841–1891) surveyed these experiences in the following words:

> While thus no actual proof of the possibility of decomposition of elements is available, and while a synthesis of elements is still further away than their real dissection, this does not at all impose the properties of the elements on the assumption of one, or perhaps a limit to speculation. It appears as the task of theoretical chemistry in this direction first to find the real law of atomic numbers, then to develop a hypothesis which is satisfactory for explaining several, primordial substances in a manner similar to that used for the carbon compounds. At any rate, it is even now established that the qualities of the elements can be related to quantities—like colors to vibrations—and that this goal of all scientific explanation of nature is also attainable with regard to the chemical elements. (6)

REFERENCES

1. Leopold Gmelin, *Hand-book of Chemistry,* translated by Henry Watts (London: The Cavendish Society, 1849), Vol. 2, p. 1.

2. See W. H. Taylor, "J. A. R. Newlands, a Pioneer in Atomic Numbers," J. *Chem. Ed.,* **26** (1949), p. 491.

3. D. I. Mendeleev, *Russ. Chem. Ges.,* **1,** 60; also in *Zeitschrift für Chemie* (1869), p. 405. V. A. Krotikov, "The Mendeleev archives and museum of the Leningrad University," *J. Chem. Ed.,* **37** (1960), pp. 625–8.

4. L. Meyer, *Die modernen Theorien der Chemie.* (2d ed.; Breslau: Maruschke & Berendt, 1872), p. 303.

5. Lecoq de Boisbaudran, "Sur la théorie de la spectroscopie," *Compt. Rend.,* **82** (1876), p. 1264.

6. V. v. Richter in *Handwörterbuch der Chemie,* A. Ladenburg. Ed. (Breslau: Eduard Trewendt, 1885), Vol. 3, pp. 604–5.

16

The Course of Chemical Change

Catalysis

Two fundamental causes for chemical change were generally accepted in the early nineteenth century: the universal motion of molecules and the specific affinities among elements. Since the particles of all matter are constantly in motion, and since they are endowed with affinities, it is surprising that many substances are apparently quite stable, at least at ordinary temperatures. Heating promotes chemical change; this was an old and generally recognized occurrence that was easily explained by the increased violence of motion. Yeast produces visible motion in a sugar-containing solution or in dough. Fermentation is chemical change, and its cause was called a "ferment." Where the increase of motion obtained by heat seemed insufficient to produce the desired reaction, it was felt that the additional motion produced by a ferment-like agent might lead to success. Alchemists thought they had found such ferments in the philosopher's stone, or elixir. Only a small quantity of ferment or transmuting agent would be necessary to change large amounts of substances. After alchemistic efforts had failed and ceased, the general idea of ferment-like action remained and came to new life through experiences gained in the combustion of gases, in the decomposition of hydrogen peroxide, and soon afterward in many other fields.

During his work on a safety lamp for miners, Humphry Davy (1) investigated the combustion of methane when the mixture of this combustible gas with oxygen was in contact with a hot metal wire. A slightly preheated platinum spiral, inserted in such a gas mixture, increased its temperature almost to white heat as though the metal itself were the combustible substance. The combustion in contact with the hot wire takes place without a flame. This is characteristic of platinum and palladium, but it is not restricted to methane. A heated platinum wire connected to the wick of an alcohol lamp starts to glow and remains glowing until all the alcohol is consumed. Paul Erman (1764–1851, Berlin) showed in 1819 that the mixture of about equal volumes of hydrogen and oxygen is ignited by platinum that has been warmed to only about 500°C.

Most of these experiments were carried out with metal wires. Platinum foil gave weaker results. Presumably the difference was caused by the smaller surface of the foil. The greatest effect was obtained with fine powder made by reducing the solution of platinum sulfate with alcohol. At room temperature this powder starts to glow when it is moistened with alcohol. The finely divided platinum converts the alcohol into acetic acid. Doebereiner (1780–1849), after 1810 professor of chemistry, pharmacy, and technology in Jena, was particularly interested in the chemical properties of platinum. A great help in this work were Goethe's curiosity and the Grand Duke's present of several kilograms of this precious metal. On a later occasion, Doebereiner stated that the times he had spent on this research were "the most delightful hours of my life." With his background as a practical pharmacist and industrial chemist, he developed practical applications of the exciting properties of finely divided platinum. He used it in a chemical air improver and in a "pneumatic lighter." The latter found particular favor. In 1828 about twenty thousand of his lighters were in use in Germany and England. (2) He had no material gain from this commercial development, but he did not mind. He liked science more than money.

Peregrine Phillips in 1831 described a different practical application in his English patent No. 6069, in which platinum in the form of wire or sponge is used for oxidizing sulfur dioxide in the manufacture of sulfuric acid. In all these cases, platinum causes combustible materials to combine with oxygen. It can also provoke the liberation of oxygen, as from hydrogen peroxide, at that time a newly discovered substance. Its discovery started with the observation by Gay-Lussac and Thenard that potassium metal forms a binoxide (peroxide) when burning in oxygen. A peroxide is also formed from barium oxide when it is in contact with oxygen at red heat. Thenard dissolved this peroxide in dilute hydrochloric acid and found that it leaves its surplus oxygen in the water. Careful operation under cooling with ice was necessary, and after a series of purifications, precipitating barium (as the sulfate), iron and aluminum (as phosphates), chloride and excess barium hydroxide (by silver sulfate), the solution contained only the hydrogen peroxide. It could be concentrated under vacuum. (3)

Hydrogen peroxide is a very unstable compound. Metals, plant fibers, and animal tissues liberate oxygen gas from it so that it reverts to water. Thenard explains in the good old manner that this is an example of the action of a particular physical force. An analogous force could be assumed to produce all the secretions in plants and animals, where an organ, "without absorbing, without yielding anything," transforms the nutrients into new products. Since this force was so mysterious, it was connected with another great mystery and thought to be electrical in nature. If that were the case, and if metals in their function as nonchanging inducers of reactions could rightly be compared with ferments, then, concluded Doebereiner, the reverse might also be true. If ferments could be replaced by metals in decomposing hydrogen peroxide, ferments should be replaceable by metals in fermenting sugar solutions. Therefore, in 1824 he tried to obtain a fermentation of a sugar solution through an electrically differing pair of metals (platinum plus zinc). Furthermore, platinum should be able to combine carbon dioxide with alcohol to the sugar from which they originated in fermentation. Another reversion, that fermenting substances could excite the combination of hydrogen with oxygen to water, as platinum does, was claimed a few years later by Théodore de Saussure (1767–1845, Geneva).

Some of the attempts to explain the activity of metals and ferments continued Lémery's speculations on the form of molecules (page 66) and recurred as late as 1875 in O. Loew's assumption that "sharp corners" of the metal break up the molecules into highly active atoms. (4) Von 1824, Christian K. Pfaff (1773–1852, Kiel) rejected mechanical theories because the action of platinum was due rather to its "particular platinum nature" than to its surface form. Michael Faraday was perhaps influenced by his previous discovery of condensation in illuminating gas (page 179) when he ascribed the increased velocity of gas reactions to condensations on the surface of the metals (1833). Doebereiner included both mechanical and electrochemical causes in his deliberations.

The old (sixteenth century) method of making ether by distilling alcohol in the presence of sulfuric acid was investigated during these years, most thoroughly by Eilhard Mitscherlich (1833). Sulfuric acid, like Doebereiner's platinum, acted without being changed or exhausted. Mitscherlich considered this as being important for more than just this one reaction. "Decompositions and combinations which are produced in this manner are very frequent; let us call them decomposition and combination by contact." (5)

Compared with the preceding picturesque assumptions, this theory sounds like a retreat to a mere statement of localization. Mitscherlich would most likely have mentioned the contact theory for the voltaic battery if it had influenced his thoughts.

In his Jahres-Bericht, dated March 31, 1835, Berzelius coordinated the experiences in this field of "action by contact." He placed particular emphasis on the processes in "living nature where we see vessels of uninterrupted continuance take up blood and from their orifices give out milk, gall, urine, etc." Sulfuric acid was shown by Kirchhoff in 1812 to convert starch into sugar, and the same is true of diastase (Payen and Persoz, page 219); the action of both is of the "same nature." A "new force for evoking chemical activity," common to organic and inorganic nature, is here recognizable. Its nature is still hidden, but a name is needed for it. "I shall, therefore, . . . call it the 'catalytic force' of the bodies, and the decomposition through it, 'catalysis'." Berzelius chose this word because of its resemblance to "analysis," which designates the separation of the components of bodies "by means of the usual chemical affinity." "The catalytic force seems to mean that bodies, through their mere presence and not through their affinity, are able to awaken the affinities which are dormant at this temperature. . . ." Thus diastase converts starch through catalytic force. This does not imply that the diastase catalytic process is the only one in plant life. "On the contrary, we have good reason to expect that thousands of catalytic processes take place between the tissues and the fluids in living plants and animals. . . ."

A new name for a "hidden force" was thus created, based on many experiments, with no theory, but with an intuitive prediction that where we now have one example we shall find "thousands." Berzelius expected that the catalytic force would prove to be "a particular kind of realization" of the electrochemical relationship. John Mercer (1791–1866) in 1842 assumed a feeble chemical affinity, and Lyon Playfair (1819–1898) in 1848 supposed an accessory affinity in catalysis. All this pointed in the same electrochemical direction. Liebig, however, declared that it was harmful for science to introduce a "new force" without a theory. His own theory was a revival of G. E. Stahl's thoughts about fermentation, in which the chemical change was attributed to a transfer of molecular excitation. Wilhelm Ostwald in 1901 said Liebig's theory was unverifiable and therefore fruitless. On the other hand, Richard Willstätter in 1927 held the lack of any hypothesis in Berzelius' concept responsible for a temporary decline of interest in catalysis. Alwin Mittasch (6) does not see such a decline in the years following 1836. The theory was expanded by Schönbein; practical applications were sought in the production of sulfuric acid, nitric acid, and chlorine. The interest in catalytic processes remained active in England, France, Germany, and Italy.

In an alcoholic solution containing potassium, benzaldehyde forms benzyl alcohol and benzoic acid. This finding by Cannizzaro (7) in 1853 was soon interpreted as an example for a general rule: An aldehyde can be disproportioned into its alcohol and its acid, the middle state of oxidation into the corresponding lower and higher states, which was then called the Cannizzaro reaction.

For the oxidation of hydrochloric acid to chlorine, Henri Deacon (1822–1876), "alkali manufacturer at Widnes," as he called himself, employed copper sulfate as "the active or catalytic substance." (8) He distributed this catalyst over a porous clay carrier. "Deacon's method of obtaining chlorine" became industrial shortly after his death.

At that time, methods for oxidizing sulfur dioxide over metallic catalysts, particularly platinum, were tried in Germany.

In France, Friedel and Crafts (9) expanded their work on the action of aluminum chloride in chemical synthesis. In 1878 they described the combination of benzene with carbon dioxide to benzoic acid, and with phthalic anhydride to benzoylbenzoic acid:

$$C_6H_5CO{\cdot}C_6H_4COOH$$

The latter formed the intermediate step for a synthesis of anthraquinone, which was important for dyestuff manufacture.

The use of catalysts such as vanadium pentoxide in the manufacture of dyestuffs from aniline and its derivatives was mentioned earlier.

The Drama of Chemical Reaction

The significance of time in chemical changes began to be recognized at the middle of the nineteenth century. Up to then it had not been entirely neglected. In 1775, C. F. Wenzel proposed the velocity of a chemical reaction as the measure of its affinity. He had, however, little success; too many exceptions limited the usefulness of such a rule, and there was not sufficient interest in the role of time to explore reasons for the exceptions. For most cases, instantaneous action seemed to be the general assumption. A parallel can be found in physiology. According to Johannes Müller in 1844, the brain and spinal cord transmit received sensations to the muscles in infinitely small and immeasurable time intervals. Hermann Helmholtz in 1850 found his colleagues very reluctant to accept his report that he had measured the interval and found it to be 0.0014 to 0.002 seconds for frog nerves 50 to 60 millimeters in length.

In his letter to Liebig of November 5, 1853, Christian Friedrich Schönbein (1799–1868, Basle) set forth his idea that a series of processes occurs from the time when reagents are brought together until the new combination is completed. Every chemical analysis or synthesis is "a drama composed of many acts," as he expressed it in 1868. The special observation from which Schönbein started out in his letter to Liebig was the discovery that oxygen forms a new modification, ozone, in the presence of phosphorus:

> Phosphorus and oxygen of the usual kind are completely indifferent to each other at ordinary temperature, and under such conditions could always remain in closest contact without undergoing a chemical combination. Following a change of the existing conditions, e.g., on diluting the oxygen strongly or mixing it with hydrogen or nitrogen gas, everything else and, particularly, temperature remaining the same, the gas, as we now know, begins to suffer a deep change in its chemical state. It becomes ozonized and only when thus changed does it acquire the ability to associate with phosphorus chemically. . . . I am greatly inclined to believe that similar events occur in all chemical combinations. . . .

It is characteristic that one special observation is felt to be "an example." Although only one experiment, it is not haphazard and unrelated, but one of the entire group of "all" experiments and therefore exemplary. There is no other proof for it than a strongly felt intuition. Many cases of such intuitive conclusions from one experiment or from a small number serve as "examples" to demonstrate the correctness of the method of generalization. The basis of using this method was not so much experimental proof as the unexpressed conviction of a unity of nature which becomes visible to us in each single observation. The systems in chemistry were built on theories for which the bases were slim, so far as "examples" were concerned, but they were limitless as being representative of all nature. Theories were formed by adding a large proportion of personal conviction to a small collection of facts. In the equation,

$$\text{Theory} = \text{Fact} + \text{Personal conviction}$$

the two members on the right change in relative value with historical time and with personality. In any democratic discussion among scholars, facts are increased and the personal part is gradually converted into human universality. This represents the attempt to approach a final proof of theory. The process, as a whole, is democratic; in its steps it is often modified by the weight of personality. The attempt could be undertaken because it started from the fundamental assumption that unity connects all substances. The few grams of one or two substances with which the experiment was carried out were representative for any larger amount of these substances. In a similar manner, a few "examples" of different kinds of substances were sufficient to demonstrate the rule that governs a whole group of different substances. The old notion that all substances contain all elements thus appears to have left a specific residue. For elements in the meaning of substances the old notion had been abolished in the "New System"; for elements in the wider sense of qualities and causes of behavior it was still active. The old universalistic concept remained in the background as an undisclosed assumption.

Alexander William Williamson (1824–1904, London) used the formation of ether as an "example" for arriving at the "broader basis of the movements of the atoms." He explained this "basis" by using a familiar substance, hydrochloric acid. There are many atoms in a liter or any sizable volume of this gas, and they are in a process of continuous change. Each hydrogen atom does not remain in quiet connection with its own chlorine atom. Our methods do not distinguish between individual HCl "atoms"; we cannot notice the exchange directly. In a mixture of HCI with $CuSO_4$, not only H and Cl but also H and Cu will change places and, thereby, partners. At high temperatures, as Rudolf Clausius pointed out (1857), the intensity of the movements increases sometimes to such an extent that the parts of the molecule remain separated from one another. Henri Sainte-Claire Deville (1818–1881, Paris) investigated "voluntary decompositions" in which the "repulsive force of heat," instead of chemical affinity, is the cause. He tried to measure the transition into a "free state" of the molecules of ammonia, water, and sodium hydroxide-hydrate and to demonstrate "that this phenomenon, which must be quite general for sufficiently high temperatures, can often be accurately measured." (10)

In the same year, Kekulé published his thoughts about addition compounds formed between reagents. His theory of the "drama" of the reactions (11) tries to prevent or avoid the erroneous idea "as if the radicals and atoms existed in a free state during the interchange, while, so to speak, on the way" to the end products. Instead, two molecules combine first, attracted by affinity, and then a redistribution of atoms takes place in this addition compound. The intermediate attraction is followed by a separation in a different direction:

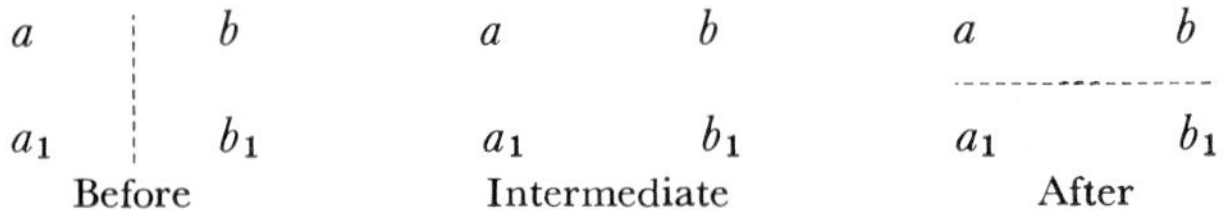

a ⋮ b	a b	a b
a_1 ⋮ b_1	a_1 b_1	a_1 b_1
Before	Intermediate	After

Actually, he replaces the difficulty of assuming a "free state" for radicals and atoms by the other difficulty of explaining the free state of the compounds aa_1 and bb_1. The relationship between the two difficulties is similar to that between Dalton's and Avogadro's views regarding atoms and molecules (page 151).

Ideas lead to programs of experiments. The two approaches to such programs were either the measurement of physical properties characteristically accompanying the chemical change or the separation of the intermediate compounds into substances. For the first approach, optical properties had been suggested since the 1830s, when Jean-Baptiste Biot (1774–1862, Paris) followed the changes in a solution of tartaric acid by observing the rotation of the plane of polarized light. Eilhard Mitscherlich predicted in 1843 that "polarized light is a means for observing the changes which take place in an atomic group when different substances act upon it." He developed a convenient apparatus for such measurements and described it in the fourth edition of his *Lehrbuch der Chemie* (1844). This was the method Ludwig F. Wilhelmy (1812–1864, Heidelberg) used for finding the laws according to which the action of acids on cane sugar takes place. (12) The change of optical rotation, in a sugar solution, called "inversion," can be described by the equation

$$-\frac{dZ}{dT} = M \cdot Z \cdot S$$

The decrease of the sugar dZ in the short time interval dT is equal to the product of the quantity of sugar Z (*Zucker*) and of acid S (*Säure*), multiplied by a factor M which is a median value of the velocity of inversion. This, according to Wilhelm Ostwald, is "the first time that the course of a chemical process has been formulated mathematically." (13)

About the function of the acid in the hydrolysis of saccharose, Löwenthal and Lenssen found in 1852 that "Every acid is active; the degree is different according to the acidity." A correlation was found here which connected a subjectively observed quality with an objectively measurable chemical activity. J. H. Jellett (1817–1888, Dublin) used measurements of optical rotation for determining the distribution of acid between optically active alkaloids (14):

Quinine + Codeine hydrochloride = Codeine + Quinine hydrochloride

J. H. Gladstone (1827–1902, London) tried to separate complicated influences on the formation of ferric rhodanide, using the red color as an indicator and measure. (15)

So far as it was considered in Wilhelmy's experiments, the inversion of cane sugar proceeds only in one direction, from the saccharose to the mixture of glucose and fructose. The reaction between an organic acid and an alcohol leads to the corresponding ester and water. This reaction, however, does not continue to completion because of the opposite tendency of the ester to split into its components. The result is an equilibrium between acid, alcohol, ester, and water.

Acid + Alcohol = Ester + Water

M. Berthelot and one of the few assistants in his laboratory work, L. Péan de Saint-Gilles (1832–1863), were attracted to the study of this reaction because, as they state, it is "of the greatest interest for the theory of affinity." It is a question of the influence of time and the overwhelming role that certain conditions of equilibrium exert, these being entirely independent of those expressed by the laws of Berthollet. The esters form a new fundamental type which is as characteristic for organic chemistry as the salt type for mineral chemistry. The reactions of the esters are models for a vast number of phenomena which recur with the same principal marks in our laboratory chemistry as in the transformation of the constituents of living organisms. (16) The laboratory and the living organisms are still the two fields in which the chemist sees his science applied, as we found it twenty-five years before in the development of catalysis. Chemical industry was not yet closely enough connected with science, or sufficiently developed, to provide corroborating comparisons.

Acids and bases combine to salts quickly in homogeneous media, such as gases or solutions, "because the substances reacting with each other form an electrically conducting chain." Ester formation is slow because it depends on diffusion. The more the reaction proceeds, the greater is the dilution of the reagents by their product, which progressively slows the diffusion. This is fortunate insofar as it allows one to use the rapid salt formation as an analytical method for determining the change of acid concentration.

A mathematical formula is used only sparingly in the lengthy treatise of Berthelot to describe the "limit" of esterifaction. The conclusion of the extensive experiments differs from the introduction.

The analogy with inorganic reactions, emphatically denied in the beginning, is re-established at the end, although the essential and differentiating influence of time is again stressed.

The driving force in the drama of chemical reaction is affinity. It is influenced by physical forces. Berthollet (page 129) had shown that cohesion and elasticity or expansion change the course of reactions when their products drop out of the solution and precipitate or when they leave it as gases. The effect of affinity depends not only upon the presence of the substances but also on their active masses. Cato Maximilian Guldberg (1836–1902) and Peter Waage (1833–1900) in Oslo, Norway (then called Christiania), saw that the quantities per volume, or the concentration of the reagents, represented the active masses. They started from an example like

$$\underset{\text{Potassium sulfate}}{K_2SO_4} + \underset{\text{Barium carbonate}}{BaCO_3} = \underset{\text{Potassium carbonate}}{K_2CO_3} + \underset{\text{Barium sulfate}}{BaSO_4}$$

They expressed a first step of generalization by substituting any substances

$$A + B = A' + B'$$

As a second generalization, they introduced the concentrations p, q and p', q' for these substances. The corresponding affinities were introduced in the third step as the factors k or k', which express the intensities, while p and q represent the active quantities. The products $k \times p \times q$ or $k' \times p' \times q'$ are therefore the forces that decide the outcome of the drama. Equilibrium means equality of these forces; when the reaction has reached a standstill, kpq is equal to $k'p'q'$, or

$$p \times q = \frac{k'}{k} \times p' \times q'$$

The concept of forces of affinity does not recur in the final result. This concept had been brought into the discussion because of its historical background. In the particular work of the Norwegian authors it brought about more difficulty than clarity. (17) When only the quantities of substances are measured, as in Guldberg and Waage's work or that of Berthelot and Gilles, the equilibrium indicates only a part of the actions of affinity. Another part that belongs to it is the change in heat. This part had been the object of important developments since about 1840. The relationship of heat and affinity required the building of a new system.

Esterifications With Dramatic Consequences

Schönbein, who sensed the "drama" involved in chemical reaction, discovered one reaction that had highly dramatic consequences. In 1846, he esterified cellulose by nitric acid and obtained a powerful explosive. This was not the first time a carbohydrate had been nitrated. In 1833 Braconnot nitrated starch, and in 1838 Pelouze investigated the reaction more deeply. Schönbein was the first, however, who pursued the technical application of his nitrated cellulose as gunpowder. Rudolf Böttger (1806–1881, Frankfurt-am-Main) worked independently in the same direction.

The year 1846 is remarkable for work on other organic esters of nitric acid. The Italian chemist Ascanio Sobrero (1812–1888) produced such esters with mannit and with glycerol.

Great industrial activities followed soon and continued in spite of many catastrophic explosions. Alfred Nobel (1833–1896, Stockholm), who lost a brother in such an explosion, invented methods for safer operations. He combined nitroglycerin with adsorbent earth materials to make "dynamite," and he obtained great success with special initiators from 1859 to 1868. The new industry led to scientific studies like those by Frederick A. Abel (1827–1902). (18)

Other inventors were intrigued by the solubility and the plastic properties of nitrocelluloses. In Newark, New Jersey, John Wesley Hyatt (1837–1920) and his brother Isaiah obtained U.S. patent 105,338 of July 12, 1870, on their discovery that the addition of camphor to nitrocellulose gives strong plastic materials; they could be molded into clear sheets for photographic purposes.

Count Hilaire Bernigaud de Chardonnet (1839–1924) studied with Pasteur who, at that time, was investigating silkworm disease. Under the lasting impression from this work, de Chardonnet developed a process for making an artificial silk by spinning a solution of "pyroxylin." Ten years after the first French patent, (19) de Chardonnet discovered that the costly and dangerous process of completely drying the nitrocellulose was not necessary; a "hydrate" containing about 25 percent water was even more soluble than the water-free product. (20)

Other methods than that of delicate nitration were found for converting cellulose into a soluble derivative from which sheets and fibers could be produced. Paul Schützenberger (1829, Strasbourg, 1897, Paris) made an acetate by heating cellulose with acetic anhydride under pressure. The method of heating under pressure had been proposed in 1682 by Denis Papin (1647?–1712).

(21) Esterifications with other organic acids followed, but industrial applications began only around 1915.

Charles Frederick Cross (1855–1935, London) and his associates discovered an esterification of cellulose that proceeds in an aqueous medium. They started from the alkali cellulose which John Mercer (1791–1866), a calico printer of Lancashire, had described in 1844 and which became the basis for the widely used "mercerization" of cotton. By treatment with carbon bisulfide, they obtained a xanthogenate which they explained as follows:

> The constitution of the derivative may be expressed by the general formula $CS\langle{}^{OX}_{SNa}$; X representing the variable cellulose unit, that is, the acting residue. This is, however, not a cellulose residue pure and simple, but an *alkali-cellulose;* a fact which is to be expected *a priori,* and is proved by treating the solution with benzoyl chloride, when cellulose is eliminated as a *cellulose benzoate.*
>
> The formula, therefore, may be written $CS\langle{}^{O\cdot(X\cdot ONa)}_{SNa}$ the sodium salt of alkali-cellulosexanthic acid. (22)

After more details had been worked out in 1900, this process became industrially important.

REFERENCES

1. Humphry Davy, "Some new experiments and observations on the combustion of gaseous mixtures with an account of a method of preserving a continued light in a mixture of inflammable gas and air without flame," *Phil. Trans.,* **107** (1817), pp. 77–83.

2. Schweigger's *Jahrbuch,* **24** (1828), p. 417.

3. L. J. Thenard, "Observations sur l'influence de l'eau dans la formation des acides oxygénés," *Ann. Chim.* (2), **9** (1818), pp. 314–7; "Suite des expériences sur l'eau oxygénée," *ibid.,* **10** (1819), pp. 114–5.

4. O. Loew, *J. Prakt. Chem.* (2), **11** (1875), p. 372.

5. E. Mitscherlich, "Über die Aetherbildung," *Pogg. Ann.,* **31** (1834), pp. 273–82.

6. J. J. Berzelius, *Jahres-Bericht über die Fortschritte der physischen Wissenschaften,* XV (1836), p. 237. Alwin Mittasch, *Berzelius und die Katalyse* (Leipzig: 1935), *Kurze Geschichte der Katalyse in Praxis und Theorie* (Berlin: 1939).

7. S. Cannizzaro, "Über den der Benzoesäure entsprechenden Alkohol," *Liebig's Ann.* (N.S.), **16** (1854), pp. 113–7.

8. Henry Deacon, "On Deacon's method of obtaining chlorine, as illustrating some principles of chemical dynamics," *J. Chem. Soc.* (N.S.), **10** (1872), pp. 725–59.

9. Ch. Friedel and J. M. Crafts, "Fixation directe de l'acide carbonique, de l'acide sulfureux, de l'anhydre phthalique sur la benzine, synthèse de l'acide benzoique, de l'hydrure de sulfophényl, et de l'acide benzoylbenzoique," *Compt. Rend.,* **86** (1878), pp. 1368–71.

10. Henri Sainte-Claire Deville, "De la dissociation ou décomposition spontanée des corps sous l'influence de la chaleur," *Compt. Rend.,* **45** (1857), pp. 857–61.

11. A. Kekulé, "Über die Constitution und die Metamorphosen der chemischen Verbindungen und über die chemische Natur des Kohlenstoffs," *Liebig's Ann.,* **106** (1858), pp. 129–59.

12. L. F. Wilhelmy, "Über das Gesetz, nach welchem die Einwirkung von Säuren auf den Rohrzucker stattfindet," *Pogg. Ann.* **81** (1850), pp. 413–28, 499–526.

13. W. Ostwald, *Lehrbuch der Allgemeinen Chemie* (Leipzig: Wilhelm Engelmann, 1896–1902), Vol. 2. Part 2, p. 69.

14. J. H. Jellett, *Transactions of the Irish Academy,* **25** (1875), p. 371.

15. H. Gladstone, "Some experiments illustrative of the reciprocal decomposition of salts," *J. Chem. Soc.* (London: 1856), pp. 44–56.

16. M. Berthelot and L. Péan de St. Gilles, *Ann. Chim.* (3), **65, 66,** and **68** (1862–3).

17. C. M. Guldberg and P. Waage, *Études sur les affinités chimiques* (Christiania: 1867) and *J. Prakt. Chem.* (2), **19** (1879), p. 89.

18. F. A. Abel, "On the manufacture and composition of gun-cotton," *Phil. Trans.,* **156** (1866), pp. 269–308.

19. Hilaire de Chardonnet, French patent 165,349 of November 17, 1884.

20. Hilaire de Chardonnet, German patent 81,599 of May 20, 1895.

21. Paul Schützenberger, "Mémoire sur les dérivés acétiques des principes hydrocarbones, de la mannite et de ses isomères, et de quelques autres principes immédiats végétaux," *Ann. Chim.,* **21** (1870), pp. 235–64.

22. C. F. Cross, E. G. Bevan, and C. Beadle, "The interaction of alkalicellulose and carbon bisulphide," *J. Chem. Soc.,* **63** (1893), pp. 837–45, esp. p. 842.

17

Physical and Chemical Energies

Heat and Affinity

The concept that heat is the result of "unnoticeable motions of the molecules of matter" had been defended by Lavoisier and Laplace toward the end of the eighteenth century and amplified by Davy, Thomas Young, and Ampère at the beginning of the nineteenth. Nevertheless heat remained on the list of chemical elements. It is one of the four "imponderable substances" in Berzelius' *Lehrbuch* of 1825. In the preceding year the final separation of heat from the system of substances had begun.

The new approach was introduced by Sadi Carnot (1796–1832, Paris), a young engineer who investigated the performance of the steam engine. His father, Lazare Carnot, had enlarged the theory of water-driven machines by two new principles. The first was that water could here be considered as a representative of any liquid; the second demonstrated that the machine works with highest efficiency when the driving liquid transfers its motion to the driven wheel in insensibly small steps and completely. Sadi Carnot used and enlarged these two principles in his ideas about the heat-driven engine. Water vapor became the representative of any gas, and the insensibly small steps of power transfer were idealized to a reversibility of a cycle of operations. The cycle becomes completely reversible when the difference in driving force is zero; however, action can take place only with at least a small difference between the forces. Thus strict reversibility exists only where there is nothing to reverse. For all real events, reversibility is a limit state which can be approached but never reached.

Such a closed cycle of reversible operations is a small world of its own. It is so constructed as to contain a sequence of events separated from all other events in the big world so that all scientific attention can be concentrated without diversion. The scientific ideal does not describe reality in all its ramifications but only a limited section from which ambient reality is more or less removed. This new insight of Carnot can be considered as one of the results that a long series of philosophical discussions had prepared for science. Boyle was only skeptical; he struggled with the concept that reality either conforms to the ideal or is entirely different from it. Leibniz resorted to an essentially impossible concept, a prestabilized harmony between ideas and realities. French philosophy showed the necessity for progressing beyond the convenient optimism that everything is at its best. Voltaire ridiculed the pretense that we are living in the best of all possible worlds by speaking about the best of the impossible worlds. The German philosopher Hegel was resigned to a nature that is powerless over its special realities.

Mathematical developments had led to a different kind of limit in the calculus. There a new mathematical element was created, a unit so small that it could serve to reconcile coarse observation of discontinuities with continuous change. Carnot discovered a concept which later on was found to be equivalent to the mathematical limit. The result was the possibility of treating thermodynamics mathematically. Joseph Louis Lagrange (1736–1813) prepared the ground for such possibilities through his general mechanics of the conservation of energy with the bold concepts of virtual velocities: "Powers are in equilibrium when they are inversely proportional to their virtual velocities taken in their own directions. As for the nature of the principle of virtual velocities, it must be admitted that it is not sufficiently clear in itself to be formed into a first principle, but it can be regarded as the general expression of the laws of equilibrium." (1) The equilibrium here considered is that of levers and pulleys; chemistry had no place in this discussion.

This was the background from which Sadi Carnot approached the question: Is steam the best means for producing power through heat? Sadi Carnot found the answer on the basis of Gay-Lussac's experiments about specific heat and the expansion of gases. The change of heat into power was recognized as independent of the medium, steam. The laws connecting heat and power were those of heat; the substance water was only an interchangeable carrier. The motive power of heat is analogous to that of a waterfall; the driving difference in the levels of water is comparable to the difference in temperatures of heat. Carnot constructed an idealized cycle of operation in which a gas expands at high temperature and is compressed to the original volume at a low temperature. The power thus obtained depends only on the difference of temperatures. In notes published posthumously by his brother, Sadi Carnot derives from "some ideas which I have formed about the theory of heat" that, in modern measurement, the mechanical equivalent of heat is 370 kg-meters. (2)

Benoît Pierre Émile Clapeyron (1799–1864, Paris) was the first to see the importance of Carnot's ideas. From discussions of Carnot's cycles he concluded that a quantity of mechanical work is of the same nature as a quantity of heat passing from a hot to a cold body. "It also follows that the work *W* developed by the transition of a certain quantity *Q* of heat from body *A*, held at the temperature t_1, to another body *B*, held at the temperature t_2, is the same for every gas or liquid, and, at the same time, that it is the greatest which can possibly be realized." (3) These temperatures are measured in degrees which are defined by the rate of expansion of air with heat. An "arbitrary series of numbered points of reference" is thus obtained. They now prove to be inconvenient because the amount of work *W* per heat unit which descends one degree in temperature is smaller at high than at low temperatures of this scale. Sir William Thomson (Lord Kelvin of Largs), working in Edinburgh, devised a scale on which all degrees have the same value; that is, a unit of heat descending from a body *A* at the temperature $T°$ of this scale to a body *B* at the temperature $(T - 1)°$ would give out the same mechanical effect whatever the number *T* is. "This may justly be termed an absolute scale, since its characteristic is quite independent of the physical properties of any specific substance." (4)

The new relationship between heat and mechanical work sought the points of independence from matter. They were strictly valid for "all" gases. The question was not raised as to how many actual gaseous substances had to be investigated in order to permit such general statements. The experiments of Boyle, Mariotte, and Gay-Lussac formed the basis. Further development gradually opened new aspects for the relationship of heat with chemical change. At first, in the work by German Henri Hess (1802–1850, St. Petersburg), a purely chemical connection was attempted.

> After the investigations concerning the definite proportions in the compounds had found such a simple expression in the atomistic theory, one discovered, first in the mineral realm, a number of analogies in the composition which were represented by general chemical formulae and thus offered several definite [typical] compositions. The discovery of isomorphism showed that most of the elements of such compounds could be replaced by others without destroying the essential character [which is now called 'type'].
>
> I soon realized that among the symptoms accompanying each

chemical combination there is an essential one which had not been sufficiently studied; I mean the development of heat. More than once I had worked on this subject, as a treatise which I presented in 1831 can testify. But it was only in 1839 that longer continued thinking made me suspect that the cases where the symptoms are the least striking may be the most instructive. After some groping, I concentrated on the study of the heat quantities which the combinations of sulfuric acid with water develop. There I saw, without

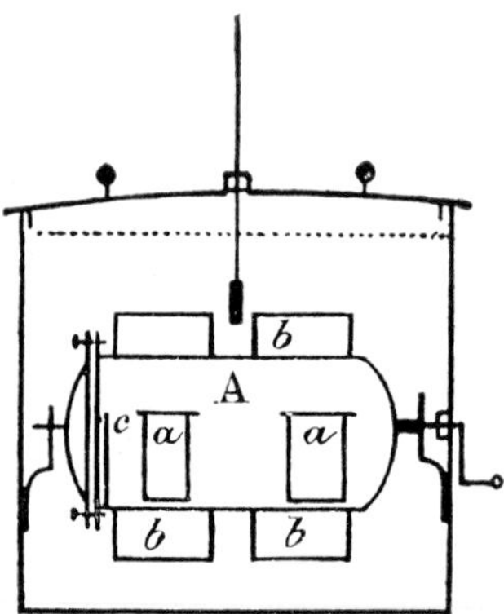

Fig. 28. Diagram of calorimeter. (From G. H. Hess, *Poggendorff's Annalen der Physik,* **50,** 1840, p. 387.)

The calorimeter consists essentially of a copper cylinder *A* with partition *c* in a water container provided with a thermometer. Copper plates *b* are attached to increase heat exchange between the cylinder contents and water. Of the reagents, that of which the larger quantity is needed is put into *A* after the cover has been removed; for the other reagent beakers *a* are used. When the cover has been closed and the unit assembled, the contents of cylinder and beakers are mixed by turning. The change of temperature is then measured.

a doubt, that the atom which is held most strongly also develops the most heat, and I was confirmed in the opinion that the quantity of developed heat could serve as a measure of affinity.

In the course of my investigations I ascertained that no matter by which way a compound may come to be formed, the quantity of heat developed through its formation is always constant; the compound may come to be formed in a direct or indirect way, at once or in different periods of time. This principle is so evident that if I did not think it sufficient in itself I should not hesitate to present it as an axion. (5)

Hess extended his experiments from mixtures of sulfuric acid with water to the neutralization of acids and alkalis, to the preparation of lead and zinc sulfates in different steps, and to the determination of the constitution of salts. His theory arose from a connection of

J. B. Richter's stoichiometric laws with the concept of a heat substance.

These investigations were concluded in 1842. In the same year, Julius Robert Mayer published his discovery that heat is a force among forces, (6) not a substance among substances. Robert Mayer (1814–1878) was born in Heilbronn and studied medicine in Tübingen. After a short period of studies in Paris (1839), he served as doctor on board a ship bound for Java. It was in Surabaya that observation of the intense red of the venous blood of the natives startled him. He connected it with Lavoisier's theory that animal heat is the result of the physiological oxidation of blood. It came to him as an inspiration that in a hot climate less combustion is required to maintain body temperature. The traditional idea that oxidation takes place in the veins helped shorten the train of thought which here found an outstanding example of the classical axiom, cause equals effect. Forces are causes, they are indestructible, transformable, imponderable. As "a practical conclusion," Mayer calculated, from data given by Gay-Lussac and by Dulong for the specific heats of gases at constant volume against those at constant pressure, the "mechanical equivalent of heat" as 1 calorie = 365 kg-meters.

Robert Mayer later extended his ideas to the conservation of force in "living nature" (1845). Here he discussed the "influence of contacts" which initiates transformations of "chemical force" into mechanical effect. Catalysis becomes an example of processes of release, about which Mayer published an article a few years before his death. "The innumerable processes of release withstand all calculations because qualities, unlike quantities, cannot be determined numerically." (7)

At the time when Mayer experienced his inspiration in Java, an English brewer, James Prescott Joule (1818–1889), measured the heat produced by voltaic electricity (1840). He was "satisfied that the grand agents of nature are, by the Creator's fiat, indestructible; and that wherever mechanical force is expended, an exact equivalent of heat is always obtained." (8)

He calculated the energy—*vis viva* in his expression—that is equivalent to the heat content of a substance, and he was amazed to find it "enormous." The scale in which the temperature is measured has to start at the absolute zero, which was, at that time, estimated as 480 degrees below the ice point of the Fahrenheit scale.

> We see what an enormous quantity of *vis viva* exists in matter. A single pound of water at 60° must possess 480° + 28° = 508° of heat; in other words, it must possess a *vis viva* equivalent to that acquired by 415.036 pounds after falling through the perpendicular

> height of one foot. The velocity with which the atmospheres of electricity must revolve in order to present this enormous amount of *vis viva,* must of course be prodigious, and equal probably to the velocity of light in the planetary space, or to that of an electrical discharge as determined by the experiments of Wheatstone. (9)

A complete exposition of the "stringent law of mechanics," namely, the conservation of force in all its applications, was the purpose of Hermann Helmholtz in a paper mainly written in 1843 and 1844. (10) "It is evident that the concepts of matter and force as applied to nature must never be separated. A pure matter would be indifferent to the rest of nature, since it could never cause a change in it or in our sensory organs; a pure force would be something which should exist and again should not, since we call that which exists matter . . . both are abstractions from reality, formed in exactly the same manner. . . ." In systems constructed of material points, all forces are "invariable attracting and repulsing forces, their intensity depending on the distance." The sum of the force of tension and that of motion is always constant. Following William J. M. Rankine (1820–1872, London) these forces were called "potential" and "kinetic" energy. Rankine also coined the name "adiabatic" for processes in a system with walls that are impermeable to heat.

Hermann Helmholtz (1821–1894) was at that time a doctor in the Prussian army. After a year of teaching anatomy to artists, 1848, he was professor of physiology in Königsberg until 1855, in Bonn, 1858, and in Heidelberg. He left in 1871 to become professor of physics in Berlin, and he finally became president of the Physikalisch-Technische Reichsanstalt in 1888. For his studies on the velocity of excitation and contraction in nerves and muscles, he constructed the myographion (1854). His physiological work which was connected with a deep relation to the arts ("The artist cannot copy nature, he must translate it") led him to comparisons between seeing and hearing and then back to studies on the course and propagation of electrical discharges. He induced Heinrich Hertz to investigate the relationships between vibrations of light and of electricity (1879–1880). Thermodynamics filled the later years of his work. In 1883 he began to advocate a government-sponsored "institute for the experimental pursuit of exact sciences and precision technique." It took five years to realize these plans. When we consider the history of our National Science Foundation, we realize that speed in such decisions has not followed the increase which has been so noticeable in everything else since 1883. Helmholtz's influence on his time can perhaps be exemplified by Adolf Trendelenburg, the philosopher of

Berlin, who declared that he had returned to mathematical studies because he wanted to be able to understand Helmholtz (1868). (11)

The development of energetics began with generalizations through which Lazare Carnot extended the functions of water to those of any other liquid, and Sadi Carnot extended the actions of steam to those of any carrier of heat. Particular substances were replaced by general relationships of actions. This process was followed by other generalizations which eliminated, in addition to substances, mechanistic hypotheses of molecular motion and material transmitters of forces. The new science of energetics did not need such hypotheses; it used the numerical relationships between different classes of events. William J. M. Rankine outlined these principles in 1855. (12)

Abstraction from special qualities of substances would have seemed like the abandonment of the task that chemistry had to perform. However, the abstraction did not consist in a negation of qualities; it had a positive side in creating a science of relationships that form a general basis for chemical qualities.

The word "force" in Mayer's and Helmholtz's deductions was not meant to designate the strict sense of this word in which it means the product of mass and velocity, but rather the product of mass and the square of velocity multiplied by ½, or $\frac{1}{2}mv^2$. William Thomson reintroduced the expression "energy" for this product, after Thomas Young had used it in a somewhat different connection in 1800. The conservation of energy was called the First Law of the mechanical theory of heat by Rudolf Clausius (1822–1888, Bonn). He derived the Second Law from the Carnot-Clapeyron principle in the following improved form: The proportion between the heat converted into work and the heat transferred from a higher to a lower temperature depends only on these two temperatures (1850). W. Thomson's formulation expressed the same meaning from a different point of view: "It is impossible, by inanimate material agency, to derive mechanical effect from any portion of matter by cooling it below the temperature of the coldest of the surrounding objects." (13) For reversible processes, and with Thomson's absolute scale of temperature, T, the Second Law can be expressed by the equation

$$\sum \frac{Q}{T} = 0$$

or, for continuous change of temperature,

$$\int - \frac{dQ}{T} = 0$$

Clausius proposed a "convenient form" of this law by introducing the symbol S, defined by the equation $dS = dQ/T$ and representing a measure for the "transformation content" of the system. He modified the Greek word for transformation slightly into "entropy" so as to make it similar to energy.

A gas automatically expands into a vacuum. The temperature does not change in this process as a whole, as Gay-Lussac had shown, but its entropy increases. This becomes obvious when the cycle is completed. The system is returned to its original condition when the gas is compressed to its original volume. Heat of compression has to be removed by a cooling system in order to restore the original temperature. From the small basis of such experiences Clausius arrived at the great generalization: The energy of the world is constant; the entropy of the world strives toward a maximum. (14)

All these derivations were based on *physical* changes, the expansion and compression of gases, the transformation of heat into mechanical work. The application to *chemical* changes was first carried out by August Friedrich Horstmann (1843–1929, Heidelberg). He started from the general law for entropy which Clausius had formulated. In a chemical equilibrium, the system of substances acquires that state among all the possible states in which the entropy is a maximum. In equilibrium, the differential dS of entropy, divided by the differential dx of the part x of the reacting substances, must therefore be equal to zero. (15) This leads to an equation connecting the heat of reaction, temperature, and volume or pressure. A simple case is the dissociation of a gas into its elements, like $HCl \rightarrow H + Cl$. This involves a number of changes of entropy.

> It is *1* decreased by the conversion of heat into chemical work; *2* increased through the greater distance between the atoms of the decomposed molecule; *3* increased, because the remaining undecomposed molecules have to move farther apart to fill the same space; *4* and *5* decreased as the number of molecules of the two products of decomposition increases and these molecules are thus crowded together.
>
> The entropy will then be greatest when as many molecules as possible are decomposed but as little as possible heat is consumed, and when, besides, the molecules of each of the three gases are removed as far as possible from one another. In general, this cannot occur at complete decomposition; therefore only a part is decomposed. (16)

Still broader and more fundamental was the application of the laws of energy given by Josiah Willard Gibbs (1839–1903, New

Haven) in *The Principles of Thermodynamics as Determining Chemical Equilibrium* (1874).

Although Dalton in 1803 and Gaudin in 1835 drew symbolic pictures of atoms and molecules, they and their contemporaries were not yet ready to carry their speculation into the actual realm of atomic dimensions. The laws found for weight and volume proportions were macroscopic. A wide gap separated these laws of chemical proportions from the explanation that they resulted from the atomic structure of matter. The gap was widened during the first expansion of analytical work on new compounds. Chemical experiences alone could not bring atoms into closer range. The phenomena observed when electricity passes through solutions led back to atomic concepts (page 142). Electricity is transported by atomic fractions of molecules. In Faraday's system these fractions with electrical charges are called "ions." On the other hand, for the influences induced by electricity flowing in conductors (metallic wires), Faraday created the notion of lines of force, which shared with the concept of electrons the character of being the final, or smallest, units, corresponding with atoms.

If experiment did not make these smallest units visible, mathematics provided the tools for calculating the mechanical interactions of the vast numbers of these units which are assumed to form visible quantities of matter and action. In 1740 Daniel Bernoulli (1700–1782) had laid the foundation for a theory of the movements of the molecules in a gas. The thermodynamic theories of the first half of the nineteenth century were amplified by the renewal of Bernoulli's approach. The mathematical treatment takes the molecules as realities, disregards their special properties at first, and finally leads back to them. Some examples will demonstrate this procedure.

Between the molecules there must be large spaces in which they move. Without knowing anything more about sizes and numbers of the molecules, the mathematician can derive relations between them. If m is the mass of one molecule and v the velocity of its progressive movement, then its kinetic energy must be $mv^2/2$. The laws of elastic shock demand that a molecule that hits a wall of its container suffers a change of its movement (mv) equal to $2mv$. A number n of molecules hitting the unit of surface wall per unit of time thus exert a pressure of $p = 2mvn$ per unit surface. A cube of 1 cm^3 contains a great number of molecules. Before we know this number, we represent it by a symbol N. The number of shocks on one wall of the cube then is Nv. The molecules hit the six walls of the cube per unit of time (one second) so that n in the above equation is $\frac{1}{6}Nv$, from which the pressure per square centimeter

$p = \frac{1}{3}Nmv^2$. The value of Nm, the mass per cubic centimeter, is the same as the specific gravity of the gas, s. Since pressure and specific gravity can be found by measurement, the velocity of the molecular movement can be calculated. For hydrogen, for example, at 0°C, $v = 184{,}000$ cm sec^{-1}.

The speed with which a gas can flow through a narrow orifice indicates the degree of inner friction between the gas molecules. A set of assumptions must be made in order to derive correlations. The assumptions themselves are tested by the outcome of the mathematical calculations. The sphere is the form of highest symmetry and easiest for calculation; therefore Clausius and Maxwell assumed spherical molecules. Mathematically derived laws of the distribution of velocities among the molecules permit us to interpret inner friction as the mean length of "free paths" between collisions of the molecules.

The speed of sound in a gas, which Adolph Kundt (1839–1894, Berlin) measured by a strikingly simple method (from 1866 to 1868), is an expression of the relationship between the specific heat at constant volume to the specific heat at constant pressure; and this relationship is based on that between energy of movement and inner energy of the molecules.

This new period of constructing molecules differed fundamentally from that of the seventeenth century. Its creators used new models for mathematical calculation and for connecting physical quantitative measurements. Chemistry had made progress by correlating substances with an assembly of qualities, where formerly each single quality had been interpreted as being due to one particular substance. Physicists now reached out for a real ultimate unit of all matter by correlating all physical properties with form of molecules and their mechanical interactions. In chemistry the new problem was to connect quality with the composition of a compound from elements, the relative position of the elemental particles in the molecule. Laws of substitution, isomorphism, and polymorphism were thus created. In physics the "mechanical" theory of heat and elasticity invited further detailed speculations. William J. M. Rankine tried to introduce a particular kind of molecular motion:

> ". . . The laws of the expansive action of heat are deduced from a mechanical hypothesis, called that of molecular Vortices. These laws are capable of being expressed and proved independently of any hypothesis; but it is nevertheless considered, that a molecular hypothesis which has already led to the anticipation of some laws subsequently confirmed by experiment, may possibly lead hereafter to the anticipation of more such laws, and may at all events be regarded as interesting in a mathematical point of view; although its

objective reality, like that of other molecular hypotheses, be incapable of absolute proof." (17)

Helmholtz (1858) assumed that molecules are vortices which, in the physiocomathematical ideal, can be deformed without losing their identity. William Thomson developed this vortex theory still further (1867).

Gibbs directed these physiocomathematical theories toward chemistry. Josiah Willard Gibbs, like Hermann Helmholtz, was the son of a philologist. While a tutor at Yale, first of Latin then of natural philosophy, Gibbs obtained a patent (U.S. No. 53,971) for an automatic brake for railroad cars. This, however, remained a solitary excursion into the field of engineering. He continued his studies in France and Germany, and he was in Heidelberg when Helmholtz taught there (1868–1869). To him, mathematics was the appropriate language for expressing physical and chemical change. Through Wilhelm Ostwald, Gibbs' memoir on thermodynamics gained the attention of the scientific world in 1887. The Phase Rule and the new science of statistical mechanics (1902) initiated far-reaching developments in science and industry. Henry Adams even tried to discover "the tendency of history" in a book entitled *The Rule of Phase Applied to History* (written 1909, published 1919).

One of the important "convenient" units that Gibbs introduced was the chemical potential. The concept of potential itself was not new. Pierre Simon de Laplace (1749–1827) had used the term with the meaning that a directed force between the unit of masses or electric charges is measured by the rate of decrease which the potential shows in that particular direction. With this mathematical foundation of force, Laplace had obtained a general formula for changes of potential in the three directions of space. In order to do that, he introduced the relation of smallest changes of potential to infinitesimal changes of distance.

The chemical potential may be defined in the words of James Clerk Maxwell (1831–1879, Cambridge):

> By differentiating the energy with respect to the volume, we obtain the pressure of the fluid with the sign reversed; by differentiating with respect to entropy, we obtain the temperature on the thermodynamic scale; and by differentiating with respect to the mass of any one of the component substances, we obtain what Professor Gibbs calls the (chemical) potential of that substance in the mass considered.

The potential of each component must be constant within a portion of mass separated from the rest of the universe and thus forming a closed system. Within such a system, temperature and pressure will not alone govern the possible events but, in addition, also those factors that result from changes of the composition of the substances. For his broad survey of all the inherent possibilities, Gibbs found it "convenient" to distinguish between the components, meaning the chemical substances, and the phases or physical states in which they are present. Thus defined, phases are the physically homogeneous and mechanically separable portions of the system. Since all gases form homogeneous mixtures, there is only one gaseous phase; liquids and solids, however, can be present in several phases. The components are the smallest number of chemical individuals by which the composition of each phase can be expressed. The degrees of variability or "freedom" of the system are determined by these influences which can be combined into a simple rule. The specific qualities of the substances do not enter into this rule. It is concerned with their chemical energies, which follow one and the same pattern. Nothing specific is said concerning these energies; it is only important that their number be the same as that of the components present in the system to be considered. If the number of components is designated as n, the variables of chemical energies are also n in number. In addition, changes of heat and of volume introduce two further variables. The degree of freedom to change in such a system is reduced by one for each phase—gas, liquid, and solid—in which the components exist and in which they have already used up one degree of freedom. When the number of phases is equal to r, the remaining number of degrees of freedom is equal to $n + 2 - r$. (18)

This is the Phase Rule. It is the strangest and most versatile equation in physics and chemistry. At first glance the concepts it combines seem to lack commensurability, which is the first requirement for an equation. Component, physical state, and conditions for equilibrium appear to be widely diverging concepts until it is understood that the Phase Rule is concerned only with the energies involved, the energies of heat, volume, and chemical affinity. That such a general rule can be formulated demonstrates the great usefulness of the concept "energy."

The men who initiated these great developments of energetics and thermodynamics saw simple experiences and thoughts as the general models and rules of all processes. Sadi Carnot was impressed by the waterfall and the thought of continuity. Robert Mayer started from the ancient idea that cause equals effect. James Prescott Joule felt that the law of conservation was "the Creator's fiat." Rudolf Clausius went from the spontaneous expansion of gases to the fundamental laws of the universe, as Louis Pasteur had done when he linked his special experience with tartaric acid salts to the asymmetry of the universe and William Thomson (Lord Kelvin) when he detected a "universal tendency toward the dissipation of mechanical energy."

Max Planck (1858–1947, Berlin) explained the "tendency" of entropy towards a maximum by a "predilection" of nature: "Among the natural processes are, for example, the conduction of heat out of a warmer body to a colder one, the generation of heat by friction or impact, and others. None of these processes can be completely reversed, each one of them provides the transition from a state of smaller predilection to a state of greater predilection of nature." (19)

Ernst Mach objected to the second law of Clausius on the ground that it expresses a mere tautology: "If the entropy of the universe could really be determined, that would be the best absolute measure of time, and the tautology in the law about the heat-death would be exposed." (20) Mach failed to consider that "the law of the heat-death" or the tendency of entropy towards a maximum contains no statement about the rate at which the process proceeds in time.

Electricity and Affinity

Electricity was first produced by rubbing glass against silk or fur. The "electrical machine" suggested to Robert Boyle "the mechanical origin of electricity," about which he wrote in 1675.

Descartes attributed the attractions and repulsions between substances near electrically charged materials or around the poles of magnets to certain "effluvia," something like a very fine, scarcely substantial fluid. This fluid was thought to emanate from the magnetically or electrically charged body so that it could act at a distance. Electricity itself could similarly be represented by a fluid, more specifically, by two fluids, one for positive electricity and one for negative.

Whether the explanation of electricity was mechanistic or materialistic, it was incomplete so long as it did not include the different behavior of substances with which electrical phenomena are connected. William Gilbert had already, about 1600, divided these substances into two general groups, the *ideoelectrics* and the *anelectrics,* of which only the first are electrified by friction. A further division of the first group was made according to the positive or negative electrical charge that they obtained by the mechanical work of rubbing.

The positive state of electrical charge was also called "vitreous," because it was obtained by rubbing glass, and the negative, correspondingly, was called "resinous" electricity. The connnection with the chemical nature of the substances was not as simple as an opposition between resin and glass. Georg Christoph Lichtenberg (1744–1799, Göttingen) assembled the relationships between 13 materials in a table.

LICHTENBERG'S TABLE OF EXCITATION, TRANSPOSED

(The marks denote the electricity of the substances under which they stand.)

	Polished Glass	Hair	Wool	Feathers	Paper	Wood	Wax	Sealing Wax	Ground Glass	Metals	Resin	Silk	Sulfur
Polished glass	0		—	—	—	—	—	—	—	—		—	—
Hair								—			—	—	
Wool	+					—		—	—		—		
Feathers	+								—				—
Paper	+	+						—	—				—
Wood	+	+	+						—			—	—
Wax	+								—				—
Sealing wax	+	+	+					0	—				—
Ground glass	+		+	+	+	+	+	+				—	—
Metals	+	+							+	0			
Resin	+	+	+							+	0		
Silk	+	+							+	+			
Sulfur	+			+	+	+	+	+	+				0

Thomas Young, who "transposed" this table, remarked: "It appears that any substance in this table, rubbed with any of the following substances, becomes positively electric; with any of the preceding, negative. This proposition is, however, liable to some modification, according to the mode of applying friction, and the degree of heat; the table also requires some further subdivision." (21)

Volta (page 135) produced a constant flow of electricity by means of his batteries. This constant flow, which he called "electrical current," was obtained by connecting two different metals by "moisture," actually a solution of acids or salts in water. Johann Ritter thought (1801) that the mechanical contact between different substances provoked the electrical action, and that its extent was determined by the chemical nature of these substances. This seemed like an impossible compromise to many physicists and chemists in the early nineteenth century. To them the contact theory, which relied on a mechanism, seemed to exclude the chemical theory, which saw the cause in the chemical nature of a system. Many experiments were designed in the expectation that they would decide for one theory and against the other. This was rarely achieved. The discussion between contactists and chemists was as lively, even as violent, as that between mechanists and vitalists in philosophy or between neptunists and vulcanists in geology. The opposite viewpoints could be clearly distinguished in words and formulated into opposite theories. When, in 1828, Auguste de la Rive (1801–1873, Geneva) showed that the electrical charge between two metals was reversed by changing the liquid medium between them from dilute to concentrated nitric acid, he saw this as proof of the chemical theory. Pietro Marianini reached the opposite conclusion from the same experiments because, according to him, the change of acid concentration influenced the surface of the metals so that the effect could be considered as conforming to the contact theory.

Quantitative measurements and an analogy between electricity and heat paved the way out of the dilemma. Electric current deviates the magnetic compass needle. The deviation was found (1820) to measure the strength of the current (Hans Christian Oersted, 1777–1851, Copenhagen). The electroscope had indicated the mere presence of positive or negative electricity; now its quantity could be determined by reading the angle of deflection of a magnetic needle. When this quantity of electricity was considered as analogous to the quantity of heat, the temperature difference which causes the flux of heat suggested that an analogous factor should be established for electricity. It flows under the action of a difference in pressure or potential. The flow of heat through a substance encounters a certain resistance which is characteristic for the particular substance. A characteristic resistance to the flow of electricity could similarly be established.

A mathematical treatment of the theory of heat was given in 1822 by Jean Baptiste Joseph de Fourier (1768–1830, Paris). Five years later, Georg Simon Ohm (1787–1854, Berlin) published a mathematical treatment of the electrical battery. (22) Electrical current he defined as the quantity of electricity per unit time and he designated it by the letter i. Its potential π is connected with the resistance r by the mathematical relation $i = \pi/r$; the electrical current is directly proportional to the potential and inversely proportional to the resistance of the circuit.

Quantitative measurements of the chemical effects produced by electricity were carried out by Michael Faraday (1791–1867, London). While learning the trade of bookbinding he became interested in the content of the books and managed to attend some of Humphry Davy's lectures. He offered his services to Davy in an application which he accompanied with a carefully illustrated transcript of the lectures. Davy accepted him as an assistant in 1813 without suspecting that Faraday would sometime be called Davy's greatest discovery. After Davy's death, Faraday advanced to laboratory superintendent and in 1825 became director of the laboratory of the Royal Institution.

His great skill in designing and performing experiments was directed by innate convictions of great general laws. He wrote, November 20, 1845: "I have long held an opinion, almost amounting to conviction . . . that the various forms under which the forces of matter are made manifest have one common origin; or, in other

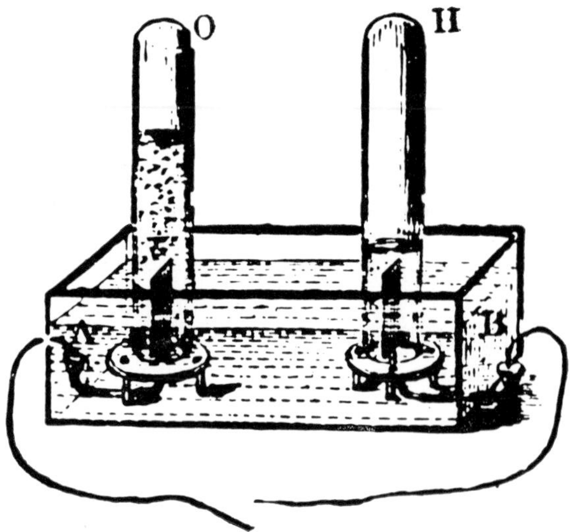

Fig. 29. Apparatus for electrolysis. (From Michael Faraday's popular lecture, "The Chemical History of a Candle," edited by William Crookes, London, 1874, p. 111.)

words, are so directly related and mutually dependent that they are convertible, as it were, one into another, and possess equivalents of power in their action." (23) Such ideas were shared by many contemporaries, and they were brought into several definite forms precisely during the period to which this statement by Faraday belongs.

Faraday found confirmation in the relationships between the quantity of electricity produced by a certain number of strokes in the electrical machine and the amount of chemical substance decomposed by it. This was directly demonstrated when he used as the substance potassium iodide soaked up in paper and compared the size and intensity of the brown spots which the liberated iodine gave on the paper when electric current was passed through it. The current from voltaic batteries decomposed chemicals "in direct proportion to the absolute quantity of electricity which passes." This experimental result definitely disproved the contact theory, which would contradict the general law of nature. Force cannot be created without either a corresponding change of acting matter or the consummation of a generating force.

> The electricity which decomposes, and that which is evolved by the decomposition of a certain quantity of matter, are alike. The equivalent weights of bodies are simply those quantities of them which contain equal quantities of electricity or have naturally equal electric powers; it being the *electricity* which *determines* the equivalent number *because* it determines the combining force. Or, if we adopt the atomic theory or phraseology, then the atoms of bodies which are equivalent to each other in their ordinary chemical action have equal quantities of electricity naturally associated with them. But I must confess I am jealous of the term *atom:* for though it is very easy to talk of atoms, it is very difficult to form a clear idea of their nature, especially when compound bodies are under consideration. (24)

The new experience needed new words for its general conception. Faraday requested advice from the Reverend William Whewell, of Trinity College, Cambridge, for the new nomenclature. The decomposition by electricity was electro-lysis, in analogy to the usual chemical ana-lysis. The metallic poles are electrodes. That surface at which the electric current, according to our present expression, "enters" the electrolyte is the anode, the other the cathode. When zinc and platinum are the two electrodes, the zinc plate forms the anode where oxygen, chlorine, etc., are evolved; these were, therefore, called "anions," i.e., the wanderers to the anode. The platinum forms the cathode, and the substances that wander to it, such as copper, silver, etc., are "cations."

Electric force was thus capable of overcoming the chemical force of affinity, and in the voltaic battery this affinity was converted into electricity. Faraday discovered other processes in which "forces of matter" are "convertible, as it were, one into another." Electricity affects magnets, as was shown by Oersted. By moving a magnet back and forth through a metal loop, Faraday obtained an electrical current. He attributed it to a transmission of energy by "lines of force" (1831). An electromagnetic field rotates the plane of polarized light. James Clerk Maxwell, who developed Faraday' theories mathematically (1855), said in the introduction to a later work (25):

> . . . Faraday, in his mind's eye, saw lines of force traversing all space, where the mathematicians saw centers of force attracting at a distance; Faraday sought the seat of the phenomena in real actions going on in the medium, they [the mathematicians] were satisfied that they had found it in a power of action at a distance impressed on the electric fluids.
>
> . . . Faraday's methods resembled those in which we begin with the whole and arrive at the parts by analysis, while the ordinary mathematical methods were founded on the principle of beginning with the parts and building up the whole by synthesis. . . . One of my principal aims [is] to communicate to others the same delight which I have found myself in reading Faraday's *Researches*. . . .

The new developments in electrochemistry soon found practical applications. Robert Hare, Jr. (26) (1781–1858), from 1818 to 1847 professor of chemistry at the University of Pennsylvania, built large voltaic batteries with 18″ × 24″ plates of zinc and copper. He connected charges of explosives to the battery by wires, and was thus able to set off explosives from a distance, even under water. Zinc-copper batteries were improved by John Frederick Daniell in London (1790–1845). A copper plate in the form of a cylinder was immersed in a solution of copper sulfate and separated from the central zinc-amalgam rod by a porous ceramic cylinder. The inside liquid was dilute sulfuric acid (1836). This battery gave a more constant current than previous devices.

Moritz Hermann von Jacobi (1801–1874, Petrograd) observed, as Daniell had before, that the copper metal deposited in the battery reproduced the details of the surface on which it was formed. This was the beginning of galvanoplastics (1837). An accidental observation that ceramic surfaces could be used as electrodes when they were made conductive by a graphite layer made it possible to reproduce plaster molds by covering them with some electrolytic metal.

The principle of the Daniell battery was used by William Robert Grove (1811–1896, London). His battery (1839) consisted of a zinc cylinder in sulfuric acid on the outside and, separated by a porous ceramic cylinder, a platinum foil in nitric acid in the center. This battery was stronger than any of the previous ones but it was expensive because of the use of platinum. Bunsen (page 265) replaced it by carbon which, properly prepared, had the chemical stability and electric conductivity required for this electrode.

R. Gaston S. Planté (1834–1889, Paris) began in 1859 to investigate a battery with lead plates in dilute sulfuric acid of about 10 percent. This soon developed into a reversible battery in which chemical affinities were converted into electricity, and the action was restored by using electrical current to reverse the chemical reactions. Initially the reverse reaction was a very costly one because it had to be energized from other primary electrochemical reactions; eventually, however, when electrochemical reactions were no longer the only source for electrical current, Planté's type of battery gained great importance and wide application.

Electrical current in a battery is a migration to the electrodes of ions present in the solution. Rudolf Clausius in 1857 showed that the positively and negatively charged parts of molecules in solution are not in fixed connection with one another. Ohm's law can be interpreted only by assuming that the ions change partners and are temporarily, between the changes, in a free state. The electric current does not produce the separation into the part-molecules, or ions, it only directs their movements. When the number n of particles moves in the positive direction, and the number n' in the negative direction, they produce a current of a strength proportional to $(n + n')$. In most cases, n will not be equal to n'. In a solution of hydrochloric acid, the hydrogen ion moves with much greater velocity than the chlorine ion. Wilhelm Hittorf (1824–1914, Münster, Westphalia) had considerable difficulty in convincing physicists that the difference in ionic mobility is consistent with the basic electrical conditions of equality between the opposite charges. While an electrical current is passing through a solution of HCl, hydrogen and chlorine are discharged at the electrodes as gases. With an arbitrary and relative figure of 100 ions of hydrogen and 100 ions of chlorine discharged, the solution directly surrounding the cathode would have 100 chlorine ions that have lost their partners; similarly, the solution at the anode would have 100 hydrogen ions without their chlorine ions as partners. However, the ions migrate during the electrolytic decomposition. Of the 100 hydrogen ions, apparently only present in excess at the anode, 80 migrated to the cathode to supply the same number of chlorine ions with their electrolytic equivalent, and during the same period of time 20 chlorine ions left and migrated to the anode to neutralize the remaining hydrogen ions there. The balance between the oppositely charged ions is thus continuously maintained. The concentrations, however, change; they increase at the anode and decrease at the cathode.

Hittorf's work on the relative mobility of ions (1853–1859) was amplified by Friedrich Kohlrausch (1840–1910, Berlin) and expressed as the law of the independent migration of ions (1867): During electrolysis each ion moves with its definite individual velocity without being influenced by the other ion of opposite charge in the solution. The method that led to this law consisted in measuring the resistance of solutions to the passage of an alternating current. A direct current would produce changes in the composition of the solution and in the potentials at the electrodes, whereas alternating current probes the state of the solution without changing it. Difficulties in the physical arrangements for testing were gradually eliminated, and by 1880 Kohlrausch's method could be used conveniently for measuring the change in electrical resistance, or its reciprocal value, electrical conductivity, that occurs when substances and conditions are varied.

Svante Arrhenius (1859–1927, Stockholm) carried out such measurements for his doctoral thesis, which he completed in 1883. Since electrical current in a solution consists in the movement of molecules or their electrically charged parts, the values measured for conductivity have to be compared for equal numbers of molecules, that is, for equivalent molecular weights. The conductivity, not of a constant volume of solution but of a constant number of molecules whatever the volume in which they are dissolved, increases as the concentration decreases; the greater the dilution, the more ions are offered by the same amount of electrolyte.

Faraday had established that the passing of electrical current through a solution is equivalent to the transfer of ions. Hittorf and Kohlrausch interpreted their results as showing that the oppositely charged ions are free to move separately with the current. Now Arrhenius concluded that the ions are present and are in this free state without the electrical event which is described and measured as current. When a salt is dissolved in water, it breaks apart into its ions. Not all the salt does that under all circumstances; part of it may remain combined. The relative amount of this part is characteristic of the chemical nature of the substance and dependant on the concentration. Therefore, measuring the equivalent conductivity meant determining the proportion of the ions actually present to the number of ions that would be present if the electrolyte (salt, etc., in the solution) were completely separated into its simple "electrolytic molecules," which is another name for ions.

This result was published at a time when other methods of investigating the state of dissolved substances had met with unexpected difficulties. Solutions exert an osmotic pressure, which Moritz Traube (1826–1894, Berlin) described (1867). The botanist Wilhelm Pfeffer (1845–1920, Leipzig) recognized the importance of this pressure in the life of plants where cell walls enclose juices, which are solutions of chemicals, and control the exchange of water and nutrients. Artificial membranes separating water from a solution of sugar in water could be constructed in such a manner as to allow only the water to pass through to the sugar solution, but not the sugar to the water. The pressure with which water is attracted to the sugar solution was found in 1877 to be directly proportional to the concentration of the sugar.

This osmotic pressure of the sugar solution is as great as the gas pressure would be if the solvent (water) were removed and the sugar were present in the same volume in the form of a gas. J. H. van't Hoff concluded that osmotic pressure is independent of the particular solvent and that it follows the laws of pressure–temperature relationship found for gases.

Thermodynamic calculation of cycles in which water is evaporated or frozen out from solutions gave mathematical formulae for the increase in boiling point and the lowering of the freezing point of solutions as compared with the pure solvent. The temperature differences were found to be directly proportional to the molecular concentration when this is expressed in molecular weights. Since the osmotic pressure is directly proportional to the molecular concentration, it can also be measured by the influence of the dissolved substance on boiling and freezing points. For example, an aqueous solution having a boiling point of $(100 + t)$°C has an osmotic pressure $P = 57.0 \times t$ atmospheres.

It was in part a rediscovery of Charles Blagden's work of 1788 when François Raoult (1830–1910, Grenoble) found in 1883 that the freezing temperature of a solution is reduced in direct proportion to the molecular concentration; so that m grams of a substance having the molecular weight M reduce the freezing point by $t = E\frac{m}{M}$ °C. The proportionality factor E is a value that van't Hoff derived thermodynamically from the heat of fusion of the solvent. The corresponding factor for the molecular increase in boiling temperature was similarly connected with the heat of evaporation of the solvent.

These relationships were beautiful in their great sweep and satisfying in showing the unity in so many different properties of solutions. But they were not quite true. The deviations of the measured figures from the theoretical calculations were particularly great for solutions of salts, acids, and alkalies.

Van't Hoff used an idealization for arriving at the basic theory. The concentration had to be extremely low. The laws were strictly valid only for a limit state in which the difference between pure solvent and solution was infinitely small. This was the same kind of limit state that formed Carnot's starting point (page 241). Real solutions, e.g., of sugar, could therefore be expected to follow the laws only in a certain approximation. For solution of salts, acids, and alkalies it was necessary to introduce a factor i of deviation. Now Arrhenius showed that this factor i was identical with the coefficient that measured the relation between active molecules and the sum of active and inactive molecules by the electrical conductivity.

In the state of utmost dilution, the coefficient i has its highest value, which means that all molecules of the electrolyte are dissociated into active parts. In higher concentrations, the relation between the actual conductivity λ to the conductivity at infinite dilution λ_∞ is $\alpha = \lambda/\lambda_\infty$. In 1887 Arrhenius declared that this ratio expresses the degree of dissociation of a solute into its ions.

The strength, or chemical affinity, of acids or alkalies in solutions, which Wilhelm Ostwald had attempted to determine, was now explained as a function of the dissociation into ions. Ostwald welcomed this explanation which Arrhenius' theory offered. Enthusiastically he combined forces with Arrhenius and van't Hoff. He saw a new science of physical chemistry emerging and became its foremost advocate and organizer. Affinity seemed now well on its way to being converted from a metaphysical notion to a measurable energy which can be accurately determined in all its various effects, whether they are found as influences in the course of chemical change or manifested as physical properties.

The coordination of experiences for many fields and many countries which resulted in the creation of this new system bears some resemblance to the history of valence in organic chemistry or that of the Periodic System of the elements. The three men who contributed most to the new development were alike in one respect, they produced important work at an early age. Van't Hoff was twenty-two when he published his theory of the asymmetric carbon atom, Arrhenius twenty-four when he conceived the new interpretation of the state of solutions; Ostwald (1853–1932) began his new approach to the problem of chemical affinity at the age of twenty-one and was a professor in Riga before he was twenty-eight. Arrhenius and Ostwald were attracted to chemistry as an art of experimenting, while van't Hoff acquired experimental skill very late in his life as a scientist. On the other hand, his theoretical work remained confined to physics and chemistry, while Arrhenius expanded his interests to medicine and astronomy and Ostwald to the philosophical aspects of the theories of energy and to the relationship of science and religion. Van't Hoff had the distinction of being the recipient of the first Nobel prize for chemistry (1901). Ostwald and Arrhenius received the prize in subsequent years. Van't Hoff was at that time free from teaching duties as a professor at the Academy of Sciences in Berlin. In 1905 Arrhenius left the chair of physics at the University of Stockholm to devote himself to the research institute of the Nobel foundation. Ostwald became professor of physical chemistry in Leipzig before he was thirty-four, but after twenty years he resigned his professorship in order to be free from academic restrictions because of his interest in philosophical monism and the science of color. He was perhaps the most impetuous of the three. His ideas came to him as inspirations, in lightning-like illuminations. In his autobiography he describes the moment in which the necessity for a radically new manner of thinking in physics opened itself up to him like a pentecostal experience of the spirit.

The new science was not born out of single experiments and dry mathematical drudgery!

Light and Affinity

Light is a substance more mobile than but just as material as air, water, or earth. This summarizes the thinking of most chemists at the turn from the eighteenth to the nineteenth century. (27) Some considered light as an element, while others speculated about its composition from caloric and oxygen. Such a composite nature of light was assumed by Étienne Louis Malus (1775–1812), one of the scientists who accompanied Napoleon during the campaign in Egypt (1798–1799), and who pursued this subject in spite of war and pestilence. Ten years later, describing his observations on the polarization of light, Malus compared the theories of Huygens and Newton and decided for the latter.

> All the ordinary phenomena in optics can be explained either by the hypothesis of Huygens, who believes they are produced by the vibration of an ethereal fluid, or according to the opinion of Newton, who believes them to be produced by the action of substances on the luminescent molecules which themselves are considered as belonging to a substance, subject to the attractive and repulsive forces which

> serve to explain the other physical phenomena. The laws relating to the course of rays in double refraction can still be explained by one or the other of the two hypotheses. However, since the observations which I just described prove that the phenomena of reflexion are different for an equal angle of incidence, which cannot occur in the hypothesis of Huygens, it is necessary to conclude not only that light is a substance subjected to the forces which animate the other substances, but in addition that the form and the disposition of its molecules have a great influence on the phenomena. (28)

It seemed obvious that light is a substance and therefore subject to the same laws as other substances, or to say with strict simplicity, "the cause of light is called light-stuff." (29) Such an anwser is as general as the question directed to the "essence" of light and the reason for its ability to combine with chemical substances. Much more was needed to explain special observations. Newton had to endow his "luminous particles" with poles and "fits of easy reflexion and transmission" in order to account for the colors which he obtained by prisms and between convex lenses of great focal lengths.

The theory of undulations explained these phenomena much better than Newton's hypothesis, especially when Thomas Young used an analogy to sound waves (1801). The thickness of the air spaces between the two lenses, at the places where the colors appeared, had been calculated by Newton. In Young's wave theory, the thickness of the air through which the wave travels can be correlated with the wavelength. The phase differences are responsible for the appearance of colors. Augustin Jean Fresnel (1788–1827, near Paris), originally a road construction engineer, published figures for wavelengths in the same year (1821) in which Joseph von Fraunhofer (1787–1826) derived similar values from measuring diffraction spectra. Since the velocity of light was known (determined by Olaf Römer in 1676), the "source of light" could now be described as a state of motion of matter which produces waves of 440 to 880 million vibrations per second. (30)

The chemical action of light on horny silver, or silver chloride, is noticeable beyond the visible violet of the sun spectrum, as J. W. Ritter discovered in 1801. An attempt that same year by Humphry Davy to use the blackening of silver salts in light for reproducing engravings failed because he found no means of fixing the image. Abandoning silver salts as the medium, Joseph Nicéphore Nièpce used resins extracted from plants and asphalt on silver or copper plates. The resins lost their solubility in proportion to the intensity of light so that the picture could be developed by solvents. This process of 1816 has recently been rediscovered. Nièpce died in

1833. His collaborator, Louis Daguerre (1789–1851), later returned to silver compounds. He deposited silver iodide by treating a polished silver plate in iodine vapor and fixed it in hyposulfite solution after it was exposed to light and the image developed by mercury vapor. Numerous variations of the processes included the steps of treating the iodized silver plate with bromine and stabilizing the image by gold chloride. The French government honored Daguerre by granting him a life pension on August 10, 1839. This can be called the official birthday of photography. It also is the year in which William Henry Fox Talbot (1800–1877, Lacock, England) discovered the advantages of silver bromide over the chloride, and the organic "revelators" (developers), of which gallic acid was the best example.

For a time the practical application of these photochemical reactions seemed more important than the theoretical relationship between intensity of light and extent of chemical change. The reaction of hydrogen with chlorine offered an impressive example for such a relationship. This reaction is explosive in direct sunlight, slower in diffused light, and scarcely noticeable in the dark, according to Gay-Lussac and Thenard (1809). This discovery was more thoroughly investigated in 1843 by John William Draper (1811–1882) in New York. A chemical reaction could serve to measure light if it could be assumed that the chemical action of the same quantity of light is proportional to the content in a light-sensitive substance. Wilhelm Constantin Wittwer (1822–1908, Regensburg) made this assumption for the solution of chlorine in water, which he investigated. However, there are many limiting conditions which have to be considered. The product of the light-reaction itself, and traces of impurities, influence the conversion of chlorine into hydrochloric acid. In the reaction between hydrogen and chlorine gas, the presence of 0.2 percent of hydrogen in excess of the stoichiometric proportion reduces the photochemical effect to 37.8 percent, and small quantities of oxygen depress this effect almost to the vanishing point.

These were results of investigations by Robert Wilhelm Bunsen and Henry Roscoe in Heidelberg (1855–1862). With pure materials there is proportionality of chemical effect to light, but even then an initial period of ten to fifteen minutes is found, during which the reaction is lagging; Bunsen called this an "induction period." Fifty years later Burgess and Chapman explained it by the presence of traces of ammonia.

The photochemical effect is connected with an absorption of light energy; this absorption was called a "photochemical extinction" of light. When the product of light intensity and time is held constant, the effect is constant. Bunsen and Roscoe compared the brightness of the sun disc with that of a flame produced by burning a magnesium wire of 0.1485 mm thickness. The visible brightness of the sun is 524.7 times that of the magnesium flame, and the chemical action is only 36.6 times greater. Another comparison shows that, by burning 72.2 grams of magnesium in ten hours, as much light is produced as by burning ten kilograms of stearin in the form of candles.

The careful attention to fine experimental details, the skill in constructing simple pieces of laboratory apparatus, and the combination of scientific accuracy with practical vision that appear in this work are characteristic of Bunsen (1811, Göttingen –1899, Heidelberg). When he discovered that freshly precipitated iron hydroxide removes arsenic from its solutions, he proceeded to investigate the use of iron hydroxide as an antidote in arsenic poisoning (1834). In Cassel, where he succeeded Friedrich Wöhler, his attention was drawn to the problems of blast-furnace operations. He not only invented methods of taking and analyzing gas samples but he also concluded his scientific analysis with specific recommendations for utilizing the carbon monoxide and the heat of the waste gases. Upon an invitation of the British Association for the Advancement of Science, he carried out a similar investigation of British blast furnaces with equally important practical results (1845).

In an attempt to analyze alkarsine, Bunsen treated this compound of alcohol and arsenic with strong oxydizing agents. An explosion occurred which damaged his right eye severely (1836). Nevertheless, during the next five years, he continued the experimental study of organic arsenic compounds which have an "almost unbearable odor." He desired to "draw these interesting substances out of the darkness to which they seemed to have been condemned by an exaggerated fear." (31)

A simple and efficient gas burner, the Bunsen burner, was a byproduct of his work on gas combustion. Many forms of gas burners had been in use, among them one that Faraday developed in 1828. In Bunsen's device, the gas enters through a narrow nozzle into a wider tube which is provided with holes in its lower part. The gas entrains the air that it needs for combustion through these adjustable holes and mixes with it in the wider tube. This burner was used as the light source in photochemical work. Bunsen planned to investigate the characteristic colors produced when certain salts are brought into this flame. His friend the physicist Gustav Kirchhoff (1824–1887, Heidelberg, later Berlin) recommended the use of spectra for better observation. Kirchhoff found an explanation for the dark lines in the sun spectrum which Fraunhofer had observed and

Fig. 30. Blast furnace. (From M. V. Regnault, *Elements of Chemistry for the Use of Colleges, Academies, and Schools,* translated by Thomas X. Betton (Philadelphia: Parrish, Dumbery, and Mears, 1852), p. 72.)

Ore and fuel (charcoal) are charged layer by layer through mouth *G* and descend through belly *A* and boshes *B* to heath *E*. Air is blown in through the nozzle at the bottom.

The carbonic acid formed in the lowest part at the highest temperature reacts with the glowing carbon above and forms carbon monoxide with consumption of heat, and the carbon monoxide reduces the oxide in the ore. The gas leaving the furnace is "cold" and highly combustible.

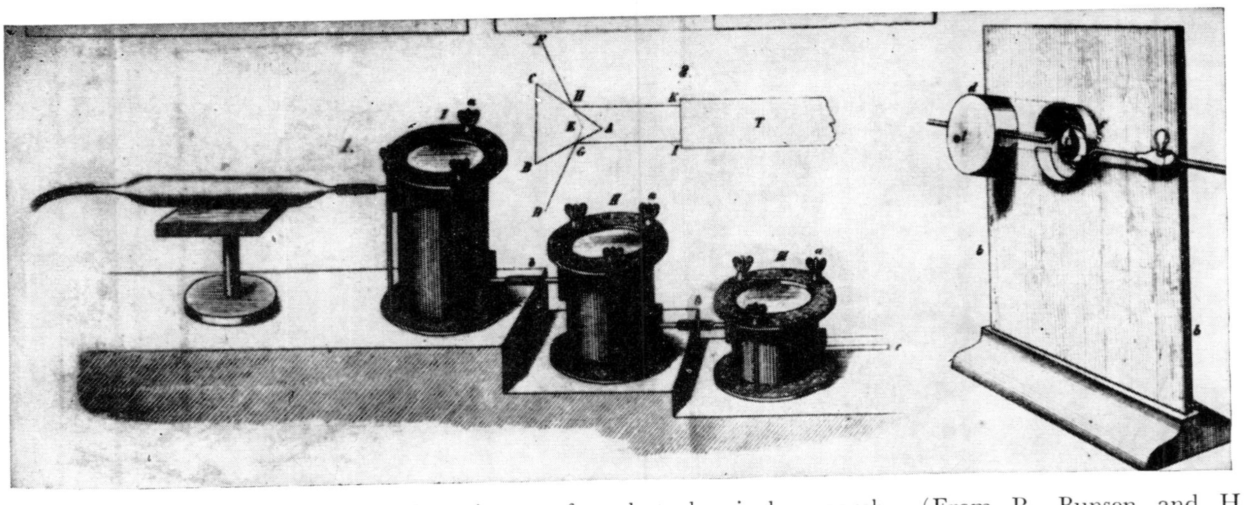

Fig. 31A. Bunsen's burner and equipment for photochemical research. (From R. Bunsen and H. Roscoe, *Poggendorff's Annalen*, **100**, 1857, p. 43, Plate I.)

At the left is equipment for purifying the mixture of hydrogen and chlorine developed in equimolecular proportions by electrolysis of a strong solution of hydrochloric acid. The three glass cylinders, are blackened on the outside, closed by glass plates, and provided with tubes for gas inlet and outlet.

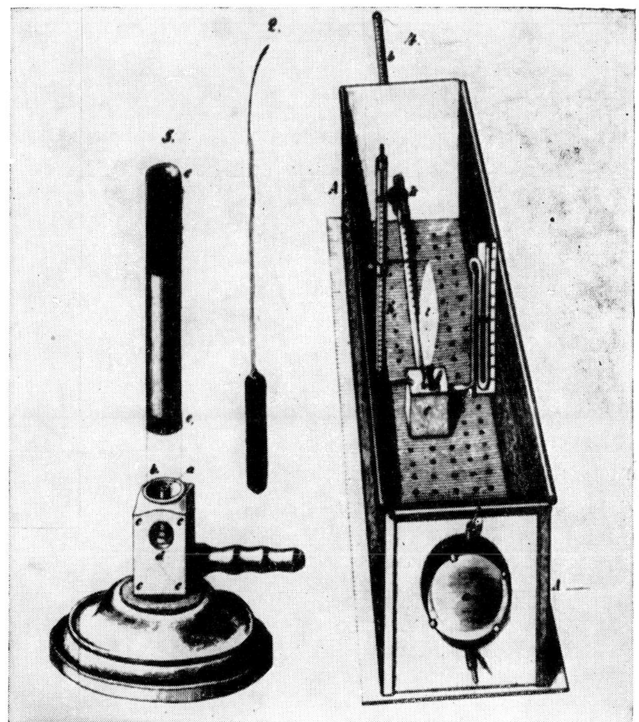

Fig. 31B. Bunsen's burner and equipment for photochemical research.

The "usual crosscut burner" (above, left) is here surrounded by a housing with holes, and thread in top hole into which the tube is fitted. The gas draws its own supply of air through the side hole *d*.

The apparatus for the illumination is shown above, right. Box *A*, blackened on the inside, contains flame *l* which can be positioned at a desired distance by means of the tube. In order to obtain a constant and reproducible light, gas pressure is measured by the gauge (right) and flame height on the scale (left). The light leaves the box through the front wall insert, which holds a heat-absorbing cylindrical glass filled with water.

measured. They are the result of specific light absorptions in the atmosphere of the sun. Kirchhoff and Bunsen reproduced the phenomenon of the Fraunhofer lines in the laboratory. All sodium salts give a yellow line in the spectrum at the place of a dark Fraunhofer line which was designated by the letter *D*. (32)

Kirchhoff's fundamental experiment consisted in viewing the white light from a source of high temperature after it passed through a flame of lower temperature which is colored by a sodium salt. The white light was obtained by heating lime in the hydrogen–oxygen flame. Goldsworthy Guerney had discovered the property of burned lime to emit a very bright light under these conditions, and through one of the frequent misnomers, this lime light was at first called Drummond light, after Thomas Drummond (1797–1840), British engineer and administrator. From the source of higher temperature, the sodium flame absorbs the light which it emits. The bright spectrum of the lime light, therefore, appears weakened or relatively dark at the place of the *D* line. Kirchhoff tested his explanation with iron, which sends out not only one but more than seventy lines, all corresponding to dark lines in the sun spectrum.

Analysis by observation of flame spectra now developed into a method of revealing unknown elements on the earth and in the stars. New dimensions in space and in sensitivity were opened up. The spectroscopic test is absolutely specific and extremely sensitive. Bunsen calculated that sodium chlorate could thus be discovered when present in less than three millionths of a milligram. For potassium, because of the place of the lines in the spectrum, the sensitivity was somewhat smaller, but a hundred thousandth of a milligram of strontium or lithium could be detected.

The spectrum of certain well waters showed two blue lines, one of which was close to but not identical with a strontium line, while the other appeared farther toward the violet. Kirchhoff and Bunsen concluded "with complete certainty" that a hitherto unknown element was thereby indicated (1861). This was expected to represent a "fourth alkali metal." A few grams of its salt were produced out of fifty tons of the water of the Dürkheimer spring. The discoverers called the new element "caesium" (Cs), "derived from *caesius,* which the ancients used to designate the blue of the clear sky."

A fifth alkali metal revealed its presence upon spectroanalysis of lepidolith, a mineral rich in lithium. Two lines were observed in the extreme red. Again referring to classical Latin authors, Bunsen called the element "rubidium."

In the same year (1861), William Crookes (1832–1919, London) tried to prepare tellurium from the residues accumulated during the production of sulfuric acid in a German plant. Since he found some difficulties in his experiments, he decided to use the new tool of spectroscopic investigation. A hitherto unknown green line in the spectrum of these residues indicated the presence of a new element. In reference to the Greek word *thallos* (green twig), he named the new element "thallium."

The elements indium (1863), gallium (1875), and scandium (1879) were similarly discovered by means of the method which Kirchhoff and Bunsen had introduced into chemistry. The discovery of a new element is always considered an event of major importance because it reveals another of the immutable building materials of nature. This importance is, however, often limited to theoretical science when the element occurs in only small quantities and is difficult to separate or to utilize.

Spectroscopy soon proved its practical value as a means of identifying well-known elements and compounds. One particular case was the control of converting pig iron into "malleable iron and steel without fuel," as Henry Bessemer (1813–1898, London) demonstrated in 1856. The carbon of the raw iron is oxidized by air which is introduced under pressure into the molten metal. It was important to stop the process just at the point when the oxidation of the carbon was terminated. An experienced observer could see the change in the appearance of the flame which occurred at that point. Henry Roscoe in 1862 recommended observation by spectroscope as more reliable.

Light and Plant Life

The relationship between animals and air was discovered much earlier than that between plants and air. Joseph Priestley found in 1772 that air which had been exhaled by animals, and thus made unsuitable for breathing, was refreshed by green plants. This did not occur without daylight. The Dutch physician Jan Ingen Housz (1730–1799) recognized that green plants did not produce dephlogisticated air when sunshine was excluded (1779). On the other hand, its production was increased when the water present in his experiments was enriched with carbon dioxide, as Jean Senebier (1742–1809) of Geneva stated in 1782. Does the plant liberate the oxygen from the water or from the carbon dioxide? Lavoisier left this question open when he summarized these findings in 1786. There is no plant life without water and carbon dioxide. These two substances decompose mutually; "the hydrogen leaves the oxygen to combine with the carbon so as to form the oils, the resins, and the plant body; at the same time the oxygen of the water and of the carbonic acid is set free in abundance, as Priestley, Ingen Housz, and Senebier observed it, and it combines with light to form oxygen gas." (33)

The origin of the hydrogen, carbon, and oxygen content of plant substances was thus explained. The transformation of those elements into resins, oils, and plant bodies could be left to the vital force. The organic force, with the aid of light, might even produce nitrogen, according to Henri Braconnot, in 1807, which is common to all the albuminous parts of a plant. These parts share with egg white the property of being coagulated by heat, acids, or alcohols according to de Fourcroy in 1789.

Théodore de Saussure (1767–1845, Geneva) was not satisfied with such explanations. They contained a conglomerate of questions to which the answers can be given only by experiments. In his work from 1797 to 1804, he postulated that plants and animals alike give off carbon dioxide constantly, in sunshine or in darkness. In the sun, plants take CO_2 from the air and exhale oxygen. An increased CO_2 content of the air which stimulates plant growth in the light damages it in the dark.

Are all parts of the sun spectrum equally effective in the assimilation of carbon dioxide? F. W. Draper in 1845 filtered the light through a yellow solution of potassium chromate and found it still active, while the blue ammoniacal solution of copper absorbed the active light. The green pigment in plants obviously served to absorb the active part of the sunlight. Pelletier and Caventou in 1818 proposed to give the name "chlorophyll" to the green substance extracted by alcohol from green leaves. Such an extraction was a doubtful means of separating a pure substance out of the aggregate of leaf substances. Berzelius raised the question of whether the green color actually belonged to the fats and waxes in the extract or whether it should be compared to a real dyestuff like indigo (1825). Separations were attempted by using different solvents, lime precipitations, and distributions of the extracted matter between ether and hydrochloric acid. Green, yellow, red, and blue colors were observed, but the analysis of these pigments gave widely differing values.

It was a great step toward chemical identification when Felix Hoppe-Seyler (1825–1895), the professor of physiology in Strasbourg, succeeded in preparing a crystallized chlorophyll (1879). He first removed the juice from leaves by pressing and washing with a mixture of water and alcohol. Subsequently digesting the green residue with warm alcohol brought the green substance into solution, together with some of the waxes and resins. The solution was then treated with bone char to absorb the chlorophyll and a somewhat similar substance which another washing with warm alcohol removed from the char. Ether or naphtha then dissolved the chlorophyll. It crystallized from such a solution upon slow evaporation of the solvent. Even then, however, it contained some phosphorus, which Hoppe-Seyler suspected of indicating the presence of lecithine in this product.

The gentle forces of specific absorption were certainly less destructive than the previously used alkalies and acids. The chemical elementary analysis was not sufficient to test whether or not the real chlorophyll was represented by the crystalline substance. The more sensitive physical measurement of the absorption spectrum which this substance gave in solution showed that it differed somewhat from the natural chlorophyll, although both had in common some of the absorption in the red part of the spectrum.

Eugen Lommel (1837–1899, Munich) studied the "optical behavior" of chlorophyll. He distinguished between the specificity and the intensity of the light. "A ray that is not absorbed (e.g., the farthest red) cannot act, however great its mechanical intensity. A ray that is absorbed completely produces only little action when its mechanical intensity is small. For the assimilation of plants, the most effective rays are those that are the most strongly absorbed by the chlorophyll and also have a high mechanical intensity. These are the red rays between B and C." (34) The thermocouple measures the intensity. The letters B and C identify the Fraunhofer lines in the spectrum.

Wilhelm Engelmann (1843–1909, Berlin) pursued this further under biological viewpoints (1882). The red lines of the spectrum proved the most effective source of energy for assimilation. By a special micro-technique, he investigated aerobic, oxygen-greedy bacteria as the indicators of the effect. A thread of a green algae (*Chladophora*) in water containing such bacteria was illuminated, and the degree of attraction to the oxygen-producing plant was observed.

The full explanation, which seemed within reach in Lavoisier's time, was later replaced by a network of problems. Even after it was established that plants use carbon dioxide in sunlight by means of chlorophyll, the question of what chemical substances were primarily produced by this reaction remained. Liebig postulated in 1843 that organic acids were formed and converted into sugar by a process of reduction. Others emphasized starch as "the first visible product of assimilation," as Julius Sachs (1832–1897, Würzburg) expressed it in 1865. (35)

In 1870 Adolf von Baeyer assumed that formaldehyde is the first product. In consecutive steps it is polymerized into sugars, starch, and cellulose (page 202). This appeared to tell the whole story, which was based on reasonable analogies but which was actually not much more than a program for future investigation. However, when the theory was formulated, it was conceived and meant as the present true picture and the culmination of all previous knowledge. Neither the formation of formaldehyde nor its actual polymerization had been observed in the green leaf. They had been found in the test tube, and from there they were projected into the living organism. In certain respects, it was a reversal of the older thinking which assumed that a particular force, specific to the organism and not reproducible outside of it, produced chemical changes of a unique character.

From the stage of glucose, other plant substances are formed. According to Armand Gautier (1837–1920), a loss of water can lead from glucose to phloroglucinol:

$$\underset{\text{Glucose}}{C_6H_{12}O_6} - 3H_2O = \underset{\text{Phloroglucinol}}{C_6H_6O_3}$$

It was clear, however, that such an overall formulation mainly served to open the door to many questions.

REFERENCES

1. Louis de Lagrange, *Mécanique analytique* (Paris: 1788), Vol. 1, p. 21. René Dugas, *A history of mechanics,* translated by J. R. Maddox (Neuchatel: Editions du Griffon, 1955), pp. 332 ff.

2. Nicolas Léonard Sadi Carnot, *Réflexions sur la puissance motrice du feu* (Paris: 1824). Republished with an appendix by H. Carnot in 1878. Frederick O. Koenig, "On the history of science and of the Second Law of Thermodynamics," *Men and Moments in the History of Science,* Herbert M. Evans, Ed. (Seattle: University of Washington Press, 1959), pp. 57–111.

3. B. P. E. Clapeyron, *Mémoire sur la puissance motrice de la chaleur* (Paris: 1833); *Poggendorff's Ann.,* **59** (1843), p. 457.

4. W. Thomson, "On an absolute thermometric scale founded on Carnot's theory of the motive power of heat, and calculated from Regnault's observations," *Phil. Mag.* (3), **33** (1848), pp. 313.

5. G. H. Hess, "Thermochemische Untersuchungen," *Pogg. Ann.,* **50** (1840), pp. 385–404; **57** (1842), pp. 560–84.

6. J. R. Mayer, "Bemerkungen über die Kräfte der unbelebten Natur," *Liebig's Ann.,* **42** (1842), pp. 233–40.

7. J. R. Mayer, "On Release" (1876). See *Mechanics of Heat* (3d ed. by J. Weyrauch, 1893).

8. J. P. Joule, "On the Caloric Effect of Magneto-Electricity and on the Mechanical Value of Heat," *Phil. Mag.,* **23** (1843), pp. 263, 369, 435.

9. J. P. Joule, *Phil. Mag.,* **27** (1845), p. 207.

10. H. Helmholtz, *Über die Erhaltung der Kraft* (Berlin: 1847).

11. Cf. Leo Königsberger, *Hermann von Helmholtz* (Braunschweig: F. Vieweg & Sohn, 1902–1903).

12. W. J. M. Rankine, *Proc. Phil. Soc. of Glasgow,* **3** (1855), p. 381.

13. W. Thomson, "On the dynamical theory of heat." *Edinburgh Trans.,* **20** (March 17, 1851), Part 2, p. 261.

14. R. Clausius, "Über verschiedene für die Anwendung bequeme Formen der Hauptgleichungen der mechanischen Wärmetheorie," *Pogg. Ann.,* **125** (1865), pp. 351–400.

15. A. F. Horstmann, "Dampfspannung und Verdampfungswärme des Salmiaks," *Chem. Ber.,* **2** (1869), pp. 137–40; "Zur Theorie der Dissociation," **4** (1871), pp. 635–9.

16. A. F. Horstmann, "Theorien der Dissociation," *Liebig's Ann.,* **170** (1873), pp. 182–210.

17. W. J. M. Rankine, "On the hypothesis of molecular vortices, or centrifugal theory of elasticity, and its connection with the theory of heat," *Phil. Mag.* (4), **10** (1855), pp. 354–63, 411–20, esp. p. 420.

18. J. Willard Gibbs, *Trans. Connecticut Ac.*, 3 (October 1875–May 1876), pp. 108–248, and (May 1877–July 1878), pp. 343–524.

19. Max Planck, "Über das Prinzip der Vermehrung der Entropie," *Wiedemann's Ann.* (N.F.), **30** (1887), pp. 562–82.

20. Ernst Mach, *Prinzipien der Wärmelehre* (Leipzig: Barth, 1919), p. 338, footnote.

21. Thomas Young, *A course of lectures on natural philosophy and the mechanical arts* (London: Johnson, 1807), Vol. 2, p. 426.

22. G. S. Ohm, *Die galvanische Kette methematisch bearbeitet* (Berlin: 1827). See also Charles G. Fraser, *Half-Hours with Great Scientists. The Story of Physics* (New York: Reinhold Publishing Corp., 1948), pp. 457 ff.

23. M. Faraday, *Experimental Researches in Electricity* (London: 1855), Vol. 3, p. 172. L. Pearce Williams, *Michael Faraday, a Biography* (London: Chapman & Hall/New York: Basic Books, 1965).

24. M. Faraday, Royal Institute, December 31, 1833; *Experimental Researches in Electricity* (London: 1839), Vol. 1, p. 256.

25. J. C. Maxwell, *A Treatise on Electricity and Magnetism* (London: 1873), p. ix.

26. See Edgar F. Smith, *Chemistry in America* (New York: D. Appleton & Co., 1914), pp. 151–205.

27. Peter Joseph Macquer, *Chymisches Wörterbuch* (Leipzig: 1788), Vol. 1, p. 629.

28. E. L. Malus, *Mém. Phys. Chim. de la Soc. d'Arcueil,* **2** (1809), pp. 261 ff.

29. M. H. Klaproth and Friedrich Wolff, *Chemisches Wörterbuch* (Berlin: 1808), Vol. 3, p. 440.

30. *Handwörterbuch der reinen und angewandten Chemie,* Begr. von Liebig-Poggendorff-Wöhler (Braunschweig: 1849), Vol. 4, p. 848.

31. R. W. Bunsen, *Pogg. Ann.,* **42** (1837), p. 145.

32. R. W. Bunsen, "Photochemische Untersuchungen," *Pogg. Ann.,* **100** (1857), pp. 43–88.

33. A. Lavoisier, "Sur la décomposition de l'eau par les substances végétales & animales," *Mém. Ac. Paris,* 1786 (1788), pp. 590–605.

34. E. Lommel, "Über das Verhalten des Chlorophylls im Licht," *Pogg. Ann.,* **143** (1871), pp. 568–85, esp. pp. 580 ff.

35. Julius Sachs, *Experimentalphysiologie* (1865). Translated by H. M. Ward, *Lectures on the Physiology of Plants* (Oxford: 1897).

Period III

Expansion of Synthesis and Analysis:

From the Latter Part of the Nineteenth Century to the Present

18

Survey of Period III

In the 1880's the century of chemistry which began with the establishment of the New System ended in a feeling of saturation. The task seemed to be completed; the goal of chemistry appeared to have been reached. At the middle of that century Liebig had already felt that advance was possible only in a new field of chemical physiology. The great laws, all of them, had been found; only routine work on the details remained to be done. The feeling was shared by many physicists and mineralogists for their own fields of science.

There had been early warnings that scientific methods, particularly the chemical method of producing pure systems, should be considered with some criticism. It was pointed out that the impurities that were discarded in the process of separation might be of greater importance than was realized at the time. These isolated pure systems, even if they were scientific, were too far removed and too artificially abstracted from life to be useful or applicable in philosophy or history. By retiring into the pure system that it had constructed, nineteenth century science was about to lose that close contact with life which the old chemistry had maintained.

The two great discoveries of the nineteenth century, energy in the physical world and evolution in the organic, seemed to offer the basis for a new outlook on life, and an attempt was made to develop it into a new religion. A new Aristotelianism appeared to be in store, a complete and stable compendium of a finite science.

This attitude, which was inherited from the previous century, changed completely during the new period. Far-reaching new discoveries demonstrated that instead of having arrived at the end of scientific expansion we were only opening up new avenues. Many of the new findings, particularly those made toward the present time, were announced as beginnings in fields in which we have "scarcely scratched the surface."

The growing success of experimental science strengthened the old philosophical rationalism and added to it the declaration that all problems can be solved by science. The declaration was meant to be reversible and to state that what science cannot solve is not really a problem but at best a relic of antiquated thinking. Expanding industrialization was in step with this new rationalism.

In contrast to this general justification of the specific means that

Fig. 32. The mill at Gary, Indiana, 1915. (From a lithograph by Joseph Pennell, 1860–1926. Plate VI in his *Pictures of the Wonder of Work.* Courtesy of the Library of Congress.) Etcher and author Joseph Pennell wrote,

". . . here, at these new works, the engineers, the steelmakers, have built mills which are nothing more than Rembrandt's mills, glorified and magnified."

science had found for itself, there persisted a general criticism of this science that never reached the reality of life and its values. This criticism did not offer a basis for changing the methods of chemistry, but it contributed to a search for itensifying chemical methods. The conclusion to which the criticism led was not that chemistry had gone too far and should revert to humanization and universalism, but that it had not gone far enough. The separation had to be still further refined in order to show all the parts of which the natural systems consisted. The finer the separations and the greater the specialization, the more complete would be the synthesis of an integrated science.

At first, however, the separation of matter into finer and finer parts seemed to lead to greater disintegration. The very solidity of substances seemed dissolved not only into molecules and atoms but also into nuclei and electrons. The greater the detail of measurement, the finer the instruments that had to be used. New mathematical methods were needed for coordinating the series of delicate instrument readings. Finally it appeared as though the concept of substances was nothing more than a superfluous duplicate for the mathematical relationships which were seen as representing all that is real. In the new search for unity, and without any irreverence, God, who had been the Chief Chemist to the late alchemists, was now felt to be the Chief Mathematician. This most recent excess of scientific revolution actually returned to the classical Greek philosophy of the reality of numbers.

In chemistry, the new unity was attained not by abandoning separation and specialization but by intensifying them. Although the atom was divided into finer parts and thus lost its original meaning, the atomistic concept was extended beyond matter to include energy. In this way even the old general dualism of matter and motion, or substance and force, was resolved into a higher unity in which matter in motion is equivalent to energy. Fire, the old representative of energy, had previously been considered the universal analyzer of matter. Robert Boyle demonstrated that fire does not have this function, and he concluded that there was no general analyzer. This was now seen in a different light. A really general analyzer had to have energy in a much higher concentration than that of ordinary fire. Under the influence of the analyzers found in the new period, even elements were separated into constituent parts by fission. Elements, like atoms, ceased to have their original absolute meaning. Synthesis, the aim which organic chemistry reached in the second half of the nineteenth century, could now be extended to the elements.

The new unity, obtained through increased specialization, disposed of many former problems in which absolute decisions seemed to be required. It did so by stating a region of indeterminacy which we reach at the absolute human limit of observation. Concepts that designated the limit of our possibilities had been constructive and useful on many occasions. The physical body, which Galileo "conceived in his mind" as free from any influence of an external force, was on the limit line of reality. Limit states that we can approach but never reach had been introduced by Carnot in thermodynamics. They were used by van't Hoff in application to the theory of solutions. On the approach to the absolute zero of temperature and pressure as well as to the absolute highest limit of velocity, new experiences of wide importance were found. The limit state of high dilution of gases under low pressures gave the first indication that the atom can be separated into a heavy electropositive and a light electronegative part. Another limit was that of the specific action of smallest quantities of matter. It had first been discovered as catalysis. Now it was specialized into actions of vitamins, hormones, biotic and antibiotic substances, or ergones and antiergones, to use Hans von Euler's collective word for substances of high biological activity.

The new chemistry of the unweighably small quantities, of which Marya Curie spoke in 1911 in connection with radioactivity, has its counterpart in the new chemistry of large commercial production. Substances of highest sensitivity are obtained by new methods of using specific adsorptions and excluding the actions of water and air, and substances of greatest stability are produced in plastics, dyestuffs, and alloys. Synthesis and analysis in the new dimensions furnish substances in which the available energy is highly specific and concentrated.

Industrialization was variously the source and the fruit of expanded research. Because the wider spread of knowledge stimulated competition, manufacturers had to continue developing their methods and products. The profits form industrialization could only be maintained, and had to be maintained, by further scientific work. Science became the reservoir from which technical progress was nourished, but the relationship was not as one-sided as this picture might indicate.

The two world wars had a profound influence on the direction of science and its industrial use. The production of chemicals on a large scale and in great variety had two opposite effects. It united the world by making faster transportation possible and tore it apart through increased demands on control over raw materials and markets for finished products. By increasing the life span of man and the growth of population, and by employing new weapons of warfare, industrialization created new problems. They were not problems for chemistry alone but at the same time for economics, ethics, law, and finally, religion. Obviously, the science that had emerged from deification and humanization cannot solve the problems of mankind without the forces to which this science owed its origin.

The primary record of the reports on all this work was kept in the "repertorium" section or reviews of many journals, but particularly by *Chemisches Zentralblatt*, *British Abstracts*, and *Chemical Abstracts* (U.S.A.). In 1907, *Chemical Abstracts* started with a staff of two and a budget of $15,500. In 1963, the staff was 4000 and the budget $4.8 million; about 10,000 journals were monitored. As of December 31, 1966, the Compound Registry at the Chemical Abstracts Service, Columbus, Ohio, listed 523,718 unique compounds; the number of assorted references was about one million.

Far less spectacular was the increase in the number of patents annually issued. In reading the table showing the number of patents granted by four great industrial countries in the nine selected years, consider the fact that the numbers are not additive for any one year. For example, in 1960 about 50 percent of all the patent applications in Great Britain were made with priorities is another country that may have led to patents there. Patents from this group, therefore, would be counted in several national lists.

NUMBER OF PATENTS ISSUED ANNUALLY IN SELECTED YEARS BETWEEN 1886 AND 1960*

Year	France	Germany	Great Britain	United States
1886	7,660	3,966	3,741	12,903
1890	9,009	9,680	10,646	25,313
1900	12,400	8,784	13,710	24,644
1910	16,064	12,100	16,269	35,141
1920	18,950	14,452	14,191	37,060
1930	24,000	26,737	20,765	45,226
1940	10,100	14,647	11,453	42,323
1950	17,800	2,383	13,509	43,129
1960	35,000	19,616	26,775	47,286

* Compiled from P. J. Federico, "Historical patent statistics 1791–1961," *Journal of the Patent Office Society*, **46** (1964), pp. 89–171.

19

Matter and Radiation

Electrical Discharge in Gases

Science and philosophy are deeply concerned with the disparity between the concepts of matter and force. Robert Greathead and Hermann Helmholtz warned in different ways, but with equal intensity, against the error of considering the difference as absolute. Leibnitz once said: Force is truly a substance, meaning that there is a region in which the two are not different. Where can that region be found?

Chemists once considered heat, light, electricity, and magnetism as substances and listed them as material elements. Physicists thought that matter was force. The opposition, and in some cases contradiction, between these extremes represented a special form of the problem of motion on which philosophers in the fourteenth century had speculated and on which Galileo had experimented. Matter in motion is action; Descartes gave the product of volume and velocity as the measure of this action, and Newton combined mass and velocity to express the "quantity of motion" or momentum, the product mc. The result of much philosophical contemplation about the meaning of motion and momentum assumed this simple mathematical form, which facilitated further development. Maxwell's theory postulated that electromagnetic waves have momentum like a mass in motion, characterized by a value of the velocity c equal to the velocity of light. If the energy of these waves is symbolized by the letter E, the momentum becomes E/c, and since a momentum is the product of mass and velocity, $E/c = mc$. As the speed with which matter moves approaches the velocity of light, matter becomes transformed into energy in the relationship defined by the formula $E = mc^2$. This conclusion, which Albert Einstein (1879–1955) developed in his theory of relativity, was based upon the experimental observation of matter in a state of motion at high speed and upon theoretical considerations which showed that the old materialistic concept of an ether had to be abandoned.

In 1845 J. P. Joule had pointed with amazement at the enormous quantity of kinetic energy—*vis viva*—contained in a substance at ordinary room temperature (page 245). He thought of a connection with the "rotation of electric atmospheres" at "prodigious" velocity, approaching that of light. Such thoughts were carried through to their full consequences in the new theory.

Experimental work was begun in the early part of the nineteenth century soon after the discovery of relationships between chemistry and electricity. The quiet discharge of electricity through metals or salt solutions at first appeared to be entirely different from the sparks and noise accompanying the passage of electricity through gases. Faraday distinguished between the conductive and electrolytic passage of electricity and the "disruptive" discharge through gases. This discharge, as William Snow Harris (1792–1867) found in 1834, required quantities of electricity in direct proportion to the pressure of the gas. By reducing the pressure, the electricity finds less resistance to its passage. After Heinrich Geissler (1814–1879) invented the mercury vapor pump, it was possible to reduce gas pressure in glass tubes to small fractions of a millimeter, atmospheric pressure normally being 760 mm of a mercury column. Electrical discharge between metallic anode and cathode inserted in such a tube produced fluorescence of the glass wall in the neighborhood of the cathode. In 1859 Julius Plücker (1801–1868, Bonn) discovered that the position of the fluorescent patches changed when a magnet was brought close to the tube. Whatever the cause of the fluorescence, it responded to a magnetic field. On the other hand, the fluorescence was caused by a radiation starting from the cathode which could be made to cast a shadow and which thus resembled light. Eugen Goldstein (1850–1930) spoke of cathode rays. He considered them as similar to rays of ordinary light, and since these were waves in the ether, according to Huygens' theory, the cathode rays should also be regarded as a "disturbance" in this universal medium which permeates all matter.

While the analogy with light could account for the straight line of propagation and the luminescence, it did not explain the deflection by a magnetic field. For William Crookes (1832–1919, London) this was the most important means for characterizing these rays. He had been led into this field of investigation through experiments which started from problems of an entirely different kind. As a student at the Royal College of Chemistry, he was asked (1850) by A. W.

Hofmann to separate the selenium from sulfuric acid sludge. The continued investigation brought him to the discovery of a new element, later named "thallium." In his efforts to determine the atomic weight of this element, he used the method of weighing under vacuum. The behavior of his balance under these conditions was perplexing until he discovered that light acted upon the metal under vacuum as though it had a pressure of its own (1874). Radiation seemed to perform a mechanical action. An analogy to Plücker's and Goldstein's experiment on cathode rays seemed to exist. The deflection of these rays by magnets was now found to change with the direction of the magnetic field. Cathode rays appeared as a stream of particles carrying a negative electric charge. By the electric discharge under very low pressure, matter was converted into a new state of radiant matter. In this fourth state, matter and energy seemed to be in a region of transition, a region which, Crookes predicted, would offer a solution to the greatest scientific problems of the future. (1)

One important step in that direction was the discovery in 1886 of positive rays by E. Goldstein. When the cathode was pierced with holes, the electrical discharge gave visible rays in a direction opposite to the cathode rays, and while these were independent of the nature of the gas in the tube, the new canal rays changed in color with change of the kind of gas.

Electrically charged atoms in solutions had been a familiar concept since Faraday's electrolytic investigations. In this concept, substance and electricity were clearly distinguished; their combination was entirely different from a new state of matter which Crookes proclaimed.

Joseph John Thomson (1856–1940, Cambridge, England) maintained the distinction between substance and electricity in an explanation of his experimental results in 1891. "We assume then that the electric field is full of tubes of electrostatic induction, that these are all of the same strength, and that this strength is such that when a tube falls on a conductor it corresponds to a negative charge on the conductor equal in amount to the charge which in electrolysis we find associated with an atom of a univalent element." (2) The "tubes of electrostatic induction" which corresponded to Faraday's "lines of force" became electric charge when they alighted on a material particle. In electrolysis, the ratio of electric charge to the mass m of a hydrogen ion was measured by the time and current in amperes required to liberate the quantity m grams of the ion in the form of the hydrogen element. One ampere current flowing for one second is equal to one tenth of the electromagnetic unit, usually designated by the letter *e*. The value of *e/m* for the hydrogen ion in solutions was 9578.5. J. J. Thomson measured *e/m* for cathode rays deflected by a magnetic field of known strength and found the ratio to be about a thousand times as great; later, improved methods gave the ratio for cathode rays as 1837 times that of the hydrogen ion. There was no hope that the mass of the cathode rays could be measured directly like that of electrolytically produced hydrogen, but connections with several other new fundamental experiences were developed.

Heinrich Rudolf Hertz (1857–1894) proved in Karlsruhe what Maxwell's theory predicted, namely, that electromagnetic waves travel with the speed and properties of light. The decisive experiments were carried out in 1888. A few years later the relationship between electromagnetism and light was demonstrated by Pieter Zeeman (1865–1943) in Leyden. Spectroscopic measurements showed a widening and splitting of the sodium and cadmium lines when the vibrations of the light were influenced by a magnetic field (1896).

At about the same time, Wilhelm Konrad Röntgen (1845–1923), a professor of physics in Würzburg, discovered that the impact of cathode rays on the glass wall of the tube formed the source of a new radiation. This radiation acted upon photographic film like light, but it also penetrated through black paper and thin sheets of metal.

Röntgen rays formed ions in the air through which they passed. These ions acted as the nuclei for condensing water vapor from a saturated atmosphere. The quantitative relationship between radiant particles and water particles was not immediately known. Assumptions had to be made as to the number of particles combined with a certain quantity of water. These assumptions could be tested by varying the experimental conditions. It was consistent with the observed proportions of electrical charge and droplet size to assume that the particles of cathode rays are much smaller than hydrogen atoms. George Francis FitzGerald (1851–1901, Dublin) suggested (1894) adopting for these particles the name "electron," which his uncle George Johnstone Stoney had originally applied to a "nonconducting part" of the atom. The atom had been conceived as an ultimate particle of matter; now a new kind of particle was postulated, with the difference that it did not refer to substances but to a structure in the ether.

The new meaning of electrons was the "discrete electric nuclei" or "centers of radial twist in the medium." The magnitude of this particle, the electron, became a measurable reality as the composite of all these theories and experiences, for which Charles Thomas Rees Wilson's (1869–1959) "cloud chamber" (1897) formed a measuring apparatus. J. J. Thomson calculated that for his value $e/m = 10^7$ in electromagnetic units, the mass of one electron was 10^{-27} grams. He estimated that the mass of the hydrogen atom was about a thousand times this figure, or 10^{-24} grams. One gram of hydrogen, or approximately 11.2 liters of this gas at one atmosphere and 0°C,

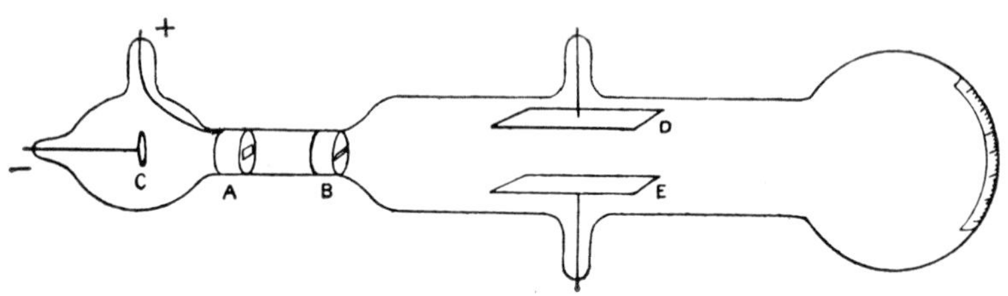

Fig. 33. J. J. Thomson's vacuum tube. (From *Phil. Mag.* (5) 44, 1897, p. 296.) He described it in 1897 thus:

"The rays from the cathode C pass through a slit in the anode A, which is a metal plug fitting tightly into the tube and connected with the earth; after passing through a second slit in another earthly-connected metal plug B, they travel between two parallel aluminum plates about 5 cm. long by 2 broad and at a distance of 1.5 cm. apart; they then fall on the end of the tube and produce a narrow well-defined phosphorescent patch. A scale pasted on the outside of the tube serves to measure the deflection of this patch. At high exhaustions the rays were deflected when the two aluminum plates were connected with the terminals of a battery of small storage-cells; the rays were depressed when the upper plate was connected with the negative pole of the battery, the lower with the positive, and raised when the upper plate was connected with the positive, the lower with the negative pole. The deflection was proportional to the difference of potential between the plates, and I could detect the deflection when the potential-difference was as small as two volts."

would thus contain 10^{24} atoms. The correction of the figure for the electron came later through experiments by Robert Andrews Millikan (1868–1953, Pasadena) who used oil droplets instead of water and showed that the electron really was the smallest amount of electricity which could not be divided further. (3)

Cathode rays now appeared as a stream of electrons liberated from the atoms. Ionization of a salt *in solution* meant a migration of electrons between the chemical components of the salt which were thereby distinguishable as negative and positive parts. Ionization of a *gas* disrupted the atom into free negative electrons and atoms deprived of their negative particles and therefore positively charged. The passage of electricity in a gas separated the atoms into parts which were there all the time, a heavy nucleus of positive charge and electrons sufficient to neutralize it. This theory of J. J. Thomson (1897) was confirmed when the canal rays were proved by Wilhelm Wien (1864–1928, Munich) to be positive particles of an e/m value about in the range of the ratio for hydrogen ions. The discovery of radioactive elements provided an entirely independent additional proof.

Radioactive Substances

Röntgen's discovery started from the accidental observation that crystals of barium platinocyanide, $BaPt(CN)_4$, were fluorescing when they were near cathode rays. (4) Some of the circumstances of the discovery were like a repetition of Galvani's (page 134) experiences, and just as upon Galvani's discovery, so now physicists from all over the world rushed into the newly opened field. Among them was Antoine-Henri Becquerel (1852–1908, Paris), whose grandfather and father were renowned physicists. In his father's collection were uranium salts which were known to fluoresce in the dark after a period of exposure to light. The source of the newly discovered X rays (Röntgen rays) was the fluorescent spot of the cathode ray tube. Was fluorescence, for instance that of uranium salts, always the source of X rays? Becquerel found in February, 1896, that the uranium salts, even without previous exposure to sunlight, acted on photographic plates through thick black paper as Röntgen rays did. The fluorescent uranium salt used in the first experiments was complex potassium sulfate. Chemical conversions showed that the activity went with the fractions that contained the uranium, and it was so specific that it had to be attributed to a new kind of radiation, called "Becquerel rays."

The only other element that exerted similar action was discovered in thorium (1898). The search for activity, guided by electric measurements, was carried on by Pierre and Marya Curie in Paris, by Ernest Rutherford in Cambridge, by Elster and Geitel in Braunschweig. The Curies used pitchblende, the uranium-bearing ore, and separated a fraction from it which was about four hundred times more active than uranium. The electrical activity radiating from this substance remained with it in all the chemical processes of dissolving and precipitating. Actually, the radiation served as the means for discovering in which part of the separated material the active substance was present. One active substance was precipitated together with bismuth. Its unique property indicated that it was a new element, and it was named "polonium" in honor of Marya Curie's native land, Poland. Another element of different radiation, which was found to precipitate with barium, was called the radiant element, "radium." Both were discovered in 1898. The Austrian government had large quantities of residues from the mines of St. Joachimstal. Silver and lead and a little uranium had been usefully extracted from the ore; the residue appeared to be worthless. A few carloads of it were now sent to Pierre and Marya Curie for large-scale work on separating the radium from it. Their success made the discarded residues worth millions of dollars.

The radiation emitted by these elements was analyzed by the methods developed for cathode rays and canal rays. These physical methods became intelligible by means of another chemical discovery which was made in these eventful final years of the nineteenth century. Lord Rayleigh (1842–1919, London) had carried out precision measurements on the density of nitrogen. He prepared this gas in two different ways: from air, by removing the oxygen, and from ammonia, by chemical decomposition. The former gave a slightly higher value than the other. Although the difference was only 1/1000 part, he was "much puzzled" because he knew that the errors of his experiments were smaller than this difference. When William Ramsay (1852–1916) was asked about this, he remembered that he had read Cavendish's account of his experiments of more than a century before. This careful observer mentioned a small gas residue remaining when nitrogen oxide, prepared from air, was absorbed in potash lye. Ramsay intuitively connected the old observation with the new. He suspected the presence of a heavier gas in the supposedly pure nitrogen from the air; Lord Rayleigh thought a lighter component went with the chemically prepared nitrogen. In the nitrogen from air, they found the heavier gas. Nothing they tried caused it to react, not even with fluorine. On the basis of the Greek word for inert, they called the new element "argon" (1895).

This experience caused Ramsay to investigate the gas that had been observed when minerals containing uranium were dissolved. It had been assumed that this gas was nitrogen, but Ramsay soon confirmed his suspicion that it was an entirely different substance. In March, 1895, he wrote as follows:

> I bottled the new gas in a vacuum tube, and arranged so that I could see its spectrum and that of argon in the same spectroscope at the same time. There is argon in the gas; but there was a magnificent yellow line, brilliantly bright, not coincident with but very close

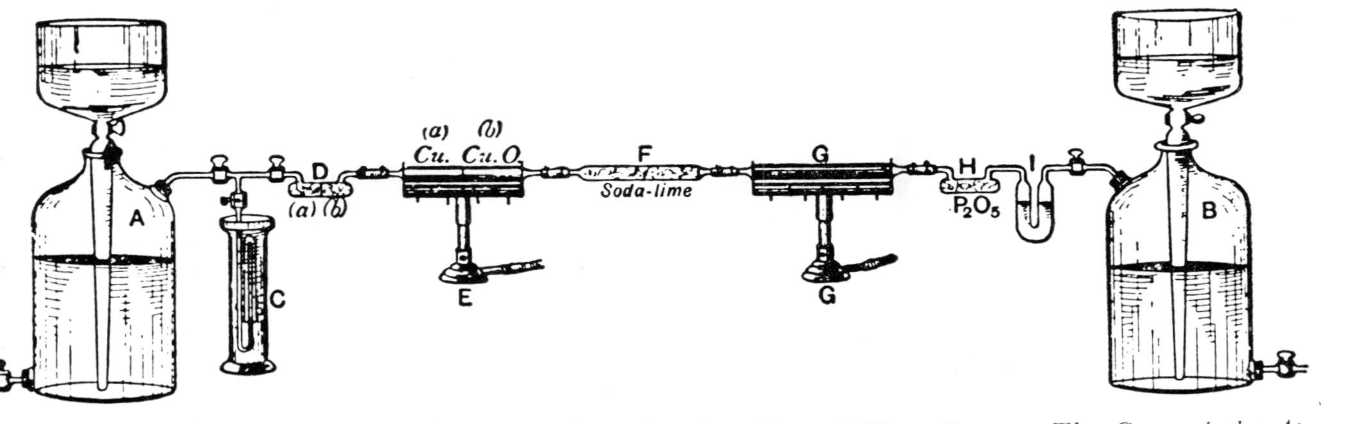

Fig. 34. Apparatus for the separation of argon from the air. (From William Ramsay, *The Gases of the Atmosphere; the History of Their Discovery*, Macmillan & Co., London, 1896, pp. 158–89). On page 159 of his *Gases of the Atmosphere*, Ramsay describes the process of concentrating argon from atmospheric nitrogen:

"Air is moved from gasholder A to another B, through a tube filled with magnesium heated to redness G, to absorb nitrogen; over red-hot copper oxide (*a*) (*b*), so that any carbonaceous matter such as dust should be oxidised to carbon dioxide and water; and these, if produced, were absorbed by placing in the train of tubes, one filled with a mixture of soda and lime F and I, to absorb any carbon dioxide which might possibly be formed, and two filled with pentoxide of phosphorus D and H, to dry the gas, so that water-vapor, carried along with the gas from the gasholders (which contained water) might be removed before the gas passed over the red-hot magnesium; for water acts on hot magnesium, forming oxide of magnesium and hydrogen, and the gas would have become contaminated with the latter had this precaution not been taken.

"The process was continued for ten days, by which time most of the nitrogen had become absorbed. The apparatus was then somewhat altered so as to make it possible to work with a smaller quantity of gas; but the tubes destined to absorb nitrogen, hydrogen, etc., were filled with the same materials as before."

> to the sodium line. I was puzzled, but began to smell a rat. I told Crookes, and on Saturday morning when Harley, Shields, and I were looking at the spectrum in the darkroom, a telegram came from Crookes. He had sent a copy here, and I enclose that copy. You may wonder what it means. 'Helium' is the name given to a line in the solar spectrum, known to belong to an element, but that element has hitherto been unknown on earth. . . . It is quite overwhelming and beats argon. (5)

Further search yielded three more inert gases from the air, "neon" (the new), "krypton" (the hidden), and "xenon" (the foreign) (1898).

Helium (He), the gas first observed spectroscopically in the sun (*helios*), has an atomic weight of 4. The positive rays given off from the new radioactive elements had an e/m value which showed that they consisted of positively charged helium. The negative radiation was similar to that of cathode rays. Besides, there was a radiation which did not carry an electric charge, and which, similar to Röntgen rays, could not be deflected by magnetic fields. These three groups of radiation were clearly distinguished by Ernest Rutherford (1902) and designated by the first three letters of the Greek alphabet, α, β, γ. An α-particle has an absolute weight of 6.6×10^{-24} grams, a β-particle 9×10^{-28}; γ-rays are characterized by a wavelength of between 10^{-8} to 10^{-9} cm.

The question arose as to whether or not these radiations were an essential property of uranium and the other new elements. A disc of platinum exposed to radium acquired an activity which persisted for some time after the radium was removed. This "induced" activity could further be traced to another new element which, although not procurable in visibly large quantities, could be condensed on a fine copper wire that was cooled in liquid air. Its optical spectrum could be measured (by Ramsay, in 1904) and its atomic weight was found is 1911 to be close to the expected value. Since radium has the atomic weight 226 and loses one helium particle in the transformation, radium emanation (later named radon) should have the atomic weight 222.

The emission of radiation is accompanied by a development of heat. The energy spontaneously developed was not, as preliminarily suspected, a transformed energy taken up from the surroundings; it was developed as a result of the decay of these heavy elements. The instable atom discharges itself of electrons and helium atoms; the γ-rays result from the recoil caused by the release of these particles at high speed. E. Rutherford and his collaborator, Frederick Soddy (1877–1956), thus explained in 1902 the process of radioactive de-

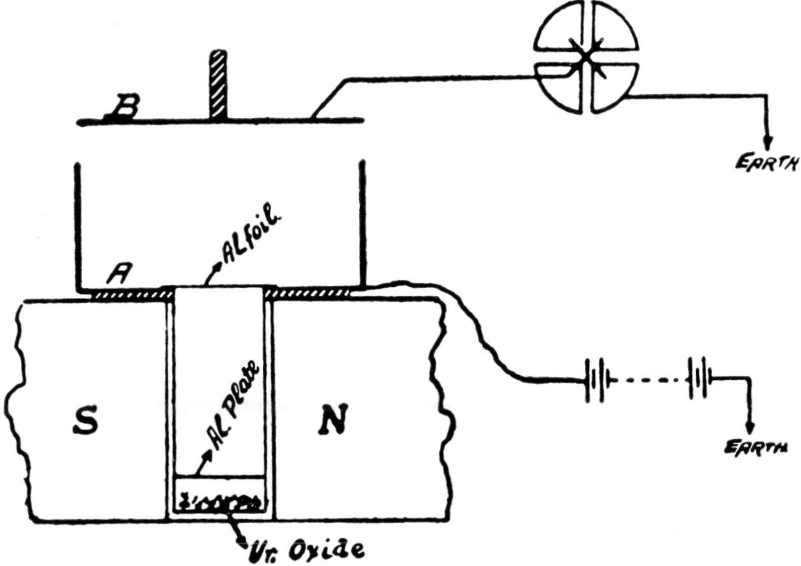

Fig. 35. Reaction of a magnetic field on uranium radiation. (From E. Rutherford, *Phil. Mag.* (6), **4**, 1902, p. 3.) The arrangement is described in *Philosophical Magazine* as follows:

"In the experiments on the action of a magnetic field on uranium radiation [in Fig. 35], a thick layer of uranium oxide was placed on the bottom of a rectangular lead box 5.7 cms. long, 1.8 cm. wide, and 4.0 cms. deep, which was placed between the flat pole-pieces of a large electromagnet. The rays, after passing out of the lead box, passed between two parallel insulated plates A and B. One of these plates A was charged to a P.D. of 50 volts above the earth by means of a battery. The other plate B was connected to one pair of quadrants of an electrometer in the usual manner."

composition. The loss of α and β particles changes the chemical nature of the atom. This was confirmed by the chemical analysis of the decay products. Radium is transformed in defined stages. After losing four α-particles, radium is changed to an element RaD which should have the atomic weight 210 (4×4 subtracted from 226). Polonium (RaF), the first to be discovered, is actually the last radioactive product of radium. Improved chemical methods for its separation were given by M. Curie and A. Debierne is 1910. It lost half of its radioactivity in 135 days. The end product of its transformation should have the atomic weight 206. That of ordinary lead is 207.18. The new product, RaG, proved to be identical in all chemical properties with lead, except for its lower atomic weight.

Isotopes

The Periodic System did not have enough room for the new elements resulting from radioactive decay. Coincidentally, our chemical methods for separating elements are not capable of distinguishing between certain elements produced by radioactive decay and the corresponding "ordinary" elements. Georg von Hevesy (1885–1966, Budapest), found in Rutherford's Cambridge laboratory that RaD and RaG could not chemically be separated from ordinary lead. Fritz Paneth (1887–1958) had similar experiences. Both could not achieve the original task of separating the two radium products from ordinary lead, but they turned failure into success in 1913 by developing a new method for using those elements as indicators of the presence of the smallest quantities of lead. The quantitative measurement of activity permitted the determination of quantities that are too small for normal chemical dosage.

The progress in the analysis of radiation indicated an increasing number of decay products. The theoretical concept of the atom structure could be elaborated beyond the original picture which Rutherford had given in 1902. In his expanded theory of 1911, a heavy nucleus of N times e charges is surrounded by N electrons. They move on concentric circles around the nucleus. While the outer of these circles may have a diameter of 10^{-8} cm, the diameter of the nucleus itself is only of the magnitude of 10^{-22} cm.

When an α-particle is split off, the nucleus loses two positive charges and four units in atomic weight. When an electron is given off (β-radiation), the weight of the product remains practically the same as that of the parent element, but the valency changes to the next higher number. The place for such new radioelements in the Periodic System in some cases coincides with the place already taken by an old element. Frederick Soddy called such elements, because they have the same place (*topos*), "isotopes" (1911). Several isotopes of uranium were found among its radioactive descendents, and others are isotopes of thorium. RaE is an isotope of bismuth, and end products of radium decay are isotopes of lead. The atomic weight in these cases is not the absolute characteristic for an element which the work of the preceding century had thought to have established.

Just before the outbreak of the war (1914), indications were found that isotopes occur not only in radioactively produced elements. Soon after the war, Francis William Aston (1877–1945, London) established this fact for the inert gas neon. The positive rays, or canal rays, produced in a modified Thomson tube containing neon at low pressure, separated under the influence of a magnetic field into two streams. These left their mark on a photographic plate, and calculation of the e/m relationship had to be interpreted as showing the presence of two kinds, or species, of neon. The atomic weights were 20 and 22, while the atomic weight of neon from the air was 20.2. At that time the basis for a theory of isotopes had been formulated with the aid of the quantum theory. The method of separating the electrically charged particles of substances according to their mass was called "mass spectroscopy." (6)

The Quantum Theory

The concept that heat is not a substance but a state of vibration in all substances had been developed during the nineteenth century. The molecular vibration causes radiation that is invisible to the eye but is measurable when converted to electricity. For example, an electric current is produced when a junction of two different metals is exposed to heat radiation. As the temperature increases, the radiation becomes visible. It starts with a dark red at about 525°C and turns "white" at over 1000°C. High temperatures are measured optically. A definite relationship between frequency of vibration, or its inverse, the wavelength, and temperature was found in 1879 by Josef Stefan, and in 1893 Wilhelm Wien derived a law of very simple mathematical form from the change of the wavelength λ of maximal intensity of radiation with T the absolute temperature: $\lambda \times T$ = constant.

The measured values of radiant energy at low temperatures differed by orders of magnitude from those calculated on the basis of classical dynamics. Max Planck (1858–1947, Berlin) therefore introduced a new hypothesis, which he first published in October 1900. To considerations of statistics and thermodynamics he added a new concept of a limit. The first step was to explain the connection between energy and temperature by considering the probabilities for the exchange of energy among systems. The states of these systems must be assumed to be governed by a great number of independent variables. The systems, Planck wrote,

> are in statistical equilibrium, when an energy transition between them does not increase the probability. Thus, if $W_1 = f(E_1)$ is the probability for the first system to have he energy E_1, and $W_2 = j(E_2)$ the probability for the second system to have the energy E_2, then the probability for both systems to have the energies E_1

and E_2 simultaneously is W_1W_2, and the condition for this to be a maximum is

$$d(W_1W_2) = 0, \qquad \text{or} \qquad \frac{dW_1}{W_1} + \frac{dW_2}{W_2} = 0$$

under the condition that $dE_1 + dE_2 = 0$.

The general condition for the statistical equilibrium:

$$\frac{1}{W_1}\frac{dW_1}{dE_1} = \frac{1}{W_2}\frac{dW_2}{dE_2}$$

By identifying the statistical equilibrium with the thermodynamic equilibrium which is characterized by equality of the temperatures, we obtain the general definition of temperature,

$$\frac{1}{T} = k\,\frac{1}{W}\frac{dW}{dE}$$

where k is given by the units of temperature. (7)

The value for the probability of a steadily changing variable can be derived from the distribution of independent elementary regions of equal probability. Maxwell and Boltzmann had assumed that these regions vary without any limit. If q designates one of the independently variable coordinates of movement in space having the impulse ("moment") p, the change of energy is the product $dq \cdot dp$, and this product was assumed to vary down to an infinitesimally small value. Such an assumption, however, led to the wrong law for the energy of radiation. Planck therefore postulated a lower limit, a finite value for the integral of this product: $\int\int dq \cdot dp = h$. Otherwise the fundamental concepts of Maxwell and Boltzmann, the statistical distribution of energies according to the general laws of probability, remained the same. With this "elementary quantum of action" (h), the mathematical formula for the relationships between energy, wavelength of radiation, and temperature was in close agreement with experimental results. By introducing the figures obtained by experimental measurements into the new formula, the numerical value of h could be calculated. $h = 6.548 \cdot 10^{-27}$ erg sec (erg seconds). One erg is the physical unit of energy equal to about one ten-billionth of one British Thermal Unit; one kilocalorie is about 42 billion ergs. So accurate were these measurements that later work confirmed them within close limits. The newest figure for h is 6.626×10^{-27} erg sec.

Radiant energy is thus found to be sent out in packages of $h \cdot \nu$, where ν is the frequency, the number of vibrations per second. As an "atom" of energy, $h\nu$ differs fundamentally from the atom of matter; h is a universal constant, whereas the atom is specific for each element. The atomic concept which corresponds in universality with the quantum is the number of particles contained in equal volumes of gases, or, generally speaking, in quantities of matter taken in the proportions of their atomic (or molecular) weights. From Planck's theory it followed that 6.16×10^{23} molecules are present in one gram-molecule (2 grams of hydrogen or 32 grams of oxygen, etc.). This figure, derived from measurements of heat radiation, was confirmed by results from many other fields of experiment. For instance, the decay of radium (atomic weight 226.5, according to M. Curie) gives 3.4×10^{10} α-particles per gram in one second (E. Rutherford). The period of decay is about 2000 years (Bertram B. Boltwood, 1870–1927, New Haven, found this in 1908), so that 1.09×10^{-11} of all the N atoms of 226.5 grams of radium are decomposed in one second. Therefore,

$$226.5 \times 3.4 \times 10^{10} = N \times 1.09 \times 10^{-11}$$

and

$$N = 7.1 \times 10^{23}$$

Uncertainties existed in the numerical value of N in 1908, but they were much smaller than the uncertainties of the atomic weights in 1808.

The quantum theory was developed in order to arrive at a law for radiant energy. The new concept of a principle of least action had to be traced to the source of this action, an oscillation of the elementary particles. The quantum-theoretical change of the atoms as oscillators with changes of temperatures was calculated by Albert Einstein. His theory of specific heat showed that the law for atomic heat, pronounced in 1819 by Dulong and Petit, becomes valid at high temperatures. The newly recognized limit of the quantum of action thus explained the limitation of an older law.

The analysis of electrical discharge through gases and of radioactive disintegration spurred the construction of models of the atom. These had to represent a structure in which a heavy nucleus of positive charge held electrons within a sphere of attraction. The rotations and oscillations within this structure had to be assumed in such manner that optical and electrical properties could be accounted for. Quantum theory divided the figurative plane of action into symbolic ellipses, defined by multiples of $qp = h$. Ellipses now took the place of the circles that Rutherford had postulated. Niels Bohr (1885–1962, Copenhagen) transformed this mathematical symbolism into a model of the atom. (8) The ellipses became the paths that the electrons described in their rotation around the nuclei of the atoms. The quantum-theoretical conditions for the radiation and absorption of energy were fulfilled if the electrons jumped from one ellipse to the next. In doing this, the energy changes from E_1 to E_2, and $E_1 - E_2 = h\nu$. The radiation produced by the jump has the frequency ν.

This theory, first published in 1913, compared the atom with a planetary system and had Kepler's astronomical laws as a basis for analogies. More directly pertinent were the laws found for the series of lines in the spectrum of the lighter elements. The electric charge of the electron became known from the measurements of the deflection of electron rays in magnetic fields; the new concepts gave a relationship between electrical potential V in volts and the frequency ν of the spectral line produced by the potential. They were confirmed in 1913 in the experiments of James Franck (1882–1964) and Gustav Hertz (1887–), a nephew of Heinrich Hertz.

For a while it appeared as though Planck's theory confirmed the explanation of reality by discrete units which atomic theory had started. The quantum as a discrete smallest unit of energy seemed to be comparable to Newton's corpuscles of light. The old controversy between Newton's corpuscles and Huygens' waves of light, which for a long time had been assumed to be resolved in Huygens' favor, seemed to return now to the preference of a concept more similar to Newton's. The real decision, however, changed the problem by removing it from the customary either-or position. The subdivision of energy into quanta brought it close to an analogy with matter at the time when the discovery of the almost massless electron brought matter close to energy. The experiments that have been carried out since 1913 showed that light is not only wave but also corpuscle, the electron not only corpuscle but also wave. According to Niels Bohr, in 1923, the two concepts are not contradictory, they are complementary. (9).

The elementary quantum of action, h, did not lose its great significance in this change; its importance was demonstrated in 1925 by the German physicist Karl Werner Heisenberg (1901–) to be more universal than had been realized before. It is a limit value of our ability to measure changes of position dq separately from changes of momentum dp. A fundamental range of indeterminacy is defined by the product $dq \cdot dp$.

Analysis and Synthesis of Elements— The New System of the Elements

The Periodic System of the elements was the result of the discovery that chemically similar elements recur at periodic intervals when the elements are arranged in the order of their atomic weights. Corresponding periodic intervals were found for such physical properties as specific gravity, hardness, and electrical conductivity. Confidence in the general rule enabled us to predict the place and properties of unknown elements. Analysis by flame spectroscopy was one of the tools by which some of the predicted elements were discovered. A rule connecting the lines in the spectrum of hydrogen was found by the Swiss physicist and teacher Johann Jakob Balmer (1825–1898, Basle) in 1885, and this rule was found to be of general importance. Balmer represented the wavelengths of the hydrogen spectrum by a formula in which a "fundamental number," arbitrarily represented by the letter h, is multiplied by a factor $m^2/(m^2 - n^2)$, where $n = 2$ and m can assume the values 3, 4, 5, and 6. The formula represented the visible part of the hydrogen spectrum accurately. Was it possible to establish a similar formula for other spectra? Could n have other values than 2? The answers to these questions came when the infrared and ultraviolet spectra could be measured.

The generalization of the Balmer formula was given by Johannes Robert Rydberg (1854–1919, Lund) and Walter Ritz (1878–1909, Göttingen). By introducing the frequency $v = 1/\lambda$, and writing $N = n^2/h$ in Balmer's formula (1910), the generalization was expressed by

$$\nu = N(1/n^2 - 1/m^2)$$

It was valid for the range from infrared to ultraviolet, where ν ranges from about 5.10^{12} to 3.10^{15}, or the wavelength from about 6.10^{-3} to 1.10^{-5} cm. An extension of this range was offered by the Röntgen rays, for which preliminary experiments indicated wavelengths of the order of 10^{-8} to 10^{-9} cm.

In the optical range of vibrations, wavelengths were measured by diffractions. The principle had been developed by Fresnel. A practical instrument consisted of a diffraction grating, a series of closely spaced rulings on a plate. Henry Augustus Rowland (1848–1901) constructed a machine for producing 43,000 divisions per inch (1882). However, this would still be a few thousand times too coarse for Röntgen rays. Max von Laue (1879–1960) calculated that the distance between the atoms in a crystal could form a three dimensional grating of the magnitude needed for diffracting these rays. In the simple case of sodium chloride, weight, volume, and number of atoms in the molecule can be calculated from the following data: The mass of one gram-molecule, the combined weights of sodium and chlorine, is 58.46; the specific gravity is 2.164. The volume of 27.48 cm^3 contains 6.07×10^{23} molecules. When each of the atoms is considered as forming the center of a cube of the size d^3, it is easily calculated that $d = 2.814 \times 10^{8}$. The first experiments carried out in Laue's Institute by Walter Friedrich and Paul Knipping in 1912 confirmed the deduction. A new method for measuring the wavelength of Röntgen rays was thus established, and it could be used in reverse to determine the structure of crystals by using X rays of known characteristics. (10)

An unknown structure, the crystal, was successfully used to measure another unknown, the wavelength, because both unknowns were united in a systematic concept. As William Lawrence Bragg said in 1922, "These two lines of investigation, into X-ray spectra and into crystal structure, are the two great branches of research to which Laue's discovery led." He said this on the occasion of accepting the 1915 Nobel Prize in physics for both himself and his father, William Henry Bragg (1862–1942, London). The delayed presentation in 1922 was made necessary by the war.

Even before Laue developed this method, Charles Glover Barkla (1877–1944) characterized Röntgen rays through absorption in aluminum. Every element, he concluded, has its own Röntgen radiation, a "characteristic radiation," as he called it.

The English physicist Henry Gwyn Jeffreys Moseley (1887–1915) used the characterization of X rays by wavelength in 1913. A spectrum of high-frequency radiation proved to be a direct function of the position of the element in the Periodic System. (11) This position had at first been considered as completely governed by the atomic weight, and it had been successfully correlated to the sequence of physical properties and chemical similarities. There were a few exceptions. According to the atomic weights, nickel, at. wt. 58.68, should precede cobalt, at. wt. 58.97, whereas according to the relationships with the neighboring elements, the sequence should be reversed. The new rule derived from high-frequency spectra showed the way out of the dilemma. The order of the elements is not primarily defined by the atomic weight but by a characteristic which Moseley called the "atomic number." The square root of the wave number, which is the reciprocal of the wavelength measured in centimeters, can be connected with the atomic number by a simple proportion, or, as Moseley expressed it, "There is in the atom a fundamental quantity which increases by regular steps as we pass from one atom to the next. This quantity can only be the charge on the central positive nucleus." This stepwise increase was connected with the structure of the electron shell around the atomic nucleus by Manne Siegbahn (1886–) and his school. Moseley was killed in action at Gallipoli in the World War.

The detailed measurement of optical and X-ray spectra calculated on the basis of quantum mechanics and the theory of relativity were represented in a structure of the electron shell. The atomic number was also the number of the electrons; their distribution on quantum shells corresponded to the periods in the system of the elements.

Table of the Elements of 1923

Like the old Periodic System, the new one contained gaps which were precisely defined. New discoveries of elements were guided by high-frequency spectrum rules which now functioned with greater precision than the rules of visible spectra did several decades earlier. An element of the atomic number 72 revealed its presence in a zircon from Norway by characteristic lines of its X-ray spectrum. Dirk Coster (1889–1950) and G. v. Hevesy called it "hafnium" because it was discovered (1922) in Copenhagen, a city whose earlier name was Hafnia. Element 43 was made artificially by bombarding molybdenum (element 42) with neutrons or deuterons (1937) and was called "technetium" (Tc). (12) The companion element 75, rhenium, of group VIIa in the Periodic System, was found through its optical spectrum at the high temperature of the electric arc (by W. Noddack in 1925).

The atomic number is identical with the electron number; the atomic weight, however, increases more rapidly than in proportion to the atomic number.

Radioactive materials and X rays have a powerful destructive action on organisms. Many of the pioneers in these fields suffered the loss of fingers, limbs, and even life because of this. In 1918 E. Rutherford found that even elements can be "destroyed" under the impact of the high energies now available. He bombarded nitrogen with α-rays from RaC and observed a radiation which had four times the penetrating power of the α-particles. He concluded that hydrogen had been split out of the nitrogen nucleus. In this result it was more surprising that the helium particle withstood decomposition than that the nitrogen did not.

TYPES OF ELECTRON SHELLS OF THE ELEMENTS

N \ n_k	1_1	2_1	2_2	3_1	3_2	3_3	4_1	4_2	4_3	4_4	5_1	5_2	5_3	5_4	5_5	6_1	6_2	6_3	6_4	6_5	6_6	7_1	7_2
1 H	1																						
2 He	2																						
3 Li	2	1																					
4 Be	2	2																					
5 B	2	2	1																				
— —	—	—	—																				
10 Ne	2	4	4																				
11 Na	2	4	4	1																			
12 Mg	2	4	4	2																			
13 Al	2	4	4	2	1																		
— —	—	—	—	—	—																		
18 A	2	4	4	4	4																		
19 K	2	4	4	4	4		1																
20 Ca	2	4	4	4	4		2																
21 Sc	2	4	4	4	4	1	2																
22 Ti	2	4	4	4	4	2	2																
— —	—	—	—	—	—	—	—																
29 Cu	2	4	4	6	6	6	1																
30 Zn	2	4	4	6	6	6	2																
31 Ga	2	4	4	6	6	6	2	1															
— —	—	—	—	—	—	—	—	—															
36 Kr	2	4	4	6	6	6	4	4															
37 Rb	2	4	4	6	6	6	4	4			1												
38 Sr	2	4	4	6	6	6	4	4			2												
39 Y	2	4	4	6	6	6	4	4	1		2												
40 Zr	2	4	4	6	6	6	4	4	2		2												
— —	—	—	—	—	—	—	—	—	—		—												
47 Ag	2	4	4	6	6	6	6	6	6		1												
48 Cd	2	4	4	6	6	6	6	6	6		2												
49 In	2	4	4	6	6	6	6	6	6		2	1											
— —	—	—	—	—	—	—	—	—	—		—	—											
54 X	2	4	4	6	6	6	6	6	6		4	4											
55 Cs	2	4	4	6	6	6	6	6	6		4	4				1							
56 Ba	2	4	4	6	6	6	6	6	6		4	4				2							
57 La	2	4	4	6	6	6	6	6	6		4	4	1			2							
58 Ce	2	4	4	6	6	6	6	6	6	1	4	4	1			2							
59 Pr	2	4	4	6	6	6	6	6	6	2	4	4	1			2							
— —	—	—	—	—	—	—	—	—	—	—	—	—	—			—							
71 Cp	2	4	4	6	6	6	8	8	8	8	4	4	1			2							
72 Hf	2	4	4	6	6	6	8	8	8	8	4	4	2			2							
— —	—	—	—	—	—	—	—	—	—	—	—	—	—			—							
79 Au	2	4	4	6	6	6	8	8	8	8	6	6	6			1							
80 Hg	2	4	4	6	6	6	8	8	8	8	6	6	6			2							
81 Tl	2	4	4	6	6	6	8	8	8	8	6	6	6			2	1						
— —	—	—	—	—	—	—	—	—	—	—	—	—	—			—	—						
86 Em	2	4	4	6	6	6	8	8	8	8	6	6	6			4	4						
87 –	2	4	4	6	6	6	8	8	8	8	6	6	6			4	4					1	
88 Ra	2	4	4	6	6	6	8	8	8	8	6	6	6			4	4					2	
89 Ac	2	4	4	6	6	6	8	8	8	8	6	6	6			4	4	1				2	
90 Th	2	4	4	6	6	6	8	8	8	8	6	6	6			4	4	2				2	
— —	—	—	—	—	—	—	—	—	—	—	—	—	—			—	—	—				—	
— —	—	—	—	—	—	—	—	—	—	—	—	—	—	—		—	—	—				—	—
118 ?	2	4	4	6	6	6	8	8	8	8	8	8	8	8		6	6	6				4	4

N. Bohr and D. Coster, *Zeitschrift fur Physik*, **12** (1923), page 344, reproduced from George von Hevesy, *Ber. D. Chem. Ges.*, **56** (1923), p. 1507.

N is the atomic number.

n_k is the symbol for the electron shells.

Bohr and Coster explain the periodicity of the chemical and optical properties of the elements by the fact

An explanation could be derived from the relativistic relationship between energy and matter, $E = mc^2$. If four atoms of hydrogen, at. wt 1.0077, formed one atom of helium, at. wt 4.002, a loss of mass occurs: $\Delta m = 4 \times 1.0077 - 4.002 = 0.029$. This corresponds to the loss of energy $\Delta E = 0.029 \times c^2$ ($c = 3 \times 10^{10}$ cm-sec^{-1}, the velocity of light). The formation of helium from hydrogen was thus calculated to develop an amount of energy equal to 6.25×10^9, expressed as calories per atomic weight. Ordinary "chemical" reactions of an exothermic nature develop less than one ten-millionth of this energy. While the details of the figures varied with new results of the determination of the atomic weights, the general conclusion remained valid.

Francis William Aston (1877–1945, Cambridge) summarized it at the end of his Nobel Prize lecture in 1922:

> Should the research worker of the future discover some means of releasing this energy in a form which could be employed, the human race will have at its command powers beyond the dream of scientific fiction, but the remote possibility must always be considered that the energy once liberated will be completely uncontrollable and by its intense violence detonate all neighboring substances. In this event, the whole of the hydrogen on the earth might be transformed at once and the success of the experiment published at large to the universe as a new star.

The time which Aston predicted began to be prepared for less than ten years later, and subsequent developments have led to a controlled release of the energy concentrated in the atoms of heavy elements. It started with the observation by Walther Bothe (1891–) and Karl Becker (1896–) in 1930, that a very penetrating radiation was emitted when beryllium was bombarded by α-particles. Irène Curie (1897–1956) and her husband, Frédéric Joliot (1900–1958) placed a block of paraffin between the irradiated beryllium and the measuring device; the registered effect was considerably greater than without the paraffin. James Chadwick (1891–), working in the Cavendish Laboratory at Cambridge, discovered the reason for this effect. The primary process consisted in the expulsion

---

that "for the outermost electron paths, the effective quantum numbers, in contrast to the main quantum numbers, change but little when going from one element to its homologous element in the next period of the system of the elements." (p. 357)

The table contains a prediction for the eagerly sought element 87 and goes far into the future by listing element number 118.

A different distribution of the electrons among the subshells started from more detailed experimental and mathematical studies of the spectra by Edmund Clifton Stoner ("Distribution of electrons among atomic levels," *Phil. Mag.*, **48** (1924), p. 719). The number of electrons for these shells is not equal, but increases by four; e.g., instead of a sequence 8, 8, 8, 8 as in the 1923 table, it is 2, 6, 10, 14.

of neutral particles of very high speed. These particles split protons out of the hydrogen contained in the paraffin. The neutral particles, called "neutrons," were not like those that Rutherford had expected in 1920 to be formed through the neutralizing combination of the positively charged proton with an electron. Chadwick said:

> I assume that the reaction is
>
> $$Be_4^9 + He_2^4 \rightarrow C_6^{12} + n_0^1.$$
>
> The masses of all the nuclei concerned are now known with reasonable accuracy; Bainbridge's measurement gives $Be^9 = 9.0132$; from Aston's measurements, $He^4 = 4.00106$ and $C^{12} = 12.0003$; and the mass of the neutron is 1.0067. . . . Assuming that energy and momentum are conserved, the velocity and energy of the neutron liberated by an α-particle of polonium (velocity $= 1.60 \times 10^9$ cm/sec, energy $= 5.3 \times 10^6$ electron volts) can be calculated. Its velocity is 4.77×10^9 cm/sec and energy 11.9×10^6 electron volts. These values are much greater than any found in the experiments described above. Neutrons of this velocity would eject protons with ranges up to about 150 cm in air, while the greatest ranges found for the protons experimentally is 70 cm, with, however, indications of ranges greater than 100 cm. (13)

The symbol for the neutron is n_0^1, indicating that it has no charge, has no place among the atomic numbers, and has nearly the mass of the hydrogen atom. Soon after Chadwick's discovery, Heisenberg showed that the neutron is part of every atomic nucleus except that of hydrogen. The number for the position of the atom is equal to the number of electrons and therefore also of the positive protons; the figure for the atomic weight is the sum of the protons and the neutrons. (14)

In 1932, protons, electrons, and neutrons became the three universal elements, the ultimate components of all substances, including the chemical elements. The long search for universal elements had started with the qualities we feel as simple and with the substances we consider as representative. Then, the action of heat on substances and of substances on each other taught that elements are specific; they are not universal because they are unchangeable. A few elements, however, proved unstable: The radioactive elements disintegrate with the release of radiations of high energy and specificity. With the use of these radiations, elements could be synthesized. Tracks observed in the cloud chamber and their mathematical treatment showed to Patrick M. S. Blackett in 1922 that an oxygen isotope was built up from alpha particles impinging on nitrogen. (15)

In 1934, Irène Joliot-Curie and Frédéric Joliot exposed a thin sheet of aluminum to the X-rays from polonium, and when these were then removed, a radioactivity remained. After dissolving the irradiated metal in aqua regia, the radioactivity stayed with the phosphate precipitated from the solution. Aluminum of atomic weight 27 had been transmuted into phosphorus of atomic weight 30, and this was the first artificially made radioactive element. (16)

In the same year, Leo Szilard (1898–1964) filed a patent in England on "Improvements in or relating to the transmutation of chemical elements," in which he claimed a chain reaction between beryllium and neutrons with the formation of helium and energy. The patent was issued in 1949 with the number 630,726.

At that time, Enrico Fermi (1901–1954) subjected practically all the common elements to the neutrons from irradiated beryllium. From uranium he obtained the isotope 235 and emitters of β-rays thought to be elements 93 and 94, establishing the first of the expected elements beyond uranium 92. To be captured by the irradiated material, the neutrons were passed through water or paraffin, with their firmly-bonded hydrogens. The neutrons were thus slowed down to "thermal" velocities in the order of heated molecules. The products were recognized and characterized only by comparing the measured radiation with the calculated values. (17)

The name technetium (Tc), the first technically made element, remained for element 43, after C. Perrier and Emilio Segrè (1902–) in 1937 established it definitely on the surface of molybdenum that had been irradiated under the cyclotron of the Radiation Laboratory at Berkeley. (18)

Irradiation by neutrons thus produced new elements synthetically: aluminum gave phosphorus, molybdenum the element 43. Fermi expected that his β-emitting elements from uranium were the elements 93 and 94, the avidly sought transuranites. Irène Joliot-Curie, Frédéric Joliot, and Paul Savitch measured a half-life of 3.5 hours for a substance that strongly resembled lanthanum; yet they thought it had been produced by a synthesis beyond uranium.

With the technique of the Joliots, Otto Hahn (1879–1968) and Fritz Strassmann obtained four products. The interpretation again was on the normal expectation. Two of these products should be isotopes of radium, yet they were inseparable from barium. (19)

Immediately after a report of this event was published, Lise Meitner (1878–1968) and Otto R. Frisch (1904–) came to a different conclusion: With Niels Bohr's model of atomic structure, a heavy nucleus could break up into two nuclei of medium weight in a process they called "fission." When barium (atomic number 56) is formed in the fission of uranium (92), the other product should be the element of atomic number 36, which is krypton. (20)

Neutrons were also released in this process. The exciting possibility existed of returning the neutrons into the process, which would then become a source of tremendously concentrated energy. The fission of one gram of U-235 would release the equivalent of 5×10^9 kCal. When hydrogen burns and the water is condensed, the heat gained is 34.18 kCal/gram.

Hahn, Meitner, and Strassmann had obtained a U-239 isotope in 1936. Edwin M. McMillan (1907–) in 1940 stated its transmutation into a new element, the long-sought 93, which he named neptunium. In the same year Glenn T. Seaborg (1912–) discovered its further change into a long-lived new element, 94, and he named it "plutonium."

Soon, several hundred laboratories and manufacturing plants in England and in the United States were joined in national efforts to take the major step from scientific work with micrograms to the industrial production of fissionable ammunition.

At Oak Ridge, Tennessee, a plant was erected in which U-235 was to be enriched. The method for separating the isotopes followed earlier attempts to achieve simpler separations by systematically repeated fractional diffusions, as William D. Harkins in 1921 had tried Sainte-Claire Deville's "hot-cold tube" technique of 1856, and as Gustav Hertz had tried with neon in 1932. Klaus Clusius (1903–) used a heated wire in a tube with cool walls in a refined arrangement so that the lighter isotope would preferentially move to the hot center. (21) At Oak Ridge, uranium hexafluoride was fractionated through fine pores in graphite walls.

At Hanford, Washington, uranium was transmuted into plutonium, at. wt. 239, by inserting "slugs" of the metal into a "pile" of graphite. The dangerously radioactive product was separated from residual uranium in operations observed through periscopes and regulated by remote control. At Los Alamos weapons were assembled from the fissionable material which, when brought together in the critical amounts and at the critical speed, exploded in a nuclear chain reaction. A few pounds of fissionable material yielded as much energy by nuclear explosion as twenty thousand tons of trinitrotoluene could develop in molecular decomposition.

After the war, nuclear reactors were constructed for weapons and for power generation. The number of reactors increased from 13 in 1950 to 43 six years later; by the end of 1966 there were about 230 power reactors. The generating capacity of the nuclear reactors in 1965 was 1045.2 net electrical megawatts, and the total capacity

Fig. 36. Charging uranium into the pile. (Courtesy of United States Atomic Energy Commission.)

UNITED STATES ATOMIC ENERGY COMMISSION, Washington 5, D.C. (AEC-52-4381)

"An operator places aluminum-jacketed uranium slugs in a fuel channel opening on the loading face of the graphite reactor. The natural uranium slugs, weighing 2.57 pounds each, are four inches long and 1.1 inch in diameter. They are placed end to end in rows of 39 to 54 in each channel. Openings in the shield are round, but each channel in the graphite cube itself is diamond shaped, with sides of 1.75 inches. Thus the slug, when in place, does not fill the channel. This permits passage of cooling air being pulled through the reactor by exhaust fans. Cooling is necessary to remove heat generated in the fission process."

of all generators was 222,285 megawatts. The quantity of uranium ore mined rose from about 3 million short tons in 1956 to a peak of 8 million tons in 1960, when world production of U_3O_8 was 41.140 tons.

From the start, one of the by-products of this development was to make isotopes available in relatively great quantity and variety. From 1946 the list included

I-131	P-32	C-14	Na-24	S-35	Ca-45	K-42
Au-198	Au-199	Fe-55	Fe-59	Co-60	Sr-89	Sr-90

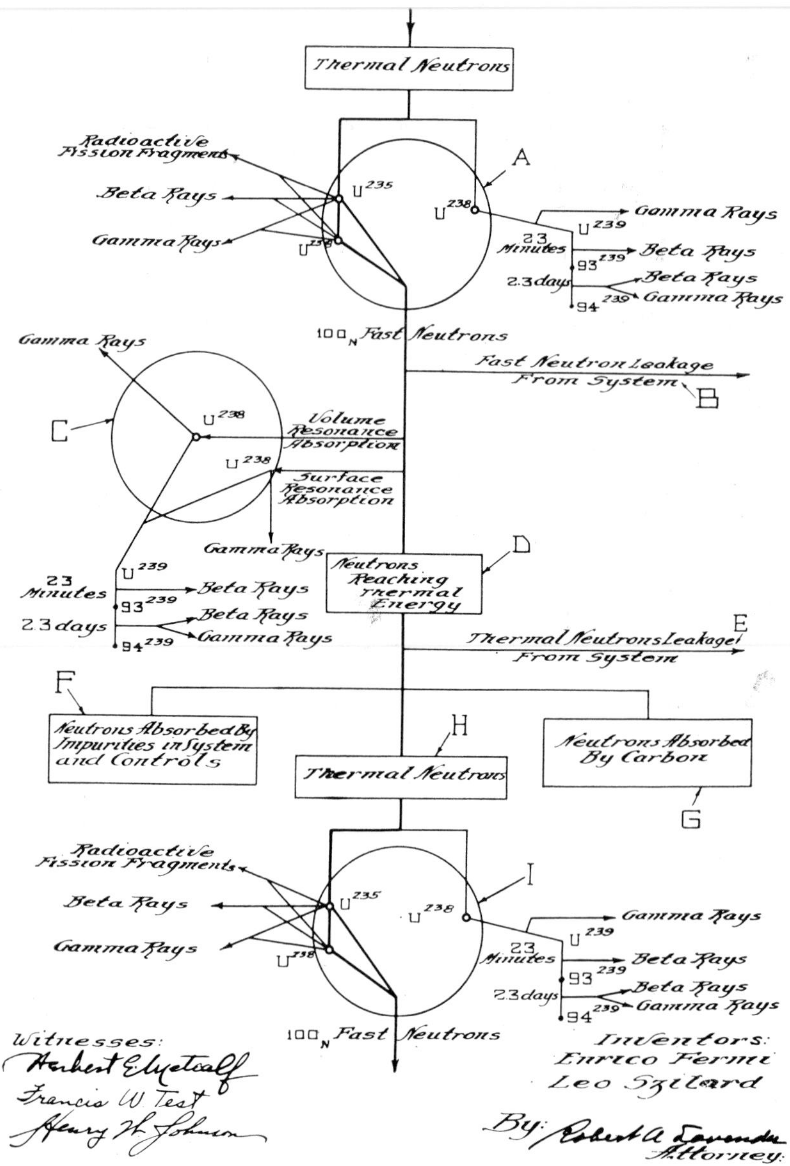

Fig. 37. Neutronic reactor. Flowsheet from the U.S. patent by Enrico Fermi and Leo Szilard, assigned to the U.S. Atomic Energy Commission. (Patent 2,708,656, Class 204-193, application Dec. 19, 1944, patented May 17, 1955.)

The patent consists of 27 sheets of drawings and 30 pages of specification and claims. Claim 8 is cited here. It is in the legal form of one sentence. The first five lines set the stage for the specific statement of "the improved

Isotopes had been used before their name as a class was proposed. In 1905 Bertram Borden Boltwood tried to determine the age of rocks from the proportion in which they contained Pb-206 and uranium. (22) The use of isotopes in chemical analysis began in 1913 (page 294) through the work of von Hevesy and Paneth. Rudolf Schönheimer (1898–1941, New York) studied animal metabolism with isotopically labelled fats from 1935 on. (23) After the war, isotopes became increasingly important in medicine for diagnosis and therapy. Industrial applications followed somewhat more slowly.

The series of "man-made" elements beyond uranium grew steadily, (24) although it has not yet reached element 118 so boldly included in the list of 1923 (page 302).

The history of the new source of energy differs characteristically from that of comparable events in previous centuries. After the introduction of gunpowder had revolutionized warfare, philosophers attacked the problems of motion with renewed vigor. The speculations of Descartes, Leibniz, and Newton developed into physical theories. After the steam engine revolutionized industry, physicists began to study the principles of energy. The theory of the steam engine led to the science of thermodynamics. The utilization of atomic energy was prepared by decades of scientific research during which the theoretical background for the conversion of matter into energy was formed.

While the number of chemical elements reached 103, many new "elementary particles" resulted from studies with the new powerful irradiations. In what sense are these particles "elementary"? Hideki Yukawa (25) felt that "an elementary particle could be defined as one that is associated with an irreducible local field. A

---

construction" that is claimed and protected by this patent. The other drawings show arrangements of the moderator and fissionable material to which other claims are directed.

"8. In a neutronic reactor having an active portion comprising a mass of moderator selected from the group consisting of graphite and heavy water, having dispersed therein a thermal neutron fissionable material containing a thermal neutron fissionable isotope and an isotope having a resonance absorption for neutrons, the improved construction wherein the thermal neutron fissionable material is aggregated in the form of bodies substantially free of moderator and of neutron absorbers other than said latter isotope, said bodies being in the moderator, geometrically spaced therein, and surrounded by the moderator, the moderator being in a substantially continuous phase, said bodies having all dimensions thereof at least 0.5 centimeter, the purity of the moderator and the thermal neutron fissionable material, the size and spacing of the bodies of fissionable material in the moderator, and the total mass of fissionable material and moderator being sufficient to sustain a chain reaction."

field is said to be irreducible if it can no longer be decomposed into parts, each of which transforms linearly by itself under Lorentz transformation." In order to reduce "infinite masses and electric charge" to "the observed finite masses and charge," it may be necessary to introduce "higher and higher derivatives of field quantities in the interaction . . . without end." With all the new mathematical tools and the theory of relativity we hope to have reached "the beginning of an attempt" at a unified theory of the new particles.

Such a unified theory would perhaps give us the elements in Robert Boyle's definition: "Certain primitive and simple, or perfectly unmingled bodies; which not being made of any other bodies, or of one another, are the ingredients of which all those called perfectly mixt bodies are immediately compounded, and into which they are ultimately resolved . . . " This definition contains only statements about "bodies;" the change that has to be introduced now is the relationship to energy and the "field."

REFERENCES

1. William Crookes, "On a Fourth State of Matter," *Phil. Trans.*, **30** (1880), p. 469.

2. J. J. Thomson, "On the illustration of the properties of the electric field by means of tubes of electric static induction," *Phil. Mag.*, **31** (1891), pp. 149–71.

3. R. A. Millikan, *Electrons (+ and —), Protons, Neutrons, Mesotrons, and Cosmic Rays* (Chicago: University of Chicago Press, 1947). The first edition of this book appeared in 1917 with the title, *The Electron.* Newly discovered particles of matter were added to the titles of subsequent editions. The most recent one, the "Revised Edition of 1947," has the title, *Electrons (+ and —), Protons, Photons, Neutrons, Mesotrons, and Cosmic Rays.*

4. See, e.g., Otto Glasser, *W. C. Röntgen* (Springfield, Ill.: Charles Thomas, 1934).

5. From Ramsay's letter of March 24, 1895. See, *Nobel, the Man and His Prizes,* edited by the Nobel Foundation (Stockholm: 1950), pp. 337 ff. See also H. Schuck, R. Sohlman, A. Osterling, G. Liljestrand, A. Westgren, M. Siegbahn, A. Schou, and N. K. Stahle, *Nobel, the Man and His Prizes,* edited by the Editors of the Nobel Foundation (Amsterdam: Elsevier, 1962).

6. Arthur J. Dempster, "Thirty Years of Mass Spectroscopy," *The Scientific Monthly,* **67** (1948), pp. 145–53. O. U. Anders, "The place of isotopes in the periodic table, the 50th anniversary of the Fajans-Soddy Displacement law," *J. Chem. Ed.,* **41** (1964), pp. 522–25.

7. Max Planck, "Irreversible Strahlungsvorgänge," *Wiedemann's Ann.,* **1** (1900), pp. 69–122; **6** (1901), pp. 818–31.

8. *Niels Bohr and the Development of Physics: Essays Dedicated to Niels Bohr on His 70th Birthday,"* edited by W. Pauli and by L. Rosenfeld and V. Weisskopf (New York: McGraw-Hill, 1955).

9. See "Fifty Years of Quantum Theory," *Science,* **123** (1951), pp. 75–101. (Max Planck's biography by Walter Meissner, articles on the quantum theory by Albert Einstein, Arnold Sommerfeld and E. Rapp, Linus Pauling, Henry Margenau.

10. William H. Bragg and William L. Bragg, *X-rays and Crystal Structure* (London: G. Bell & Sons, Ltd., 1915).

11. H. G. Moseley, "The High Frequency Spectra of the Elements," *Phil. Mag.,* **26** (1913), p. 1024; **27** (1914), p. 703. John L. Heilbron, "The work of H. G. J. Moseley, " *Isis,* **57** (1966), pp. 336–64.

12. J. C. Hackney, "Technetium—element 43," *J. Chem. Ed.,* **28** (1951). pp. 186–89.

13. J. Chadwick, "The neutron," *Proc. Roy. Soc.,* A **142** (1933), pp. 1–25, esp. p. 9.

14. W. Heisenberg, "Bau der Atomkerne," *Z. f. Physik,* **77** (1932), pp. 1–11; **78** (1932), pp. 156–64; **80** (1933), pp. 587–96.

15. P. M. S. Blackett, "On the analysis of α-ray photographs," *Proc. Roy. Soc.,* A **102** (1922), pp. 294–318; William D. Hawkins and R. W. Ryan, "A method for photographing the disintegration of an atom, and a new type of ray," *J. Am. Chem. Soc.,* **45** (1923), pp. 2095–107.

16. Irène Curie and Frédéric Joliot, "Un nouveau type de radioactivité," *Compt. Rend.,* **198** (1934), pp. 254–56.

17. Enrico Fermi, *Collected papers,* Vol. 1: *Italy, 1921–38,* edited by Edoardo Amaloi, Enrico Persico, Franco Rasetti, and Emilio Segrè, Academia Nazionale dei Lincei (Chicago: Chicago University Press, 1962).

18. C. Perrier and E. Segrè, "Some chemical properties of element 43," *J. Chem. Phys.,* **5** (1937), pp. 712–6; **7** (1939), pp. 155–6.

19. Otto Hahn, *A Scientific Autobiography* (New York: Charles Scribner's Sons, 1966); translated from the German edition (Braunschweig: 1962) by Willy Ley.

20. L. Meitner (Stockholm) and O. R. Frisch (Copenhagen), "Disintegration of uranium by neutrons: A new type of nuclear reaction," *Nature,* **143** (1939), pp. 239–40; O. R. Frisch, "Physical evidence for the division of heavy nuclei under neutron bombardment," *ibid.,* p. 276.

21. K. Clusius, "Verfahren zum Zerlegen von Gasgemischen durch thermische Diffusion," German patent 701,016 of Jan. 7, 1941; application, Apr. 3, 1938.

22. B. B. Boltwood, "The origin of radium," *Phil. Mag.* (6), **9** (1905), pp. 599–613.

23. R. Schönheimer and D. Rittenberg, "Deuterium as an indicator in the study of intermediate metabolism III. The role of the fat tissues," *J. Biol. Chem.,* **111** (1935), pp. 175–81.

24. Glenn T. Seaborg, *Chem. & Eng. News,* **24** (1946), p. 1192. Glenn T. Seaborg, *Man-Made Transuranium Elements* (Englewood Cliffs, N.J.: Prentice-Hall, Inc., 1963). Manson Benedict, "Chemical industry and nuclear energy," Perkin Medal Address, *Chem. & Ind.,* April 2, 1966, pp. 564–8.

25. Hideki Yukawa, "Attempt at a unified theory of elementary particles," *Science,* **121** (1955), pp. 405–8.

20

Chemical Bond and Physical Form

Affinity and Valency

Early investigations of matter in a state in which it radiates, or of radiation which is carried by particles of matter, were regarded as being in the field of physics. For the most part, chemists were little influenced by this work in their search for systematic coordination in the field of "purely" chemical reactions. In this field, substances react with substances and the "natures" of these substances have full play. They are influenced by physical conditions; Berthollet had tried (1801) to explain the results of affinity as governed by the physical attributes of elasticity and solubility.

In the seventeenth century the chemist had been a "philosopher by fire"; in the nineteenth century he arrived at truly philosophical conclusions about heat in relation to affinity. They led to new forms for two basic laws:

1. The law of constancy and conservation, as expressed, for example, by Germain Hess in 1840.

2. The law of change and the tendency toward a maximum, as formulated for chemical reactions by Berthelot in 1864 and for entropy by Clausius in 1865. Constancy and tendency were combined in affinity.

A deep feeling of the mystery of affinity, combined with the joy of doing things with his hands, started Wilhelm Ostwald (1853, Riga –1932, Leipzig) on a lifelong search. As a student in Dorpat he read Julius Thomson's book on *Thermochemistry*. It came to him as an inspiration that any other property could serve as well as the heat of chemical reactions to measure the effects of affinity. He selected density and the refraction of light because he had the equipment to measure the change of these properties during chemical reactions. As professor of chemistry in Riga (1882) he investigated the reaction in which an ester is split, or hydrolized, into its component parts, alcohol and acid. Berthelot had used this type of reaction to derive rules of chemical equilibria (page 236). Ostwald was interested in the function of the mineral acid that produces the splitting of the ester. The technique was again very simple; as the reaction proceeded, acid was generated. The amount of the known solution of an alkali needed to neutralize a portion of the reacting mixture thus gave the equivalent amount of acid, and the change of this amount in relation to the time intervals traced the rate at which the reaction proceeded. Another previously investigated reaction was later included, the splitting of sugar (saccharose) into glucose and fructose, which could be observed by the change of optical rotation in a polarimeter.

Such reactions served Ostwald as the means for measuring and comparing the chemical "strength" of the acids that produced the change. These acids did not themselves change in the reaction; they were catalysts in the sense that Berzelius had defined and that Ostwald now (from 1888 on) endeavored to express more clearly. His earlier (1878) measurements of densities and volumes in relation to chemical change had induced him to speak of a new branch of volumetric chemistry. With the same urge to generalize, and from the conviction that each series of particular observations revealed a general systematic connection, he now erected a more definite theory of catalysis than Berzelius had given. It was the same tendency from which his great textbook of chemistry began to take shape after 1880.

Ostwald belonged among those great teachers of chemistry who spent most of their teaching effort in providing the systemization of knowledge so that others could transmit it to their students. Ostwald himself did more of his teaching in books than in classrooms. He resembled Liebig in this respect, and he was quite different from such great creators of schools as Robert Wilhelm Bunsen, Adolph Baeyer, and Emil Fischer, who never spent much time writing textbooks. Ostwald could have seen here an example of the validity of the law of the conservation of energy in the fields of mental activities, one of the favorite subjects of his later years. A man who spends much of his energy in providing texts has little energy left to propound them himself!

In 1884 Svante Arrhenius published his doctoral thesis on the electric conductivity of electrolytes. A new way of measuring the "strength" of acids—and of alkalies, too—was here developed. The chemical picture for the relationships of affinities was given in 1887 by the theory of dissociation in which ions existed in the solutions of electrolytes before any electric current passed through them. The year 1884 also brought the publication of van't Hoff's studies on chemical dynamics. (1) Here the experimentally derived law of mass action (see Guldberg and Waage, page 237) was projected into mathematical form in which it was combined with the general law of gas behavior, $p \cdot v = R \cdot T$, correlating the changes of pressure p and volume v with the absolute temperature T by the "gas constant" R. The combination became fruitful through the application of Carnot cycles to chemical reactions. The equilibrium constant k in the Guldberg-Waage equation was now connected with the energy relationships in the reaction

$$\ln k = \frac{Q}{RT} + \frac{\Sigma C_v}{R} \ln T + \frac{\Sigma S'}{R}.$$

The natural logarithm of k can thus be seen as having been determined by functions of the heat of reaction Q, the sum of the specific heats C_v at constant volume, and the sum of the entropy constants S' of the partners in the reaction. The change that the equilibrium undergoes when the temperature is changed and the volume kept constant could be generally expressed as a change in the direction in which heat is absorbed. When temperature is kept constant and the pressure is increased on the reacting system, the equilibrium will tend to change towards the reduction of volume. Henri Le Chatelier (1850–1936) generalized this law of the mobile equilibrium still further (2): Any change of one of the factors of the equilibrium of a system produces the reaction which causes that factor to change in a direction opposite to that which was originally applied.

It was significant for the new approach to the dynamics and kinetics of chemical reactions when van't Hoff replaced the equal sign = by arrows pointing in both directions ⇆ when writing a chemical "equation." Physicists had long considered the solidity of matter to be a function of the constant and rapid movement of its particles. With the new sign, chemists expressed the movements of the substances participating in an equilibrium. And at the time, when physicists obtained new insight into the structure of matter by investigating gases under extremely low pressure, chemists like van't Hoff derived general laws of solutions by considering the limit of lowest concentrations.

All these efforts had the same goal, the use of physical measurements and concepts to arrive at the meaning and effect of chemical affinity. Ostwald organized these efforts in establishing a physical chemistry. He brought the outstanding researchers in this field together on the editorial board of a new journal devoted to physical chemistry. There had long been journals and annals that combined physics with chemistry in their title. The new *Zeitschrift,* which started in February 1887, was to promote physical viewpoints and methods in a chemistry that thereby should become "general" beyond the individual substances.

At the University of Leipzig, where he was professor from 1887 until he resigned in 1906, Ostwald created a center of this physical chemistry, at first against strong resistance from "pure" chemists. His former assistant Walther Nernst (1864–1941) started a second center at Göttingen in 1890, and other institutes of physical chemistry were organized soon afterwards.

The newly cultivated field of science spread its influence to industrial chemistry. Its greatest success there was the solution of the old problem of synthesizing ammonia. (3) The theory stated that one volume of nitrogen combines with three volumes of hydrogen to produce two volumes of ammonia:

$$1N_2 + 3H_2 \rightleftharpoons 2NH_3$$

Avogadro's theory, combined with the principles developed by van't Hoff and Le Chatelier, led to the conclusion that pressure should influence the formation of ammonia from its elements in a favorable direction. The calculation that Fritz Haber (1868–1934, Karlsruhe, then Berlin) carried out had to be corrected according to a third law of thermodynamics, which Walther Nernst derived in 1906.

This was a law for the approach to the absolute zero of temperature. The difference between free energy of a system A, like the heat of reaction, and the total energy U tends to disappear as the temperature approaches absolute zero, at least insofar as the change of these energies with change of temperature is concerned. The mathematical expression for Nernst's law is that, for T approaching zero,

$$\frac{dA}{dT} = \frac{dU}{dT}$$

This law for an apparently remote limit state had many consequences for practical conditions. In the special case of the synthesis of ammonia, it stimulated new efforts after the first discouraging results in 1905. High pressure (200 atm, or 2,800 psi) and high temperature alone were, however, insufficient to produce a noticeable degree of reaction. A catalyst was necessary, and though iron worked at temperatures of about 700°C, catalysts were sought that would be active at one or two hundred degrees less. With platinum or metals from the platinum group, the equilibrium was sufficiently shifted to ammonia formation for a satisfactory output per time and volume of the reaction vessel to make ammonia synthesis industrially interesting. Carl Bosch (1874–1940, Heidelberg) and Alwin Mittasch (1869–1953), together with a large group of chemists and engineers, developed the process to production scale at the Badische Anilin- und Soda-Fabrik in Ludwigshafen. When Bosch described this work in his Nobel Prize lecture in 1932, he mentioned that about 20,000 experiments on the action of catalysts had been made. The conversion of ammonia into nitric acid by catalyzed combustion had been started by Wilhelm Ostwald in 1901 and began to be carried out industrially in 1906.

The continuous operation with gases at high temperatures and pressures required the use of many kinds of instruments, including those for automatic gas analysis, for measuring and proportioning gas streams, and for regulating and monitoring pressures and temperatures. Companies like the Badische Anilin- und Soda-Fabrik organized new departments for designing and constructing instruments. Chemists and engineers had long worked together; now, the need for the new profession of chemical engineer arose for the tasks of equipment design, control, and maintenance. This represented something like a parallel to the combination of physics and chemistry into a physical chemistry or chemical physics.

The new unification that developed out of increased specialization found expression in the concept of unit processes or unit operations. They explored and created the common features in energy exchange, or crystallization, or distillation, applied to different chemicals. This can be considered as the industrial counterpart to the emphasis on a "general" chemistry that would perhaps better be called unified chemistry, because instead of dealing in generalities it seeks the specific unifying characteristics of the individual substances.

The practical consequences of the theory of affinity were to be seen in the First World War—its extent and fire power would not have been possible without synthetic ammonia and nitric acid.

Hydrogenation in Organic Chemistry

Scientific and industrial interest in the reactions of unsaturated organic substances with hydrogen brought far-reaching developments at the end of the nineteenth century. Paul Sabatier (1854–1941) "thought, and I still think, . . . that the real cause of the catalytic action of porous platinum is not a simple phenomenon of physical condensation which produces a local rise in temperature, but that it is a real chemical combination on the surface of the metal with the free gas." In analogy with experiments that Moissan and Moureu had carried out on acetylene, Sabatier, together with Jean-Baptiste Senderens, tried ethylene (C_2H_4). This gas was brought into contact with freshly prepared fine powders of nickel or cobalt at 300°C. A vivid reaction took place, char was deposited, and ethane, C_2H_6, was produced. Obviously, part of the ethylene had been decomposed into carbon and hydrogen, and the hydrogen had combined with another part of the ethylene (1897). Higher yields of the hydrogenation product were obtained when the hydrogen was supplied to begin with. A number of unsaturated organic substances could thus be hydrogenated, and the general principle was announced early in 1901: "Pass the vapors of the substance, together with an excess of hydrogen, over freshly reduced nickel kept at a convenient temperature (150°–200°C)." (4)

Only one year later a patent on the "hardening" of fats by catalytic hydrogenation appeared. (5)

Hydrogenation for "liquefying" coal was the aim of work that Friedrich Bergius (1884–1948) started in 1913 and later extended to heavy mineral oils.

A synthesis of methanol in the catalyzed reaction of carbon monoxide with hydrogen, from about 1923, became a powerful competitor of methanol produced by wood distillation. At pressures of one to fifteen atmospheres, the reaction can be directed to the production of light and heavy hydrocarbons. This synthesis, developed by Franz Fischer (1877–1947, Mülheim-Ruhr), Hans Tropsch, and their associates, contributed greatly to the German supply of motor fuel and lubricants during the war.

Valences and Electrons

In these reactions, unsaturated valences are connected with hydrogen. Carbon monoxide, for example, contains carbon bound together with oxygen, $C=O$. This leaves two of the normal four valences of carbon free. The addition of hydrogen in the methanol reaction would, therefore, be represented by

$$\begin{array}{c} | \\ C{=}O \\ | \end{array} + 2H_2 = \begin{array}{c} H \\ | \\ C \\ | \\ H \end{array}\!\!\begin{array}{l} \diagup H \\ \\ \diagdown OH \end{array}$$

In van't Hoff's theory of 1874, the carbon atom is represented in the center of a tetrahedron from which the valences extend to the corners. This figurative representation was sufficient for the chemistry of organic compounds for a long time. All the conclusions drawn from this figure were in agreement with the observations and even with the predictions. A theory of a cyclic arrangement of carbon atoms to carbon compounds could be gained from it. The stability of the benzene ring, the relative instability of other rings, could be explained by the angle that the valences formed in these configurations. Adolph Baeyers strain theory (1885) for the valences forced out of the arrangement in the regular tetrahedron was successful. Not only did the heats of formation increase for "strained" compounds, the index of refraction also showed abnormalities where double bonds occurred.

Yet the simple representation of a valence by a straight line, indicating one indivisible unit, did not seem adequate for a special group of organic compounds. In these compounds, like butadiene,

$$\overset{1}{H_2C}{=}\overset{2}{CH}{-}\overset{3}{CH}{=}\overset{4}{CH_2}$$

a sequence of two double bonds is interrupted by one single bond. These compounds were considerably more reactive at the two ends than the formula would lead one to expect. Johannes Thiele (1865–1918) concluded in 1899 that the distinction between single and double bonds was exaggerated. Valences should be divisible and in this case they should be so divided as to leave more unsaturation at carbons 1 and 4.

$$\underset{|}{CH_2}{-}CH{-}CH{-}\underset{|}{CH_2}$$

The index of optical refraction again conformed to the assumption that such compounds with "conjugated" double bonds were in an exceptional state.

This theory proved to be more remarkable for partitioning the valence than for explaining the behavior of a large group of conjugated compounds. Experimental results obtained with inorganic compounds led Alfred Werner (1866–1919, Zürich) to another and more fundamental attack on the previous concept of valency. Platinum chloride, $PtCl_4$, can add two molecules of hydrochloric acid or of ammonia. The four valences of platinum should be saturated by the four chlorine atoms, and yet there was more affinity available to form crystallizing compounds with the other molecules. Previous attempts to show the arrangements of the atoms in these molecules had been based on mere formalism. Measurements of electric conductivity in solutions of the compounds, and replacements of some of the atoms by others in analogy to the methods used in organic chemistry, gave an experimental approach to the molecular structure. The solution of the problem required a new general theory, since the previous concepts of valency were insufficient. After the normal or principal valences were saturated, there remained a certain number of auxiliary valences by which the platinum could bind the ammonia. Isomerisms between these complex compounds could be explained as interception (*Einlagerung*) or as addition of the complex-forming molecules. Optical activity was found in certain compounds of platinum and cobalt. Werner had previously extended van't Hoff's theory of the asymmetric carbon atom to the nitrogen atom (1890). Now he constructed three-dimensional geometric models for his new metal compounds and founded the stereochemistry of inorganic substances.

The division of valences into principal and auxiliary types was made for the special cases from which the investigation started. Werner considered it as only preliminary. A generalized theory, in his opinion, should be based on a uniform field of valency which the combining atoms divide among themselves. (6)

Such a general theory could be seen as desirable, but it could not be carried out in detail with the chemical experience of the time. The electrochemical dualism of Berzelius seemed to offer more tangible possibilities. While the attraction between positive and negative "atoms" lingered in perhaps every chemist's mind, a professor at the Technische Hochschule of Breslau, Richard Abegg (1869–1910), developed a compensation rule: "Every element is endowed with a positive and a negative maximal valency; the sum of both valences is always 8." (7)

Abegg published this conjecture about an internal compensation at the time when the old dualism between the elements was converted into a dualism within the atoms (Rutherford, 1902, 1911). To begin with, sodium was not positive nor chlorine negative. When they combine, sodium loses an electron to the chlorine and then both assume the function of oppositely charged ions. Bohr's theory could be used for the teleological explanation of these events. The chlorine atom has 17 electrons, seven of them in the outer shell. With the electron taken from sodium, it could complete its outer shell to the number 8, which characterizes the chemically stable, completely saturated atom of the next inert gas, argon. This structure seemed the goal that the chlorine atom desired to attain. In this theory, the elements are endowed with a tendency to complete an inner atomic structure, a new expression in physical terms of the old idea that connected affinity with something akin to human will and love.

Walther Kossel (1888–1956, Berlin) saw what Abegg had missed, the importance of the electron shell around the atoms:

> If the valence activity in polar compounds is conceived completely as electro-valency, that is, as an exchange of known electron numbers, then it can be shown that the order of valences in the Periodic System leads to a very simple law, namely, that the very pronounced valence characters of those elements that are close to a noble gas are to be considered as following from the tendency to reach the electron number of these stable neighboring atomic forms by adding or relinquishing electrons, or at least not to exceed these atomic forms.

He presents the following table and schematic drawing for the first few elements (8):

KOSSEL'S PERIODIC TABLE (1916)

	H 1 (1)							
He 2 (2, 0)	**Li** 3 (2, 1)	**Be** 4 (2, 2)	**B** 5 (2, 3)	**C** 6 (2, 4)	**N** 7 (2, 5)	**O** 8 (2, 6)	**Fl** 9 (2, 7)	**Ne** 10 (2, 8)
Ne 10 (2, 8, 0)	**Na** 11 (2, 8, 1)	**Mg** 12 (2, 8, 2)	**Al** 13 (2, 8, 3)	**Si** 14 (2, 8, 4)	**P** 15 (2, 8, 5)	**S** 16 (2, 8, 6)	**Cl** 17 (2, 8, 7)	**Ar** 18 (2,8,8)
Ar 18 (2,8,8,0)	**K** 19 (2,8,8,1)	**Ca** 20 (2,8,8,2)	**Sc** 21 (2,8,8,3)	**Ti** 22 (2,8,8,4)	**V** 23 (2,8,8,5)	**Cs** 24 (2,8,8,6)	**Mn** 25 (2,8,8,7)	

Note: The underlined digit stands for the number of electrons in the outermost shell.

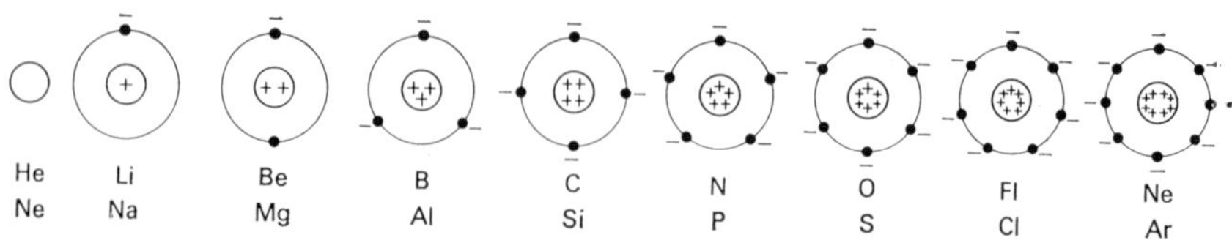

Affinity as a tendency is here combined with the perfection of electronic structure, and the polarity in the dualism of Berzelius vanishes behind the desire for symmetry.

Gilbert N. Lewis (1875–1946, Berkeley, California) avoided speculations about "tendencies" and developed ideas like those of Abegg in work summarized in 1916, which Irving Langmuir (1881–1957) continued in greater detail. They wrote formulas in which the simple straight line for the valence bond did not appear; instead, dots indicating the valence electrons surrounded the connected atoms.

The publications of Kossel and Lewis coincided in 1916. In 1926, publications on electronic valence theories coincided in greater number. Christopher K. Ingold (1893–), with E. H. Ingold, developed a theory of "electronic strain," a late sequence of Adolf Baeyer's strain theory of 1885 and its extension in depth and generality. The year before, Samuel Abraham Goudsmit (1902–) and his fellow student in Amsterdam, George F. Uhlenbeck, had proposed a new kind of axial rotation for the electron, the "spin," for which the quantum numbers could be ½ and −½, in apparent contradiction of the whole-number rule for the quanta but in agreement with the mathematical treatment for the wave accompanying and representing the electron as a particle. With special attention to the spin, Werner Heisenberg in 1926 calculated a vibratory motion of the valence electrons that corresponded to an acoustical resonance. Paul Adrien Maurice Dirac (1902–) published his derivation of resonance in the same year.

Kekulé had defended his benzene formula as delineating only an extreme limit state of a continuous vibration. Baeyer had drawn formulas for dyestuffs in which at least one of the components vibrated between limits presented by the picture drawn with the static valence lines. Arthur Hantzsch (1857–1935, Leipzig) considered the valence bonds of tautomeric compounds as partially in one, partially in the other configuration. These thoughts now acquired mathematical forms, derived from the combination of quantum theory, wave mechanics, Bohr's theory of atomic structure, and probability calculations.

In all these mathematical derivations, intuition played an important role. This is clearly expressed in 1925 by Wolfgang Pauli (1900–1958), when he formulated a new rule: "When in the atom an electron is present for which the quantum numbers in the outer, strong field have definite values, then this place is 'taken'." Pauli added: "We cannot give a precise derivation for this rule, but it seems to present itself of its own very naturally." (9) The rule was generally confirmed, and it was called Pauli's exclusion principle.

The intuition that united results "obtained from the quantum mechanics and from a theory of paramagnetic susceptibility" enabled Linus Pauling (1901–) to describe "the nature of the chemical bond" in terms of probable locations of electrons in their shells. Though the classical valence line had to be replaced by complex valence fields, the lengths and the angles of the chemical bonds were given in precise figures. (10)

Affinity and Surface

The electronic concept of valency located affinity in the electrons of the outer shell of the atom structure. A "hidden quality" was thus brought into the light of science as a definite part of the substance, just as, for example, acidity was removed from the old concept of a "primitive acid" to the function of an ionizable hydrogen atom as part of the molecule of an acid. In both cases the new development was the result of coordinating many new experiences and had, therefore, many consequences besides solving an old problem. Since electrons could be expelled, or at least loosened, out of the atomic spheres, it was concluded that electrons might be active in the physical processes of adhesion and adsorption. The widened new concept of valency, amply demonstrated by Alfred Werner, contributed to the development of a theory of catalysis. The surface of specially prepared metals was assumed to be the source of residual valences which, according to Irving Langmuir, provide the force for adsorption (1916). The molecules of a gas, for instance, hydrogen, thus influenced by surface valences of a finely divided metal, acquire a particular state of condensation and affinity. Later on, Langmuir found that the emission of electrons from tungsten surfaces at high temperatures is greatly influenced by adsorbed films of thorium. Under certain conditions this electron emission can be a hundred thousand times as great as that from a pure tungsten surface. Results of these theoretical studies were applied in the construction of incandescent lamps.

The activation of affinities at the surface of finely divided metals extends to the hydrogen that is present in the molecules of organic substances. Heinrich Wieland (1877–1957, Munich) saw in the activation of hydrogen the primary cause for catalyzed oxidations. In a reversal of the current theories, after 1912 he emphasized dehydrogenation as the decisive first event in oxidation. Even the conversion of a metal, such as zinc, into its oxide, can be explained as a loss of hydrogen, with water as an essential participant in the reaction:

$$Zn + H_2O = Zn(OH_2) = ZnO + H_2$$

This partial return to the phlogiston theory—in which hydrogen represents phlogiston—offered an explanation for the influence of water on combustion. The explosive combustion of carbon monoxide readily occurs in the presence of water vapor but requires very high initiating temperatures in its absence. In 1880 Harold Baily Dixon (1852–1930, London) first described this influence of water. Herbert Brereton Baker (1862–1935) continued this research, and Wieland formulated the chemical steps as follows:

1. $CO + H_2O = HCO \cdot HO$
2. $HCOOH = H_2 + CO_2$
3. $H_2 + \frac{1}{2}O_2 = H_2O$

In the first step, carbon monoxide combines with water; the addition compound rearranges its atoms to formic acid, which disintegrates in the next step into hydrogen and carbon dioxide. It is the hydrogen that is oxidized. The reformed water then acts again on CO. The combustion of CO is thus a chain reaction which, as Fritz Haber found (1896), could be substantiated by the spectroscopic analysis of flames.

In his studies of the reaction between hydrogen and iodine, Max Bodenstein (1871–1942, Berlin) found that the wall of his glass vessel influenced the results. (11) Adsorption was suspected as the cause. Irving Langmuir explained the general basis as follows:

> ". . . Gaseous molecules impinging on a solid or liquid surface do not in general rebound elastically from the surface, but condense on it, and are held or adsorbed on the surface by forces similar to those holding the atoms or group molecules of solid bodies. If these forces are weak, the "life" of the adsorbed molecules on the surface is short, so that the number of molecules adsorbed at any one time is relatively small. . . ." (12)

The study of photochemical reactions brought a renewed and refined theory about the chain of events. In 1912, Albert Einstein derived a simple formula connecting the number N of molecules reacting when light of vibration number ν brings the quanta $h\nu$ into a system and thereby provides the energy Q:

$$N = Q/h\nu$$

Emil Warburg (1846–1931, Berlin) considered this law of the photochemical equivalent as analogous to Faraday's law of the electrochemical equivalent, with one difference: Einstein's law gives only the number of absorbing molecules without relating what they will do, whereas the electrical elementary quantities will act to charge or discharge. In the reactions he tested, Warburg found the photochemical equivalents predicted by the theory. (13) The reaction between hydrogen and chlorine, however, digresses from the law by many orders of magnitude.

Walther Nernst in 1913 presented the following scheme for this reaction:

1. $Cl_2 + h\nu = 2Cl$
2. $Cl + H_2 = HCl + H$
3. $H + Cl_2 = HCl + Cl$

1^2. $Cl + H_2 = HCl + H$

A chlorine molecule dissociates into two atoms by using up the energy supplied in the form of light and in the quantity $h\nu$; a free chlorine atom then splits a molecule of the hydrogen into one HCl and one H which is reactive enough to split a chlorine atom out of a chlorine molecule. The initial shock which caused the dissociation of a chlorine atom thus started a long sequence of reactions.

Cyril Norman Hinshelwood (1897–1967) and his collaborators at the University of Oxford applied the idea of reaction chains in explaining the influence of certain solids on the course of the combination between hydrogen and oxygen. At the relatively low temperatures around 500°C, powdered silica accelerated the reaction very much. "At high temperature, the normal catalytic effect of the wall of the reaction chamber gives place to a negative effect, which may be due to the catalytic destruction of an autocatalyst for the principal reaction, or the interruption of 'reaction chains' or to both causes." (14) The effect may be similar to that of "anti-knocks" in the combustion of fuels in the cylinder of a motor. Such studies on combustion of gaseous hydrocarbons were pursued by Nikolaj Nikolajevitj Semenov (1896–) and his group. (15)

The adsorption of dissolved substances on solid surfaces had long been noticed and used in industry. Fritz Paneth tried to define the solid surfaces by measurement with radioactive indicators. (16) In continuing such studies, Isaac M. Kolthoff (1894–) found that the adsorption of a dyestuff such as Ponceau 2R from aqueous solution on lead sulfate involves an ion exchange: "The adsorbed Ponceau ions replacing sulfate ions at the surface of the lattice." (17*a*) With

Wool Violet 4BN, he said, "There is one dye ion adsorbed per 1.6 lead ions in the surface." (17*b*).

$C_{41}H_{45}N_3O_7S_2Na_2$, mol. wt. 801.

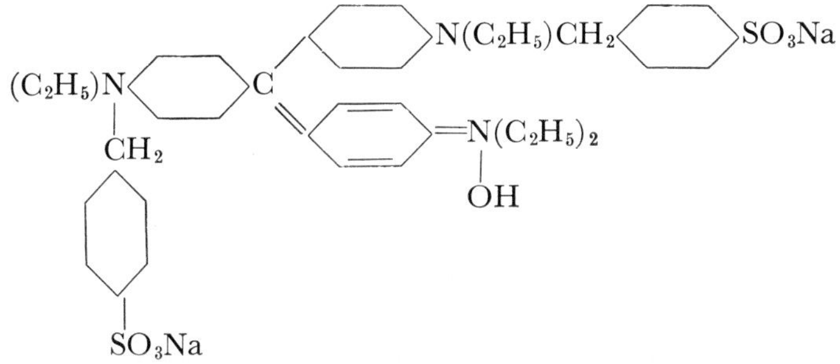

$N(C_2H_5)CH_2$ SO_3Na

$(C_2H_5)N$ C

$=N(C_2H_5)_2$

CH_2

OH

SO_3Na

Wool violet 4BN according to I. M. Kolthoff

The exchange of ions between a dissolved substance and the surface of a solid material became an effective and gentle means for separating and purifying sensitive substances. Synthetic resins were prepared with reactive groups for specific tasks. The method of ion exchange on surfaces proved particularly useful when products occurred or were first made in very low concentrations, for example, biologically active fermentation products.

The Colloidal State of Matter

The recognition of a particular form of distribution of matter in solution originated in experiments on the flow of gases through narrow openings. Thomas Graham (1805–1869, Glasgow), a professor at London University from 1837 on, found in measurements of different gases that this flow, called "diffusion," occurred at rates that were inversely proportionate to the square root of the density of the gases (1833). The diffusion of liquids was the next subject of his investigations. The idea that a substance dissolved in water, or another liquid, would behave as if the substance were in the form of a gas may have caused him to extend his investigations from gases to solutions. Salts diffuse out of their solutions into surrounding water with different speeds, and they can be separated accordingly. Graham found, about 1850, that albumen and gum arabic diffuse much more slowly than salts. When he separated solutions from water by means of a membrane, he observed that dissolved glue did not go through the membrane into the water; it did not dialyze. He recommended making the membrane from vegetable parchment, which is obtained by dipping paper briefly into concentrated sulfuric acid or zinc chloride. Crystallized substances, for instance salts, dialyze readily. Glue served as the model substance for the nondialyzing substances. The Greek word for glue is *kolla;* hence the name "colloidal," or glue-like, for the nondialyzing substances. This name was retained even for such entirely different materials as silica, when it was produced in 1862 from sodium silicate by acid in an instable solution.

A colloidal state of matter was now defined as one that can be distinguished from the crystallized state by dialysis. The solutions of the former were called "sols." There were also other characteristic properties. Sols of gold shatter incident light. Faraday had observed it, and his successor as Director of the Royal Institution, John Tyndall (1820–1893), investigated it more systematically (1869). The Tyndall effect became a means of characterizing colloid states.

Richard Adolf Zsigmondy (1865–1929, Göttingen) had become interested in the luster colors produced by spreading mixtures of gold and certain metal oxides on porcelain and heating to a red glow. This old technique now led to a scientific approach to the riddles of Kunckel von Löwenstjern's ruby glass (1679) and Andreas Cassius' purple (1685). Zsigmondy and H. Siedentopf, working in Jena in 1903, constructed an ultramicroscope in which the object was illuminated through a narrow slit at right angles to the direction of the microscope. With this tool, the formation and particle sizes of colloidal solutions could be observed.

The colloidal state of matter now became a particular state of distribution or dispersion. A new branch of science, between physics and chemistry, began to define its realm by abstracting the quality of the dispersed substance and the nature of the dispersing medium. It was a region intermediate between genuine solutions with particles to one millionth of a millimeter, and dispersions with particles of over one millimeter. Colloidal solutions proper were assigned a particle size range of one millionth to one thousandth of a millimeter; beyond this was the field of emulsions and suspensions in solids, liquids, or gases.

One of the general conclusions from studies of the colloidal state was a proof for the reality of atoms and molecules. Jean Perrin (1870–1942) applied the laws of ideal gases (Avogadro) to emulsions which he made by adding water to alcoholic solutions of a resin, particularly mastix. From the size of the particles, measured microscopically, and their distribution along a small column, he calculated the Avogadro number N of particles that form one unit, not in grams but in molecular weight. This number turned out to be the same as that found by all other then available methods, 67 to 68 $\times$ 10^{22} molecules. Nevertheless he concluded:

> We must always be able to express a visible reality without the aid of invisible elements. This is actually very easy to do. We only have to eliminate the invariant number N from the p equations used for its determination so as to obtain $(p - 1)$ equations in which all directly observable properties occur and which result from the connections between the properties which are, primarily, entirely independent of one another (like, for example, the viscosity of the gases, the Brownian movements, the blue color of the sky, the spectrum of the black body, and radioactivity). (18)

Wilhelm Ostwald had objected for a long time to the atom theory, contending that it was an unnecessary and unproved duplication of experimental results. Perrin refuted the second of these objections, but in part at least confirmed the first.

Colloidal solutions are unstable; flocculations or gelatinizations occur unless "protective" colloids are present. The electrical charge appeared as one of the factors that decide about their existence. Leonor Michaelis (1875–1949, New York) found for protein sols that changes of electrical charge precipitated the protein outside a range of a stable "isoelectric" equilibrium (1910). The correlation between osmotic pressure and electrical conductivity does not hold true for the colloidal solutions as it does for the genuine ones. James W. McBain (1882–1953, Stanford, California) found this particularly true for soap solutions. In 1918 he introduced the term "colloidal electrolytes" for those "in which one of the ions is partially or wholly replaced by conducting charged colloidal particles or micelles." (19)

In the language of colloid science, washing uses the dispersing action of certain substances on the dirt particles. They have to be removed from the tissue to which they adhere, and they have to be kept from resettling. The organic acid in the soap is essential for this effect. In 1913 Albert Marie Joseph Reychler (1854–1937) published his studies on cetylsulfonic acid and its sodium salt as washing agents (20). At a concentration of 0.2 percent in water, the acid behaved like a soap in emulsifying fat and foaming. This was interesting but not surprising. Bile was long known as fat-emulsifying material, and since Hermann Kolbe's work of 1862, taurine, a component of bile, had been acknowledged as a sulfonic acid: $H_2NCH_2CH_2SO_3H$. At least since 1883, the old additive in dyeing, Turkey red oil, was known to be a sulfonic acid made from castor oil. Depending on the method of sulfonation, the product contained sulfonic acids with the C—SO_3H group and sulfate esters with the —C—O—SO_3H group.

Industrial interest in sulfonation products as wetting and washing materials developed somewhat slowly. When fats as raw material for soap became scarce in Germany during the World War I, the effort was toward making organic carboxylic acids from hydrocarbons, especially paraffin, by oxidation. With manganese compounds as the catalysts, fatty acids from propionic to decylic were obtained. (21)

Soon after the war, increasing demands for emulsifiers and detergents in home and industry went parallel with a growing availability of raw materials from synthesis, based on natural gas and petroleum. Alcohols, esters, ethers, and salts of sulfonic acids and sulfates became industrial products in a great variety of compositions. Under the label "surface-active agents," or surfactants a production of about 1200 million pounds is listed for 1958, 2120 million pounds for 1964.

With dispersed oil and gas bubbles, the usual separation of heavy ores from the lighter silicates, the "gangue," was reversed. The result was a "paradox," a process of flotation that brought the heavy particles to the surface as a swimming froth to be skimmed off, while the gangue was removed as a mud below. The origins of the process were embroidered by legends; the further developments were carried by "practical" men with intuitive convictions about the right approach, and this led to litigation concerning the validity of the patents that began to appear in 1886. T. A. Rickard, editor of the *Mining and Scientific Press,* San Francisco, characterized the situation in 1916 as follows: "The litigation, which is now a serious obstacle to the free development of the process, has arisen largely from confusion of ideas as to the underlying causes of flotation. The patentees did not understand the phenomena with which they played. Those to whom they sold their patents knew still less. The interpretations of attorneys and judges have elucidated the law but confused the physics." (22) Nevertheless, large tonnages of ores, particularly sulfidic ores, were separated by flotation processes.

After commercial success was assured, scientific investigation was considered worthwhile. Through the combination of oils with surfactants and specific "collecting" agents, the method of flotation became applicable to a wide variety of ore separations.

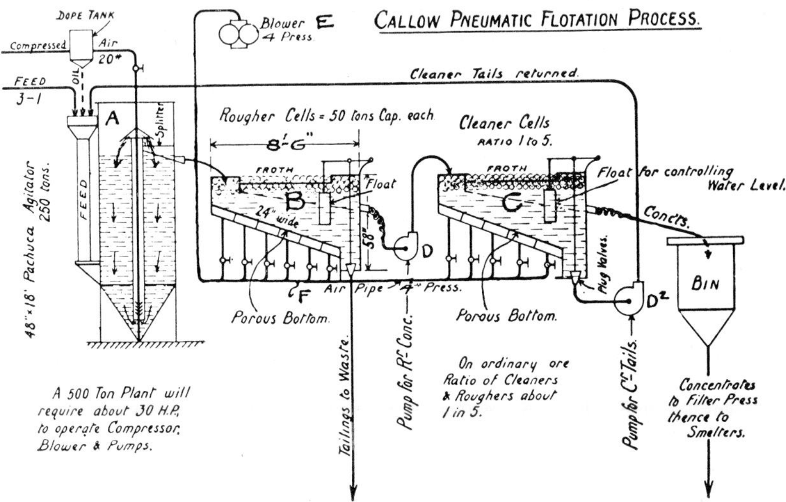

Fig. 38. Diagram of J. M. Callow's flotation process for copper ores. (From the *Mining and Scientific Press,* May 29, 1915, San Francisco.)

A standard cell has a capacity of 33–75 tons of ore per 24 hours. Refined pine oil is added at "as low as" 0.13 lb per ton of ore. Air at 15 psi is pressed in at a rate of 6–10 ft^3/ft^2 of blanket surface. The process was installed for the National Copper Co. in Mullen, Idaho, in Feb. 1914.

REFERENCES

1. J. H. van't Hoff, *Études de Dynamique Chimique* (Amsterdam: Frederick Muller & Co., 1884).

2. Henri Le Chatelier, *Recherches sur les Équilibres Chimiques* (*Extraits des Annales des Mines,* Paris: 1888).

3. A. Mittasch, *Geschichte der Ammoniaksynthese* (Weinheim: Verlag Chemie, 1951). A. Mittasch, *Salpetersäure aus Ammoniak* (*ibid.,* 1953).

4. From P. Sabatier's Nobel Prize lecture, 1912.

5. German patent No. 141,029 (1902), inventor, Karl Peter Wilhelm Theodor Normann.

6. Alfred Werner, *Neuere Anschauungen auf dem Gebiete der anorganischen Chemie* (Braunschweig: Vieweg, 1909). Translated by E. P. Hedley, with the title, *New Ideas on Inorganic Chemistry* (New York: John Wiley & Sons, 1911). George B. Kauffman, *Alfred Werner, Founder of Coordination Chemistry* (New York: Springer-Verlag New York Inc., 1966).

7. R. Abegg, "Valenz und periodisches System," *Z. anorg, Chem,* **39** (1904), pp. 330–80.

8. W. Kossel, "Über Molekülbildung als Frage des Atombaus," *Ann. der Physik* (4), **49** (1916), pp. 229–362, esp. pp. 230, 352.

9. W. Pauli, "Über den Zusammenhang des Abschlusses der Elektronen-

gruppen im Atom mit der Komplexstruktur der Spektren," *Z. Physik,* **31** (1925), pp. 763–83; in *Collected Scientific Papers* (New York: Interscience, 1964), Vol. 2, p. 225.

10. Linus Pauling, *The Nature of the Chemical Bond* (Ithaca, N.Y. Cornell University Press, 1939; 3rd ed, 1960). C. K. Ingold, *Structure and Mechanism in Organic Chemistry* (*ibid.,* 1953).

11. Max Bodenstein, "Über die Zersetzung des Jodwasserstoffs in der Hitze," *Z. phys. Chem.* **13** (1894), pp. 56–127; "Zersetzung und Bildung von Jodwassertoff," *ibid.,* **22** (1897), pp. 1–33.

12. I. Langmuir, "The adsorption of gases on plane surfaces of glass, mica, and platinum," *J. Am. Chem. Soc.,* **40** (1918), pp. 1361–1403.

13. E. Warburg, "Quantentheoretische Grundlagen der Photochemie," *Z. Elchem.,* **26** (1920), pp. 54–59 (summary of work started in 1912).

14. F. Paneth and W. Thimsen, "Über die Adsorption von Farbstoffen an Kristallen," *Chem. Ber.,* **57** (1924), pp. 1215–21; F. Paneth and A. Radu, "Über die Adsorption von Farbstoffen an Diamant, Kohle, und Kunstseide," *ibid.,* pp. 1221–5.

15. C. N. Hinshelwood and H. W. Thompson, "The kinetics of the combination of hydrogen and oxygen," *Proc. Roy. Soc.,* **A118** (1928), pp. 170–83, esp. p. 183.

16. N. N. Semenov, Nobel Prize lecture, 1956.

17*a.* I. M. Kolthoff and Charles Rosenblum, *J. Am. Chem. Soc.,* **55** (1933), pp. 2664–72. 17*b.* I. M. Kolthoff, W. von Fischer, and Ch. Rosenblum, *ibid.,* **56** (1934), pp. 832–36.

18. Jean Perrin, "The Proofs for the Real Existence of Molecules." In *Le Conseil Solvay* (1911). *Abh. der Bunsen-Gesellschaft* No. 7 (Halle: Wilhelm Knapp, 1914), p. 205.

19. James William McBain, Elfreida Victoria Cornish, and Richard Charles Bowden, "Studies of the constitution of soap in solution: Sodium myristate and sodium laurate," *J. Chem. Soc.,* **101** (1912), pp. 2042–56; "The hydrolysis of soap solutions measured by the catalysis of nitrosotriacetonamine," *ibid.,* **113** (1918), pp. 825–32; with A. V. Pitter, "The relative concentrations of various electrolytes required to salt out soap solutions," *ibid., 1926,* pp. 893–8.

20. A. Reychler, "Cetylsulfonic acid," *Bull. Soc. Chim. Belgique,* **27** (1913), pp. 110–6.

21. C. Kelber, "Die Oxydation von Kohlenwasserstoffen mit Sauerstoff. Die Oxydation von Paraffin," *Chem. Ber.,* **53** (1920), pp. 66–76.

22. T. A. Rickard, *The Flotation Process* (San Francisco: Mining and Scientific Press, 1916), p. 34.

21

Inorganic Chemistry

Metals and Alloys

Technical developments have influenced our lives so deeply that the modern age has been variously called the Age of Electricity, of Plastics, or of Wood. Sometimes the advance of the aluminum, magnesium, and sodium industries has been considered sufficiently important to indicate an Age of Light Metals. Actually, industrial production has been growing in so many directions since the late nineteenth century that none of these names could be justified—except the most recent one, the Age of Atomic Energy.

In this country the statistics of mineral products show that the dollar value of the annual production of metallic products was about equal to that of fuels from about 1880 to 1910. From then on the value of the annual fuel production increased steadily over that of the metallic products and reached over $10 billion in 1948 when the metallic products were about $3.5 billion.

In the absolute quantity produced, iron remains the predominant metal; with regard to the rate of growth, however, aluminum is first. United States production of new magnesium metal ("primary" production) amounted to only about 280 short tons in 1930, rose to 170,000 tons in 1943, and declined abruptly after the war to about 5,300 tons in 1946. From 1950 on, the production of magnesium rose considerably, though not consistently; in 1965 it reached 81,361 tons in the United States, an estimated 174,000 tons in world production.

The figures for the less common metals indicate the development of metal alloys. The improved stability that iron obtains through the addition of chromium was reported in 1821 by Pierre Berthier (1782–1861, Nemours). Faraday worked with steel of high chromium content in his search for better instruments and reflecting mirrors in 1822. A British patent of 1872 (No. 1923) claimed alloys

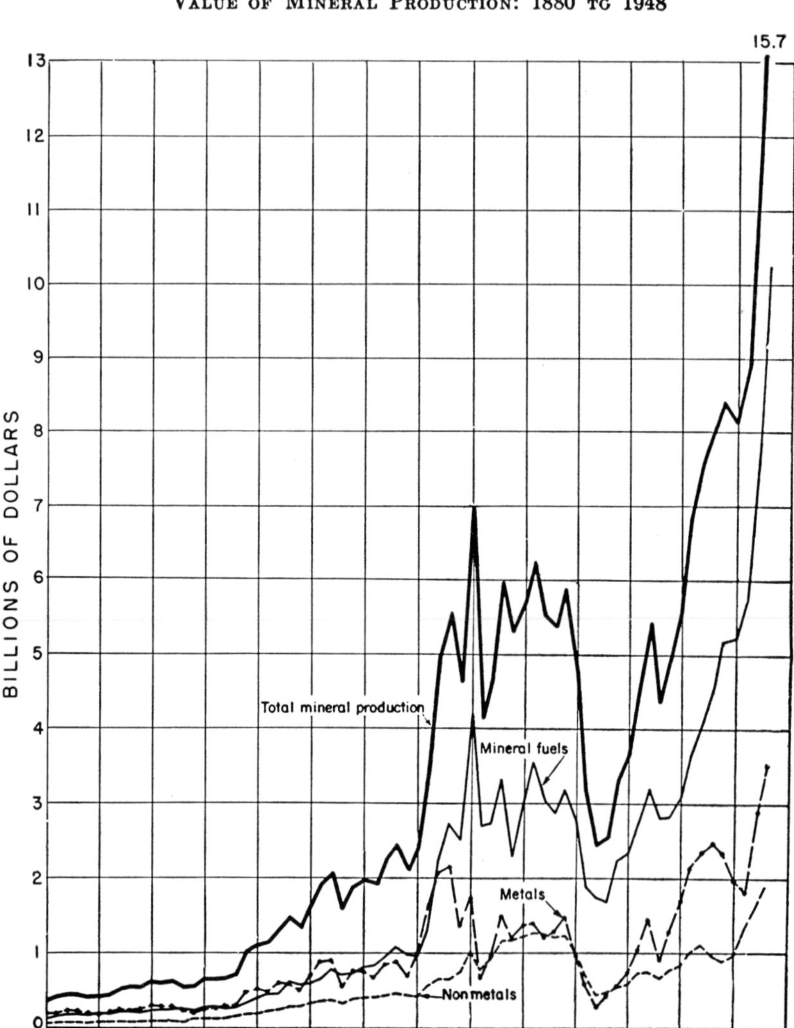

Fig. 39A. Value of mineral production, 1880–1949. (From *Statistical Abstracts of the United States,* 1950, p. 690.)

The curves show the influences of the World War I, the Depression (as of 1932), and World War II.

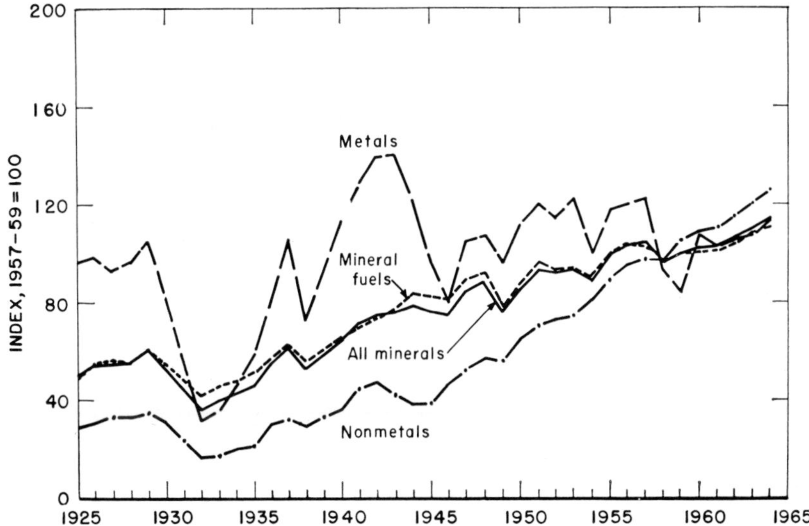

Fig. 39B. Indexes of physical volume of mineral production in the United States, 1925–64, by groups. Index numbers 1947–1949 = 100. (From Minerals Yearbook 1964, Vol. 1, Fig. 1, p. 4. Bureau of Mines, Division of Minerals.)

containing 30–35 percent chromium and 1.5-2 percent tungsten. In this country, Elwood Haynes (1857–1925) brought out alloys (1912) which he called "stellite" for high-speed cutting tools. Cobalt, chromium, and tungsten were used. At the Friedrich Krupp Works in Essen, Germany, Benno Strauss (1873–1944) produced chromium-

SOME OF THE METALS PRODUCED IN THE UNITED STATES
(in thousand short tons)

Year	Aluminum	Pig Iron	Copper	Lead	Zinc
1880	—	4,295	30	96	25
1890	0.03	10,307	130	158	64
1900	2.5	15,444	303	280	124
1910	17.7	39,580	540	393	269
1920	69.0	41,357	604	485	463
1930	114.5	35,562	607	608	498
1940	206.3	46,204	909	517	675
1945	495.0	53,224	783	441	765
1950	719	66,400	1,100	508	843
1955	1,566	79,264	999	479	964
1960	2,014	66,501	1,080	382	800
1965	2,754	88,185	1,352	148	1,005

nickel steels from 1912 on. In Sheffield, England, Harry Brearley (1) (1871–) had nonrusting knives made from chromium steel alloys in 1913.

The use of molybdenum, vanadium, and nickel in alloys of low-carbon steel (carbon below 0.7 percent) gave special properties of hardness and resistance to chemicals of high temperatures. Silicon made iron resistant even to hydrochloric acid.

The properties of aluminum were found to be very greatly influenced by other metals. A hardenable alloy (duralumin) discovered by Alfred Wilm (1869–1937, Berlin) contained 4 percent copper, 0.5 percent magnesium, 0.6 percent manganese, about 1 percent silicon, and 0.3 percent iron (1906). Fine crystals of the compound $CuAl_2$ were formed in the hardening operation. Later alloys, without copper, owed their improved qualities to the presence of Mg_2Si in the aluminum. In 1898 osmium was introduced to replace carbon as the filament in electric light bulbs by Carl Auer (1858–1929), who was knighted in 1901 and given the title "von Welsbach". Auer had investigated rare earths in Robert W. Bunsen's laboratory in 1884. He found a practical use for his scientific research. The brilliant light which some of the mixtures of these earth oxides showed in the flame of the Bunsen burner suggested to him the use of such mixtures in gas illumination. The gas mantle which he finally developed consisted of thorium oxide to which 1 percent of cerium oxide was added. Alloys containing rare earth metals and iron proved to be pyrophoric (1904), giving off brilliant sparks when struck by steel. They found application in cigarette lighters and tracer shells.

An alloy of iron with 35.6 percent nickel was shown by Charles Edouard Guillaume (1861–1938, Sèvres) to differ from all metals in remaining invariable in dimension within relatively wide temperature changes. For this alloy, called "invar," he found a companion, "elinvar," which keeps the same elasticity at changing temperatures.

Nickel was prepared by Murray Raney (1885–1966) in a form in which it is highly active as a catalyst for hydrogenation. He first produced an alloy with aluminum and decomposed it with alkali which dissolves the aluminum (1925). In a survey of his work, Raney said: "It is in the preparation of catalysts that the chemist is most likely to revert to type and to employ alchemical models. From all the evidence, it seems that work should be approached with humility and supplication, and the production of a good catalyst received with rejoicing and thanksgiving." (2)

Auguste J. Rossi (1839–1926), who came to New York from France, extolled the benefits to be derived from alloying iron with titanium. (3) From 1893 on, Nicolas Siemionovitch Kurnakow

Fig. 40. Casting sodium bricks. (Courtesy du Pont de Nemours & Co.)

Here, at Du Pont's Electrochemicals Department plant at Niagara Falls, N.Y., molten sodium is running into iron molds where it solidifies rapidly into bricks. The sodium later enters into the manufacture of other chemical products.

(1860–1941, Leningred) studied the "complex metallic bases," including mercury with cesium or rubidium, and lead with tellurium or indium. (4) The qualities sought in developing new alloys were corrosion resistance and mechanical strength combined with convenient workability, and, most recently, stability at very high temperatures. The great variety of iron and copper alloys with nickel, chromium, molybdenum, and silver (5) has been increased by including several of the formerly "rare" metals, such as columbium, zirconium, or niobium. Large quantities of titanium are used in the structure of airplanes.

Heavy Chemicals

Sometime around 1880, chemical industrial production began to increase at a higher rate than ever before. The causes for this growth are so interlocked that the few figures to be mentioned here represent the result of many influences.

The first decades of this period saw no major war, and during World War I, material played an increasingly larger part due to the preceding industrial development. Populations increased, and complete expectation of life—as it is called in vital statistics—rose. Figures for the state of Massachusetts give male life expectancy at birth as 41.75 years in 1880 and 59.29 years in 1930 (43.50 years and 62.63 years, respectively, for females). In the field of finance, it is significant that the value of the minted gold in Germany was 1300 million marks in 1876, and 4800 million marks in 1911, when deposits in American banks were $941.4 and $7963 million, respectively.

Another complex result, more directly pertinent to the production of heavy chemicals, i.e., basic chemicals produced in large quantities, is represented by the consumption of commercial fertilizers in the United States, as shown by the table. From 1880 to 1930 this quantity increased by a factor of 11.5, while the population rose from about 50 million to about 123 million. In 1960, about 2.9 times as much fertilizer was produced as in 1930; the population had grown to about 180 million.

For sulfuric acid, calculated as 100 percent, the production was 0.338 million short tons in 1899, 2.84 in 1931, 17.9 in 1960, and

COMMERCIAL FERTILIZERS CONSUMED IN THE UNITED STATES*

Year	Thousands of Tons	Nitrogen Content (in percent)	Phosphoric Oxide Content (in percent)	Potassium Oxide Content (in percent)
1880	753	2.6	9.3	1.7
1890	1,390	2.7	9.5	2.2
1900	2,730	2.3	9.1	3.2
1910	5,547	2.6	9.0	3.8
1920	7,296	3.1	9.1	3.5
1930	8,425	4.5	9.4	4.2
1940	8,656	4.9	10.7	5.1
1950	20,345	6.1	10.4	6.8
1960	24,374	12.4	10.9	8.9

* Source: Historical Statistics of the United States 1789–1945, U.S. Department of Commerce, Bureau of the Census; for the method of calculating the tonnages of fertilizer components see: U.S. Dept. of Agriculture, Circ. # 315, p. 19 (1945). Source from 1950 on: *Statistical Abstracts of the United States, 1966.*

All content figures have been calculated in percent to conform with the method of tabulation in the *Statistical Abstracts of the United States, 1966* (87th annual edition).

24.8 in 1965; for "synthetic" soda (at 58 percent Na_2O) the corresponding figures were 0.39, 1.51, 4.56, and 4.93 million tons.

This rise in chemical production was connected with developments in the building of machinery and containers, in transportation and consumption. The basis, however, was formed by discoveries of new principles, studies of new reactions, and developments of processes. The history of some of these discoveries in the manufacture of sulfuric acid, soda, and electrolytic products will be briefly sketched here.

Sulfuric Acid and Soda

The starting material for sulfuric acid is sulfur dioxide, a product of the direct combustion of sulfur either in the form of the element or of metal sulfides. Nitric acid serves as the means of combining the dioxide with more oxygen to the trioxide which dissolves in water, forming sulfuric acid. This was the basis for the "chamber process," carried out in large chambers, the walls of which were lined with sheets of metallic lead.

The use of lead chambers started in England (1746), and that country remained the largest producer of sulfuric acid for about a century and a half. In 1878, when the total European production was about a million tons, England produced 60 percent of it. At that time the need for highly concentrated sulfuric acid began to increase. The primary product of the chamber process was an acid of about 62.5 percent which required a costly step for concentration. One hundred kilograms of 94 percent sulfuric acid in 1878 had cost 5.5 German marks, while 100 percent acid sold for 20 marks. The synthetic dyestuffs industry used acid which contained dissolved sulfur trioxide, so-called "fuming sulfuric acid," and its price was about three times that of the 100 percent acid.

Differences in price stimulated the search for more economical methods for producing the highly concentrated acids. Attempts to oxidize sulfur dioxide by air in contact with platinum "in a finely divided state" (6) had been made in 1831 by Peregrine Phillips (1778–1851) in England. The idea was pursued by many chemists, among them William Petrie, who specified in his patent the use of "platinum in such a state as to expose a large surface with very little bulk, such as . . . filaments of asbestos coated with platinum wire. . . ." (7) Platinum distributed on asbestos fiber was the catalyst that Clemens Winkler used in his work which he described in 1875. Winkler (1838–1909) had started as a mining engineer and had later studied chemistry under Kolbe, who came from Bunsen's laboratory. Bunsen's methods for gas analysis were further developed by Winkler. He felt well equipped to carry his process for the catalytic production of fuming sulfuric acid from the laboratory to production scale. The difficulties encountered in this undertaking, however, proved to be too great. Winkler returned from industrial development to scientific work. He discovered an element in 1886 which he called "germanium."

An individual inventor needed the technical and financial support of a large organization in order to develop his findings into a commercial process. Rudolf Knietsch (1854–1906) had this support in the Badische Anilin- und Soda-Fabrik at Ludwigshafen. Basic studies of the equilibrium in the oxidation reaction showed that the process should work. The platinum catalyst, to which the purified sulfur dioxide gas was carried through lead pipes, was efficient enough in the laboratory. In larger-scale tests, the activity of the catalyst was quickly extinguished, even when all known precautions were taken to purify the gas. It was known that arsenic, this poison for organisms, was also harmful to the catalyst. The hot sulfur dioxide gas was cooled slowly to provide a good aggregation of the particles of entrained matter, and it was washed repeatedly to remove soluble impurities (1898). All this was not enough until the source of the poisoning effect was found in impurities of the iron used for the piping in the plant. Another new feature became dominant, the heat of reaction which had formerly been disregarded. Scientific work in thermochemistry found its industrial application in a carefully regulated heat balance. (8)

After this contact process had proved successful, much work was done on new catalysts. Platinum in a variety of forms, and also vanadium pentoxide, were tried (1899). Many costly patent suits marked the way of the new process which soon brought Germany into first rank among the European producers of sulfuric acid. In the 1930's the total production in the United States was about equally divided between chamber and contact-process output. The great expansion during the war years was mainly in favor of contact processes.

The manufacture of soda by the Leblanc process required much hand labor, gave hydrochloric acid as a troublesome by-product, and converted most of the sulfuric acid into the undesirable calcium sulfide in its "tank waste." An analysis of the product made in 1860 showed its actual Na_2CO_3 content as only 28 percent; other sodium salts and much CaS were present.

The great demand for soda from the industries of soap, glass, and paper-pulp manufacture stimulated attempts to produce soda by a different method, one long-known in the laboratory: the precipitation of sodium bicarbonate from salt solutions by ammonium bicarbonate,

$$H_2O + NH_3 + CO_2 + NaCl = NaHCO_3 + NH_4Cl$$

The bicarbonate would have to be heated for conversion into the "calcined" soda. The scheme looked simpler than that of the Leblanc process, but several trials ended in failure. Industrial chemistry still was the work of "philosophers by fire," operations in aqueous systems had much less support from traditional experience.

Ernest Solvay (1838–1922, Brussels) was not deterred by the failure of others and by his own initial difficulties. His difficulties were far from being solved when he obtained a Belgian patent in 1861. He saw that the process had to be at least partially continuous and cyclic with regeneration of the ammonia. New equipment and new thinking in material balances were necessary for success. For the absorption of the carbon dioxide in ammoniated brine, Solvay and his associates built an absorption tower with perforated plates at several levels, but the perforations became ineffective through clogging with the precipitated bicarbonate. The regeneration of the ammonia by heating its chloride solution with magnesia posed its particular problems. Nevertheless, the economic outlook was bright enough to warrant all efforts for developing the new technology.

Soda in the 1860s had a market price of 750 francs per long ton, equivalent to \$150 at that time. Solvay estimated that he could produce it for \$35. In June 1866, when the year's production of Leblanc soda was about 50,000 tons in all countries put together, Solvay's plant in Belgium first reached 1.5 tons per day. From then on the expansion was rapid. Ingenuity in developing production equipment, greater availability of ammonia as a by-product from coal distillation, and organizational skill brought Solvay soda to equal rank with Leblanc soda in 1887, when the total soda production reached one million tons. In 1922 the production in the international Solvay concern was over 3.5 million tons at an average price of less than \$20 per ton. (9)

In 1964, when United States production was close to 4.5 million long tons, an additional 1.2 million tons of soda was supplied from "natural" sources, mainly in Wyoming and California.

Electrochemical Products

Electricity produced by chemical reactions in batteries like those of Grove and Bunsen (page 258) was used to some extent in the galvanoplastic deposition of metals from their solutions. An electrochemical industry began to develop after more efficient generators of electricity had been built. Such generators were provided through the electrodynamic principle which Werner von Siemens and, almost simultaneously, Charles Wheatstone discovered in 1867, and the dynamoelectric machine of Zénobe Théophile Gramme in 1869. At first, however, electricity was so expensive that it could be used only for very valuable materials. In 1872 Gramme built a machine for Christoffle, in Paris, to be used for silver plating. Silver and copper refining on a large scale was carried out by means of electricity after 1875.

The principles of converting salt into sodium hydroxide and chlorine by electrolysis were contained in Faraday's and Hittorf's work, but an industrial application was declared impossible and uneconomical as late as 1888. Three years before, Julius Stroof, in Griesheim near Frankfurt, had already started to produce caustic soda electrolytically. An "artificial" coal electrode, made on the principle of Bunsen's electrode, was used, and the solution on the cathode was separated from that at the anode by a diaphragm prepared from cement. Berzelius had used mercury as the cathode, the negative pole, because it dissolved the alkali metal. Hamilton Young Castner (1859–1899), of the United States, built an electrolytic cell with a mercury cathode. It was introduced in England in 1897 and at Niagara Falls in 1901. The sodium amalgam formed in this cell was decomposed with water and an iron cathode in a second operation which furnished hydrogen as a by-product.

In Aussig, Austria, diaphragm and mercury were replaced by an arrangement in which an inverted bell jar separated the carbon anode from the metal cathode. The sodium chloride solution was kept flowing from anode to cathode so as to counteract the changes caused by the different speeds of ionic migration (1904).

Chlorine, the gas produced at the anode, was converted into chlorinated lime. In 1890 Germany imported about 7,000 tons more chlorinated lime than it exported; ten years later its export exceeded imports by 30,000 tons. (10)

Perhaps the first production of an organic substance by an electrolytical method was that of iodoform from sodium iodide and alcohol (by Ernst Schering in 1884). Electrochemical reductions (nitrobenzene to aniline) and oxidations (gluconic acid from glucose, Horace J. Isbell and Harriet L. Frush, 1931) offered gentle and easily regulated methods for organic chemistry.

In the electrochemical processes, solution of high concentrations were often used. The relationships expressed by Faraday's law were generally confirmed, but the theories of dissociation and conductivity, developed for ideal solutions and low concentrations, could not be applied without considerable modification. Those theories from the late years of the preceding century now proved to be approximations. "At high dilutions, these approximations introduce small errors of the same order of magnitude and of opposite sign, so that the agreement of the Ostwald dilution law with the earlier measurements on weak electrolytes was sufficiently close to be considered a triumph of the Arrhenius theory of electrolytic dissociation." (11)

Viscosity, which Ostwald later considered as an influencing factor, was not solely responsible for the deviations in concentrated solutions Instead of modifying the basic simple assumptions empirically, Peter Debye and Erich Hückel developed new fundamental concepts. The ions should not be considered as really independent from one another. An ion was visualized in 1923 as surrounded by an ionic atmosphere of oppositely charged ions. Even if a simple model were assumed in which ions are represented by rigid, unpolarizable spheres, it was necessary to consider attractions between oppositely charged ions, according to the attraction between positively and negatively charged bodies which Coulomb had formulated. In the theory of Niels Bjerrum (1879–1958, Copenhagen), which was expanded by Raymond M. Fuoss (12) and Charles A. Kraus (1875–1967), the association by coulombic forces is intermediate between complete dissociation and complete electronic linkage. If C^+ represents the cation, A^- the anion of singly charged elements, the relationship is given in the equilibrium:

$$\underset{\text{Dissociated}}{C^+ + A^-} \rightleftharpoons \underset{\text{Associated}}{[C^+A^-]^\circ} \rightleftharpoons \underset{\text{Undissociated}}{CA}$$

In the 1880s, when Svante Arrhenius in Stockholm was developing a theory of electrolytic dissociation, Henri Moissan (1852–1907) in Paris was discovering how to produce elementary fluorine by electrolysis. In a U-tube of platinum, which also served as the cathode, he cooled hydrogen fluoride to $-50°$ and introduced the anode through an insulating stopper made from fluorspar. He announced his success on June 26, 1886.

On July 9, 1886, Charles Martin Hall (1863–1914, Oberlin, Ohio) filed his U.S. patent application for a "Process of reducing aluminum from its fluoride salts by electrolysis," which was issued on April 2, 1889, No. 400,664. He claimed the electrolysis of a fused bath containing "the fluorides of aluminum, potassium, and lithium." At about the same time, Paul Louis Toussaint Héroult

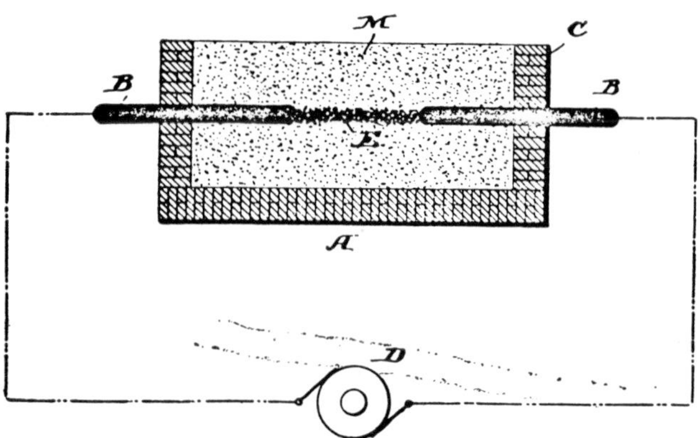

Fig. 41. E. G. Acheson's Electric Furnace. (Drawing from Acheson's U.S. patent 492,767.) *A,* furnace, lined with fire brick. *B,* electrodes. *D,* dynamo. *E,* conducting core. *M,* mixture for reaction.

(1863–1914) developed a similar process for the electrolytic production of aluminum.

Henri Moissan also showed that high temperatures can be obtained by passing strong electric currents through poorly conducting materials. Edward Goodrich Acheson (1856–1931) at first worked with Thomas Edison at Menlo Park, New Jersey, on the development of carbon filaments for electric lamps. From 1892 on, Acheson invented processes of making a silicon carbide and, later, graphite in electric furnaces. In his U.S. patent No. 492,767 of February 28, 1893 (application filed May 10, 1892), he heated a mixture of carbon, silica, clay, and salt and obtained a new, hard material to be used as an abrasive: "It thus appears that the material which I have designated as carborundum is practically a new compound . . . and its purity is represented by the formula SiC . . . silicide of carbon or carbide of silicon" (from page 2 of the patent). Acheson promoted his inventions with great energy. He traveled far to demonstrate his products, made contracts for their production and use, and accepted honors as a great inventor. (13)

More important than the carbide of silicon was the carbide of calcium. It was an easily "portable" source of acetylene for the lamps on bicycles and the first automobiles, before acetylene became a chemical raw material. Two German chemists, Adolph Frank (1834–1916, Charlottenburg) and Heinrich Caro (1834–1910, Dresden) together found the long-sought way of "binding" the nitrogen of the atmosphere by treating calcium carbide with it in the presence of moisture. (14) Calcium cyanamide was developed as a fertilizer and as a source of cyanamide.

For the generation of electricity by means of chemical reactions, William White Jacques, of Newton, Massachusetts, tried a new approach. He obtained British patent 4788 of April 25, 1896, on "An improved electric battery, and method or process of converting the potential energy of carbon or carbonaceous materials into electrical energy," of which claim 10 says: "As a generator of electricity by the chemical combination of carbon with the oxygen of air, an oxidizable electrode of carbon or carbonaceous materials, an electrolyte of molten sodium or potassium hydroxide continuously impressed with oxygen by a blast of air, a collecting cathode not chemically acted upon by said impressed electrolyte when the circuit is completed, a containing vessel of iron and means for maintaining the electrolyte in a molten condition." He recommends using pure iron; a carbon content reduces the efficiency of the generator. The voltage of this first fuel cell was low. (15)

REFERENCES

1. Harry Brearley, *Knotted String, Autobiography of a Steelmaker* (New York: Longmans, Green & Co., 1941).

2. Murray Raney, "Nickel catalysts," *Ind. Eng. Chem.,* **32** (1940), pp. 1199–1203; U.S. patents 1,563,587 of Dec. 1, 1923, and 1,914,473 of June 27, 1933.

3. A. J. Rossi, address of acceptance, on receiving the Perkin Medal, *Ind. Eng. Chem.,* **10** (1918), pp. 138–95, 141–5.

4. Leon Dlougatch, "Nicolas Siemionovitch Kurnakow," *Revue de Métallurgie,* **22** (1925), pp. 650–62, 711–32.

5. See, e.g., M. G. Fontana, "New alloys for severe corrosion service," *Chem. Eng.,* October 1946, pp. 114–5; "Corrosion resistance of copper and copper alloys" (Material supplied by the American Brass Co., Waterbury, Conn.), *Chem. Eng.,* January 1951, pp. 108–12.

6. Peregrine Phillips, Vinegar Maker, "Manufacture of sulphuric acid," British patent 6096, issued July 15, 1931.

7. William Petrie, "Improvement in the manufacture of sulphuric acid," British patent 590, issued Jan. 11, 1852.

8. R. Knietsch, "Über die Herstellung von Schwefelsäure nach dem Contact Verfahren," *Chem. Ber.,* **34** (1901), pp. 4069–115.

9. C. S. Glenn, "Ernest Solvay, father of the alkali industry and social crusader," *Sci. Monthly,* **73** (1951), pp. 114–20. L. F. Haber, *The Chemical Industry During the Nineteenth Century, A Study of the Economical Aspect of Applied Chemistry in Europe and North America* (Oxford: Clarendon Press, 1958).

10. Benno Lepsius, "Die Elektrolyse in der chemischen Grossindustrie," *Chem. Ber.,* **42** (1909), pp. 2892–916.

11. Herbert S. Harned and Benton B. Owen, *The Physical Chemistry of Electrolytic Solutions* (New York: Reinhold Publishing Corp., 1943), p. 206.

12. R. M. Fuoss, "Properties of electrolytic solutions," *Chem. Reviews,* **17** (1935), pp. 27–42.

13. *An Autobiography by Edward Goodrich Acheson,* published in 1910. Republished with preface and addendum by Raymond Szymanowitz (Port Huron, Mich.; Acheson Industries, 1965).

14. O. Kühling, Über die aus Erdalkalikarbonaten, Kohle, und Stickstoff entstehenden Produkte," *Chem. Ber.,* **40** (1907), pp. 310–9.

15. About further developments, see, e.g., *Fuel Cell Systems,* Advances in Chemistry, No. 47 (Washington, D.C.; American Chemical Society, 1965).

22

Organic Chemistry

Links between Inorganic and Organic Chemistry

In the course of the nineteenth century, analogies between inorganic and organic substances frequently gave the answers to decisive questions. On one festive occasion, Adolphe Wurtz exclaimed: "There is but one chemistry!" (1) That was when he had extended his study of ethylene oxide to the polyethylene glycols and saw their analogy to the polysilicates and the polystannates.

The link that Wöhler had discovered by his "synthesis" of urea remained without practical consequence for more than 80 years, until the technical problems of ammonia synthesis had been solved. Bunsen's work on the kakodyl series and its organic compounds of arsenic was an isolated achievement. Frankland, however, derived general theories from his experiments on zinc alkyls and corresponding compounds of tin and antimony.

Perhaps the first to use metal-organic compounds as a means for organic synthesis were Georg Wagner (1849–1903, Warsaw) and Alexander Saytzeff (1841–1910, Kazan, Russia). From ethyl formiate, they produced "a new isomer of amyl alcohol" by a reaction with zinc ethyl (2):

1. Addition:

$$HCO{\cdot}OC_2H_5 + Zn\begin{cases}C_2H_5\\C_2H_5\end{cases} = HC(C_2H_5)(ZnOC_2H_5){\cdot}OC_2H_5$$

2. Exchange:

$$HC(C_2H_5)(ZnOC_2H_5){\cdot}OC_2H_5 + Zn\begin{cases}C_2H_5\\C_2H_5\end{cases}$$
$$= HC(C_2H_5)_2(ZnOC_2H_5) + Zn\begin{cases}C_2H_5\\OC_2H_5\end{cases}$$

3. Hydrolysis:

$$HC(C_2H_5)_2(ZnOC_2H_5) + 2H_2O = HC(C_2H_5)_2{\cdot}OH + Zn(OH)_2 + C_2H_6$$

Philippe Antoine Barbier (1848–1922, Lyons) tried this method for converting methylheptenone

$$\begin{array}{l} CH_3\text{—}\underset{\displaystyle |\atop\displaystyle CH_3}{C}\text{=}CH\text{—}CH_2\text{—}CH_2\text{—}\underset{\displaystyle |\atop\displaystyle CH_3}{CO} \end{array}$$

into dimethylheptenol

$$\begin{array}{l} CH_3\text{—}\underset{\displaystyle |\atop\displaystyle CH_3}{C}\text{=}CH\text{—}CH_2\text{—}CH_2\text{—}\underset{\displaystyle |\atop\displaystyle CH_3}{C}(OH)\text{—}CH_3 \end{array}$$

When the zinc compound did not work, Barbier used the analogous magnesium compound. The thought of doing that was perhaps inspired by much earlier work of Auguste Cahours (1813–1891, Paris), who had included magnesium ethyl in his study of metal-organic compounds. (3) Barbier suggested to his student Victor Grignard (1871–1935, Nancy) that he continue this work for his doctoral dissertation. Grignard heated magnesium in the form of turnings with isobutyliodide. The reaction became manageable when he added ethyl ether, naturally with the exclusion of moisture. The metal dissolved by combining with the organic iodide, and its ethereal solution reacted easily with alcohols, aldehydes, ketones, and acids. (4) Through the addition of ether, Grignard made the organic magnesium compounds widely useful as agents in organic synthesis.

Cahours had also mentioned a few alkyl compounds of aluminum; for these, however, the scientific and technical importance began after a long interval and surpassed that of the magnesium compounds from about 1950 on.

Another link between the two branches of chemistry was established with the finding that carbon is not alone in forming optically active compounds. Le Bel had tried to obtain such compounds from ammonium, in which the four hydrogen atoms were replaced by four different alkyl groups, but his work of 1891 was not confirmed. With improved methods of separation, especially the use of D-camphor-β-sulfonate, William Jackson Pope (1870–1939, Cambridge, England) resolved the optical isomers of benzylphenylallylmethyl ammonium. In 1900, Pope, who had studied under Henry Edward Armstrong (1848–1937, London) who in turn had been a pupil of Frankland, showed that sulfur, too, can be an "asymmetric" center. For elements from beryllium and boron to iridium and platinum, optically active compounds were prepared.

These new findings widened the basis for the discussion of structure and symmetry, such as that by Frans Maurits Jaeger (1877–1945,

Groningen). At the first "Conseil de Chimie" under the sponsorship of Ernest Solvay in 1922, Jaeger called "the doctrine of the asymmetric atom . . . no longer opportune. . . . The only condition for optical activity is that the arrangement of the atoms in question has no other elements of symmetry than simple axes of rotation. The presence of any other elements of symmetry makes the considered atomic arrangement identical with its image, and the molecule is no longer to be resolved into two enantiomorphic isomers. Therefore, the enantiomorphic molecule can have a high symmetry; Pasteur's term dissymmetry is thus a better choice than the term asymmetry" (Institut International de Chimie, Solvay, 1925, ref. 7, pp. 162 ff.).

Valence, Structure, and Color

The period beginning about 1880 brought a fundamentally new science of the elements and atoms. Organic chemistry, however, could continue to build its systems on the foundations laid during the earlier parts of the nineteenth century. All the elements, and even their isotopes, could be explained with the neutron, the proton, and the electron as structural units, and the arrangements of the electrons were found to be governed by laws that excluded a great number of purely mathematical combinations. All the organic compounds could be defined by the number and the arrangement of the atoms of carbon and a few other elements, mainly hydrogen, oxygen, and nitrogen, in the molecule of the substances. Since about 1870 it had become necessary to include the arrangement of the atoms in three-dimensional space as one of the variables, and the concept of valence had to be enlarged by finer differentiations. Fundamentally, however, the principles of organic chemistry remained unchanged. The number of pure organic substances separated from natural materials and produced by artificial synthesis grew into many hundreds of thousands. The more chemical reactions that were found for the identification and production of compounds, the easier it became to determine the chemical structure of highly complex substances and to reach a final proof for the structure by synthesis in well-defined steps.

The meticulous care in developing methods for analysis, separation, and synthetic production of new substances had its reward not only in gaining a satisfactory scientific system but also in a great extension of practical use as dyestuffs, plastics, motor fuels, and in the chemical production of highly specific materials for food and health.

The principle of organic chemistry, that a pure substance is defined by reproducibility in a definite atomic structure of its molecule, had to be maintained and aligned with the concepts of oscillations and vibrations developed in physical chemistry. Invasions of these concepts into organic chemistry occurred at various times. The first invasion used a weak spot in the theory that every compound had one definite arrangement of the atoms in its molecule. When Adolf Baeyer, in the continuation of his indigo studies, investigated the chemical reactions of isatin, he found (1882) that two structural formulae were indicated for this one compound by its reactions. With acetylating agents, it reacted according to Formula I; with silver and methyl iodide, according to Formula II. Once this exceptional case was established, a search for analogies began. The exception to the old rule could be validated only by being made part of a new rule.

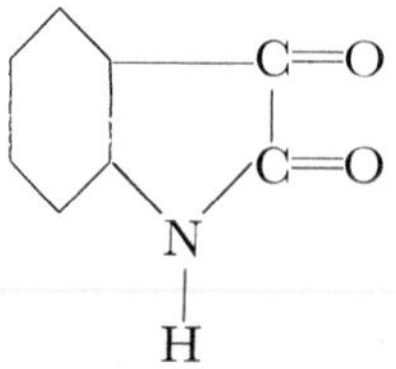

C=O, C=O, N, H

Isatin I

C=O, C—OH, N

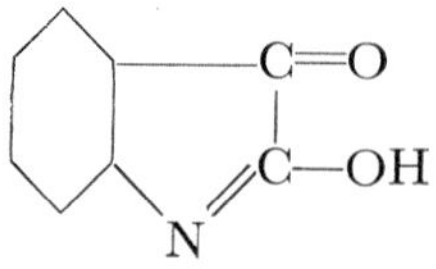

Isatin II

So long as only this particular set of reactions was considered, the structure could be explained as varying with the conditions of the chemical change, following the way that Berzelius had recommended in a similar difficulty (page 180). But times had changed.

The techniques of separating isomers were finer; the identification by chemical reaction could be amplified by the measurement of physical properties in which the substances were observed without chemical influences and compared with a large group of other substances.

Conrad Laar (1853–1929, Bonn) tried to develop such a new rule. The configurations

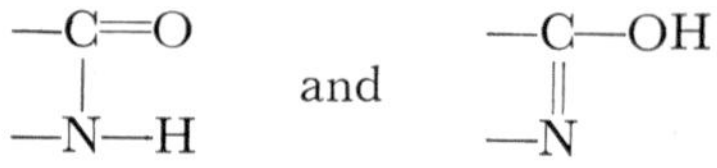

$$\begin{array}{c} -C{=}O \\ | \\ -N-H \end{array} \quad \text{and} \quad \begin{array}{c} -C-OH \\ \| \\ -N \end{array}$$

Model I

$$\begin{array}{c} -C{=}O \\ | \\ {=}C-H \end{array} \quad \text{and} \quad \begin{array}{c} -C-OH \\ \| \\ {=}C \end{array}$$

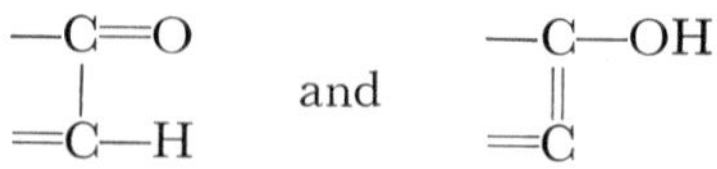

Model II

appeared in other newly discovered compounds. Apparently hydrogen could oscillate between two positions and form pairs of compounds which Laar in 1885 called "tautomeric." The models shown above represent the extremes between which the oscillation takes place.

It was first shown for compounds corresponding to Model II that the two forms could be separately identified. Transitions from one form to the other, and equilibria conditions, were established for them by Ludwig Claisen (1851–1930, Kiel) and Wilhelm Wislicenus (1861–1922, Tübingen). The principle of definite constitutions was confirmed, the invasion repelled. The victory brought a definite gain to organic chemistry. The rigidity of the concept of molecular structure was cautiously modified. In the pictorial representation of this structure, the lines indicating valence bonds were broken up. Werner's distinction between primary and auxiliary valences and Thiele's partial valences had their successors in Hugo Kauffmann's (b. 1870) theory of split valences (5) which gave, for example, the following drawing for phenol:

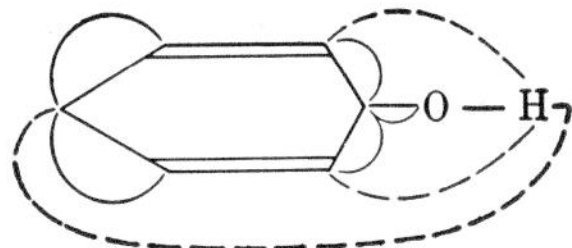

The splitting of the hydrogen valence between oxygen and carbon atoms of the benzene ring was offered as an explanation for the acidity of phenol, which is much greater than the acidity of alcohols without a benzene ring, e.g., C_2H_5OH (ethyl alcohol). Kauffmann further read into his formula the presentation of the influence that the introduction of an —OH group has on the visible color of aromatic compounds.

Carl Graebe and Carl Liebermann had concluded from their studies of quinone and alizarin that "the physical property of color depends upon the manner in which oxygen or nitrogen atoms are grouped, that in the colored compounds these elements are in a more intimate bond to each other than in the colorless compounds." (6) A simple example for this rule was azobenzene (Formula I), which is yellow-red. When the "more intimate" double bond between the two nitrogen atoms is opened by adding hydrogen, colorless hydrazobenzene (II) is formed:

$$C_6H_5{-}N{=}N{-}C_6H_5$$

(I) Azobenzene

$$C_6H_5{-}\underset{H}{\underset{|}{N}}{-}\underset{H}{\underset{|}{N}}{-}C_6H_5$$

(II) Hydrazobenzene

Otto N. Witt (1853–1915, Berlin) distributed the color-forming effect over two factors: One was the chromophore, for example, nitrogen or nitrogen with oxygen, in the "more intimate" double bonds; the other a contributing or enhancing factor, the auxochrome. A hydroxyl group can function as an auxochrome (1876, further developed in 1888).

The cause of the color, formerly seen in the presence of the old color-giving element sulfur, was now attributed to constituent parts of the molecule and their combined influence. H. Kauffmann in 1911 made a further distinction between independent chromophores like the nitroso-group N=O, and dependent chromophores like C=O, which need additional chromophores to be effective. The cumulation of such groups, their intimate neighborhood, was decisive. Acetone, CH_3—CO—CH_3, is colorless; diacetyl CH_3—CO—CO—CH_3, is yellow; triketopentane CH_3—CO—CO—CO—CH_3 is orange-red. Benzophenone is colorless; an additional bond between the two benzene rings produces an orange color in fluorenone:

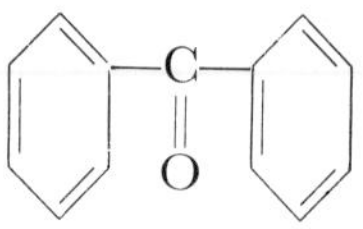

Benzophenone

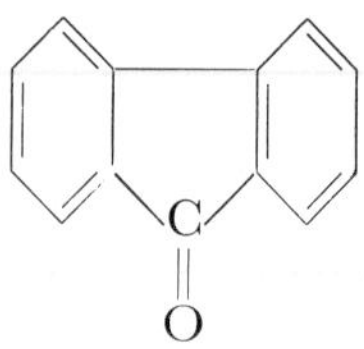

Fluorenone

The rule was confirmed in many cases but it did not cover all colored compounds adequately. The important group of dyestuffs derived from triphenyl methane was best explained by assuming that

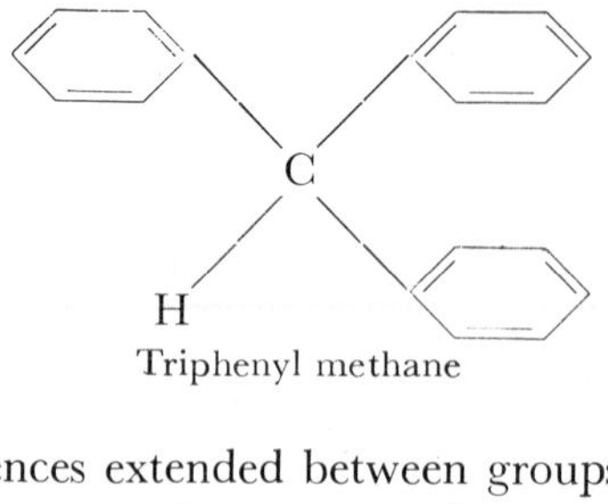

Triphenyl methane

partial, or split, valences extended between groups which in the older theory would have appeared as separately saturated. The salts of crystal violet were thus represented by a formula with partial valences between the amino groups. In addition, the acid radical X was

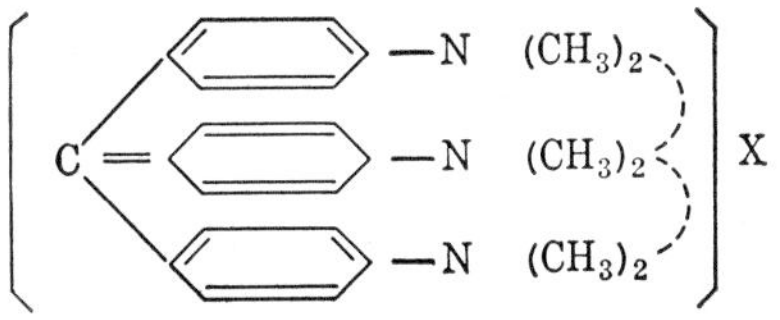

—N $(CH_3)_2$
C —N $(CH_3)_2$ X
—N $(CH_3)_2$

Crystal violet (Arthur Hantzsch, 1919)

here seen as bound by the entire basic molecule, not by one specific part of it as the older theory would have prescribed.

Much thinking and a great amount of experimental effort resulted in adding a few small broken lines to the picture by which atomic relations in the molecule of this dyestuff were symbolized. A great deal of chemical history was compressed into such a picture. Its great beauty was not static, and it did not only indicate what this one substance, crystal violet, "really" was, but it also contained the directions for further conclusions. As it was derived from theories and experiences concerning methane, benzene, quinone, substitutions by additional groups and comparisons with other colored substances, it pointed the way to the construction of other dyestuffs. The construction could start on paper. There was sufficient basis for predicting properties of molecules to be built, and sufficient freedom in expecting and utilizing differences between the predicted and the observed results. Since cumulation of "intimate" bonds should deepen the color, benzene would be replaced by naphthalene, azo-groups would be multiplied, auxochromes would be introduced.

Such formulations went beyond the "classical" concept that valences are simple and indivisible bonds between the atoms of a molecule. By the end of the nineteenth century, this concept, only about thirty years old at that time, lost its strict validity and became merely an approximation to the truth. New experiences brought other modifications of relatively young theories.

From 1896 on, Paul Walden (1861–1957, Tübingen) studied conversions of optically active substances into their antipodes, for which the atoms had to move much more freely in the molecule than was usually assumed. Rearrangements of the atoms in the otherwise constant molecule followed complicated rules: André Job (1870–1928) (7) and Marc Tiffeneau (1873–1946, Paris) sought to elucidate the mechanics and energetics of this "chemical mobility" within the molecule.

Since about 1892, John Ulric Nef (1862–1915) had argued for the recognition that carbon can exist with two free valences in certain reactive compounds. Thus, he wrote: "The aldehydes, R—CH:O, as has long been known, reduce Fehling's solution and silver solutions with great ease. This is due to the presence of oxyalkylidene particles,

R
>C=, which burn at the expense of the oxygen in the water." (8)
HO

In 1900, Moses Gomberg (1866–1947, Ann Arbor, Michigan) described "a case of trivalent carbon;" it was the highly reactive triphenylmethyl, which he obtained from the removal of the bromine in triphenylbromide by reaction with silver. (9)

An accumulation of phenyl groups on the carbon atom increases the stability of its trivalent state in the compounds that Wilhelm Schlenk (1879–1943) and his associates in Berlin synthesized; (10) for example:

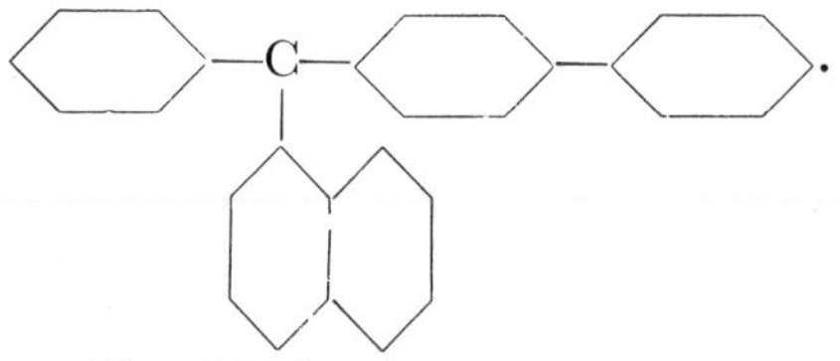

Phenyl-biphenyl-α-naphthylmethyl

As a result of the greatly increased activity in organic chemistry near the turn of the century, other "classical" assumptions about valence states were changed. Usually, the start was a particular experiment; its generalization was met with doubt, and this led to a program of wider research. One of the serious beginnings for the theory that oxygen can be quadrivalent was the study of dibenzalacetone, the condensation product from acetone and benzaldehyde:

$$C_6H_5CH:CHCOCH:CHC_6H_5$$

Claisen dissolved this faintly yellow compound in concentrated sulfuric or hydrochloric acid. These solutions were deeply colored. Claisen therefore concluded (1884) that the oxygen of the central CO group had combined with one equivalent of the acids and become quadrivalent. The two changes, of color and of valence state, explained each other.

For the valence change of the oxygen in dimethylpyrone, John Norman Collie (1859–1942) and T. Tickle in London pointed to an analogy with the nitrogen in dimethylpyridine, then spelled "pyridene" (11):

```
    H    Cl                         H    Cl
     \  /                            \  /
      NH                              O
     /  \                            /  \
CH3·C    C·CH3                 CH3·C    C·CH3.
    ||   ||                        ||   ||
    HC   CH                        HC   CH
     \  /                           \  /
      CO                             CO
```

Dimethylpyridone hydrochloride   Dimethylpyrone hydrochloride

Adolf Baeyer in 1902 gave the name "oxonium" to those compounds with oxygen in the higher valence state. For the ether-compound in Grignard's reagent he proposed the formula (12):

```
C2H5\     /MgCH3
     >O<
C2H5/     \I
```

From measurements of freezing point depressions and electric conductivities, Arthur Hantzsch concluded soon thereafter that oxonium salts can exist in solution.

Loaded with phenyl, nitrogen becomes bivalent in $(C_6H_5)_2N$ and quadrivalent in its oxide, as Heinrich Wieland (1877–1957, Munich) found in 1911 (13):

```
H5C6\      /C6H5        H5C6\
     >N—N<        → 2        >N
H5C6/      \C6H5        H5C6/
```

$$(C_6H_5)_3C—C(C_6H_5)_3 \rightarrow 2(C_6H_5)_3C$$

These new findings enlarged rather than displaced or invalidated the older theories. The physical properties that served to identify these new substances were, as always before, in precise relationship to definite chemical structures. Arthur Hantzsch (1857–1935, Leipzig) emphasized this particularly for the optical properties. No chemical change takes place without its optical equivalent, and no essential change in optical properties occurs without a corresponding chemical change. When a dyestuff, like congo red, turns blue through the presence of acid, or red under the influence of alkali, a change within the molecule must be the cause. This was successfully proved against a physical explanation which started from an apparently logical assumption that the physical change in color must have a physical cause in particle size or surface developments. The chemical explanation of this color change prevailed, just as it had prevailed about a hundred years before, in the theory of electrochemical phenomena.

Because organic chemists at university laboratories were completely immersed in building their scientific systems, the industrial chemists could construct substances for commercial production. The effect of this development on national economy can be appreciated from the statistical figures in the tables.

GERMAN TRADE IN INDIGO

Year	Import	Export
	(In million marks)	
1896	20.7	6.4
1911	0.446	41.8

VALUE OF GERMAN EXPORTS IN 1912

	In million marks	In long tons
Alizarin	23.64	11,589
Indigo	45.21	24,827
Other tar dyestuffs	133.76	59,696

The scientific investigation of dyestuffs was based on their relationship to many other substances; the industrial production of dyestuffs was connected with increases in coal-tar distillation, increases in the manufacture of sulfuric acid, nitric acid, and hydrochloric acid, and the development of equipment and apparatus for producing and packaging on a large scale.

The availability of synthetic dyestuffs had a remarkable influence on the development of medical chemistry. Anatomists used dyestuffs to make tissue preparations more distinguishable under the microscope. Paul Ehrlich (1854–1915, Frankfurt-am-Main) learned this technique as a student of medicine. At first he was less concerned with the chemical constitution of these dyes than with their fixation by the tissues. A pigment becomes a dyestuff when it has an affinity for the material to which it is applied. Acid pigments dye silk and wool, but cotton needs an intermediary, a metal compound which serves as a mordant. Ehrlich was impressed with Paul Schützenberger's theory that animal fiber acts as a mordant. The poisonous

Fig. 42. Parts of the indigo manufacturing plant of the Badische Anilin- und Soda-Fabrik, about 1920. (From a privately printed book, *Die Badische Anilin- und Soda-Fabrik,* p. 76.)

action of alkaloids had been explained by their elective affinity for protein. Ehrlich felt intuitively that an analogy existed between the chemical combination of alkaloids with living protein and the elective coloring of tissue by dyestuffs (1878). He used methylene blue (which Heinrich Caro had discovered in 1876) to stain bacteria and cell nuclei selectively (1881). Soon after Robert Koch described (1882) his discovery of the tubercle bacillus, Ehrlich was able to show him an improved method for staining it. Besides elective affinity between tissue and dyestuff, there is also specific chemical action which is caused by the oxygen demand of the living cell. This demand can be great enough to take oxygen out of the dyestuff and to reduce it to its colorless leuko-form (page 210). It was known that indophenol blue yielded its oxygen more readily than alizarin blue. Ehrlich used this known difference in 1885 as a method for comparing the avidity for oxygen in specific parts of the organism. The reaction in the living body, *in vivo,* occurred with water-insoluble dyestuffs, while reactions in the test tube, *in vitro,* prefer solutions. The old adage that substances do not react unless dissolved was therefore changed by Ehrlich for organic reactions: Substances do not act unless fixed. For this fixation of substances to tissues, he developed a working hypothesis which was too crude and much misunderstood, yet useful in many respects.

In this region of supposed chemical reactions with unknown and certainly complex factors in the organism, the analogies had to be bolder than in a field where scientific data were more closely planted. Since the azo-dyestuff trypan red protected mice against the results of infection by trypanosomes (the microorganisms causing sleeping sickness) Ehrlich concluded that the double-bound nitrogen group in this dyestuff caused the beneficial effect. Arsenic is related to nitrogen in the periodic system. Would the substitution of nitrogen by arsenic have particular effects?

The organic arsenic compound called atoxyl had just (1905) been successfully tested by Paul Uhlenhut (1870–1957) against the sickness of chickens caused by spirilla. For humans, atoxyl proved to be too poisonous. This substance, which Ehrlich and Alfred Bertheim (1879–1914, Frankfurt-am-Main) proved to be arsanilic acid (aniline substituted by arsenic acid), did not have the analogous azo-like structure that was sought. Ehrlich found it in patient experimentation, to which he was led by an original bold analogy. Compound number 606 in the series of experiments, containing two arsenic atoms with a double bond between them, first synthesized in 1909, was effective against spirilla and against spirochaeta, the protozoan producing syphilis.

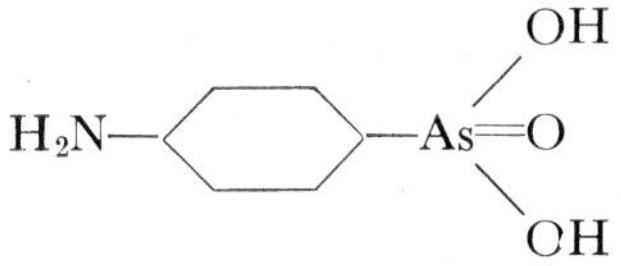

Arsanilic acid

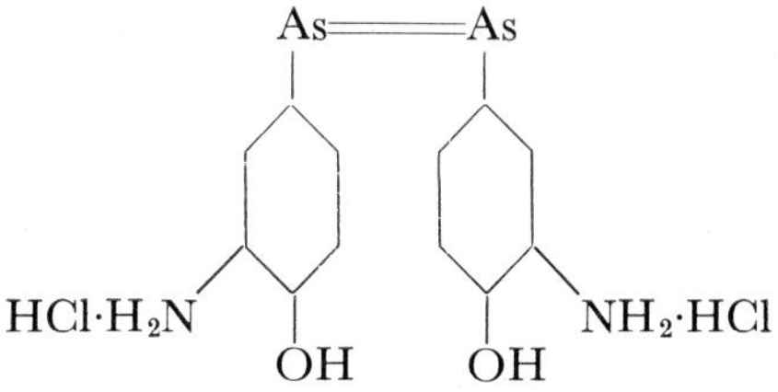

Salvarsan, Arsphenamine, Compound 606

The thought that connected dyes with therapeutic agents had roots deeper than logical argument. The shared protein nature of wool and muscle fiber was considered sufficient to conclude that a substance with an "elective" affinity to one would also attach itself to the other. While lacking any hint at the required specific medical activity, the thought had its great successes. Two examples will be cited here.

The first is connected with modified dyes derived from "acridine," a name that Carl Graebe and Heinrich Caro had given in 1870 to an "acrid" substance extracted from coal tar. Its formula as an analogue of anthracene was established much later:

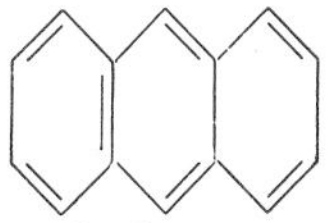

Anthracene

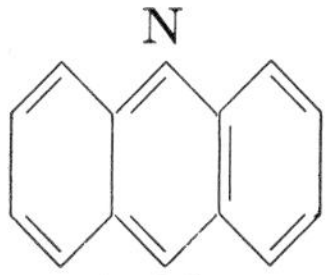

Acridine

Modified acridinium dyestuffs were valuable additives in topical wound dressing: trypaflavin was discovered by L. Benda in 1912 and rivanol by Roser and Jensch in 1922.

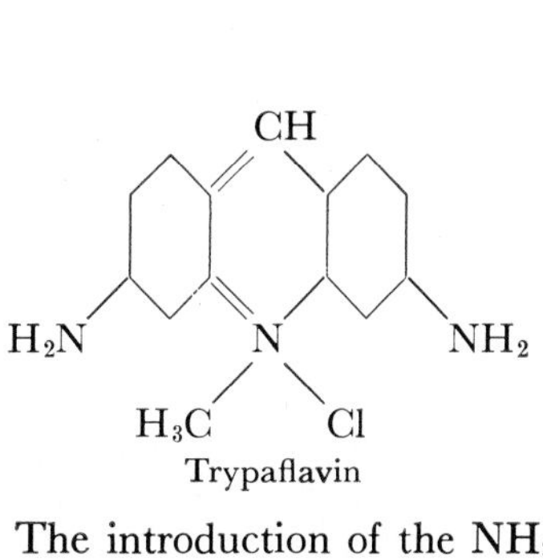

Trypaflavin

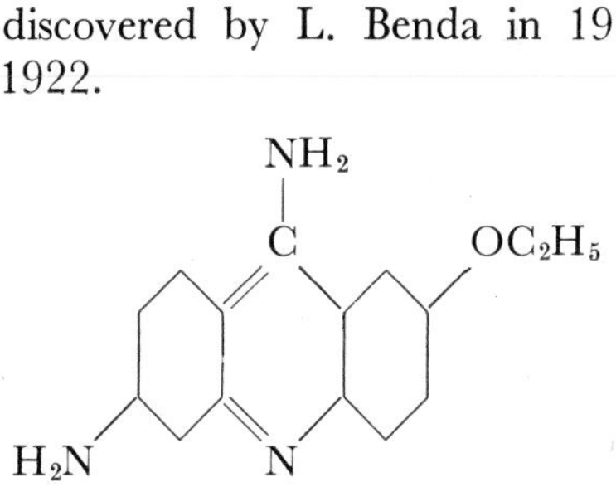

Rivanol

The introduction of the NH_2SO_2 group gave azo dyestuffs greater fastness on wool. This was interpreted as showing an increased "affinity for protein molecules." In 1930, Fritz Mietzsch (1896–1958, Elberfeld) thereupon introduced this sulfonamide group into azo dyes and found one of them highly effective against streptococcal infections; it was named Prontosil rubrum:

$$HCl \cdot H_2N-C_6H_3(NH_2)-N=N-C_6H_4-SO_2NH_2$$

Prontosil

Several other such dyes were synthesized and patented. (14) This work was done at the I. G. Farbenindustrie works at Elberfeld. In the laboratory of Ernest Fourneau (1872–1949) at the Pasteur Institut in Paris, the simple, colorless *p*-aminobenzenesulfonamide

$$H_2N-C_6H_4-SO_2NH_2$$

Sulfanilamide

was shown to be as effective as the complex dyes. (15) That conclusion, however, was a kind of idealization. Sulfonamides, popularly called sulfa drugs, were synthesized in thousands of variations, and many of them found specific medical applications.

Complex Metal-Organic Compounds and Natural Dyestuffs

The success in producing synthetic dyestuffs and in recognizing the chemical structure of alizarin and indigo demonstrated that organic chemistry was on the right path. This had been seriously questioned at various times during the nineteenth century. Objections were raised against "the hairsplitting of the organic chemists," as William Robert Grove called it, and against the unnatural substances produced for no other apparent purpose than to satisfy the demands of a paper-and-desk chemistry. Such criticism came mostly from the ranks of physicists and physiologists, while organic chemists found that to come closer to nature they had to increase the hairsplitting. The methods had to be more gentle, the separations more delicate in the approach to the chemistry of the two most important natural pigments, the green chlorophyll of plants and the red hemine of blood.

Physical methods had been introduced into chlorophyll research at an early stage. David Brewster (1781–1866, Edinburgh) described the optical absorption spectrum of his chlorophyll product in 1834. The difference of color between arterial and venous blood invited spectroscopic investigation. When Claude Bernard observed the action of carbon monoxide on hemoglobin, he measured the displacement of oxygen by the poisonous gas and described the accompanying color change by the characteristic absorptions in the spectral light (1857).

Chemical reactions with acids and alkalies gave a number of

different products from chlorophyll, but their relationships found various interpretations. The blood pigment was converted by Ludwig Teichmann in 1853 into crystallized derivatives by treatments with salt and acetic acid. They were certainly not identical with the natural substances.

Instead of strongly reacting chemicals, Armand Gautier (1837–1920, Cannes) used absorbent charcoal in his attempts to separate pure chlorophyll from alcoholic leaf extracts. But charcoal was too strong an absorbent; Michael Tswett (1872–1920, Warsaw) replaced it by calcium carbonate, which selects the dyestuff more exclusively. The gentle method of selective absorption helped to solve the problem of separating highly sensitive substances without changing them. Chlorophyll is sensitive even to the action of alcohol used apparently as a mere solvent. This was shown by Richard Willstätter (1872–1942). He approached the investigation of chlorophyll with the experiences gained in his work on quinones in Adolf Baeyer's laboratory in Munich. The alkaloid cocaine had been another subject of Willstätter's studies. These led him to a new concept of its chemical structure. A by-product of this scientific work was the partial synthesis of one of the alkaloids that accompany cocaine in nature. It was soon manufactured industrially.

When Willstätter turned from quinones and cocaine to chlorophyll, he improved the conditions under which chlorophyll could be separated. He refined the methods for distribution of the pigment in various solvents, which Gregor Kraus had attempted, and of separating its components by adsorption, which Michael Tswett had first described in a publication of 1906. (16) Petroleum ether extracts only the yellow carotenoids from dried green leaves; when as little as 1 percent alcohol is added to the solvent, it extracts also the chlorophyll. Tswett attributed this effect to a release of adsorbed chlorophyll by the alcohol, and he continued from there to a study of adsorptions.

> If a petroleum ether solution of chlorophyll is filtered through a column of an adsorbent (I use mainly calcium carbonate which is stamped firmly into a narrow glass tube), then the pigments according to the adsorption sequence, are resolved from top to bottom into various colored zones, since the stronger adsorbed pigments displace the weaker adsorbed ones and force them farther downwards. This separation becomes practically complete if, after the pigment solution has flowed through, one passes a stream of pure solvent through the adsorbent column. Like light rays in the spectrum, so the different components of a pigment mixture are resolved on the calcium carbonate column according to a law and can be estimated on it

> qualitatively and also quantitatively. Such a preparation I term a chromatogram, and the corresponding method, the chromatographic method. (17)

After a slow start, the recognition of this method as highly valuable spread into many fields of research and technology. After 1950, its application was expanded from solutions to gases. A great development of instrumentation made it possible to analyze small quantities of complicated mixtures in a very short time by various methods of gas chromatography.

From this point of view, the quantities with which Willstätter had to work were quite enormous. An enzyme, chlorophyllase, is present in grass and leaves. It causes exchange of the ethyl alcohol, used in laboratory operations as a solvent, for another alcohol, phytol, which forms part of the chlorophyll molecule. Willstätter explained:

> The method of our investigation was to arrive at the peculiarities of its constitution, without first isolating and investigating chlorophyll itself, on two ways of degradation, namely, by exploring the two series of derivatives which are produced by the reaction with acids (olive-colored compounds) and with alkalies (chlorophyll-green carbonic acids). Thus by splitting with acid we are able to safeguard that component of chlorophyll which is separated by alkali. . . . On the other hand, the alkali derivatives of the dyestuff must retain a characteristic atom group which is destroyed by acid so easily and with such striking change of color. (18)

Magnesium, in an amount of nearly 3 percent, was established as an important part of the chlorophyll molecule. Magnesium is stable toward alkali, easily removed by acids, and bound not by the carboxyl group but by nitrogen. The nature of this bond was understandable on the basis of Werner's theory of primary and secondary valences. The basic structure of chlorophyll was closely related to that of the red pigment in hemoglobin. This was shown by the preliminary formulas for two products of gentle degradation (19):

```
                                          CH=CH
                                          |    |
  CH3·C—CH                                C————C
      ‖    \\                            //    ‖
      ‖      >N                        N<      ‖
      ‖     /   .                     .  \     ‖
  C2H5·C—C       .                  .     C————CH
          \\      .               .      //
            >C————.———————————.———C<
          /        .         .       \\
  C2H5·C=C           .     .           >C====C·C2H5
      |    \                           /       |
      |     >N————Mg————N<             |       |
      |    /                \          |       |
  CH3·C=C                    C=========C·CH3
          |                  |
         CH3                CH3
```

Ätiophyllin, $C_{31}H_{34}N_4Mg$

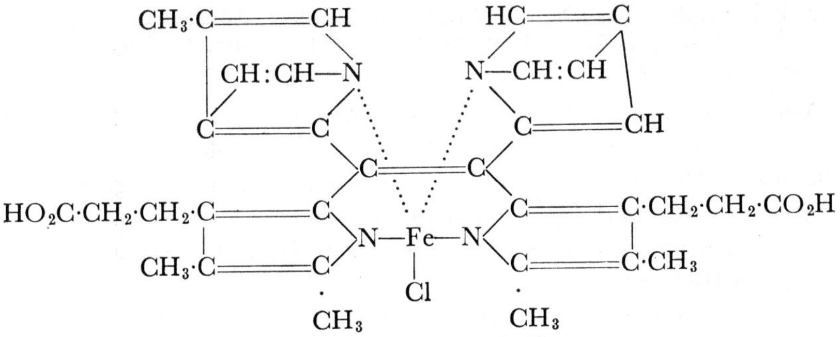

Hämin, $C_{33}H_{32}O_4N_4FeCl$

Anthocyanidine

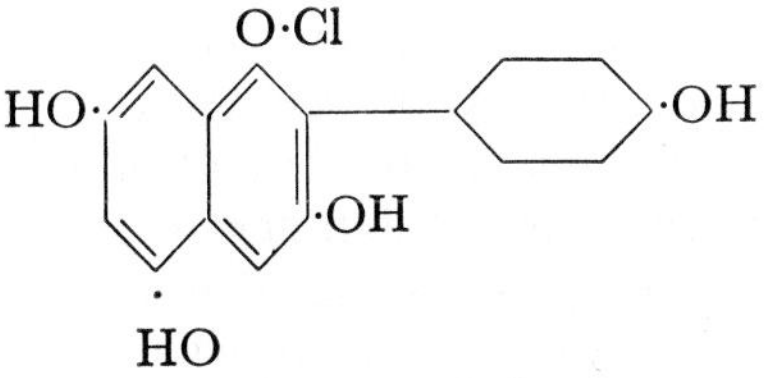

Pelargonidinchloride

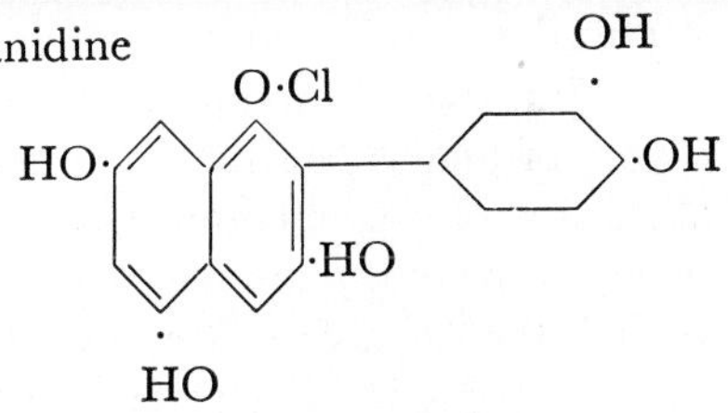

Cyanidinchloride

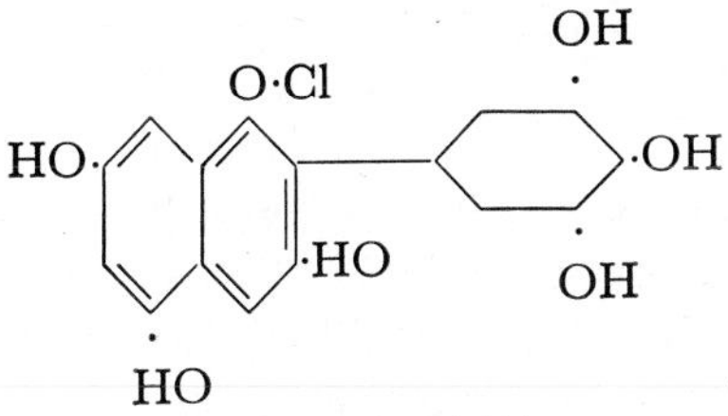

Delphinidinchloride

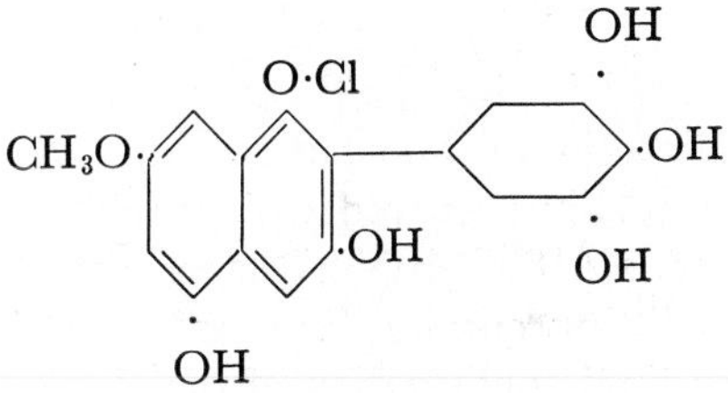

Myrtillidinchloride

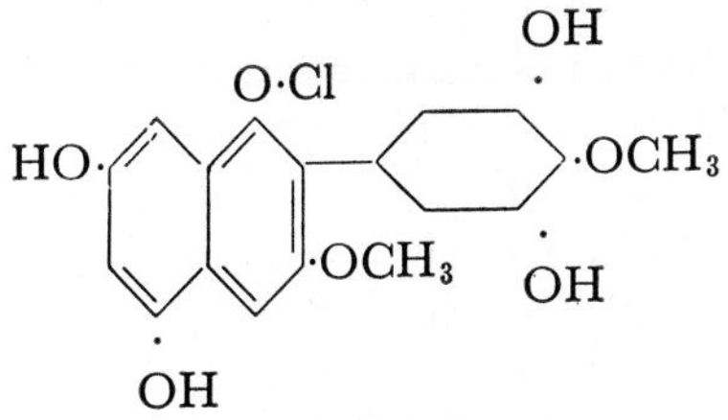

Oenidinchloride

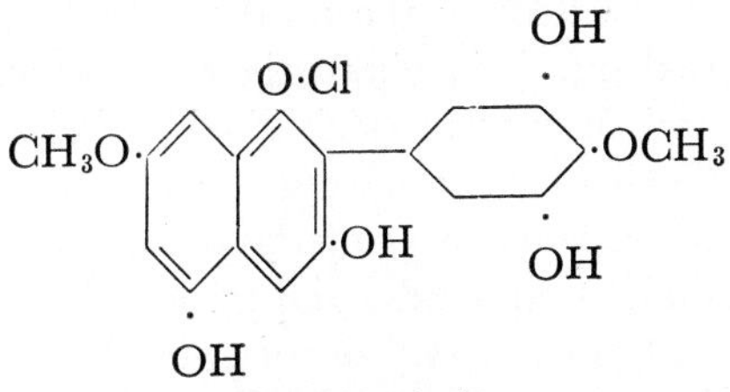

Malvidinchloride

Willstätter published his first report on chlorophyll from the laboratory of the Polytechnicum in Zurich in 1906. He continued it with many collaborators in Berlin-Dahlem at the Kaiser Wilhelm Institute for Chemistry, and in Munich after he became the successor of his old friend and teacher Adolf Baeyer (1916). In Dahlem he began to include the pigments of flowers and fruits. The materials were harvested from small plantations on the institute grounds, and great care was taken to exclude deterioration between collection and investigation. The new group of dyestuffs, the anthocyanins, showed a uniform principle of structure. Slight chemical changes in the molecule were found to account for the great variety of color in flowers. They differed chemically from chlorophyll, and they did not have its important function in the conversion of carbon dioxide and water into carbohydrates, to which Willstätter devoted intensive study (1918).

While there was no doubt that plant colors were due to the presence of chemically definable pigments, it appeared quite uncertain whether enzymes were substances, in the chemical meaning of the word. Enzymes were known by their specific catalytic action. The "active" part of a muscle tissue or a plant juice could be separated from inactive admixtures, but it was enveloped in greater mystery than "ordinary" chemical substances by its sensitivity to acidity or alkalinity of the medium and to heat. Diatase, from malt, was a widely used enzyme, but was it a substance? Willstätter was convinced that it was. Methods for measuring enzymatic action and concentrating it in a smallest amount of substance, separated from the natural material, gave results that confirmed his conviction. In his book on enzyme studies (20) he reported that enzyme purity could be increased many hundreds of times compared with the raw materials. The purifications were obtained with silica and alumina, specially prepared with specific adsorptive qualities. James B. Sumner's (1887–1955, Ithaca, New York) discovery in 1929 of the urea-splitting enzyme "urease" from jack beans in crystallized form gave a final confirmation of the chemical concept of enzymes as substances.

The chemistry of the anthocyanins was confirmed and further elaborated by the synthesis that Robert Robinson (1886–) carried out. At about the same time, the yellow pigments from carrots and lilies were established as belonging to a different group of great biochemical importance, the "carotenoids." Experiences in the field of terpenes, new methods for chemical synthesis by means of magnesium compounds, and improved analytical procedures were combined with measurements of refraction and absorption of light and with further developments of separation by adsorption. Thus the chemistry of the carotenoids took shape in the 1930's in work concentrated at the laboratories of Richard Kuhn (1900–1967), Willstätter's former student, in Heidelberg, and in Zurich at the laboratories of Paul Karrer (1889–), who had studied under Alfred Werner and had worked with Paul Ehrlich.

The constitution of hemin was cleared up in all details and verified by synthesis by the long work of Hans Fischer (1881–1945) in Munich, who died just before he could complete the same task for chlorophyll. This purely theoretical work had an unexpected industrial consequence. During the synthetic production of phthalimide by condensation of phthalic anhydride with ammonia in the plants of Scottish Dyes, Ltd., a dark blue "impurity" was often formed. The product contained iron from the reaction vessel. The basic information on hemin and chlorophyll made it possible to explore the chemistry of the blue "impurity" and to start the development of a new group of synthetic dyestuffs of exceptional stability, the phthalocyanines, a work that has been going on since 1928. Reginald Patrick Linstead (1902–1966, London) elucidated the chemistry of these phthalocyanines, and J. Monteath Robertson included them in his X-ray studies of organic compounds. In 1935 Robertson arrived at the following alternative structures for phthalocyanine (I and II) and for the copper compound (III and IV). In I and III there is an orthoquinonoid formation at *A* that is absent in II and IV, but this difference should not be taken too seriously:

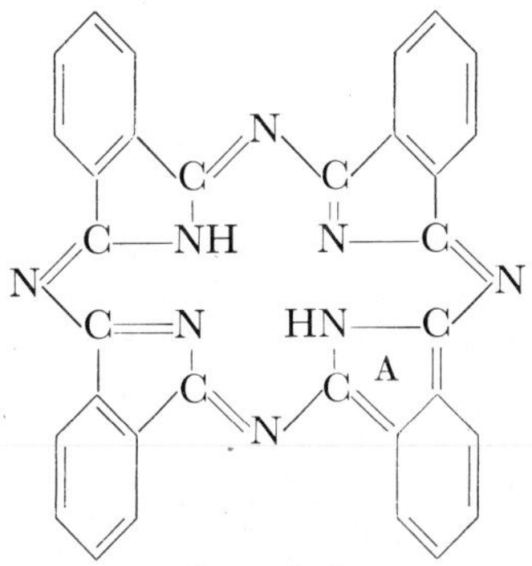

Formula I

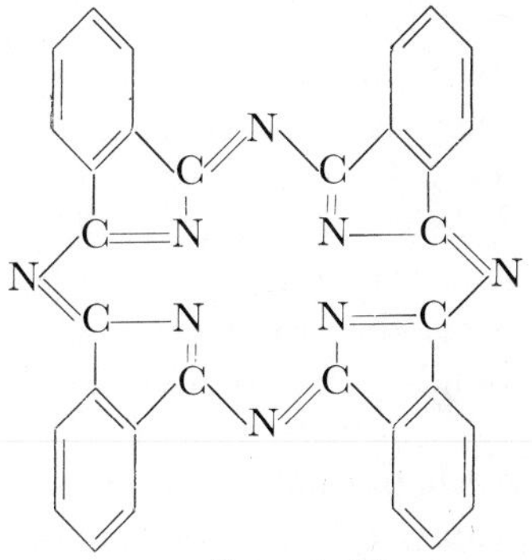

Formula II

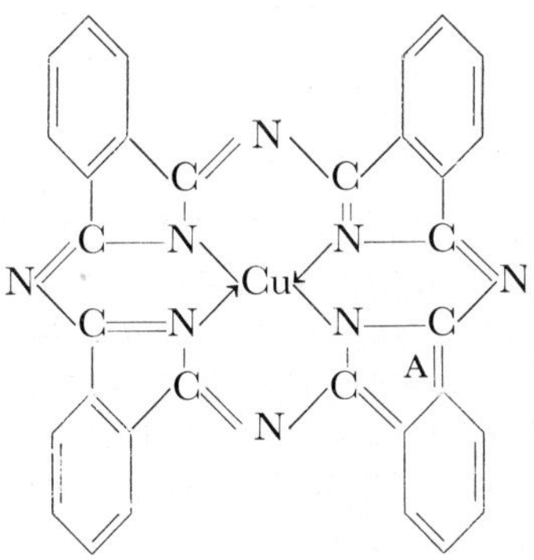

Formula III

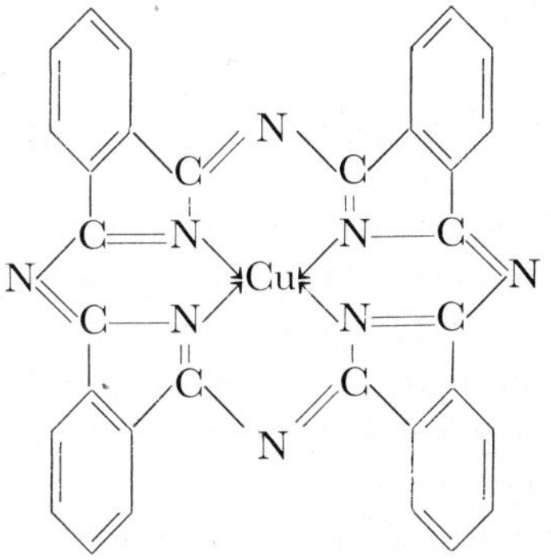

Formula IV

A few difficulties remain with regard to the fine structure. Formulæ (II) and (IV), which contain no imino-hydrogen and represent the metal atom as bound by four coordinate links, are perfectly centro-symmetrical and thus completely satisfy the crystal evidence; but Linstead shows that the chemical evidence and the physical properties of the copper compound are rather definitely in favour of (I) and (III), which necessitate one *o*-quinonoid and three benzenoid rings. The difficulty of reconciling these formulæ with the centro-symmetry display in the crystal is not, however, very great. The problem is analogous to that encountered in reconciling the ordinary Kekulé formula for benzene to the centro-symmetry displayed by symmetrically substituted benzene derivatives in the crystalline state. In the phthalocyanine structure we must regard the whole molecule as one continuously conjugated system, so that the *o*-quinonoid ring does not possess a definite location in the structure. This is not in conflict with the chemical evidence.

United States production of phthalocyanine dyes was about 10,000 pounds in 1941, 754,000 in 1958, and very nearly two million pounds in 1964.

The metals in complex organic bonds do not react in the normal way; they are "masked," as Carl Liebermann said. (22) Werner's theories led to intensified studies, such as those by Paul Pfeiffer (1875–1951, Bonn). Pfeiffer synthesized complexes of copper, nickel, or iron and cyclic aldehydes or ketones with hydroxy or amino groups in the ortho position. (23) Industrial application of such compounds followed with some delay. Although the catalytic effect of metals, in trace amounts, on the oxidative deterioration of fats and hydrocarbons had been known for some time, the inactivation of these catalysts by complexing began to be practiced mainly after 1940, but then the number of compounds and the fields of their use grew rapidly. (24)

Purines, Proteins, and Carbohydrates

The excretion of uric acid (page 182) had its physiological origin in proteins. Medical interest in the chemistry of uric acid was as great as the purely chemical one, particularly since an alkaloid, caffein, was closely related to uric acid. Besides, the alkaloid theobromin from cocoa forms caffein by introducing a methyl group, as Liebig's pupil A. F. L. Strecker (1822–1871) showed in 1861. Transformations by chlorine and methyl substitutions in the molecule of uric acid were the procedures by which Emil Fischer established the structural relationships of these substances. This work, which began in 1882, was complicated by the tautomerism of uric acid.

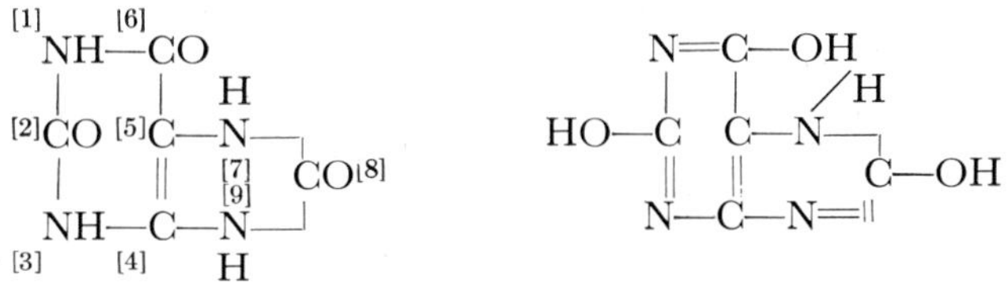

```
[1]     [6]
 NH—CO                           N=C—OH
 |    |   H                      |  |  /H
[2]CO [5]C—N—┐              HO—C  C—N—┐
 |    ||  [7] CO[8]              ||  ||     C—OH
 |    ||  [9]                    N—C—N=┘
 NH—C—N—┘
[3]  [4]  H
```

Besides, it proved very difficult to obtain specific reactions in position [8]. In 1897 the formula that Ludwig Medicus had anticipated twenty-two years earlier was proved. The methyl group that causes the difference between theobromin and caffein was located in position

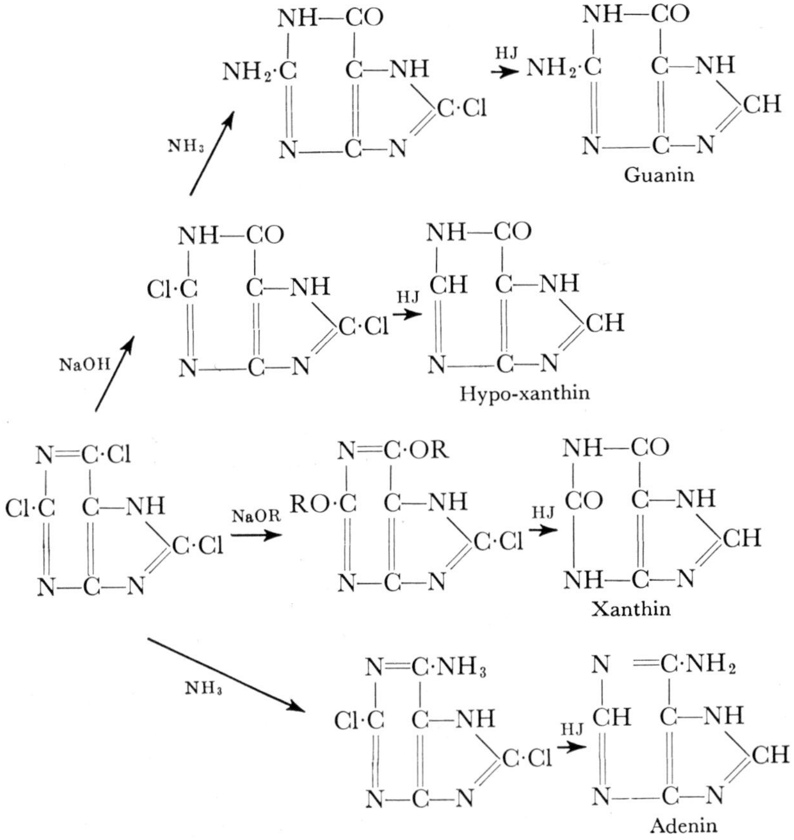

```
                 NH—CO                      NH—CO
                 |    |                     |    |
             NH2·C    C—NH      HJ      NH2·C    C—NH
                 ||   ||    \   →           ||   ||   \
                 ||   ||     >C·Cl          ||   ||    >CH
        NH3 ↗    N————C—N   /               N————C—N  /
                                                Guanin

         NH—CO                  NH—CO
         |    |                 |    |
     Cl·C     C—NH          HJ  CH   C—NH
         ||   ||   \        →   ||   ||  \
         ||   ||    >C·Cl       ||   ||   >CH
 NaOH ↗  N————C—N  /            N————C—N /
                                 Hypo-xanthin

     N=C·Cl                  N=C·OR                 NH—CO
     |  |                    |  |                   |    |
 Cl·C   C—NH        NaOR RO·C   C—NH         HJ     CO   C—NH
     ||  ||   \      →       ||  ||   \      →      |    ||   \
     ||  ||    >C·Cl         ||  ||    >C·Cl        |    ||    >CH
     N—C—N    /              N—C—N    /             NH—C—N    /
                                                      Xanthin

          NH3 ↘              N=C·NH3                N  =C·NH2
                             |  |                   |   |
                         Cl·C   C—NH          HJ    CH  C—NH
                             ||  ||   \       →     ||  ||   \
                             ||  ||    >C·Cl        ||  ||    >CH
                             N—C—N    /             N———C—N  /
                                                      Adenin
```

[1]. Caffein without the methyl in position [7] was identified with another alkaloid, theophyllin. Adenin, an alkaloid found in tea extract, could be structurally derived from the tautomeric form of uric acid, with hydrogen in place of its hydroxyls and with an amino group on carbon [6]. All these substances could be considered as derivatives of a *purum uricum,* which Fischer called "purine." He finally prepared it in 1898 by reducing the iodinated uric acid with zinc. (25) The demands of the chemical formulations were met. Pure substances were found which the system of organic chemistry permitted to be formulated on paper. A number of natural products were identified with their position in this system.

All those sytematic connections appeared at first as purely theoretical, but they influenced that other system of facts which is called "applied" or "practical." Julius von Mering had expected to obtain a sedative or sleep-inducing substance by attaching methyl groups to urea. Emil Fischer constructed a diethyl derivative of barbituric acid instead. It was successful as a medicament under the name "veronal" (1904) and, modified by substitution of a phenyl for one of the ethyl groups, as "luminal" (1906).

A few of the products obtained by the hydrolysis of proteins were known by analysis and synthesis. Jacob Volhard (1834–1910), Liebig's pupil and later his son-in-law, identified "sarkosin" (from Greek *sarx,* flesh) by synthesis from chlorinated acetic acid and methylamine ($H_2N—CH_3$):

$$\begin{array}{l} \;\;\mathrm{H} \\ \mathrm{HC—COOH} \\ \;\;\;| \\ \mathrm{HN—CH_3} \end{array}$$

in 1862. Hippuric acid is a benzoyl derivative of aminoacetic acid (glycine), as Victor Dessaignes (1800–1885, Paris) proved by synthesis in 1853. Theodor Curtius (1857–1928, Heidelberg) discovered that this synthesis also leads to products of higher condensation (1882). Amino acids can be esterified in the usual reaction with alcohol, containing as a catalyst hydrochloric acid. This acid combines with the amino group and can be removed by digestion with silver oxide. The method found by Theodor Curtius in 1883 was delicate and costly. When Emil Fischer substituted sodium hydroxide, under controlled conditions, for the silver oxide, he made it possible to obtain the esters of amino acids quickly and inexpensively. The esters were easily separated in pure form by distillation (1901).

The stereoisomers of the amino acids could not, however, be separated in the usual way. The influence of the basic amino group weakened the acidity of these acids so that they did not form salts with the optically active alkaloids. A preliminary reduction of the influence of the amino group was necessary. It was achieved by introducing acetyl groups in place of hydrogen in the amino group. The separation into the optical antipodes thus became feasible. Optically active alkaloids formed characteristic salts, and the optically active amino acids could be recovered from them. Hydrolysis of casein by sulfuric acid of 25 percent strength, and then with concentrated hydrochloric acid, gave a number of different amino acids, of which Emil Fischer and his collaborators identified and separated 70 percent. The knowledge of the products of hydrolysis opened the way toward synthesis. In 1907 Fischer succeeded in combining, in a chemically controlled manner, eighteen amino acid fractions to a peptide of molecular weight 1213. While excited reporters announced that the "greatest riddle of life" had been solved, Fischer knew and emphasized that no real protein had yet been produced artificially, not even silk fibroin, which appeared to be one of the simplest proteins. And while biologists had reason to doubt that the methods used in the investigations were adequate for the synthesis of a natural protein, Fischer's former pupils continued to explore the relationships between amino acids and the products of their syntheses. Emil Abderhalden (1877–1950, Halle) combined chemical with physiological research on the nutritive importance of each amino acid. Max Bergmann (1886–1944, Dresden, New York) extended it in physiocochemical directions and applied the methods, particularly to the investigation of hide and leather.

With the construction of purine as the "pure" model for a number of alkaloids, Emil Fischer used the same method as Wöhler and Liebig had used in 1838 with their urilic acid for the substances chemically related to uric acid. The perception of a unifying link in different substances again started an eventful search, when Johann Friedrich Miescher (1811–1887, Basle) in 1868 established the term "nuclein" for substances separated in a certain way from the nuclei of cells, e.g., of yeast, and Albrecht Kossel (1853–1927, Heidelberg) in 1879 obtained what he named "nucleic acids" from nuclein. Purines, phosphoric acid, and carbohydrates together formed these nucleic acids; their detailed elucidation thus depended on the developments in the chemistry of the carbohydrates.

One of the pure organic chemical substances produced in large quantities and at low cost is the crystallized sugar, saccharose, from beets and sugar cane. World production of this sugar was 10.8 million tons in 1895, 34.5 million tons in 1935. (26) Prices fluctuated under the influence of taxation and government regulation. (27) From the turn of the century to World War I, the price per pound was listed between 3.5 and 4.5 cents, including 1.685 cents duty. Great improvement in technical equipment, particularly for cane sugar, kept production increasing after the war.

Consumption of sugar in the United States has amounted to about a hundred pounds per person in recent years. Molasses, a by-product of sugar manufacture, formed an important raw material for the production of alcohol by fermentation. Between 1901 and 1926 the quantity of molasses used for alcohol production rose from 14 million to about 240 million gallons. The increase did not continue; influenced by the larger crops of other agricultural products, it declined in some of the later years.

Other carbohydrates produced in nearly pure form on a large scale are cotton, wood cellulose, and starch.

WORLD PRODUCTION OF CARBOHYDRATES
(in million short tons)

	1955	1958	1964
Sugar	42.9	50.9	63.7
Cotton	10.7	11.0	13.1
Wood Cellulose		37.1	58.5

Source: *Statistical Abstracts of the United States:* 1966, pp. 897, 914. The figure for Wood Cellulose excludes the U.S.S.R.

World production of starch (exclusive of the Soviet Union and its sphere of influence) was 4.050 million tons in 1963, about 58 percent from corn and 31 percent from potatoes.

The separation of two starch components, which Anselm Payen had already attempted in 1838, became more definite through the work of Léon Gervais Marie Maquenne (1853–1925, Paris): "Starch paste consists essentially in a perfect solution of amylose, thickened by an insoluble mucilage to which we have given the name amylopectin." (28) The names were derived from the Greek word for starch, *amylon*. Both components yield glucose on hydrolysis with acids or with the enzyme diastase.

Saccharose is easily hydrolyzed to the simpler sugars, glucose and fructose. This relationship was not adequately explained by the formula that Rudolf Fittig (1835–1910, Strasbourg) proposed in 1871:

$$C_6H_7\left\{\begin{array}{l}O\\(OH)_4\end{array}\right.$$

$$C_6H_7\left\{\begin{array}{l}O\\(OH)_4\\O\end{array}\right.$$

This juxtaposition of the C_6 sugars did not account for the fact that saccharose is a nonreducing sugar. Glucose and fructose reduce alkaline copper or silver solutions, due to the combination of aldehyde and hydroxyl groups. Saccharose does not have a free aldehyde group. Bernhard Tollens (1841–1911, Göttingen) therefore suggested in 1883 that the two parts are connected by a carbon-to-carbon bond. A. Wurtz had pointed to this possibility a few years before on the basis of an analogy to ethylene oxide and propylene oxide. A. Colley in 1870 had formulated glucose with an oxygen bridge between two different carbon atoms:

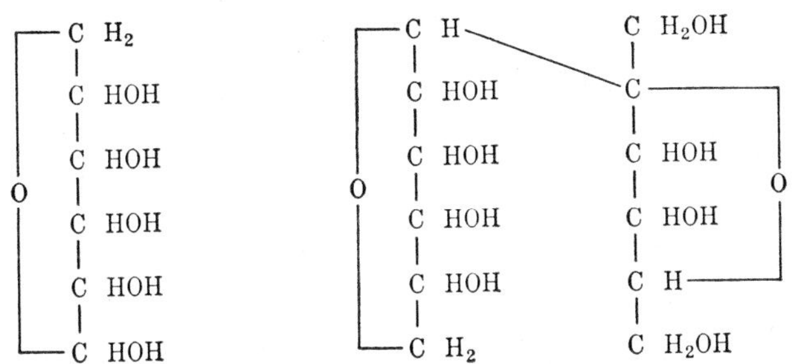

Colley's glucose formula

Tollens' saccharose formula

The oxygen bridge could explain why glucose does not readily give all the usual aldehyde reactions. The written formula showed, however, that much of it was still mere conjecture. If there were an oxygen bridge, it could connect any pair of the carbon atoms; and if there were a linkage as shown in the saccharose formula, the ease with which it is separated in hydrolysis would be without analogy. Besides, definite steric arrangements had to be found in order to explain the optical activity of the sugars.

An approach to these problems was facilitated by a new specific reaction which Emil Fischer found. Phenylhydrazine, $C_6H_5NHNH_2$, which he discovered in the course of his work on diazotation (1875), combined with simple sugars and gave crystallizable compounds. This proved to be a reaction by which these sugars could be separated and characterized. Reaction with methyl alcohol under precisely defined conditions gave derivatives which could be separated into optical isomer. The alcohol reacted with the aldehydic oxygen. These compounds, called "glucosides," existed in two complimentary asymmetric forms which were distinguishable by enzymes (Edward Frankland Armstrong, in 1901). (29) Definite assignment of the relative positions for the hydrogen and hydroxyl groups around the carbon atoms was the goal. In order to reach it, comparisons between all the known simple sugars were necessary. Reactions such as those that Heinrich Kiliani found in oxidation or in combination with prussic acid were used to arrive at a three-dimensional model of the sugars. Projection of the tetrahedral structure on the plane of paper gave Fischer the sterical formula for the dextrorotatory glucose in 1891 (39):

$$
\begin{array}{rl}
 & \mathrm{H} \\
 & \mathrm{C^1{=}O} \\
 & | \\
\mathrm{H} & \mathrm{C^2OH} \\
 & | \\
\mathrm{HO} & \mathrm{C^3H} \\
 & | \\
\mathrm{H} & \mathrm{C^4OH} \\
 & | \\
\mathrm{H} & \mathrm{C^5OH} \\
 & | \\
\mathrm{H} & \mathrm{C^6OH} \\
 & \mathrm{H}
\end{array}
$$

D-Glucose

Even then the formula was not complete. The oxygen bridge had to be provided. In accordance with Baeyer's strain theory, it was assumed that it combined carbon 1 with carbon 4. The two methyl glucosides were then assigned by Fischer the following structural formulas:

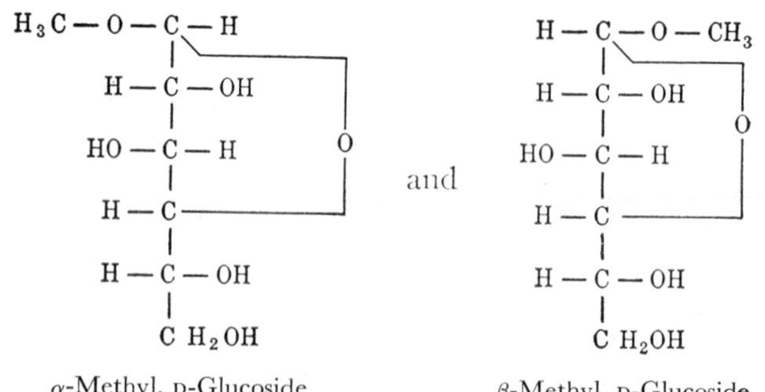

α-Methyl, D-Glucoside β-Methyl, D-Glucoside

By oxidation in the aldehyde position to the corresponding acid, rearrangement by aqueous pyridine, and reduction back to the aldehyde by means of sodium amalgam, the predicted series of pentoses was realized. For the names, the letters were rearranged like the hydroxyl groups:

```
    CHO            CHO            CHO            CHO
     ·              ·              ·              ·
   H | OH         H | OH        HO | H         HO | H
  HO | H         HO | H         HO | H         HO | H
  HO | H          H | OH        HO | H          H | OH
     ·              ·              ·              ·
   CH2·OH         CH2·OH         CH2·OH         CH2·OH
  Arabinose       Xylose         Ribose         Lyxose
```

Ribose is the pentose sugar in the nucleic acids studied by Phoebus Aaron Theodor Levine (1869–1940, New York); they are combined "mononucleotides" like inosinic and guanylic acid (31*a*):

```
                                                         N—C—N
                         H    H    H                   //  ||  ||
      /OH                ·    ·    ·              CH<      ||  ||
O=P———————O—CH2—CH—C———C———CH————————N—C  CH
      \OH                |    ·    ·    |                   |   |
                         |   OH  OH    |O                 OC—NH
                         |_____________|
                          Inosinic acid

                                                      N—C—N
                       H   H    H                   //  ||  ||
      /OH              ·   ·    ·              CH<      ||  ||
O=P———————O—CH2—C—C———C———CH————N—C  C(NH2)
      \OH              |   ·    ·    |                |   |
                       |  OH  OH    |O              OC—NH
                       |____________|
                        Guanylic acid
```

In the years 1920 to 1930, Horace S. Isbell (1898–   ) and Claude S. Hudson (1881–1952, Washington, D.C.) reduced the uncertainties of this model still further. The properties of the acids obtained by oxidation could best be explained with an oxygen bridge linking carbons 1 and 5. The perspective formula of W. N. Haworth (1883–1949, Birmingham) gave a truer representation of the glucose molecule (1929):

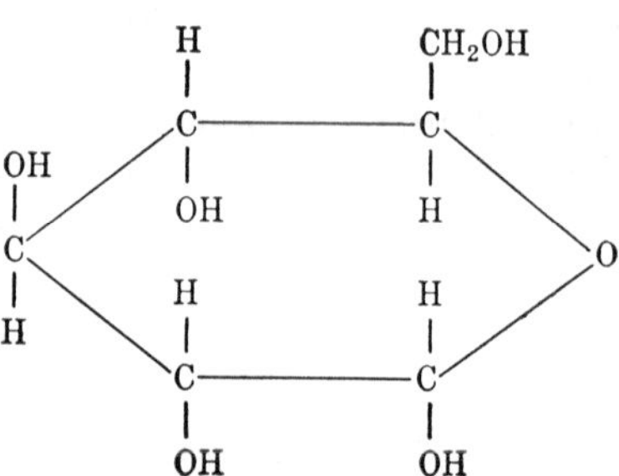

Haworth's glucose formula

These formulations expressed many relationships between derivatives and the large group of other sugars. The saccharides, which are composed of several simple sugar, offered additional problems.

By complete hydrolysis, starch can be converted into the same simple sugar, glucose, as cellulose. A gradual hydrolysis, however, gives starch in the form of the "double" sugar, maltose, when cellulose forms cellobiose. The difference between these two bioses was completely explained by Haworth as one of the steric arrangements. The question of how many molecules of glucose, or maltose and cellobiose, respectively, were combined in starch and in cellulose remained.

The question could be formulated because of all the preceding work on molecular structure and the theory of polymerism; the answer could be approached by combining many experimental methods and coordinating their results. Röntgen spectra revealed to R. Herzog a crystalline structure in cellulose. The viscosity of dissolved cellulose derivatives, particularly the nitrates and acetates, could be interpreted in its functional indication of the size of the molecules. The rate at which cellulose splits into simple sugars under the influence of dilute acids could be regarded as being related to the degree of polymerization, according to Karl J. Freudenberg (1886–). Purely chemical methods were designed to show whether the glucose molecules were arranged in chains or in rings. A chain has end groups which differ from the links; a ring consists of equal members. Models were built to show mechanically possible molecular structures and to indicate experiments for their verification.

The many-sided efforts, especially from 1925 to 1935, to elucidate the structure of cellulose and starch led to the concept of the macromolecule. Hermann Staudinger (1881–1965, Freiburg) converted these substances into derivatives and reconstituted them without change in their properties. The derivatives were therefore "polymer-analogues." The chemical unit that can pass unchanged through chemical operations shows itself to be held together by ordinary valences, a molecule in these cases formed of hundreds of glucose parts. Freudenberg had proved that the glucose units in cellulose formed a next higher unit of cellobiose, and Haworth had shown its structure as a 4-glucosidyl-glucose. The chemical "formula" for cellulose, therefore (with the value of x up to 1000 for "native," undegraded products), was

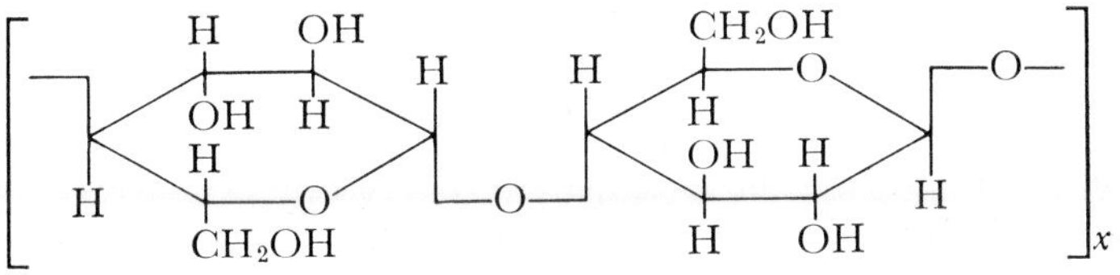

H OH CH$_2$OH
H H O O
OH H H
H OH H
H O O H
CH$_2$OH H OH
x

Its steric arrangement was revealed by the X-ray spectra.

By extraction with dilute aqueous alkali solutions, Braconnot in 1811 obtained from mushrooms a substance which he named "fungin." This name was changed in 1823 to "chitin," from the Greek word meaning armor. The choice of this word proved particularly appropriate when Berthelot found the same substance in the shell of lobsters. G. Ledderhose, working in Hoppe-Seyler's laboratory, treated it with hydrochloric acid, which split off acetic acid and converted the substance into the hydrochloride of a glucosamine (1876). Oswald Schmiedeberg (1839–1921, Strasbourg) prepared the free amine in 1891.

In mucus and cartilege, amines of glucose and other hexoses were discovered, especially by P. A. Levine. (31*b*) The acetylglucosaminyl group, derived from

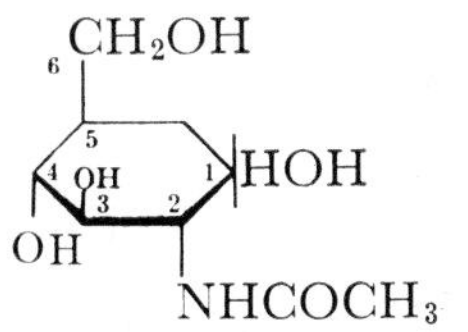

^{6}CH$_2$OH
5
4 OH 3 2 1 HOH
OH
NHCOCH$_3$

N-acetyl-D-glucosamine

is present in the blood-group substances, which Karl Landsteiner (1868–1943, New York) first described in 1900. (32)

Around 1860 Paul Schützenberger heated cellulose or sugar with ammonia and obtained something resembling an albuminoid. He thought he had thereby confirmed the hypothesis of Thomas Sterry

Hunt (1826–1892, New York) expressed in the formula:

Albuminoids = Cellulose + Ammonia − Water

Other chemists were not as ambitious to synthesize proteins and sought, instead, to find characteristic color reactions. Mulder gave the name "xanthoproteinic acid" to the "yellow acid" that Fourcroy and Vauquelin had seen when they brought proteins together with nitric acid. After Mulder's work of 1837, Nicolas Auguste Eugène Millon (1812–1867) in Paris described a test with an acidic solution of mercury nitrate containing nitrous acid, which gave a red color with proteins (1851). Particularly valuable among many other color tests was that discovered by Siegfried Ruhemann (1859–1943, Cambridge, England). He was studying derivatives of 1,3-diketohydrindene. Among them was the triketohydrate,

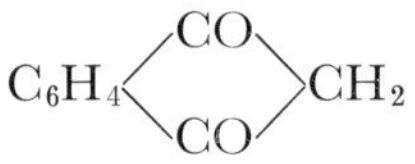

$$C_6H_4\begin{matrix} CO \\ CO \end{matrix}CH_2 \qquad\qquad C_6H_4\begin{matrix} CO \\ CO \end{matrix}C(OH)\cdot CN$$

1,3-diketohydrindene 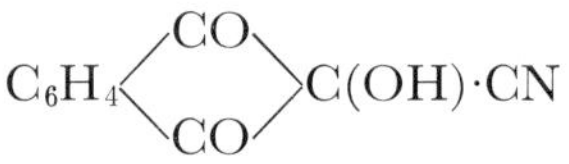 — Cyanhydrine of triketohydrindene

which he characterized by the product of its reaction with hydrocyanic acid, and which gave a blue color with α-amino acids $R \cdot CH(NH_2) \cdot COOH$. He published this study in 1910. (33) Recently, Frederick Sanger (1918–) found in 1-fluoro-2,4-dinitrobenzene a reagent that gave crystallized compounds with amino acids, and with their help he succeeded in identifying the sequence of the amino acids in insulin. (34)

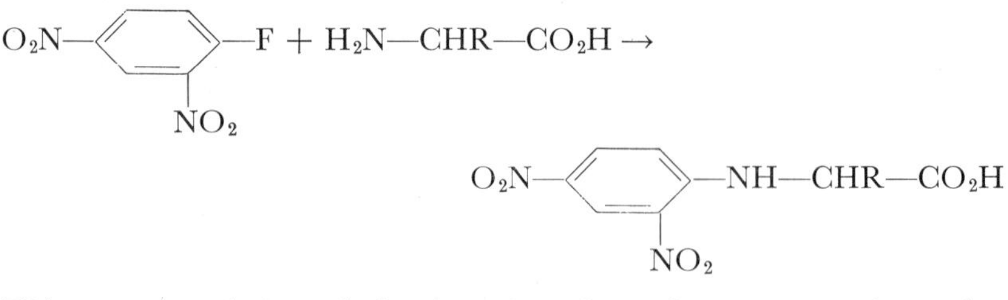

$$O_2N\text{—}C_6H_3(NO_2)\text{—}F + H_2N\text{—}CHR\text{—}CO_2H \rightarrow O_2N\text{—}C_6H_3(NO_2)\text{—}NH\text{—}CHR\text{—}CO_2H$$

This represented the culmination of work on the structure of proteins that had been the goal for many decades. (35)

Synthetic Polymers

The extensive scientific research on high polymers was to a considerable extent supported by a new chemical industry which had its origin in several ingenious discoveries and which needed more basic information as it grew. The first of these discoveries consisted in a mere mixture. In 1868 John Wesley Hyatt found that a nitrocellulose, "pyroxilin," acquired greatly improved plastic properties when it was mixed with camphor and a little alcohol. In 1897 W. Krische and A. Spitteler observed that casein can be hardened and made more permanent by a treatment with formaldehyde. Reactions between phenol and formaldehyde, which A. Baeyer had studied in 1878, were found by Leo H. Baekeland (1863–1944) to offer great industrial possibilities. Baekeland had studied and taught chemistry in Ghent before he came to New York in 1889. His first great success was the photographic paper "Velox" that was printable in artificial light. He demonstrated molded articles and varnishes prepared from phenol-formaldehyde resins in 1909. In 1918, at the end of the war, a large surplus of phenol was on hand. It amounted to over twenty thousand tons. This was soon consumed in manufacturing the new resins for which the expanding production of cabinets for radio receivers offered a great market.

Alfred Einhorn (1857–1917, Munich) described methylol compounds of urea in 1908, but the development of urea-formaldehyde resins began only about ten years later. These and the phenol-formaldehyde resins could be prepared in an intermediate form and mixed with wood flour or mineral fillers. Heating in molds under pressure then converted them into the final, irreversibly "set" products.

Attempts to produce "synthetic" rubber began in 1912, mainly in Germany and with the aim of independence from importations. Polymerization of butadiene with sodium ("Natrium") gave a kind of rubber which the Badische Anilin-und Soda-Fabrik sold under the name Buna. The polymerization of styrene and indene

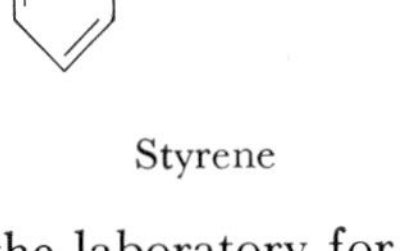

—$CH{=}CH_2$

Styrene

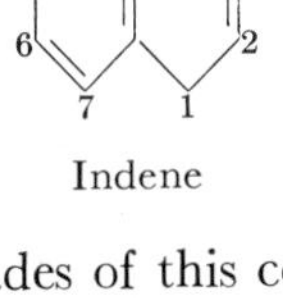

4 5 3 6 2 7 1

Indene

remained in the laboratory for the first decades of this century. The theory for these polymerizations first used Kekulé's ideas of intermediary addition compounds with the catalysts, although it was pointed out that the conditions of these reactions precluded actual addition compounds. (36) The widening of valence theory, the experience with "free" radicals, and the recognition of macromolecules led to new concepts of polymerizations.

Another new concept emerged from the effort to prevent a polymerization. In 1920 François Charles Léon Moureu (1863–1929,

Paris) published the results of his war work on acrolein. For its use as a lacrimator, it had to be kept monomeric. Moureu and his group achieved this by counteracting the effect of oxygen. Small proportions of hydroquinone or naphthols acted as "antixodiants," or better, antioxygens. The use of specific antioxygens spread to the protection of rubber, gasoline, lubricating oil, and more recently, foods as well.

The successful poly-condensation by means of formaldehyde gave mainly materials for molding. For films and fibers, cellulose remained the basis for chemical modifications. Carboxymethylcellulose, from the reaction with monochloroacetic acid under alkaline conditions, became a competitor to methyl cellulose in 1934 for use

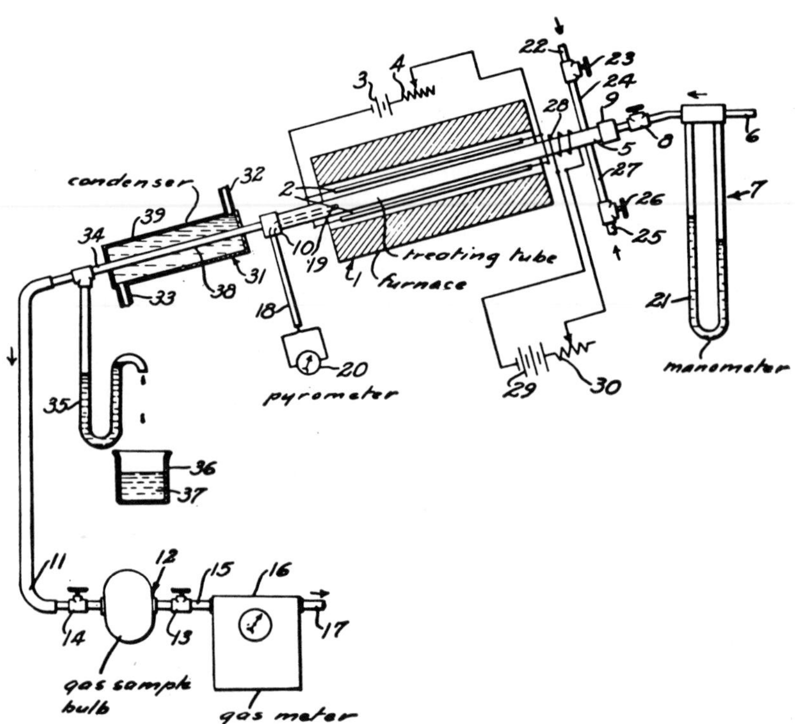

Fig. 43. Laboratory apparatus for producing acetylene from other hydrocarbons, according to Robert G. Wulff, U.S. patent 1,843,965, filed Oct. 1, 1928.

Steam from *22* and hydrocarbon from *25* pass through treating tube *5*. The mixture is heated to over 1500°F by coil *28* and heating elements *2* in the furnace. The products are quickly cooled, separated from condensate *35*, passed through gas meter *16*, and through *17* to storage.

as a textile finish, soap additive or substitute, and general thickener. These developments were more influenced by the technical progress in producing high-grade cellulose than in its scientific elucidation.

At about that time, interest in the true polymerization of unsaturated hydrocarbons turned to small molecules, especially to acetylene as the most versatile starting material. Ample quantities were available from calcium carbide; an additional source was the partial oxidation of other hydrocarbons, as by the Wulff process. The technique of partial oxidation had first been developed (1905) for the production of formaldehyde from methanol. During the following twenty-five years, this technique was extended to naphthalene and the xylenes for the production of phthalic acids. Special problems remained with the highly sensitive and explosive acetylene. The addition of hydrochloric acid to vinyl chloride, of hydrocyanic acid to acrylonitrile, looked obvious on paper but required good engineering on a large scale. The development of polymers derived from acetylene was a special feature in the work of the I. G. Farbenindustrie A.G. in the late 1930's. The polymerization of styrene was also actively pursued.

In England, polyethylene became a technical product in 1936; it was produced under high pressures, with oxygen from the air as the carefully controlled catalyst. The partial oxidation of paraxylene to terephthalic acid—"tere-" because this phthalic acid was first obtained from terpenes—provided the skeleton in the polyesters from which terylene fibers started their great industrial life in 1941.

At the Wilmington, Delaware, laboratories of E. I. du Pont de Nemours & Co., William Hume Carothers (1895–1937) combined vinylacetylene with HCl to get a product that he called "chloroprene"

$$CH_2{:}\underset{}{\overset{\overset{\displaystyle Cl}{|}}{C}}{\cdot}CH{:}CH_2$$

Chloroprene

because of its analogy with isoprene, and polymerized it to a strong rubber. Shortly thereafter, he and J. W. Hill condensed polyamides with polycarboxylic acids to polymeric polyamines, which after 1935 became industrial products under the generic name of nylon (37):

. . .—NH—R—CO—NH—R′—CO—NH—R—CO—NH—R′—CO—. . .

Silk (polyamide)

. . .—O—R—CO—O—R—CO—O—R—CO—O—R—CO—O—R—CO—. . .

Polyester (from hydroxy acid)

. . .—O—R—O—CO—R′—CO—O—R—O—CO—R′—CO—

Polyester (from dibasic acid and glycol)

. . .—O—R—CO—NH—R′—CO—NH—R′—CO—O—R—CO—. . .

Mixed polyester-polyamide

During World War II, copolymers of butadiene and styrene, for special uses also with acrylonitrile, supplanted natural rubber and were later developed on their own merits. The handling of the starting materials and the testing of the products were carefully planned, but the methods of polymerizing and the selection of catalysts were often the results of accidents.

Avery A. Morton (1892–) described it as an accident that he found the catalytic action of amylsodium on butadiene. (38) He stirred a solution of butadiene in pentane into amylsodium dissolved in isopropyl ether, and "within seconds . . . a band of rubber completely insoluble and nonswelling in all common solvents . . wrapped around the propeller." Generalizing from sodium to alkali metal, and from amyl to olefin, he coined the name Alfin for this group of polymerization catalysts.

Karl Ziegler (1898–) had been studying metalorganic compounds for years when an accidental discovery in his institute at Mülheim (Ruhr) in 1954 showed that alkylaluminum compounds with a small impurity of nickel catalyzed the polymerization of ethylene at normal atmospheric pressure. This led to the deliberate addition of titanium salts to trialkylaluminum and the production of polyethylenes of very high molecular weight without the use of high pressures. (39)

The United States production of polystyrenes rose from about 10 million pounds in 1942 to 495 in 1946, 800 in 1953, and 1728 in 1964. Again in millions of pounds, vinyl resins, including copolymers, rose from 530 in 1954 to 870 in 1958 and to 2050 in 1964; polyesters from about 117 in 1958 to 316 in 1964. The rise in polyolefins was equally spectacular, from 865 million pounds in 1958 to about 2900 in 1964. Among other newcomers were the silicone resins, the polyurethans, the epoxies, the acrylics, and the polyamides derived from caprolactams. Plastics derived from cellulose had a somewhat modest share, with about 161 million pounds in 1964. The invention and production of auxiliary materials, like plasticisers, antioxidants, and other protective agents, expanded similarly.

During these developments, and to a great extent responsible for them, scientific research was expanded to the correlation of spectroscopically evaluated atomic bond strengths with the macroscopic behavior of materials and the regulation of the spatial arrangement in the macromolecules to produce stereospecific polymers. Hermann Mark (1895–) contributed greatly to the first, Giulio Natta (1895–) to the second of these advances.

Ethereal and Mineral Oils

ETHEREAL OILS. Turpentine and the oils obtained from plants by steam distillation are composed of carbon and hydrogen. A connection between these ethereal oils and india rubber (caoutchouc) came to light when Charles Greville Williams (1829–1910) obtained as a product of its thermal decomposition a low-boiling hydrocarbon which he named "isoprene" without giving any reason for his choice. He stated the unsaturated character and a "polymeric relation between isoprene and caoutchin" in his work of 1860. Gustave Bouchardat,

$$\begin{array}{l} H_3C \searrow \\ \quad\quad\quad C\text{—}CH\text{=}CH_2 \\ H_2C \nearrow\!\!\!\nearrow \ \ (2) \quad (3) \quad\ (4) \\ (1) \end{array}$$

Isoprene

(1842–1918) confirmed this "relation" by making a rubber from isoprene (Paris, 1879). The chemical formula for this oil, C_5H_8, suggested to Berthelot that it was the simplest type of terpene. The polymerisation of isoprene gave terpenes of the formula $C_{10}H_{16}$ and sesquiterpenes, $C_{15}H_{24}$, built from three molecules of isoprene. Gustave Bouchardat actually produced terpenes from isoprene by heating it, under pressure, to temperatures of 280°C (1879).

When Kekulé converted the terpene, from which this group of hydrocarbons received its name, into "cymene" (1872), he showed that terpene is a benzene derivative with a methyl and an isopropyl group, present, as in cymene, in para position. Menthol from peppermint leaves and camphor from the wood of the camphor tree (*Cinnamomum camphora*) are solids at ordinary temperatures, "coagulated" ethereal oils, in the language of the seventeeth century.

Kekulé found that camphor, a ketone, can be converted into *p*-cymene (and carvacrol, a derivative of menthol), and he formulated camphor accordingly. Stepwise oxidation showed, however, that the carbon atoms of the methyl and isopropyl groups were not freely attached to the hydroaromatic ring, but formed a second ring within it. C. Julius Bredt (1855–1937, Aachen) introduced the concept of the bicyclic structure with his camphor formula (1893). Synthesis verified this structure. A synthetic production of camphor had been sought for a long time; Berthelot had produced it from the hydrochloride of pinene, the main constituent of pine oils, by oxidizing the intermediately formed camphene (1869). Scientific and economic interests were combined in these efforts to manufacture a substance on which Japan had a monopoly and which was used in medicine and in the plastics industry.

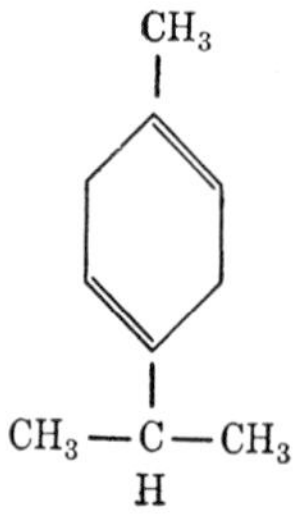

Terpene
Kekulé (1872)

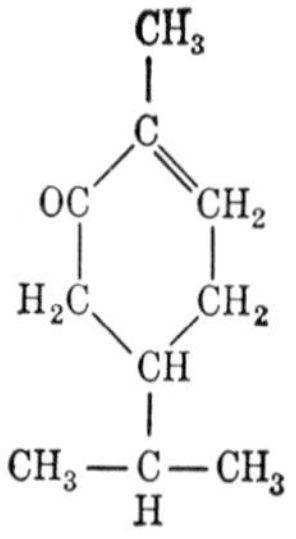

Camphor
Kekulé (1873)

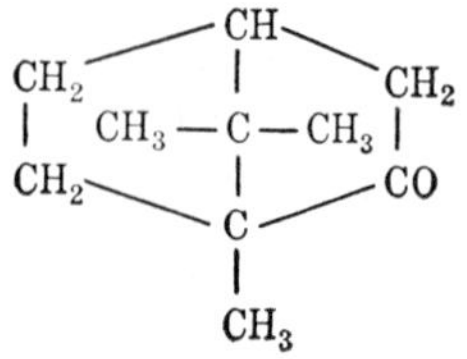

Camphor
Bredt (1893)

These dual interests supported each other in the systematic work on terpenes to which Otto Wallach (1847–1931, Bonn) devoted a life-time of research. Industry needed methods for identifying ethereal oils by the pure substances that could be separated from them. Falsification could thus be detected; new compositions could be produced. A comparison of the new system of ethereal oils with the plants from which they came showed that chemically similar substances could be obtained from botanically different sources.

William Augustus Tilden (1842–1926, London) obtained crystallizing products from terpenes when he combined them with nitrosylchloride. He described the reaction in 1875, the year in which Emil Fischer discovered phenylhydrazine. The nitrosylchloride method became as helpful in terpene chemistry as the phenylhydrazine method in the study of carbohydrates.

The isoprene rule, which Berthelot had formulated and which Wallach confirmed, found a new and wider application by Leopold Ruzicka (1887–). The following is one of his examples for "the regular coordination" of three isoprene molecules to farnesol or cadalin (40):

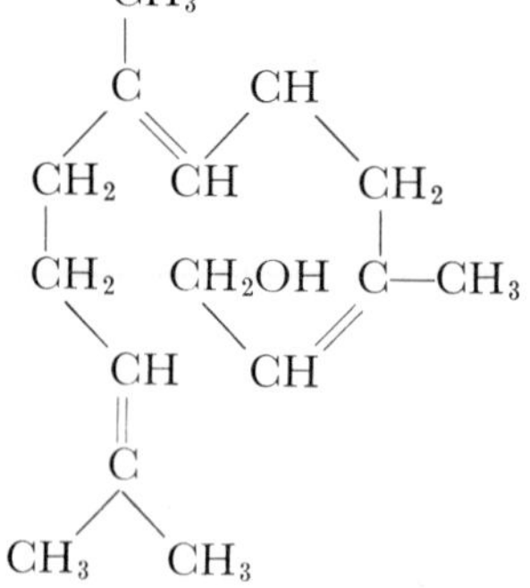

Farnesol

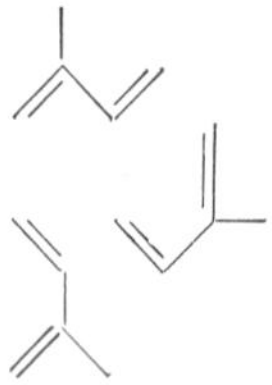

Three
Isoprene Molecules

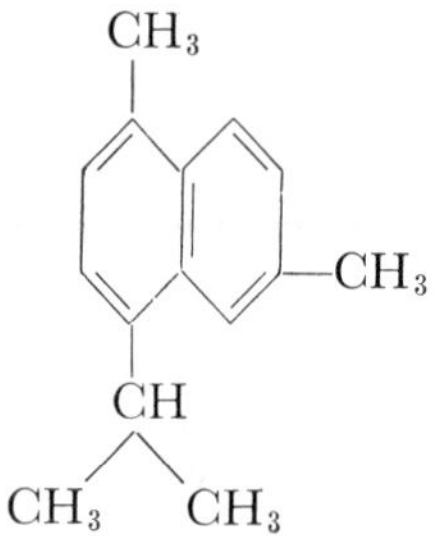

Cadalin

In the unsaponifiable matter from the oils, particularly from the liver of elasmobranch fish such as sharks and rays, Ian Morris Heilbron (1886–1959, London) found a highly unsaturated hydrocarbon, "squalene." Paul Karrer synthesized it by treating farnesyl bromide with magnesium. (41) Squalene is built from isoprene units, in a symmetric arrangement of "head to tail" (carbons 1:4) and "tail to head" (carbons 4:1) arrangements: (1:4)—(1:4)—(1:4)—(4:1)—(4:1)—(4:1):

H_3C CH_3 CH_3 CH_3 CH_3 CH_3 H_3C CH_3

Squalene

Mineral Oils. While the production of mineral-energy fuels has increased greatly during this century (Fig. 44), the production from waterpower has been constantly low. During the first two decades of this century, the mineral-energy fuels produced in the continental United States came from bituminous coal and lignite, whereas in subsequent years crude petroleum and natural gas were the growing sources.

The world production of crude petroleum increased tenfold from 1910 to 1949 and threefold during the subsequent 25 years. From

PRODUCTION OF CRUDE PETROLEUM

(in million barrels of 42 U.S. gallons)

Year	United States	World	United States (in percent)
1910	210	328	64.0
1919	378	556	68.0
1929	1,007	1,486	68.0
1939	1,265	2,006	60.6
1949	1,840	3,398	54.2
1960	1,575	7,689	33.5
1964	2,785	10,328	27.0

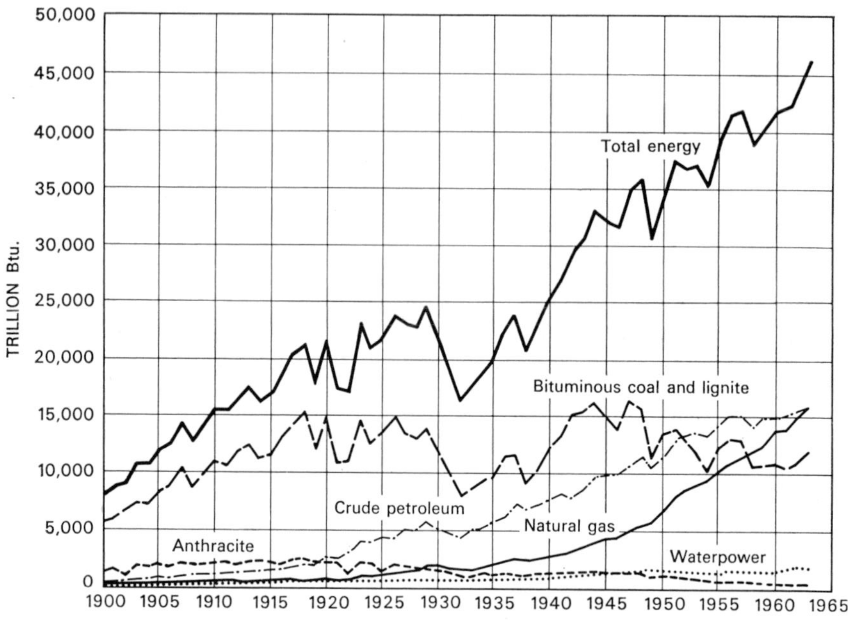

Fig. 44. Production of mineral-energy fuels and energy from waterpower in the continental United States, 1900–1963. (From the 1963 *Minerals Yearbook,* Vol. II: Fuels, U.S. Department of the Interior, Bureau of Mines.)

the early drillings in Rumania in 1857 and in the United States in 1859 to the end of 1955, about 3768 billion gallons of petroleum were taken out of the earth, 2210 billion of them in this country. (42) For 1964 alone, the corresponding figures were 444 billion gallons for the world, 116 billion for the United States.

For the separation of the crude petroleum, with its composition varying with the geographic origin, into fractions for fuels, solvents, tars, and asphalt, distillation was only a first step. Refining operations used treatments with sulfuric acid, adsorption on clays and carbons, or extractions by solvents. Lazar Edeleanu (1861–1941) developed the extraction of aromatic compounds by liquid sulfur dioxide in 1907. Toluene for TNT (trinitrotoluene) was in very short supply during World War I. Heat treatments, as by the Burton process (Fig. 45) increased the yields in motor fuels.

Old-timers at the drilling rigs know many tales about improvements that resulted from unscheduled changes of operating conditions by a negligent night crew. In general, however, this industrial development was closely linked with scientific research. This is particularly true of the catalytic processes, to which Vladimir N. Ipatieff (1867–1952, Chicago) contributed prominently. With the use of specific catalysts, the yields in aliphatic and aromatic compounds could be tailored to many requirements. (43) In the Houdry processes, silicates were the preferred catalysts. (44)

Catalysts were also added directly to the gasoline, especially tetraethyl lead, which Thomas Midgley (1889–1944, Columbus, Ohio) introduced in 1923. The single invention of tetraethyl lead increased the available horsepower of the automobile engines made in the year 1941 by an amount equal to seventy-five Boulder Dams! (45)

As lubricants, mineral oils were originally regarded as substitutes for vegetable oils. In automobile races, castor oil was the preferred lubricant as late as 1936. Scientific research on lubrication received

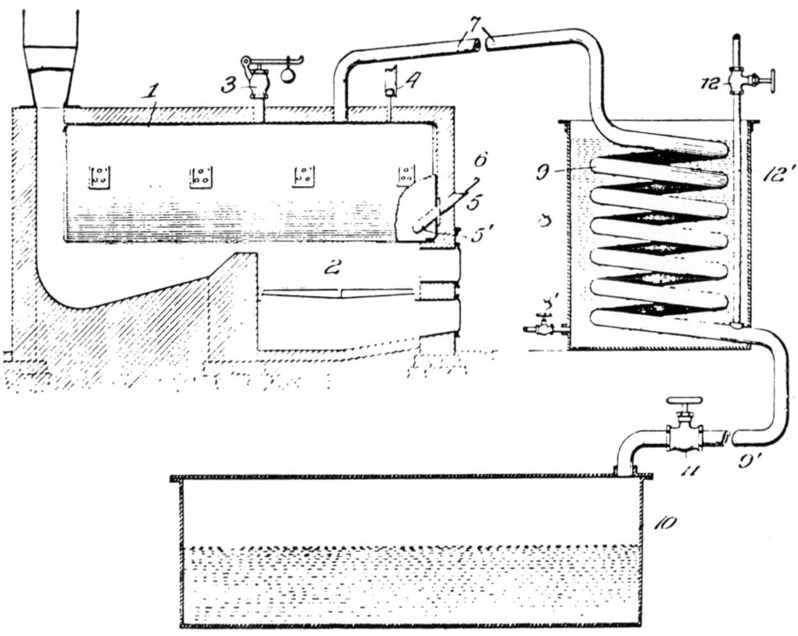

Fig. 45. "Manufacture of Gasolene" according to William M. Burton, U.S. Patent 1,049,667, filed July 3, 1912.

Petroleum distillates with boiling points above 260°F are heated, under pressure, to 315°–425°F through fire chamber *2* in boiler *1* equipped with safety valve *3,* pressure gauge *4,* and thermometer *6* in well *5.* A conduit *7* leads the vapors to condenser *8* through coil *9* into receiver *10* for the condensed product. Valve *11* is opened from time to time to release the product of low boiling point manufactured by the process.

a new impulse through the expansion of automobile production. Terms like "unctuousness," "oiliness," "lubricity" were used to indicate a property that was gradually correlated with molecular form, viscosity, surface tension, and film strength. Results were rather confusing for a long time. Lubricating oils were compounded with substances that would extend their usefulness over a wide range of temperatures and reduce secondary changes through oxidation. It was said in 1937 that "the crankcase oil of the future should be made with the same precision and understanding that metallic alloys are made today." (46)

Lubrication at the interfaces in motors is one of the important conditions for energy generation; the other condition, still more generally important, is the air used for combustion and for carrying its products. With the growth of industrial operations, we have become increasingly concerned with the need to keep air pollution down. Mainly from combustion, about 40 million tons of sulfur dioxide were discharged into the air over the United States in 1967. Here are new tasks for chemical engineering.

REFERENCES

1. Adolphe Wurtz, "On oxide of ethylene, considered as a link between organic and mineral chemistry," A discourse delivered to the Fellows of the Chemical Society of London, June 5, 1862, *J. Chem. Soc.,* **15** (1862), pp. 387–406, esp. p. 406.

2. G. Wagner and A. Saytzeff, "Synthese des Diäthylcarbinols, eines neuen Isomeren des Amylalkohols," *Liebig's Ann.,* **175** (1875), pp. 351–74.

3. A. Cahours, *Ann. Chim.* (3), **58** (1860), pp. 5–82.

4. Victor Grignard, "Combinaisons organo-magnésiennes mixtes et leur application à la synthèse d'acides, d'alcohols, et d'hydrocarbones," *Ann. Chim.* (7), **24** (1901), pp. 433–90.

5. Hugo Kauffmann, *Die Valenzlehre* (Stuttgart: Ferdinand Enke, 1911).

6. C. Graebe and C. Liebermann, "Über den Zusammenhang zwischen molekularer Constitution und Farbe bei organischen Verbindungen," *Chem. Ber.,* **1** (1868), pp. 106–8.

7. André Job, "La mobilité chimique," in *Institut International de Chimie Solvay, Premier Conseil de Chimie* (Paris: Gauthier-Villars, 1925), pp. 284–319.

8. J. U. Nef, "On the fundamental conception underlying the chemistry of the element carbon," *J. Am. Chem. Soc.,* **26** (1904), pp. 1549–79, esp. p. 1572 f.

9. M. Gomberg, "An instance of trivalent carbon: triphenyl methyl," *J. Am. Chem. Soc.,* **22** (1900), pp. 757–71.

10. Wilhelm Schlenk, "Beiträge zur Kenntnis der Valenz des Kohlenstoffs, Arsens, und Siliciums," *Liebig's Ann.,* **394** (1912), pp. 178–222, esp. pp. 208 ff.

11. J. N. Collie and Thomas Tickle, "The salts of dimethylpyrone, and the quadrivalence of oxygen," *J. Chem. Soc.,* **75** (1899), pp. 710–7.

12. A. Baeyer and Victor Villiger, "Über die basischen Eigenschaften des Sauerstoffs," *Chem. Ber.,* **35** (1902), pp. 1201–12.

13. H. Wieland, "Tetraphenylhydrazin und hexaphenyläthan," *Liebig's Ann.,* **381** (1911), pp. 200–16.

14. Fritz Mietzsch, "Zur Chemotherapie der bakteriellen Infektionskrankheiten," *Chem. Ber.,* **71** (1938) pp. A15–28.

15. J. Trefouel, Mme. J. Trefouel, F. Nitti, and D. Bovet, "Action of *p*-aminophenylsulfamide in experimental streptococcus infections of mice and rats," *Compt. Rend. Soc. Biol.,* **120** (1935), pp. 756–8.

16. Trevor Robinson, "Michael Tswett," in *Chymia,* **6** (1960), pp. 146–61.

17. M. Tswett, "Physikalisch-chemische Studien über das Chlorophyllproblem. Die Adsorptionen," *Ber. d. deutschen Botanischen Gesellschaft,* **24** (1906), pp. 316–23, esp. p. 322, cited in the translation by Laszlo Zechmeister, *Annals of the New York Academy of Sciences,* vol. 49, Art. 2 (New York, Feb. 10, 1948), p. 146; M. Tswett, "Adsorptionsanalyse und chromatographische Methode, Anwendung auf die Chemie des Chlorophylls," *ibid.* (1906), pp. 384–93.

18. Richard Willstätter, *Aus meinem Leben,* Arthur Stoll, Ed. (Weinheim: Verlag Chemie, 1949), p. 175. "Über Pflanzenfarbstoffe," *Chem. Ber.,* **47** (1914), p. 2831–74.

19. From R. Willstätter, *Chem. Ber.,* **47** (1914), p. 2872.

20. R. Willstätter, *Untersuchungen über Enzyme* (Berlin: Julius Springer, 1928).

21. J. M. Robertson, "An X-ray study of the structure of the phthalocyanines. Part I. The metal-free, nickel, copper, and platinum compounds," *J. Chem Soc.,* 1935, pp. 615–21, esp. p. 618. Frank H. Moser and Arthur L. Thomas, "Phthalocyanine compounds," *J. Chem. Ed.,* **41** (1964), pp. 245–9.

22. Carl Liebermann, *Chem. Ber.,* **18** (1885), p. 1974; *ibid.,* **41** (1908), pp. 1436–44.

23. P. Pfeiffer, E. Breith, E. Lübbe, and T. Tsumaki, "Tricyclische orthokondensierte Nebenvalenzringe," *Liebig's Ann.,* **503** (1933) pp. 84–130.

24. Roger W. Watson and Theodore B. Tom, "Relation of structure and effectiveness in copper deactivation," *Ind. Eng. Chem.,* **41** (1949), pp. 918–23; R. L. Smith, "Properties and applications of sequestering agents," *Chem. & Ind.,* Nov. 10, 1956, pp. 1284–91.

25. Emil Fischer, "Synthesen in der Puringruppe," *Chem. Ber.,* **32** (1889), pp. 435–504.

26. See *Statistical Abstracts of the United States* (1950), p. 636.

27. See John E. Dalton, *Sugar, a Case Study of Government Control* (New York: The Macmillan Co., 1937).

28. L. Maquenne, "Recherches sur l'amidon," *Ann. Chim.* (8), **2** (1904), pp. 109–34; *Bull. Soc. Chim.,* **35** (1906), pp. i–xv, quotation from p. xiv.

29. E. F. Armstrong, *The Simple Carbohydrates and the Glycosides* (London-New York: Longmans, Green & Co., 1910).

30. C. S. Hudson, "Emil Fischer's discovery of the conformation of glucose, a semicentennial retrospect," *J. Chem. Ed.,* **18** (1941), pp. 353–7; "Historical aspects of Emil Fischer's fundamental conventions for writing stereo-formulas," *Advances in Carbohydrate Chemistry,* **3** (1948), pp. 1–22.

31a. P. A. Levine and W. A. Jacobs, "Über die Hefe-Nucleinsäure," *Chem. Ber.,* **42** (1909), pp. 2474–8. 31b. P. A. Levine, Hexosamines, Their Derivatives, and Mucins and Mucoids, Monograph No. 18, The Rockefeller Institute for Medical Research (New York: 1922).

32. Winifred M. Watkins, "Blood-group substances," *Science,* **152** (1966), pp. 172–81.

33. Siegfried Ruhemann, "Triketohydrindene hydrate," *J. Chem. Soc.,* **97** (1910), pp. 2025–31; R. S. Morrel, "Siegfried Ruhemann," *J. Chem. Soc.,* 1944, p. 46; Robert West, "Siegfried Ruhemann and the discovery of ninhydrin," *J. Chem. Ed.,* **42** (1965), pp. 386–7.

34. Frederick Sanger, "Amino acid sequence in the glycyl chain of insulin," *Biochem. J.,* **53** (1953), pp. 355–74.

35. H. B. Vickery and Thomas B. Osborne, "Review of hypotheses on the structure of proteins," *Physiological Reviews,* **8** (1928), pp. 293–446.

36. Eduard Färber, "Die Zwischenstufen bei chemischen Umwandlungen," *Naturwiss.,* **8** (1920), pp. 322–7.

37. H. F. Mark and G. S. Whitby, *Collected Papers of Wallace H. Carothers on Polymerization* (New York: Interscience, 1940). W. H. Carothers and Julian W. Hill, "Studies of polymerization and ring formation. XV. Artificial fibers from synthetic linear condensation superpolymers," *J. Am. Chem. Soc.,* **54** (1932), pp. 1579–87.

38. Avery A. Morton, Eugene E. Magat, and Robert L. Letsinger, "Polymerization. VI: The Alfin catalysts," *J. Am. Chem. Soc.,* **69** (1947), pp. 950–61.

39. Karl Ziegler, "Aluminium-organische Synthese im Bereich olefinischer Kohlenwasserstoffe," *Angew. Chem.,* **64** (1952), pp. 323–9; Karl Ziegler, Heinz Breil, Heinz Martin, and Erhard Holzkamp, "Polymerization catalyst," U.S. patent 3,113,115 of Dec. 3, 1963; German application, Jan. 19, 1954; G. Natta and I. Pasquon, "The kinetics of the stereospecific polymerization of α-olefins," *Advances in Catalysis* (New York, 1959), Vol. 11, pp. 1–66.

40. Leopold Ruzicka, Jules Meyer, and M. Mingazzini, "Höhere Terpenverbindungen III," *Helv. Chim. Acta,* **5** (1922), pp. 345–68.

41. Paul Karrer and A. Helfenstein, "Synthese des Squalens," *Helv. Chim. Acta,* **14** (1931), pp. 78–82.

42. John S. Glover and Rudolph L. Lagai, *The Development of American Industries—Their Economic Significance* (4th ed.; New York: Simmons–Boardman Publishing Corp., 1959).

43. Robert M. Love and Reuben F. Pfennig, "Aromatics from petroleum," *Progress in Petroleum Technology,* Advances in Chemistry Series, No. 5 (Washington, D.C.: American Chemical Society, 1951), pp. 299–309.

44. A. G. Oblad, T. H. Milliken, Jr., and G. A. Mills, "Chemical characteristics and structure of cracking catalysts," *Advances in Catalysis* (New York: Academic Press, Inc. 1951), pp. 199–247.

45. R. E. Wilson, "Technology as a multiplier of our natural resources," *Chem. and Eng. News,* **22** (1944), p. 784.

46. George M. Maverick and R. G. Sloane in *Symposium on Lubricants* (Philadelphia: American Society of Testing Materials, 1937), pp. 33 ff.

23

Biochemistry

Problems in a Chemistry of Life

In the first part of the nineteenth century, chemistry was divided into an inorganic and an organic branch. At first, organic chemistry received its methods and ideas from the elder sister; later, the relationship was to a considerable extent reversed. Towards the end of the nineteenth century, the influence of physics and physiology, neighbors of chemistry in the system of sciences, became strong enough to justify the establishment of the new branches of physical chemistry and biological chemistry.

In the beginning it was advantageous to stress the distinctions among the four branches. Gradually, and especially after about 1920, it became apparent that the connection among them was important. The methods developed in one branch were used as tools in the others. Theories about chemical constitution and action, whether gained from physical concepts or from analogies to organismic behavior, were extended to all branches.

Among these four branches of chemistry, biochemistry has a special position at the borderline of physiology and medicine. This position carried practical problems, for example, when the Nobel Prize Committees had to decide in which field to place the work deemed deserving of a prize. Greater were the conceptual difficulties when biochemistry was burdened with the task of providing a complete and exclusive "explanation" of life. Paracelsus proclaimed that the ripening of fruit was the work of a natural alchemy. At his time, that was a glorious discovery; later on it became as questionable and ambiguous as a "force of life."

In the middle of the last century, G. J. Mulder (page 218) showed that the knowledge we can acquire by studying the components of saliva and their action is science but quite different from nature. The gap between science and life is wide; it is not filled by postulating a force of life. M. Berthelot, therefore, advised us "to ban life from all explanations relative to organic chemistry." (1) Organic chemists followed this advice, but physiologists and biologists objected to it. Gustav von Bunge (1844–1920), professor of physiology in Basel, defended vitalism as "the only correct way . . . to start from what we know, our interior world, in order to explain what we do not know, the exterior world." (2) And Hans Driesch, professor of biology in Cologne, saw no other way out of the difficulty than to introduce the force of life again, in the form of an Aristotelian entelechy, as "a real element of nature." (3)

At the turn of the century new efforts to "ban life" from our explanations of enzyme or vitamin action were necessary and successful. The question remained whether we had to do the reverse and exclude chemistry from an explanation of life. Can we conceive a chemistry of life as a real part of life, not only as an artificial abstract of it? In 1904 Raphael Meldola (1849–1915, London) answered the question optimistically, although somewhat ambiguously: "But although the doctrine of a special 'vital force' has received its deathblow from the hands of modern science, and although there is no warrant for the belief that the physics and chemistry of animals and plants is ultrascientific, yet it must not be lost sight of that the synthetical possibilities of the living organism have brought us face to face with modes of chemical action of which we are as yet profoundly ignorant." (4)

Paul Ehrlich explained some of these modes by a dualism of receiving and impinging forms. Starting "from what we know," he and Julius Morgenroth (1871–1924) introduced another, basic dualism derived from dread and desire, in the specific directions of "horror autolyticus" and "ictus immunisatoris." (5) The science of immunology establishes these expressions of life and follows their results.

After forty years of extensive research, ambiguity remained in the optimistic forecast that Erwin Schrödinger (1887–1961) gave: ". . . living matter, while not eluding the 'laws of physics' as established up to date, is likely to involve 'other laws of physics' hitherto unknown, which, however, once they have been revealed, will form just as integral a part of this science as the former. . . ." (6)

The general problem of a chemistry of life was often hidden from sight by an abundance of special new discoveries, but the relationships thus establish the kind of scientific system which remains distinct from nature. Mulder saw this clearly. Hans A. Krebs (1900–) stated it with special reference to the study of carbohydrate oxidation, this basic process in respiration and muscular activity which we try to explain by intermediate chemical reactions:

> Physiologically, most intermediates exist only transitorily, i.e., in minute quantities. Moreover, they only occur intracellularly. These circumstances preclude their identification under "physiological" conditions. To investigate intermediary metabolism, the concentration of the metabolite must be artifically raised, or poisons must be added, and/or the tissue has to be removed from its normal site and to be perfused, or sliced, or minced, or extracted. The statement, therefore, that the evidence is valid for living tissues under "physiological" conditions always implies the assumption that the reactions occur under conditions different from those of the experiment. As far as one can see, this state of affairs is bound to persist, and for this reason the theory of intermediary reaction mechanism is bound always to remain a theory. (7)

Instead of despairing that we shall ever reach the goal, we can hope for improvements in the future and blame the present difficulty on a passing imperfection. This attitude is implied in the words of Albert Szent-Györgyi (1893–): "There is no doubt in the author's mind that the real nature of life will remain a closed book as long as we try to approach it only with ideas of 'classical' chemistry." (8) There is no gratitude for what has been achieved when only the absolute is considered.

In the course of such theoretical work, biochemists discovered new facts about nutrition, about substances essential for health, and about medicines and medications. The science of the chemistry of life did not penetrate the "secret" of life; there is much more to life than mere chemistry. But there is a part of life that can be grasped by chemical means, and there are chemically defined substances that can change the course of essential processes in living organisms.

Biochemical Methods

The extreme specialization of research in biochemistry developed through an integration of methods from all fields of physics and chemistry. It is impossible to state a quantitative relationship between specialization and integration, and it is scarcely true that one was exactly complementary to the other. A wide knowledge of methods became as essential for a good biochemist as the correct philosophy was for the doctor, in Paracelsus' opinion.

In the progress of the art of purifying organic substances, attention was focused on those parts that formerly were only unknown impurities. The quantities of new substances discovered in this way were sometimes very small. Analysis, and especially combustion, to find the proportions of the elements, carbon, hydrogen, and others, in the substance destroyed at least several tenths of a gram. In his work on bile acids, Fritz Pregl (1869–1930, Graz, Austria) felt the need for a less wasteful method. In the first decades of our century he developed a method of combustion that gave accurate results with one hundredth of the usual quantities. Methods of microanalysis were also worked out for inorganic substances and for the determination of molecular weights. Specific adsorbents were found for separating closely related sensitive substances without chemical changes. The old adsorbent, charcoal, found successors in synthetic resins which were produced with a variety of adsorbent properties. They could be used to separate closely related organic substances from one another or to remove ions from solutions. Application to scientific research was extended to industrial operations in the sugar industry and in the production of medicaments.

Machines in which centrifugal force is used for separating solids from liquids had been introduced into the sugar and starch industries at about the middle of the last century. Applications of centrifugal machines to biological research began in 1889. Theodor Svedberg (1884–), a professor in Upsala, Sweden, conceived the idea that by increasing the speed of rotation a centrifugal separation of large, heavy molecules should be possible even if they are dissolved. The technical difficulties in constructing a high-speed or ultracentrifuge were great. Theodor Svedberg solved many of them during his visit as a guest researcher and lecturer at the University of Wisconsin in 1922–1923.

> The procedure was based on the fact . . . that it should be possible to determine the mass of heavy molecules by measuring the sedimentation equilibrium in the ultracentrifuge.
>
> When a solution is centrifuged in a closed cell for a sufficiently long time, a state of equilibrium is finally reached when sedimentation and diffusion balance each other. To determine the molecular weight, it is therefore necessary only to measure the relation between the concentration of the solution at two points situated x_1 and x_2 cm from the center of rotation, and to know the temperature, the speed of the centrifuge, the partial specific volume of the solute, and the density of the solvent.
>
> The formula holds only for dilute solutions. In the case of concentrated solutions, the formula for the molecular weight will include the expression for the partial specific free energy of the solute. (9)

The separation was observed by means of a special optical arrangement through which photographs of the small amount of solution could be taken while it was under the influence of many thousand times the usual field strength of gravity.

The migration of molecules under the influence of an electrical potential is governed by many factors from which that of the size and shape of the molecule can be separated. A method was developed, particularly by Arne Tiselius (1902–) in Svedberg's institute, that used this property for characterizing highly complex substances through electrophoresis.

The use of radioactive isotopes was first introduced into inorganic chemistry as an analytical tool (p. 294). Radioactive carbon, phosphorus, and iodine gave otherwise unobtainable information about the processes of assimilation in plants and metabolism in animals. In addition to these new methods, refinements of the older techniques of drying or distilling in a high vacuum were developed for laboratory research and industrial production.

New types of resins as adsorbents made chromatography more specific. Fluorimetry attained a sensitivity of 10^{-8} moles per liter, and amounts of 10^{-11} moles were identifiable. For the measurement of radio frequency energy absorbed by magnetic nuclei, apparatus came into use about 1953. (10) Microanalytical methods were refined to an ultra-micro range by Karl Linderstrøm-Lang (1896–1959) at the Carlsberg Laboratory in Copenhagen to help the biochemist. Volumes down to 1 μl (one millionth of a liter) could be "comfortably" handled. A balance consisting of a fine quartz fiber a few millimeters in length as the "beam" gave weighings accurate to 4×10^{-12} grams—about the weight of one red blood corpuscle.

The general methods of radioactive labeling took such special biochemical applications as marking the sulfur in proteins by S^{35} or the nucleins by P^{32}.

With such biochemical methods, Hershey and Chase (11) in 1952 established that bacteriophages inject their specific deoxyribonucleic acid into the bacteria that they "eat up" while multiplying.

Fermentations and Enzymes

Fermentation was a central subject of the controversy between vitalists and mechanists. Pasteur saw in it a form of life; when microorganisms lack oxygen, they resort to fermentation (1861). Liebig considered it an example for the rule that substances communicate their own state of motion or activity to other substances with which they are in contact. The chemical way out of this insoluble either-or controversy was indicated by Moritz Traube (1826–1894). Chemistry has to look for the substances in the microorganisms that are responsible for the actions (1874).

This program was logically sound. In the historical development, however, it was not the logical and systematic approach that led to the solution. It was obtained through accidents and by observers who had sufficient experience to interpret them.

Eduard Buchner (1860–1917, Munich) planned to prepare medically useful products from bacteria by treatment with alkalies. In order to preserve a juice pressed out of yeast, he added a concentrated solution of sugar to it (1896). He was surprised to notice a slow fermentation in this mixture. When he found that no yeast cells were present, he knew that he had made an important discovery. He followed it through systematically. His main object was to separate the fermentative effect from the life of the microorganism.

Yeast can be killed by alcohol or acetone; it can be ground to destroy the cells and squeeze out the juice. The lifeless products obtained from the yeast are still able to produce fermentation.

Not all the activity of living yeast was recovered in these products. Arthur Harden (1865–1940, London) used yeast killed and liquefied by self-digestion (autolysis), boiled a portion of this liquefied yeast, added it to the mixture, and thus obtained a rate of fermentation about as high as that of living yeast. This result was very unexpected, since the boiling should destroy any remainder of "life." A similar effect was obtained by the addition of potassium phosphate to the cell-free juice. On the other hand, an addition of phosphates to living yeast had little influence on the rate of fermentation. Apparently the living organism had an enzyme, phosphatase, which provided the required phosphate by mobilizing it from organic compounds. To reach such a conclusion, Harden had to consider alcoholic fermentation as a sequence of several enzymatic processes.

The decomposition of a hexose sugar was not even roughly presented by the usual chemical formulation; an intermediate formation of a phosphate of the hexose preceded the splitting into alcohol and carbon dioxide. This discovery of 1905 was confirmed by the separation of hexose phosphates from fermenting solutions in substantial quantities.

Several methods were known to convert yeast into a liquid that contains the fermentative agent. Buchner called this agent "zymase," but Harden's investigations taught that this was not one single enzyme. It was expected that the enzymes producing hexose phosphate and splitting it again were accompanied by others that were responsible for the further steps in the changes from sugar to alcohol and carbon dioxide. Some details of these changes came to light when it was found that pyruvic acid is fermented by yeast. Pyruvic acid, the product of pyrolysis (splitting through heat) of the acid of grapes, named *uvic* acid or, more commonly, tartaric acid, contains an arrangement of carbon, hydrogen, and oxygen close to that in alcohol. Fermentation of this acid consists in the liberation of carbon dioxide; the rest of the pyruvic acid should then be acetaldehyde.

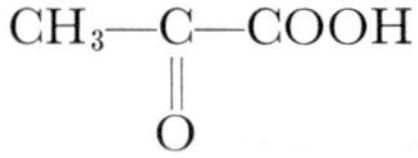

$$CH_3{-}\underset{\underset{\displaystyle O}{\|}}{C}{-}COOH \qquad\qquad CH_3{-}\underset{\underset{\displaystyle O}{\|}}{C}{-}H$$

Pyruvic acid 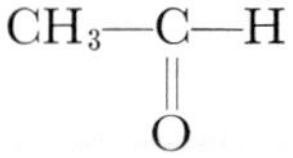 — Acetaldehyde

If pyruvic acid were an intermediate product in sugar fermentation, aldehyde should precede alcohol. To prove that this is so, Carl Neuberg (1877–1956, Berlin, New York) added sodium sulfite to fermenting liquors because it was known that sulfite combines with aldehydes. The sulfite would thus stabilize any formed aldehyde which in the normal course of fermentation would be reduced to alcohol. The hydrogen that would normally be used for the reduction would then be available to reduce another split product of the sugar, containing a chain of three carbon atoms, to glycerol. The prediction was found fulfilled. During World War I fermentation of sugar with the addition of sulfite became a method for producing glycerol on an industrial scale. Aldehyde, the cornerstone of the theory, was an undesirable by-product in industry.

While fermentation of sugar by yeast was thus forced into new paths, fermentation by other microorganisms was also developed on an industrial scale. Butanol and acetone were manufactured with the use of *chlostridium butylicum*. The process was developed by Chaim Weizmann (1874–1952) in 1916. It spread from wartime England to France and America during the Second World War.

Bacteria that convert sugar into lactic acid were used at the start of preparing mashes for alcoholic fermentation. The preliminary acidification helped to keep down "infection" of the yeast by other microorganisms. The production of lactic acid itself by fermentation was carried out on a modest scale; world production, half of it German, was estimated at 6000 tons in 1929, compared with over a million tons of industrial alcohol (excluding wine, beer, and liquors).

The scientific importance of lactic acid fermentation was much greater than this proportion of production rates might indicate.

Lactic acid is formed in a muscle when it performs work. In the presence of oxygen, this lactic acid disappears again and it seems as though it were an intermediary stage in the oxidation of glucose which supplies the chemical energy for muscle action. Otto Meyerhof (1884–1951) found in 1920, however, that the additional oxygen consumed during work was only sufficient for oxidizing one-sixth to one-quarter of the lactic acid formed. Most of it disappears in the rest period of the muscle through a resynthesis of glycogen. Phosphoric acid plays an important part in these changes. Muscle contains phosphates of the amino acids and purines, among them creatine and adenosine, and, instead, arginine in the invertebrates. The

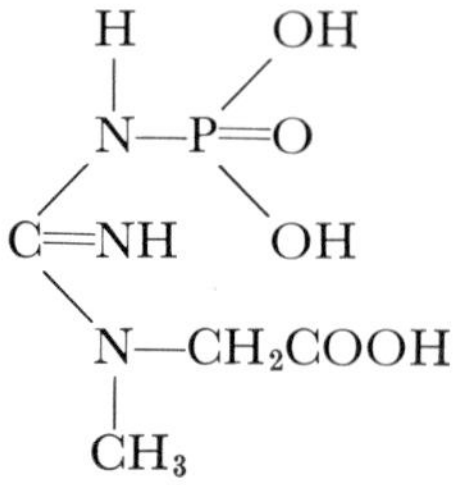

```
    H    OH                           OH
    |   /                            /
    N—P=O                      NH—P=O
   /    \                     /      \
  C=NH   OH                  C=NH     OH
   \                          \
    N—CH2COOH                  NH
    |                          |
    CH3                        CH2
                               |
                               CH2
                               |
                               CH2
                               |
                               CHNH2
                               |
                               COOH
```

Creatine phosphate 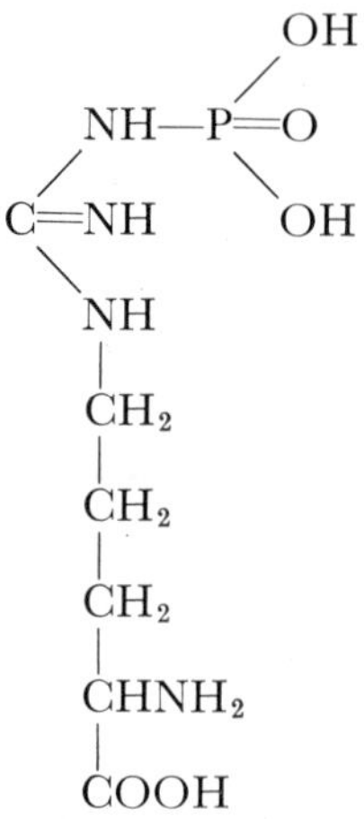 — Arginine phosphate

chemical reactions that the muscle converts into mechanical work involve changes of these phosphates. On the basis of these experiences in muscle chemistry, the process of the fermentative breakdown of glucose appeared as a chain of reactions in which phosphate bonds were formed and opened, while oxidations and reductions occurred with the fractured parts of the hexose molecule. These concepts arose from investigations made in the 1930's. More details are still being brought to light. More and more they seem to complicate our picture of that apparently simple conversion of sugar into alcohol and carbon dioxide, but we now recognize that the new knowledge connects fermentation with the other fundamental process of life, which is respiration. Enzymes form the connecting link.

Enzymes, as catalysts in life processes, share with other catalysts the two outstanding characteristics of sensitivity and specificity. In some respects, metallic catalysts are so similar to enzymes that Georg

Bredig (1868–1944) felt justified in considering the former as "inorganic ferments" (1901). If there was any "riddle" here, it was not a riddle of life; it seemed on the way to being reduced to pure physical chemistry. Iron salts catalyze the decomposition of hydrogen peroxide (Schönbein, 1863), and iron is an essential element in the red blood pigment. Oxidizing enzymes were therefore considered as acting through their iron content. Willstätter showed in 1917 that this is not true for peroxydase, but Otto Warburg (1883– , Berlin) rediscovered the importance of iron in experiments which started in 1914 and were rounded out in 1925.

> The new development of the enzyme problem begins with an accident. In experiments on the respiration of the sea-urchin egg, carbon dioxide was to be determined by liberating it through tartaric acid. It turned out that tartaric acid, when it came into contact with the cell substance, was oxidized by the oxygen of the air. The cell substance, therefore, contains a catalyst which burnt the otherwise stable tartaric acid. This catalyst was boilproof, even heatproof; it was nothing else than iron which occurs in traces in the substance of the sea-urchin egg. (12)

Charcoal from hemin was a model of the oxidizing ferment; it contained iron and nitrogen and it transmitted ordinary oxygen to amino acids and other organic materials to complete combustion at normal organismic temperatures. Small amounts of iron-containing enzymes were measured by their specific absorption of light.

Otto Warburg and Erwin Negelein found that carbon monoxide retards respiration in the dark and that light overcomes this effect. They remembered the work of Ludwig Mond (1839–1909, London) on the decomposition of iron carbonyl in light (1891), and of John Scott Haldane (1860–1936) on the similar action of light on the compound of hemoglobin with carbon monoxide (1897). They concluded therefore that the reversible bond of carbon monoxide on the respiratory enzyme extends to its iron. Spectroscopy in the range of 2500–6000 Angstroms showed them Fe-cysteine and Fe-porphyrine as the active centers.

While this was being discovered in Berlin, David Keilin (1887–1963) at Cambridge, England, investigated muscle preparations and living organisms (wax-moths) under the Zeiss microspectroscope. In 1925, he discovered a pigment that changes color during oxidations and reductions: ". . . this pigment is not a simple compound, but a complex formed of three distinct hemochromogen compounds . . . not yet completely elucidated. I propose therefore to describe it under the name of Cytochrome, signifying merely 'cellular pigment' . . . Cytochrome is distinct from muscle-hemoglobin [also called myochrome, or myoglobin], and both pigments can be easily seen in the same muscle of a bird or a mammal." (13) Keilin stated that yeast grown under conditions of rapid multiplication under strong aeration, so-called baker's yeast, contained a much higher proportion of cytochrome than brewer's yeast.

A yellow enzyme was isolated from yeast by Warburg in 1932. Its components were a yellow pigment and a complex protein (H. Theorell, 1935). The yellow pigment was also found in milk and thus received its name "lactoflavin." This pigment and its naturally occurring phosphate compound have vitamin B_2 activity; combination of the phosphate with the colloidal protein component is necessary for the enzyme activity (Richard Kuhn, 1936).

Many single enzymatic steps were distinguished in fermentation, respiration, assimilation, and muscle activity, and relationships between enzymes, vitamins, and nucleic acids began to emerge. These developments had little influence on the industries that were producing ethyl alcohol by fermentation and growing yeast. The operational improvements came from general chemical and technical advances, but these improvements did not contribute to the development of alcohol by fermentation but to its production by synthesis from ethylene. This began very modestly in 1934, grew slowly during the next ten years, and continued faster after the war, while alcoholic

ANNUAL ALCOHOL PRODUCTION IN THE UNITED STATES

(in million U.S. gallons at 60°F
containing 50 percent ethanol by volume)*

Year	Fermentation	Synthesis
1934	229.5	12.1
1941	438.6	70.5
1945	1017.0	113.4
1950	320.5	201.2
1954	264.3	299.3
1964	289.2	549.8
1966	340.8	548.6

*As recorded by the Alcohol and Tobacco Tax Division, Internal Revenue Service, U.S. Treasury Department. (Multiplication by 1.89266 converts the official proof gallon into liters of actual ethanol.)

fermentation retreated. These events are indicated in the table, which shows the annual United States production of alcohol during this period.

Just when alcoholic fermentation started to decline, fermentation began to gain new importance for the production of biotic and antibiotic substances.

Vitamins—Biotic and Antibiotic Substances

By the middle of the nineteenth century the main constituents of our food had been recognized as belonging to three chemical groups, carbohydrates, proteins, and fats. Liebig distinguished between two physiological kinds of nutrients. The first, called "plastic," served for building and maintaining the body substance; the second, called "respiratory," was used as a fuel for maintaining body temperature. Muscular work was assumed to be produced only from the protein materials in the food. This preconceived idea caused extended controversies. Eduard Friedrich Wilhelm Pflüger (1829–1910, Bonn) found one way to its solution in the comparison of the carbon dioxide exhaled with the oxygen respired. The stoichiometrical relationship of CO_2 to O_2, the respiratory quotient, is equal to unity for carbohydrates, 0.7 for fats, and 0.8 for proteins. The method was not simple to employ. It had been first conceived by Lavoisier and Laplace (1780), and it found its most thorough elaboration after many intermediate attempts by Wilbur O. Atwater (1844–1907) and Francis G. Benedict (1870–1957), in Boston, after 1898.

The results of all these measurements were summarized by Max Rubner (1854–1922, Berlin) in 1902: "The intake of food . . . always gives an effect which corresponds to the quantity of food consumed." (14) There are no mysterious effects that are large in comparison with the cause. The energy of food is the physical value determined as calories in combustion. This summary of about one hundred and twenty years of research on food and nutrition appeared just at the time when new discoveries proved it too general and incomplete.

That something was missing in our knowledge of these relationships was first pointed out for milk. J. B. Dumas had noticed the bad effects of "synthetic" milk during the siege of Paris in 1870 and concluded: "No conscientious chemist can assert that the analysis of milk has made known the products necessary to the life which that aliment contains." (15)

In Java, Christian Eijkman (1858–1930, Utrecht) studied the symptoms and causes of a serious disease, beriberi. In 1897 he found that hens kept on a diet of polished rice developed a paralysis similar to that of beriberi, and that they could be cured by adding the rice polishings to their diet. The usual explanation for sickness was an active agent, a poisonous substance. Eijkman suspected that polished rice contained some poison which was counteracted by the bran. It took only a short time to reverse the explanation, at least partially, and to demonstrate that the absence of the beneficial substances contained in the bran was responsible for beriberi.

Purified nutrients are deficient in some essential factor that yeast needs for its growth. E. Wildiers in 1910 brought the allusion back to "life" by calling this factor "bios." For rats, the declining rates of growth produced by highly purified food materials could be restored to normal by the addition of very small quantities of milk, according to Frederick Gowland Hopkins (1861–1947, Cambridge). Milk and eggs were the remedies for pellagra that Joseph Goldberger (1874–1929, Washington, D.C.) found in his 1913 investigation in the southern United States. The disease was thus caused by a deficiency in the diet and not by bacteria.

Calories and the chemically known components of food had to contain mysterious "factors" in order to maintain the normal rate of life. Not quantities, but unknown qualities seemed to be required. Casimir Funk (1884–1967, London) designated them as "vitamines" (1912), but they were not amines in the chemical meaning of the word. They are not alkaline. Jack Cecil Drummond (1891–1952, London) therefore in 1920 suggested a change which was important, although it consisted only in omitting the last letter in the word "vitamine" to indicate "a neutral substance of undefined composition." Although the assumption of (chemical) neutrality could not be maintained, the progress from "factor" to substance soon became an experienced reality. However, not only one substance was involved. In the same way that Berzelius concluded from the knowledge of one ferment that "thousands" would be found, the biochemists expected not one but a number of vitamins. Elmer V. McCollum (1879–1967) in Madison, Wisconsin, proposed to designate them alphabetically. The fat-soluble vitamin, which was first investigated, thus became vitamin A. The vitamin that prevents nervous deterioration, or neuritis, was historically next and it received the letter B as "the antineuritic vitamin." Drummond's antiscorbutic vitamin

C was isolated in 1919, and this was followed by discovery of the antirachitic vitamin D in 1922.

When K. Huldschinski healed rachitic children by irradiation with ultraviolet light (1918), and when an ultraviolet irradiation of fodder was discovered to be effective against nutritional deficiencies (Madison, Wis., Harry Steenbock and E. B. Hart, 1923), the substance was sought that caused the effect. Research in this country and in England and Germany led to the isolation and production of vitamin D from irradiated ergosterol. Color and measurement of the specific absorption of light were also used as guides in studying other vitamins.

In 1923, Herbert M. Evans (1882– , at Berkeley, California) assisted by Katharine S. Bishop, announced the "existence of a hitherto unknown dietary factor essential for reproduction." The Greek vocabulary helped to name this "carrier of fertility" tocopherol. This antisterility factor, which in 1924 B. Sure (1892–1960) designated as vitamin E, proved to have some chemical similarity to vitamin A. "Both vitamins A and E are derived from unsaoponifiable portions, the former industrially from marine animal livers, the latter from vegetable sources. Both have long chain alcohol groups, the former in connection with a β-ionone ring structure and the latter with chroman ring structure. The semblance, however, ends there." (16)

```
        H     O
        |     ‖
        C     C
      //  \  /  \
H—C       C      C—CH3        CH3           CH3            CH3            CH3
  |       ‖      ‖            |             |              |              |
H—C       C      C—CH2—CH═C—(CH2)3—CH—(CH2)3—CH—(CH2)3—CH—CH3
      \\  /  \  /
        C     C
        |     ‖
        H     O
```

Vitamin K_1
(2-methyl-3-phytyl-1,4-naphthoquinone, from the leaf of alfalfa)

In experiments on the biosynthesis of cholesterol started in 1926, Henrik Dam (1895–) in Copenhagen raised chicks on fat-free diets, produced by extracting the fat with organic solvents. After a few weeks, the animals suffered severe bleeding on breast, wings, and feet. Addition of vitamin C, or of selected salts, did not help. Dam concluded that the extraction had removed an essential food ingredient together with the fats. The curative effect of the extracted material proved that it contained "an hitherto unknown anti-hemoragic factor." In 1934, Dam proposed to call it vitamin K. How fortunate that the extraction and the evaporation of the solvent had not destroyed the "factor!" In 1939, Edward A. Doisy (1893–)

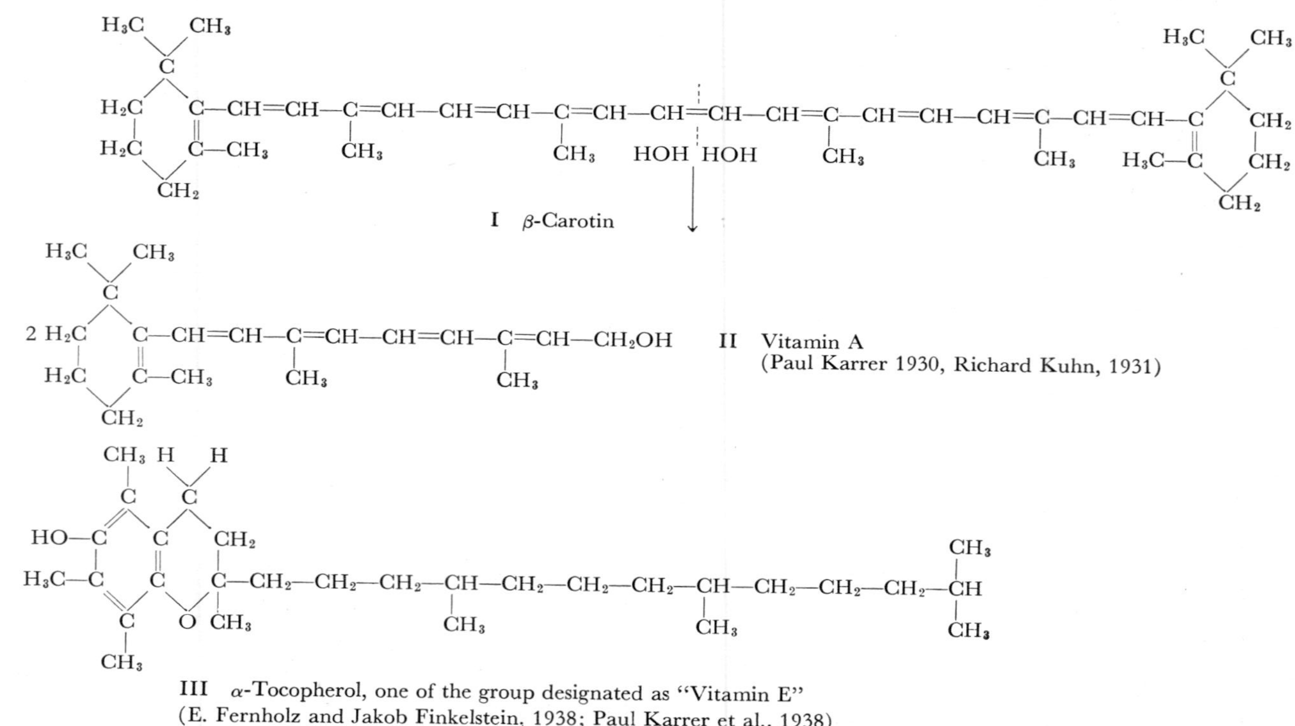

I β-Carotin

II Vitamin A
(Paul Karrer 1930, Richard Kuhn, 1931)

III α-Tocopherol, one of the group designated as "Vitamin E"
(E. Fernholz and Jakob Finkelstein, 1938; Paul Karrer et al., 1938)

prepared it in pure, yellow crystals from fats and putrified fishmeal, Paul Karrer, from alfalfa. Their syntheses confirmed its chemical structure as based on 1,4-naphthoquinone, with substituents varying between the vitamin K products from different sources.

In his Nobel prize lecture, Paul Karrer stated in 1937: ". . . Not ten years have passed since the time when some scientists questioned the material specificity of the vitamins and thought that a special state of matter, a special colloidal nature, was the cause for the peculiar vitamin effects that had been observed." A similar phase had occurred in the discussion about what the enzymes "really" are. Beyond that, the discussion was part of the controversy between mechanists and chemists that recurs on many occasions and at many times. It originates in the usual tendency towards seeking explanations by one simple and universal idea, and it ends successfully in the recognition that neither one of the opposing ideas can stand alone.

Helmholtz had shown that with regard to force and matter, but the general insight was never sufficient; it had to be reached and defined again for every specific subject. Seen in another connection, the tendency towards a simple universality appears as the metaphysics that science continually tries to overcome but will never eradicate. This conclusion from past events becomes metaphysical itself through the word '"never" which extends beyond the reach of "all" experience.

Attention had been drawn to needed "factors" by the sickness their absence produced, and confirmation depended on demonstrating their curative effects. The method was somewhat different for the substances that determine organic development, such as the "organizers" of Hans Spemann, and for the growth factors that were gradually recognized, first for bacteria and plants. Roger John Williams (1893–) described such a growth factor in 1933. He called it "pantothenic," from the Greek *pantothen,* "from everywhere," because he concluded from his findings that its presence was universal. Actually, he had first obtained it from cultures of Aspergillus niger, and the growth it stimulated was that of yeast. (17)

Pantothenic acid was later found to be a derivative of β-alanine, $H_2NCH_2CH_2COOH$:

```
      OH   CH3  OH   O    H    H    H
      |    |    |    ||   |    |    |       O
H-----C----C----C----C----N----C----C----C//
      |    |    |              |    |      \
      H    CH3  H              H    H       OH
```

Pantothenic acid

Some of these substances of great and specific biological action have an amazingly simple structure. A single-celled organism from the group of the algae, *Chlamydomonas engametos,* developed male characteristics when one molecule of a terpene (4-oxy-β-cylo-citral) was present per cell (Richard Kuhn, 1939–1941).

Lactic acid-producing groups of bacteria, lactobacilli, became indicators for specific biotic substances. Rhizopterin, produced by *Rhizopus nigricans,* has to be present only in a concentration of 34 billionths of a milligram per milliliter to effect the growth of *Lactobacillus casei* (E. L. Rickes et al., 1947).

Another group of growth factors was discovered in the foliage of many plants; its first representative was therefore called "folic acid." Like rhizopterin, folic acid is a derivative of the pterines, substances that Heinrich Wieland and especially Clemens Schöpf (1899–) in Darmstadt had prepared from the pigments in the wings of butterflies (Lepidoptera).

The group of B vitamins contains members that occur in yeasts. Vitamin B_{12}, however, is mainly produced in the liver. George B. Minot (1885–1950), William B. Murphy (1892–) at Harvard, and George H. Whipple (1878–) at Rochester showed its effects in curing anemias. The deep red vitamin B_{12} contains cobalt in complex bond to carbon and nitrogen. (18) Cobalt, which is highly poisonous in any sizable amounts, is necessary to life when present in traces. For the traces of other poisonous elements, for example boron, molybdenum, or zinc, that are essential in fertilizers for plants, a similar explanation is not yet available.

The rapid advance of vitamin chemistry between 1920 and 1940 was made possible through the previous "hairsplitting" of the organic chemists and through the combination of methods developed in physics and biology. At first the advance seemed to bring increasing specialization and complication in a field that the science of the nineteenth century apparently had simplified into far-reaching general laws. As research proceeded, however, new connections were discovered. The way from living yeast to zymase and to the recognition of this "ferment" as a system of enzymes and coenzymes, and the way from a vitamine to a large group of different vitamins, came together and now indicate a possible juncture. "Every vitamin is a part of a co-enzyme," according to Otto Meyerhof.

For example, Hans von Euler-Chelpin's coenzyme A consists of a thioethanolamine group (A) connected with pantothenic acid (B) which is in turn linked through a diphosphate group to adenylic acid (C):

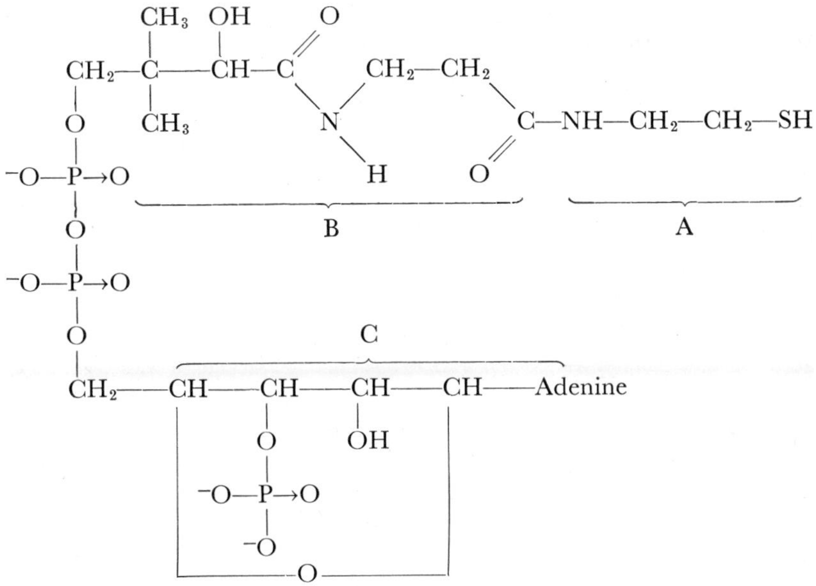

```
                CH3  OH        O
                 |    |       //
        CH2—C——CH—C          CH2—CH2
         |       |        \  /          \
         O      CH3         N             C—NH—CH2—CH2—SH
         |                   \          //
    -O—P→O                     H        O
         |        \___________________/   \____________/
         O                   B                    A
         |
    -O—P→O
         |
         O                        C
         |        ______________________________
        CH2———CH———CH———CH———CH———Adenine
               |        |       |        |
               |        O      OH        |
               |        |                |
               |   -O—P→O                |
               |        |                |
               |       -O                |
               |________________O________|
```

Structure of coenzyme A

When Pasteur and Joubert observed in 1877 that the growth of anthrax bacillus was inhibited by infections with air-borne micro-organisms, they felt that this indicated therapeutic possibilities. Fifty years later, Alexander Fleming (1881–1955, London) found that a staphylococcal culture, accidentally infected by spores of a species of *Penicillium,* showed signs of dissolution.

> It is certain that every bacteriologist has not once but many times had culture plates contaminated with molds. It is also probable that some bacteriologists have noticed similar changes to those noted above, but that, in the absence of any special interest in naturally occurring antibacterial substances, the cultures have simply been discarded.
>
> It was, however, fortunate that . . . I was always on the look-out for new bacterial inhibitors, and when I noticed on a culture plate that the staphylococcal colonies in the neighborhood of a mold had faded away, I was sufficiently interested in the antibacterial substance produced by the mold to pursue the subject. (19)

Harold Raistrick (1890–) and C. Thom identified the species as *Penicillium notatum,* which had first been described in 1911 by

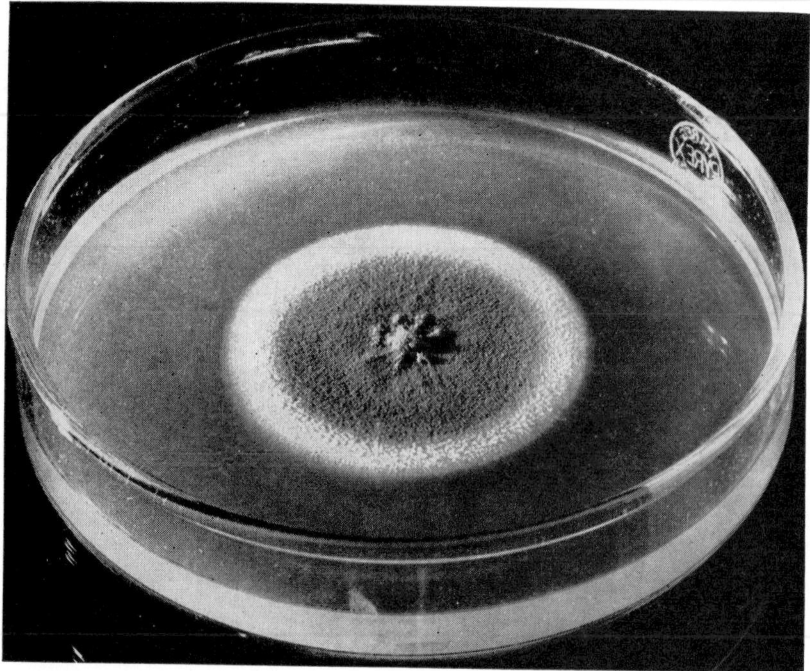

Fig. 46. The producer of penicillin Colony of *Penicillium notatum* on agar in petri dish. (Courtesy E. R. Squibb & Sons.)

R. Westling of Upsala. From 1930 on, cultures were distributed, but little more was done until ten years later. The group led by Howard Walter Florey (1898–1968) and Ernst Boris Chain (1906–) at Oxford extracted penicillin from larger cultures and successfully treated patients. Fleming gives the following account of the great event that accelerated further developments:

> My first experience of treating a patient with concentrated penicillin was in the summer of 1942. A middle-aged man with streptococcal meningitis appeared to be dying in spite of sulphonamide treatment. The streptococcus was sensitive to penicillin and Florey was good enough to give me his whole stock of penicillin to try on this, the first case of meningitis to be treated. After a few days treatment with intramuscular and intrathecal injections the patient was out of danger and he made an uneventful recovery.
>
> The result was so dramatic that penicillin was brought to the attention of the Minister of Supply, who immediately called a

meeting of everyone interested—academic and industrial. This became the Penicillin Committee, under the Presidency of Sir Henry Dale, which furthered the production of penicillin in Great Britain and which exchanged information freely with the American authorities. (20)

New strains of Penicillium were developed for aerated and submerged growth instead of surface growth. The water in which corn had been steeped proved to be a valuable additive to the nutrients. The method of separation of the penicillin out of its high dilution in the fermented broth used solvent extraction, partition chromatography, and finally drying from the frozen state, as had just been invented for blood plasma. Complete drying of the heat-sensitive product was necessary; even a small moisture content led to rapid destruction of its bioactivity.

The yellow, crystalline product contained several derivatives of the same fundamental lactam. The most active proved to be the benzyl derivative, named penicillin G:

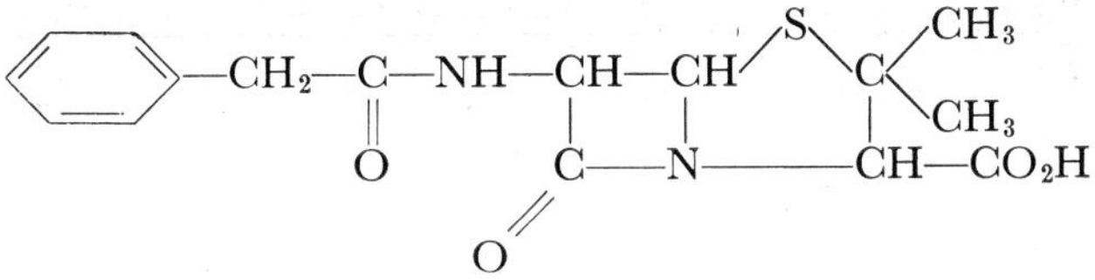

```
                                            S     CH3
                                          /   \  /
(C6H5)—CH2—C—NH—CH—CH            C
           ||        |       |              |  \
           O         C——N————CH—CO2H  CH3
                    //
                   O
```

Penicillin G

It was reasonable to assume that the production of antibiotics was not the exclusive privilege of a *Penicillium*. A world-wide search for "molds" began, and sometimes a successful producer was discovered right in the soil of the backyard or on a molded patch of a piece of melon. A *Streptomyces,* named *venezuelae* because it came from a mulched field somewhere in Venezuela, produced a peculiar, chlorine containing "chloromycin," or chloramphenicol, a derivative of nitrobenzene:

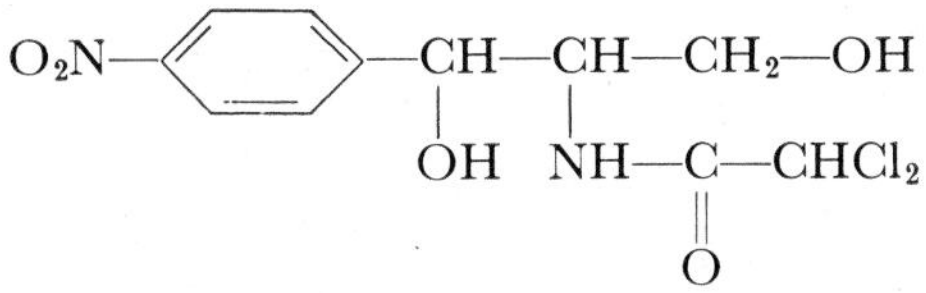

```
O2N—(C6H4)—CH—CH—CH2—OH
             |      |
            OH   NH—C—CHCl2
                    ||
                    O
```

Chloramphenicol

It was first synthesized commercially in 1948.

From another type of *Streptomyces,* "terramycin," or oxytetracyclin, was isolated:

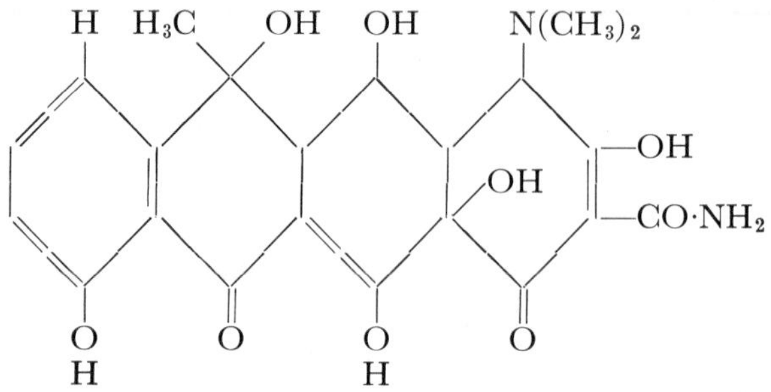

H H_3C OH OH $N(CH_3)_2$

—OH

OH

$—CO{\cdot}NH_2$

O O O O

H H

Terramycin (oxytetracyclin)

Streptomycin, which Selman A. Waksman (1888–) developed from a *Streptomyces* griseus in the early 1940's at Rutgers University, New Brunswick, N.J., proved particularly valuable through its wide spectrum of antibiotic action. One of its components is a rare 3-methylpentose, streptose. It also contains two guanidine groups:

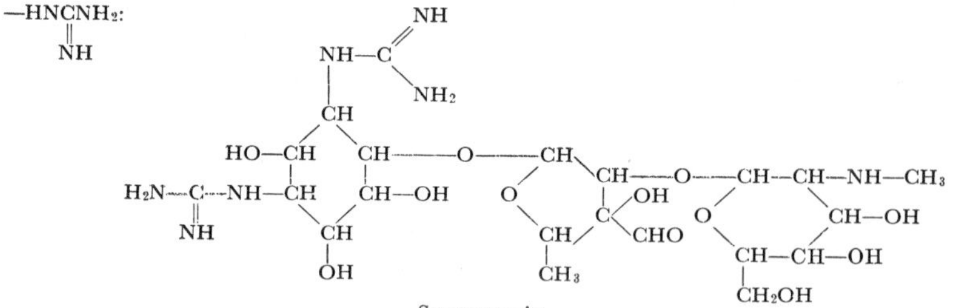

$—HNC(=NH)NH_2$:

NH

NH—C

NH_2

CH

HO—CH CH——O——CH

CH——O——CH—CH—NH—CH_3

H_2N—C—NH—CH CH—OH O OH

C CH—OH

NH CH CH CHO O

CH—CH—OH

OH CH_3 CH_2OH

Streptomycin

The number of microbially produced antibiotics has been continually increasing, concurrent with improvements in the techniques for isolating special strains, creating conditions favorable for their growth and combining methods for producing the antibiotics in high purity. The great variety in their chemical structure precluded a theoretical generalization. The time for concepts such as those of Ehrlich and Morgenroth, *horror autolyticus* and *ictus immunisatoris,* has passed—or perhaps has not yet returned.

It was, however, a time for industrial production and increasingly wide application. In 1953 the production of antibiotics for medical and agricultural uses was 1.63×10^6 pounds with a sales value of

$231 million; included were 372 trillion units of penicillin salts. The corresponding figures for 1964 were 6.5×10^6 lb at $386 million and 1,202 trillion units. Vitamin production was 7.2×10^6 lb in 1956 and 14.1×10^6 in 1964, about half of it vitamin C. The costliest to produce per unit was vitamin B_{12}: The 202 kg produced in 1956 were worth $22.6 million, the 398 kg of 1964 $6.9 million.

Hormones

At the beginning of the nineteenth century (1802), F. M. X. Bichat proclaimed that all physiological processes are directly caused, i.e., without any intermediaries, by the tissues of the organism. Georges Cuvier (1769–1851) identified the entire animal with its nervous system; all physiological processes are actions of the nerves. The concept of the immediate action of tissues or nerves began to be changed when the general importance and wide distribution of ferments, or enzymes, was recognized by Berzelius in 1836. The new trend progressed through Claude Bernard's investigations. In 1855 he distinguished between two kinds of secretion by the glands, the external secretion, which extracts substances from the blood, and the internal, which delivers substances into the blood. Ivan Petrovich Pavlov (1849–1936) showed that the mere sight or smell of food can start the secretion of digestive juice, and he explained it by nervous impulses sent out from the brain.

Exactly one hundred years after Bichat's publication, a decisive experiment proved that nerves can be by-passed in exciting the pancreas gland to secrete its juice into the blood stream. William M. Bayliss (1860–1924) and Ernest H. Starling (1866–1928), working at Oxford in 1902, extracted a substance from mucous intestinal membrane by digesting it with acid. This substance acted directly on the pancreas gland. Since there was one such substance, there should be many more of the same kind. In the way in which Berzelius had established the general concept of catalysts, Bayliss and Starling in 1904 introduced "hormones," from the Greek *hormōn,* "awakening," or "inducing," as the designation for substances in the juices of inner secretion. At the time of these experiments, one substance had become chemically known to which the definition of a hormone could be applied. This substance had been isolated from the glands adjoining the kidneys, the adrenals, and had therefore been called "adrenalin." In the years 1901 to 1904 its chemical structure was found to be as shown.

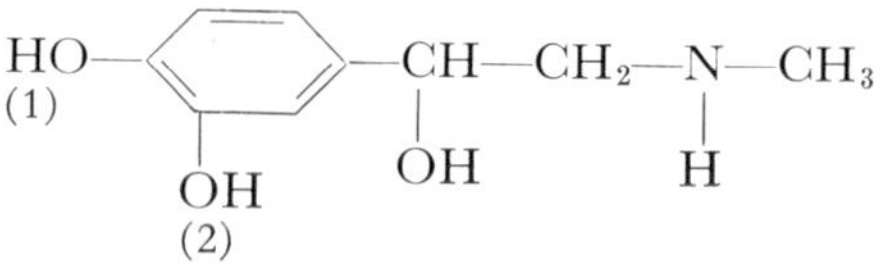

HO—(benzene ring)—CH—CH$_2$—N—CH$_3$ with OH (2) on the ring, OH on CH, and H on N; HO marked (1)

Adrenalin
(Epinephrine)

Adrenalin (also called epinephrine) increases the excretion of glucose in the urine, as it occurs in diabetes. The role of the pancreas in diabetes was clearly shown by J. v. Mering and his collaborators in 1889. A structure in the pancreas, "islets" (*Inseln*) as Langerhans had called them (1869), were assumed to play a predominant part in this function of the gland. Efforts to extract the active substance began in 1898. They were vitiated by a protein-splitting enzyme, trypsin. The attempts to overcome this enzyme action finally succeeded. Frederick Grant Banting (1891–1941) and Charles H. Best (1899–), in John James Richard Macleod's laboratory at Toronto in 1922, extracted a pure hormone, insulin, and showed its efficiency in regulating the sugar utilization in diabetics.

The pituitary gland excretes hormones which are antagonistic to insulin. Bernardo Alberto Houssay (1887– , Buenos Aires) found that the injection of pituitary extracts causes diabetes by destroying the pancreas. The chemical basis for these hormone actions is the influence on the formation of hexose phosphate, which is the first step in sugar conversion in digestion as well as in fermentation (Carl F. and Gerty T. Cori).

Extracts from the cortex, the outer part of the adrenals, showed influences on the metabolism of salts, carbohydrates, and proteins. These influences were more complex than was at first assumed. They began to be recognized about 1930. The hormones from the adrenal cortex were identified as steroids and called "corticosterones."

Efforts to separate these hormones and define them chemically started in 1935, led by Edward C. Kendall (1886–) at the Mayo Foundation in Rochester, Minnesota, Oskar Wintersteiner (1898–) at Columbia University, and Tadeus Reichstein (1897–) in Zürich. Reichstein isolated substances which he first designated by letters A to R. The knowledge of cholesterol and cholic acids helped in developing the chemical formulation for the hormones of this group (21). A partial synthesis was achieved in 1946. A few years later, Robert B. Woodward (1917–) led the group that accomplished the complete synthesis of cortisone. (22)

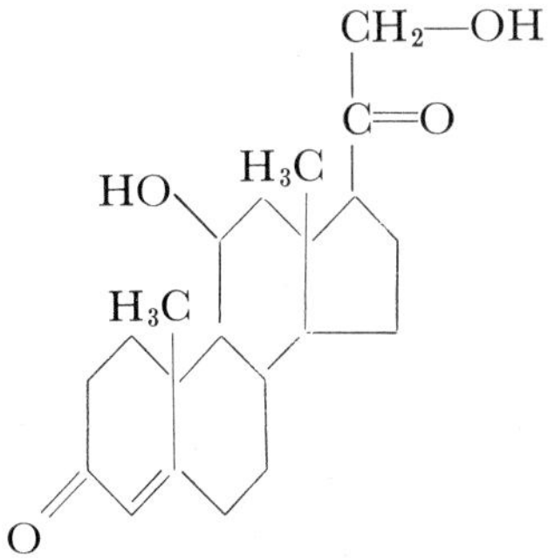

CH_2—OH | C=O | H_3C | HO | H_3C | O

Corticosterone

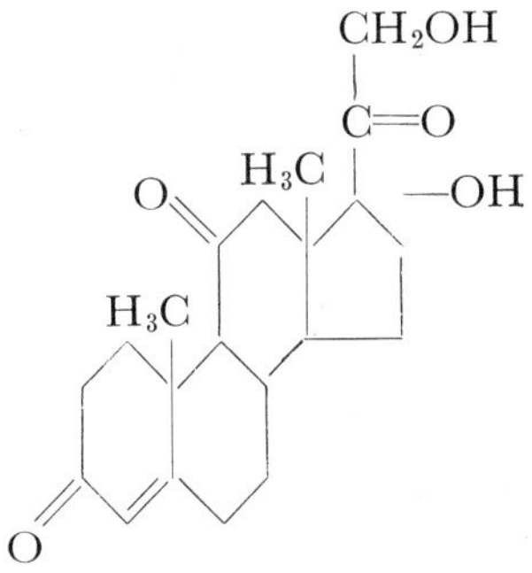

CH_2OH | C=O | H_3C | —OH | O | H_3C | O

Cortisone

From urine and the sex organs hormones were obtained that had a specific effect on plant growth and the sexual development of animals. Edward A. Doisy (1893–   ) in St. Louis, Mo. and Adolf Butenandt (1903–   ) in Berlin and Dahlem independently obtained the first pure sex hormone in crystallized form in 1929. It was isolated from the follicle, hence its name "folliculin." Sexual development of the uterus in a castrated mouse was caused by 0.025 millionth of a milligram of this hormone. "Testosterol," which acts as a male sex hormone, was isolated from urine. The activity contained in 150 cc of urine was concentrated into 0.3 milligrams by chemical purification. Another male sex hormone, "androsterone," was synthetically produced by Leopold Ruzicka by a method that gave complete information about its chemical structure. A most surprising fact, established by Butenandt in 1938, was the close chemical relationship between male and female sex hormones; a very slight structural change in the molecule converts one into the other.

Among the folk medicines of undefinable origin, there were several with hormone action. The leaves of the blueberry plant have long been used for insulin-like action on blood sugar. Ephedra equisetina, or sinosa, a small bush of the gymnosperm class, furnishes ephedrine, which is similar to epinephrine, though less effective in raising the blood pressure:

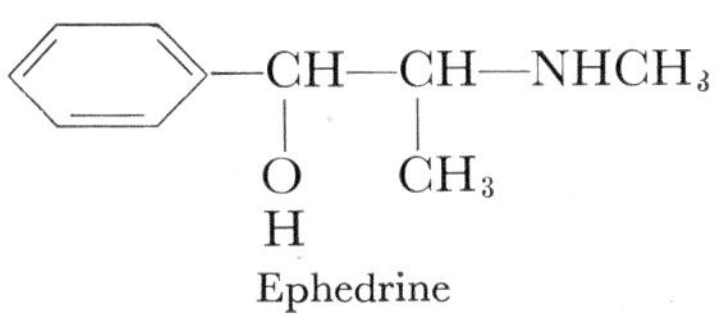

C_6H_5—CH(OH)—CH(CH_3)—$NHCH_3$

Ephedrine

In 1921, the plant physiologist Gottlieb Haberlandt (1854–1945) published his studies on "wound hormones" of plants. Cells proliferate on the surface of a cut in order to "heal" the wound, e.g., on a sliced potato. This does not occur when the surface is rinsed in water. Haberlandt concluded that the rinsing washes away the wound hormones. (23) The general concept of hormones made it convenient to classify an unknown but necessary "cause" of cell growth. More positive examples came from the study of fungi. When they grow, they produce an excess of growth-producing "agents" over what they need for themselves. In this respect, the suspected hormones resembled enzymes such as diastase, produced in excess by sprouting barley. A similar enzyme was found in the 1870s when the pancreas was investigated. This enzyme was separated by rubbing the pancreas with glycerol. The enzyme was named "trypsin," from the Greek term, "to wear down." The amino acid that the action of trypsin made appear (Greek *pheinein*) from proteins received the name "tryptophan." Alexander Ellinger (1870–1923, Frankfurt-am-Main) in 1904 derived the following formula as the most plausible for tryptophan (24):

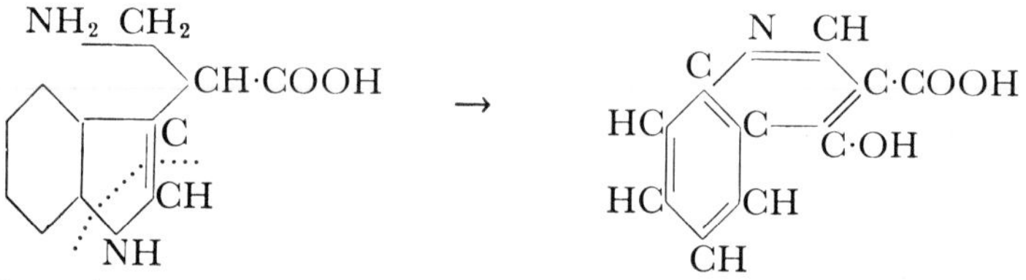

NH_2 CH_2 — CH·COOH; C; CH; NH → N CH; C; C·COOH; HC; C—C·OH; HC; CH; CH

Tryptophan when fed to dogs, forms Kynurenic acid

Ellinger could also have used the finding by F. Gowland Hopkins and Sidney M. Cole in 1903 that tryptophan is converted into indoleacetic acid under the influence of Escherichia communis. About thirty years later, this acid was one of those that Fritz Kögl (1897–) discovered among growth hormones for plants; they are developed in the growing tip of the coleoptile of oats. (25) Frits Warmolt Went and Kenneth V. Thimann (26) discussed the aspects of "evocators," organizers, stimulants, and "auxins" to the exclusion of "field" theories and concluded that auxins produce a "master reaction."

Japanese mycologists and biochemists had for many years been interested in phytohormones produced by fungi. From *Gibberella fujikuroi* (*Fusarium moniliforme*), a fungus growing on rice, E. Kurosawa in 1926 and especially T. Yabuta in 1939 developed extracts containing hormones of great growth-promoting activities, the group of gibberellins. These fungi were first grown in surface cultures and later with the greatly improved techniques that had been worked out for submerged growth of Penicillium. (27) These fungi produce hormones and poisons together, and the application of too much growth hormone can itself act as a poison for the plant.

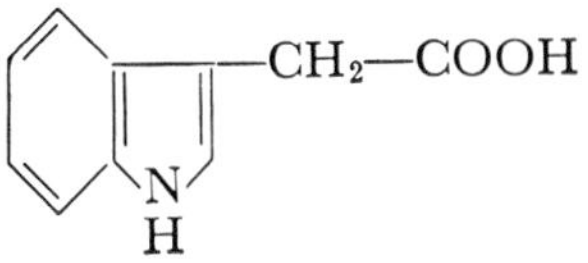

Indoleacetic acid

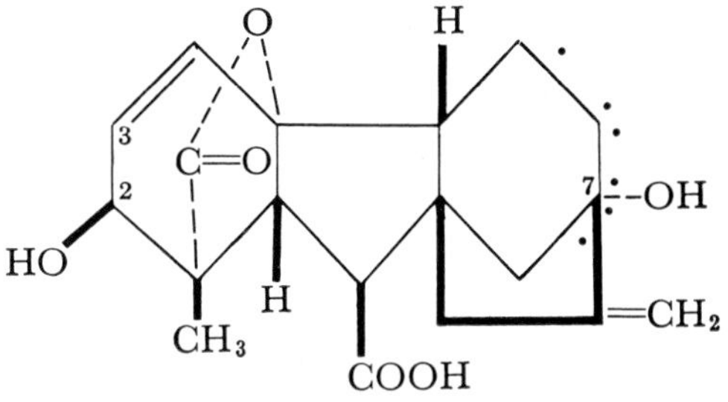

Gibberellic acid

Poisons and Medicaments

Whether a substance is detrimental or beneficial may depend on the relative quantity that is administered to an organism. Two examples from old and recent times will illustrate this: Paracelsus used toxic alkaloids and mercury salts for successful medications. A growth-promoting substance like 2,4-D (2,4-dichlorophenoxyacetic acid) becomes a weed killer when "too much" of it is applied.

Zinc sulfate is generally toxic for living organisms. In very small proportions, however, it increases the growth of certain strains of *Aspergillus,* as Felix Victor Raulin (1815–1905, Paris) discovered in 1869. He started a field of study that was expanded by Wilhelm Pfeffer. Vitamin D was the first substance for which the excess was found to have the opposite of the desired effect.

In 1929 W. Lange described diisopropyl phosphorofluoridate of

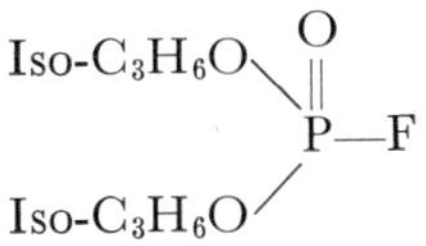

Diisopropyl phosphorofluoridate

which small quantities act very strongly on the human organism. This phosphate ester paralyzes, with fatal results, and yet it later became a remedy for a grave nerve disease. The development of an explanation started from the work of Otto Loewi (1873–1961) in Graz, Austria, on the transmission of nerve impulses. (28) In 1921 Loewi found that the stimulation of an isolated frog's heart could be transmitted by a liquid to a second heart. The fluid used for perfusing the first heart was brought into contact with the second heart and acted there very similarly to a vagus stimulation. The active "vagus substance" thus proved to be separable from the nerve, its product but not its exclusive property. Loewi, in connection with work by Henry Dale (1875–1968) in London, identified the active substance with acetyl choline.

The specific role of acetyl choline in transmitting nerve impulses was elucidated in connection with work on the electric organ of the squid. David Nachmansohn at Columbia University found in his studies, starting in 1937, that the electric organ is rich in an enzyme that hydrolyzes this ester:

$$(CH_3)_3N(OH)\text{—}CH_2{\cdot}CH_2{\cdot}O{\cdot}OCCH_3 \xrightarrow{\text{cholinesterase}} (CH_3)_3N(OH)\text{—}CH_2CH_2OH + CH_3COOH$$

The renewed acetylation is energetically coupled with the conversion of adenosine triphosphate into the diphosphate, a reaction that is fundamental for many biochemical processes:

$$\text{Adenine—pentose—O—}\underset{\underset{O}{\|}}{\overset{\overset{OH}{|}}{P}}\text{—O—}\underset{\underset{O}{\|}}{\overset{\overset{OH}{|}}{P}}\text{—O—}\underset{\underset{O}{\|}}{\overset{\overset{OH}{|}}{P}}\text{—OH} \quad \text{Adenosine triphosphate (ATP)}$$

$$+ H_2O \downarrow$$

$$\text{Adenine—pentose—O—}\underset{\underset{O}{\|}}{\overset{\overset{OH}{|}}{P}}\text{—O—}\underset{\underset{O}{\|}}{\overset{\overset{OH}{|}}{P}}\text{—OH} \quad \text{Adenosine diphosphate (ADP)} + H_3PO_4$$

The interfering alkyl phosphates are bound to the enzyme and thus block its action. (29) An agent that releases the block by decomposing the enzyme complex was found in certain pyridine derivatives, especially pyridine aldoxime methiodide. (30)

Strychnine, eserine, and prostigmine act exclusively by paralyzing the enzyme acetylcholinesterase. D. W. Woolley concluded in 1945 that pharmacological actions can generally be explained as effects on enzyme systems.

An amine that causes spasms of smooth muscle, e.g., of intestines or the uterus, was derived from "histidine," the amino acid to which Alfred Kossel gave this name in allusion to the Greek *histos,* "tissue."

Advances in histology and new techniques in tissue culture at the beginning of this century made it possible to study the effects of histamine and its synthetic antagonists.

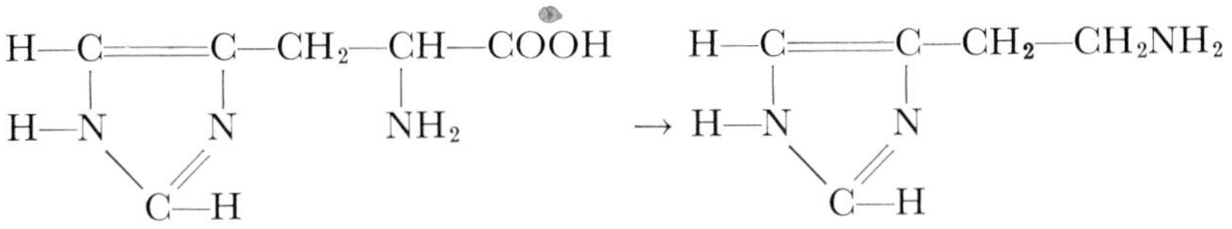

$$\text{H—C}{=}\text{C—CH}_2\text{—CH(NH}_2\text{)—COOH (ring: H—N, N, C—H)} \rightarrow \text{H—C}{=}\text{C—CH}_2\text{—CH}_2\text{NH}_2 \text{ (ring: H—N, N, C—H)}$$

Histidine Histamine

Daniel Bovet summarized (in Rome, 1950) some of the relationships between chemical structure and antihistamine action. (31)

Histaminic action is also exerted by extracts from ergot, in which Charles Tanret (1847–1917, Paris) found ergosterol. (32) Ergot belongs to the group used in folk medicine, of which the following may be mentioned here: The American mandrake, also called May apple, is a remedy used by the Penobscot Indians of Maine; its alcoholic extract, podophyllin, is included in the British Pharmacopeia of 1953. Rauwolfia was named in honor of Leonard Rauwolf, who in 1582 published his medico-botanical studies on expeditions to Asia and Africa. From *Rauwolfia serpentina* a research group at the Ciba Pharmaceutical Company isolated an alkaloid and named it *reserpine,* as an irregular form of *serpentina.* (33) The chemical structure of these and other natural active agents formed the model for great, diversified synthetic productions of medicaments.

Extremely small quantities of biotic and antibiotic substances exert great biological influence. These substances belong to groups that differ widely in chemical structure and in their effect on organisms. It has therefore proved impossible to arrive at a general theory. Whenever the attempt was made to reduce the explanation to simple physiochemical relationships, it was soon found that at best a preliminary and limited rule had been obtained. Ehrlich's theories were working hypotheses, helpful only when used with caution. A theory of narcosis, which Hans Horst Meyer (1853–1942, Vienna) pointed out in 1899 and which Charles Ernest Overton (1865–1933) tried to extend (1901), was based on the solubility of narcotic substances in the fat-like, lipoid component of organismic cells. Again it was found that the theory was only approximately true.

Reactions between chemicals remain in the realm of substances; reactions of chemicals upon organisms go beyond chemistry because the effect is produced by stimulating a complex of biological processes. This fundamental difficulty of generalization in biochemistry can still be described in the words of Johannes Müller (1801–1858), the great physiologist who was professor in Bonn and after 1833 in Berlin:

> In the chemical experiment, the reagent of known nature is contained in the product which it forms with the unknown substance or its parts. The reagent does not only incite the product. The product belongs to the reagent as much as to the unknow substance. Experiment in physiological matters, however, becomes indefinite because the answer of living nature to the action of the reagent does not contain the known reagents as an essential part. Because all substances, all stimulations which act upon the organism, incite in it not what they themselves are but something different from them, the life energies of the organism. (34)

In spite of its general terms, this explanation is too narrow for the experiences of chemistry in our century. Great influences exerted by the smallest quantities of specific substances have been found in alloys and colloids as well as in organisms. A broad fundamental theory correlates a small difference of atomic mass with a vast amount of energy, and the introduction of an almost inconceivably small unit of energy, the quantum, has helped to solve many scientific problems. These problems, however, are far apart from those of biochemistry at the present time, or, as Niels Bohr expressed it, "Just as the relativity theory has taught us that the convenience of distinguishing sharply between space and time rests solely on the smallness of the velocities ordinarily met with compared to the velocity of light, we learn from the quantum theory that the appropriateness of our usual causal space-time descriptions depends entirely upon the small value of the quantum of action compared with the actions involved in ordinary sense perceptions." (35) As our "ordinary sense perceptions" are sharpened and refined by widening experiences with specific biochemical agents, we may hope to find new approaches to general theories for the great effect of the small quantities.

The biochemical studies of the effects of poisons and medicaments have been carried out on many levels of organisms. In the great specialization of these studies, an integration to the understanding of life has remained the aim. Jacques Monod (Pasteur Institute, Paris) devoted much of his work to the lowly *Escherichia coli* and the substances that activate or inhibit its enzyme and gene systems. He found the result "interesting primarily because it proposes a functional correlation between certain elements of the molecular structure of proteins and certain of their physiological properties, specifically those that are significant at the level of integration, of dynamic organization, of metabolism." (36) A century ago, Berthelot advised to "eliminate" life from organic chemistry. He meant that organic chemical facts should not be explained by life. Now the two have come together again, and biologists are warning us against trying to explain all of life by organic chemistry alone.

REFERENCES

1. M. Berthelot, *Chimie organique fondée sur la synthèse* (Paris: 1860), Vol. 2, p. 653.

2. G. Bunge, *Lehrbuch der physiologischen und pathologischen Chemie* (Leipzig: F. C. W. Vogel, 1887), p. 14.

3. Hans Driesch, *The Science and Philosophy of the Organism* (The Gifford *Lectures,* University of Aberdeen, 1907–1908).

4. Raphael Meldola, *The Chemical Synthesis of Vital Products* (London: 1904), Introduction, p. iv.

5. Paul Ehrlich and Julius Morgenroth, "Studies on hemolysins, 5th communication," *Berliner klinische Wochenschrift,* 1901, No. 10; also in *Studies in Immunology by Paul Ehrlich and his Collaborators,* collected and translated by Charles Bolduan (2nd ed; New York: Wiley & Sons, Inc., 1910), pp. 82 ff., 364 ff.

6. Erwin Schrödinger, *What Is Life?* (Cambridge: The University Press, 1944), p. 68.

7. H. A. Krebs, *Advances in Enzymology,* Nord and Werkman, Eds. (New York: Interscience Publishers, 1943), Vol. 3, p. 220.

8. A. Szent-Györgyi, "Introduction," *Advances in Chemical Physics* (New York, John Wiley & Sons, Inc. 1964), Vol. 7, p. xii.

9. The Svedberg and Robin Fåhraeus, "A new method for the determination of the molecular weight of the proteins," *J. Am. Chem. Soc.,* **48** (1926), pp. 430–8.

10. Kai Ulrik Linderstrøm-Lang, by John T. Edsal, in *Advances in Protein Chemistry,* **14** (1959), pp. xiii–xxiii.

11. A. D. Hershey and M. Chase. "Independent functions of viral protein and nucleic acid in growth of bacteriophage," *J. Gen. Physiol.,* **36** (1952), pp. 39–56.

12. O. Warburg and E. Negelein, "Fermentproblem und Oxydation in der lebenden Substanz," *Zeitschr. Elchem.,* **35** (1929), pp. 928–35.

13. D. Keilin, "On cytochrome, a respiratory pigment common to animals, yeast, and higher plants," *Proc. Roy. Soc.,* B**98** (1925), pp. 312–39, quotations from pp. 314, 338.

14. M. Rubner, *Die Gesetze des Energieverbrauchs bei der Ernährung* (Berlin: Deuticke, 1902).

15. J. B. Dumas, "The constitution of blood and milk" *Phil. Mag.,* **42** (1871), p. 129.

16. Morris Ant and Erwin Di Ctan, "Vitamin E in rheumatic diseases," *Ann.* N.Y. Acad. Sci. **52** (1949), pp. 374–9.

17. Roger J. Williams, Carl L. Lyman, George H. Goodyear, John H. Truesdail, and Duncan Holaday, " 'Pantothenic acid,' a growth determinant of universal biological occurrence," *J. Am. Chem. Soc.,* **55** (1933), pp. 2912–27.

18. Dorothy Crowfoot Hodgkins, Jenny Pickworth, and J. H. Robertson (Oxford University), R. J. Prosen, R. A. Sparks, and K. N. Trueblood (University of California, Los Angeles), "The structure of vitamin B_{12}. II. The crystal structure of a hexacarboxylic acid obtained by the degradation of vitamin B_{12}," *Proc. Roy. Soc.,* A**251** (1959), pp. 307–52.

19. A. Fleming, *Brit. Med. Bull.,* **2** (1947), p. 4. A. Fleming, H. W. Florey, D. C. Bodenham, and Eliot C. Cutler, "Discussion on penicillin," *Proc. Roy. Soc. Med.,* **37** (1944), pp. 101–12.

20. Alexander Fleming, "History and development of penicillin," in A. Fleming, Ed., *Penicillin, Its Practical Application* (London: Butterworth; St. Louis: C. V. Mosby Co., 1946), pp. 15 ff.

21. T. Reichstein, "Über Bestandteile der Nebennierenrinde," *Helv. Chim. Acta,* **19** (1936), pp. 29–63; 1107–26; *ibid.,* **21** (1938), pp. 1197–1210.

22. R. B. Woodward, Franz Sondheimer, David Taub, Karl Heusler, and W. M. McLamore, "The total synthesis of Cortisone," *J. Am. Chem. Soc.,* **73** (1951), p. 4057; "The total synthesis of steroids," *ibid.,* **74** (1952), pp. 4223–51.

23. G. Haberlandt, *Wundhormone als Erreger von Zellteilungen* (Berlin: Bornträger, 1921), reprinted from *Beiträge zur allgemeinen Botanik,* **2,** No. 1.

24. A. Ellinger, "Über die Constitution der Indolgruppe im Eiweiss (Synthese der sogen. Skatolcarbonsäure) und die Quelle der Kynurensäure," *Chem. Ber.,* **37** (1904), pp. 1801–8.

25. F. Kögl, "Discussion meeting on growth factors," *Proc. Roy. Soc.,* **124** (1937), pp. 1–23.

26. F. W. Went and K. V. Thimann, *Phytohormones* (New York: Macmillan Co., 1937).

27. F. H. Stodola, *Source Book on Gibberellin, 1828–1957* (Washington, D.C.: Agricultural Research Service, U.S. Dept. of Agriculture, 1958).

28. Otto Loewi, "Über humurale Übertragbarkeit der Herznervenwirkung," *Pflüger's Archiv,* **189** (1921), pp. 239–42. "Chemical transmission of nerve impulses," *Am. Scientist,* **33** (1945), pp. 159–74.

29. David Nachmansohn, "Chemical factors controlling nerve activity," *Science,* **134** (1961), pp. 1962–8.

30. Irwin B. Wilson and Sara Ginsberg, "A powerful reactivator of alkylphosphate-inhibited acetylcholinesterase," *Biochem. and Biophys. Acta,* **18** (1955), pp. 168–70.

31. Daniel Bovet, "Introduction to antihistamine agents and Antergan derivatives," *Ann.* N.Y. Acad. Sci. **50** (9) (1950), pp. 1089–1126. (Conference held October 1947.)

32. Charles Tanret, "Sur un nouveau principe immédiat de l'ergot de

seigle, l'ergostérine," *Compt. rend.,* **108** (1889), pp. 98–100; "Sur l'ergostérine et la fongistérine," *ibid.,* **147** (1908), p. 75–7.

33. J. M. Mueller, E. Schlittler, and H. J. Bein, "Reserpine, the sedative compound from Rauwolfia serpentina" (in German), *Experientia,* **8** (1952), p. 338.

34. Translated from J. Müller's inaugural lecture, October 19, 1824.

35. N. Bohr, "The quantum postulate and the recent development of atomic theory," *Nature,* **121** (1928), pp. 580–90.

36. Jacques Monod, "From enzymatic adaptation to allosteric transitions," *Science,* **154** (1966), pp. 475–83, esp. p. 482.

List of Periodicals Cited

For extensive lists of chemical periodicals see:

E. J. Crane, Austin M. Patterson, and E. B. Marr, *A Guide to the Literature of Chemistry* (2d ed., New York: John Wiley & Sons, 1957).

Chemical Abstracts (Washington, D.C.: American Chemical Society, 1961). pp. 1j–397j, and annual supplements.

EXPLANATIONS OF ABBREVIATIONS USED IN THIS BOOK

Liebig's Ann.
Annalen der Chemie. Founded (1832) as *Annalen der Pharmacie.* From 1840 to 1873 under the title *Annalen der Chemie und Pharmacie, vereinigte Zeitschrift des Neuen Journals der Pharmacie für Aerzte, Apotheker und Chemiker, und des Magazins für Pharmacie und Experimentalkritik* (Berlin: Verlag Chemie GmbH.).

Poggendorff's Ann.
Annalen der Physik und Chemie. Formerly *Annalen der Physik* and issued as *Annalen der Physik und Physikalischen Chemie* from 1819 to 1824. See Gren's *J. der Physik.*
Ann. Chim.
Ann. de Chim. Phys.
Annales de Chimie et de Physique. After 1914 separated into *Annales de Chimie* and *Annales de Physique* (Paris: Masson & Cie.).

Ann. N.Y. Acad. Sci.
Annals of the New York Academy of Sciences (New York: published by the Academy).

Ann. Sci.
Annals of Science, a Quarterly Review of the History of Science Since the Renaissance (London: Taylor & Francis Ltd.).

Bull. Soc. Chim.
Bulletin de la Société Chimique de France (Paris: Masson & Cie.).

Angew. Chem.
Zeitschrift für angewandte Chemie. After 1946, *Angewandte Chemie* (Weinheim: Verlag Chemie Gmb.H.).

Bull. Inst. Hist. Medicine.
Bulletin of the Institute of the History of Medicine, now *Bulletin of the History of Medicine* (Baltimore: The Johns Hopkins Press).

Chem. Abstr.
Chemical Abstracts (Washington, D.C.: The American Chemical Society).

Chem. Ber.
Berichte der Deutschen Chemischen Gesellschaft (Gesellschaft Deutscher Chemiker; Weinheim/Bergstr.: Verlag Chemie GmbH.) Vol. 1, 1868. After 1945, the title was changed to *Chemische Berichte* while continuing the numbers; thus, Vol. 81 has the date 1948.

Chem. Rev.
Chemical Reviews (Washington, D.C.: American Chemical Society).

Chem. Ztg.
Chemiker-Zeitung.

Compt. Rend.
Comptes Rendus hebdomadaires des Séances de l'Académie des Sciences (Paris: Gauthier-Villars).

Crell's Ann.
Chemische Annalen für die Freunde der Naturlehre, Arzneigelahrtheit, Haushaltungskunst und Manufacturen, ed. Lorenz von Crell (Helmstädt, C. G. Fleckeisen) 1784–1804.

Gren's J. der Physik.
Gren's Journal der Physik, founded 1790, continued since 1799 as *Annalen der Physik* by Ludwig Wilhelm Gilbert, after his death in 1824 continued by J. C. Poggendorff.

Helv. Chim. Acta.
Helvetica Chimica Acta (Basel: Swiss Chemical Society).

Ind. Eng. Chem.
Industrial and Engineering Chemistry (Washington, D.C., American Chemical Society).

Isis.
Isis. An International Review Devoted to the History of Science and Civilization. Official Quarterly Journal of the History of Science Society (founded by George Sarton; Cambridge, Mass.; from Vol. 55, No. 180, 1964, on; Robert P. Multhauf, Ed.; Berkeley: University of California Press).

J. Am. Chem. Soc.
Journal of the American Chemical Society (Washington, D.C.: American Chemical Society).

J. Chem. Ed.
Journal of Chemical Education (Easton, Pa.: American Chemical Society).

J. Chem. Soc. London.
Journal of the Chemical Society (London).

J. Chim. Phys.
Journal de Chimie Physique et de Physicochimie Biologique (Paris).

J. Phys.
Journal de Physique (Paris: Société Française de Physique).

J. für Chem. und Phys.
Journal für Chemie und Physik, Ed., Johann Salomo Christoph Schweigger, 1811–1825.

J. Prakt. Chem.
Journal für Praktische Chemie (Leipzig: Johann Ambrosius Barth Verlag).

Mag. f. Pharmacie.
Magazin für Pharmacie und die dahin einschlagenden Wissenschaften (Karlsruhe: C. F. Müller).

Mém. Ac. Paris.
Académie des Sciences, Paris, starting 1666 as *Histoire de l'Académie Royale des Sciences,* since 1790, *Mémoires de l' Académie des Sciences.*

Mém. de la Soc. d' Arcueil.
Mémoires de physique et de chimie de la Société d' Arcueil (Paris, J. J. Bernard) 1807-1817.

Mém. Inst. Nat.
Mémoires de l' Institut National de France.

Nature.
Nature, A Weekly Illustrated Journal of Science; later, *A Weekly Journal of Science* (London: Macmillan & Co., Ltd.).

Naturwiss.
Die Naturwissenschaften (Berlin: Springer Verlag).

Osiris.
Osiris. Commentationes de Scientiarum et Eruditionis Historia Rationeque (Bruges: The Saint Catherine Press).

Phil. Mag.
Philosophical Magazine (London: 1798–1814). Later, *Philosophical Magazine and Journal* (1814–1827). Then, *Philosophical Magazine or Annals of Chemistry, Mathematics, Astronomy, Natural History and*

General Science (1827–1832). *The London and Edinburgh* (to 1840), later, *The London, Edinburgh and Dublin Philosophical Magazine and Journal of Science.* Since 1945, *The Philosophical Magazine, A Journal of Theoretical, Experimental and Applied Physics* (London: Taylor & Frances Ltd.).

Phil. Trans.
Philosophical Transactions of the Royal Society of London, founded 1665.

Poggendorff's Annalen.
See *Annalen der Physik und Physikalischen Chemie.*

Proc. Am. Ac. Arts Sc.
Proceedings of the American Academy of Arts and Sciences (Boston).

Proc. Phil. Soc. Glasgow.
Proceedings of the Philosophical Society of Glasgow (Glasgow).

Proc. Roy. Soc.
Proceedings of the Royal Society of London.

Science.
Science. Published by the American Association for the Advancement of Science. (Lancaster, Pa.: Business Press; from Vol. 130, 1959, in Washington, D.C.)

Scientific Monthly. Official publication of the American Association for the Advancement of Science (Washington, D.C.).

Trans. Connecticut Ac.
Transactions of the Connecticut Academy of Arts and Sciences (New Haven, Conn.: Yale University Press).

Z. anorg. Chem.
Zeitschrift für anorganische Chemie, founded 1892 by Gerhard Krüss; since Vol. 92, 1915, *Zeitschrift für anorganische und allgemeine Chemie* (Leipzig: Johann Ambrosius Barth Verlag).

Zeitschr. Elchem.
Zeitschrift für Elektrochemie und Angewandte Physikalische Chemie, Bunsen Gellschaft, Ed. (Berlin: Verlag Chemie). After Vol. 51 of 1945, Vol. 52 appeared in 1948, published by Verlag Chemie GmbH., Weinheim/Bergstrasse. With Vol. 67 (1963) the *Zeitschrift* appeared under the new title: *Berichte der Bunsengesellschaft für physikalische Chemie (früher Zeitschrift für Elektrochemie).*

Index